John Murray, Sir Robert Lambert Playfair

Handbook for travellers in Algeria and Tunis : Algiers, Oran, Tlemçen, Bougie, Constantine, Tebessa, Biskra, Tunis, Carthage, etc.

John Murray, Sir Robert Lambert Playfair

Handbook for travellers in Algeria and Tunis : Algiers, Oran, Tlemçen, Bougie, Constantine, Tebessa, Biskra, Tunis, Carthage, etc.

ISBN/EAN: 9783337208479

Printed in Europe, USA, Canada, Australia, Japan

Cover: Foto ©Andreas Hilbeck / pixelio.de

More available books at **www.hansebooks.com**

HANDBOOK FOR TRAVELLERS

IN

ALGERIA AND TUNIS

ALGIERS, ORAN, TLEMÇEN, BOUGIE,
CONSTANTINE, TEBESSA, BISKRA, TUNIS, CARTHAGE,

ETC.

BY SIR R. LAMBERT PLAYFAIR, K.C.M.G.

AUTHOR OF 'HANDBOOK (MURRAY'S) TO THE MEDITERRANEAN;'
'TRAVELS IN THE FOOTSTEPS OF BRUCE;'
'THE SCOURGE OF CHRISTENDOM,'
ETC.

FOURTH EDITION, THOROUGHLY REVISED.

WITH MAPS AND PLANS

LONDON:
JOHN MURRAY, ALBEMARLE STREET.
1890.

THE ENGLISH EDITIONS OF MURRAY'S HANDBOOKS MAY BE OBTAINED OF THE FOLLOWING AGENTS.

Belgium, Holland, and Germany.

AIX-LA-CHAPELLE	} MAYER.	HEIDELBERG	. MOHR.
		LEIPZIG	. BROCKHAUS.—TWIETMEYER.
AMSTERDAM	. MULLER.—ROBBERS.	MANNHEIM	. BENDER.—LOFFLER.
ANTWERP	. MERTENS.	METZ	. ALCAN.
BADEN-BADEN	. MARX.	MUNICH	. MACKERMANN.—KAISER.
BERLIN	. ASHER,—MITSCHER AND ROSTELL.	NÜRNBERG	. SCHRAG.—ZEISER.
		PESTH	. HARTLEBEN.—RATH.
BRUSSELS	. KIESSLING.	PRAGUE	. CALVE.
CARLSRUHE	. A. BIELEFELD.	ROTTERDAM	. KRAMERS.
COLOGNE	. DUMONT.—SCHAUBERG.	STRASSBURG	. TRÜBNER.
DRESDEN	. BURDACH.—PIERSON.	STUTTGART	. METZLER.—NEFF.
FRANKFURT	. JÜGEL.	TRIESTE	. COEN.—SCHIMPFF.
GRATZ	. LEUSCHNER AND LUBENSKY.	VIENNA	. GEROLD.—DRAUMÜLLER.
THE HAGUE	. NIJHOFF.	WIESBADEN	. KREIDEL.
HAMBURG	. MAUKE SÖHNE.		

Switzerland.

BÂLE	. GEORG.—AMBERGER.	LUCERNE	. GEBHARDT.
BERNE	. JENT & REINERT.—SCHMIDT, FRANCKE, & CO.	NEUCHATEL	. GERSTER.
		SCHAFFHAUSEN	. HURTER.
COIRE	. GRUBENMANN.	SOLEURE	. JENT.
CONSTANCE	. MECK.	ST. GALLEN	. HUBER.
GENEVA	. SANDOZ,—H. GEORG.	ZURICH	. MÜLLER.—SCHMIDT.—MEYER & ZELLER.
LAUSANNE	. ROUSSY.		

Italy.

BOLOGNA	. ZANICHELLI.	PARMA	. ZANGHIERI.
FLORENCE	. LOESCHER & SEEBER.—FLOR & FINDEL.	PISA	. NISTRI.—JOS. VANNUCCHI.
		PERUGIA	. VINCENZ.—BARTELLI.
GENOA	. GRONDONA.—ANTOINE BEUF.	ROME	. SPITHÖVER, — PIALE. — LOESCHER.
LEGHORN	. MAZZAJOLI.		
LUCCA	. BARON.	SIENA	. ONORATO PORRI.
MANTUA	. NEGRETTI.	TURIN	. MAGGI. — L. BEUF. — BOCCA FRÈRES,—LOESCHER.
MILAN	. SACCHI.—HOEPLI.		
MODENA	. VINCENZI AND ROSSI.	VENICE	. ONGANIA.—MEINERS.
NAPLES	. HOEPLI.—FURCHHEIM.	VERONA	. MÜNSTER.—MEINERS.
PALERMO	. PEDONE.		

France.

AMIENS	. CARON.	LILLE	. BÉGHIN.
ANGERS	. BARASSÉ.	LYONS	. AYNÉ.—SCHEURING.—MÉRA.
AVIGNON	. CLÉMENT ST. JUST.	MARSEILLES	. CAMOIN FRÈRES.—MEUNIER.
AVRANCHES	. ANFRAY.	NANTES	. PETIPAS.—POIRIER LEGROS.
BORDEAUX	. CHAUMAS. — MÜLLER. — SAUVAT.—FERET.	NICE	. BARBERY,—GALIGNANI.
		ORLEANS	. GATINEAU.—PESTY.
BOULOGNE	. MERRIDEW.	PARIS	. GALIGNANI.—BOYVEAU.
CAEN	. BOISARD. — LEGOST. — CLERISSÉ.	PAU	. LAFON.
		RHEIMS	. BRISSART BINET.—GEOFFROY.
CALAIS	. RIGAUX CAUX.	ROUEN	. LEBRUMENT.—HAULARD.
CANNES	. ROBAUDY.	ST. ÉTIENNE	. DELARUE.
CHERBOURG	. LECOUFFLET.	ST. MALO	. HUE.
DIEPPE	. MARAIS.	ST. QUENTIN	. DOLOY.
DINANT	. COSTE.	TOULON	. MONGE ET VILLAMUS.
DOUAI	. JACQUART.—LEMÂLE.	TOULOUSE	. GIMET ET COTELLE.
GRENOBLE	. VELLOT ET COMP.	TOURS	. GEORGET.
HAVRE	. BOURDIGNON.—FOUCHER.	TROYES	. LALOY.—DUFEY ROBERT.

Spain and Portugal.

GIBRALTAR	. STATIONERY DEPÔT.	MADRID	. DURAN.— FUENTES Y CAPDEVILLE.
LISBON	. LEWTAS.		
	MALAGA	. GARCIA TABOADELA.	

Russia, Sweden, Denmark, and Norway.

ST. PETERSBURG	. WATKINS.—WOLFF.	ODESSA	. CAMOIN.
MOSCOW	. GAUTIER. — DEUBNER.—LANG.	CHRISTIANIA	. BENNETT.
		STOCKHOLM	. SAMSON & WALLIN.—FRITZ.

Malta.
CRITIEN.—WATSON.—CALLEJA.

Ionian Islands.
CORFU . J. W. TAYLOR.

Constantinople.
WICK & WEISS.

Greece.
ATHENS, KARL WILDBERG.

Alexandria.
PENASSON.

Cairo.
LIVADAS.—BARBIER.

India.
CALCUTTA—THACKER, SPINK, & CO. | BOMBAY—THACKER & CO., LIMITED.

PREFACE TO THE FOURTH EDITION

IT is not yet three years since the third edition of this Handbook was published, and already the immense extension of railway communication in the Colony has rendered it out of date.

The line from Algiers to Tunis has been completed; a new one has opened out Biskra, which is now within twelve hours of the sea. This cannot fail to become one of the most important winter stations in the basin of the Mediterranean. Another conducts to Tebessa and its wonderful Roman ruins; Bougie, the starting-point for the Chabet Pass, can be reached in one day from Algiers; the line to Tlemçen, the African Granada, is almost entirely finished; and the last one opened, from Mostaganem to Tiaret, renders easily accessible a country full of archæological interest

The Handbook has been thoroughly revised, and matters of an ephemeral nature, including information relating to hotels, etc., have been relegated to an Index and Directory.

R. L. P.

ALGIERS, *October* 1889.

In most instances throughout this volume the metric system has been adopted in preference to the English one. The following tables may be found useful by those whose minds have not yet become habituated to this more rational standard :—

5 centimètres	=	2	inches.
10	,,	4	,,
15	,,	$5\frac{7}{8}$	,,
20	,,	$7\frac{7}{8}$	,,
25	,,	$9\frac{7}{8}$	,,
30	,,	$11\frac{7}{8}$	,,
35	,,	$13\frac{3}{4}$	,,
40	,,	$15\frac{3}{4}$	,,
45	,,	$17\frac{7}{8}$	,,
50	,,	$19\frac{5}{8}$	,,

1 mètre	=	3	feet	$3\frac{3}{5}$	inches.
2	,,	6	,,	$7\frac{1}{5}$	,,
3	,,	9	,,	$10\frac{4}{5}$	,,
4	,,	13	,,	$2\frac{2}{5}$	,,
5	,,	16	,,	6	,,
6	,,	19	,,	$9\frac{3}{5}$	,,
7	,,	23	,,	$1\frac{1}{5}$	,,
8	,,	26	,,	$10\frac{4}{5}$	,,
9	,,	29	,,	$8\frac{2}{5}$	,,
10	,,	33	,,	0	,,

1 kilomètre	=	$\frac{5}{8}$	miles.
2	,,	$1\frac{1}{4}$	,,
3	,,	$1\frac{7}{8}$	,,
4	,,	$2\frac{1}{2}$	,,
5	,,	$3\frac{1}{8}$	,,

6 kilomètres	=	$3\frac{3}{4}$	miles.
7	,,	$4\frac{3}{8}$	,,
8	,,	5	,,
9	,,	$5\frac{5}{8}$	,,
10	,,	$6\frac{1}{4}$	,,

1 hectare = $2\frac{1}{2}$ acres.

The sign Θ after the names of Roman remains indicates places always interesting to the archæologist, but in a less degree to the ordinary traveller.

CONTENTS

SECTION I
INTRODUCTORY INFORMATION

SECT.		PAGE	SECT.		PAGE
1	Routes—London to Algeria	1	9	Government of Algeria	65
2	Climate of Algeria	2	10	Sport	67
3	Season for Travelling—Choice of Residence	5	11	Zoology	70
4	Railways	6	12	Geology, Mineralogy, Hot Springs, etc.	75
5	Population and Races	6			
6	Native Languages	12	13	Colonisation, Cereals, Fruit and Vegetables, Flora, Agriculture, Forests, etc.	81
7	General Description of Algeria and Tunis	12			
8	Historical Notice of Algeria and Tunis	20	14	Archæology	89

SECTION II
ALGERIA

	PAGE
CITY OF ALGIERS	93
EXCURSIONS IN THE ENVIRONS OF ALGIERS	105
A FORTNIGHT'S TOUR IN ALGERIA	112

ROUTES

ROUTE		PAGE	ROUTE		PAGE
1	Algiers to *Philippeville, Bône,* and *Tunis* by sea	113	9	Algiers to *Aumale* and *Bou Saâda*	163
2	Algiers to *Cherchel* and *Tipasa*	133	10	Algiers to *Oran* by rail	165
3	Algiers to *Coleah* and the *Tombeau de la Chrétienne*	137	11	Philippeville to *Constantine* by rail	184
4	Algiers to *Rovigo* and the baths of *Hammam Melouan*	140		City of Constantine	185
5	Algiers to *Teniet-el-Ahd*	141		Excursions in the Neighbourhood	197
6	Algiers to *Tizi-Ouzou* and *Fort National*	143	12	Constantine to *Algiers,* by the *Chabet el-Akhira*	199
7	Algiers to *El-Aghouat*, through the Gorge of the Chiffa, Medeah, and Boghari	147	13	Bougie to *Beni-Mansour* and on to *Algiers* by rail	202
8	Algiers to *Constantine* by rail	155	14	Constantine to *Batna* and *Biskra*	204

ROUTE	PAGE	ROUTE	PAGE
14 Excursions in the Neighbourhood of Batna	206	23 Oran to *Tlemçen*	254
15 Biskra to *Tuggurt*	217	24 A Tour through the centre of Oran to *Mascara, Sidi bel Abbès, Tlemçen, Lalla Marnia, Nedroma,* and *Nemours*	265
16 To *Tebessa*	221		
17 Tebessa to *Souk-Ahras,* by *Khamisa*	228	25 St. Barbe de Tlelat to *Sidi bel Abbès* by rail [thence to *Tlemçen* by diligence], on to *Ras el-Ma*	268
18 To *Aïn-Beida*	234		
19 Constantine to *Bône* by rail	236		
20 Excursion through the Kabylia of Djurdjura from *Bordj bou-Arreredj* to the *Oued es-Sahel* and *Fort National*	242	26 Arzeu to *Mascara, Saïda, Mecheria* and *Aïn-Sefra* by rail	272
21 Algiers to *Ténès* by *Orléansville*	246	27 Oran to *Beni Saf, Nemours,* and the Frontier of Morocco	279
22 Mostaganem to *Tiaret* by rail	247		

SECTION III

TUNIS

ROUTE	PAGE	ROUTE	PAGE
REGENCY OF TUNIS	284	30 Tunis to *El-Kef via* Souk el-Arbâa	308
THE GOLETTA	286		
CITY OF TUNIS	286	31 Excursion to *Bizerta* and *Utica*	309
CARTHAGE	291		
Excursion to the Bardo and the Roman Aqueduct beyond *Manouba*	297	32 Excursion to *Zaghouan* and *Oudena*	312
Excursion to *Hammam el-Enf*	298	33 Voyage along the Coast of Tunis from the Goletta to the *Island of Djerba*	317
Best Route from Tunis to *Algiers*	298	34 Susa to *Kerouan*	328
28 Bône to *Tunis* by rail	299	35 Excursion from Kerouan to *Sbeitla*	331
29 Excursion in the Country of the Khomair	305		

GLOSSARY OF ARABIC WORDS xi
APPENDIX—List of Consuls, and Bibliography . . . 334
INDEX AND DIRECTORY 341

LIST OF MAPS AND WOODCUTS

ALGIERS AND ITS ENVIRONS . *To face*
TOWN OF ALGIERS . ..
HARBOUR OF PHILIPPEVILLE .
    ,,   BÔNE .
    ,,   LA CALLE
ORAN AND ITS ENVIRONS
PLAN OF CONSTANTINE .
THE DJEDARS .
PLAN OF BENI SAF .
TRAVELLING MAP OF ALGERIA .
MAP OF TUNIS . .
TUNIS AND ITS ENVIRONS

GLOSSARY OF ARABIC WORDS USED IN THIS BOOK.

Ab, Aboo, Abou, Bou, father, possessor of.
Abd, slave. Pl. *Abid*.
Abiad, white. Fem. *Baida*.
Abiar. Pl. of *bir*, well.
Achour, tax.
Agha (Turk.), lord.
Ahel, people.
Ahmer, red. Fem. *Hamara*.
Ain, eye, spring. Pl. *Ayoun*. Dimin. *Aouina*.
Ainab, grapes.
Ait. Kabyle for *Beni*, children of.
Akhal, black. Fem. *Kahala*.
Akhdar, green. Fem. *Khadara*.
Alfa, see *Halfa*.
Amala, province.
Amin, head of a *Djemäa*.
Anchir, see *Henchir*.
Annab, jujube, Zizaphus.
Aoud, horse.
Aradh, earth.
Arbäa, four, Wednesday, 4th day.
Arch, tribal land.
Areg, sandhill; *Berr-el-Areg*, country of sandhills, the desert.
Asfel, low. Fem. *Safala*.
Azel, Government land.
Azib, encampment.

Bab, gate. Pl. *Biban*.
Bach-Agha, governor of a certain number of tribes.
Badia, country, opposed to town.
Baghal, mule.
Bahr, sea; *Bahira*, small sea or plain.
Bedoui, bedouin. Pl. *Bedou*.
Beit, house; *beit-esh-shäar*, hair house = tent.
Beled, town. Pl. *Buldan*. Dimin. *Belida*.
Ben, Ibn, son. Pl. *Beni*.
Berd, cold.
Berr, country, region.
Beylick, belonging to Government.
Bir, well. Pl. *Abiar*. Dimin. *Bouir*.
Birkeh, lake, pond.
Blad, more correctly *Belad*, country.
Bordj, castle; *Bordj-el-fanar*, lighthouse.
Bou, see *Ab*.

Caftan, Turkish dress.
Chaiba, ravine.
Chaouch, attendant on Bureau Arab, corresponding to Indian *Peon*.
Chebaka, net. Pl. *Chebabik*.
Chott, salt lake.
Couscous or *Couscousou*, a farinaceous food used by the Arabs; Kabyle, *Sksou*.

Dar, stone house; *Dar-es-Sanaa*, manufactory.
Daradja, step; *Droudj*, stairs.
Defla, oleander.
Dekhla, pass, gorge.
Deshera, village.
Dhara, north.
Dhaya, pool, marsh.
Dhib, jackal. Pl. *Dhiab*.
Dhiffa, repast offered to guests.
Diss, coarse grass.
Djamäa, mosque, village council.
Djaneb, side.
Djebel, mountain.
Djebeli, mountaineer.
Djedar, wall. Pl. *Adjdar*.
Djehad, war against infidels.
Djelad, tanner.
Djenan, garden.
Djenoub, south.
Djerid, palm branch, country of palms.
Djidid, new.
Djir, lime.
Djisr, bridge.
Djizira, island. Pl. *Djezair*; *el-Djezair*, the islands = Algiers.
Dom, dwarf palm.
Douar, group of Arab tents or families.
Doula, state, government.

El-, The.

Faras, mare.
Fedj, pass, col.
Ferka, section of a tribe.
Fernan, cork tree.
Fodha, silver.
Fokani, upper.
Fondouk, inn.

GLOSSARY OF ARABIC WORDS

Foum, mouth, opening.
Fourn, oven.

Ghaba, forest.
Ghar, cave.
Gharab, west.
Gharsa, plantation.
Ghazala, gazelle. Pl. *Ghozlan*.
Ghorfa, grotto.
Goum, more correctly *Koum*, body of Arab soldiers.
Gourbi, Arab hut.
Guetar, small wells.

Habs, prison.
Hadari, Arab living in town.
Haddad, blacksmith.
Haddid, iron.
Hadj or *Hadji*, pilgrim to Mecca.
Hadjara, stone. Pl. *Hadjar*.
Hafra, excavation.
Hai, living.
Halak, throat, canal.
Halfa, esparto grass.
Hamma, warm spring.
Hammam, bath.
Harah, quarter of a city.
Hassi, little well.
Henchir, farm, Roman ruins.
Hezzam, girdle.
Hout, fish.

Ibn, see *ben*.
Ighil, Kabyle for ridge.
Imam, leader of prayers in a mosque.

J, see Dj, usual French orthography.

Kadi, native judge.
Kaffir, infidel.
Kaid, head of a tribe.
Kalâa, fort.
Kantara, arch, bridge.
Kasba, citadel.
Kasr, palace.
Kebila, tribe. Pl. *Kebail*.
Kebir, great.
Kedim, old.
Kef, hill, mount.
Kelb, dog.
Kermia, fig.
Khadem, slave, servant.
Khames, lit. one-fifth; tenants who are remunerated with one-fifth of the produce of land for its cultivation.
Khaukh, peach.

Khazna, treasure.
Khaznadar, treasurer.
Kheit, thread, rope worn by Arabs as a head-dress.
Kheneg, defile.
Khouan, more correctly *Akhouan*, pl. of *Akh*, brother; member of a religious confraternity.
Kibla, direction of Mecca in a mosque.
Kibrit, sulphur.
Korn, horn.
Kotan, cotton.
Koubba, a dome; generally applied to tombs of Mohammedan saints.
Koudia, small hill.
Koum, mound.
Kubr, tomb. Pl. *Kubour*.
Kulb, heart.
Kusab, a reed.
Kusr, palace.

Lela, lady.

Ma, water.
Mäaden, a mine.
Mabrouk, blessed.
Mafrag, bifurcation.
Maghreb, sunset, west.
Maiz, goat.
Makam, place.
Makbara, cemetery.
Makhzen, magazine, civil Spahi.
Man-oura, victorious.
Marabout, more correctly *Marabet*, a person devoted to religion. Pl. *Marabatin*.
Mäaskara, camp.
Matmor, silos.
Mechera, ford.
Medina, city.
Medjez, ferry.
Medressa, college.
Mehalla, camp.
Melâh, *mâleh*, salt, *adj*.
Melh, salt, *subs*.
Melk, freehold property.
Melouan, coloured.
Memleka, kingdom.
Menara, minaret.
Menzel, place.
Merdj, meadow.
Meridj, swamp.
Mersa, anchorage.
Mesjid, mosque.
Messaoud, happy.
Mezrag, a lance.

Mimbar, pulpit.
Moghreb, west; the West country, namely, the Barbary coasts.
Mokaddem, head-man; generally used for the chief of a religious body.
Moulai, my Lord.

Nadour, observatory.
Nahr, river.
Nakhala, date tree.
Nemel, ant.
Nouba, garrison.

Omm, mother.
Ou, the Berber equivalent of *Ben*, son of.
Oued, river, valley.
Oulad. Pl. of *Walad*, son.
Oumena. Pl. of *Amin*, q. v.
Oust, middle, waist; central court in a house.

Rahim, merciful.
Rahman, compassionate.
Raïs, captain.
Rakham, marble.
Ramla, sand.
Ras, head, cape.
Razzia, more correctly *Ghazzia*, plundering expedition.
Roumi, lit. Roman; used to express Christian.

Stada, happiness.
Sabegha, tribal land.

Safel, lower part.
Saharidj, cisterns.
Saheb, owner, companion.
Sahel, coast.
Sakia, canal for irrigation.
Sebala, fountain.
Sebkha, salt lake.
Sebt, seventh, Saturday.
Sedra, zizaphus or jujube tree.
Seghir, small.
Seil, torrent.
Sekkin, knife.
Seksou, Kabyle name for couscous.
Shaham, fat, grease.
Shirk, east.
Si or *Sidi*, my Lord.
Silos, underground receptacles for corn.
Skiffa, vestibule of a Moorish house.
Smala, small fort occupied by Spahis.
Sof, league, confraternity.
Souk, market.

Täam, food; couscousou.
Towil, long. Fem. *Towila*.

Zab. Pl. *Ziban*, an oasis watered by a river.
Zan, an oak.
Zaouia, college, convent, or place of refuge for poor scholars or religious mendicants.
Zeitoun, olive.
Zekka, tax on cattle.

SECTION I

INTRODUCTORY INFORMATION

	PAGE		PAGE
1. Routes — London to Algeria	1	8. Historical Notice of Algeria and Tunis	20
2. Climate of Algeria	2	9. Government of Algeria	65
3. Season for Travelling — Choice of Residence	5	10. Sport	67
		11. Zoology	70
4. Railways	6	12. Geology, Mineralogy, Hot Springs, etc.	75
5. Population and Races	6		
6. Native Languages	12	13. Colonisation, Agriculture, Forests, etc.	81
7. General Description of Algeria and Tunis	12	14. Archæology	89

§ 1. Routes—London to Algeria.

The direct route from England to Algeria is through Paris and Marseilles. The traveller can either reach the latter place by the ordinary route, *via* Lyons, or by the more picturesque one passing through Clermont-Ferrand and Nimes.

From Marseilles excellent steamers of the *Transatlantique Company* (6 Rue Auber, Paris; 12 Rue de la République, Marseilles) run daily to Algiers, and to various other parts of the colony, as well as to Tunis. These departures are so numerous, and so much liable to change, that the traveller should consult the time-tables of the Company. The voyage to Algiers occupies from 24 to 36 hours, varying with the vessel and the state of the weather, and costs £4. Cheaper but less comfortable vessels of the *Compagnie Mixte* (9 Rue Rougemont, Paris; 54 Rue Cannebière, Marseilles), and of the *Société Générale de Transports Maritimes à Vapeur* (3 Rue des Templiers, Marseilles), also run weekly between Marseilles and Algiers.

Vessels of the *Holt* or *Ocean Line*, of *J. Moss and Company*, and of *Messrs. Papayanni*, leave Liverpool frequently. Information regarding them may be obtained from Messrs. Gellatly, Hankey Sewell, and Co., Pall Mall, London, and 1 Fenchurch Street, Liverpool, who will also forward heavy luggage.

Travellers will be saved much trouble and inconvenience if they procure all necessary tickets before leaving London. They are recommended to Messrs. T. Cook and Son (Ludgate Circus, Charing Cross, and 35 Piccadilly), who, besides supplying tickets, are always ready to furnish the traveller with all information he may require. Office in Algiers in Square Bresson.

[*Algeria.*]   B

§ 2. CLIMATE OF ALGERIA.

The traveller coming to Algiers with the idea that he is to find a rainless and almost tropical winter, will certainly be disappointed. For this he must go to Egypt, where fertility is not dependent on rainfall. At Algiers he will find the best winter climate on the western shores of the Mediterranean, but it will not be without a due proportion of rain and cold.

June, July, August, September, are practically rainless, and the two last extremely hot.

October and November give what would be counted the loveliest summer weather in England, with occasional, and probably very heavy, rains.

December, January, February and March are not unlike an English autumn, with a double allowance of sunshine, and of rain also, and none of its dampness.

April and May, again, give the most perfect English summer weather, with but very little rain, and are certainly the most enjoyable months in the year.

The seasons are, however, extremely variable. During the many years which the writer has spent in Algiers, no two winters have been alike, and a high functionary once remarked to him that he had spent thirty years in Algeria and had seen thirty exceptional winters.

Usually the rain falls heavily when it falls at all, and is seldom of long duration. The fine drizzling rain so common in the north of Europe is here of rare occurrence, and in the neighbourhood of Algiers itself the soil is of so absorbent a nature, and the ground so steep, that the moment the rain ceases and the sun has reappeared, the roads dry, and delicate invalids can take their exercise in the open air. But once or twice in the course of the season a bout of rain and wind must be expected which will continue two or three days. Even in these cases the air is not damp, and wet objects not actually exposed to the rain will become dry when it is falling most heavily. Rain falls on the average on about 80 days out of the 365; but not more than one quarter of these could with any propriety be termed "wet days." To ensure a fine harvest, at least 36 inches of rain are required; and for visitors the rainier seasons are found the most enjoyable, dust being, in Algiers, even in winter, a far greater annoyance than rain. It may be added that about 60 per cent of the rain usually falls at night. The average in Algiers is about 29 inches. The first rains after the long summer drought, which are also the heaviest downpours, occur, sometimes in September, generally about the middle of October, and produce an instantaneous change in the climate. December is usually the wettest month of the twelve on the coast of Algeria; on the high ground in the interior the most abundant rains are expected in the spring; but any month from October to March *may* be the wettest of some particular season.

Frost and snow are in Algiers so rare as to be almost unknown, though hailstorms are frequent. But on the High Plateaux, and on the most elevated inhabited parts of the Tell, the frost is severe, the snow lies long and deep, while the highest mountains retain some snow patches as late as the beginning of June.

§ 2. CLIMATE OF ALGERIA

The rain, the wind, and the cold generally come from the N.W. The N.E. wind, so dreaded in Europe, is here almost unknown, and harmless when it does come. There is absolutely nothing at Algiers answering to the terrible mistrale of the Riviera. The north winds, tempered by 500 miles of sea, have had all mischief extracted from them in their passage; and the cold which comes with or after the rain has none of that searching keenness so disagreeable in winds blowing directly from snowy mountains. The sirocco, or desert wind, is in winter merely a pleasantly warm, dry breeze; in spring and autumn it can be disagreeably hot, but its terrors are reserved for the summer months. Fortunately it does not often last more than three days at a time, but during its continuance the thermometer will rise about 100° in the shade on the sea-beach, and much higher a little distance inland; the sky becomes dim; the air is charged with fine sand, vegetable life seems to become extinguished, or at least suspended, and it is by no means an uncommon event to see a whole field of vines withered in a moment by a blast of this burning wind.

When the sirocco is not blowing, the nights, even during the hottest season, are cool and refreshing, and dews are copious.

There can be no doubt that Algiers is the best winter residence within easy range of England. It is not so warm and agreeable as Madeira or Egypt, but it is preferable to any place on the north shore of the Mediterranean, and it has the great advantage of being within four days' easy journey of London. Whatever a climate can do for a sick person Algiers ought to accomplish, but it cannot work a miracle.

Dr. Jackson, in his *Medical Climatology*, justly remarks:—

"As a resort from the inclement seasons of Northern Europe, for persons threatened with pulmonary consumption, Algiers is deservedly in good reputation. The climate is far from being of a relaxing character; on the contrary, it combines with its usual mildness and equability a decidedly bracing and tonic influence. Consumptive patients, in whom there is a well-marked deposit of crude tubercle, may pass one or more winters in Algiers with advantage, under circumstances which afford nature the most ample leisure for repairing the disorganised structure. The sooner the patient is placed under its influence the more likely is the result to be beneficial. But when the disease has gone beyond what I have mentioned, when the patient is obviously sinking under the malady, Algiers is not to be recommended."

It is cruelty for the physician to recommend such to quit the comforts of his own home and the society of friends in the hope of restoring health, a hope which he well knows to be fallacious.

For some heart diseases the climate of Algiers is remarkably efficacious, even more so than for pulmonary complaints.

As a rule the patient should not prolong his stay after the first heats of summer have commenced, yet it ought to be known that some of the most remarkable cures that have been effected here have been in the case of those who have spent two winters and the intervening summer in Algiers.

The following tables will give a more accurate idea of the climate of Algiers than any mere description of it:—

TABLE OF TEMPERATURE (Fahrenheit) compiled from Observations made, under the Algerian Government, at the Military Hospital of Algiers (Hôpital du Dey), during 13 years from 1865 to 1877. The thermometers are placed about 300 yards from the sea-beach, about 50 feet above the sea-level, and about 6 feet from the ground.

	Hottest Day, *i.e.* Highest Maximum in 13 years.	Coldest Night, *i.e.* Lowest Minimum in 13 years.	Coldest Day, *i.e.* Lowest Minimum in 13 years.	Warmest Night, *i.e.* Highest Maximum in 13 years.	Average Maximum in 13 years.	Average Minimum in 13 years.	Average Mean Temperature in 13 years.
January	77	32	48	62	60½	48	54
February	75	32½	48	63	62	48½	55½
March	82½	34	51	66	64	50	57
April	95½	37	50	70	68½	53½	61
May	89½	45½	57	72½	73½	58½	66
June	101	53	66	75	78½	63½	71
July	102	57½	75½	77	84½	69	76½
August.	111	56½	75	82½	86½	70	78
September	109	53½	68½	79	83	68	75½
October	97	44	61½	79	75½	61	68½
November	84½	40	53½	68½	66½	54	60½
December	77½	34	50	66	61½	48½	55

N.B.—On the sides and top of the hills about Mustafa it would be necessary to add about 3 degrees to extremes of heat, and subtract about 4 degrees for extremes of cold.

TABLE OF RAINFALL (reduced to English inches) compiled from Observations made, under the Algerian Government, at the Military Hospital of Algiers (Hôpital du Dey), during 14 years from July 1864 to June 1878. The rain-gauge is about 300 yards from the sea-beach, about 50 feet above the sea-level, and about 15 feet from the ground.

	Average Rainfall in 14 years.	Highest Rainfall in 14 years.	Lowest Rainfall in 14 years.	Average number of days on which a measurable quantity of rain has fallen.	Greatest number of such days.	Least number of such days.	Heaviest Rainfall in 24 hours in the 14 years.
January	3·64	7·66	·28	10	17	2	3·30
February	2·40	5·49	·06	7	16	2	1·48
March	3·97	9·17	·56	12	23	4	1·89
April	2·02	4·20	·04	6	12	1	1·46
May	1·21	2·78	·04	5	11	1	2·05
June	·91	3·43	·04	3	9	1	2·13
July	·09	·46	..	1	3	0	·32
August	·40	4·04	..	1	5	0	3·98
September	1·21	7·00	..	3	10	0	2·25
October	3·72	10·06	·35	8	13	3	2·84
November	4·01	7·00	1·16	10	19	4	1·77
December	5·42	8·38	·68	13	20	1	1·91
Total	29·00			79			

The average rainfall of Algiers may be estimated at 788 mil. = 29 inches ; that of Oran at 510 mil. = 19 inches ; at Constantine there is about 644 mil. = 24 inches, but much less on the High Plateaux of that province. For instance, the average at Setif is only 644 mil. = 24 inches ; Batna, 412 mil. = 15 inches ; whereas on the coast it is much greater, 1189 mil. = 44 inches at Bougie ; 945 at Djedjehy = 35 inches ; 789 at Philippeville = 29 inches ; and 842 at La Calle = 31 inches.

Three meteorological departments have been established by Government, at Algiers, Oran, and Constantine, and 44 stations have been provided with instruments. These extend to the border of the Sahara on the one hand, and from Sfax to Mogador on the coast. The observations are centralised every day at Algiers, and published in the evening.

§ 3. Season for Travelling—Choice of Residence.

The best season for visiting Algeria is from the beginning of November to the end of May. During January, February, March, and part of April, a good deal of rain may be expected, and many of the routes are then difficult, if not impossible. Still, short excursions may be made at any time when the weather appears settled. November and December are good months for travelling in the interior, but not nearly so much so as April and May, when all nature is bright with the hues of spring and the most gorgeous wild flowers. Beyond all doubt May is the finest month in the year, but the days are somewhat hot, and walking in the sun oppressive.

The only recommendation which it is necessary to give regarding clothing is, that the traveller should bring and wear exactly the same garments as he would use in England at a corresponding season. The cold, of course, is much less in Algeria, but it is felt more.

Visitors to Algeria may be divided into two categories, the tourist and the invalid ; the former will not care to remain very long in one place, and need only consult his own inclination as to a choice of residence. To the latter, however, this question is a very serious one. He generally comes abroad at great personal inconvenience, and he is willing to sacrifice every consideration to the vital one of health. He will almost certainly select Algiers itself as his residence, and he will do well to avoid the town as much as possible, and live in the country. In most cases the higher up he rises on the Mustafa hill, the better and purer is the air. The writer is almost inclined to say *the warmer is the climate*, for though houses on the highest level are more exposed to the wind, they escape the damp vapour which frequently clings to the valleys below, and they are more thoroughly exposed to the sun. The ascent is hardly an objection, as it is balanced by the advantage that, once on the summit, an invalid can walk for miles almost on level ground, amongst a never-ending variety of shady lanes, whereas lower down his rambles must be entirely on the public road, and either up or down hill.

There are numerous villas situated in beautiful gardens in the environs of Algiers, and several excellent hotels and pensions.

The best locality for a winter residence is the slope of Mustafa Supérieur, and along the road leading thence, past the Colonne Voirol towards El-Biar.

Rents have risen considerably of late, and it is hardly possible to obtain the smallest furnished villa with a garden there under 3600 f. for the season of six months, and they range from that sum up to 8000 or 10,000 f. In less desirable quarters, such as the village d'Isly, the Agha, Mustafa Inférieur, and St. Eugène, the prices are lower, but the houses are not so good, and those localities are far less healthy and enjoyable.

English visitors reside generally in the country hotels in preference to those in the town; the former are in every respect more healthy and enjoyable, though perhaps a little more expensive. For more precise information regarding houses, servants, etc., visitors may apply to Mr. Dunlop, 13 Rue d'Isly, house and general agent. He also keeps a butcher's and grocer's shop, where visitors are sure to find all they can possibly require.

§ 4. RAILWAYS.

The railway system of Algeria has made rapid progress of late years. The aim of the administration is to have a central line from Tunis to Morocco, passing through the most important points in the interior, and various subsidiary lines joining this with the sea.

The lines actually open are indicated in the body of the work.

§ 5. POPULATION AND RACES.

The population of Algeria, according to the census of 1881, was as follows:—

	French.	Jews.	Spaniards.	Italians.	British.[1]	Germans.	Other Europeans.	Mohammedans.	Total.
Algiers	98,807	11,582	42,043	8,489	3,738	1,186	3,671	1,082,156	1,251,672
Oran	70,577	14,588	68,383	4,149	477	2,017	12,425	592,708	767,322
Constantine	64,555	9,495	3,894	21,055	11,187	998	6,232	1,174,002	1,291,418
Totals	233,939	35,665	114,320	33,693	15,402	4,201	22,328	2,848,866	3,310,412
	269,604			163,415					

In comparing the census of 1881 with that of 1876, there appears an increase of 442,786 in favour of the former year; an increase which is apparent in every class of the population, except Germans, in which there is a decrease of 2312.

The two principal divisions into which the Mohammedan races inhabiting Algeria may be divided are the Berbers and Arabs. The former is a branch of the great aboriginal people which inhabited the north of Africa as far south as the Soudan, Egypt, Nubia, and as far as the west shore of the Red Sea.

[1] Includes Maltese and natives of Gibraltar.

But the word *Berber* is an inaccurate one; it was quite unknown to the ancients, who always designated the aboriginal races by specific names, such as *Lybians, Numidians, Massylians*, etc. It was the Arab conquerors who first united them all by using the term Berber, meaning to imply people whose language they could not understand; they themselves never recognised the appellation, and do not use it now.

Distinct bodies of this race still exist, especially in the more inaccessible parts of the country; but, for the most part, they have become amalgamated with the Arabs, and have lost both their distinctive character and language. This blending of the native races with their conquerors took place at two distinct epochs, the first after the brilliant conquest of North Africa by the Arab warriors in the 7th century (see p. 31), and the second after the more serious invasion of an immense Arab population in the 11th century (see p. 32).

The most important branches of this people still retaining anything like purity of origin or distinctive language, are the *Kabyles* and the *Chawia*— the latter are described farther on; the former, who inhabit the mountainous districts nearer Algiers, and with whom the traveller comes more frequently in contact, deserve a separate description.

The Kabyles. (Arab. *Kabail*, pl. of *Kabila*, a tribe.) This name is given to the people of Berber origin who inhabit the mountains of the littoral; the *Beni-Manassir*, to the south of Cherchel, and various tribes bordering the Metidja, are as much Kabyles as the mountaineers of Djurdjura. Kabylia proper, however (see p. 14), has a population of about 200,000, less than a tenth of the whole native inhabitants of Algeria.

It is certain that this race has at various epochs been much mixed with other elements, and the *débris* of the Greek and Roman colonies must have constituted a considerable portion of this mixture. The religious persecutions of the Arians and Donatists, which so effectually prepared the way for Islamism, no doubt drove many of the poorer members of these colonies for safety to the mountains, where they soon became mixed up with the aboriginal inhabitants. There can still be traced among their customs the traditions of Roman law and municipal institutions, and one frequently meets amongst them types, easily recognisable, of the Latin and Germanic races. Some have supposed that the crosses which Kabyle girls are in the habit of tattooing on their faces and arms are remnants of the Christian faith; as also the very different position occupied by the women to that usual in Mohammedan countries.

Many of their families no doubt had European ancestors, dating from long after the extinction of the Romans; their own traditions assert this fact, and the beauty of the women of *Aït Ouaguennoun*, which is proverbial in the country, is regarded as a proof of their foreign origin. The Arab element amongst them was introduced later, less by actual conquest than by the moral influence of Islamism, and the institution of slavery has had the effect here, as in all Mohammedan countries, of introducing black blood into the mixture.

Kabylia, having preserved its independence for centuries, has always afforded a safe retreat to political and criminal refugees; they were received with an unquestioning hospitality, and ended a career of adventure in these peaceful retreats. The secret of their origin has died with them, but their traces remain in the fair complexion, blue eyes, and red hair, everywhere found in the country, which certainly do not belong to African or Asiatic races.

In almost all their essential characteristics the Kabyles are the very opposite of the Arabs. They never mount on horseback; they are not nomades or pastoral; but they are strong and industrious, excellent farmers, cultivating their land with the care usually bestowed on market-gardens. They are industrious mechanics, and manufacture several articles, such as pottery and jewellery, with great taste and elegance.

One of their most distinguishing characteristics is intense patriotism. This is manifest in all their institutions, but especially by a custom which prevailed amongst them in times of danger, or invasion by a foreign enemy. A number of the youth enrolled themselves in a sort of forlorn hope called *Imessebelen* (pl. of *Messebel*), whose duty it was to sacrifice their lives for the protection of their country. The prayers for the dead were read over them before going into action, from which they could only return victorious. If they were killed their bodies were buried in a cemetery apart, which was ever after used as a place of prayer, and considered as peculiarly deserving of veneration. Were one of them to escape with the loss of honour from the field, he and all his kindred would for ever be held in contempt as outcasts.

Moreover, the Kabyle character lends itself more readily to social progress than that of the Arab: he is less distrustful, more industrious, and less disposed to that life of lazy indifference which is characteristic of the latter. He is surrounded on all sides by European colonisation, and willingly frequents the farms of colonists in search of work; while the greater part of the Arabs live in isolated tribes, and have rarely an opportunity of seriously appreciating the advantages of civilisation.

The Kabyles all belong to the Mohammedan religion, and to the orthodox *Maleki* rite—that is, they have adopted the doctrine of the Imam Malek as their interpretation of religious civil law. (See also p. 15.) Their dress is of a whitish hue, sometimes black and white, and consists of the *haik* over the *chelouka* or woollen shirt which extends below the knee. They wear a small skull-cap on the head, generally a complicated mass of rags fastened with cord on their feet, and usually the *burnous* when travelling.

Numerically the most important class of the native population are the

Arabs, who are, as their name implies, of Arabian origin, and date back from the Arab occupation of the country in the 12th century. They took possession of the most accessible portions, and drove the original owners, the Berbers, into their mountain fastnesses.

At the present day they are far less advanced than the Kabyles; they retain the habits, ideas, and nomadic life of the most primitive times, and if they have emerged from barbarism, they have certainly not attained civilisation.

They are divided into tribes, some of which are of ancient origin, but many are of a much more recent date, and some are simply aggregations of groups, as natural as possible, made by the French to facilitate the operations of the *Bureau Arabe*.

Each tribe is commanded by a *Kaid*, whose duty is to exercise surveillance over it, carry out the orders of the French authorities, arrest malefactors, and collect taxes, for which he receives a certain percentage ; he listens to all complaints, and either himself redresses the aggrieved or submits the case to the administrator of his circle. He is responsible for the good order and loyal conduct of his tribe. These Kaids are always nominated by the French, and are usually chosen from the most influential families. Thus, in time of peace, they greatly aid the French authorities, though they are dangerous to a corresponding degree in time of war or insurrection. Attempts have been made to place men of inferior birth, but of approved fidelity, in these posts, but the experiment has never succeeded ; the moment an insurrection breaks out, their power is defied, and whether the great families are in office or not, if they rebel, the tribe is sure to follow them.

The tribes are divided into a greater or less number of *Ferkats* or sections, according to their importance, each of which is administered by a *Sheikh*. These are all under the orders of the Kaid, who has a lieutenant or Khalifa to aid him.

The *Ferkat*, again, is composed of several *Douars*, composed of the tents of a certain number of persons more or less nearly related to each other. The *Ferkat* is a political or artificial group, the *Douar* is essentially a family one.

The union of several tribes is called a *Bach Aghalik*, the *Bach Agha* being the highest native dignity conferred by the French. These, however, are being suppressed as vacancies occur.

Justice is administered among the Arabs by *Cadis*, who have districts containing two to four tribes, and who perform their functions under the surveillance of the *Bureaux Arabes* in military territory, or of the Administrator where civil jurisdiction prevails.

The Arabs are essentially a nomade race, living in tents, which they change from place to place as the pasturage around them is consumed. They are not fond of hard work, and the men at least do not engage in industrial pursuits ; agriculture is the labour they prefer to all other. The theft of a plough is sacrilege, the manufacture of one a pious work.

The nomade existence is not without its advantages among a people so primitive and so filthy in their habits. The moving about their flocks from place to place serves to manure the ground, and prevent its utter exhaustion ; and where men and animals all live together, the constant striking and pitching of their tents conduces to cleanliness and to the destruction of a portion at least of the vermin with which they are infested.

The land tenure in Algeria has hitherto been such as to prevent the purchase of it by intending colonists. It was divided into four categories :—

Beylick ; the undoubted property of the State at the time of the conquest.

Azel ; belonging also to the State, but let to natives from a more or less remote period.

Melk ; freehold, possessed by private persons with regular titles.

Arch or *Sabegha ;* land not subdivided into small holdings, but belonging in common to a tribe. Thus, though a tribe of a hundred people had a thousand acres of land, and each would possess ten, they had no particular ten, and might cultivate their proportion one year in the east and another in the west of the allotment. In many tribes the chiefs of the *Douars* hold in hereditary usufruct a great proportion of the land where they are settled. These allotments are called *Mechtas*, and are subdivided amongst *Khamès*, who, as their name implies, receive as their profit one-fifth of the crop. This collective possession of the soil has the effect of strengthening the tribal bonds under the power of its chief, but it prevents good cultivation or any hope of increased civilisation amongst the Arabs. They cannot be expected to spend more money or labour than is absolutely necessary in tilling lands from which they may be removed next year. They cannot plant trees or build permanent houses, without a certainty of being allowed to enjoy the fruit of their labour.

To remedy this evil, a most important law was passed on the 26th of July 1873, constituting individual property amongst the Arab tribes (it had already existed in Kabylia), and enabling each individual to sell the portion of common land to which he may be personally entitled ; but the application of the law is fraught with numerous difficulties, and it has made but little progress.

The female in Arab society occupies a situation similar to what she fills in all Mohammedan countries ; amongst the rich she is the slave of her lord's pleasure, amongst the poor she is the household drudge, and the manufacturer of almost everything required in daily use.

The national food of the Arabs (and indeed of the Kabyles too, under the name of *scksou*) is *couscous* or *täam*. This is simply the semolina of hard wheat granulated by a peculiar process, which is one of the special accomplishments of the women. It is placed in a perforated dish, and cooked by the steam ascending from another vessel below it, containing water, meat, vegetables, and aromatic plants, which are subsequently eaten with it. Very frequently the dish is eaten without meat, but with an extra allowance of butter, red pepper, tomatoes, etc. Milk is drunk at almost every meal, sometimes fresh, more frequently sour and curdled. In the larger towns, the Arab bread made in the shape of round cake is excellent, but amongst the tribes it is by no means appetising ; it is usually made of half-ground flour, sometimes of vetch, Indian corn, or other grain.

The head of the Arab is shaven except for a tuft of hair at the back, by which he hopes to be drawn into paradise, and is always covered with the *haik*, bound round with cords of camel's hair and falling round the back and sides of his head and under the chin. He wears the white *burnous*, and occasionally a coloured one over it, slippers on his feet, or sometimes high red leather boots, and bare legs.

Moors.—The term Moor, as used at the present day, is one of European invention, and has no Arabic equivalent. It can have no other signification than that of a native of Mauritania, and as such could not properly be applied to the Arabs who overran the country and invaded Spain. The nearest Arabic equivalent to it is *Hadar*, applied to those of Arabic descent who have for generations lived in houses and towns, in contradistinction to the nomades who dwell in tents. In this sense the term Moor is used by the French, and includes all Arabs who lead a settled life, and occupy themselves in commercial pursuits rather than in agriculture. They are generally handsome, with oval pale faces, aquiline noses, and large dark eyes, and have rather an effeminate appearance. In intercourse with strangers they are polite and courteous; and in character, lazy and indolent to excess. They have very little occupation, being principally employed in embroidery, weaving, distilling perfumes, and attending to their bazaars.

The Moor's dress is conspicuous for its bright colours: it consists of a waistcoat and jacket, generally of silk, and ornamented with braid, and the *burnous;* the head, in the case of the younger men, is covered with the fez only, but this is supplemented in the elder by a turban. They wear voluminous trousers—not divided—of linen or of some soft woollen material extending below the knee, and slippers. Their women, when seen out of doors, are attired in a creamy white *haik* reaching below the knee, full white linen trousers fastened at the ankle, and slippers. Their heads and faces are covered, the eyes only being visible.

The Turks and Koulouglis.—The latter is the name by which the children of Turkish fathers and Moorish or slave mothers were known. The greater number of the Turks were sent back by the French on taking possession of Algeria, and their descendants have got mixed up in the general population, so that these races no longer exist in Algeria.

The Jews are said to have established themselves on these shores after the destruction of Jerusalem, but it is more probable that they did so on their banishment from Italy in 1342, and from various other countries during the following thirty years. Under the Turkish government they were permitted the free exercise of their religion, but were exposed to every species of indignity, and arbitrarily condemned to torture and death on the slightest provocation.

They are here much the same as in other parts of the world, the apparent aim of their existence being money-getting. The females, when young, are remarkable for their beauty; but the men, although possessing handsome features, have not a prepossessing expression of countenance.

The elder members of the community still retain the native dress, the women wearing a straight silk gown and silk handkerchief bound tightly round the head, but the rising generation have adopted European costume, since a decree of the Government of the National Defence in 1871 declared them French citizens.

Besides the above other races may be seen in Algiers—amongst them the **Beni M'zab,** a dark-skinned people from the Sahara, south of El-Aghouat. They belong to the **Ibadhi** sect, the most distinguished member of which is the Sultan of Zanzibar. Their women never leave their native oases. They wear an easily-distinguished, sleeveless garment of many colours, and are generally employed as butchers, sellers of fruit, vegetables, charcoal, etc. The **Negroes** are descendants of former slaves; they whitewash houses, and their women are sellers of bread; they are generally dressed in checked blue and white duster-material, and are conspicuous for their ugliness. The **Biskris** come from the neighbourhood of Biskra, and are employed as water-carriers, sweeps, etc.

§ 6. NATIVE LANGUAGES.

The native languages of Algeria are a corrupt form of Arabic, spoken by the Arabs, Moors and Jews ; and a dialect of the Berber used by the Kabyles and Chawia.

Written Arabic is the same everywhere, but the vulgar Arabic of Algeria is a patois contaminated by words and hybrid expressions borrowed from all the languages of Europe, a relic of the now extinct *lingua Franca*, mixed with others of Turkish and Berber origin, and simplified by the elimination of certain of the more complex grammatical rules, such as the dual number, the feminine of verbs and pronouns, etc.

The Kabyle language, though undoubtedly a dialect of Berber, is by no means a pure one ; it is greatly mixed with Arabic, and already many French words have been introduced. It has no written character, and all the literature it possesses is transmitted orally. The Kabyles have also the peculiar habit of employing conventional languages, similar to thieves' slang in England, for the purpose of disguising their conversation in the presence of strangers. Nearly every profession has one peculiar to itself.

§ 7. GENERAL DESCRIPTION OF ALGERIA AND TUNIS.

This portion of North Africa, though still supposed to consist of two separate countries, one a French colony and the other a protected state, may now be treated as a whole, and the time is not far distant when even the nominal frontier will disappear, or at most exist as the limit between two departments of the mother country.

Algeria is bounded on the W. by the Empire of Morocco : it is comprised between long. 2° 20' W. and 8° 35' E. ; and between 37° 5' and 32° 0' N. lat. Its greatest length is about 620 miles ; its greatest breadth, 250 miles ; and its area is calculated to be about 150,000 square miles.

This area, however, is merely a rough approximation to the truth, as the Southern limit of the country has never been defined with any degree of accuracy. The Western boundary was fixed by the treaty with the Emperor of Morocco of the 18th March 1845. The *Oued Kiss*, opposite the *Zaffarine Islands*, was accepted as a starting-point, instead of the *Molouia*, the ancient *Malua* or *Molocath*, which from the remotest antiquity had been considered as the boundary between *Mauritania Cæsariensis* and *Tingitana*, the present Empire of Morocco, and which is only separated from it by 12 kil. of sandy beach. An opportunity was also lost of securing the *Zaffarine Islands*, which were unoccupied at the time of the conquest, and which were taken possession of by Spain only a few hours before a French expedition sent from Oran with a similar object arrived at the spot. The actual French boundary runs from the *Kiss* in a south-easterly direction as far as *Ain Sfissifa*, a little south of the 33d parallel of latitude—a purely imaginary line. The scientific frontier,

§ 7. GENERAL DESCRIPTION OF ALGERIA AND TUNIS

which the French hope one day to attain, would start from the mouth of the *Molouia*, follow the course of that river to the watershed of the country about 33° N. lat., and then continue along the course of the *Oued Gheir*, an important river, till its junction with the *Zouzfana*, a little north of *Igli*, between the 30th and 31st parallels of latitude. The district thus gained would contain the valuable strategic positions of *Oujda* and *Figuig*, and would be within easy distance of the great oasis of *Tafilalet*.

The French Sahara contains the oases of the *Oulad Sidi Cheikh*, the *Ksours*, the *Souf*, and lately the oases of the *Beni M'zab* have been annexed.

Provinces.—Politically Algeria is divided into three provinces or departments—Algiers, Oran and Constantine. The first has 5 arrondissements—Algiers, Milianah, Medea, Orleansville and Tiziouzou. Oran also has 5—Oran, Mostaganem, Tlemçen, Sidi Bel Abbès, and Mascara. Constantine has 6—Constantine, Bône, Philippeville, Bougie, Guelma and Setif.

The **Province of Constantine** forms the eastern part of the colony, from the border of Tunis on the east to the Province of Algiers on the west : it is separated from the latter by a line from Cape Corbelin (Ras Bezerka) between Dellys and Bougie, running southwards, by no means very straight or well defined.

This province contains the scantiest population of the three, but its soil is the most fertile, its minerals the most abundant, its forests the most extensive, and its climate the most varied. In extent it occupies more than half the surface of Algeria, and its native population is much less nomade than that of the two other provinces. The Berbers of the Aurès and Grand Kabylia occupy permanent villages, composed of stone houses, and are extremely attached to their native soils.

The **Province of Oran** occupies the western part of Algeria, and is contiguous to the empire of Morocco. The area of such portions of it as are capable of colonisation, including the Tell and part of the High Plateaux, is about 38,200 square kilomètres, or nearly 9½ millions of acres.

The distinguishing feature of the province is the very narrow extent of the Tell, not exceeding on the average 80 kilomètres.

The hills which run along the coast are not as a rule high. These are the *Dahra*, between Tenès and the Chelif ; *Karkar*, or the Mountain of Lions, between Oran and Arzeu ; *Mediouna*, between Oran and the Tafna. The most important mountain in the interior is *Djebel Amour*, in the Sahara.

The principal rivers are the *Tafna*, the *Macta*, the *Sig*, the *Habra*, the *Mina*, and the *Chelif*.

The country is rich, but much drier than the two other provinces ; consequently good harvests are rarer. It is full of mineral wealth and valuable marbles, and is the chief place whence *Alfa* fibre is exported.

The **natural divisions** of the country also are three, viz. the Tell, a strip of undulating cultivated land extending from the sea-shore to a distance varying from 50 to 100 miles inland ; the High Plateaux ; and the Desert of Sahara. The course of the **Atlas Mountains**, which approach within 30 miles of the city of Algiers, is from S.E. to N.W., their ridges sloping towards the Mediterranean, and enclosing several plains, such as the Metidja, lying between Algiers and Blidah, that of the Chelif, etc. They have a course

§ 7. GENERAL DESCRIPTION OF ALGERIA AND TUNIS

of about 1500 miles, from Cape Nun, on the Atlantic Ocean, to which they give its name, to Cape Bon, in Tunis. In Morocco they rise in some places above the line of perpetual snow, the highest of them being estimated at from 11,000 to 12,000 feet. The Atlas range is not conspicuous for lofty peaks like the Alps, most of their summits being rounded.[1]

The following are the highest points throughout the colony of Algeria:—

Chellia, in the Aurès range	7,611 ft.
Tamghout Lalla Khadidja, Djurdjura range .	7,542 ,,
Djebel Ksel, in the Sahara	6,594 ,,
Djebel Touilet Makna, in Djebel Amour .	6,561 ,,
Kef Sidi Omar, in Ouarsensis . . .	6,500 ,,
Babor, in the Kabylia of Bougie . . .	6,447 ,,
Ta Babort, contiguous to it	6,465 ,,
Toumzait, near Tlemçen	6,018 ,,
Dira, near Aumale	5,934 ,,
Zakkar, near Milianah	5,184 ,,
Edough, near Bône	3,294 ,,

The **hydrographical system** of Algeria is by no means so simple as in other countries, where a system of rivers restores to the sea the water which the sun has taken from it. Here a very small portion of the country is subject to the ordinary laws; in the rest the waters either return to the clouds without passing through the sea, or circulate in vast subterranean lakes.

The watershed of the **Tell** is perfectly regular; the sources of the principal streams are situated high up, either on its southern border or on the first terraces of the High Plateaux, and, in spite of the meanderings, often necessitated by the nature of the ground, they are generally short. The Chelif alone has a length of 244 miles, the next most considerable are the Mafrag and Seybouse, the Oued el-Kebir, the Makta and the Rammel, which during flood-time discolour the water for several miles at sea, and have not the strength in summer to force themselves a passage through the banks of sand accumulated in their estuaries by the currents along the coast.

Alluvial plains of any considerable extent are rare in Algeria; they do not form, as elsewhere, in the estuary of a large river. Parallel to the sea, they stretch between the foot of the mountains and the isolated groups of hills, once probably islands, such as those at La Calle to the north of the plain of Tarf, Edough in the plain of Bône, the Sahel at Algiers, and the mountain of Lions in the plain of Oran. Rivers traverse these without draining them, and any depressions in their surface are occupied by marshes and shallow lakes, either fresh or salt. The lakes of Oubeira and Tonègue near La Calle are sheets of fresh water, as were those of Oued el-Maiz in the plain of Bône, and Lake Halloula in the Metidja, now dry.

The most interesting part of the Tell is the great mountain range inhabited by the **Kabyles**; this may be divided into two very distinct portions, the first comprising the lower part of the Oued es-Sahel, and which may be called the Kabylia of Bougie; the second, the Kabylia of Djurdjura, which bounds the

[1] For altitudes in Algeria see MacCarthy, "L'Année Géographique," 1872, p. 76.

former on the west, and which is separated from it by the range whose majestic peaks, covered with snow during six months in the year, form such conspicuous objects in the landscape seen from Algiers. It extends as far west as the Col des Beni-Aïcha, or Menerville, 34 miles from Algiers.

Both speak the same language, a dialect of Berber, build villages, cultivate the olive and fig trees, and have many customs in common; nevertheless they have a totally different administration. The Kabylia of Bougie, like all the other valleys, has been subject to frequent invasions. The Turks, who substituted their rule for the ancient government of the country, introduced the system of great commandments, and imposed upon the vanquished, hitherto governed by their own customs, the orthodox jurisdiction of the Kadis.

The Kabylia of Djurdjura, bristling with savage and rugged mountains, had never before 1857 abdicated its independence. Entrenched in their villages, perched on the crests of almost inaccessible mountains, its inhabitants saw every attempt at invasion arrested at their feet, in the valleys of the Sebaou and Issers, unable to penetrate their country. The French conquest respected their institutions, which were of a democratic nature; each village, though attached to its tribe by the bonds of a common origin, preserved its entire liberty of action, and formed a sort of political and administrative microcosm. In the village the power lay in the hands of all; the *Djemâa* (assembly) met once a week, and was composed of all men capable of bearing arms. It deliberated under the presidency of an *Amin*, elected every year by itself; it took cognisance of all questions, was sovereign judge, and enforced its own decisions.

Here, as amongst all Berber nations, were developed the institutions of *Sofs* (leagues), which divided each village, each tribe, and even each confederation. The *Sofs* do not represent any political party, like the majority and minority in a European nation. They do not originate in any theoretic ideas, and have not for their object the maintenance or overthrow of any particular form of government. They had their origin in the necessity for protection, and constituted before the conquest a mutual association, destined to cause the rights of an oppressed majority to be respected by a powerful and overbearing minority. The *Sof* lent its aid to such of its members as found themselves the victims of injustice; and if it could not obtain reparation or a peaceful settlement of the dispute, had recourse to force. Civil war broke out, and spread from village to village, and from tribe to tribe, and did not ordinarily stop without the intervention of one of the Marabouts. These are descendants of reputed saints, and owed to their origin and their neutrality an influence which they employed in re-establishing peace.

The French conquest, in substituting a regular power for the irregular action of these parties, and in repressing the appeal to arms, destroyed at a single blow the power of the *Sofs* and the influence of the Marabouts, already discredited by the very fact of the conquest. They had preached the Holy War, and promised victory in the name of the saints interred in their mountains, whose influence was to a great extent the cause of their own prestige. In the day of battle the most ardent of these Marabouts were compelled to flee the infidel invaded with sacrilegious foot their most venerated shrines, their powerlessness was evident, and their influence disappeared. The religious confraternities, and especially that of Sidi Mohammed ben Abd-er-Rahman Bou-Koberain (he who has two tombs), began to exercise the power which the Marabouts had lost. The partisans of Kabyle independence, and the discontented of all classes, habituated to the strife of *Sofs*, and searching a new opening for their energy, rallied round an institution which flattered their pride by making them the equals of the Marabouts, and permitted them to rise to the highest grades despite their ignorance and obscure birth. The Marabouts constituted a caste, an aristocracy, based on the prestige of an extinct power. The order of Sidi-Mohammed, essentially of a levelling character, was admirably adapted to suit the democratic spirit of the Kabyles; it was, moreover, a national order, as the founder was born a century ago in their own mountains. The statutes of the order are cleverly framed to impose upon the brethren (*khouan*) the most absolute obedience, to surround them with mysticism, and to make them the devoted instruments of their chief. Soon the affiliated began to be counted by thousands in both sections of Kabylia, especially in the Oued es-Sahel, where, previous to the insurrection of 1871, dwelt the Sheikh el-Haddad, an old man, eighty-five years of age, almost paralysed, but possessing an unbounded influence over his followers.

This society was the more dangerous to the French, as its members, blindly obedient, could be excited to rebellion in a moment, without allowing the slightest precursory sign to reveal the danger, a result which actually happened during the insurrection of 1871.

That insurrection induced considerable modification in the ancient organisation of the Kabyle tribes, and freed the French from the engagements which they had contracted at the conquest of Kabylia to respect the laws and customs of the people. The base of that organisation was the village, or cluster of villages, which had a sovereign *djemäa*, under the presidency of an *amin*, elected by themselves; the union of several such communes formed the tribe, at the head of which was an *Amin-el-Oumena*, elected by the *amins*. The new organisation destroys the power of the *djemäa* and substitutes an *amin* appointed by the French for one elected by the *djemäa*. It replaces the tribe by the *Section*, composed of several tribes, and places the whole under the civil authorities and the common law.

The region of the **High Plateaux** extends longitudinally from E. to W., and is formed by vast plains separated by parallel ranges of mountains. These terraces increase in height as they recede from the Tell, and again decrease as they approach the Sahara, thus forming a double series of gradients, of which the highest is 3000 or 3300 ft. above the level of the sea, much higher indeed than the summit of the hills which bound it. The spurs or projections from the mountains cut up each of these stages into a series of basins like the Hodna, in which the depressions are occupied by lakes, generally salt, known by the name of *Chotts* or *Sebkas*. This region is subject to alternations of intense cold and extreme heat; rain-water is less copious than in the Tell; instead of sea-breezes, it receives the hot blast of the desert, and it is entirely devoid of trees save on the south side of the high mountain ranges. During seasons of copious rain, however, and in places capable of irrigation, it produces abundant crops of cereals, but otherwise it presents to the weary eye of the traveller an unbroken stretch of stunted scrub and salsolaceous plants, on which browse the sheep and the camel, the wealth of the wandering Arab.

The disposition of the soil, and the existence of veins of permeable rock of a concave form, gave rise to the supposition that there existed subterranean sheets of water in several parts of the High Plateaux. Acting on this theory, artesian wells were sunk; and in many instances these brought to the surface copious supplies of water, which here is verdure and life.

Regular as is the general character of the High Plateaux, they still present several anomalies. On the southern border, the lower terrace, instead of forming a basin, presents here and there slopes, down which the water flows to the north, and thus becomes the source of several rivers in the Tell.

Towards the centre the basin of Sersou, filled of old by a vast lake, the traces of which are plainly visible, is now drained by the river Ouassel, which has forced itself a passage near Bokhari, between the excavated plateau of Sersou and the foot of the last mountains of the Tell. On quitting the High Plateaux this river becomes the Chelif, the most important in Algeria.

Towards the south-east the basin which might have been expected to exist is replaced by the immense mountain of Aurès, of which the central peak attains an altitude of 7611 ft. This protuberance takes the place of a depression; and, instead of a salt lake, we find a mountain covered with cedars and alpine vegetation. On the north the Aurès has only moderate slopes, which convey its waters into the Chotts of the neighbouring plateau. Towards the south it is prolonged almost in a straight line, and descends like a precipitous wall to the Sahara, which stretches at an immense distance below it.

In the west of Algeria the centre of the country bristles with mountains, which adjoin the great snowy **range of Deren.** The southern slopes give rise to immense rivers, amongst them the Oued Gheir, which the French expedition under General Wimpffen reached in the spring of 1870, and which, in their admiration, the soldiers compared to the Meuse.

The Sahara.—Popular belief pictures the Sahara as an immense plain of moving sand, dotted here and there with fertile oases; and the old simile of the panther's skin is still with many an article of faith. A few details are necessary to dispel this poetical but false idea.

The desert in Algeria consists of two very distinct regions, which we shall call the Lower and the Upper Sahara: this a vast depression of sand and clay, stretching on the east as far as the frontier of Tunis; that a rocky plateau, frequently attaining considerable elevation, extending on the west to the borders of Morocco.

The former comprises the Ziban, the Oued Gheir, the Souf, and the Choucha of Ouargla. On the north it is bounded by the mountain-range of Aurès and the foot of the mountains of Hodna and Bou-Kahil; on the east it penetrates into the Regency of Tunis; on the south it rises in a slight and almost insensible slope towards the country of the Touaregs; and on the west

[*Algeria.*]

it stretches in a point along the Oued Mia as far as Golea, after which it turns towards the north along the plateau of the Beni M'zab.

The Oued Gheir, the Souf, N'gouça, and the greater part of the Ziban, have a less elevation than 360 feet; Biskra and Ouargla are hardly higher, while the Chott Melghigh and part of the Oued Gheir are below the level of the sea.

The Chott Melghigh, which occupies the bottom of the depression, is sunk in the gypseous soil, and forms a sheet of water salter than the sea. It is of no great depth, and in summer, owing to evaporation, it is partly covered with a thick and brilliant coating of crystals; so that the eye can scarcely distinguish where the salt terminates and the water begins. The bottom is an abyss of black and viscous mud, emitting an odour of garlic, due possibly to the presence of bromides. Nevertheless it is not without veins of more solid ground, forming natural causeways, on which the people of the country do not hesitate to trust themselves.

The rivers of the Auresic system, essentially torrential in the mountains when confined within steep and narrow gorges, serve to irrigate the oases, where their waters are retained and absorbed by means of dams. That which percolates through these and forms streams lower down their courses is again absorbed by the *Sakias* or canals of irrigation. It is only after the copious rains of winter, and the melting of the snow in the mountains, that their beds are filled, and their waters reach the Chott.

The smaller springs and streams which have their origin at the foot of the mountains are always absorbed by the oases or by the cereals which the inhabitants of the Ziban cultivate wherever a thread of the precious liquid is found.

On the west the Oued Djedi joins the Chott; it rises on the southern slopes of Jebel Amour, fertilises the oases of El-Aghouat, and, skirting the plateaux of the higher Sahara, traverses the lower Sahara from west to east. It is only in the upper part of its course that this Oued is a permanent stream; lower down its water is to a great extent dried up by the solar rays or absorbed by barrages; the rest disappears in the permeable strata, or filters through the sand and flows along the clayey bottom which underlies it.

Like the rivers of the Aurès, but even more rarely than these, its course is only filled by the melting of the snows, or during the heavy rains on the High Plateaux.

The foregoing remarks apply equally to the other rivers which, rising in the eastern part of the higher Sahara, flow towards the region of N'gouça.

In the south the Oued Mia presents always the appearance of a dry watercourse, below the sand of which water flows along an impermeable bed. The same may be said of the Oued Gghaghar, whose source, never yet visited by Europeans, is in the Touareg country.

From time immemorial artesian wells have existed here, and have everywhere spread with their waters life and wealth.

The water, which in the lowest part of the depression is found at a depth of 20 mètres, is, at the edges of the basin, 50, 60, or 100 mètres from the surface of the soil.

Its existence, however, is not only indicated by artesian wells; through-

§ 7. GENERAL DESCRIPTION OF ALGERIA AND TUNIS

out the whole extent of the Oued Gheir, and even to the south of it, depressions are found full of water, which appear to be, as it were, the spiracles of the subterranean lake; they are styled by the natives *bahr* (sea); the French call them *gouffres*.

In the Souf the water circulates close to the surface of the soil, enclosed in a sandy substratum, which is concealed by a bed, more or less thick, of sulphate of lime, crystallised on the upper surface and amorphous in the lower part. One has only to penetrate this layer of gypsum to create a well.

When it is intended to plant a date-grove, the industrious *Souafa* remove the entire crust of gypsum, and plant their palms in the aquiferous sand beneath. Their green summits rise above the plain around, thus forming orchards excavated like ants' nests, sometimes 8 mètres below the level of the ground.

This complicated distribution of water in the lower Sahara gives rise to the different kinds of oases.

Running streams, dammed by barrages and distributed in canals, make the river oases (Ziban).

Water absorbed by permeable strata constitutes (1) the oases with ordinary wells (Oulad Djellal, etc.); (2) oases with artesian wells (Tuggourt, N'gouça, Ouargla, etc.); (3) the excavated oases (Souf).

Sometimes two systems are found united in the same place.

The higher Sahara extends from the western limits of the lower one to within the frontiers of Morocco; to the south it reaches beyond Goleah, and on the north it is bounded by the last chains of the High Plateaux.

It is principally composed of rocky steppes, only the depressions between which are filled with sand.

Towards the east descends almost perpendicularly from north to south a large promontory which rises below El-Aghouat to nearly 2900 ft., and sinks gradually towards Goleah, separated from the plateau of Tademait by a sort of isthmus 1200 ft. high. It is in this plateau that the Oued Mia and its affluents arise, which, in French territory at least, contain only slight infiltrations of water under a sandy bed.

In the centre the rocky plateaux fall rather abruptly, as far as the zone of the *Areg*, or country of sand-hills, occupying a depression, the bottom of which is about 1200 ft. above the sea.

Finally, towards the extreme west, where the chains of the High Plateaux descend lower, the Saharan plateaux also descend farther south, leaving between them numerous valleys.

In each of these three divisions the water-system is different. The eastern promontory, the crests of which are directed towards the west, sends out no spurs towards the zone of the *Areg;* but it is furrowed towards the east by immense ravines, of which the principal bear the names of Oued Ensa and Oued M'zab. Rain seldom falls in the lower part; and the southern *crevasses* are almost always deep ravines, without water or vegetation. Even in the upper part it is only during severe storms, and when more than usually abundant snow has melted on the High Plateaux, that the waters pouring on the Sahara unite in the deep defiles, forming a mighty wave, which during twenty-four or forty-eight hours precipitates itself into the estuaries of the lower Sahara. When this torrent has passed, nothing remains in its dry bed save a few pools where the gazelle drinks, and a slight subterranean percolation which serves to supply the few wells at which the caravans draw water.

These periodical inundations are quite inadequate to supply the Beni M'zab, who have established gardens in the very beds of the great ravines which dominate their seven cities. In vain they treasure up a store in their reservoirs; they are obliged to have recourse to deep wells cut in the rock, which collect the infiltration of water in the calcareous strata.

Above the promontory it is only El-Aghouat and Ain Madhi, situated in a depression at the foot of the mountains, that can utilise almost at all seasons of the year, by means of barrages or dams, the upper waters of the Oued Djedi, which flow from east to west.

In the middle, Brezina and several oases placed at the very foot of the mountain-range can also irrigate their date-groves with running water; but farther south the water flowing along the rocky plateaux encounters the moving sands of the Areg, which arrest its course and cause pools or marshes (*Dhaya*), neither usually very large nor very deep. These little Chotts present the same phenomena as the greater depressions in the lower Sahara; their ancient banks, now quite dry, attesting a very marked decrease in the volume of their waters.

Towards the east, on the other hand, where the mountains in the plateaux rise to a greater height than 2900 ft., and present a vast surface, the ravines are the beds of veritable rivers, which render abundant irrigation possible, and, uniting in two principal streams, form the Oued Messaoud, which descends southwards to an unknown distance.

Such is the upper Algerian Sahara, of which the greatest depression does not descend to within 1300 ft. of the sea, while in the lower one there is not a single point attaining that altitude. In the one the plateau is the prevailing feature, in the other the depression; here rocks abound, there they are entirely absent. As to moving sand, which the Arabs compare to a net, it occupies a sufficiently extensive zone in both regions; but still it does not cover one-third part of the Algerian Sahara.

§ 8. Historical Notice of Algeria and Tunis.

The ancient territorial distribution of the native races in North Africa cannot be traced to a period much anterior to the Romans, as they were for the most part nomades; ancient geographers indeed divide them into certain great masses, such as Lybians, Numidians, Mauri, etc., but the limits of these were very indeterminate, though roughly approximating to the more modern divisions of the country.

The Phœnicians established on the sea-coast numerous cities, some of which were commercial entrepôts, others principalities founded by exiled

§ 8. HISTORICAL NOTICE OF ALGERIA AND TUNIS

members of their community, all, however, finding in commerce an inexhaustible source of riches and prosperity.

The word Africa was at first applied by the Romans to that portion of it with which they were best acquainted, the *Africa Propria*, or *Africa Provincia*, corresponding roughly to the Carthaginian territory erected into a Roman province after the third Punic war, B.C. 146. It was subsequently extended to the whole continent. The territorial subdivision of North Africa from Egypt to the Atlantic varied considerably at different epochs. The most eastern portion, the Cyrenaica, had its limits so clearly defined by nature that it varied little except in its form of government. It remained a kingdom till B.C. 74, when it became a Roman province. Then came the proconsular province of Africa, which included the Syrtica Regio, or that part of the coast from the Syrtis Major (*Gulf of Sidra*) and Syrtis Minor (*Gulf of Gabes*) or Tripolitana and Byzacena, the former representing the modern Tripoli, and the latter, with Zeugitana and the territory of Carthage, corresponding to the modern Regency of Tunis.

Then followed Numidia, corresponding to part of the French province of Constantine contained between the Tusca or *Oued ez-zan* and the Ampsaga or *Oued el-Kebir*.

From Numidia to the Atlantic the country was known generally as Mauritania. About B.C. 46 it was divided into Mauritania Orientalis and Mauritania Occidentalis, separated by the river Molochath (the modern *Moulouia* near the frontier of Morocco). Subsequently, about A.D. 297, into Mauritania Setifensis, from Numidia to Icosium (*Algiers*); Mauritania Cæsariensis, thence to the Molochath, and Mauritania Tingitana; corresponding roughly to the French provinces of Algiers and Oran, and the Empire of Morocco.

The interior region was divided into—

1. Lybia Deserta, comprising Phazania, the country south of the Cyrenaica and Syrtica Regio.
2. Getulia to the south of Numidia and Mauritania.
3. Æthiopia and the Troglodytæ south of all these.

The word Mauritania was derived from its inhabitants, the Maurusii or Mauri, a branch of the great Berber nation, which extended from the Atlantic Ocean to beyond the banks of the Nile. Many conjectures have been made as to their origin. Sallust records that a great horde of Asiatics, led by Hercules, crossed over from Spain, and, on landing, inverted their boats and used them for houses, thus supplying the original model of the Numidian dwelling. Procopius asserts that in his time two pillars existed at Tangiers containing the record, "We fly from the robber Joshua, the son of Nun." The modern word *Zenata*, applied to the people of Berber origin who occupy the region between the desert and the High Plateaux, is merely the Arabic form of the radical from which *Canaanite* is derived. The Arabian geographers are unanimous in ascribing an Eastern origin to this people; but one thing is certain, that at a very early period the Phœnicians formed a number of colonies along the coast, the most important of which was Carthage, which created itself an imperishable name, and long disputed with Rome the government of the world.

Its origin is very obscure, but all the world knows[1] the beautiful fable of Virgil, how Dido or Elissa, daughter of Belus, king of Tyre, escaped from the power of her brother Pygmalion with the treasures for which he had murdered her husband; and, with a band of noble Tyrians who shared her flight, how she touched at Cyprus and carried off eighty maidens to be the wives of her followers, and then landed at a spot on the coast of Africa, near which Tunis and Utica (*the ancient*) were already built, marked out by nature as the site of a mighty city; how she entered into treaty with the natives, and purchased from them as much land as could be covered by a bull's hide, but craftily cut the hide into the thinnest of strips, and so enclosed a space of 22 stadia, on which she built her city, which retained its name of Byrsa (*Bull's hide*); how the city grew by the influx of people from the neighbouring country and by the adhesion of older Phœnician colonies, especially Utica; how its prosperity excited the envy of Hiarbus, king of the Lybians, who offered Dido the choice of war or marriage, and how to avoid both alternatives she stabbed herself on a funeral pyre which she had erected to the honour of her husband's memory.

The introduction of Æneas into the story is a poetic license on the part of Virgil, unwarranted by any authority in the original legend from which he derived his information. The real derivation of the word Byrsa is from the Phœnician word *Bozra*, a fortress; and Carthage was merely one, though the principal one, of many colonies founded by the Phœnicians, which itself subsequently sent out other colonies westwards, and spread in every direction the influence of its own high civilisation and commercial enterprise.

It is hopeless in such a work as this to attempt a detailed history of Carthage and the Carthaginians, to follow Hanno (B.C. 446) in his voyage to the Gulf of Guinea, Hamilcar (B.C. 481) in his disastrous expedition to Sicily, or the invasion of Africa by Agathocles (B.C. 310-306).

The **First Punic War** was a contest between Carthage and Rome for the possession of Sicily, and though virtually decided by the fall of Agrigentum (B.C. 262), the great resources of Carthage prolonged it twenty-three years later. It cost Carthage not only Sicily itself, but the dominion of the sea, and placed Rome more on an equality with her as a naval power.

The **Second Punic War** lasted from B.C. 218 to 201, and resulted in the utter prostration of Carthage, the loss of her fleets and of her possessions out of Africa.

A new and important State sprang up on the western confines of Carthage under Roman auspices, governed by Masinissa, ever ready to pick a quarrel with her, and give Rome a pretext for her destruction.

Masinissa was son of Gala, king of the Massylians, the easternmost of the two great tribes into which the Numidia of that day was divided. At the instigation of Carthage, his father had declared war on Syphax, king of the neighbouring tribe of Masæssylians, who had lately entered into an alliance with Rome. Masinissa was appointed by his father to command the invading

---

[1] As the traveller does not generally carry with him a library of reference, the writer has not hesitated in this compilation to borrow largely from Gibbon, Smith, and other standard authorities.

§ 8. HISTORICAL NOTICE OF ALGERIA AND TUNIS

force, with which he totally defeated Syphax. In B.C. 212 Masinissa was in Spain supporting the Carthaginians with a body of Numidian horse, and he shared in the defeat of Hasdrubal by Scipio at Silpia in B.C. 209.

After that battle he went over to the Romans, actuated, it is said, by resentment against Hasdrubal, who having first betrothed to him his beautiful daughter Sophonisba, subsequently bestowed her hand upon Syphax, who henceforth became a staunch ally of the Carthaginians.

After the death of Gala, and during the absence of Masinissa, the Massylian kingdom had become a prey to civil dissensions, in which, however, Syphax at first took little part; he was even disposed to acquiesce in the elevation of his old rival Masinissa to the throne, had not Hasdrubal warned him of the danger of such a course. But he yielded to the suggestion of the Carthaginian general, and assembled a large army, with which he invaded the territories of Masinissa, defeated him in a pitched battle, made himself master of the whole country, and established himself at the capital of Numidia, Cirta, the modern Constantine.

Masinissa now commenced a predatory warfare against his rival, in which he gained occasional advantages, and was still able to maintain himself in the field until the landing of Scipio in Africa, B.C. 204. Syphax supported Hasdrubal with an army of 50,000 foot and 10,000 horse, with which he assisted at the siege of Utica. The whole of the Numidian and Carthaginian armies, however, were overthrown and destroyed by the Roman general, and Syphax himself and a few followers barely succeeded in escaping to Numidia, where, shortly afterwards, he fell into the hands of the Romans, and subsequently graced the triumph of his conqueror previous to ending his days in prison.

Masinissa, who had allied himself to Scipio, and had been instrumental in defeating his rival, obtained possession both of Cirta and Sophonisba. Scipio, however, demanded her as a prisoner of the Roman senate, whereupon Masinissa sent her a cup of poison, which she at once drank, merely remarking that she would have died with more honour had she not wedded at her funeral.

To console Masinissa for his loss, and to recompense him for his services, Scipio conferred on him the title and insignia of royalty, and the possession of his hereditary dominions, which honours were immediately ratified by the senate.

About B.C. 203 Hannibal returned to Africa after his extraordinary campaign of fifteen years in Italy. He landed at Leptis, whence he proceeded to Hadrumetum (*Susa*). Masinissa hastened to the support of his benefactor Scipio, and a decisive action was fought at a place called Naragara, not far from the city of Zama. Hannibal displayed all the qualities of a consummate general, but his elephants, of which he had great numbers, were rendered useless by the skilful management of Scipio, and the battle ended in his complete defeat; he himself with difficulty escaped the pursuit of Masinissa, and retired to Hadrumetum.

All hope of resistance was now at an end, and he was one of the first to urge the necessity for peace. A treaty was concluded by which he saw the whole purpose of his life frustrated, and Carthage effectually humbled before her irresistible rival. Even his wise administration could not save her; he was denounced by the opposite faction, proscribed by Rome, and forced to fly to the court of Antiochus the Great, in Armenia, in B.C. 195, whereupon his party became extinct, and the influence of Rome supreme, even within the State.

Third Punic War.—Half a century passed without any further rupture between the two republics, but the elder Cato never ceased to denounce Carthage, and to represent her destruction as necessary to the permanence of the Roman power. His inveterate hatred proved triumphant, and war was declared. The Carthaginians were divided by factions and intestine strife, and in no condition to withstand the invaders. Still, for a time, Carthage held out. But when (B.C. 146) Emelianus Scipio, the second Africanus, came to direct the siege, operations were conducted with renewed vigour. Little by little the vast city fell into his hands, till at last only the great temple of Esculapius remained to be taken. It was defended by Asdrubal, with whom were about 900 followers. Asdrubal in the basest manner purchased personal safety by deserting his post and surrendering himself to Scipio. But his wife and children, and the greater number of the defenders, scornfully refused to follow his example, and preferred setting fire to the building and perishing in the flames.

Scipio destroyed the ports and the fortifications of Carthage; some of the public buildings were burned by the inhabitants themselves; but it is probable that the destruction of the city was more apparent than real, and that, despite of the heavy curses pronounced on any who might attempt to rebuild it, it began to rise, to a certain extent, from its ruins, even before the time of the Gracchi (B.C. 116).

The whole coast of Africa, however, from Egypt to the Atlantic, became subject to the Romans. Carthage was stripped of her glory, and many of her inhabitants were driven elsewhere. The country generally fell back under the rule of its native governors, and Masinissa made Cirta his royal residence. He died in B.C. 148, leaving his throne to his son Micipsa.

In B.C. 116 a **Roman Colony** was established at Carthage by Caius Gracchus. It continued in a languishing condition till the time of Julius Cæsar and Augustus, when the city was rebuilt under the name of Colonia Carthago, and it continued the first city in Africa till a comparatively modern period. As the senate abstained from all endeavours to extend its conquests in Africa, the country enjoyed uninterrupted peace till the death of Micipsa in B.C. 118. He divided the kingdom between his two sons, Adherbal and Hiempsal, and his nephew Jugurtha. The last had already distinguished himself in Spain, under Scipio Africanus Minor, and was an ally of Rome; but on his having deposed and assassinated both his cousins contrary to the orders of the Senate, they declared war against him, B.C. 111. Albinus was first sent over to Africa, but he was probably bribed, and certainly defeated, by Jugurtha, at Suthul, and compelled to evacuate Numidia.

Q. Cæcilius Metellus was sent to succeed him as proconsul, B.C. 109. He was a man of stainless integrity and high talents; but though he compelled

Jugurtha to deliver up a considerable quantity of treasure, arms, horses and elephants, he was powerless to obtain possession of his person. He followed him to Thala, which stronghold he succeeded in taking after a siege of forty days; but Jugurtha succeeded in effecting his escape with part of his treasure, while the Roman deserters in his army, with the remainder of it, shut themselves in the palace, which they set on fire, and perished in the flames.

Marius, the legate of Metellus, and chief leader of the popular party in Rome, was elected consul in B.C. 107, and charged with the conduct of the war against Jugurtha. In the following year (B.C. 106) Jugurtha was surrendered to him by the treachery of Bocchus, king of Mauritania, and having subsequently adorned his conqueror's triumph, he was thrust into prison, where he died of starvation on the sixth day.

After this the crown of Numidia was given to Juba, son of Hiempsal, whose reign was short and troubled. Africa had now become the stronghold of the Pompeian faction. Pompey indeed was no more; but his two sons were here, Scipio, his father-in-law, Cato, Labienus, Afranius, and other devoted adherents, who all united with Juba in continuing the conflict in Barbary.

Cæsar himself came to Africa for the purpose of finally subduing the Pompeian faction. His talents and good fortune produced their wonted effect. He landed at Hadrumetum (*Susa*) with a force of only 3000 foot and 150 horse. There he was joined by P. Sittius, a former accomplice of Cataline, who was well acquainted with the country and the native tribes. Having failed to take this city, he marched to Ruspina (*Monastir*), and shortly after (B.C. 47) ensued the great and decisive battle of Thapsus (*Ras Dimas*), in which the Pompeian party was utterly defeated, with a loss of 10,000 men. Cæsar then took Utica, where Cato, who commanded it, committed suicide. Scipio also killed himself. Afranius was killed by Cæsar's soldiers. Labienus, Varus, and the two sons of Pompey escaped into Spain. King Juba set out for Zama with his friend Petreius. There he had collected all his household and treasures, and hoped to perish with them; but, being refused admittance, he and Petreius agreed to fight together, so that one at least might fall with honour. Petreius was quickly killed, and Juba, having in vain essayed to make away with himself, got a slave to despatch him.

Bocchus and Bogud, kings of Mauritania, who had alternately fought under the banner of the two great rivals, also lost their lives, and their dominions, and thus the whole of North Africa fell into the power, and became an integral portion, of the Roman empire.

Numidia was placed (B.C. 46) under the government of Sallust, who plundered the country in a merciless manner to enrich both himself and his patron, but who did good work for posterity by collecting materials for his celebrated history of the Jugurthine wars. Cirta, the capital, was made a colony to recompense the partisans of Publius Sittius, who had rendered Cæsar such important services, and it was named Cirta Sittianorum or Cirta Julia, which names it retained until the beginning of the 4th century.

But though Africa was thus reduced to the condition of a Roman province, the emperor knew better than to confide the government of these turbulent countries entirely to Roman officers.

The young Juba had been carefully educated at Rome, where he attained a high literary reputation. He is frequently cited by Pliny, who describes him as more memorable for his erudition than for the crown he wore. Plutarch also calls him the greatest historian amongst kings.

In the year B.C. 26 Augustus, wishing to give to the people of the late monarch a sovereign of their own race, fixed upon this son of Juba. He married him to Selene, daughter of Anthony and Cleopatra, and restored to him the western portion of his father's dominions, trusting to his thorough Roman education to secure his submission, and on the prestige of his race and name to win the affections of the Numidian races, and to hasten their fusion with the conquering nation.

He removed his capital to the ancient Phœnician city of Iol, to which he gave the name of Julia Cæsarea.

He died in A.D. 19, leaving a son, Ptolemy, the last independent prince of Mauritania, who was far from sharing the high qualities of his father.

His reign was characterised by debauchery and misgovernment, and the Mauritanians were not slow to rise in revolt under the leadership of Tacfarinus. This war lasted for seven years, shortly after which Tiberius died, and was succeeded by Caligula, who summoned Ptolemy to Rome, and, after having received him with great honour, caused him to be killed, as he thought that the splendour of his attire excited unduly the attention of the spectators. It is more likely that he desired to appropriate the wealth that Ptolemy was known to have accumulated. This murder was followed by a serious revolution in Mauritania, which lasted several years.

The whole country, which heretofore had comprised sundry kingdoms, states, and principalities, henceforth became provinces of the Roman Empire governed by prætors and proconsuls, who seemed to have farmed it very much for their own benefit, and to have submitted the inhabitants to the utmost amount of exaction which they were able to bear.

Sometimes their complaints reached the senate, as in the case of the proconsul Marius Priscus and his lieutenant Hostilius Firminus, in the reign of Trajan, who were prosecuted before the Emperor himself by Tacitus and Pliny the younger, and condemned to exile.

The next 300 years were the most prosperous in the history of North Africa, and it is to this epoch that most of the splendid remains still existing in Algeria and Tunis belong. The African provinces were most important to the empire, which drew from them its richest stores, and had little to pay for defence. The details, however, which have reached us of this epoch are of the most meagre description. Insurrections were of frequent occurrence, and the peace of the country was only the more troubled by the **Introduction of Christianity**, the lawless and hot-blooded natives ranging themselves on the side of the various sects, and constantly resorting to violence to maintain their views. Thus, though they contributed some shining names to the army of martyrs, they helped far more to swell the bands of the persecutors.

One of the insurrections amongst the native tribes was suppressed by Hadrian in person (122) when he came to visit this portion of his dominions. He made a second visit to Africa three years later (125), when he bestowed

§ 8. HISTORICAL NOTICE OF ALGERIA AND TUNIS

many important benefits on the province, such as the aqueduct of Carthage, and the great road thence to Theveste.

The Moors continued to trouble the public peace in the reign of Antoninus, who drove them into the Atlas, and compelled them to sue for peace (138). But they broke out once more under Marcus Aurelius, and actually pushed their incursions across the Mediterranean into Spain (170).

On the accession of Septimius Severus (173), himself an African, a native of Leptis, he sent troops over to prevent his rival Pescennius Niger from taking possession of the proconsular province. Macrinus, who attained the purple by the murder of Caracalla (217), was a native of Mauritania Cæsariensis. Elagabalus, who succeeded him (221), was a son of Sextus Varius Marcellus, formerly governor of Numidia, and commandant of the Third Legion, Augusta, at Lambessa. It appears as if Africa had the privilege at this time of conferring the purple, if not on its actual children, at least on those who made it the country of their adoption. The case of the Gordians offered a striking example of this.

Gordian the elder, who in 229 had been the colleague of Alexander Severus in his third consulate, was sent in the following year (230) by the Senate as proconsul to Africa, and his son was subsequently appointed, by the same body, his lieutenant. Several years passed in peace under his government, when the murder of Alexander Severus (235) and the accession of the brutal Maximinus completely changed the aspect of the country.

A more rigorous procurator sent by him was killed by the Africans, who compelled Gordianus to accept the purple, which he did at Thysdrus in February 238, he being then more than 80 years of age. His son was also declared emperor conjointly with him, and as soon as they had appeased the first tumult of election, they removed their court to Carthage, and sent a deputation to Rome to solicit the approbation of the senate. This body warmly espoused their cause, but before their confirmation was known in Africa the Gordians were no more.

Capelianus, governor of Mauritania, with a small force of veterans, and a great host of barbarians, marched upon Carthage. The younger Gordian sallied out to meet him; but his forces were quite undisciplined, and his valour only served to obtain for him an honourable death on the field of battle. His aged father, whose reign had not exceeded 36 days, put himself to death on the first news of the defeat (March 238), whereupon Carthage opened its gates to the conqueror. The death of Maximin took place in the same year. Maximus and Balbinus were very soon after slain by the soldiery, and the grandson of the aged Gordian was carried to the camp, and saluted as Emperor. He in his turn was assassinated by his army in Mesopotamia before he had attained the age of 19 years, in March 244.

Gibbon observes: "While the Roman Empire was invaded by open violence or undermined by slow decay, a pure and humble religion gently insinuated itself into the minds of men; grew up in silence and obscurity, derived new vigour from opposition, and finally erected the triumphant banner of the Cross on the ruins of the Capitol."

Nothing is certainly known of the **African Church** till the end of the 2d century. The 3d century, however, was its time of greatest trial and glory. Its members seemed endowed with the greatest fervour and devotion, and the most extravagant honour was attached to the outward acts of martyrdom and confessorship.

The names of 580 sees between Cyrene and the Atlantic have been handed down to us by ecclesiastical historians. But its greatest glory is to have produced three men, Tertullian in the 2d century, Cyprian in the 3d, and Augustine in the 4th.

The most celebrated martyr of the African Church was Cyprian, Bishop of Carthage, who was beheaded by order of the proconsul Galerius in 257.

In the year 296, under the government of Diocletian, Maximian, Galerius, and Constantius, the whole of Africa from the Nile to the Atlas was in arms. A confederacy of five Moorish nations issued from their deserts to invade the peaceful provinces. Maximian, in whose special charge Africa was, hastened to the scene of insurrection, and the progress of his arms was rapid and decisive. He vanquished the fiercest barbarians of Mauritania, and removed them from their mountains, the reputed strength of which had inspired them with a lawless confidence.

In the early part of the reign of Constantine arose the schism of the Donatists, which, though springing from small beginnings, grievously afflicted both Church and State for upwards of a century.

Mensurius, Bishop of Carthage, dying in 311, the greater part of the clergy and people chose in his place the Archdeacon Cæcilianus, who, without waiting for the Numidian bishops, was at once consecrated by those of Africa alone. The Numidian bishops, who had always been present at the consecration of a bishop of Carthage, were highly offended at being excluded from the ceremony, and summoned Cæcilianus to appear before them to answer for his conduct. On his refusal, they held a council, declared him unworthy of the episcopal dignity, and chose Majorinus, his deacon, as his successor in office.

The most violent of these Numidian bishops was Donatus, of Casæ Nigræ, from whom some have supposed that the whole faction was named; but there was another prelate of the same name, who succeeded Majorinus at Carthage, and received from his sect the name of Donatus the Great: hence it has been a question from which of these the name was derived.

The controversy spread rapidly through all the provinces of North Africa, which entered so zealously into the ecclesiastical war that in most cities there were two bishops, one at the head of Cæcilianus's party, and the other acknowledged by the followers of Majorinus.

The Donatists brought this controversy before the Emperor Constantine in 313. After three separate inquiries, the case was given against them, and the emperor deprived the Donatists of their churches, and sent their seditious bishops into banishment. They, however, resisted his decree, and retired in large numbers to the Atlas Mountains. In 348 they defeated an army sent for their forcible conversion, and remained for a century the scourge of the neighbouring provinces, being urged by frantic fanaticism to constant revolts and ravages.

In 326, when the whole empire was united under the sceptre of Constantine, that monarch constituted four prætorial prefectures, and Africa was comprised, with Italy and the intermediate islands, as one of these great territorial divisions. In the distribution which he made of his empire in 335, Africa was given to Constans, together with Italy and Illyria.

Valentinian succeeded to the empire in 364, and apportioned the East to his brother Valens, reserving the West to himself. Africa was at this time in a deplorable condition of anarchy, aggravated by the feebleness and rapacity of its governor, the Count Romanus. Leptis and Tripoli were sacked by the Asturians, and Ruricius, the governor of the latter city, was executed on a false charge at Setifis.

The insurrection of Firmus, chief of one of the most influential tribes of the Mauri, caused the emperor to despatch Count Theodosius for its repression in 369. Romanus was sent in disgrace to Rome, but it was not till after a long and harassing series of campaigns that Firmus, driven to extremity, committed suicide, and Theodosius returned in triumph to Setifis.

On the death of Valentinian, on the 17th November 375, the sceptre of the West remained in the hands of his son Gratian, with whom his brother Valentinian II. was associated as colleague. Africa was apportioned to the latter, a child of four years of age. Maximus obtained the throne by putting Gratian to death in 383, and in 388 was recognised in Africa, which he exhausted by his exactions. Theodosius, who had succeeded Valens in the East, put him to death, and eventually reunited the whole empire under his sceptre, in which condition it remained till his death in 395, when it was divided between his two sons, of whom the younger one, Honorius, became the Emperor of the West, and of Africa, under the tutelage of the celebrated Vandal captain, Stilicho.

At this time Gildon was military governor of Africa, which had groaned under his yoke for twelve years; not daring to declare himself actually independent, he attempted to effect the same result by placing himself under the protection of the Empire of the East (397); but Stilicho was not of a character to suffer this disguised defection, and having in his employ an irreconcilable enemy of Gildon in his brother Mascezel, whose children the former had recently put to death, he entrusted to him the command of a body of troops, which landed in Africa, attacked Gildon between Theveste (*Tebessa*) and Ammaedara (*Hydra*), and utterly defeated him. Gildon, abandoned by his followers, embarked on board a vessel to seek a refuge in the East, but being driven by contrary winds into the harbour of Tabarca, he was taken prisoner, and put an end to his life by hanging himself in 398.

Africa returned to its allegiance to Honorius, and the post which Gildon had occupied of *Magister utriusque militiæ per Africum* was suppressed, and a new system of separate civil and military government was organised.

But the period was passed when administrative reforms could have any effect, and the country, weakened by so many disturbances between opposing sects and races, became an easy prey to the enemies now pressing the Roman Empire on every side. The opportunity for invasion was given during the minority of Valentinian III. through the jealousy of the two great pillars of the State, Ætius and Boniface. The former, enraged at his rival being appointed governor of Africa, brought false charges of disloyalty against him, which at last drove Boniface into the very acts of treason of which he had at first been unjustly accused. He called to his assistance **Genseric, king of the Vandals** in Spain, who landed in Africa A.D. 429, and was speedily joined by troops of native Moors and the wild bands of the Donatists. With these formidable allies he marched through the country, devastating it on every side. In spite of the late repentance of Boniface, he seized the six Roman provinces one after another, and in 439 Carthage, which had been again restored to the position of the second city of the West, fell into his hands.

Genseric now commenced to consolidate his power in Africa. In order to prevent the Romans from attaining any footing in the country he destroyed nearly all the fortresses which they had built. Born a Catholic, he embraced the Arian heresy, and persecuted his former brethren with all the malignant zeal of an apostate, and he gave, by his maritime expeditions, a new turn to the wild spirit of his people, who were the earliest predecessors of those pirates and corsairs that were the scourge of the Mediterranean before the French conquest.

Procopius, the historian of Justinian's wars against the Vandals, relates of Genseric that his orders to his steersmen were: "Turn your sail to the wind, and it will lead us against the objects of God's anger." He ravaged the coasts of Sicily and Italy, and in A.D. 455 enjoyed a fourteen days' sack of Rome, bringing back immense treasures and 60,000 prisoners.

Amongst these treasures were the golden candlesticks and the holy table of the temple, brought to Rome by Titus; these were afterwards rescued by Belisarius, taken to Constantinople, and sent by Justinian to the Christian Church at Jerusalem, after which there is no record of their fate.

In 476, after a vain attempt to re-conquer the African provinces, the Eastern Empire was obliged also to humble itself before the Vandals, by securing to them in a treaty Sardinia, Corsica, the Balearic Islands and Sicily.

Genseric died A.D. 477; and under his successors the rough Northmen fell into the luxurious habits of the Romans they had conquered, and the **Byzantine Empire** took advantage of the first pretext for a fresh invasion. This was offered in the reign of Justinian, when Gilimer, having deposed his relative Hilderik, assumed the crown of Africa. A large fleet and army were sent from Constantinople under command of Belisarius, who landed at Carthage in A.D. 533. He completely routed the Vandal forces on the first encounter, and compelled their sovereign to flee for refuge to Numidia. For a time Gilimer retrenched himself in Mons Papua (*Edough*), near Bône, but he was soon compelled to surrender, and was carried by his conqueror to Constantinople, near which he remained in honourable retirement for the remainder of his life. Belisarius was succeeded in Africa by the most illustrious of his generals, the eunuch Solomon, who restored all the most important strongholds, and after a short and brilliant career was killed before the walls of Tebessa in a fruitless endeavour to repress an insurrection of the warlike Berber hordes of that neighbourhood. The Vandal power was destroyed, but

§ 8. HISTORICAL NOTICE OF ALGERIA AND TUNIS

that of the Byzantines was never thoroughly established; it rested not on its own strength but on the weakness of its enemies. The soldiers of the lower empire held, it is true, the towns on the coast and many important fortresses, but the fertile plains were in the hands of the native races, and in many places became desert in consequence of the tremendous decrease in the population caused by successive wars.

In the next century the country suffered invasion from a new quarter.

In the twenty-seventh year of the Hedjira (A.D. 647) the Khalif Othman determined to effect the conquest of Africa, and on the arrival of the Arab army in Egypt a detachment was sent on to Tripoli. The Patrician Gregorius was at this time governor of Africa. He had been originally appointed by Heraclius, Emperor of the East, whose father had held the same office, and who himself had started from Africa on the expedition which resulted in the overthrow of the Emperor Phocas and his own elevation to the purple. Gregorius subsequently revolted from the Byzantine Empire, and by the aid of the native Africans made himself independent sovereign of the province.

Ibn Khaldoun says that his authority extended from Tripoli to Tangiers, and that he made Suffetula (*Sbeitla*) his capital.

The command of the expedition was given to the brother of the Khalifa, Abdulla Ibn Säad, under whose orders were placed the *élite* of the Arab troops, to whom were added 20,000 Egyptians. The number of the whole force did not certainly exceed 40,000 men. On entering the country occupied by the Romans, the Arab general sent on a detachment to Tripoli commanded by Ez-Zohri. On their arrival before the city they found it too strong to be carried by assault, and they continued their march to Gabes.

A message was sent to Gregorius offering him the usual conditions—to embrace Islamism or to accept the payment of tribute, both of which he indignantly refused. The invaders continued their march till they met the Byzantine army on the plain of *Acouba*, situated about a day and a night's march from Sbeitla.

The army of Gregorius is said to have numbered 120,000 men, but this immense multitude was probably composed of naked and disorderly Moors or Africans, amongst whom the regular bands of the empire must have been nearly lost.

For several days the two armies were engaged from dawn of day till the hour of noon, when fatigue and the excessive heat obliged them to seek shelter in their respective camps.

The daughter of Gregorius, a maiden of incomparable beauty, fought by her father's side; and her hand, with 100,000 dinars, was offered to whomsoever should slay Abdulla Ibn Säad. The latter retaliated by offering the daughter of Gregorius and 100,000 dinars to any one who would slay the Christian prince, her father. The combatants had been in the habit of discontinuing the battle every day at noon, but on one occasion the Mohammedan leader, having kept a considerable portion of his troops concealed and in reserve, recommenced the action with these at mid-day, and utterly defeated the Christian force. Gregorius and a vast number of his followers were killed, the camp was pillaged, and the beautiful daughter of the prince was captured and allotted to Ibn ez-Zobeir, who had slain her father.

Shortly afterwards Ibn Säad and his followers returned to the East laden with spoil; their invasion had been a purely military one, and they were unencumbered either with women or cattle.

In 665 Moaouia ben el-Hodaidj brought another army from the East, and on this occasion the Mohammedans retained what they again conquered, and the province of *Ifrikia* was formed and placed under the command of Okba bin Nafa. The Moors and the Berbers adopted without trouble the name and religion of the Arabs; and fifty years afterwards a Mussulman governor reported that there was no longer cause to raise the tax imposed on Christian subjects. Thus was swept away the African Church, which had been adorned by the names of Augustine, Tertullian, and Cyprian.

In the reign of the caliph Walid, A.D. 711, on the invitation of Count Julian, governor of Ceuta, and the small part of the country held by the Visigoths of Spain, the Arabs advanced farther west, and the valiant General Tarick, landing at Gibraltar (*Djebel Tarick*), carried the Crescent into Europe. Multitudes of the Moors followed the Arabs into Spain, and the Europeans gave the African name to their Asiatic conquerors.

During the next century the provinces of Africa were under the rule of Emirs appointed by the caliphs. They made their capital at Kairouan in Tunis, and were constantly employed in struggles with the Arab governors and Berber chieftains who ruled under them. In 800 hereditary power was conferred by Haroun er-Rashid on Ibrahim, son of Aghlab, and eleven of his descendants reigned after him, till in 910 a powerful rival rose among the Berbers who inhabited the province of Constantine. This was Abou Mohammed Obeid-Allah, who claimed to be a descendant of Fatima, daughter of the Prophet, and, surrounded by mystery and marvellous legends, he soon overthrew the Aghlabites; and his successors, pushing their conquests farther east, established the dynasty of the Fatimite caliphs at Cairo. In 944 Ziri, governor of Aschir, one of the provinces of Central Mogreb, built the town of Algiers; and the Fatimite caliph assisted him to establish an hereditary throne for his race, which ruled until Rodger, king of Sicily, took Tripoli from Hassan Ben Ali, and the dynasty of the Zirites came to an end. The Hammadites, a branch of the same family, held the province of Constantine; and the Moravides, or *Marabatin*, a tribe of military saints from the south, seized Oran and invaded Spain, 1055.

About this time occurred **the great Arab Immigration**. It was no brilliant and ephemeral conquest, like that of Sidi Okba: the land was overrun by a foreign people, who speedily absorbed the Berber nation or drove the remains of it into the mountains. The tribes of Hillal and Soleim had inhabited the deserts of the Hedjaz, where they existed as much by brigandage as by the produce of their flocks. When the Fatimites undertook the conquest of Syria, they encountered the most determined resistance from these tribes. Subsequently El-Aziz had them banished to Upper Egypt, whence they soon found their way into, and overspread the whole country between Egypt and the Atlantic. Ibn Khaldoun, speaking of these nomades, likens them to a cloud of locusts, destroying everything over which they passed. Their lawless character soon caused them to be expelled from all the great centres of habitation, whereupon they took to the country, where their descendants exist in the same nomade condition at the present day.

The Moravides of the west were displaced by the Almoahades (*El-Moahidin*, those who attest the unity of God), another sect of warriors who arose in the mountains of Morocco, conquered the Hammadites in 1153, and drove the Sicilians from Tripoli in 1160. The Almoahades remained in power till 1270, their capital being Tlemçen ; they were then overthrown by the Beni-Zian, a desert tribe, who in a short time obtained possession of the whole of Central Moghreb, with the exception of the larger coast towns, which succeeded in maintaining themselves as independent powers.

One of the most important of these was **Algiers**, built on the site of the ancient town of *Icosium*. This name does not often occur in history. Pliny, however, mentions that the Emperor Vespasian created it a *Latin* city,—a title somewhat higher than Italian and less than Roman.

During the Christian epoch mention is made of a Donatist Bishop of Icosium, Crescens, in 411, and of another, Laurentius, in 419, the latter of whom was one of the three legates from Mauritania Cæsariensis sent to the Council of Carthage. Nevertheless, it was a city of no great importance, probably a mere station between the more considerable cities of Iol and Rusgunia.

In the tenth century of the Christian era Bologguin, son of Ziri, was authorised by his father to found three towns, viz. Milianah, Lemdia (now Medeah), and *El-Djezair Beni-Mezghanna* (meaning "The Islands of the Children of Mezghanna"), abbreviated to *El-Djezair* (Algiers), which last was founded in the year 944.

In 1067 El-Bekri mentions it as then containing many splendid monuments of antiquity, some of which were brought to light in digging the foundations of the modern city ; but scarcely anything, with the exception of a few inscribed stones, has been preserved : one of these, however, bears the important word *Icositanorum*.

Almost since the foundation of Algiers an uneasy feeling existed regarding the part she was destined to play in the world's history. The Spaniards were seriously occupied in attempting to drive the Moors from their own country, but as soon as they became aware of the rising importance of this city (in 1302), they despatched four vessels to reconnoitre it ; finding it simply a fortified enclosure, without any commerce, they contented themselves with taking possession of a small island in front of the harbour, subsequently called the *Peñon* or *Bordj el-fanal*. During the next eighteen years commerce began to spring up, and the Spaniards themselves were well content to find a market at their doors whence they could draw their supplies.

In 1342 the Jews were expelled from **Italy**, in 1380 from Holland, and from many other countries about the same period ; it is possible that they contributed to increase the population, and to extend the trade of the infant city.

After the expulsion of the Moors from Spain (1505), they sought an asylum on the coast of Africa, but they could not long remain there in peace, and very soon adopted the profession of pirates, seeking thus to harass their hereditary enemies and ruin their commerce. To stop their depredations Ferdinand V. prepared a descent on the coast of Africa. On the 15th of September 1505 Don Diego of Cordova took possession of Mersa el-Kebir, and four years later, on the 18th of May 1509, the Cardinal Ximenes, who had instigated Ferdinand to undertake the war, came in person to direct the siege, and take possession of the town of Oran. The king himself lacked funds for the enterprise; but these were supplied by the Cardinal; and the expedition, in consequence, gained the name of the "Crusade of Ximenes de Cisneros," and was regarded as a holy war, all who fought in it having indulgence from certain fast days for the remainder of their lives. After the capture of Oran, Cardinal Ximenes charged Don Pedro Navarro, who had rendered important services during the expedition, to take possession of several ports on the littoral which had been in the habit of welcoming and protecting the Moorish pirates. On the 1st of January 1510 he set sail for Bougie, which he took without much difficulty. Dellys, Mostaganem, and Tlemçen, not being in a condition to offer any serious resistance, became tributary to Spain.

Algiers also consented to pay an annual tribute, and to promise that corsairs would not be permitted to enter the harbour or dispose of their plunder in the town. To ensure these conditions he built a fort on the Peñon, part of which still exists, and serves as base to the lighthouse.

About this time (1510) commenced the remarkable career of the brothers Barbarossa, as they are usually styled by Europeans, but not, as is supposed, from the red colour of their beard; the word is merely a corruption of the Turkish name of the elder brother **Baba-Aroudj**, who with **Kheir-ed-din**, were sons of Yakoot Reis, captain of a galley belonging to the island of Mytelene; according to others of a potter there. They associated themselves with a number of other restless spirits, and soon found themselves at the head of a piratical fleet, consisting of twelve galleys and many other smaller vessels, with which they came to seek their fortune on the coast of Barbary.

On entering Tunis with a cargo of plunder and slaves, they made magnificent presents to the reigning prince Mulaï Mohammed, of the dynasty of Beni Hafes, and obtained permission to establish their headquarters in his dominions.

As we have said, the town of Bougie was at this time occupied by the Spaniards, and one of their first exploits was to try to recover it for the Mohammedans; they attacked it, but without success, in 1512, on which occasion Aroudj lost an arm.

Two years later (1514) they took Djedjeli from the Genoese, capturing 600 slaves and an immense amount of booty.

The renown which the brothers had acquired in fighting against the Christians induced the Emir Salem ben Teumi of Algiers (1516) to implore their assistance to dislodge the Spaniards from their position on the Peñon. Aroudj gladly accepted the invitation, and, leaving his brother with the fleet, marched on Algiers with a force of 5000 men. He was hailed as a deliverer, but he soon made himself master of the town, put Salem ben Teumi to death, and proclaimed himself king of Algiers in his stead.

In 1517 he occupied Medea and Tlemçen, which places he added to his dominions. At the same time his fleets continued to infest the coasts of Spain and Italy, and so frequent and cruel were their devastations that Charles V. at the beginning of his reign (1518) despatched a body of troops to the governor of Oran sufficient to attack him. At first Aroudj shut himself up in the Mechouar of Tlemçen, but being forced to evacuate it, and being hotly pursued by the Spaniard Martin d'Agole, he died on the banks of the Rio Salado or river of Ouchda, about 92 kil. west of Oran, in the country of the Beni Moussa.

Kheir-ed-din succeeded his brother, but, seeing himself menaced by the Spaniards on the one hand and by the native Algerians on the other, he placed himself under the suzerainty of the Sublime Porte, and was named Pacha by Selim I. He afterwards defeated, near the Balearic Islands, the Spanish Admiral Portundo, and in 1530 captured the Fort Peñon, which the Spaniards had held for thirty years, and put its governor to death.

He connected it to the mainland by a mole, in which work 30,000 Christian slaves were employed for three years, and surrounded the town with a wall.

Kheir-ed-din now (1518) conceived the project of taking possession of the kingdom of Tunis, by far the most flourishing country at that time on the coast of Africa, and the state of intestine strife prevailing there opened to him an easy means of effecting his purpose.

Mulaï Mohammed, the last prince of the Beni Hafes dynasty, which had existed in an uninterrupted line for three centuries, died in 1525, leaving a numerous family of sons by different wives. Mulaï Hassan, one of the youngest, owing to the intrigues of his mother, had been chosen as his successor. It is alleged that he poisoned his father. Certainly he put to death all those of his brothers whom he could get into his power; but Reshid, one of the oldest, succeeded in escaping to the Arabs in the interior, and with their support for a long time disputed his brother's right to the throne.

He eventually took refuge at Algiers, and implored the protection of Kheir-ed-din, who, seeing the great advantage which might accrue to himself by supporting his title, received him with every mark of friendship and respect. He easily persuaded Reshid to accompany him to Constantinople, and induced Sultan Soliman to equip an expedition for the conquest of Tunis, which done, the unhappy Reshid was thrown into prison, whence he never again emerged.

After ravaging the coast of Italy the fleet anchored at Bizerta, where it was warmly received; the inhabitants even proposed to co-operate with him, but their offer was not accepted, and Kheir-ed-din proceeded without loss of time to the Goletta, the fort at which place soon fell into his hands. He gave out that the object of his appearing on the scene was to reinstate Reshid on his father's throne, on which the inhabitants of Tunis, weary of Mulaï Hassan's government, expelled the latter from the city, and opened their gates to his brother. But when the new prince did not appear the people began to suspect the corsair's treachery. Kheir-ed-din did not leave them long in doubt, but informed them that the Beni Hafes had ceased to reign, and that he had come in their place as representative of the Sultan. The inhabitants flew to arms, and surrounded the citadel into which Kheir-ed-din had led his troops; but he had foreseen such an attack, and was not unprepared for it, and the artillery on the ramparts soon overpowered the ill-directed musketry fire of his assailants, and compelled them to retire with a loss, it is said, of 3000 killed.

His first care, after having taken possession of Tunis, was to put his new kingdom in a proper state of defence. He strengthened the citadel which commanded the town, fortified the Goletta in a regular manner at vast expense, and made it his principal arsenal and the station of his fleet. He won over the warlike tribes of the Drid and Nememchas by liberal presents, and succeeded in introducing a Turkish garrison into the holy city of Kerouan, the second capital of the country.

Mulaï Hassan fled for safety to Constantine (1535), where he made the acquaintance of a renegade Genoese, named Ximea, by whose advice he demanded the aid of **Charles V.**, and engaged to second his operations with a contingent of Arabs. Daily complaints were brought to the Emperor of the outrages committed by the Barbary pirates on his subjects, both in Spain and Italy, and the glory to be obtained by ridding the world of this odious species of oppression induced him to turn a willing ear to the representations of the dethroned prince, and to conclude a treaty with him for the invasion of Tunis. He drew contingents for this purpose from every part of the empire: a Flemish fleet brought a body of German infantry; the galleys of Naples and Sicily brought well-trained bands of Italians; the Pope rendered all the assistance in his power; the Knights of Malta, sworn enemies of the infidel, equipped a small but efficient squadron; the Emperor himself embarked at Barcelona with the flower of the Spanish nobility, and a considerable flotilla from Portugal under the command of Don Luis, the Empress's brother; Andrea Doria conducted his own galleys, the best appointed in Europe, and commanded by the most skilful officers. Doria was appointed high-admiral of the fleet; and the command of the land forces, under the Emperor, was given to the Marquis de Guasto.

On the 16th of July 1535 the fleet, consisting of nearly 500 vessels, and 30,000 regular troops, set sail from Cagliari, and after a prosperous voyage arrived at the site of Carthage, where a landing was effected without difficulty.

In the meantime Kheir-ed-din had not been idle: he called in his corsairs from their different stations; he drew from Algiers what forces could be spared, and enlisted the assistance of the African princes by representing Mulaï Hassan not only as a vassal of a Christian prince, but himself an apostate from El-Islam. Twenty thousand Moorish horse were soon collected at Tunis; the Goletta was strongly fortified, and, as the Emperor had command of the sea, the Turkish galleys were sheltered in the canal which connects the lake of Tunis with the sea, which canal was widened for the purpose, and a constant service of boats was established to supply the garrison of the Goletta with supplies.

Notwithstanding an obstinate resistance, the Goletta was taken by assault on the 25th July; the garrison retired to Tunis, and the Emperor became master of Kheir-ed-din's fleet, arsenal, and 300 brass cannon, which were planted on the ramparts. The Emperor immediately marched on Tunis, completely overthrowing Kheir-ed-din, who advanced with a large force to oppose him. Ten thousand Christian slaves confined in the citadel effected their liberation and sided with the invaders, and Charles became master of Tunis. For three days the town was given over to pillage, and it is said that 30,000 of the inhabitants perished, and 10,000 more were carried off as slaves. Mulaï Hassan took possession of a throne surrounded by carnage, abhorred by his subjects, and pitied even by those who had been the cause of those calamities.

He was obliged to sign a treaty, dated 5th August 1535, acknowledging that he held his kingdom in fee of the Crown of Spain, agreeing to pay 12,000 crowns for the subsistence of the garrison at the Goletta, and to send every year to the Emperor twelve horses, and as many falcons, as a token of vassalage. He also agreed to free all Christian slaves in his dominions, allow perfect liberty of religion, the exclusive right of fishing for coral to the Spaniards, and undertook that no corsair should be admitted into any of his ports.

The Emperor left a garrison of 200 men in his citadel of Tunis, and retired to the Goletta, and thence to his former camp at Carthage; and having left orders for the construction of a new fort at the Goletta, he set sail for Europe. On his way he took possession of the ports of Bizerta and Bône, in which latter town he left a garrison of 1000 men.[1]

Kheir-ed-din effected his escape (1536), but was immediately recalled to Constantinople, where he died in 1546.

Six very remarkable contemporary paintings illustrative of this expedition are extant, and were exhibited by Her Majesty the Queen to the Society of Antiquaries at London on the 8th May 1862. They represent:—

1. Landing of the expedition near Carthage. 2. Attack on the Goletta fort, and skirmish with the Turks. 3. Capture of the Goletta fort. 4. Advance on Tunis and defeat of the Turks. 5. Capture and sack of Tunis. 6. Convention with the Turks and departure of the army. The paintings are attributed to an artist named Jan Cornélisz Vermeyen, who is represented in one of the paintings as making his drawings. These interesting works of art were discovered in the Castle of Greinberg on the Danube and taken thence to Coburg. Through the influence of the late Prince Consort they were cleaned and repaired by M. Eichener of Augsburg, and subsequently brought to England for a time, when they were returned to Coburg. One of the pictures is of peculiar interest, as it gives an undoubted representation of the St. Ann, the curious *Carrack* of the Knights of St. John.

1537. Several of the cities of Tunis, amongst others Susa and Kerouan, revolted against Mulaï Hassan, who was forced once more to apply to Charles

[1] Consult Robertson's "History of the Reign of Charles V."

V.; by his command the Viceroy of Sicily sent an expedition against Susa in 1537, which, however, proved unsuccessful.

Two years later (1539) Andrea Doria reduced the principal cities on the coast—Kelibia, Susa, Monastir, and Sfax—to the authority of Mulaï Hassan, and Monastir received a garrison of Spanish soldiers.

Mulaï Hassan resolved to crush the insurrection by the reduction of Kerouan, against which he marched with a considerable force of native troops and the Christian garrison left behind by Charles V., but the former nearly all passed over to the enemy, and he was glad to get back to Tunis accompanied only by his Spanish allies. No sooner was the Spanish garrison withdrawn from Monastir (1540) when that town, as well as Susa, Sfax, and Kelibia, again revolted, and placed themselves under the protection of the celebrated corsair Draguth, an officer trained under Kheir-ed-din, and scarcely inferior to his master in bravery, talent, and good fortune. After a year, however, Doria again appeared on the coast and drove off the Turks.

1542. The precarious terms on which he held his power induced Mulaï Hassan to proceed in person to Europe, to solicit once more the help of the Christians. During his absence his son Mulaï Hamed usurped the kingdom, and on his father's return with a small body of followers, the son overcame the father in battle, and, having put out his eyes, permitted him again to return to Europe, where he shortly afterwards died.

Algiers still continued in the state of independence in which it had been left by Kheir-ed-din, who was succeeded in the government by Mohammed Hassan, as Pacha, in 1536. He was a renegade eunuch, who had passed through every stage in the corsair's service, and had acquired such experience in war that he was well fitted for any station which required a man of tried and daring courage. He carried on his piratical depredations against the Christian states with even more audacity and success than his master. Repeated and clamorous complaints reached the Emperor that the commerce of the Mediterranean was greatly interrupted by the corsairs of Algiers, which, since the capture of Tunis, had become the common receptacle of freebooters. Moved partly by these considerations, and partly with the hope of adding further glory to his last expedition to Africa, Charles issued orders (1541) to prepare a fleet and an army for the invasion of Algiers.

He was deaf to the advice of his faithful admiral, Andrea Doria, that he should not expose his armament to destruction by approaching the dangerous shores of Algiers at an advanced period of the year. His resolution was as inflexible as his courage was undaunted: and even a prince less adventurous might have been excused for his confidence in so splendid an array.

It consisted of 20,000 foot and 2000 horse, Spaniards, Italians, and Germans, mostly veterans, together with 3000 volunteers, the flower of the Spanish and Italian nobility, and 1000 men sent from Malta, led by 100 of the knights of St. John.

He sailed from Porto Venero, in the Genoese territories, and, having touched at Majorca, arrived before Algiers on the 20th October 1541. At first the roll of the sea and the vehemence of the wind would not permit the troops to disembark, but at last the Emperor seized a favourable opportunity and

§ 8. HISTORICAL NOTICE OF ALGERIA AND TUNIS

landed them without opposition between Algiers and the mouth of the Harach, on the spot now occupied by the Jardin d'Essai.

To oppose this mighty army Hassan had only 800 Turks and 5000 Moors, partly natives of Africa and partly refugees from Spain. He returned, however, a fierce and haughty answer when summoned to surrender.

But what neither his desperate courage nor skill in war could have done, the elements effected for him. On the nights of the 24th and 25th violent rain began to fall, which rendered the firearms of the invaders useless; the Turks, taking advantage of the storm, pursued the Christians with such impetuosity that they were compelled to retreat. One hundred and forty of the vessels were wrecked by the same tempest. The survivors were embarked on board the remainder at Cape Matifou on the 1st, 2d, and 3d of November, notwithstanding the earnest advice of Cortez, the conqueror of Mexico, who felt confident that a second attempt would be more successful. The Emperor was the last to embark. He arrived at Bougie on the 4th, remained there till the 17th, and arrived in Spain on the 1st of December, having lost a third of his army and more than a third of his fleet.

In 1542 Hassan, Pacha of Algiers, attacked and massacred the tribe of the Zouaoua, who had furnished 2000 men for the army of Charles V. His successor was Hassan, son of Kheir-ed-din, who continued in power until 1552, when Salah Raïs, an Arab of Alexandria, was made Pacha. He retook Bougie from the Spaniards (whose governor, Peralta, was beheaded at Valladolid), united the towns of Tlemçen and Mostaganem to the regency of Algiers, and died of the plague at Matifou in 1556.

The next Pacha, Mohammed Kordougli, was assassinated in the Koubba of Sidi Abd-el-Kader, in the same year, by Youssef, who succeeded him, but only reigned six days, when he died of the plague.

After several short and unimportant reigns, Mohammed, son of Salah Raïs, was created Pacha in 1566. He made some additions to the town, and built several new forts, and was succeeded in 1568 by Ali el-Euldj el-Fortas, a celebrated pirate, whose reign was passed in a succession of wars against the neighbouring nations. After him came Arab-Ahmed, 1572 to 1574; and Ramdan, a renegade Sardinian, 1574 to 1576; both of whom added to the fortifications of the town. At this time there were not less than 25,000 Christian slaves in bondage in Algiers.

In the next forty years as many as eighteen different Pachas reigned; their governments being distinguished only by wars, assassinations, extortion, and tyranny.

The history of the country now becomes very obscure. Internally the Turks extended their conquests over the whole of the Barbary States, even as far south as the desert. They divided Algeria into the three "Beyliks" of Oran, Constantine, and Titeri, the regency still having its capital at Algiers. With regard to the outer world, the history of the State is but that of the large towns, which sent out their pirate vessels even as far as the North Sea, and became so powerful in the Mediterranean that none of the European States escaped the disgrace of paying at times a regular tribute to secure safety to their mariners.

Amongst other captives, in the year 1555, was Cervantes, who remained in captivity five years and a half. He was taken prisoner on the voyage from Naples to Spain by a squadron of Algerine galleys, commanded by Amant Mame, and fell to the lot of Dali Mame, a Greek renegade, captain of one of the galleys. His freedom was purchased by the *Padres Redemtores* on the 19th September 1580. He has described some of the miseries to which he was subject in the story of "The Captive" in *Don Quixote*. A grotto is pointed out in the "Propricté Sabatery," near the Jardin d'Essai, where Cervantes and his companions resided after their flight from Algiers and before being actually freed. Many of the Christians, hopeless of regaining their liberty, renounced their religion, and some rose to high places in the State, several even becoming Deys. It is said that in 1640 there were 3000 renegade corsairs in the Algerine fleet; a large proportion, no doubt, tempted to join by the chance of enriching themselves which such a trade offered.

An **English Consulate** was established at Algiers towards the end of the 16th century. John Tipton, who held the office in 1580, was perhaps the first consul ever regularly appointed with a commission and an exequatur, and there has been an almost uninterrupted succession ever since.[1]

Very early in the 17th century the Algerines began to substitute square-rigged vessels for the galleots which they had been in the habit of using. Sir Francis Cottington, writing from Madrid to the Duke of Buckingham in 1616, says: "The strength and boldness of the Barbary pirates is now grown to that height, both in the ocean and Mediterranean seas, as I have never known anything to have wrought a greater sadness and distraction than the daily advice thereof. Their whole fleet consists of 40 sail of tall ships of between two and four hundred tons a piece."

About this time a prize was made on the coast of France which had the effect subsequently of bringing hope, comfort, and deliverance to many a weary Christian slave. A young man of the name of Vincent de Paul embarked on board a vessel at Marseilles bound for Narbonne. It was taken by three Barbary pirates in the Gulf of Lyons, and all on board carried to Tunis. Vincent de Paul was at first sold to a sailor, who soon parted with him. He was subsequently purchased by an Arab doctor, with whom he remained from September 1605 till August 1606, when his master died, leaving him to a nephew, who soon after sold him to an Italian renegade.

St. Vincent was the cause of this man's return to Christianity, and they both escaped in a boat to France in July 1607. In 1625 St. Vincent laid the first foundation of his mission, which continued without interruption in Algeria and Tunis, till the former country became a French possession. Indeed, it exists there at the present time, engaged in other works of piety and charity.

1616. Mustafa Pacha (Algiers). At this time Louis XIII. complained to the Porte at Constantinople, in consequence of the behaviour of the Pachas, and sent to the galleys some Algerine captives who had escaped from Spain into France. In return the Pacha imprisoned M. de Vias, the French consul

---

[1] For an account of British relations with Algiers from this time till the French conquest, see the author's "Scourge of Christendom." Smith, Elder and Co. 1884.

at Algiers, who had to purchase his liberty by payment of large sums of money, and in 1618 was succeeded by M. Chaix, previously vice-consul. In March 1619 a treaty of peace was signed between Louis XIII. and the Pacha, Hussein.

1621. Kader Pacha (Algiers). Hostilities again commenced with France, and some Algerine envoys were put to death at Marseilles, in retaliation for which M. Chaix was killed.

In 1620 **Sir Robert Mansel**, vice-admiral of England, was sent to make a demonstration against Algiers. The royal navy was not yet, however, sufficiently large to rely on its own resources, and in this, the only warlike operation undertaken by it during the reign of James I., the greater number of vessels employed were hired from private merchants. It consisted of eighteen ships, six belonging to the king and twelve hired ones, and so greatly had the size of British ships increased during late years, that the smallest of the royal vessels was 400 tons burden, and carried 36 guns. The expedition itself was productive neither of benefit nor glory. It was thus described by Mr. Secretary Burchell: "Such was the ascendant Count Gondomar, the King of Spain's ambassador, had at the court of King James I., that at his solicitations a squadron of men-of-war was sent to the Mediterranean, commanded by Sir Robert Mansel, to bring the Algerines to reason, by whom the Spaniards were daily most insufferably molested. That commander appeared before Algiers; but he had not much reason to be satisfied at the success he there met with, and in return for the civility of his visit, his back was scarce turned but those corsairs picked up near forty good sail belonging to the subjects of his master, and infested the Spanish coasts with greater fury than ever."

The narrator of this expedition, who was on board one of the vessels, mentions that while they were still in the harbour conducting their fruitless negotiations, two British vessels were brought in as prizes by the "Turkes Pyrates," and there is no mention made of any demand for their restitution. The admiral had sent the King's letters to the Dey in charge of Captain John Roper, who was detained until a consul should be appointed. The nomination of this consular officer is more curious than flattering to our national dignity. The historian of the expedition says: "The 6th (December 1620) after long debating, finding the Turkes perfidious and fickle, as well as detaining our messenger who delivered His Maiestie's letters, notwithstanding we had sufficient hostages for him, as in breaking all other promises, in the end it was agreed thus: upon leaving a consull with them they would let our messenger come aboord againe. Whereupon the admirall sent a common man[1] well cloathed, by the name of a consull, whom they received with good respect, and sending our messenger aboord, received their owne pledges and delivered us some 40 poor captives, which they pretended was all they had in the towne. This was all we could draw from them."

1628. The Dutch Admiral Lambert arrived in 1624 with six vessels to demand the restitution of certain captured slaves and ships, which was at first refused by the Divan; but after Lambert had hanged at the yard-arms of his vessels the pirates in his power, his demands were granted. In 1628 Sanson

[1] Mr. Richard Ford.

Napollon concluded a peace with the Pacha Hussein-Khodja on behalf of the French, in which slaves were exchanged; this peace cost them £270,000. In the same year the Koulouglis revolted, and were nearly all massacred.

The audacity of the Algerine pirates at this time was unparalleled, their prizes amounting to, it was said, about 20,000,000 francs. The Christian powers of Europe having constantly endeavoured to exterminate them without success, had now nearly all adopted the expedient of paying tribute to the Pacha to escape their depredations, which they carried as far as the North Sea.

Even the shores of England were not respected. An incident which occurred a few years earlier deserves to be recorded, in the words of the principal actor in it, the **Rev. Devereux Spratt**[1]:—

"October 23d, 1640.—The horrid rebellion of Ireland brake forth, and in it God's severe judgements upon the English Protestants, there being not less than 150,000 murdered as by public records appears. . . . I returned to Ballybegg, where I remained in the discharge of my calling until the English army came to carry us off. . . . Then at Corke I petitioned the Lord Inchaquin, who gave me a pass for England; and coming to Youghole in a boate I embarked in one John Filmer's vessell, which set sayle with about six score passengers; but before wee were out of sight of land wee were all taken by an Algire piratt, who putt the men in chaines and storkes. This thing was so greivious that I began to question Providence, and accused Him of injustice in His dealings with me, untill ye Lord made it appear otherwise by ensueing mercye. Upon my arrivall in Algires I found pious Christians, which changed my former thoughts of God, which was that He dealt more hard with me than with other of His servants. God was pleased to guide for me, and those relations of mine taken with me, in a providential ordering of civil patrons for us, who gave me more liberty than ordinary, especially to me, who preached the Gospel to my poor countrymen, amongst whom it pleased God to make me an instrument of much good. I had not stayed there long, but I was like to be freed by one Captain Wilde, a pious Christian; but on a sudden I was sould and delivered to a Mussleman dwelling with his family in ye towne, upon which change and sudden dissappointment I was very sad. My patron asked me the reason, and withall uttered these comfortable words, 'God is great,' which took such impression as strengthened my faith in God, considering thus with myself, shall this Turkish Mahumetin teach me, who ame a Christian, my duty of faith and dependence upon God?

"After this God stirred up ye heart of Captaine Wilde to be an active instrument for me at Leagourno in Italy, amongst the merchants there, to contribute liberally towards my randsome, especially a Mr. John Collier. After the captaine returned to Algires he paid my randsome, which amounted to 200 cobs. Upon this a petition was presented by the English captives for my staying amongst them; yt he showed me, and asked what I would do in ye case. I tould him he was an instrument under God of my liberty, and I would be at his disposeing. He answered, Noe. I was a free man, and should be at my own disposeing. 'Then,' I replyed, 'I will stay,' consider-

[1] The MS. of this diary is in the possession of his descendant, Admiral Spratt, R.N.

ing that I might be more servisable to my country by my continuing in enduring afflictions with the people of God than to enjoy liberty at home."

Shortly before the outbreak of the Civil War an Act of Parliament was passed by both Houses "whereby they did manifest unto the world their resolution of undertaking that Christian work of the **Redemption of the Captives** from the cruel thraldome that they lay under." For some time, however, all action in this respect was necessarily intermitted. In the year 1645 the Parliament sent out "a ship of strength called the *Honour*, laden with a Gargasoon of money and goods to a great value," in charge of their special agent, Edmond Casson, who was authorised to treat for the liberation of the English captives at Algiers. Unfortunately this vessel was destroyed by fire in the harbour of Gibraltar, but in the following year (1646) another similar vessel, called the *Charles*, was despatched. The parliamentary report of the mission thus relates the result :—

"In prosecution of which orders the said agent, ship, and goods proceeded on the voyage, and God hath so blessed the work that they arrived in safety at Algeir, where after a long and difficult treaty, the register of the captives was taken, wherein are enrolled the names of all that are upon that place, and the price for their ransome agreed on, as they first cost in the market. That Gargasoon of money and goods hath by the agent been so well managed, that 244 persons, men, women, and children are redeemed and sent home in the said ship, the *Charles*. The agent is constrained to stay there until such time as the remainder are likewise redeemed, in preparation to the despatch whereof two ships are now preparing to be sent thither with a greater Gargasoon than before." Casson died at Algiers in 1654.

In 1637 some French vessels took possession of two Algerine pirate ships, on board of one of which was the new Pacha, Ali, coming from Constantinople. In return, Youssef seized M. Pion, the French consul, and an agent named Mussey, both of whom narrowly escaped being burnt alive. At this time Algiers possessed 300 pirate vessels, and in the same reign the town was nearly destroyed by an earthquake.

In 1655 took place **Blake's celebrated action at Tunis**, one of the grandest feats in English naval history. There were long accounts to settle with that regency for its piratical conduct towards British vessels, and there was a strong suspicion that many unhappy captives languished there in slavery. He first made his appearance at the Goletta, but, failing to obtain any satisfaction for his just demands, he broke off negotiations, proceeded to Cagliari for provisions, and on the 3d of April again appeared off Porto Farina, the winter harbour and principal arsenal of the Bay of Tunis, where his fleet was anchored inshore under the guns of the batteries; these were strengthened for the occasion, and further protected by a camp of several thousand horse and foot.

At daybreak on the 4th of April, Blake, with his whole squadron, consisting of the *St. George*, his own flag-ship, the *St. Andrew*, carrying the flag of Vice-Admiral Badly, the *Plymouth*, *Newcastle*, *Taunton*, *Foresight*, *Amity*, *Mermaid*, and *Merlin*, rode into the bay, and, divine service having been performed, coolly proceeded to anchor as close to the great batteries on shore as they could float. In a short time the whole artillery of Porto Farina, not less than 120 guns of large calibre, opened fire upon the fleet, which fiercely replied against its solid masonry. The conflict was still undecided when Blake sent his boats under cover of the smoke to burn the corsair vessels. The whole of the nine large ships of war were speedily in flames. In four hours from the first broadside the work was done, the pirate vessels were utterly destroyed, the batteries on shore were silenced, and the walls of Porto Farina were so much injured that the works could easily have been carried by assault, had Blake deemed it advisable to do so. But his aims were accomplished, and the lesson then read to the Tunisians made his subsequent negotiations with other Barbary States a matter of little difficulty. When the English squadron anchored off Algiers to demand restitution of property and the liberation of English slaves it met with little opposition, and a bargain was made for the ransom of all the captives at a fixed price.

1661. Disputes between the Governments of Algiers and Great Britain became very frequent about this time, as the fear of our power had been so much lessened by Blake's death that the corsairs had again begun to commit depredation on our shipping. Mr. Pepys tells us how he went to the Fleece tavern to drink, and remained till four o'clock, telling stories of Algiers and the manner of life of slaves there, and how Captain Mootham and Mr. Dancs (father of the Archbishop of York), who had been both slaves there, did make him fully acquainted with their condition, how they did eat nothing but bread and water, and how they were beat upon the soles of their feet and their bellies at the liberty of their patron.

In that year the Earl of Sandwich was sent by Charles II. to bring over the Queen from Portugal, and at the same time to settle the matters in dispute at Algiers. In the latter mission he was quite unsuccessful. Pepys observes, "The business of Algiers hath of late troubled me, because My Lord hath not done what he went for, though he did as much as any man in the world could have done." And later, that early in 1662 letters came from "My Lord" that "by a great storm and tempest the whole of Algiers is broken down and many of their ships sunk into the Mole, so that God Almighty hath ended that unlucky business for us, which is very good news."

This no doubt disposed the Pacha to conclude a peace with England, which was done by Admiral **Sir John Lawson** on the 23d April 1662.

In 1663 Lawson again proclaimed war on Algiers, in consequence of some English vessels having been captured, and the refusal of the Dey to make restitution for the goods which had been taken out of them, together with the imprisonment of the consul. Peace was concluded by Admiral **Sir Thomas Allen**, on 30th August 1664, on the basis of the last one. A treaty of peace between France and Algiers was signed in 1666, by which all Algerine privateers were furnished with a free pass by the French consul; but it was broken in 1667 by Ismaïl sending some ships against the French to the siege of Candia. He was finally beaten by the Marquis de Martel, and peace re-established.

In 1669 an officer named Khelil proposed to the Janissaries or Turkish militia that the power should no longer be solely in the hands of the Pachas, who were becoming unbearable through their tyranny, but that their interests should be represented by an Agha, elected by themselves.

The Pacha was retained out of respect to the Sultan, but he was not permitted to interfere in State affairs, though allowed an appanage suitable to his rank. This plan was adopted, and the reigning Pacha, Ibrahim, thrown into prison, and Ismaïl appointed in his stead. The originator of the plan, Khelil, was made Agha, and shortly after assassinated in 1670.

In 1669 war was again declared between England and Algiers, and Sir Thomas Allen was once more charged with its conduct. This expedition was no more successful than the previous one, if we except the brilliant episode of **Sir Edward Spragg's** action at Bougie, where the principal fleet of the pirates was assembled, protected by a strong boom thrown across the entrance of the harbour. Sir Edward broke the boom, silenced the batteries, and captured or burnt the whole of their shipping. The Algerians rose in revolt against their Government on receiving news of this disaster, and put the reigning Dey, Ali Agha, to death, making at the same time ample submission to the English admiral.

In 1675 the Dutch offered large sums for the purchase of peace, but their terms were not accepted by the Divan at Algiers. Even as regards England they seemed not to have had a sufficiently severe lesson, for in 1677 it was found necessary to send **Admiral Herbert** against them with another squadron, but the mere sight of his force recalled to their minds so lively a recollection of the chastisement they had received from Sir Edward Spragg that they at once submitted, and, though they plundered every one else, it was some time before they ventured to insult the British flag. But the mere fact of keeping Englishmen in bondage did not seem to have been considered "an insult to the British flag" in those days.

The **piratical search for slaves** was in fact an organised system. The Turks considered it lawful to keep all Christian prisoners in bondage, and entirely at the mercy of their respective masters. The answer of the Dey to the remonstrances of an English consul was, "Know you not that my people are a company of rogues, and I am their captain?" Not only were all prisoners of war so treated, but it was the constant habit of the Dey, on any European State attempting reprisals, to send to the galleys the consul of that country, and all merchants and crews of vessels who were bold enough to have visited his ports for the purpose of commerce. On many occasions hundreds of these peaceful traders were killed, and the consuls also treated with great barbarity, being burnt alive, or blown from the mouths of cannon; while, in one instance, on the approach of a French fleet, their representative was thrown towards them from a mortar. The number of whites kept in slavery is astonishing. In 1646 it was reckoned that there were not less than 20,000; in 1768, 1500 Christians were redeemed by Spain alone; and when Lord Exmouth finally destroyed the pirate navy in 1816, he obtained the liberty of 3000. These are some of the most striking instances; but hundreds of captives were annually ransomed by their respective nations, or by societies formed for the purpose. Many priests nobly devoted themselves to ministering to the slaves, even voluntarily going to the galleys for the sake of being with them. Several of these, who were killed among the other victims of the Turks, have been canonised.

War again broke out with Algiers, and lasted for five years. It is stated on excellent authority that between the years 1674 and 1681 five or six thousand English slaves were brought into Algiers, and about 350 vessels captured, and at the peace of 10th April 1682 the Dey refused to surrender a single English slave, leaving the general to bargain with their several masters as best he could for their ransom.

The treaty then signed between Charles II. and the Government of Algiers contained a clause to the following effect : " The King of Great Britain shall not be obliged by virtue of this treaty to redeem any of his subjects now in slavery, but it shall depend absolutely upon His Majesty or the friends or relations of the said persons in slavery to redeem such as shall be thought fit, agreeing to as reasonable a price as may be with their patrons or masters for their redemption, without obliging the said patrons against their will to set any at liberty." This treaty, which may be seen in vol. i. of Hertslet's Compilation, page 58, is probably the most degrading one ever concluded between Great Britain and a foreign power; nevertheless this provision was renewed by James II. on 5th April 1686, and by George II. on 18th March 1729. The condition of the slaves was most pitiable. Such as belonged to the Dey were imprisoned in the *Bagnio*. They had a ration of black bread and a little soup once a day; they were compelled to labour incessantly, some at the quarries outside the town; others were harnessed to stone carts like mules; many had to labour at the ovens where bread was made for the Janissaries, and their lot was even more miserable than the others; the least wretched were the skilled artisans, but these found it almost impossible to obtain their freedom, so useful were they to the State. Such as were owned by private individuals were even more unfortunate than the others, being treated worse than beasts of burden, and liable to every species of cruelty and torture that their pitiless masters could devise. The only consolation left to them was the ministration of the Catholic missionaries, who spent their time, and often sacrificed life itself, in solacing their misfortunes.

In August and September 1682, and again in 1683, the French **Admiral Duquesne** appeared before Algiers with a strong fleet, and commenced to bombard the town; it was the first occasion of shells being used for such a purpose, and they not only committed great ravages in the town, but so terrified the Dey that he consented to deliver up 546 French slaves. This enraged the Turks beyond endurance. The Dey, Baba Hassan, was murdered, and Mezzo-Morto elected in his stead. His first act was to threaten Duquesne to blow away every Frenchman from guns if the attack was renewed—a threat which he carried into execution by thus disposing of M. Le Vacher, the French consul and Vicar-Apostolic, together with twenty other Frenchmen.[1] In 1684 a humiliating peace was concluded, nominally for 100 years.

In 1688, in consequence of some raids made upon French, English, and

[1] The immense cannon from which these unfortunates and many others were blown away was called by the Turks *Baba Merzouk* (Father Fortunate), and by the French *La Consulaire*. It is now preserved as a trophy on the Place d'Armes at Brest.

Dutch ships, and the imprisonment of the French consul, M. Piolle, the town was bombarded by the **Duke d'Estrées**. Mezzo-Morto was wounded, and M. Piolle and forty Frenchmen were blown from the mouths of cannon. From this period to the end of the century the country was in a state of anarchy, many Deys being appointed, and immediately afterwards assassinated. The city was constantly ravaged by the plague, it being said that in 1698, 24,000, and in 1702, 45,000 persons died of this malady.

The successive attempts of various European nations to suppress this nest of ruffians having thus proved completely futile, they were all in turn obliged to buy peace, and even to submit to the additional disgrace of paying part of their tribute in cannon, bombs, and other munitions of war. The conditions imposed on the Danes may be cited as an instance in proof. Peace was accorded to them only on condition of immediately delivering to the Dey twenty 24-pounder guns, twenty 12-pounders, four iron mortars, 6600 shells, 20,000 cannon balls, 20,000 lbs. of powder, 50 masts, 100 yards, 20,000 lbs. of tar, 10,000 lbs. of resin, 2000 planks, 40 cables, and further paying him annually, 10,000 lbs. of powder, 4000 balls, 25 masts, 50 yards, 12 cables and 24 hawsers.

One can understand how, receiving such presents every year, frequently augmented at the caprice of the Dey, the State of Algiers was able to strengthen itself, so as to become the scourge of Europe.

In 1710 a new revolution gave to the Algerian Government the constitution which it continued to hold until the French conquest. The Janissaries obtained the Sultan's consent that the Dey elected by themselves should be named Pacha, and that the Sublime Porte should have no other representative in Algiers. From this moment it became in reality an independent State, and in connection with Constantinople was restricted to the despatch of a present, its exchange for the Caftan of Investiture on the accession of a new Dey. In the same year the Dey of Oran made an expedition against Algiers, but was defeated on the banks of the Harrach, and beheaded.

1716. The town partially destroyed by an earthquake.

1719. Mohammed, Pacha Dey, renewed the treaty of peace with France.

The year 1726 was celebrated for the unusual cold, Algiers being in that winter covered with snow.

1732 to 1748. Ibrahim ben Ramdan, Pacha, during which period frequent struggles with Tunis took place.

On the 1st of February 1748 Ibrahim ben Ramdan, Pacha of Algiers, died, not without suspicion of poison.

1748 to 1754. To him succeeded Mohammed Kodja, surnamed the *one eyed*, who had the reputation of being just, humane, and superior to all the other aspirants to the throne.

In 1752 and 1753 there was a serious outbreak of plague at Algiers. In April of the latter year 400 died in the city, in June 1700, and as many in July, but it was much more at many other cities of the regency, especially Djidjelly, La Calle, and Constantine. In 1754 and 1755 there were only a few isolated cases at Algiers, but in 1756 this scourge seemed inclined to make up for its inaction during the two previous years, and by the end of August 10,000 had died in the city alone.

1754 to 1766. On the 11th of December 1754 the Dey and his Khaznadar were both assassinated, and Baba Ali was elected in the place of the former. He was a man entirely wanting in good sense and capacity. He at once recommenced the war with the Dutch, who were fain to conclude an onerous and humiliating peace. He rendered himself popular by encouraging piracy and other crimes. He took Tunis, which was given up to pillage. The French consul was sent to the Bagnio, as many of his predecessors had been, and only released on payment of a large sum of money. One of his successors was similarly treated. The Bey required some of the European States to renew their consuls every three years, on account of the presents which he was accustomed to exact on such occasions; and others, like Venice, he actually compelled to pay him an annual tribute.

From 1762 to 1765 **James Bruce** of Kinnaird, the well-known African traveller, held the office of British Consul-General at Algiers. After resigning office he made extensive explorations in Algeria, Tunis, Tripoli, and the Pentapolis, where he made accurate drawings of all the Roman remains of any consequence in those countries. A selection of these was published, after the lapse of more than a century.[1]

1766 to 1791. Baba Ali Dey died on the 2d February 1766, and was quietly succeeded by Mohammed ben Osman, who had occupied the place of treasurer to his predecessor. He governed his people sagely and well during twenty-five years, and did what a Dey of Algiers could to restrain the piratical tendencies of his subjects within due limits.

In no former reign had there been so many conspiracies against the Dey's life, but none of them were successful. He was exceedingly exacting in his negotiations with European States, and managed under one pretext or another to lay them all under contribution to him.

In 1775 took place the unfortunate Spanish expedition against Algiers, commanded by the **Count O'Reilly**. It consisted of 51 vessels and about 24,000 troops. They left Carthagena on the 23d June, and arrived before Algiers on the 31st June and 1st August. They landed to the east of the river Harrach, and the first division at once commenced its march towards the town. They were so harassed, however, by the enemy, who had taken up advantageous positions all along their route, that they became thoroughly discouraged, and when subsequently they were charged by a troop of camels, they retreated in the utmost confusion to their vessels. The loss acknowledged by the Spaniards was 218 officers and 2589 men killed and wounded, besides which the army abandoned 18 pieces of artillery and a great number of arms and munitions of war.

Another naval expedition was sent against Algiers in 1783, which bombarded the town, killing about 300 persons and destroying about as many houses. A third and even more futile attempt was made in the following year. Subsequently, in 1785, they concluded a peace with the Dey, for which they were content to pay a million piastres and a vast amount of military stores.

[1] "Travels in the Footsteps of Bruce in Algeria and Tunis." By the Author.

§ 8. HISTORICAL NOTICE OF ALGERIA AND TUNIS

In April 1786 the **plague** again broke out ; it lasted eighteen months, and carried off more than a third of the population. It was calculated that during the first fifteen months 35,600 Mohammedans, 2300 Jews, and 620 Christian slaves, in all 38,520, perished.

In 1789 the French entered into a new treaty with the Dey at the price of most humiliating concessions, the negotiators consoling themselves with the fact that Louis XIV., after three expeditions against Algiers, had been compelled to purchase an equally inglorious peace.

1791 to 1799. In July 1791 Mohammed ben Osman died, and Baba Hassan was proclaimed Dey. His first act was to demand a frigate from the French to convey his ambassador to Constantinople, and to inform the consuls that in future the annual presents or tribute should be doubled. It never seemed to occur to any European power to dispute the orders of this despot, although compliance with them only made him the more exacting. Whenever he was in want of money he declared war on some European power, and forced it to purchase peace at an extravagant price. Venice, Spain, Holland, Portugal, Denmark, and Naples, were thus treated, and even America followed their example. Small wonder then that at this time the Dey's treasury was reported to contain 4 millions sterling !

Nevertheless at this time the power of the Algerine State was by no means formidable. Shaw states that in 1732 they had only half a dozen ships of from thirty-six to fifty guns, and not half that number of brave and experienced captains. The whole land force in Turks and Koulouglis was not more than 6500, of whom one-third were old and worn-out, and though the seaward defences were pretty strong and carefully looked after, those on the landward side were quite insignificant. Even sixty years later, though they had accumulated an immense supply of naval stores of all kinds, there is no reason to suppose that they were substantially stronger, or that any of the principal nations of Europe would have had the least difficulty in extirpating them. The fact was that the nations of Europe were too much occupied in fighting amongst themselves to be able to pay much attention to Algiers, and each was very well content that the Algerines should prey on the commerce of its neighbours if only its own remained secure.

1799 to 1805. On the 15th May 1799 Baba Hassan died, and was succeeded by his nephew Mustafa, an ignorant and avaricious person, who commenced his reign by the pillage of his predecessor's family, the consuls as usual being laid under contribution. In 1800, in consequence of the French occupation of Egypt, the Dey arrested all the consular establishment of that nation, the priests and many others, who were at once put in chains, and kept in the Bagnio for thirty-three days. On the 30th September 1800 the great Napoleon agreed to a peace at the price of oblivion for the past and a payment of 300,000 piastres to the Dey ; but this not being approved of by the Sultan, the French consul and all his countrymen were ordered to quit the regency, and left on the 30th January 1801. They were not allowed to return till after the conclusion of the preliminaries of peace between England and Turkey on the one hand, and France on the other, towards the end of the year.

[*Algeria.*]

The **United States** had at this time (1800) a considerable trade with the Mediterranean, and the Algerines were not backward in falling upon the unsuspecting and unarmed Americans, capturing their ships and casting the crews into bondage.

Immediately after the peace of 1783, when the United States became an independent nation, Algiers declared war upon them. In 1785 two American vessels were captured in the Atlantic Ocean. In 1793 eleven more prizes were made, and then the number of American citizens in slavery at Algiers exceeded a hundred. Colonel Humphreys, American minister at Lisbon, was charged by the President to negotiate with the Barbary States, and he despatched Mr. Joseph Donaldson for that purpose to Algiers. He then negotiated a treaty of peace, by which the Americans bound themselves to pay to the Dey the sum of 721,000 dollars, partly as ransom for American captives, and partly as gratification, presents, etc., to the Government of the regency. It was further agreed that the American Government should pay an annual tribute of 22,000 dollars in munitions of war and marine stores, which sum, in consequence of the arbitrary value fixed on the various articles, was almost doubled in reality.

In the month of October 1800 the United States 32-gun frigate *George Washington*, commanded by Captain Bainbridge, was lying at anchor in the roads of Algiers. The Dey considered this a fine opportunity to get the presents which he, as well as the heads of the other regencies, annually paid to the Sultan, conveyed to Constantinople. He made a requisition for the services of the frigate for this purpose, and the commandant, though most unwillingly, thought that he could not avoid performing the duty. This conduct deeply wounded the susceptibility of the Americans, but the President thought it more prudent to follow the example of older and richer States in Europe, and make the best terms he could with the Algerines.

The influence of France now began to wane in Algiers. The defeat of Trafalgar destroyed its marine and its commerce, and made England undisputed mistress of the seas. The French were expelled from La Calle, and the exclusive privilege of coral fishing conceded to the English for a period of ten years at a rent of 267,000 f. per annum.

1805 to 1808. On the 12th of September 1805 Mustafa was murdered by the Janissaries and replaced by Ahmed Khodja. The first thirty days of his reign were marked by the spoliation of the Jews, and the most frightful massacres; the usual presents from the consuls were exacted with the utmost rigour, and in one week he extorted from Spain 12,000 piastres, Holland 40,000, America 100,000, Austria 50,000, and England 10,000.

1808 to 1809. Ahmed Dey was killed on the 7th of November 1808 by the relations of those whom he had massacred on his accession, just as he was on the point of escaping to France with his ministers and treasures; his successor, Ali ben Mohammed, only lived a few months, being in his turn assassinated on the 7th of February 1809.

1809 to 1815. Hadji Ali, his successor, commenced his reign with an act tantamount to a declaration of war with France. He demanded an exorbitant sum from the consul, and not only imprisoned him, but also M. de Berthemy, aide-de-camp to Napoleon, and M. Arago, the celebrated astronomer, then on a purely scientific mission to Algiers. They only purchased their release after three months' captivity by the payment of a large sum of money.

1812. In 1812 the Government of Algiers again declared war on the United States. It is believed that the Regency adopted this step on the advice of certain Jews, who, seeing the increasing importance of the American mercantile marine, thought that Algiers might as well obtain a share of this commercial prosperity by the simple expedient of plunder. The moment chosen for this step was the 17th July 1812, when the *Alleghany*, an American vessel, arrived at Algiers with the annual tribute. The Dey showed the greatest dissatisfaction at the articles of which it was composed. He ordered the consul to pay the tribute in money for the future ; and, together with his family and all American citizens, to quit the regency by the 25th of the same month. The consul did all he could to persuade the Dey to reconsider this decision, but without effect ; he was actually compelled to leave. In the month of September following an American vessel was captured, and the President endeavoured in vain to obtain the release of the captives by paying their ransom. The Dey refused to enter into any negotiation on the subject, declaring that he considered American slaves as beyond price.

The Congress of the United States could no longer tolerate such behaviour or support the idea of remaining tributary to Algiers. Accordingly, in May 1815 **Captains Bainbridge** and **Decatur** and **Mr. William Shaler** were chosen by the President to proceed to Algiers with a squadron, and on their arrival there they at once made a demand for a modification of all existing treaties. The Algerines were confounded at this step, and, as it happened that all their vessels were then out cruising, they accepted almost without discussion the conditions dictated to them, and the treaty was signed on the 30th of June. On the same day Mr. Shaler landed as Consul-General of the United States at Algiers.

Commodore Decatur then proceeded towards Tripoli and Tunis, and compelled the governments of those regencies to comply with his demands.

1815 to 1817. In the middle of March 1815 Hadji Ali was murdered by his soldiery, and his successor Mohammed only survived him a fortnight, he having been arrested and strangled in prison. Omar ben Mohammed, Agha of Spahis, was the next Dey. He was born in Mytelene, and was forty-three years of age when he came to the throne. He is represented as having been singularly handsome in appearance, and of great natural intelligence, sober and continent in his life, and of a courage so renowned that it gained him the name of "the terrible."

In the beginning of 1816 **Lord Exmouth** was ordered to proceed to the various Barbary States to claim the release of all Ionian slaves who had then become British subjects, and to make peace for Sardinia. He was also permitted to make peace for any other States in the Mediterranean who should authorise him to do so. He had no difficulty in obtaining the liberation of the Ionians, and he also effected the freedom of the Neapolitans and Sardinians, the former paying a ransom of 500 and the latter 300 dollars a head.

The fleet then sailed for Tunis and Tripoli, where Lord Exmouth concluded treaties with the Beys, entirely abolishing the institution of Christian slavery.

He again visited Algiers and attempted to enforce a similar demand, but the Dey answered as a man confident in his strength to resist it. Lord Exmouth assured him that he formed a very inadequate idea of a British man-of-war, and declared that if hostilities should become necessary he would engage to destroy the place with five line-of-battle ships.

On his way back to the ship Lord Exmouth and suite were very roughly handled by the Algerines, but eventually the Dey consented to treat on the subject in England and at Constantinople. Lord Exmouth, having no authority to enforce his demands, was fain to be content with this, and returned to England. But before he arrived, news came that while he was still at Algiers on the 23d of May, the crews of the coral fishing-boats at Bône had gone on shore to attend mass, it being Ascension Day, when they were attacked by a large body of Turks and barbarously massacred.

The British Government, justly considering that these barbarians, whose existence was a reproach to the civilised world, had filled up the measure of their crimes by this outrage, determined to exact complete submission or inflict the most signal vengeance.

The ancient harbour of Algiers was then very much as it now appears in the plan, without of course the jetties, which have been added by the French. The entrance was not more than 120 yards wide. All around bristled with fortifications and artillery. The lighthouse battery had 50 guns in three tiers; at the extremity of the rock was a battery with 30 guns and 7 mortars in two tiers; the mole itself was filled with cannon in a double tier; the eastern batteries next the lighthouse had an inner fortification with a third tier of guns, making 66 guns in those batteries alone. The islet had in all 220 guns, besides 300 more in the various batteries along the coast-line opposite to it.

Nelson, in a conversation with Captain Brisbane, had named 25 line-of-battle ships as the force that would be required to attack them. Lord Exmouth was offered any force he required, but he determined to take no more than the number he had mentioned to the Dey, five ships of the line, to which, however, were added three heavy and two small frigates, four bomb vessels, and five gun-brigs.

On arrival at Gibraltar on the 5th of August he found a **Dutch squadron**, consisting of five frigates and a corvette, commanded by Admiral van Capellan, who, on learning the object of the expedition, solicited and obtained leave to co-operate.

On the 27th the fleet arrived opposite Algiers, and a flag of truce was sent on shore to communicate the ultimatum of the British Government, and demand the immediate liberation of the consul, who had been imprisoned in irons.

No answer was given, when the fleet bore up and each vessel proceeded to take up its appointed station. The flag-ship, the *Queen Charlotte*, anchored half a cable's length from the mole head, her port battery flanking the batteries from the mole head to the lighthouse. A gun was now fired from the upper tier of the eastern battery, a second and a third followed, the remainder being drowned by the thunder of the *Queen Charlotte's* broadside.

The enemy now opened fire from all their batteries, while the rest of the British squadron took up their position at the entrance to the mole. The Dutch squadron with admirable gallantry went into action under a heavy fire before the works to the south of the town. On the opposite side of the lighthouse were placed the bomb vessels, while the flotilla of gun, rocket, and mortar boats was distributed between the line-of-battle ships and the entrance to the mole.

Soon after the battle became general, the enemy's flotilla of gunboats advanced, when a single broadside sent 33 out of 37 to the bottom. The whole of the Algerian frigates were burnt at their anchors and blown up, and by ten o'clock at night it was felt that the objects of the attack had been attained. The fleet had fired 118 tons of powder, 50,000 shot (weighing more than 500 tons of iron), besides 960 13- and 10-inch shells. The sea defences of Algiers, with a great part of the town itself, were shattered and crumbled to ruins. In the British ships 123 men were killed and 690 wounded, while the Dutch had 13 killed and 52 wounded. Lord Exmouth escaped narrowly: he was struck in three places; a cannon shot carried away the skirts of his coat, and another broke his glass. The losses of the Algerians were estimated at 7000. On the following morning the Dey acceded to all Lord Exmouth's demands, namely:—

1. **The abolition of Christian slavery for ever.**
2. The delivery of all slaves in the dominion of the Dey.
3. The repayment of all money received by him for the redemption of slaves since the beginning of the year.
4. Reparation and a public apology to the consul.

The total number of slaves liberated, including those freed a few weeks before, were—

At Algiers	1612
Tunis	781
Tripoli	580
Total .	3003

The **battle of Algiers** forms a class by itself amongst naval victories; it was a new thing to place a fleet in a position surrounded by formidable batteries. Nor was it less happy in its results: it broke the chains of thousands, it gave security to millions, and it delivered Christendom from a scourge and a disgrace.

1817 to 1818. On the 3d of September 1817 Omar Dey was murdered, and succeeded by Ali Khodja, who, to save himself from sharing the fate of so many of his predecessors, left his palace in the city and took up his residence in the Casba, at the summit of the town, whither, on the previous night, 350 mules had transported his treasure, estimated at 300 millions of francs.

In the spring of 1818 the plague again made its appearance, and amongst its victims was the Dey, who died on the 1st of March.

1818 to 1830. No sooner was the breath out of his body than the Divan proclaimed Hussein-Khodja, minister of the interior, Dey in his place, and he was the last who ever sat on the throne. He speedily turned his attention to the reconstruction of the fleet burnt by Lord Exmouth, and in 1820 he had 44 vessels, manned by 1560 sailors.

Since the treaty made by Lord Exmouth the Dey found it impossible to obtain Christian slaves for his public works; he was therefore driven to fill his Bagnio with Kabyles, and even the private servants of the consuls were not spared. The British consulate was violated in the search for certain Kabyles; this brought about a rupture between Great Britain and Algiers, and the consul, Mr. McDonell, was forced to embark and leave the place. In July 1824 a naval division of 6 sails appeared before the place, while 10 more remained out at sea. There was a slight engagement which lasted three hours, but the Dey persisted in his refusal to receive Mr. McDonell. Algiers was blockaded till the 24th, when there was a second engagement. Eventually the affair was patched up, and Admiral **Sir H. Neale**, who commanded the squadron, made two concessions to the Dey, the weaker that they were secret,—namely, that the British flag should not be hoisted on the English consulate in Algiers, and that Mr. McDonell should not return as consul.

When Mr. St. John succeeded him all the disgraceful ceremonies in the intercourse between the representative of Great Britain and the Turkish authorities were continued. The consul was obliged, the moment he came in sight of the Dey's palace, to walk bareheaded in the hottest sun; in waiting for an audience he had to sit on a stone bench in the public passage; he could not wear a sword in the Dey's presence, nor ride to the palace, though his own servants, if Mohammedans, might do so.

In spite of the chastisement inflicted by Lord Exmouth, and the daily threat made by the representatives of European nations at Algiers, their corsairs continued to infest the seas till the very last; and after the abortive attempt of the English to secure the return of their consul, the audacity and perfidy of the Algerian Government knew no bounds, and the most solemn treaties were regarded as so much waste paper.

The subject of the dispute which eventually accomplished its downfall was the claim of a Jew named Bacri, on account of stores supplied to the French Government during Napoleon's wars. This had been regulated by common accord at 7 millions of francs; and, at one of the interviews which the consul had with the Dey on the subject, the latter is said to have struck him on the face with his fan.

This conduct, for which he refused to make any reparation, served as an excuse to the French Government to send an expedition against Algiers; and the town was blockaded during three years in so inefficient a manner as to excite the ridicule of the Turkish officials.

On the 14th of June 1830 a French army, commanded by **General de Bourmont** and **Admiral Duperré**, consisting of 34,000 men, landed, with little opposition, at Sidi Ferruch. It is worthy of remark that all previous attacks on Algiers had been made from the east; and that the suggestion to effect a landing at this point was first made in the work of Mr. Shaler, Consul-General of the United States at Algiers,[1] a suggestion which was followed exactly by the invading force. On the 19th of the same month the battle of Staouëli was fought, and on the 24th that of Sidi Khalef.

On the 4th of July the French arrived in front of the town, and opened fire on Fort l'Empereur, which was abandoned at 10 A.M. by its garrison, who set fire to the powder magazine. The Dey now sent for the British Consul-General, and requested him to go to the French camp and ascertain the commander-in-chief's conditions.

These were that the town should be surrendered at 10 o'clock the next morning, whereupon the Dey's person and property should be respected. On the following day, 6th July, the Dey signed this convention, and at 1 P.M. the French troops entered the town and took possession of the forts.

Hussein Pacha embarked at Algiers on the 10th, with a suite of 110 persons, of whom 55 were women. He first fixed his residence at Naples, and subsequently at Leghorn, and eventually in Egypt. Mohammed Ali Pacha received him with the consideration due to his rank and misfortunes, when one day, after a private audience, Hussein retired to his private apartments, and died, it is said, a few hours afterwards, in violent convulsions.

At the conquest the Regency was considered in a flourishing condition, and nearly 2 millions sterling were found in the Turkish treasury, a sum more than sufficient to defray the expenses of the war; nevertheless the united value of the imports and exports at Algiers did not then exceed £175,000 per annum. Algiers, Blidah, Cherchel, and Bône, were the only really flourishing towns of the Deylick; all the rest of the Tell, with the exception of Kabylia, was occupied by the petty clients of a limited number of rich families, who thought much more of defending their crops against the attacks of their neighbours than of advancing the public prosperity. Each tribe lived apart on its own resources, ever on the alert to repel assailants; there was no such thing as a commonwealth, no means of communication, and hardly any commercial transactions.

The French army, being firmly established at Algiers, began at once to extend its operations. General de Bourmont sent in the same month an expedition to Blidah, and took temporary possession of Mersa el-Kebir to the west, and Bône to the east. Upon the revolution of July, and Louis Philippe's acceptance of the crown, it became doubtful whether the conquest of Algeria would be carried on, and the generals withdrew their troops from all the towns excepting Algiers. In September, however, Marshal Clauzel, under the orders of the new authority in France, replaced General de Bourmont. The policy of Marshal Clauzel was to place tributary Beys in the different towns; but the natives, who had at first received the French without suspicion, now made a vigorous resistance.

The most serious opponent whom the French had to encounter was the well-known **Abd-el-Kader**, a man described by Marshal Soult as one of the only three great men then living, all Mohammedans, the other two being Mohammed Ali, Pacha of Egypt, and Schamyl.

[1] "Sketches of Algiers." Boston, 1826.

Abd-el-Kader was born in 1808, in the plains of Ghris, near Maskara. His father, Mahi-ed-Deen, belonged to a family of *Cherfa*, or descendants of the Prophet, and was himself renowned throughout Northern Africa for the piety of his life and his active charity.

When Abd-el-Kader was about 19 years of age his father took him to perform the pilgrimage to Mecca and Medina, and to visit the tomb of Sidi Abd-el-Kader El-Djilani, at Baghdad. They performed a second pilgrimage to Mecca and Medina, and returned to their native country after an absence of two years.

After the fall of Algiers, the order which the Turks had managed to preserve by terror amongst the Arab tribes gave place to anarchy; one tribe rose against another, private vengeance or a thirst for plunder filled the country with marauders, the markets were abandoned, well-disposed persons withheld their produce, and famine threatened to succeed plenty.

The inhabitants of Tlemçen implored the Sultan of Morocco to send a prince of his family to become their Sultan, but the diplomatic efforts of the French prevented the realisation of this project. Si Mahi-ed-Deen was next proposed, but he excused himself on account of his great age, and all he would consent to do was to take command of the Arab tribes sent to disturb the French in their new possession, Oran. Here it was that Abd-el-Kader began to be distinguished, and before he had attained his twenty-fourth year he was hailed by the warlike tribes of Hachems and Beni Amer as their Sultan, and immediately proceeded to Maskara to proclaim and preach the *Djehad*—holy war against the infidel. Thence he despatched his emissaries to invite all the tribes around to send contingents to his forces, and appointed January 1833, before the walls of Oran, as the time and place for opening the campaign. He expected that few save his own followers would accept the invitation, but he made his attack nevertheless, and though he was repulsed he proved his own earnestness, and sealed, as it were, the covenant with the blood of his family, his nephew having been killed by the French. The next few months were occupied by him in attempting to bring about a spirit of unity amongst his tribes; and his absence from the neighbourhood of Oran induced the commandant of that place, General Desmichels, to commence the offensive, which he did by the occupation of Arzeu and Mostaganem. Abd-el-Kader tried in vain to prevent it, and spent the rest of 1833 in consolidating his own power by the occupation of the important city of Tlemçen. A series of engagements followed, and prisoners were captured on both sides; the first overtures of peace, however, came from the French; and on the 4th of February 1834 a treaty was concluded between General Desmichels and Abd-el-Kader, in which the position of the Emir was distinctly recognised, but no recognition on his part of the sovereignty of France was even implied. The form of the treaty displayed the most culpable negligence; each of the contracting parties drew up a paper of conditions, which was signed by the opposite party; and it was only the French paper, signed by the Emir, which received the ratification of Louis Philippe. This was, however, unknown to Abd-el-Kader, who believed that his terms were as binding on the French as their terms were on him.

The Emir had now time to turn his undivided attention to the organisation of his own government; he received considerable presents of arms and ammunition from the French, and began to raise a standing army, and to crush one by one the rivals who had hitherto refused to recognise his supremacy; and in a short time he was undisputed master of the entire province of Oran, which he held not so much by his sword as by the love and admiration of all those wise enough to prefer order to anarchy.

The tribes in the other provinces began to turn their eyes towards so prudent and powerful a chief. A deputation from Medeah implored him to undertake the government of Titeri, which he did, and installed Khalifas of his own as governors of Milianah and Medeah. To the latter place the **Governor-General d'Erlon** sent a mission under Captain St. Hippolyte, with presents, offering to substitute another treaty for that concluded by General Desmichels. The Emir suddenly resolved to return to Maskara, and induced the French mission to return in his suite, which produced an immense effect in his favour amongst the Arab tribes. Immediately on his arrival there he dismissed the mission with a statement of the conditions on which he would consent to treat with the Governor-General, which were in effect a mere revival of those in the Desmichels treaty.

It was not long after this ere hostilities again broke out between Abd-el-Kader and the French; the pretext was afforded by two important tribes placing themselves under the protection of the French at Oran, which was considered by the Emir as a breach of existing conventions.

Then came the disastrous expedition against Constantine (q.v.), and shortly afterwards the celebrated treaty of the Tafna (30th May 1837), by which France abandoned to the Emir nearly the whole of the province of Oran and two-thirds of that of Algiers, reserving only to themselves Oran, Mostaganem, and Arzen, with their territories in the former; and in the latter Algiers, the Sahel, and the Metidja, including Koleah and Blidah.

This state of things could not last long, and when the French had taken Constantine, a dispute regarding the limits of the Metidja and the advance of the army under **Marshal Valée** and the Duc d'Orléans through the Portes de Fer, were considered by the Emir as a breach of the treaty. The French were nothing loth to extricate themselves from a position which had become exceedingly inconvenient, and on their part commenced offensive operations.

Once more Abd-el-Kader raised the standard of a holy war, and massacres of Europeans took place throughout Algeria. In return the French generals extended their conquests on every side. Cherchel fell, Medeah and Milianah were once more occupied, and a desultory warfare was carried on till 1841, when **General Bugeaud** became governor. He commenced a campaign in which the Prince de Joinville and the Ducs d'Aumale and de Nemours served under him. In July Tekedemt, Bokhari, Taza, and Saïda, towns on which Abd-el-Kader depended, were destroyed, and he was hunted through the country, till, his camp being taken, he was driven to take refuge in Morocco at the end of 1843. The Sultan of that country made him caliph of one of his border provinces, and his attacks upon the French while in this position involved his protector in a war. This war terminated in a great victory of the French, 14th August 1844, where General Bugeaud won for himself the title of Duc d'Isly, and, by a treaty in March 1845, Abd-el-Kader lost his asylum in Morocco. He did not on this account relinquish his endeavours to harass the invaders of his native country, but took advantage of the discontent which was fomented in Algeria by Bou-Maza (the man with the goat) to join forces with him ; and when his partisans were crushed at the combat of Aïn-Kebira, 13th October 1845, he sought the support of a new Sultan of Morocco. This ally was defeated, 24th March 1846, by General Cavaignac, and Abd-el-Kader, deserted by his adherents, who began to lose their superstitious reverence for him and to tire of his imposts, was driven from mountain to mountain, showing to the last an indomitable courage. Surrounded on every side by enemies, and with numbers reduced to his mere personal following, he gave himself up, on 21st December 1847, to General de Lamoricière, at Sidi Brahim. His submission was received by the **Duc d'Aumale**, then governor of Algeria, on the 23d ; and two days later he was despatched to Toulon with his family and servants. He remained there till 2d November 1848, when he was removed to the castle of Amboise, near Tours, and was released by Louis Napoleon, 16th October 1852, after swearing on the Koran never again to disturb Algeria. He went at first to Broussa, and being driven thence by an earthquake, went to Constantinople, and subsequently settled at Damascus, where he died.

The struggles of the natives did not cease with the subjection of Abd-el-Kader, though previously Si Hamed-ben-Salem, his caliph, and Bel-Kassem, second in command, had given themselves up; and in the same year Bou-Maza and Mulaï Mohammed, an agitator of Kabylia, surrendered, and promised to use their influence on the side of peace. The troubles in France during 1848 encouraged the Arabs to make fresh efforts in all the three provinces, but they were put down by timely severities. The hardy natives of Kabylia continued to give the most trouble, and the successive expeditions against them might be illustrated by as many tales of daring and devotion as of cruelty. It was not till the end of 1857 that the French spoke of the mountainous region as entirely subject to them. Among the generals who rendered themselves celebrated in these campaigns are the names of Changarnier, Cavaignac, Pélissier, Canrobert, Saint-Arnaud and MacMahon. The resistance each year grew less and less, and the colonists were established on a firmer footing.

The years 1866 and 1867 were the most disastrous since the French conquest. A prolonged and excessive drought produced a failure of crops all over the country ; dried up the sources of the springs ; whole tribes were deprived of their means of subsistence, while the stagnant and polluted water, which alone they could procure for drinking purposes, induced a visitation of cholera which carried off tens of thousands.

One of the severest invasions of locusts ever known, which occurred in 1866, caused the destruction of much of what the drought had spared, and in January 1867 an earthquake destroyed several villages in the Metidja, and seriously injured many more. Not less than 200,000 perished during these two years from the effects of pestilence and famine.

In 1871 a serious **insurrection** broke out, but before commencing a narrative of it, it is necessary to glance at the state of Algeria and the events which transpired there after the declaration of war between France and Germany. At that period the colony was perfectly tranquil, and even the defeats sustained by French arms in the opening battles of the campaign did not materially alter the aspect of affairs, but rather created a desire amongst the native races to avenge their brethren who had fallen fighting side by side with their conquerors. But after Sedan a very marked change began to appear. The fall of the Emperor was sincerely regretted by the great Arab chiefs, who had been his honoured guests at Compiègne; while the excited condition of the public press, and the impolitic measures of the government of Tours and Bordeaux, especially the naturalisation *en masse* of the Jewish inhabitants, inspired them with serious fears for their own position.

On the other hand the colony was entirely denuded of troops, and the old and experienced officers of the Bureau Arabe had almost all quitted their posts for active service in France.

The first act of the insurrection took place in January 1871, at Souk Ahras, where a Smala of Spahis mutinied, and being joined by the adjacent tribes, more or less connected with them by family ties, devastated the farms around, murdered some of the colonists, and endeavoured ineffectually to obtain possession of the town. The insurgents were speedily repulsed by a column from Bône, and obliged to seek refuge in Tunis.

About the same time the wandering tribes occupying the Oued-el-Kebir between Philippeville and the sea broke out and attacked the little town of El-Mila; a detachment from Collo soon suppressed the disturbance. No sooner was it put down than it broke out again in the south and south-east, where Mahi-ed-Deen, son of the Emir Abd-el-Kader, and Ben Chohra, an old Algerian insurgent who had taken refuge in Tunis, had circulated letters amongst the tribes exciting them to revolt. The column which had restored order at El-Mila marched to the frontier, overthrew the rebels before Tebessa, and drove their leaders to the south.

This insurrection could not fail to produce a corresponding effect in the desert; old family feuds and rivalries broke out under the pretext of combating the insurrection, one chief waged war against another; numerous razzias were made, and very soon the whole Sahara was in flames.

Tuggurt was besieged by the Cherif Bou Choucha, as was also Ouargla; the garrison of the former place was massacred, the property of the State was plundered, and order was not perfectly restored there till quite the end of the year, when all the rest of the country had been pacified. Bou Choucha remained at liberty in the oases of Ain Salah till April 1874, when he was taken prisoner by Said, brother of the Agha of Ouargla.

This insurrection was embarrassing to the French, but it was not of extreme gravity, as the events of the south, dependent as it is for supplies on the Tell, can never exercise a serious influence on the general condition of Algeria. The situation of the colony therefore was critical, but not seriously compromised, when the preliminaries of peace with Germany were signed. Already some troops had arrived, and the return of the prisoners of war would soon place an army of seasoned veterans at the disposal of France. This was the time selected for the outbreak of a violent aggression, which might have been serious some months before, but of which the issue could never be doubtful from the moment that France was able to dispose of all her resources. The affairs of the Commune at Paris might have inspired some hope of success, but this could not have been foreseen when the events about to be related occurred.

The village of Bordj-bou-Arreredj, the scene of the first serious devastation of the insurgents, is situated about 72 kilomètres from Setif, in the middle of the tribe of the Hachems, and is the European centre nearest to the territory in which Si Mohammed ben El-Hadj Ahmed El-Mokrani exercised his authority.

He had been for many years Kaid of his tribe, but to augment his prestige, and in the hope of making him a faithful vassal of France, he was promoted to the dignity of Bach-Agha of the Medjana. His influence was very great: he was an intimate personal friend of some of the most distinguished French generals, and had been a frequent guest at the imperial fêtes at Compiègne. He, like many others, took great umbrage at the changes which had taken place in the government of Algeria, especially at the substitution of a civil commissaire of the republic for a governor-general such as Marshal de MacMahon; and when a decree was signed by M. Cremieux circumscribing his command, and constituting part of his territory civil, he is said to have exclaimed: "If my position is to depend on a Jew I renounce it, though I am willing to support anything from one who wears a sword, even if he use it on me." Another cause which probably led this great chief into rebellion was the embarrassed condition of his affairs. Treated like a prince in Paris, he had spent large sums of money in the most lavish manner; loan succeeded loan; ruin appeared inevitable; and he not improbably hoped in some manner, hardly defined to himself, to retrieve his position by force of arms.

Another great chief was Si Mohammed Said ben Ali Cherif, Bach-Agha of Chellata, possessing almost as much influence in Kabylia as Mokrani did in the Medjana, and far more venerated than he, being the lineal descendant of a celebrated saint. He had, however, of late years lost a considerable amount of his prestige, and with it the offerings which the faithful used to bring to the shrine of Chellata, owing to the correspondingly increased power obtained by the superior of the order of *Khouans*, the chief of the religious confraternity of Sidi Mohammed bou Koberain, the Sheikh Mohammed Amzian ben Ali el-Haddad, or the blacksmith. The sons of this Sheikh, M'ahmed and Azziz, enjoyed nearly as great power as their father: the former, a religious fanatic, had already played a part in a previous insurrection; the latter—younger, dissipated, and ambitious—was ready to join in any scheme likely to gratify his vanity or increase his importance.

It was necessary, however, for the common cause that the old rivalry between these two houses should disappear, and through the mediation of Mokrani a reconciliation took place between Ben Ali Cherif and Ben el-Haddad. It was then arranged that Mokrani should be chief of the plain, Si

Azziz of the insurgents, and that Ben Ali Cherif should remain with the French authorities at Algiers, to communicate all that transpired there.

On the 18th February five Europeans were murdered at the Portes de Fer, where some roadmaking was going on, and a month later Mokrani sent in his resignation as Bach-Agha, and followed this up by a formal declaration of war.

He then laid siege to the town of Bordj-bou-Arreredj, pillaged all the outlying farms and buildings, and even drove the garrison into the fort, whereupon the town was occupied by the enemy, plundered, and set on fire. The insurgents adopted every means, some of them, such as mining, hitherto unheard of in Arab warfare, to reduce the place, but in vain. After a siege of twelve days, during which time there was much bloodshed and suffering, and the town reduced to a heap of ruins, the fort was relieved by a column from Setif.

It would be tedious to follow all the operations which ensued. Mokrani succeeded in destroying isolated posts and houses, burning villages, and massacring colonists surprised in the open country or on the roads; but all his efforts to take fortified places failed, and everywhere in the field his men were defeated with great slaughter. The French, at one time reduced to the defensive, had begun to assume the offensive—it was at this moment, when the insurrection appeared almost overcome, that, like a train of gunpowder, it spread over Kabylia at the voice of the Sheikh el-Haddad.

This remarkable man was held in the utmost veneration from Morocco to Tunis: his limbs were completely paralysed; he had passed the last twenty years of his career in a small, dark, filthy cell, where the pious came in crowds to see him through a small window in the side, happy if they were permitted to kiss the hem of his garment.

His sons placed themselves at the head of vast hordes of Kabyles. Bougie, the seaport of the district, was besieged and entirely cut off from all communication with the interior, from the 18th April to the 30th June. The farms, oil mills, public buildings, and everything belonging to Christians throughout Kabylia, were destroyed. Dellys and Djidjelly were in like manner invested, and all the outlying farms ruined. Fort National (then called Fort Napoleon), the French stronghold in Western Kabylia, supported a siege of sixty-three days with great courage and endurance. The garrison of Tiziouzou was likewise blockaded in the fort, and the village destroyed. The village of l'alaestro was attacked and burnt after a short but heroic resistance; nearly all the males, fifty-four in number, were massacred, and forty individuals, of whom thirty-two were women and children, were carried off, and only released at the termination of the campaign, after twenty-two days' captivity.

But now the affairs of the Commune at Paris being over, reinforcements began to arrive from France, the beleaguered towns were relieved, the principal leaders were taken prisoners, and such as escaped were pursued as far as the desert, when they were forced to surrender.

The decisive battle of Mokrani's campaign took place at Souflat, thirty miles from l'alaestro, where his forces were routed and he himself killed.

His death was as noble as his life had been; he had promised General Durrieu, the acting Governor-General, that he would remain faithful to France so long as she should be at war, and it was not till peace had been signed that he sent a formal declaration of war, resigned his functions, gave up his cross of the Legion of Honour, and permitted forty-eight hours to elapse before commencing hostilities. Now that he had staked and lost his all, pursued in every direction by French columns, seeing that the whole colony was being covered with troops, nothing remained for him but an honourable death. He descended from his horse at the battle of Souflat, and on foot at the head of his men he fell pierced with a ball in the forehead.

One more outbreak took place to the west of Algiers, in the mountain district inhabited by the Beni Manassir, between Milianah and the sea. Cherchel was blockaded for a month. The inland village of Zurich, which had been hurriedly protected by a stockade, was gallantly defended during many days by thirty militia and forty military prisoners, most of whom were enfeebled by fever; but, despite the vast disparity of combatants, every village, however slightly fortified, held out successfully, though all the intervening farms, about eighty in number, were sacked and destroyed, and the guardians murdered.

By the middle of August 1871 the insurrection was thoroughly extinguished, and such of the principal leaders as were not killed in action were reserved for future trial, and those who had not participated in any actual massacres were treated with great leniency.

The submission of the revolted tribes, however, was only accepted on the condition that they should consent to disarmament and to the imposition of a war contribution, which was fixed at 30 millions of francs. A general sequestration of landed property was also ordered, but the owners were permitted to resume possession of it in many instances on comparatively easy terms. From this a liberal allowance was made to those who had lost either property or near relatives in the insurrection. The farms and villages were rebuilt on a better scale, the population was increased by the arrival of numerous immigrants, principally from Alsace and Lorraine, and numerous centres were created even in the heart of Kabylia.

An **insurrection** broke out in the **Aurès** mountains in May 1879, in the territory of the Touaba, or Oulad Daood; it was headed by an obscure Marabout named Mohammed bin Abdulla, imam of the Mosque of Hammama, who succeeded in collecting round him a band of discontented Chaouia and vagabonds of all sorts. The commandant of Batna sent two native horsemen to apprehend him, which they actually did, but they were cut to pieces by his followers, and the Marabout was rescued. This was the commencement of hostilities. The insurgents then attacked the Smala of Si el-Hachemi, son of the Kaid Bou-Dhiaf, at Medina; he was not strong enough to resist them, and retired to Batna. They then proceeded to the village of T'Kout, in the Bordj of which resided the Kaid Bachtarzi, him also they killed, but they spared his followers, on condition that they recognised the divine mission of the Marabout. On this becoming known at Batna, the commandant ordered Si Bou-Dhiaf, Kaid of the Oulad Daood, to proceed against the insurgents. He had no force save twenty or thirty followers, to whom were added an officer of the Bureau Arabe, and a few Spahis. On the night following their arrival at their first halt, near Hammama, they were attacked by the Marabout's forces, and although Bou-Dhiaf defended himself with the traditionary courage of his race, killing four enemies with his own hands, he was slain, and his troops had to retreat, leaving their dead, wounded, and baggage in the hands of the insurgents. Emboldened by success, they proceeded to attack the Bordj of Si Bel Abbas, Kaid of the Oulad Abdi ; he himself was absent, but it was occupied by his son Si Lahsen and a few retainers. It was speedily taken, and the young chief and his retainers were massacred. Recruits now began to join the standard of the Marabout from every direction, but the authorities were alive to the importance of the movement, and columns began to advance towards the Aurès from Constantine, Batna, and Biskra. An action took place at El-Arbaa, between an advance guard of the Batna column and 1500 insurgents ; the latter were completely routed, leaving 400 of their number dead on the field. The French penetrated to the very heart of the mountains, pacified the country, and compelled its inhabitants to agree to the terms proposed by the Governor-General, namely, the delivery of hostages, the payment of an indemnity, and the surrender of the principal instigators. The insurgents fled before the French troops to the south, till at last in an attempt to reach Negrine the remainder of these unfortunates, to the number of three or four hundred, perished of thirst and fatigue in the Sahara. The Marabout succeeded in reaching the Djereed of Tunis, but he was subsequently delivered up to the French, and, with his principal accomplices, was tried by a court-martial at Constantine. He and twelve others were condemned to death, twenty-six to various periods of imprisonment, and sixteen were acquitted.

In 1879 a commission was formed at Paris to study the question of railway communication between Algeria and Senegal by the Soudan ; several scientific expeditions were organised ; amongst others, **Colonel Flatters** explored the country between Tuggurt and the 26th degree of N. latitude. In the following year he was again sent to complete the task which he had so successfully commenced. His mission left Ouargla on the 4th of December 1880, and consisted of 11 French, 47 native tirailleurs, 32 camel drivers, 8 Chamba guides, and a certain number of Touaregs, together with 100 riding camels and 180 camels of burden. It followed the Oued Mya, and thence directed its course towards the Sebkha of Amad-Ghor, passing by Hassi-Messeguem and Amguid ; up to that time everything went well, and the last news received from it was dated 29th January 1881.

On the 28th of March following, four of the survivors reached Ouargla, and brought the intelligence that at four days' march from Hassiou, Colonel Flatters had been led into an ambush, that part of the mission had been massacred, and that all the camels had been carried off. The survivors, fifty-six in number, of whom five were French, endeavoured to retreat to Ouargla, a distance of 1500 kilomètres, without means of transport, and almost without provisions. Harassed by the Touaregs, and dying of hunger, they lost many of their number, but the *débris* of the mission still continued to advance, under the command of Maréchal-des-Logis Pobeguin, the last surviving Frenchman. The Khalifa of Ouargla hastened to send out an expedition in search of these unfortunate people; they were found in the month of April at Hassi-Messeguem; the party then consisted only of twelve; no Frenchman had survived. In addition to these twelve men and the Chamba guides, who had disappeared on the day of the massacre, seventeen men turned up afterwards.

Shortly after this the assassination of **Lieutenant Weinbrenner** became the signal for assassination in the south of Oran. A clandestine emigration was observed in the direction of the Tunisian Djereed; in May disturbances were signalled in Djebel Amour, and a small column was sent out from El-Aghouat in the direction of Aflou and Tadjerouna. It here received considerable reinforcements, and inflicted a severe lesson on the El-Aghouat Ksel, which restored confidence amongst the tribes in the department of Algiers. This was followed by the despatch of a column to visit successively M'zab, Metleli, Goleáh, and Ouargla; it returned to El-Aghouat on the 1st of February.

Early in April the Bach-Agha of Frendah reported to the French authorities that disaffection existed amongst the tribes at Tiaret, Geryville, and Saida, and that it was being fomented by a Marabout named **Bou-Amama Bel-Arbi**, who belonged to the great religious family of the Oulad Sidi Cheikh. This fanatic gave himself out as the agent of God destined to drive the French out of the country of the Arabs: orders were given to arrest him, and it was in attempting to execute these that an officer of the Bureau Arabe at Geryville, M. Weinbrenner, was massacred, with nearly all his escort, on the 22d of April; at the same time the telegraph between Geryville and Frendah was cut. This was the signal for a general insurrection in the south; *goums*, or columns of Arab horsemen, sent to attack the insurgents, deserted to or fled before them. On the 11th and 12th of June they made a rapid attack on the workmen, nearly all Spanish, engaged in collecting Alfa grass to the south of Saida, and massacred great numbers of them. This created a panic amongst the Spanish colony, and in a few days 10,000 of them fled from Algeria to their native country, whence, however, they very soon returned.

In July the well-known Si Suleiman ben Kaddour appeared on the scene, and collected around him many tribes which had not joined Bou Amama, and thenceforth he became the veritable chief of the insurrection.

Military operations against the Arabs at such a time and place were almost impossible. As soon as the weather began to get cool, expeditionary columns scoured the country in every direction, and did what was practicable towards restoring order, but the chiefs of the insurrection never were captured.

In one of these expeditions Colonel Negrier committed an act which the Arabs will never pardon or forget; he destroyed the tomb of Sidi Cheikh, the great saint of the Sahara, and transported his ashes to Geryville. This act gained him great popularity with the extreme party in Algeria, and it was never formally repudiated by Government; but some time after the tomb was reconstructed, and the saint's bones once more deposited in it, at the expense of the State.

In November 1882 the territory of the **Beni M'Zab** (see pp. 11, 19) was annexed to Algeria, and taken possession of by a column under the command of General the Prince de la Tour d'Auvergne. The reason assigned was that sanguinary struggles were constantly taking place there, and that it had become a rallying point for all the disaffected tribes in the south.

§ 9. GOVERNMENT OF ALGERIA.

Before the German war the military rule in Algeria had as an essential character the union of the command of the troops and the political and administrative authority in one person. This régime reached its culminating point under Marshal de MacMahon in the subordination of the prefects to the generals commanding the divisions or provinces, but its want of success ended in predisposing the *Corps Législatif* against it, and in the session of 1870 it was decided to introduce to a certain extent civil government. The revolution of September 1870 hastened the fall of the military authority, and the Government of the National Defence fixed the basis of civil government, and removed Algeria from the control of the Minister of War. The office of sub-governor was entirely abolished, and a civil governor-general appointed, under whom the government of the whole colony was centralised at Algiers. At first a separate general officer was appointed to command the entire military and naval forces, having under him generals commanding the three provinces. Subsequently, the first appointment was abolished, and each of the generals commanding provinces was made independent of any central authority and subject only to the Minister of War in Paris. The inconveniences of this system were so strongly felt during the administration of the first civil governor, that although the principle was not modified, a military officer, **General Chanzy**, was appointed to the office of civil governor-general, and invested with the chief command of the military and naval forces.

On the fall of Marshal de MacMahon's government, **M. Albert Grévy** was sent as civil governor-general and *commandant des forces de terre et de mer*. He was received with enthusiasm by the colony, not only on account of his relationship to the President of the Republic, but as the representative of an entirely new state of things, to introduce civil government and the common law in supersession of the arbitrary rule of the Bureau Arabe. On his departure, after two years and a half government, it was the universal opinion of the colony that his resignation was the only satisfactory act of his career. He was succeeded by **M. Tirman**, who was not invested with any military powers.

The old institution of *Bureaux Arabes*, now called the *Service des Affaires Indigènes*, was placed, by a decree dated 12th May 1879, under his direct control, although a small and yearly decreasing extent of territory is still administered by the military authorities, represented by the commandant of the 19th Army Corps.

This service consists of—1. A Central Bureau at Algiers; 2. Divisional Bureaux at Algiers, Oran, and Constantine; 3. Sub-divisional Bureaux; 4. Bureaux of Circles; and 5. Bureaux of Annexes. The departments of the Interior, Justice, Public Worship, Finance, Postes, Public Instruction, Commerce, Agriculture, and Public Works, are each under their respective Ministers in Paris; but these have conferred on the governor-general the power to dispose of the whole or part of the credits given to them by the budget in order to provide for the expenses of the government-general in Algeria.

Each of the three provinces or departments is administered by a prefect, as in France, but always under the superior authority of the governor-general.

The governor-general is further assisted by a council of government composed of the principal civil and military authorities, which studies the various projects brought forward, and gives its advice to the Government; a superior council, meeting once a year, to which delegates are sent by each of the provincial general councils, is charged with the duty of discussing and voting the colonial budget.

Algeria sends three senators and six representatives to the National Assembly—namely, one of the former and two of the latter for Algiers, Oran, and Constantine.

Each department or province in Algeria has a general council composed exclusively of French and natives; the foreign element permitted under the Empire is now excluded. The number of each council is fixed at 36—namely, 30 ordinary members, French citizens, elected in Algeria, and 6 native assessors, named by the Minister of the Interior.

In the growing necessity which is now felt for extending civil government in Algeria, the *rôle* played by the army in times past should never be overlooked; its results are written in the great works everywhere carried out by it. After the conquest it pacified the country, and gave its first administration, such as it was, and such as circumstances permitted. Now that mission is to a certain extent accomplished; still purely civil government is only practicable in the districts entirely pacified, and containing a considerable European element.

The military force in Algeria constitutes the 19th Corps d'Armée of France. In time of war it can be divided in two; 8 regiments of infantry, 2 regiments of artillery, 2 of cavalry, 1 battalion of engineers, can be mobilised and used for active operations in Europe. It consists of 4 regiments of *Zouaves*, 3 regiments of *Tirailleurs indigènes*, 6 battalions of *Chasseurs a pied*, 3 battalions of *Infanterie legère d'Afrique*, 1 Foreign Legion—in all 53 battalions of infantry; 4 regiments of *Chasseurs d'Afrique*, 3 regiments of *Spahis*, 1 brigade of Hussars—in all 52 squadrons; 16 batteries of Artillery, and a certain number of Companies of Discipline. In 1884 the effective of all these forces amounted to 53,647 men and 14,850 horses. Frenchmen born in the country, or electing to reside in it for ten years, are only compelled to serve one year in the army instead of the longer period in force in France.

Of this force the only strictly local and native forces are the Spahis and Tirailleurs indigènes, or *Turcos*. The latter approach very nearly to the Native Infantry in India, the former to the Irregular Cavalry.

Of the Spahis a certain number are stationed in advanced posts in military territory, where each man (with the exception of such Europeans as may join the corps and officers) has a piece of ground allotted to him, which he is permitted to cultivate for his own use, free of taxation ; the other squadrons are lodged in government barracks. The regiments are recruited by volunteers, who may be either married or single, but no difference is made in their duty on this account; they must also each have a good horse and produce a certificate of unexceptionable conduct. The period of service is four years, which may subsequently be extended by periods of from two to four years. No squadron can be composed of natives belonging exclusively to one tribe. Before they can be admitted to squadrons located in *Smalas* as above described, they must have served at least two years in barracks. Frenchmen may be admitted on the same conditions as natives, except that no concession of land is made to them. Natives cannot rise above the rank of Captain-commandant.

§ 10. Sport.

The shooting season opens about the middle of August, and closes in the beginning of February, except for birds of passage, which may be shot from the 15th of March till the 15th of April. No one is permitted to shoot without a license ; persons desiring to obtain one should apply at the consulates of their respective nations. This applies principally to civil territory ; in military districts the authorities are by no means particular ; still the law is the same in both.

The shooting in the immediate neighbourhood of Algiers is not good, the country is becoming too settled ; still there are places within easy range of town where hares and partridges may be found in considerable abundance. Snipe and wild ducks are abundant in the eastern part of the Metidja ; woodcock can usually be met with in the marshes between the Maison Carrée and the Gué de Constantine, in December, and wild boar almost everywhere.

For larger game the traveller must go farther off, and ought to obtain the co-operation of the Arabs of the district. But travellers coming to Algeria with a sole view to sport will certainly be disappointed.

The Government allows the following sums for the destruction of wild animals :—

Lions, 40 f. each ; panthers, 40—cubs of each, 15 f. ; hyenas, 15 ; and jackals, 2 f.

The following table is interesting, showing the numbers of each kind killed in Algeria from 1873 to 1884 :—

Animals.	1873	1874	1875	1876	1877	1878	1879	1880	1881	1882	1883	1884	Totals.
Lions	7	9	9	16	12	24	11	10	1	3	2	..	104
Lionesses	3	14	12	11	9	7	11	6	5	1	1	1	81
Whelps	1	..	1	5	2	3	3	..	..	..	2	..	17
Panthers	91	93	109	111	126	121	135	100	71	48	56	34	1,095
Do. young	8	9	8	3	17	30	15	12	5	4	..	8	119
Hyenas	220	200	217	194	241	156	114	144	64	132	102	104	1,882
Jackals	2528	2773	2916	3648	2919	2760	2175	2900	501	1468	1013	1584	27,185
Totals	2858	3098	3272	3988	3326	3098	2464	3169	647	1656	1176	1728	30,480

Lion and Panther Hunting.—The presence of a lion or panther is soon known by the numerous ravages committed amongst the flocks and herds in the district. The men of the tribe then assemble, and fix the day for hunting it. In the meantime eight or ten are appointed to watch its movements, and decide on the best method of attack. On the day appointed all come well armed. Five or six of the bravest and most agile are selected to undertake the dangerous task of forcing the beast to quit its lair. The tribe now divides itself into seven or eight groups, which surround the place where it is known to be, each group being connected with the next one by skirmishers. Those selected to attack now advance, accompanied by dogs, carefully examining every bush, and keeping themselves ready for any eventuality. The outer circle is gradually contracted, the dogs commence to howl and bark, and very soon the exact spot where the animal is concealed becomes known.

It generally remains stretched on its belly, its head resting on its fore paws, till the dogs are within a few paces; it then makes a bound on the nearest dogs, who usually pay for their temerity with their lives. While occupied with them it is attacked by the Arabs from every direction, but at a respectful distance, and is soon riddled with balls.

If it is killed outright the delight of the Arabs is boundless, but if only wounded they have to look out for their own safety; if there is a horseman amongst them, it is generally on him that the beast fixes his attention; and he requires a good eye, and his horse a sure and rapid foot, to effect an escape, while those on foot finish him off.

The lioness has her young ones about the end of January, and these remain with her, and, like her, make their voices heard at the first approach of danger. She defends them bravely, which the female panther does not always do. Ambuscades are also much used for shooting wild animals. A hole is dug, the bottom of which is an inclined plane of 45 degrees, just large enough to contain a man. The huntsman enters it, the top is covered over with boughs of trees and a thin layer of earth, leaving only a small hole for air and for the muzzle of his gun. In front of this is tied an animal, either living or just killed, care being taken that the ambuscade should be well to leeward of the direction in which the beast is expected to arrive.

Pitfalls are also constructed for large animals in the shape of an inverted funnel, covered over like the ambuscades, and generally placed behind some natural obstacle which the lion would have to clear at a bound to reach the animal used as a decoy, generally a goat or sheep fastened to a picket.

Wild Boar Hunting.—The wild boar commits great destruction in cultivated fields, which it grubs up in search of the roots of arums and other bulbous plants, and it equally devours the grain when it reaches maturity. It is as much to extirpate them as to obtain their flesh that the Arabs chase the wild boar, which they do either from ambuscades or in the open field. When they wish to have a *grande battue* they collect three or four hundred men, of whom fifteen or twenty are well armed. The beaters drive the boars towards them, and sometimes a considerable number are killed and young ones captured.

Gazelle Hunting.—Gazelles are hunted either from ambuscades or by riding them down. In the former case a certain number of persons conceal themselves behind brushwood or natural inequalities of ground, while others on horseback go out in search of a herd of gazelles and try to drive them to where their companions are posted. In the latter case, two or three men on horseback follow the flock at a gentle trot till the animals are tired, when, at a given signal, they gallop in amongst them, and when at forty or fifty paces distant fire at them with slugs; each Arab frequently kills his two beasts.

Bustard Shooting.—The bustard is found on all the plains of the south, and even in some parts of the Tell in the hot season; its flight is heavy, though tolerably long sustained. As soon as it perceives a man it tries to conceal itself behind a tuft of alfa or tall grass, follows every movement of the sportsman, and rarely allows him to get within shot except during the hottest part of the day, when it almost allows itself to be ridden over. The bustard in its flight has always an inclination to go in a circular direction; the Arab takes advantage of this peculiarity by getting beyond it, and, without appearing to follow it, endeavours to make it describe a gradually decreasing circle till he gets within range. He usually tries to hit it on the wing, in the hope of breaking a leg or a wing, as its plumage is so thick that it is exceedingly difficult to kill when running.

The lesser bustard, or *Poule de Carthage*, is common, and affords excellent sport.

Falconry.—The best falcons are found in Jebel Amour or the Sahara. Immediately a falcon is snared, its master covers its head with a leathern hood, and perches it on his shoulder, taking care to sew a thick pad of leather on that part of his *burnous*. It is left two days without food, and then it is fed on fresh raw meat, with the head uncovered. This is repeated twice every day, and in the intervals its master does all he can by caresses to tame it, and accustom it to captivity. In two or three months he begins to accustom it to search for its own food while still attached to him by a thin string; and even on the mornings of the days when it is subsequently to be employed, he endeavours to let it see and almost attack a living quarry.

The falcons principally used by the Arabs are the Saker (*Falco sacer*), the Lanner (*Falco lanarius*), the Barbary Falcon (*Falco barbarus*), and the Peregrine (*Falco peregrinus*), all of which species breed in the country.

The trade of tamer of falcons is hereditary in certain families, and it is only the highest ranks of Arabs who can afford to indulge in this luxury. The falconers usually form part of their retinue.

An expedition of this nature is usually a great fête in an Arab tribe; it is frequently arranged to celebrate a marriage, or the visit of a person of distinction. A day is selected when the atmosphere is perfectly clear. The falconers are mounted on horseback, generally with three falcons, two on the shoulders and one on the head. Forty or fifty horsemen place themselves in a single line, thirty or forty paces apart, while others on foot beat the ground between them.

It is usually in the great plateaux of the south, covered with alfa, that this sport is practised. The moment a hare is started the falcons are unhooded, and allowed to see their prey. They at once soar into the air out of sight; the horsemen start off at full gallop, with loud cries; the birds poise themselves for a moment in the air, and then descend with deadly aim on their victim, which would soon be torn to pieces did the falconers not rush forward and regain their birds.

Not only hares, but partridges, bustards, flamingoes, and other large birds are thus hunted, and so precious are well-trained falcons that they are transmitted from father to son, and no money would tempt an Arab to part with one. The casual visitor to Algiers must not count on being able to enjoy much of this sport, unless he is on terms of intimacy with some of the superior French officers in the south of the colony, who might perhaps be induced to organise a day's "*Chasse aux faucons*" for his amusement.

Partridge Shooting.—The Arabs have several strange methods of shooting or killing partridges. One is to take advantage of the propensity which these birds have to huddle together in case of danger. An Arab covers himself with the skin of a lion, panther, jackal, etc.; and when he sees a covey frightened at his approach he fires into the middle of them, and not unfrequently kills eight or ten at one shot. They are also frequently able to attract them at night by means of a lantern, and kill them with sticks.

§ 11. ZOOLOGY.

The **Fauna** of Algeria does not differ materially from that of the Mediterranean system in general. In the eastern portion it resembles that of Sicily and Sardinia, while in the west it approaches more nearly still to that of Spain. The presence of European birds in Algeria is of course easily explained; but there are many mammalia, fish, reptiles and insects common to both countries. Some of these are no longer found in Southern Europe, such as the lion, panther, serval (*Felis serval*), hyena, jackal, golden fox (*Vulpes niloticus*), genet (*Genetta afra*); but abundant evidence of the existence of these in remote ages is found in the caverns of the south of France. One species of genet, however (*Viverra genetta*), is very common in Spain, and the jackal (*Canis aureus*) is abundant in some provinces of European Turkey. The progress of civilisation in Europe has caused their disappearance, while Mohammedan barbarism has favoured their multiplication in Africa, a country little inhabited, and abounding in flocks and herds.

The lion is hardly ever found in the mountains of Kabylia, except sometimes in the Oued es-Sahel. Its favourite haunts are in the neighbourhood of Jemmapes, between Philippeville and Bône, and the back of the Djurdjura range, between the Oued es-Sahel and Aumale; it is now, however, rapidly approaching extinction. The panther is found more or less frequently all over the country, as are various other species of the cat and dog tribe. Mouflons or wild goat (*Ammotragus tragelaphus*) and gazelles are common in the south. The Algerian monkey (*Inuus ecaudatus*) is found from the gorge of the Chiffa as far as the eastern limit of Kabylia. Their depredations are sometimes very serious, and the natives use every means in their power, short of shooting them, to drive them away. They entertain a superstitious dread of killing these animals, as they believe them to be the descendants of members of the human race, who, having incurred the Divine anger, were deprived of speech.

In the forest of the Beni Saleh, in the province of Constantine, red deer (*Cervus barbarus*) are still to be found, but they are becoming rarer every year, owing in a great measure to the destruction of the forest land by fire; there is too much reason to fear that they will soon become extinct. They may be found in the forest of Beni Saleh, and in the vicinity of Ghardimaou on the Tunisian railway.

One of the most important animals in Algeria is the camel, and the Arabs reckon their wealth by the number they possess. These animals, which live thirty or forty years, are not usually worked before five years of age, nor after twenty-five. They are docile and domestic, and are of incalculable value as beasts of burden in the desert, where no other animal could live for so long without water—one supply of which, every five or six days, suffices for them. They have also been successfully employed by the French generals as a means of transport for troops; but they can only be used in the Sahara, as north of the Atlas the climate is too cold. A good camel will carry a load of from 500 lbs. to 800 lbs., or even more, for a distance of 30 or 40 miles in a day. There is a larger variety, called by the Arabs "Mehari," which has hardly any hump, and which is used more for speed than for carrying burdens. It is capable of performing a journey of 80 to 100 miles, for several days in succession, keeping at a trot the whole distance. The food of the camel is grass and branches of trees, and sometimes barley and dates. When they are past work they are fattened for killing, the flesh being considered good and wholesome, especially the hump, which is the choicest part. The skin is used for several purposes, and the hair is used for weaving into various tissues, especially Arab tent cloth. The milk of the camel is a staple article of food amongst the Arabs.

The native cattle of Algeria are of excellent quality as a stock on which to graft the better European varieties. They are hardy, and support admirably the alternations of heat and cold, wet and drought, to which they are exposed in the pasture-lands of the High Plateaux.

One of the great sources of wealth in this colony is its sheep, which are bred on the High Plateaux, where agriculture is impossible. Before the conquest the Arabs reaped hardly any advantage from their flocks, as they were to a great extent cut off from a market on the coast by the rapacity of the intervening tribes. For some years after the conquest two or three shillings was considered a fair price for a sheep; even in 1866 one could be purchased at the market of Bou-Farik, close to Algiers, for from nine to eleven shillings; now a similar beast fetches sixteen to twenty shillings, and when sent by rapid steam transport to France, it realises from thirty-two to forty in the Paris market, where during the summer more than 20,000 are sent every month.

Regarding the horse, the reader cannot do better than study the excellent work of General Daumas, "Les Chevaux du Sahara."

The **Ornithologic fauna** of the coast district of Algeria closely resembles that of Southern Europe, though even in that portion of the country some birds are found whose occurrence in Europe rests upon very slender evidence; amongst these may be mentioned the Tchagra Shrike, the Dusky Ixos, the Ultramarine Titmouse, the Algerian Chaffinch, and Moussier's Redstart, all of which species are to be frequently met with in the neighbourhood of Algiers, and are often brought to the market of that city. In the High Plateaux and the Sahara many species of birds unknown in Europe occur, and the province of Constantine is especially rich. Amongst the more conspicuous birds of the mountains may be mentioned the Lämmergeyer, the Imperial, Tawny, Golden and Bonelli's Eagles, and the Bald Ibis; whilst the Houbara Bustard, the Demoiselle Crane, and various species of sand grouse, occur in the vast plains of the interior.

Ostriches are found sparingly in the northern part of the Sahara, and more plentifully farther south, but are every year becoming more rare. They are gregarious, living in herds of five or six individuals. An ostrich skin with the feathers is worth on the spot from £10 to £25; but it is very seldom that one can be obtained that has not been more or less thinned by the Arabs. Ostriches, when pursued, always run in circles, so that while one party of horsemen follows the herd, another rides at right angles to a place affording a good look-out, endeavouring to discover the route taken by the birds. If they succeed in this they pursue them, and usually run down one or more, although some of their horses frequently fall exhausted before the chase is over. When running at full speed they can easily outstrip the horses, their stride being from 25 to 28 feet! Ostrich eggs are excellent eating. The shells are sold in Algiers, some coloured and mounted for ornament only, and others made into sugar-basins, cups, etc.

Fish.—Every species of fish that is found in the Mediterranean is caught off the coast of Algeria, among the most important of which are the tunny, sardine, sole, mullet, besides shellfish in great variety; the Algerian prawns, especially those of Bône, being of enormous size and delicate flavour.

The fresh waters of Algeria contain twenty-one species of fish, none of which are of much value from an economic point of view, with the exception of two species of barbel and the common eel. Of the number five are peculiar to Algeria: the trout (*Salmo macrostigma*), which loves the cool and limpid water of the Oued Z'hour and its affluents, flowing over beds of granite and gneiss through cool shady forests in the vicinity of Collo—this is the most southern of the salmon family; the *Tellia apoda*, a small cyprinodon, destitute of ventral fins, which has no known habitat save the spring of Bou-Merzug, from which it never strays more than half a mile; the *Leuciscus callensis*, which peoples all the lakes and springs in the east of Algeria; the *Barbus setifensis*, which is found everywhere; and the *Syngnathus algeriensis*, peculiar to the Seybouse and the two streams which unite to form it, the Oued Cherf and the Bou-Hamdan; and a species of *Chromis* (*C. tristramii*) from the desert.

The fish fauna of the Tell and High Plateaux belongs exclusively to the Mediterranean system; the Sahara alone is linked to Africa by its *Chromidæ*.

Several attempts have been made to introduce other species as articles of food. The Arabs have never shown a very great liking for fish, and have never attempted to naturalise them, except in the case of the goldfish, which was prized rather for its beauty than for its economic value.

The first attempt to introduce European species since the French conquest was made in 1858 by MM. Kralik and Cosson, who brought to Constantine a barrel of young carp and the ova of various Salmonidæ. The latter were successfully hatched, and the young fish developed rapidly in the pure water of the cistern in which they were placed; but no sooner were they launched into the water of the river Roumel than their bodies and eyes seemed to get covered with a sort of calcareous film, and they speedily died. The carp, on the contrary, have succeeded admirably in the Basin of Djebel Wahash, and have multiplied amazingly. Some were put into the Roumel; but the Zouaves, informed of their translation, immediately set to work to catch them, and soon destroyed these new denizens of the river.

Attempts at pisciculture have also been made in the province of Algiers, where carp and, more recently, tench have succeeded perfectly in reservoirs.

At this point, however, the experiment has remained stationary, and no effort to naturalise the fish thus bred has been made. The question, as far as relates to the Salmonidæ, appears easy to resolve, after the experience gained at Constantine. Fish of this family require fresh and clear water not charged with calcareous deposits. These conditions are only possible on certain points of the littoral, particularly in Eastern Kabylia, and partly in that of Babor, where the streams rise on the sides of high mountains, preserving a temperature nearly constant, flowing on a bed of gneiss, granite, or schist, and protected from the rays of the sun by shady forests.

Unfortunately, on the whole of the littoral of the provinces of Constantine and Algiers, the mountain-range is broken up into an infinite variety of little basins, very steep, which only supply running water from autumn till June. An extensive zone of acclimatisation cannot, therefore, be anticipated for the salmon family; and the small volume of water in those streams will not permit the introduction of the larger species; but the Algerian trout may well be employed to people the few suitable rivers where it does not already exist.

In this zone also an attempt might advantageously be made to introduce fish of other families, especially of the Percidæ, which delight in clear and limpid water. In the province of Oran these might succeed in the upper part of the Tafna, which flows over a bed of rocks and gravel.

In other parts of the country, where even the most important streams sink, during the hot season, to a mere series of pools connected by shallow rills thoroughly heated by the sun's rays, the carp and tench offer the best chances of success. The latter (which, in Europe, inhabits muddy marshes almost dry in summer, without detriment to the quality of its flesh) might endure as well as the barbel the calcareous salts which the majority of rivers in Algeria hold in solution, the rather that they would be free from their natural enemies the larger crustaceans and voracious fishes.

It is by no means uncommon for fish to be ejected by artesian wells; and this has formed the subject of numerous speculations. It has been concluded that these fish inhabited the vast subterranean sea which occupies the bottom of the Saharan depression; and it has been asked how, if they were destined to live in perpetual obscurity, they were not destitute of eyes like the Sirens of the grottoes of Carniola or the Crustacea of the Mammoth Cave in the United States?

We have already noticed the existence, from Biskra as far as Temacin, of *bahrs* or *gouffres*, which communicate with the underground sheet of water, and occupy too great a surface to be regarded as the enlarged apertures of fallen-in wells. All these apertures are inhabited by considerable numbers of Cyprinodons and Chromidæ. There they live freely exposed to air and light, and breed under normal conditions. Their underground life is merely an episode, and, as it were, an incident in the voyages which they undertake between one *bahr* and another. When they reach the neighbourhood of a well they are forced up with the water or obey an instinct to mount to the surface.

Snakes of various species occur throughout Algeria, but the only venomous one is the *Cerastes*, or horned viper, found commonly in the Sahara, but sometimes also in the High Plateaux. The tortoise, chameleon, scorpion, and a large species of lizard, called by the Arabs "Deb," are also found.

Mention must also be made of the **Locusts**, which are one of the plagues of Algeria. They appear every few years; and four serious incursions have taken place since the French conquest.

These invasions take place under a double form: first, dark clouds of adult insects darkening the sun, and appearing like a thick fall of snow, come from the direction of the High Plateaux. These soon commence to lay their eggs in any light sandy soil they can find, and in thirty or thirty-five days afterwards the young insects or *criquets* commence to appear. These are far more destructive than the parents, and under their attacks vegetation of every kind disappears as by magic. They usually appear towards the close of the hot season, and the first rain or cold of autumn causes them all to disappear.

The first serious invasion of locusts was in 1845, and did considerable damage; but as European cultivation was not then in a very advanced state its effects were not seriously felt. The second was in 1866, and left deeper traces for several years, both from the immense number of insects which remained, and from the permanent injury done to vegetable life, which has been estimated at £800,000. The third was in 1874, less calamitous than the others, owing to the vigorous measures taken to destroy both the adult insects, the eggs, and the criquets. The fourth is devastating Algeria at the present moment (1889), and no one can predict when it may terminate. During 1888 it prevailed over an area of 300,000 hectares, containing a population of 700,000 souls; the estimated value of the loss sustained being 25 millions of francs. In 1889 this is expected to be much greater.

The inhabitants of the desert, however, do not regard these insects with the same dread as do those of more fertile districts; for them they are a precious manna sent by Providence; they collect them with care, dry and salt them, and devour them with as much relish as a Londoner does shrimps at Margate.

§ 12. Geology, Mineralogy, Hot Springs, etc.

Geology.—The **Crystalline rocks**, including granite, gneiss, and mica-schist, are but slightly developed as regards superficial extent, though they attain a considerable thickness. They seem to be confined to the neighbourhood of the coast, on or near which they are found in small patches, and at distant intervals all the way from Tetuan and Ceuta, in Morocco, to the frontier of the Tunisian territory. There is a patch near Nemours, not far from the west frontier of Algeria, and others at Algiers, the Djurdjura mountains, Djebel Goufi (Cape Bougiaroni), and Djebel Edough, between Philippeville and Bône. The **Palæozoic rocks** also attain a considerable thickness, though with a small superficial development; and as fossils have not yet been discovered in them, their age is not accurately known, but they are thought to belong to the Silurian epoch. They consist for the most part of much altered limestones, associated with schists; in places of argillaceous or arenaceous schists with quartzite. They are found in the neighbourhood of the coast, usually at the spots where the crystalline rocks show themselves.

Upon these palæozoic rocks rest unconformably at certain places a considerable thickness of red conglomerates, coarse sandstones, and arenaceous slates. They are non-fossiliferous, and may be either Devonian or Permian. **Jurassic strata** are only found in scattered patches in the two eastern provinces of Algeria, but in the province of Oran they are extensively developed. The former seem, from the fossils which their limestones and dolomites contain, to blend together the three divisions into which the lias can usually be separated. In the province of Oran, above these liassic strata, are others nearly 2000 ft. thick, which fall into the Kelloway, Oxford clay, and Coral rag divisions of the Middle Oolite. It seems that the Lower and Upper Oolite are not represented, and the next beds are those that belong to

The **Cretaceous formation**, which in the provinces of Constantine and Algiers are so well developed that some geologists believe all the divisions into which the formation is distinguishable in France are to be found here. The Neocomian division, which is chiefly composed of sandstones and marls, with a thickness of more than 1000 ft., is seen at a number of detached points, extending from Tunis to Morocco. The mountainous district near Cherchel and Milianah is composed of these beds, which hereabouts reach the coast. The greater part of the hill of Chennoua, east of Cherchel, consists of inferior cretaceous rocks.

The middle and upper divisions of the cretaceous formation cover a large extent of surface in Algeria, and in many districts the beds are much inflexed and dislocated. M. Coquand, who has examined the geological features of Constantine, states that he has met with five stages of the lower chalk, seven of the middle chalk, and four of the upper chalk, with their characteristic fossils. The upper divisions are but feebly developed in the Oranese Tell, but in the south of the province it occupies a considerable superficies.

Commencing the Tertiary beds with the Nummulitic division of the Eocene, rocks of that formation have been found at many detached points, but not to extend over a wide surface of the country. In the province of Constantine there are patches in the High Plateaux and in the mountainous region bordering them on the south. A more northerly band of patches is seen passing by the mountains of Babor (between Djidjelly and Bougie), Djurdjura, Bouzegza (the striking hill seen from Algiers in the south-east), Chennoua (seen from Algiers in the west), and Cape Tenès. In the province of Oran only a few small fragments have been discovered. The beds of the **Miocene** epoch are extensively developed in Algeria. The lowest division is well seen at Tiziouzou (Djurdjura), and on the flanks of the Atlas between Blidah and El-Affroun; also at Milianah and Tenès, all in the province of Algiers. The next stage is susceptible of division into several groups, one of which is the exact equivalent of the faluns of Touraine, abounding in **Ostrœa crassissima**. The cedar forest of Teniet-el-Ahd stands above beds of this division, the Helvetian group of continental geologists. A third stage, which does not contribute to the constitution of the Atlas ranges, but is only found at their feet, is chiefly composed of marls and sandy limestones or molasse. These beds are well developed in the Sahel of Algiers. In this district we find first a coarse sandstone with clypeastus, then a thick deposit of marls, which in places are rich in shells, and at the top a molasse with *Terebratula ampulla*.

The **Pliocene** epoch is represented in the province of Oran by sandstones with many recent shells, which sometimes attain a thickness of 150 m. (plateau of Mostaganem, valley of the Chelif, etc.) In the other provinces such beds are as yet unknown.

Beds of the **Quaternary** epoch (applying the term to all deposits posterior to the last Alpine dislocations) cover very large spaces in Algeria, and offer problems which will require much study on the part of the geologist. The lowest division consists of a thick deposit of pebbles surmounted by beds of gravel, above which is an argillaceous deposit. These beds are posterior to the latest basaltic rocks, and they have been subjected to a movement of elevation. The immense extent covered by these deposits in the interior of the country is very remarkable, as well as the height to which they reach on the Plateaux. They appear to be of precisely the same nature as those extending over enormous spaces in the Sahara. Their origin remains an unsolved enigma. One point, however, is clear: they do not belong to a deposit, originally continuous and afterwards dislocated, but they were accumulated by atmospheric agencies in separate basins of greater or less extent. In the coast region the plain of the Metidja and the valley of the Chelif afford examples of these wonderful accumulations of transported materials. The Metidja plain has been bored to the depth of **600 ft.** without reaching the limit of the quaternary deposits.

In addition to these subaerial deposits there are raised beaches to be seen at intervals all along the coast, from Tunis to the Atlantic border of Morocco, showing that the land has been elevated a few feet in recent times, for the fossils thus brought into view belong to the existing fauna of the Mediterranean.

Finally, there is the earthy matter deposited in the great depressions,

Introd. § 12. GEOLOGY, MINERALOGY, HOT SPRINGS, ETC. 77

called by the Arabs **Sebkas** or **Chotts**. These are hollows, frequently of a great size, which in some cases are filled with water, in others permanently dry. The deposit alluded to is of a more or less argillaceous and very fine material. It is often stratified, the beds being sometimes a few yards in thickness. In it are found shells of terrestrial molluscs of living species.

Though the sedimentary deposits above described constitute the most prominent features of the geology of Algeria, **Eruptive rocks** are not wanting in this country. It is true their mineralogical character is not always easy to determine; but we may admit, in general, that many of those rocks have a great affinity with melaphyrs and basalts, whereas others belong to diorites, dolorites, porphyries, and trachytes.

In the province of Oran basalts are common, particularly between Oran and Tlemçen, but it is in the province of Algiers that eruptive rocks have been most studied. They appear there either like gigantic dikes, disposed on more or less regular lines, directed generally from east to west, or they are scattered about like isolated islands. The first are for the most part represented by a chain of mountains or hills—such are the two eruptive ranges between Milianah and Cherchel—of which the one follows the northern slope of the *Sra Kebira*, and the other (to the north of the first) extends from the chain of *Djebel Souma*, nearly to the small town of *Zurich*. Farther to the north, the shore between Cherchel and the Oued Arbil is more or less chequered by numerous volcanic outbursts, which, without following uninterrupted lines, follow the direction of the shore, and consequently range equally from east to west. Among those volcanic manifestations must be mentioned a kind of **peperino** which occurs in the neighbourhood of Cherchel, where, on both sides of the *Oued el-Hachem*, the tertiary regularly-stratified deposits present a curious alteration in the structure and the mineralogical composition of the rock; for not only are these tertiary strata highly indurated, as if they had been exposed to the action of fire, but they include a quantity of little dark-greenish fragments, different from any rock occurring on the surface of the country. It is therefore probable that the agent which converted those tertiary strata into a volcanic conglomerate, reminding us of the *peperino* of Rome and Naples, was of a subterraneous nature, the more so as a dark-greenish rock, very like a diorite, composes the superior part of the mountain Djebel Arujaud, situated to the west of Cherchel, near the mouth of the Oued Masselmun. The *peperino* of Cherchel occurs equally in the plain of Metidja.

The three above-mentioned zones (Sra Kebir, Oued-Arbil, and the shore of Cherchel) constitute the chief linear ranges of volcanic rocks in the province of Algiers; but, as we have already stated, except those linear (or nearly so) volcanic expansions, the country in question is chequered by numerous volcanic outbursts scattered about promiscuously. Such are the local outbursts which generally mark the site of hot springs so abundant in this country, and among which the *Hammam Melouan* is one of the most remarkable. An important local volcanic outburst is offered by the mountain *Zakkar Gharbi* (to the north-west of Milianah), crossed by a porphyric dike of a whitish colour more than 8 kilomètres in length. It is chiefly composed of felspar, including crystals of quartz, small lamellæ of mica, and some other minerals in less quantities. It may perhaps not be quite without the limits of our subject to remark that the vegetation observed on this large dike consists almost exclusively of the *Cistus ladaniferus*, a fact which offers a curious exemplification of the peculiar connection between the chemical composition of the soil and its vegetable character.

It is highly probable that all the above-mentioned volcanic rocks in the provinces of Oran and Algiers are contemporaneous, or nearly so, and there cannot be any doubt about their age, for they have all protruded through the tertiary deposits of the country, and therefore are of a post-tertiary epoch. One of the numerous instances which prove this statement is offered by the *peperino* of the plain of Metidja, where, on many points, this volcanic conglomerate is covered by the quaternary deposits, which, moreover, frequently include fragments of the volcanic rocks of the country.

It is most likely that these may be discovered in other parts of Algeria; but in the present state of our knowledge we must limit ourselves to those positively ascertained. At all events, the concentration of volcanic rocks in the province of Algiers, and in the proximity of the town, may account for the frequent earthquakes to which Algiers, Blidah, Djidjelly, etc., are subject.

This rapid sketch cannot be closed without inquiring into the part which the phenomenon of **glaciation** may have played in the geological history of Algeria—a phonomenon which has given rise to a greater amount of controversy than perhaps any other fact of Natural Philosophy. It is true Algeria has not yet been sufficiently explored to yield a satisfactory answer to this important question; nevertheless many of its regions have been carefully studied by able geologists, such as MM. Coquand, Ville, and Pomel, from whose observations all traces of the glacial epoch could not have escaped had they existed. It seems, therefore, very probable that Algeria has not been exposed to the glacial period. This fact is of great importance, because it adds another large country to the number of those which do not offer any trace of a geological phasis considered by so many natural philosophers as having invaded the greatest part of our globe—a hypothesis which loses ground as our geological investigations gain in extension. So, for instance, no positive trace of the glacial period has hitherto been ascertained in European Turkey, Greece, in the Caucasus, in the Himalayan mountains, in Thibet, or in China; neither did M. de Tchihatchef discover any in the Altaïen mountains of Siberia, or on any point of the large peninsula of Asia Minor, which during six years he crossed in every direction. Like all those countries, Algeria seems to have escaped the action of the glacial period, *in spite of the proximity of other countries invaded by it*, an exemption which has a striking parallel in Asia Minor; for the northern shores of this peninsula are separated only by a distance of about 500 kilomètres from the southern limit of the erratic blocks in European Russia, which do not go beyond the latitude of 51 degrees, a distance almost equal to that between Land's End and the Pentland Straits. It will easily be admitted that if one of these two extremities of England were now to be buried under a thick permanent crust of ice, such an event would have a great effect upon the opposite extremity, whatever might be the nature of the intermediate space, whether land or water, for in the first case traces of ancient moraines, as well as furrowed and scratched surfaces of rocks, would indicate the former existence and movement of glaciers ; and, in the second case, erratic blocks and *debris* would have been transported from one point to the other by floating masses of ice. The absence in Asia Minor of any traces of the intense cold which during the glacial period prevailed through almost the whole of European Russia is particularly striking, when we consider that now, when the large Russian plains are no longer covered with glaciers, but merely exposed to the atmospheric current coming directly from the Arctic region, they exercise a strong influence on the climate of the Black Sea, of the northern shores of Asia Minor, of the Bosphorus and of Constantinople. This refrigerant action manifests itself not only by the depression of the annual, and particularly of the winter temperature, much lower than that of any countries placed under the same latitude and under similar topographical conditions, but also by the curious phenomenon of congelation, of which the Black Sea, the Bosphorus, and even the Dardanelles have offered several instances, for M. de Tchihatchef has shown that this fact has occurred no less than *seventeen* times during the historical period.[1]

All these extraordinary phenomena receive a new support from Algeria, for the littoral of Africa is separated from Southern France and Italy, where the glacial period has left unmistakable traces, by a distance still smaller than that between Asia Minor and Southern Russia. Therefore the absence in Algeria of any well-ascertained traces of the glacial epoch is a most important contribution to the argument which may be alleged in favour of the statement—that the glacial period, far from possessing a *general* character, is less remarkable for its *extension* than for its *localisation*, and took place not only independently of temperature and geographical position, but rather in a most striking opposition to such conditions, so that the extension of glacial phenomena has been checked or favoured by causes hitherto inaccessible to our knowledge, and at any rate very different from those admitted by the theories of many geologists belonging to the school of glacialists.

MINERALOGY.

During the last 30 years numerous concessions of **Iron, Lead, Copper**, and other minerals have been made, but the working of them has not always been attended with success, principally owing to the want of adequate means of transport. The mineral wealth of Algeria appears to be boundless ; **calamine** or **carbonate of zinc, cinnabar** or **sulphide of mercury**, various **ores of copper**, and **argentiferous lead ore**, are found in great abundance, especially in the province of Constantine. But the most valuable mineral of Algeria is its iron, which is found close to the sea, throughout nearly the whole littoral. The quality is exceptionally rich and good ; it is nearly devoid of sulphur, arsenic, and phosphorus ; the proportion of metal in the ore is sufficient to enable it to pay a heavy freight to Europe, and in much

[1] *Vide* "Asie Mineure," vol. ii. (Climatologie), pp. 25-67, by P. de Tchihatchef ; and "Le Bosphore et Constantinople," pp. 268-318, by the same author.

of it there is a large proportion of manganese, which is of the greatest value in the reduction of the metal.

Algeria possesses immense quantities of **Salt**. In *Routes* 12 and 21 will be found a description of two remarkable mountains of rock-salt; and there are many enormous salt lakes and marshes, some of them being hundreds of square miles in area, which could be made to furnish almost any quantity. Many different kinds of **marble** are found, some of it of excellent quality, such as the white, gray, red, green, rose-veined, etc. The quarry of so-called **Algerian onyx** at Aïn Tekbalet was formerly worked by the Romans. More than sixty ancient quarries have recently been found near Kleber, in the province of Oran, yielding the long-lost Numidian marbles formerly so highly prized. They are of a richness and beauty quite unequalled in any other part of the world. **Building-stone** is abundant; also freestone, gritstone, gypsum, potters' and brick clay, and slate.

Hot Springs.

There are numerous thermal springs in Algeria, but few of them are as yet turned to any account. Those principally used are:—

The **Hammam R'hira**, the Roman Aquæ Calidæ, near Bou Medfa, on the railway to Oran. Traces of the ancient Roman town still exist; and there is a large and commodious establishment there. Temp. about 115° Fahr.

The **Hammam Melouan**, in the valley of the Harrach, much frequented by the natives, who have implicit belief in the efficacy of the waters. Temp. 103° Fahr.

The **Hammam Meskoutin**, near Guelma. These are the most remarkable of any of the hot springs of Algeria. The waters contain a great deal of carbonate of lime in solution, which, gradually depositing, has formed a large rock, from the top of which the springs issue. They are the hottest of all the sources in the country, the temperature being 203° Fahr.

The **Hammam** at the **Portes-de-fer**, containing 22 centigrammes of sulphate of soda per litre of water, and having a temperature of 158° to 170° Fahr., is excellent in cases of cutaneous diseases.

The **Ain M'kebrita**, 50 kil. S.E. of Constantine, which, though not very warm, is rich in sulphur and chloride of sodium.

The **Bain de la Reine**, 3 miles from Oran, where there are bath-houses. The waters, which rise in a grotto, have a temperature of about 125° Fahr. Besides those here mentioned, many other mineral springs, both hot and cold, exist, which are less frequented. (See the various localities indicated.)

Earthquakes.

Algeria is subject to earthquakes, which frequently occur, and are occasionally very severe. One occurred in 1716, and continued with intervals for a whole month. In 1825 Blidah was entirely destroyed by one, and, according to Consul-General Thomas's report, more than 14,000 of the inhabitants perished; and again, in 1867, the same town and several surrounding villages were partially thrown down. The town of Djidjelly was also destroyed by the same cause in 1855. A very severe one occurred at M'sila in the end of 1885.

§ 13. Colonisation, Agriculture, Forests, etc.

Colonisation.—The colonisation of Algeria is a splendid work still far from completion. A long extent of seaboard, rich soil, boundless material wealth, a fine climate, magnificent scenery, the most favourable geographical position conceivable,—all these ought to secure for it a brilliant future.

France has indeed done much for it, and the world owes her a debt of gratitude for having converted a country which on the sea-coast was a nest of pirates, and in the interior a chaos of anarchy, into a colony, not yet indeed as prosperous as it ought to be, but still an infant of fair promise, requiring only tranquillity and population to make it what it once was, the granary of Southern Europe.

Like the conquest of a country, colonisation should proceed inland from the sea. At first on the littoral there were low plains, marshy and hot, the nurseries of malarious fevers. These are now to a great extent drained, and long culture has rendered them comparatively healthy; trees have everywhere been planted, and it may be now said that the plains have been conquered to colonisation, and the higher and more healthy lands are now open to it.

An exception may perhaps be made to a certain extent in the plain of the Chelif. The agricultural produce of a country does not entirely depend on the fertility of its soil; the hygrometrical condition of its climate is equally important. Thus the plains of the Metidja and Chelif have equally good soil, but in the first, rain is more abundant, and the sea-breezes afford a certain quantity of moisture; the consequence is that its harvests are generally good, and population can always find the means of increasing. But in the plain of the Chelif rain is more scarce, the air drier, owing to the sea-breezes being shut out by a range of hills along the coast, and good harvests are not obtained more than once in three years.

Evidently the only means of remedying this, and opening out this great plain to colonisation, is by constructing dams or *barrages* to irrigate the land, and by planting trees on a grand scale wherever possible.

This plain contains 500,000 acres of land of the first quality, of which 200,000 are capable of being irrigated. Colonisation is here represented by but few centres of European population, of which the European inhabitants hardly exceed 4000, the natives being scarce in proportion. Nevertheless, a railway and a good road traverse this valley for a length of 200 kilomètres, and several barrages have been constructed. In the present condition of this plain it would be inhumanity to create many villages, the heat of summer there being intense, and the absence of all shade greatly increasing the fatigue of labour; wherever trees have been planted their influence on the climate has been considerable, and there has been a perceptible decrease of temperature.

From 1833 to 1844 absolutely nothing was done towards colonisation; between the latter year and 1848 the villages of the Sahel and of the Atlas were laid out, and many of them finished. Marshal Bugeaud conceived the idea of converting his soldiers into colonists; he gave them lands, supplied them with the mules of his train, and built them the necessary public edifices; but a year after not one of them remained; they had sold both land and beasts and disappeared, none can say where.

After the revolution of 1848 the *Assemblée Nationale* voted with enthusiasm the sum of £1,000,000 sterling for the purpose of establishing agricultural colonies in Algeria, and for the relief of the workmen of Paris thrown out of employment, nearly all of whom were strangers to such work. The number of immigrants who availed themselves of this arrangement was 10,376, and 41 colonies were created, having an area of about 140,000 acres. The expense of these colonies was very considerable, and amounted to about £8000 for every 100 souls.

After the insurrection of 1871 the Government of Algeria decreed the confiscation of the land belonging to all the insurgents, but, unwilling to apply this punishment too rigorously and depopulate the country, a compromise was effected; the State took possession only of such portions as were necessary for the creation of new villages in the heart of the insurgent districts, and allowed the original proprietors to retain a large proportion of their possessions, exception being made to the great leaders of the insurrection, who, as might be expected, possessed some of the finest land in the colony—notably in the Oued es-Sahel, or valley of Bougie, and in the Medjana.

The number of douars whose land was thus sequestrated was 321, namely, 132 in the province of Algiers, and 189 in that of Constantine; of these 154 purchased back their land for sums of money, 121 sacrificed a portion of the land itself, and 46 paid partly in money and partly in land. The total amount in money received was 8,637,000 f. and in land 288,968 hectares, while the war contribution exacted from the insurgents was little short of the sum originally demanded, 30 millions of francs.

In 1873 a large number of families from Alsace and Lorraine were induced to emigrate to Algeria through the action of the *Société protectrice des Alsaciens-Lorraines*, presided over by the Comte d'Haussonville. 670 families arriving without means of any kind were provided with concessions of land, houses, seed, and the means of living comfortably till after the first harvest. Others having some small means of their own received liberal assistance to enable them to settle under favourable conditions in the country, and large concessions were given from the sequestrated land to older colonists.

The result from 1871 to 1883 may thus be summarised. The area of land devoted to colonisation is 475,807 hectares, of which 347,268 has been given to individuals and the rest to communes. The value of this land is estimated at 43,267,991 f. The state has expended for the installation of colonists 16,568,507 f. The number of individual concessions is 12,270, and the number of families settled on them is 10,030. Of this number, 3474 having failed to comply with the conditions of their grants, these were revoked and reconceded to 3526 new families. Of the 10,030 families originally provided for, 5837 were still resident on their concessions, 718 had let their land, and 1418 had sold it.

Cereals.—The principal cereals grown are wheat, barley, and rye, but agriculture may still be said to be in its infancy. In England the mean produce of land may be taken at 25 bushels an acre ; in France it is about 14 ; but in Algeria, in spite of the natural richness of the soil, the average yield, under European culture, is only 8 or 9 bushels, while the Arab rarely obtains more than six times the amount of seed corn. The reason of this is that the land has never been deeply ploughed ; it is not manured, and little or no care is taken to free it from the noxious weeds which choke the corn and exhaust the soil. In the Tell, the region most favourable for agriculture, there are more than 30 millions of acres, of which not more than 10 or 12 millions are planted with cereals. The total production of the colony in an average year is about 350 millions of bushels. The wheat, and especially the *hard wheat*, is much sought for in Europe for the manufacture of macaroni, vermicelli, etc., on account of the large quantity of gluten which it contains. The barley is the species called *Hordeum hexasticum*, and is principally used as food for cattle. A smaller quantity of oats, maize, and beans is also grown ; but the soil and climate of Algeria seem peculiarly suitable for fruits and vegetables, which are produced in perfection. In December and January the fields are filled with all those which are seen in Paris and London only in spring and summer. Owing to the increasing competition of India and America the cultivation of cereals can hardly prove remunerative in this country, and land has consequently become depreciated, in some places to the amount of 25 per cent.

Fruit and Vegetables.—Among the more important are peas, beans (of which there are many different kinds), cauliflowers, turnips, parsnips, carrots, gherkins, beetroot, cucumbers, gourds, artichokes, asparagus, mushrooms, pimento (or red pepper), lettuces, onions and potatoes, which last yield two crops yearly. Among the fruits are apricots, strawberries, plums, melons, water-melons, cherries, bananas, pomegranates, pears, apples, etc. Many of the vegetables are gathered all the year round. Madder, henna (used for dyeing the nails), colza, opium, saffron, balm, aniseed, and many peculiar species of plants are also cultivated.

The fig is found everywhere, but especially in the mountains of Kabylia, up to 3800 ft. above the sea ; it forms one of the staple articles of food amongst the Kabyles, who eat it in great quantities when fresh, and dry numbers of it for winter use ; it is also exported for the distillation of a spirit much in use amongst the Jewish community.

The orange tribe grow admirably, and are most productive in many parts of the colony ; the best places for their culture are at the foot and in the gorges of mountain ranges, where the air is fresh and cool, and abundant means of irrigation obtainable ; they cannot be grown successfully at a greater elevation than 500 feet above the level of the sea. Many other fruits of an intertropical origin flourish in the same region, such as the banana, the guava, the aligator pear (*Persea gratissima*), the loquat (*Eriobotrya japonica*), and several others.

§ 13. COLONISATION, AGRICULTURE, FORESTS, ETC. *Algeria*

The date-tree (*Phœnix dactylifera*) is only cultivated in and near the Sahara, of which it has rightly been called the king; without it the entire desert would be uninhabited and uninhabitable. The 33d parallel of latitude appears to be the limit north of which it will not ripen its fruit save under very exceptional circumstances. It requires not only abundant irrigation, but great solar heat; the Arabs say that it stands with its feet in the water and its head in the fires of heaven. The love of the Arab for this precious tree may well be imagined, growing as it does in the sand, contenting itself with water so saline as to destroy ordinary vegetation, giving a grateful shade when all around is burnt up by the ardent heat of summer, resisting the winds which bend but cannot break its flexible stem, affording a fruit sought for in every part of the world, and not only sufficing for the food of the producer but affording a valuable means of exchange by which he may supply all his other wants.

The male tree of course bears no fruit; it has merely a bunch of flowers enclosed until maturity within a spathe. The females have also bunches of flowers, which, however, cannot become developed into fruit until fecundated by the pollen of the male flower. To ensure this result the Arabs ascend the trees in the month of April, and insert into every female spathe a portion of the pollen of the male flower. The fruit then begins to swell, and forms long clusters weighing from 20 to 40 lbs., each tree producing from 100 to 200 lbs. in a season. To multiply the date-tree the Arabs do not sow the seed, as they could not then be sure of the sex of the trees; they prefer to plant the suckers from the base of a female tree, whence the name *Phœnix*; these become productive in about eight years, but do not attain full fruition before twenty or twenty-five. The trees are about 45 ft. high, and as they are planted very close together they afford a dense shade, in which, however, the air circulates freely, so that all kinds of fruit, vegetables, etc., can be cultivated below them. The trees will live for about 200 years, but they are not worth preserving after a century. When they are no longer valuable for the fruit, the sap is extracted to make a kind of insipid wine; and the heart or cabbage of the tree is also eaten. They are then cut down, and the wood, although very inferior in quality, is here valuable, where no other kind can be procured. The roots are used for fencing and roofing, and the leaves are made into mats, baskets, sacks, and cord.

Like all other species of cultivated plants, the date-tree has numerous varieties. In the oases of the Ziban alone seventy distinct varieties are recognised.

The trees come into flower in spring, in March or April, and the fruit is ripe about October.

Tobacco is cultivated with great success, the produce being extremely good; and the Reports of the Juries of the Exhibitions of 1851 in London, and 1855 in Paris, were both most favourable. Indeed, the tobacco of Algeria is said to be finer and of better quality than even that of America. Flax and hemp also are grown to a considerable extent, and cotton has been tried with success; it was cultivated in the Tell by the Turks before the French conquest. At the London Exhibition of 1851 no fewer than eleven prizes were granted to samples of cotton from Algeria. Still this country is never likely to become a great cotton-producing one ; there is not sufficient land capable of irrigation, and labour is so scarce that almost any other kind of culture is more remunerative.

But perhaps the most promising culture in which the colonist can engage is that of the vine. M. Dejernon, who was sent by the French Government to report on the subject, thus states his general impressions regarding it : "In my eyes the vine is a providential plant for Algeria ; it prospers everywhere, in the worst land, on the most burning soil. In the three provinces I have not found a spot which is unfit for it ; everywhere also, but especially on the littoral, I have tasted wine rich in alcohol, and which would have had precious qualities if only it had been better made. The vine will become the fortune of the country. . . . Algeria possesses in its geological structure, in the rays of its sun, in the currents of its air, in its topographical details, those precious qualities which give to the products of the vine their tone, their colour, their delicacy and limpidity. It can produce an infinite variety of wines, suited to every constitution and to every caprice of taste."

The disaster of France was Algeria's opportunity. The cultivation of the vine in France suffered so much by the ravages of the Phylloxera that immense tracts of country, once the richest vineyards in the world, were dug up and put under cultivation with cereals, which did not yield more than a fraction of their former revenue.

To protect the cultivation of the vine in Algeria from this scourge, a decree was passed on the 24th June 1878, prohibiting the importation of cuttings, vine leaves used as packing, fresh fruit and vegetables, and trees and plants of every description. Potatoes only are allowed to be introduced, after having been thoroughly washed. Nevertheless all precautions have failed to prevent the importation of the disease ; it has been observed in various places, especially at Philippeville ; the most active measures are adopted for its detection and eradication when observed, and during 1888 it was not noticed in any new place.

In 1888 an area of 88,326 hectares was planted in vines, and the quantity of wine produced was little short of 3 millions of hectolitres. The quality is as good as the quantity is considerable ; not only does the colony produce sufficient for its own consumption, but great quantities are exported to Bordeaux, whence, after some manipulation, it is exported as the celebrated vintage of that country. Quantities are also sent to other places in the south of France, mixed with wine manufactured from dry raisins and sold in Paris as Algerian wine.

Another important production of Algeria is a natural one, Alfa fibre (Arab. *Hulfa*) or Esparto grass, under which name are confounded several species of gramineæ, and especially the *Stipa tenacissima*, Linn., or *Macrochloa tenacissima*, Kunth., and the *Lygeum spartum*, Linn. The former is the *Hulfa* of the Arabs, the latter the *Esparto* of the Spaniards. Both are abundant in Algeria, but the first is almost the sole vegetable of the High Plateaux ; it occurs in the greatest quantities, and is principally exported from Algeria. It is calculated that the area of these High Plateaux is about

27 millions of acres, of which surface not less than 16 millions of acres are covered with *Halfa*.

It is almost all exported to England for the manufacture of paper, and Mr. Edward Lloyd, who first organised this trade, is undoubtedly one of the greatest benefactors to Algeria. During 1887 upwards of 2,250,000 metric quintals were gathered, principally in the department of Oran.

The fibre made from the leaves of the dwarf palm, called *Crin végétal*, is also coming into great demand in the European markets, especially in Germany. It is used both for the manufacture of paper and for stuffing furniture, but for the latter purpose the principal objection is its strong fœtid odour, which hitherto has not been successfully removed.

Flora of Algeria.—The first idea of the traveller in reaching Algiers is the dissimilarity between the vegetation he sees and that which he has left behind. Instead of the familiar hawthorn hedges he finds enclosures surrounded by the agave and prickly pear; ancient olives and masses of lentisk festooned with clematis; fields covered with narcissus, iris, various kinds of ophris, and generally bright with flowers of every hue; shady nooks in which grow the African cyclamen with its marbled leaves; in less cultivated ground dwarf palm, arbutus, tree-heath, and cistus form a *makis* in nowise less beautiful than that for which Corsica is so celebrated; while in the gardens, roses, geraniums, violets, and all manner of cultivated flowers bloom throughout the winter. But soon this idea is weakened; he sees that the vegetation is purely European in its character, and almost every plant he finds is a native of Southern Europe, though growing here with greater luxuriance. The flora of Algeria consists of about 3000 species, of which not more than 450 are indigenous to the colony, and of this number 100 are peculiar to the Sahara.

Until quite lately there was no good work on the botany of Algeria, easily accessible to the traveller. The monumental works of Desfontaines and Cosson are of course the great standards, and Munby's *Catalogus Plantarum in Algeriâ sponte nascentum* contains a tolerably accurate list, but there was great need of something in the form of a scientific and descriptive catalogue. This has now been supplied by two local botanists, professors in the École de Médecine, whose work[1] will be universally hailed as a most valuable contribution to Algerian literature.

System of Agriculture.—The system of agriculture pursued by the natives differs considerably in different regions; the Kabyles cultivate their land much more intelligently and carefully than the Arabs. The usual agrarian measure amongst the Arabs is the extent which can be ploughed during a season by one plough and two oxen: this varies, according to the nature of the soil, from 25 to 50 acres. The season for ploughing commences immediately after the first rains of autumn, usually in October or November, and continues till February, and even later for some crops if abundant rain has fallen.

[1] "Flore de l'Algérie, ancienne Flore d'Alger transformée, contenant la description de toutes les plantes signalées jusqu'à ce jour comme spontanées en Algérie. Par Battandier et Trabut, Professeurs à l'École de Médecine et de Pharmacie d'Alger. Algiers: 1st Part, 1888; 2d Part, 1889. Each 4 frs. To be continued."

Introd. § 13. COLONISATION, AGRICULTURE, FORESTS, ETC. 87

When the proprietor does not himself farm his own land, he lets it to a *khamis* (or one-fifth); that is, to a farmer who pays the owner four and retains for his own use one-fifth of the crop. The owner, however, is bound to supply oxen for ploughing, seed corn, and advances of money until harvest.

Other arrangements are common, chiefly amongst Europeans, where the proprietor receives two-thirds or one-half of the crop, according to the amount of aid he renders to the tenant.

In the High Plateaux agriculture is carried on under very different conditions. If the soil has not been thoroughly saturated there, the cultivator hardly obtains the amount of his seed corn ; but after a rainy winter, or where irrigation is possible, the whole region is covered with the most exuberant vegetation. One grain produces from 150 to 200 heads of corn, and the cultivator is largely indemnified for the losses of the previous year. A curious botanical curiosity was sent to the Governor-General of Algeria in 1862 from M'sila,—a plant of wheat, produced from a single grain, having 400 ears of corn. The fertility of this district has been celebrated from the earliest times, and Strabo asserts that it often produced two crops a year, and in some places yielded 240 times the amount of seed sown. Pliny confirmed these assertions, and cited the instance of a plant of wheat sent to Nero with 340 ears upon it. The natives construct rude barrages to collect the rain water and utilise the overflow of the river, and several Artesian wells have been sunk by the French, and everywhere with success.

Forests.—The extent of forest land in Algeria, according to the latest statistics, is as follows :—

Departments.	State Forests.	Communal Forests.	Total.
	Hectares.	Hectares.	Hectares.
Algiers . . .	436,780	22,735	459,515
Oran	564,784	15,628	580,412
Constantine .	963,873	41,260	1,005,133
Totals . .	1,965,437	79,623	2,045,060

The area of state and communal forests consists of the following trees :—

	Hectares.
Aleppo pine	813,665
Maritime pine	536
Ilex	604,954
Cork	277,886
Chêne zeen (*Q. mirbeckii*) . . .	62,585
Cedar	42,882
Thuya	24,039
Miscellaneous	245,060
Total	2,071,607

There are also about 314,000 hectares of private forest.

The total number of trees of every description is estimated at 12,000,000.

The most valuable timber trees are—

The Cork oak (*Quercus suber*). It is stripped of its bark every eight or ten years in the summer months; but it is allowed to reach the age of fourteen or fifteen years untouched. Incisions are made longitudinally and transversely on the trunk, when the cork can be removed in large squares. This operation is called "démasclage." The cork obtained the first time is thin and hard, and is chiefly used for the manufacture of lamp-black, for painting. The produce of the second and third cuttings is also inferior, after which the cork is of the best quality. The trees usually furnish fifteen or twenty harvests, and should produce each time an average of 100 to 150 lbs. of cork, although as much as 900 lbs. is sometimes obtained from one tree.

The Chêne zeen (*Quercus mirbeckii*), used as timber for building purposes, railway-sleepers, etc. It affects cool, moist situations, and is found in an extensive zone of the Tell, from La Calle as far as Tlemçen.

The Chêne vert (*Quercus ilex*), also a valuable timber.

The chestnut-leaved oak (*Q. castaneæfolia*) occurs only in the mountains, and never descends lower than 3000 ft. above the sea.

The sweet acorn oak (*Q. ballota*), a handsome tree, which grows abundantly in poor soil and at all altitudes, and produces a large harvest without labour or expense. The acorn is eaten roasted; the Kabyles also grind it, and make couscous with the flour. This acorn has lately been largely exported to Europe for the adulteration of coffee.

Amongst the Coniferæ are the atlas cedar (*Cedrus atlantica*), the principal forests of which are in the Aurès mountains, near Batna and at Teniet-el-Ahd, the trees there rising sometimes to the height of 80 ft., with a girth of 20 ft. The *Abies* or Pinsapo of Babor. The Aleppo pine (*Pinus halepensis*), producing about £40,000 worth of resin annually. The Thuya or Atlas cypress (*Callitris quadrivalvis*), the trunks of which are almost imperishable, and the roots of which afford one of the richest and most beautiful of ornamental woods. There are two species of juniper, and tamarisks are found on the margins of salt lakes.

There is a very handsome ash (*Fraxinus australis*), indigenous to the Atlas, and a pistachio (*P. atlantica*) peculiar to it.

The olive is only grown to perfection in Kabylia, commencing at an elevation of about 2600 ft. above the sea; the trees as a rule receive very little care, and, as a consequence, they do not yield an abundant harvest oftener than once in two years. The fruit is small, but the oil is of an excellent quality. The tree grows, and even bears abundantly, in regions lower down; but there it is apt to suffer from the heats of summer, and the fruit is liable to be injured by the attacks of an insect, the *Dacus oleæ*, which cause it to fall before maturity. It has been calculated that there is in Algeria sufficient land, admirably adapted for its cultivation, to contain 100 millions of trees, which would yield 100 million litres of oil, worth annually 800 millions of francs, which result could be obtained in about twenty-five years.

The forests throughout Algeria, and to a much greater degree in Tunis have been greatly injured by periodical conflagrations caused by the Arabs, in some cases out of motives of enmity towards the French, in others for the sake of obtaining better pasturage for their flocks ; the most destructive were in 1865, during the insurrection of 1871, in the month of April 1873, and in the summer of 1877. The surface more or less damaged by fire is, on an average of the last five years, about 28,000 hectares per annum.

The question of the *reboisement* of Algeria is therefore one of the most important matters that can engage the attention of the State. To effect this by planting the trees indigenous to the country would certainly be a long and costly operation ; but with the Australian species, remarkable for their rapid growth, the question becomes much more easy of solution. Thanks to the indefatigable perseverance of three men, Messrs. Rammell, Cordier, and Trottier, veritable benefactors to this country, Algeria has been endowed with a precious boon, the introduction of the eucalyptus, a tree which, by reason of its rapid growth and its property of absorbing miasma, will undoubtedly exercise a powerful influence in changing the climate both of dry and malarious parts of the colony. Many species have been tried, but the most generally successful are the red-gum of Australia (*Eucalyptus resinifera*), the Tasmanian blue-gum (*E. globulus*), and the *E. Colossea*.

It is impossible to foresee to what size these trees may attain in Africa, but in Australia they sometimes reach a height of 300 ft., and are hardly less in circumference than the giant Wellingtonias of California. Some of the Australian acacias and casuarinas are hardly less valuable than the eucalyptus, but none of them can be cultivated with success at a greater altitude than 1500 ft. above the sea.

§ 14. ARCHÆOLOGY.

To the student of history, the archæologist, and the philologist, Algeria and Tunis offer a vast field for exploration and research, and, what is so difficult to find elsewhere, one whose riches are far from being exhausted.

All over the former country, but especially in the province of Constantine, are scattered prehistoric monuments ; assemblages of rude stones, dolmens, cromlechs, excavations in the rock ; in fact almost every known variety of Megalithic remains.

Some of these are close to Algiers, near Guyotville ; others at Djelfa.

In the province of Constantine are the monuments of Ras-el-Akba, between Guelma and Constantine ; of Bou-Merzouk ; of Roknia, near Hamman Meskoutin ; at the foot of the Beni-Saleh mountains in the Oued Besbes ; south of La Calle ; at Foum-el-Mabrek and N'guib, near Bône ; at Gastel, between Souk-Ahras and Tebessa ; near M'daourouch ; and all over the country of the Nememcha and the Aurès mountains. A manufactory of flint instruments was found near Negrin at the ruins of Besseriani (*Ad majores*).

Leaving this prehistoric period, we find abundant traces of Phœnician occupation, if not in actual ruins, at least in the names of places, especially seaports, showing that the Phœnicians created commercial establishments all along the north coast of Africa, wherever a creek promised shelter for their frail but adventurous barques. The Carthaginians, who followed in their steps, founded cities farther inland, and several Punic inscriptions have been found at a considerable distance from the sea.

Then followed the long and bloody wars which terminated in the ruin of Carthage and the occupation of her colonies by the Romans, about the middle of the second century, B.C.

These were at first left under the government of native princes, such as Masinissa, Bocchus, and Juba, the first and last of whom erected those gigantic sepulchres, the Medrassen and the Tombeau de la Chrétienne, near Batna and Algiers. Subsequently, about A.D. 40, the country was reduced to the condition of a Roman province.

Magnificent ruins remain to attest the glory of this epoch : temples dedicated to every deity in heathen mythology, theatres, triumphal arches, architectural details in the purest style of art, mosaics of rich colour and varied design, baths, monumental fountains, and hydraulic works, all testifying to the vast extent and solidity of the Roman sway in Africa.

The early Christian epoch is equally well represented by basilicas transformed into churches, inscriptions containing the name of Christ, Christian symbols and monograms, the graves of bishops, saints and martyrs, and above all the scenes consecrated by the life, ministry, and death of Saint Augustine, and his no less saintly mother, Monica—of that friend of his youth and of his old age, Alypius of Tagaste ; of his no less beloved friend Possidius, who subsequently became his biographer. Here also may be studied with advantage the scenes of those frantic theological wars which caused the downfall of the African Church.

The next epoch was more marked by destruction than construction. Count Boniface, governor of Africa in the fourth century, having conceived the idea of rendering himself independent of Rome, called in the Vandals to assist him ; they came, and soon made themselves masters of the country. At first they well sustained their destructive reputation, but subsequently they so lost their vigorous and warlike habits that Belisarius, at the head of a small phalanx of well-disciplined soldiers, had little difficulty in destroying them, and annexing Africa to the Eastern empire. The Byzantines under Solomon, the lieutenant and successor of Belisarius, commenced to restore the most important military buildings throughout the country, such as those at Tebessa, M'daourouch, and elsewhere, still in good preservation, and unmistakably renewed with older Roman materials.

When intestine feuds and disputed successions had wrought the ruin of the Eastern empire, Africa was thrown into such a state of confusion as to pave the way for the most marvellous conquest that the world's history contains.

A mere handful of Arab soldiers under Okba ben Nafa, with the sword in one hand and the Koran in the other, overran and conquered North Africa, from the Nile to Tangiers. Many vicissitudes took place, and Okba himself was killed ere this conquest was consolidated, but eventually all the native races adopted the new religion, and became more or less assimilated to the Arabs. Many of them no doubt passed over into Spain with Tarek, whose name lives imperishably in GIBRALTAR (the mountain of Tarek), although he himself shared even a worse fate than his predecessor, Belisarius.

The epoch of the first Mohammedan invasion is well marked by the tomb of Okba, near Biskra, which still bears what is probably the oldest Mohammedan inscription in Africa, if not in the world—*This is the tomb of Okba ben Nafa: may God have mercy upon him !*

The descendants of these conquerors did great things in the land of their adoption : they founded important kingdoms, of which that of Tlemçen is pre-eminent, both from its past history and the splendour of its existing monuments. They encouraged art, science, and literature, and attained a degree of splendour hardly inferior to that of the Romans.

This progressing civilisation, however, was checked by the invasion of a horde of savage nomades from Arabia, who devastated the country and forced the aboriginal inhabitants to take refuge in their mountain fastnesses, and even to found new colonies beyond the great desert, such as Timbuctoo and Senegal.

At the end of the fifteenth century the Moors expelled from Spain found a shelter in Algeria, where they were speedily followed by their conquerors. These were not always victorious, but they succeeded in forming a few colonies on the coast, the ruins of which exist in great abundance at Oran, Bougie, and even at Algiers.

We need not here dwell on the Turkish period, which has been described elsewhere, and which has hardly yet passed into the realms of archæology, but there is much, especially in its domestic architecture, to delight and interest the tourist.

We have said sufficient to show that there are few countries offering a wider field of study to the archæologist, or of instruction to the general traveller, than Algeria and Tunis.

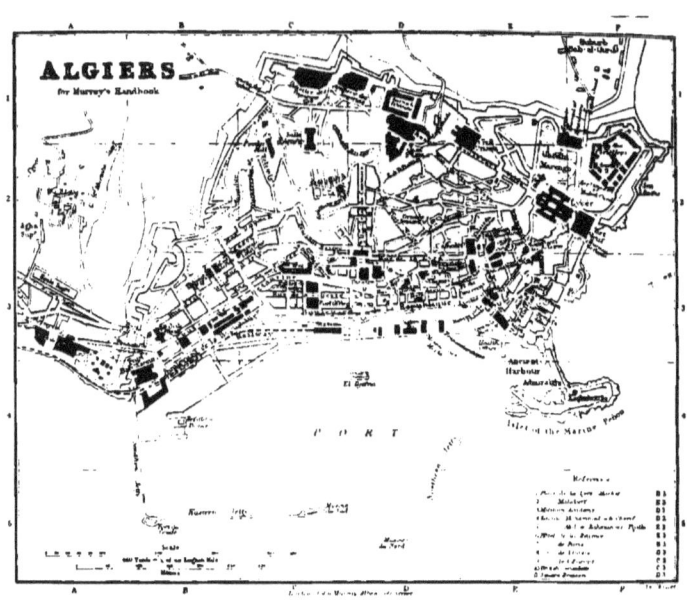

SECTION II

ALGERIA

CITY OF ALGIERS

FORTIFIED place of the first class, seat of the Government-General, and of the various other high civil and military authorities of the colony. Residence of Admiral commanding the Marine in Algeria, an Archbishop, and of the various Consuls-General and Consuls of foreign powers.

Court of Appeal, Council of Mohammedan Law, Tribunal of First Instance, two Justices of the Peace, Chamber and Tribunal of Commerce.

Chief place of the department or province. Prefecture, Headquarters of the 19th Corps d'Armée, of the division and subdivision of Algiers.

Population of the Province:—

French	98,807
Jews	11,582
Mohammedans	1,082,156
Foreigners	59,127
Total	1,251,672

Population of the city of Algiers, including the suburb of *Bab-el-Oued* and the *Faubourg d'Isly*, but excluding the *Village d'Isly*, *El-Biar*, *Bou-Zarea*, *Mustafa*, and *St. Eugène:*—

French	29,052
Jews	5,350
Europeans of foreign origin	15,506
Mohammedans	21,431
Total	71,339

El-Biar:—

French	658
Jews	19
Foreigners	357
Mohammedans	1238
Total	2272

Bou-Zarea:—

French	245
Jews	2
Foreigners	804
Mohammedans	558
Total	1609

Mustafa and the Village d'Isly:—

French	8612
Jews	135
Foreigners	724
Mohammedans	4147
Total	13,618

St. Eugène:—

French	868
Jews	412
Foreigners	454
Mohammedans	612
Total	2346

ALGIERS, the ancient *Icosium*, is situated on the western shore of the bay of the same name, 500 m. S. of Marseilles. The town, which is triangular in form, is built on a slope of the *Sahel*, the name given to a chain of hills running along the coast for a considerable distance towards the W. The view, when approaching it from the sea, is most beautiful. It appears from a distance like a succession of dazzling white steps or terraces rising from the water, which, contrasting with the bright green background of the Sahel, explains the origin of the Arab comparison of Algiers to a diamond set in an emerald frame.

The shores of the bright blue bay are dotted here and there with white villages, French villas, and Moorish palaces, appearing in the midst of the richest and most luxuriant verdure, some placed high up on the slopes of the hills, and others standing on the water's edge. Beyond is the verdant plain of the Metidja, stretching away in the distance to the foot of the Atlas range, whose summits form a magnificent background to the whole picture, which will bear comparison with any in Europe. The writer always maintains that the finest view in the Mediterranean is from the Greek theatre of Taormina, and the next finest is from his own windows at El-Biar.

Algiers is divided into two distinct parts, the modern French town and the ancient city of the Deys.

The **Modern Town** consists of regular streets and squares, fine public buildings, and modern hotels, and is well lighted with gas. The *Place du Gouvernement* is a fine large square, in which the principal streets, Rue Bab-Azoun and Rue Bab-el-Oued, join, planted on three sides with a double row of plane-trees. In front of the Hôtel de la Régence is a group of palm and orange trees, and a remarkably fine clump of bamboos, surrounding a fountain. Towards the eastern side is a bronze equestrian statue of the Duke of Orleans by Marochetti. It was cast out of the cannon taken at the conquest of Algiers. The bas-reliefs on the pedestal represent on the N. the taking of the citadel of Antwerp ; and on the S. the passage of the Col de Mouzaïa. This Square is the fashionable resort for evening promenade, when it is crowded with loungers of every grade and race. A military band performs here occasionally.

The *Place Bresson*, opening like the preceding on to the Boulevard de la République, has a pleasant garden in the centre. The *Place Bab-el-Oued*, or Place d'Armes, is a triangular space near the shore, adjoining the Arsenal. This was the site of the ancient Moorish cemetery ; the N. side was reserved for the interment of the pachas, and in the middle was the fort "des vingt-quatre heures," rendered celebrated as the place of martyrdom of Geronimo (see p. 98). This was also the ordinary place of execution, both under the Turkish Government and for the first years which followed the conquest. On one side of this place is the Jardin Marengo, which commands a fine view. The other principal squares of the French town are the *Place Mahon*, adjoining the Place du Gouvernement ; the *Place de Chartres*, used as a market-place ; the *Place de la Lyre*, in which is a covered market ; the *Place d'Isly*, in the centre of which stands a bronze statue of Marshal Bugeaud, by M. Dumont ; and the *Places Randon*, and *Malakhoff*. The *Rue Bab-el-Oued* (River Gate), and *Rue Bab-Azoun* (Gate of Grief), both leading from the Place du Gouvernement, are the two most important streets of the city, and contain the best shops. Among the other principal streets of this quarter are the *Rues de la Lyre, de Chartres, Juba, de la Marine*, and *d'Isly*, some of which are arcaded on both sides—a great advantage in this climate, as the pedestrian is thereby enabled to reach any part of the town without being much exposed to the sun in summer or to the rain in winter. The *Boulevard de la République* is built on a series of arches at the head of the cliff, and extends all along the front of the town. On one side it is bordered by handsome buildings, while a wide promenade runs along the other, overlooking the bay, harbour, and shipping. The Quay and Railway Station are about 40 ft. below, and are reached by two inclined roads leading from the centre of the Boulevard. This work was constructed by Sir Morton Peto, to whom the town transferred the concession for 99 years, which had been granted to it by the Imperial decree of 1860. The first stone was laid by the

Emperor on the 17th September 1860, and the work was completed in 1866, at a cost of about £300,000. It is still the property of an English company. It is composed of two tiers of vaults, forming about 350 warehouses and dwelling-houses, the whole occupying an area of 11 acres, and extending over a frontage of 3700 ft.

The **Old Town**, inhabited chiefly by Arabs and Jews, lies on the steep hill rising behind the Rues Bab-Azoun and Bab-el-Oued, and is the very opposite of the French town already described. At the apex of the triangular-shaped mass of white houses stands the *Kasba*, or Citadel, about 400 ft. above the shore.

The **Streets** are very narrow, tortuous, and irregular, often ending in a *cul de sac*, and are so steep as to be inaccessible for carriages. They are cool and shady, owing to their extreme narrowness. The longest of them, the Rue de la Kasba, is ascended by 497 steps. These streets are joined by many alleys just wide enough to pass through, and the whole labyrinth is terribly confusing to the stranger; many of the Arab names have been retained, but so travestied as hardly to be recognisable; thus *El-Akhdar* (the Green) becomes *Locdor*; *Souk-el-Djamäa* (Market of the Mosque) is changed into *Soggemah*, etc.

The Moorish **Houses** are perfectly symbolical of the private life of the occupants: everything like external decoration is studiously avoided, while the interior is picturesque and elegant. The outer door usually gives entrance to a vestibule, or *skiffa*, on each side of which is a stone bench divided off like stalls by marble or stone columns, supporting the graceful flat arch peculiar to Algiers. Here it is that the master receives his male friends. Beyond this is the *oust*, or open court, the *impluvium* of the Romans, and the *patio* of the Spaniards, generally paved with marble, tiles, or bricks, having an arcade all round, formed by the pillars and the horseshoe arches which support the upper gallery.

The pavement of the court enclosed by the arcade is usually sunk a few inches, in order to carry off the rain-water. In this central court the great domestic festivities, such as marriage, circumcision, etc. are held. The rooms around it are more or less of a public character; at least they are not used as dwellings by the family; they are usually kitchens, storerooms, baths, etc. The more private apartments are all above, leading off from the upper gallery, which is similar to the lower one, but having the pillars joined by an elegant wooden balustrade, just high enough to lean on. The rooms have generally large folding-doors reaching from the floor to the ceiling, with a smaller aperture in each leaf, which may be used when it is too cold to keep the whole open. The interiors are whitewashed, and have generally a dado of tiles 3 or 4 ft. high along the walls. The ceilings are sometimes handsomely sculptured, but more generally they exhibit the naked rafters of thuya or kharoob wood, pine, or cedar. It was the small scantling of this, in times when the communication with other countries was less easy than it is at present, that regulated the width of Moorish rooms, seldom more than 12 ft.

One of the principal features of Moorish houses in town, rising as they do one above the other, is the flat terraced roofs, from which a magnificent view is obtained of the city, the harbour and shipping, and the distant mountains. Under the Turkish Government these were reserved for the women alone, who used to visit each other by climbing over the parapets which divided the houses. No Christian male (the consuls excepted) was ever permitted to go on his own terrace during daylight.

Dr. Shaw, consular chaplain at Algiers about 1720, and whose travels and researches in Barbary are deservedly esteemed for their accuracy and fidelity, illustrates many passages of Scripture by a reference to Moorish architecture. For instance, *the middle of the house* (Luke v. 19), where our Saviour was in the habit of giving instruction to His disciples, was no doubt the hollow Moorish court or *oust* (literally, waist, middle). This in summer was covered over with a curtain running on ropes, to which the Psalmist may have alluded in speaking of *spreading out the heavens like a curtain*. The prophet Jeremiah exactly describes Algerian houses when he says that they *were ceiled with cedar and painted with vermilion*. Any one who has seen a Moorish court can understand the allusion to Samson having pulled down the pillars in the Temple of Dagon, while *three thousand persons were on the roof to see him make sport*.

Some of the Moorish houses best worthy of a visit in town are the palaces of the Governor-General and Archbishop, and the Library in the Rue de l'Etat-Major; the Government offices near the Prefecture, formerly the British Consulate; and in the country, the Governor-General's summer palace; the Château d'Hydra, belonging to Mr. Eyre Ledgard, in which there is a priceless collection of ancient tiles; and the magnificent property of Mr. Macleay at El-Biar.

The **Shops** in the native quarter are merely recesses or small chambers in the walls of the houses, and in them is carried on the process of manufacturing some of the articles which are exposed for sale in the shops of the French town below. Here may be seen the embroiderer at work with his gold and silver thread, the shoemaker with kid slippers of every colour and variety, the pedagogue with his school of young Moors, the worker in gold and silver, the barber shaving Moorish heads or chins; and the cafés where the natives sit cross-legged drinking coffee, and while away their time in smoking and playing draughts. Indeed, a walk through the old town is of greater interest to the stranger than any of the sights of modern Algiers. But perhaps what most strikes the traveller from Europe on first walking through the city is the variety and picturesqueness of **Costumes** (see also Introd. pp. 8, 10, 11) he meets in the streets. French soldiers and officers, Zouaves and Turcos, with their smart uniforms; the Jew, with dark-coloured turban, jacket and sash, blue stockings and shoes; the Moor, in smartly embroidered jacket, full short trousers, and white stockings; bare-legged Arabs, wrapped in their white burnous: Mozabites, with their coats of many colours; Negroes from the Soudan; Spaniards and Maltese, all jostle one another in the crowded streets; while Moorish women, dressed in white, with full trousers, slippers, and their faces covered to the eyes, mingle with ladies in fashionable modern toilets, and with Jewesses whose jaws are bound with a muslin handkerchief, and whose straight silk robes reach from the neck to the slippered feet.

CHURCHES.

Church of England.—The Church of the Holy Trinity, at the Port d'Isly, was erected in 1870 by subscription of the winter visitors, for whose use it is intended. It was consecrated by the Bishop (Harris) of Gibraltar, on the 1st January 1871. The patronage is vested in the Bishop of Gibraltar.

There is no endowment whatever, the church and chaplaincy being entirely dependent on voluntary offerings. The offertories as a rule go to the support of the church, but on certain occasions, of which notice is given, they are applied to other purposes, especially to the relief of poor British subjects, of whom there are a very large number in the Colony, and who receive most thankfully the aid which comes to them from the English Church through the Consul-General. One-half of the seats are free; the remainder are appropriated at a charge of £1 per sitting for the season. The building, though not very attractive outside, is one of the most interesting of its kind out of England.

A dado has been erected all round the church, with a more elaborate reredos behind the altar, composed of alternate slabs of different kinds of Numidian marbles and breccias (see p. 273), framed in bands of *giallo antico* and *breccia dorata*, surmounted by a frieze of smaller tablets of rose-coloured marble. In the nave and baptistery these contain memorial inscriptions. The following are some of the historical tablets:—

The first is in memory of John Typton, Consul here in 1580, the first native-born Consul ever appointed by England in any country.

1584. Lawrence, Master of Oliphant, the Master of Morton, and other banished Scottish gentlemen enslaved at Algiers, whence they were probably never released.

1620. Sir Robert Mansel, Vice-Admiral of England, sent by James I. against Algiers, in command of the first English Fleet that had entered the Mediterranean since the crusades.

1631. Two Algerine pirate vessels landed in Ireland, sacked Baltimore, and carried off its inhabitants to slavery in Algiers.

1639. William Okeley, taken prisoner by pirates. He and six other Englishmen, after much suffering, escaped to Majorca in a canvas boat.

1644. Edmund Casson, Envoy from the Parliament to Algiers, effected the liberation of many hundred British captives. He died here in 1655.

"January 5th, 1644. Gyles Parke, son of John of Holkar, and Elizabeth Gordon, daughter of Lord Vicount Kentmeere, married in Algear, by Mr. Spratte, Minister."

"October 21st, 1645. Elizabeth, daughter of the said Gyles Parke, baptized in Algier, in Barbary."

The last two are extracts from the parish register of Cartmel, in Lancashire. It has been found impossible to identify the "Lord Kentmeere" therein mentioned; but there was a Viscount Kenmure, whose family name was Gordon.

1654. Blake, after his great victory at Tunis, effected the liberation of all Christian slaves on the Barbary coast.

1660. Murrough, Earl of Inchiquin, Viceroy of Catalonia, while exiled during the Commonwealth, and his son Lord O'Brien, afterwards Governor of Tangier, were taken by corsairs near the Tagus, and sold into captivity at Algiers.

1670. Admiral Sir Edward Spragg destroyed the Algerine fleet at Bougie, and released a number of Christians.

1723. Thomas Betton, member of the Ironmongers' Company, probably himself a captive, left half of his large fortune for the redemption of slaves in Barbary.

1800. Ida, daughter of Admiral Ulric, Consul-General of Denmark, born 1800, married Consul-General M'Donell. The dramatic story of her escape, disguised as a midshipman, with her child concealed in a basket of vegetables, before the bombardment in 1816, is told in Lord Exmouth's Dispatch. She subsequently married the Duc de Talleyrand-Perigord, and died at Florence, 6th October 1880.

Many other historical events are recorded; then follow a series of tablets commemorating such of our countrymen as have died here since the French occupation.

All the windows have been filled in with stained glass, generally with memorial brasses attached, to commemorate historical personages or private individuals. The large circular window at the west end is in memory of the English who perished in captivity during the time of the Deys. It represents the deliverance of St. Peter from prison by the angel, and bears the inscription, "Lord, show Thy pity on all prisoners and captives." One in the nave is in honour of Bruce, the African traveller, Consul-General here from 1762-65. Another commemorates the gallant exploit of Lord Exmouth in 1816, who by his great victory liberated 3000 Christian captives, and for ever abolished slavery in the Barbary States. That next to it is devoted to his brave companion in arms, the Dutch Admiral Van Capellan: the cost of this was defrayed partly by his daughter, and partly by the Princes of Holland. Next to it is one in memory of Mademoiselle Tinné, grand-daughter of Admiral Van Capellan, murdered by the Touaregs near Tripoli; and so on.

On the walls are several mural tablets; one contains a list of all the Consuls and Consuls-General since 1580; another is in memory of the learned Dr. Shaw, Consular Chaplain at Algiers from 1719-31, and subsequently Regius Professor of Greek at Oxford; a third is in honour of Mr. William Shaler, Consul-General of the

[*Algeria.*]

United States, who during all the troublous times preceding and subsequent to Lord Exmouth's operations, when our Consul was imprisoned and in chains, and when he and his family were subsequently expelled by the Dey, rendered most eminent services to them and to the British nation. A smaller tablet in coloured marble commemorates the last visit to Algiers of a most faithful servant of Christ, Edward Steere, Bishop of Zanzibar. But perhaps the most interesting of the tablets is that which records the good deeds of the Rev. Devereux Spratt (see p. 42).

The last addition is the most beautiful of all; the whole of the walls and the reveals of the windows in the apse and choir have been covered with marble mosaics, executed by Mr. Burke, the eminent decorator of the Guards' Memorial Chapel, Chester Cathedral, etc. This was our local celebration of Her Majesty's Jubilee. Our American friends co-operated heartily in the work, and two identical tablets of Numidian marble have been erected in the nave; one records the fact that the decoration of the church was completed on the occasion of the Queen's Jubilee: "In humble gratitude to Almighty God for His preservation of her to her faithful subjects, during a long and glorious reign." The other commemorates two illustrious citizens of the United States, Commodore Decatur and Captain Bainbridge, and ends with a paragraph from the pen of Bishop Potter of New York, which has profoundly touched every English heart:—

"This tablet is erected, June 20, 1887, by citizens of the United States, grateful for the privilege of associating this commemoration of their countrymen with the Jubilee of that illustrious sovereign Lady, Queen Victoria, who has made the name of England dear to children and to children's children throughout all lands."

The church is the only place at Algiers which Englishmen can really call their own. The idea of making it a sort of National Walhalla will commend itself to most people, and the relatives of such as may die here will be glad of the opportunity of commemorating their departed friends in a place where the record will be read during all future times.

There is a **Scotch Presbyterian** church on the road between Algiers and Mustafa Supérieur, erected entirely at the expense of an esteemed resident, Sir Peter Coats.

The **Cathedral of St. Philippe** (*Roman Catholic*), built on the site of the Mosque of Hassan, named after the Pacha who built it in 1791, is situated in the Place Malakoff, next to the Governor-General's palace. The Archbishopric was created in 1867. The exterior of the cathedral is quite modern, and the colours are crude and unpleasing; it is a very unsuccessful attempt to combine Moorish with Christian architecture. The principal entrance, which is reached by a flight of 23 steps, is ornamented with a portico, supported by four black-veined marble columns. The roof of the nave is of Moorish plaster work, and rests on a series of arcades, supported by white marble columns, several of which belonged to the ancient Mosque. Some of the modern Moorish work is good; the pulpit is the *mimbar* of the original mosque spoilt by French millinery. The choir is ornamented with four large gray marble columns on bases of porphyry. There are some tolerable stained-glass windows, and several separate chapels. In that to the right on entering is the white marble tomb containing the bones of St. Geronimo. His history and the account of his martyrdom are given by Haedo, a Spanish benedictine who published a topography of Algeria in 1612. This work was carefully studied by the late M. Berbrugger, curator of the library, who drew public attention to the story, in the vague hope that the body might one day be found. It is as follows: During an expedition made by the Spanish garrison of Oran in 1540, a young Arab boy was taken prisoner and baptized under the name of Geronimo. When about eight years old he again fell into the hands of his relations, with whom he lived as a Mohammedan till the age of twenty-five years, when he returned to Oran of his own accord, with the intention of living thenceforth in the religion of Christ. In May 1569 he accompanied a party of Spaniards who embarked in a small boat to make a *razzia* on the Arabs in the vicinity. The expedition was chased by a Moorish corsair, and all the members taken prisoners and carried to Algiers. Every effort was made to induce Geronimo to renounce Christianity, but as he persisted in remaining steadfast in the faith, he was condemned to death, and sentenced to be thrown alive into a mould in which a block of *béton* was about to be made. *His feet and hands were tied with cords,* the cruel sentence was carried out, and the block of concrete containing his body was built into an angle of the fort, "des vingt quatre heures," then in course of construction. Haedo carefully recorded the exact spot, and added, "We hope that God's grace may one day extricate Geronimo from this place, and reunite his body with those of many other holy martyrs of Christ, whose blood and happy deaths have consecrated this country."

In 1853 it was found necessary to destroy this fort, and on the 27th of December, in the very spot specified by Haedo, the skeleton of Geronimo was found enclosed in a block of *béton*. The bones were carefully removed, and interred with great pomp in the cathedral. Liquid plaster of Paris was run into the mould left by his body, and a perfect model of it obtained, showing not only his features but the cords which bound him, and even the texture of his clothing. This interesting cast of the dead martyr may be seen in the Government Library and Museum, Rue de l'État-Major.

Nôtre-Dame-des-Victoires, Bab-el-Oued, formerly a mosque, built in the 17th century by Ali Bitchenin, a Christian slave converted to Mohammedanism.

Sainte-Croix, formerly the mosque called Djamäa el-Kasba Berrani, stands facing the Kasba in the street of the same name.

St. Augustin.—A handsome church, built in 1878, in the Rue de Constantine.

The **Church of the Jesuits,** in the Rue des Consuls.

The **French Protestant Temple,** in the Rue de Chartres.

The **Synagogue,** in the Rue Caton, is a handsome edifice in the Moorish style.

Nôtre Dame d'Afrique. See *post*.

MOSQUES.

It is said that there were in Algiers before the French conquest more than a hundred mosques; a great number of which were, however, merely "koubbas" or tombs of "marabouts," or Arab saints. These last generally consist of a small isolated domed structure containing the tomb, which is protected by a wooden grating. These koubbas are used as places of prayer, especially in the country, where no real mosques exist. They are sometimes incorrectly given the name of marabouts by the French. The word *marabet* really means one who is bound or devoted to religion, and ought to be applied to the man and not to the tomb.

There are now but four mosques regularly used for Mohammedan worship in Algiers. These are all accessible to Europeans, but visitors ought to remove their shoes at the entrance, out of deference to the feelings of those for whose use they are intended, and who prostrate themselves on the floor during prayer. The principal is

The **Grand Mosque,** or Djamäa el-Kebir, in the Rue de la Marine, the most ancient in Algeria, said to have been founded in the 11th century. An inscription on the *mimbar* or pulpit in Cufic characters proves the fact of the building having existed in A.D. 1018, while a marble slab in one of the walls records that the minaret was built by Abou Tachfin, king of Tlemçen, in 1324. The interior consists of a square whitewashed hall, divided into aisles by columns, united by semicircular Moorish arches. These columns are wrapped round to a height of 5 or 6 ft. with matting, which is likewise spread over the floor. At one end is the *mihrab*, a niche in the wall, which serves to indicate the direction in which Mecca lies. The general appearance is bare, the only decoration being the suspended lamps, and the *mimbar* or pulpit for the Imam. One part of the mosque serves as a court of justice, where ordinary cases are heard by the Cadi. The exterior presents, towards the Rue de la Marine, a row of white marble columns supporting an arcade, in the centre of which, before the entrance, stands a marble fountain. The worshippers in this mosque are of the Maleki rite, the only one represented in Algiers prior to the conquest by Aroudj.

The **New Mosque** Djamäa el-Djedid, or Mosquée de la Pêcherie, is situated at the corner of the Rue de la Marine and the Place du Gouvernement. It was constructed, according to a very doubtful tradition, in 1660, by a Genoese architect, who was subsequently put to death by the Dey, in consequence of having built it in the form of a Greek cross. It is surmounted by a large white cupola, with four smaller ones at the corners. The interior is much like that before described, bare and whitewashed, with mats round the columns and on the floor. There is, as in all other mosques, a fountain at the entrance, which the Mohammedans use for their ablutions before prayer. The square tower, or minaret, is about 90 ft. high, and contains an illuminated clock. This mosque is used by the "Hanefi" sect. It contains a magnificently illuminated copy of the Koran, in folio.

The **Djamäa Safir**, in the Rue Kleber, and the **Djamäa Sidi Ramdan** in the street of that name, are so like those already described that it is unnecessary to do more than mention their names.

The Beni M'zab have a mosque for themselves in the Rue de Tanger.

The **Zaouia of Sidi Abd-er-Rahman eth-Thalebi**, overlooking the Jardin Marengo, is well worth a visit. It contains the tomb of that saint, who died in 1471; around him are buried several Pachas and Deys, commencing with that of *Khadar Pacha*, A.D. 1605, and terminating with that of Ahmed, last Dey of Constantine. Lights are kept constantly burning on the saint's tomb, which is hung with variously-coloured silk drapery; and offerings in the shape of lamps, banners, ostrich eggs, etc., are suspended from the roof. The proportions and details of the minaret and doorway beneath it should be noticed. After the Grand Mosque it is the most ancient religious building in Algeria, always of course excepting the tomb of *Sidi Okba* near Biskra, which dates from the 7th century.

There are many more of these koubbas in Algiers, but they resemble each other so much that a notice of one will suffice.

RELIGIOUS AND OTHER CEREMONIES.

The fanatic religious performances of the **Aïssaoui**, or votaries of the religious confraternity of Sidi Mohammed bin Aïssa, occasionally take place in the native quarter of the town, and indeed can always be got up for a consideration. (*Commissionaires* at the various hotels in town know how to accomplish this.) These commence by the beating of drums and tambours, after an interval of which, one of the Aïssaoui, being inspired, rushes with a yell into the ring formed by the spectators, and begins a frantic dance, the body being swayed backwards and forwards, and contorted with fearful violence. He is soon joined by others, who continue their maniacal gestures and cries until they fall exhausted, or are stopped by the Mokaddam (head of the order). The next proceeding consists of forcing out the eyes with iron spikes, searing themselves with red-hot iron, eating live scorpions and serpents, chewing broken glass and the leaves of the prickly pear, etc., all of which acts seem to be performed under the influence of fanatical mania, the performers being apparently insensible to pain. The sight is well worth seeing *once*, for those who have tolerably strong nerves, but few persons would care about witnessing an Aïssaoui fête a second time.

Very curious **sacrificial rites** are celebrated on the seashore near St. Eugène every Wednesday morning at sunrise, by some of the lower classes of natives, the object of which is to cure diseases, and to obtain various benefits. To effect this, they slaughter a fowl or lamb, after certain incantations and burning of incense, and smear themselves with its blood, in which the virtue is supposed to reside. If the dying bird flutters in the water, it is hailed as a good omen. Persons of different races in Algiers take part in these ceremonies, which must not, however, be supposed to have anything to do with the true Mohammedan worship. It is a very ancient ceremony, and was minutely described by Père Dan in the beginning of the 17th century, who says, "Elles couppent la teste à un coq, dont elles font découler le sang dans ce mesme feu, et en abandonnent la plume au vent après l'avoir rompuë en plusieurs pieces qu'elles sement de tous costez et en jettent la meilleure partie dans la mer."

The Negroes also perform sacrifices in the Arab town annually on the feast of the Prophet's birthday, the *Moulid en-Nebbi*, which occurs on the 12th of the month *Rabia el-owel*. They are curious, but disgusting.

PUBLIC BUILDINGS, INSTITUTIONS, ETC.

Four **Aqueducts** supply the city with water. They were erected in 1622 by Hussein Pacha, and are called the aqueducts of *Hamma*, of *Telemli*, of *Aïn Zeboudja*, and of *Bir Trariah*.

A **Barrack**, formerly used by the Janissaries, now serves the same purpose for French troops in the Rue de la Marine. The barrack in the Kasba was formerly the palace of the Pacha. The largest barrack is the *Caserne d'Orléans*, N. of the Kasba, which can contain an entire regiment.

Baths. See Index.

The **General Cemetery** of Algiers and St. Eugène is on the road to the latter village, opposite the Fort des Anglais. It is in the usual French style, certainly not pleasing to English eyes. A portion of it, corresponding to the ancient consular cemetery under the Turkish Government, has been appropriated for the use of the consular corps and their families, and no interment in it is permitted without the sanction of the dean of that body, at present the English Consul-General.

A little farther is the **New Cemetery** belonging to the *Jews*, their ancient one having been taken for public purposes.

The **Cemetery of the Commune of Mustafa** is on the top of the hill above the Champ de Manœuvres ; access is obtained either by Fontaine-blene or by the Colonne Voirol. A portion of this has been appropriated for the use of the English and American community, and was consecrated by the Bishop of Gibraltar in 1871. It has been planted with shrubs and flowers, and is carefully tended at the cost of the English residents.

There are two **Mohammedan Cemeteries**, one at Mustafa (see Arab Cemetery, p. 108), and the other near the Kasba.

Champ de Manœuvres. See p. 108.

The **Club (Officers')**, next to the theatre, occupies part of the site of one of the Janissaries' barracks. It contains a monument of historic interest, a Moorish fountain, with twisted columns, regarding which M. Feraud tells the following anecdote : When General de Bourmont left Toulon for Algiers he took with him a number of printed proclamations, announcing to the Arabs that he came to deliver them from the oppressive yoke of the Turks, and to suppress piracy. Some one was required to distribute these documents, and the interpreter, George Garoné, volunteered for the dangerous service. He was landed on the coast on the night of the 13th June 1830, that before the debarkation of the French army. He was arrested and taken before the Pacha at Algiers, who ordered his head to be sawn off on the edge of this fountain, which then decorated the Court of the Kasba.

Club (English). The great *desideratum* at Algiers has always been some place where English and Americans might meet together, and enjoy something like social life. Thanks to the public spirit of a few of the principal residents, a club of unusual excellence has been (1889) established in the Villa de Royer at Mustafa Supérieur. It is situated in beautiful grounds, with lawn-tennis courts, and is abundantly supplied with current literature. This is strongly recommended to all visitors. (See also Index.)

Club Alpin, Section de l'Atlas, 2 Rue Juba.

Educational Establishments. — The superior course of instruction at Algiers consists of a School of Law, with twelve professors; a School of Medicine, also with twelve professors; a School of Science, with six; and a School of Letters, with seven professors, located in a large and handsome college at the Agha. Very interesting lectures are given in the School of Letters on the history, antiquities, geography, and languages of N. Africa.

The **Zoological Station** is an adjunct of this school, and is situated near the admiralty. It is intended for serious study, and not for popular amusement. It has an aquarium, well-arranged laboratories, a zoological library, and all that is necessary for the study of minute marine organisms of every description. The great feature, however, is the apparatus for instantaneous microscopic photography by means of electric light.

The **Lycée**, in the Place Bab-el-Oued, receives both Europeans and natives.

The course of instruction is precisely similar to that of all other Lycées in France; but the great objection to it is the mixture of races amongst the pupils, Christians, Jews, and Mohammedans being all educated together.

There is a **Petit Lycée** for younger children in the country at Ben Aknoun.

There are many other schools, both Catholic and laic, in various parts of the town and country. The best girls' schools are the convents of the Sacré Cœur at Mustafa Supérieur and of the Doctrine Chretienne in town.

The modern **Gates** are the *Passage de Constantine*, close by Fort *Bab-Azoun*; the *Port d'Isly*, just above the former; the *Porte du Sahel*, leading from the upper town towards the W.; and the *Porte Bab-el-Oued*, leading to St. Eugène and Pointe Pescade.

The **Hospital (Military), or Hôpital du Dey**, is situated outside the town at a distance of about a kilomètre, in the beautiful gardens which surround the country residence of the last Dey. It is well protected against the violent N.W. winds of winter by the hill of Bou-Zarea, and is open to the refreshing sea-breezes so necessary in the summer months. This magnificent establishment is well worthy of a visit, and the *économe* in charge will gladly give the necessary permission on application. It consists of numerous series of buildings, spacious, lofty, and well lighted, capable of containing 600 or 700 beds, or even more on an emergency, fitted with every requisite that the present advanced state of hygienic science can devise; baths of every description, covered promenades fitted as smoking galleries, with comfortable seats, and decorated with tropical plants; separate lodgings in the Dey's villa for officers, a chapel, and laboratories of various kinds. It would be difficult to find in any part of Europe a hospital better conducted, or fitted up more carefully with everything likely to restore the health or minister to the comfort of the patients.

The **Hospital (Civil)** is at Mustafa Inférieur, and can make up 450 beds. It is visited by the best French doctors in Algiers. The patients are attended by Sisters of Charity, as well as by the regular hospital nurses.

Jardin d'Essai. See *post*.

Library and Museum. — (Hours when open, see Index.) This building, which is the ancient palace of Mustafa Pacha, is in the Rue de l'Etat-Major.

The library contains 20,000 volumes and pamphlets, and 700 Arab manuscripts; also a curious and useful collection of maps and plans, most of which refer to Algeria. The Museum is on the ground-floor, and is open at the same times as the Library. There are a few pieces of ancient sculpture, amongst others a torso of Venus, found at Cherchell; a statue of Neptune, larger than life-size; a group of a Faun and Hermaphrodite, similar to one existing at Rome, and figured in Clarac, *Musée de Sculpture*, Pl. 671, No. 1736. There are also two sarcophagi of the early days of Christianity, discovered at Dellys. One has sculptured representations of Daniel in the lions' den, and Shadrach, Meshach, and Abed-nego in the furnace. The second is much finer, and contains representations of several scenes in New Testament history, such as the miracle of Cana in Galilee, of the loaves and fishes, etc. Each scene is placed between two Corinthian twisted columns. There are also some good fragments of mosaic work, including a Bacchus, and a piece of inlaid flooring. A plaster cast of the print left by the body of St. Geronimo in the block of concrete is also to be seen (see p. 98). There is also a collection of medals and old Algerian money. Some of the best sculptures and mosaics have been removed to Paris. The present curator is the well-known Algerian scholar, M. MacCarthy, whose courtesy to the English visitor is proverbial.

Library (English). See Index.

Markets. See Index.

The **Palace of the Governor-General**, in the Place Malakhoff, was formerly the house of Hassan Pacha. The white marble columns which form the peristyle are handsome; so are also the pillars of the *salle-à-manger*. The drawing-room is decorated in a very ornate Moorish style.

The **Palace of the Dey**, now summer palace of Governor-General at Mustafa Supérieur.

Shops and Bazaars.—The best shops for European goods are in the Rues Bab-el-Oued, Bab-Azoum, de la Lyre, and de Chartres. They are usually good, and hardly dearer than in France. Meat is excellent, and about the same price as in England. Game is abundant and very good. Vegetables, fruit, and flowers are cheap, and most excellent. Every sort of clothing can be bought of good quality and at reasonable prices in the streets above named. Photographs are good.

The bazaars where the best articles of Arab and Moorish manufacture can be obtained are in the Passages leading from the Place du Gouvernement to the Rue de Chartres, and in the Rue de la Lycée.

Of the many establishments devoted to the sale or manufacture of what are called *objets arabes*, none is more worthy of a visit than that of Madame Benaben, grand-daughter and successor of Madame Luce, in the Rue Bruce, nearly opposite the Cathedral. The latter lady devoted her whole life to two most laudable objects—the perpetuation of the exquisite embroidery for which Algiers has always been famous, and which, but for her, would now have become an extinct art; and the endeavour to teach Arab women to gain their livelihood in an honest manner. In their youth they are taught to work at the establishment, and when they marry and settle in life they continue to work at home, and bring the produce of their industry there for sale. Such thoroughly good "woman's work" is worthy of the highest praise and encouragement. Another person who has had the merit of perpetuating an art which had almost become extinct is M. Marlier in the Rue Jenina. He makes most beautiful trays and other objects in brass, and has a true feeling for Moorish art.

The traveller must beware, if he be dealing with Moors, and Jews especially, of giving the sum first asked; these always put on an increased price in the expectation of being beaten down. For further particulars see Index.

Theatres. See Index.

THE HARBOUR.

The **Inner Harbour** of Algiers, originally made by Kheir-ed-din in 1518, consisted of a mole connecting the town with the rocks on which the lighthouse now stands, but on which *Fort Peñon* stood formerly. The *Lighthouse* is octagonal in form, and was built in 1544 by Hassan Pacha, on the old Spanish basement. The summit of the tower is about 120 ft. above the sea-level, with a fixed light, and can be seen for 15 m.

In the Bureau de la Marine (formerly a Turkish prison), on the N.E. side of the harbour, is a picturesque doorway, ornamented with marble inlaid with colour of the 17th century.

The present harbour, commenced in 1836, is formed by continuing this mole towards the S.E. A similar mole beginning near the Fort Bab-Azoun runs E. for some distance, and then, turning N., terminates within about 350 yards of the preceding, the entrance to the harbour being between the two. At each extremity stands a fort. These breakwaters are interesting as being the first experiment tried of constructing such works with blocks of concrete. The harbour has an area of 90 hectares (222 acres), and an average depth of about 40 ft.

Two docks have been constructed, capable of containing the largest vessels.

There are two basins for discharging ships near the centre of the quays, which extend along the edge of the harbour for a distance of about 700 yards; the arches under the Boulevard de la République are used for warehouses and various other purposes.

In excavating for the present streets in the marine quarter, the foundations of the ancient town of *Icosium* were laid bare. A Roman street existed where the Rue de la Marine now lies; and two Roman cemeteries were discovered near the Rues Bab-el-Oued and Bab-Azoun. Icosium was probably not a large town, and all traces of it have now disappeared.

FORTIFICATIONS.

Of the ancient fortifications of Algiers, the chief are :—

The **Kasba**, or **Citadel**, situated on the highest point of the city, was commenced by Aroudj in 1516 on the site of an older building, and its history was the history of Algiers down to the conquest, at which period it was still the palace of the Deys, and was defended by 200 pieces of artillery. Here it was that the last Dey gave the now historical blow with his fan to the French Consul, which cost him his dominions. It was much injured by the French after the siege, a road having been cut right through the centre, the mosque turned into a barrack, and the rest of the building appropriated to military purposes. The enormous treasure found here was stored in vaults, traces of which are yet to be seen, and the ancient door lined with sheet-iron still exists, above which is a wooden gallery where the beacon and banner were displayed. There is also a minaret, and some marble columns and arches, which belonged to the ancient building. But the historical pavilion where the *coup d'éventail* was given has been allowed to fall into decay, and the walls have everywhere been despoiled of their beautiful tiles by the military engineers.

The **Fort de l'Empereur**, so called from being built on the spot where Charles V. pitched his camp during his disastrous attack on Algiers, after his retreat. It was constructed in 1545 by Hassan Pacha, the son and successor of Kheir-ed-din, and for a long time it bore his name. It is situated above the Kasba and without the town, the whole of which it commands. It was here that General de Bourmont received the capitulation of the Dey of Algiers. It was blown up by the French when they took Algiers, and is now used as a prison for officers.

The **Fort des Anglais**, which was built in 1825, as a protection against future bombardments by the English; the **Fort de l'Eau**, 18 kil. from Algiers, between that place and Matifou. There is a fort erected on Cape Matifou, and another on the Pointe Pescade. At the end of the Boulevard de la République stands the **Fort Bab-Azoun**, now connected with the line of works; it was built by Hussein Pacha in 1851; and on one side of the Place Bab-el-Oued is the **Fort Neuf**, both now used as military prisons. In 1540 a wall was built by the same Pacha, which was in some places of great thickness. It was surmounted by battlements, and pierced with loopholes, and extended from the Kasba to the Fort Neuf on one side, and to the Rue de la Lyre on the other. This has been almost entirely destroyed to make room for modern improvements.

Modern Defensive Works. — The French line of works, consisting of a rampart, parapet, and ditch, strengthened by bastions, commences above the Kasba in the quarter of the Tagarins, and stretches to the sea on either side, terminating in the Place Bab-el-Oued to the N.; and in the Fort Bab-Azoun, towards the S.

The improved means of attack of late have rendered these fortifications comparatively useless, and, doubtless, their demolition is merely a question of time. They occupy a space of 180 acres, and cost originally about 8,000,000 f. The peninsula of the admiralty is also strongly fortified.

Important isolated works have been constructed on the heights of Bou-Zarea, in the Valée des Consuls, above the Jardin d'Essai, and on the heights above the English Church to the S. of the town. These are all armed with improved modern artillery.

MUSTAFA SUPÉRIEUR.

Persons who intend spending more than one or two nights in Algiers are recommended to stop at one of the hotels (see Algiers, in Index) at **Mustafa Supérieur**, which is within easy access (2 m.) of the town by omnibus every half-hour, or by carriage (3 f.) Mustafa Supérieur is well situated on the slopes of the hills S. of Algiers amongst gardens and pine woods, and commands extensive views; and being at a considerable elevation above the sea, it has the great advantage of being fresher and more healthy than the town. This neighbourhood, with the adjoining plateau of **El-Biar** (300 ft. above the sea), is the favourite residence of winter visitors to Algiers. Besides the best hotels there are here numerous Moorish and French villas in beautiful gardens, with magnificent views of sea and land. It is hardly possible to find a more delightful residence in any part of the Mediterranean.

Hotels, English Club, Omnibuses, etc., see Index.

EXCURSIONS IN THE ENVIRONS OF ALGIERS.

1. El-Biar and Bou-Zarea.
2. Colonne Voirol, Birmandrais, Ravine of Femme Sauvage and Jardin d'Essai.
3. La Trappe, Sidi Feruch, Guyotville, Pointe Pescade.
4. Nôtre Dame d'Afrique, and Valley of Consuls.
5. Maison Carrée.
6. Fonduk and Barrage of Khamis.
7. Cape Matifou and Rusgunia.
8. Gorge of Issers, Palaestro, and Dra el-Mizan.
9. Blidah and Gorge of Chiffa.
10. Hammam Rir'ha.
11. Milianah.
12. Fort National.
13. Teniet el-Ahd (Cedar Forest).
14. Cherchel and Tombeau de la Chrétienne.

(1.) To **El-Biar** and **Bou-Zarea**. — The traveller may either ascend by the Mustafa road, passing the Governor-General's palace, and turning to the right at the Colonne Voirol, or he may follow the Tournant Rovigo, pass the Kasba, and the reservoirs for supplying the upper part of the town with water, and leave Algiers by the Porte ud Sahel. We shall assume that he takes the latter route. There are several omnibuses daily to El-Biar and Bou-Zarea, but it is best to take a carriage, fare 7 f.

3 kil. FORT L'EMPEREUR. See p. 104.

[1 kil. A bridle path to the right leads down the FRAIS VALLON, a picturesque and shady ravine, in which are situated the mineral springs of *Aoun*

Srakna, reputed to be of considerable medicinal value. The path ends at the Cité Bugeaud, the faubourg of Bab-el-Oued.]

5 kil. **El-Biar** (Ar. *The Wells*). A long straggling village lying for some distance along the road. The commune extends as far S. as the Colonne Voirol, and is the most charming and healthful part of the environs of Algiers. It contains many of the best villas occupied by English residents during the winter season, amongst others that of Sir Lambert Playfair, H.M. Consul-General; the Château d'Hydra (Mr. E. Ledgard), and the beautiful house and grounds of Mr. Macleay.

There are also several convents; one to the W. of the village is that of the *Bon Pasteur*, a reformatory and refuge for women, as well as an asylum for children. Nearer the Colonne is an orphanage for girls, belonging to the Sisters of St. Vincent de Paul; still farther on, another belonging to the same sisterhood for boys; and between the two the head establishment of the *Frères de la Doctrine Chrétienne*, who have primary schools for boys all over the colony.

A large house just outside the village on the left (Maison Couput) is that in which Maréchal de Bourmont established his headquarters, and where the final surrender of Algiers was agreed to, through the mediation of Mr. St. John, the British Consul-General.[1]

6 kil. *Château Neuf*, a wayside *auberge*. Here the road bifurcates; the lower branch leads to *Ben Aknoun* (8 kil.), once a Jesuit orphanage, now the Petit Lycée, for a younger class of boys than those received in town. Here also are the springs of *Aïn Zeboudja*, whence the upper part of Algiers is supplied with water; and *Deli Ibrahim* (11 kil.), where is a Protestant orphanage. The upper branch leads to Cheragas (12 kil.).

7 kil. From the latter of these branches the Chemin Vicinal de la Bou-Zarea turns sharp off to the right.

[1] See "Scourge of Christendom," p. 319.

About half way to the village is a vast building, erected for a lunatic asylum, now occupied as an *École Normal*.

9 kil. **Bou-Zarea**, a small European village situated on a mountain of the same name 1150 ft. above the sea. The native village is about 1 kil. farther on to the left. It contains several koubbas, notably that of *Sidi Naâman*, situated in enclosures of prickly pear, amongst which are dwarf palms of such unusual height as entirely to belie their name. The summit of the hill is occupied by a cemetery, whence a glorious panoramic view is obtained of the country in every direction.

[From this point a road, rather rough, but practicable for light carriages, leads to GUYOTVILLE, 9 kil. farther on. About half way, to the N. of the road, is the forest of *Aïn-Beïnan* (see p. 109), whence the high road to Algiers may be reached near Cape Caxine, at a point distant 11 kil. from the city.]

The traveller should return by a lonely tortuous road leading to the faubourg of Bab-el-Oued. After passing the village, to the E., the road bifurcates; the upper branch conducts to the *Observatory*, 1700 mètres from the village, built in an open space of about 12 acres in extent, 350 mètres above the level of the sea, where once stood a Turkish fort. Probably no observatory in the world is more favourably situated, while the buildings and instruments are worthy of it and of France. One of the instruments is of historical interest; it is a reflecting telescope constructed by the celebrated Léon Foucault with his own hand. The Director, M. Trepied, is most courteous to visitors. The lower branch leads to the town; about a third of the way down is the *Hospice des Vieillards*, kept by the *Petites Sœurs des Pauvres*, an excellent charity, well worthy of a visit. About 100 old men and women find an asylum here, and as it is entirely supported by voluntary contributions, donations, either in money or old clothing, are gratefully received.

(2.) To the **Colonne Voirol, Birmandraïs**, Ravine of the **Femme Sauvage**, and back by the **Jardin d'Essai** (6 f.)
The road leaves the town by the Porte d'Isly, and passes through the district of *Mustafa Supérieur*.
4 kil. The summer *Palace of the Governor-General*.

5½ kil. The **Colonne Voirol**. A small village named from the column which records the construction of the road by General Baron Voirol. He was the last of the *commandants en chef* of the army of Africa, and it was under his administration in 1833 that France finally determined to retain possession of Algeria.

[A road to the right leads to **El-Biar**. There are numerous beautiful walks in the neighbourhood.]

8 kil. **Birmandraïs**, a pretty little village in a well-wooded hollow. The proper orthography is *Bir Mourad Raïs*, "well of Mourad the captain," a celebrated renegade Flemish corsair.

[3 kil. farther, on the high road, is the village of **Birkhadem**, "the well of the slave," so called from a picturesque Moorish fountain in the market-place. In the fort above the village is a military penal establishment, and there is an interesting female orphanage for girls on the cross road leading hence to Koubba.

Instead of driving down the valley of the Femme Sauvage, the traveller may vary the excursion by returning from Birmandraïs through Koubba and the Ruisseau. There is a lovely shady road which passes through *Vieux Koubba*, 3 kil. from Birmandraïs; 2 kil. farther on is the new village of **Koubba**, the principal feature of which is the *Séminaire* or Ecclesiastical College, containing two branches, one for about 30 boys, and the other for an equal number of older students, who are usually deacons or sub-deacons. In the centre of the building is the church, the immense dome of which is one of the most prominent objects in the landscape seen from Algiers and Mustafa. The place owes its name to a small Mohammedan *koubba* or tomb, situated in the garden, now converted into a chapel. The grounds are very extensive, and chiefly laid out in vines. On the north side there is a fine *Chemin de la Croix*, with chapels, grottoes and sculptured stations. In the village is a statue to one of the finest of the old type of Algerian soldiers, General Margueritte, killed at Sedan. It is the work of Albert Lefeuvre.]

At Birmandraïs, close to the church, the road to the Ruisseau branches off to the left, through the beautifully wooded valley of the **Femme Sauvage**, so named after a young lady, by no means shy, who kept a café restaurant in this ravine shortly after the French conquest. It joins the high road below at the 6th kilomètre from Algiers.

Turning now to the W., we reach the **Jardin d'Essai**, a garden of about 200 hectares in extent. This was commenced in 1832, and while it remained in the hands of Government it was kept up with great care, but at a great expense; now it is in the hands of the *Compagnie Générale Algérienne*, and the commercial element is more considered than the advancement of science. Still it is a delightful promenade, and it contains a most interesting collection of plants, both in the open air and in greenhouses. Ornamental plants are cultivated in great numbers and exported to the principal cities of Europe. The avenues of planes, palms, bamboos, and magnolias are especially worthy of notice.

On the opposite side of the road, on the slope of the hill, is another and most attractive portion of the same garden, principally devoted to Australian plants, such as eucalyptus, araucarias, acacias, etc., the whole crowned by a beautiful wood of Canary pines. There is a fine old Moorish house in it. The gardens are open to the public; and at the *Café des Platanes*, just by the entrance, coffee and other refreshments may be obtained.

It was here that the Emperor Charles V. commenced on the 23d October 1541 to disembark his army of 24,000 men, the *débris* of which were re-embarked on board such of his vessels as escaped the tempest eight days later at Cape Matifou. In the Propriété Sabatery close by is a grotto in which Cervantes and his companions are supposed to have resided for some time.

Here it may be well to give some account of the company to which this garden has been let for a nominal rent of 1000 f. a year. A convention was passed between the *Société Générale Algérienne* and the Imperial Government in 1865, stipulating that it was to have a capital of 100 millions of francs, to be devoted exclusively to industrial and agricultural works, the exploitation of mines and forests, the erection of barrages and irrigational canals, the establishment of manufactories, etc. It was to lend a further sum of 100 millions of francs to the State, to be applied in similar works of public utility, and the Government made over to the company 100,000 hectares (250,000 acres) of the best land in the colony at a nominal rent of 1 f. per hectare per annum during 50 years. The company totally failed in all these conditions; it confined itself to financial operations, mostly *out of* Algeria, and met with serious losses. In 1878 it was liquidated, and a new society called the *Compagnie Générale Algérienne* took its place, with no more change than is expressed by its title.

On the S. of the road farther on (4½ kil. from Algiers) is an Arab Cemetery, in which is the small *Koubba of Sidi Mohammed ben Abd-er-Rahman bou Koberain*, "the man with two tombs." It was he who founded the religious confraternity which bears his name, and to which a vast number both of Kabyles and Arabs are affiliated. After having made a voyage to Egypt, he inhabited Algiers under Baba Mohammed Pacha, and subsequently died in Kabylia, in the country of the Beni Ismail, a branch of the Guechtoula, of which he was a native, and there a tomb was raised over his remains. The Algerians caused the body to be carried off and interred where it now lies, and the excitement caused by the act was only appeased by giving out that the body of the saint had been miraculously doubled, and rested in both tombs. Great numbers of Moorish women visit this cemetery every Friday afternoon.

Farther on, to the N. of the road, is the **Champ de Manœuvres**, used as a racecourse and exercising ground for troops. It is large enough to allow 25,000 men to be reviewed at once. Here commences **Mustafa Inférieur**, on the lower slope of the hill on which Mustafa Supérieur is situated. Beyond this is the **Agha**, containing manufactories and workshops, cart and carriage factories, corn and saw mills, gasworks, etc., and the female prison in the buildings of the old Lazaretto.

(3.) To **La Trappe, Sidi Feruch, Guyotville**, and **Pointe Pescade** (20 f.)

Drive by El-Biar to Château Neuf, as in excursion (1); 6 kil.

12 kil. **Cheragas**, situated at the entrance to the plain of Staouëli. The country round is very fertile, and there are several distilleries here for making essence of geranium and other scents.

17 kil. **La Trappe de Staouëli.** The Trappists obtained leave from the Government in 1843 to build a monastery, and were granted about 2500 acres of the surrounding land, which was then almost a wilderness, but which has been transformed by their exertions and industry into a fertile country, producing vines, oranges, fruit-trees, and all species of cereals and vegetables. There are two corn-mills, the water for driving which is brought by an aqueduct 30 ft. in height.

The monastery itself is a rectangular building, containing a courtyard surrounded by cloisters, and a chapel which occupies one wing of the building. The walls are covered with inscriptions calling to mind the miseries of life, among which may be seen the following: "S'il est triste de vivre à la Trappe, qu'il est doux d'y mourir." To the left is the farm, containing the stables and sheds for the large flocks and herds of the establishment, and to the right are the various workshops, the forge, bakehouse, wheelwrights' and carpenters' shops, wine vaults, dairy, etc. The cemetery is close at hand.

Facing the monastery, in the midst of a clump of palm-trees springing from a single root, stands a statue of the Virgin, *Nôtre Dame de Staouëli.* The monastery is built on the spot where the battle of Staouëli was fought between the French and Turks on 19th June 1830. The number of monks is about 100.

The small town of Staoueli is 1¼ m. N. of La Trappe.

25 kil. **Sidi Feruch**, more correctly *Sidi-Furrudj*, celebrated as the landing-place of the French army on 14th June 1839, is an elevated peninsula, stretching 1000 yards into the sea, on the top of which stood a round tower built by the Spaniards, and called *Torre Chica.*

Here was the koubba of the saint, regarding whom the following legend is told: "A Spanish captain coming one day to the spot found the holy man asleep, and carried him on board his vessel to sell him in Spain, but notwithstanding that the wind was favourable and filled his sails, the ship remained immovable. The Christian understood that this was a miracle, and ever afterwards remained the devoted friend and follower of Sidi-Furrudj. Both friends were buried in the same grave."

In 1847 the remains of the two friends were disinterred, and reverently buried by the French authorities in the cemetery of Sidi Mohammed at the Oued Aggar at Staouëli.

The small village was founded in 1844, and for some time was an important place for the sardine fisheries, but was afterwards nearly abandoned. The new barrack, capable of accommodating 2000 men, is a substantial building in the fort. The principal entrance is ornamented with sculptured trophies of peace and war. On the marble slab is the following inscription:—

Ici
LE 14 JUIN 1830,
PAR L'ORDRE DU ROI CHARLES X,
SOUS LE COMMANDEMENT DU GÉNÉRAL DE
BOURMONT,
L'ARMÉE FRANÇAISE
VINT ARBORER SES DRAPEAUX,
RENDRE LA LIBERTÉ AUX MERS,
DONNER L'ALGÉRIE À LA FRANCE.

Here was found a chapel in memory of St. Januarius with the inscription:—

HIC EST JANVARI
ET FILLII EJVS MEMORIA,
QVI VIXIT ANNIS XLVII MENSIBVS V
DISCESSIT IN PACE VI... ANNO PROVINC.
CCCCX.

Return by the sea coast, passing **Guyotville**, 15 kil. from Algiers. This village is named after Comte de Guyot, director of the Interior from 1840 to 1846, built in 1845 on the site of an Arab village, Aïn-Beïnan. It is one of the most prosperous villages in the vicinity of Algiers. Just beyond it on the sea-shore are some curious Roman quarries. Turning off here to the left, the road to Cheragas crosses an undulating and partly uncleared country. About half way, and a little more than a mile to the W., in the Oued Beni Messous, are about a dozen megalithic monuments still entire, and a considerable number in a less perfect state of preservation. These consist of dolmens—large tabular stones, supported on four upright ones. Several interesting objects have been found in those that have been opened, such as bones, pottery, bronze ornaments, etc., which may be seen at the rooms of the Société de Climatologie, Rue Bruce.

Cape Caxine, 12 kil. from Algiers. On the summit is a lighthouse, with a revolving light of the first order, visible at a distance of 24 m.

At 10½ kil. from Algiers, to the S. of the road, is a charming forest of **Aïn-Beïnan**, about 100 hectares in extent, planted by the Department of Forests in 1867-70; it consists of Aleppo pines, eucalyptus of various species, casuarinas, cork oak, Australian acacias, and other trees. It is full of beautiful views, and is a favourite place for picnics. At the *Maison Forestière* is a spring of good water. There is a rough road, practicable for light carriages, from this place to Bou-Zarea.

At 6 kil. from Algiers is **Pointe Pescade** or *Mersa-ed-Deblan*, a reef of rocks running out into the sea, on which stands the ruins of the fort of the same name, built in 1671 by El-Hadj Ali Agha, and restored in 1724 and 1732. Behind it are the ruins of another fort, now utilised as a custom-house station, said to have been the residence of Baba Aroudj (*Barbarossa*).

There is an excellent restaurant here, at which fish dinners and breakfasts can be obtained.

At 3 kil. from Algiers is **St. Eugène**, a village principally occupied by Jews; it is rarely used by winter visitors, as the situation is less healthy than Mustafa Supérieur, and there are scarcely any walks save along a crowded and dusty public road.

2½ kil. from Algiers is the general cemetery, and then follows the **Cité Bugeaud**, or faubourg of Bab-el-Oued.

Omnibuses run every few minutes from the Place du Gouvernement to St. Eugène, and even farther.

(4.) To **Nôtre Dame d'Afrique** and the **Valley of Consuls**. (4.50 f. to the church.)

A rather steep drive from the gate of Bab-el-Oued, passing behind the Military Hospital, leads to **Nôtre Dame d'Afrique**, conspicuously placed on a shoulder of Mount Bou-Zarea, having a magnificent view of the city and the sea. It is built in the Romano-Byzantine style of architecture, and has by no means an unpleasing effect. The walls of the interior are covered with votive offerings of all kinds, amongst which those of sailors predominate; indeed, this class of the community has made the church particularly its own. Above the altar is a *Black* Virgin, and around the apse the inscription, "Nôtre Dame d'Afrique priez pour nous et pour les Musslemans."

Every Sunday a ceremony is performed which has no parallel perhaps in any other church in the world. About 3½ P.M., after vespers, the clergy chant the prayers for the dead, and go in procession to the point overhanging the sea, where before a catafalque the officiating priests perform all the ceremonies over this vast grave, which the church appoints for ordinary funerals.

There is a curious statue of the Archangel Michael in this church, made of solid silver, valued at about £4000; it belongs to the confraternity of Neapolitan fishermen, and is enclosed within a rail of gilt iron at the W. end of the church.

Beyond Nôtre Dame d'Afrique is the *Valée des Consuls*, so called from having been the favourite residence of those functionaries during the time of the Deys. The farthest off house on the road was the British Consulate, figured in Mrs. Broughton's book. Half way between this and the church, on the N. side of the road, is the *Petite Séminaire* and Cardinal Lavigerie's country residence, on the site of the old French Consulate. Opposite to it, on the S. side of the road, is the old American, and a little higher up the Sardinian Consulate. The drive here is exceedingly beautiful; and as it has been very little changed, it gives a good idea of what the environs of Algiers were like during the time of the Deys. From the Séminaire a footpath leads to Bou-Zarea.

(5.) To **Maison Carrée** by the lower road, N. of the Jardin d'Essai.

2 kil. *Mustafa Inférieur*.

4 kil. The *Abattoir*, to the S. of road.

5 kil. *Jardin d'Essai*.

5½ kil. *Village of Hussein Dey*.

6 kil. Artillery *Polygon*, or practice ground.

11 kil. **Maison Carrée**. The old Turkish fort on the top of the hill, from which this village derives its name, and which is now used as a native prison, was built in 1721 by the Dey Mohammed Effendi, to prevent the landing of an enemy at the Harrach. It was rebuilt by Yehia Agha on a greater scale in 1826, to serve as a starting-point for the various excursions made by the Turks in the interior.

Near the village is the Convent of the White Fathers, a missionary order established by Cardinal Lavigerie for the conversion of the remote regions of Central Africa. They wear the Arab costume, learn the Arabic language, and accustom themselves to live entirely like natives. An attempt to send them through the Sahara signally failed, they were assassinated on their way, and they have since been sent into the interior of the continent from Zanzibar.

They have created an important agricultural establishment here, and are especially celebrated for the cultivation of vines.

In connection with this establishment are orphanages both here and at St. Charles, between Koubba and Birkhadem.

(6.) To **Fonduk** and the **Barrage of the Khamis**.

Omnibuses run twice a day to Fonduk (32 kil., 1.50 f.); but the best means of doing the excursion is to take the earliest train in the morning to Maison Blanche; the omnibus from Algiers arrives a few minutes later, and the traveller can continue in it to Fonduk. He can obtain a carriage at the *Hôtel Gessin* to visit the barrage (5 f.), and return in time for the omnibus which leaves for Algiers at 2½ P.M., arriving at 6 P.M.

Fonduk is not a particularly prosperous village, but it hopes to improve its condition when the barrage is finished. It owes its name to an Arab caravanserail which existed on the spot. About 1 kil. to the S.E. are the ruins of a large fort built in the first year of the French occupation. The village is picturesquely situated on the left bank of the river Khamis, at the foot of the first slope of the Atlas.

About 7 kil. farther up a dam or barrage has been built at a cost of 2 millions of francs. It has a height, equal to the breadth of its base, of 35 mètres; the foundations are 6 mètres deep, and repose on an impermeable stratum; the construction is of solid rubble, built with hydraulic cement; the wall exteriorly rises in a curve, and has a width at the top of 4.75 mètres; the total length is 165 mètres. This dyke will contain an immense body of water, covering an area of 100 hectares, and with a depth of 35 mètres at the barrage. But it is in a deplorable condition of neglect. Although commenced in 1869, it is far from being finished; the sluice-gates have not been erected, the canals for irrigation are not made, and the overflow on the right bank of the river has not been arranged. This indeed appears to be the weak point of the work.

The rock here is so friable that it is by no means improbable that an unusual fall of rain may result in the whole structure being carried away, as in the case of Perrigaux and St. Denis du Sig. Perhaps this may explain the otherwise unaccountable delay in utilising what has caused such an immense expenditure. The barrage, however, is well worth a visit, as it is the only important irrigational work in the province of Algiers.

In the mountain of *Bou-Zigza* (1032 mètres), near Fonduk, are some gorges which would repay exploration. There is a bridle path from Fonduk, passing this mountain, and terminating at Palaestro.

4 kil. E. of Fonduk is the thriving village of *Arbatach*, founded in 1878.

(7.) To **Cape Matifou** and the **Ruins of Rusgunia**.

This may be done, if desired, by public conveyance, as omnibuses perform the journey twice daily in three hours.

18 kil. *Le Fort de l'Eau*, built in 1581, by Djafar Pacha. It owes its name to a famous well of water within the walls. The village close to the Fort was founded in 1850, chiefly by the Mahonnais, natives of Minorca. The land was then densely covered with brushwood; five years later it was thoroughly cleared, and now numerous *Norias*, each one irrigating six acres of land, have converted it into a productive market-garden, yielding easily an annual out-turn of £30 an acre.

20 kil. *La Rassauta*. In 1836 a Polish General, the Prince de Mir, obtained from the Government the grant of a large tract of land near this place, for the purpose of trying some experiments in agriculture, which, however, were not successful.

21 kil. *L'Oued Khamis*, where there is a small battery.

26 kil. *Rusgunia* ruins. This Roman city occupied in ancient times a circular area of great extent; and the mosaics, medals, columns, etc., which have been found scattered around seem to indicate that Rusgunia was an important colony. The *débris* of this

city was extensively used as building material for Algiers.

The following inscription on a stone from these ruins, which is now built into the roof of a vault, used as a wine store, by the Intendance Militaire, almost below the statue of the Duc d'Orleans, proves the identity of Rusgunia:—

L. TADIO L. FIL. QUIR.
ROGATO
DEC. AED. IIVIR IIVIR
Q. Q. RUSG ET RUSG.
CONSISTENTES OB
MERITA QUOD FRU-
MENTUM INTULERIT
ET ANNONAM PAS
SV .... CIT INCRESCERE
AERE COLLATO.

"To Lucius Tadius, son of Lucius Quirinus, called Rogatus, the Decurions, Ædiles, Duumvirs, and the quinquennial Duumvirs of Rusgunia, and the inhabitants of Rusgunia, on account of his merit in furnishing corn, and contributing to the public stores. By subscription."

27 kil. *Matifou*, a small hamlet founded in 1853, on a promontory known to the natives as Temendafoust. The ruined fort was built by Ramdan Agha in 1661, when Ismaïl was Pacha; and from it was fired the salute on the arrival of a new Pacha of Algiers. A short distance off is a fountain called in Arabic "*Ishrub wa harab*," signifying "Drink and go away." The caution was given because of the prevalence of fever, which seldom spared those who slept near by. It was at Matifou that the Emperor Charles V. re-embarked after his disastrous expedition against Algiers in 1541.

Near the end of the Cape is the Lazaretto built on the appearance of cholera at Toulon and Marseilles in 1884.

(8.) To the **Gorge of the Issers**, **Palaestro**, and **Dra el-Mizan**. Train in 3½ hrs. to Palaestro; fair accommodation (Rte. 8).

(9.) To **Blidah** and the **Gorge of the Chiffa**. Train to Blidah in 2 hrs. This excursion may be done from Algiers and back in one day (Rte. 7).

(10.) To **Hammam Rir'ha** (Rte. 10).

(11.) **Milianah**. Train to Affreville in 4 to 6 hrs.; thence diligence to 8 kil. Milianah (Rte. 10).

(12.) **Fort National**. (Magnificent views of Kabyle mountains). Train in 4 or 5 hrs. to Tizi Ouzou (fair accommodation); thence drive of 3 hrs. to Fort National (Rte. 6).

(13.) **Teniet el-Ahd**. (Cedar Forest). Train in 4 to 6 hrs. to Affreville; diligence thence to 59 kil. Teniet el-Ahd (Rte. 5).

(14.) **Cherchel** and **Tombeau de la Chrétienne**. Train to El-Affroun in 2 to 3 hrs. (The traveller should write beforehand to keeper of Hôtel d'Orient at Blidah for a carriage to meet him at El-Affroun station to drive 32 kil. to Cherchel (good accommodation). The Tombeau de la Chrétienne may be visited by making a slight detour from the direct road (Rtes. 2 and 3).

A FORTNIGHT'S TOUR IN ALGERIA.

Many travellers when leaving Algiers, probably for Italy, *via* Tunis, have only a short time at their disposal, and are anxious to employ it to the best advantage. The following route is recommended; it will enable them to see rapidly all that is most interesting in the colony, and to reach Malta within a fortnight.

First day—To **Bougie**, either by sea or by railway (p. 114).

Second day—By carriage, through the **Chabet** (Rte. 12); sleep at **Kharata** (or the traveller can go direct to Setif in one day by diligence).

Third day—Continue drive to Setif, and on by railway to **Constantine** (*q.v.*)

Fourth day—At Constantine.

Fifth day—To **Biskra** by railway.
Sixth day—At Biskra.
Seventh day—Return to **Batna**, and visit **Lambessa**.
Eighth day—Visit ruins of **Timegad** (p. 208).

Ninth day—Visit **Cedar Forest**.
Tenth day—To **Hammam Meskoutin** by railway.
Eleventh day—To Tunis, and within the fortnight the traveller can embark there either for Malta or Marseilles.

A TOUR IN THE PROVINCE OF ORAN.

Some travellers on leaving Algiers proceed westwards, to Spain or Gibraltar; to such, if they are not afraid of a few days' travel in diligences, Route 21 is strongly recommended. It can be done in five days' actual travel, and a few more would be pleasantly and profitably spent at Tlemçen.

NEW MAP OF ALGERIA.

A new and very beautiful Map of Algeria is now being published at the *Dépôt de la Guerre* at Paris, on a scale of 1 to 50,000, or 1·4 inch to the geographical mile. When complete it will consist of 327 sheets. The hill work is shown by a combination of shading and contours which is very effective. It is printed in three colours, and every detail is shown. It costs only 1 f. per sheet.

ROUTES.

ROUTE 1.

Algiers to Philippeville, Bône, and Tunis by Sea.

STEAMERS, both of the Transatlantique Company and of the Navigation Mixte, or Touache, do the voyage each way once a week. The latter goes no farther than Bône.

The steamer on leaving Algiers takes an easterly course towards *Cape Matifou*, where there is a fixed white light on a masonry tower seen 8 m. off; the passage across the bay affording a splendid panoramic view of the city and suburbs. A short distance beyond the cape are some rocks called by the Arabs *Mersa Toumlilin*, where the French steamer "Sphinx" was wrecked in 1845.

From Matifou the coast is low and uninteresting as far as

44 naut. m. **Dellys.** Pop. 3000.

[*Algeria.*]

The modern town is picturesquely situated on a plateau, and, like all the towns on the coast, faces the E.
The Arab town is to the N. of the modern one.
During part of the winter the harbour is almost inaccessible, though tolerably sheltered from the N.W. To the S. and W. it is surrounded by slightly elevated hills detached from the last counterforts of the range which runs along the coast; it is therefore only partially sheltered from the N., the N.E., and E. winds.
French Dellys contains large regularly-built streets, and a pretty square planted with trees. The town is surrounded by a wall, pierced with loopholes.
There is a handsome *mosque*, which was built by the French in exchange for the ancient one given up to them by the natives; also a church, a free

1

school, a large hospital, and barracks for 800 men. The Arab town is ill-built, dirty, and crowded.

A school of *arts et métiers* has been established here, to replace that destroyed at Fort National during the insurrection of 1871. The building is very conspicuous from the steamer on approaching Dellys from the W.

From the lighthouse to the end of the promontory there is a splendid view of the coast, which is here bold and rockbound. The soil is particularly favourable for cultivation, and the climate is considered exceedingly healthy.

Dellys is built on the site of the Roman town of *Rusenrium*, the ancient ramparts of which are still visible on the western side. In 1857 a fine marble sarcophagus was discovered, which is now in the museum at Algiers. Rusenrium was finally destroyed by an earthquake, and Dellys was built from its ruins.

55½ m. *Cape Tedles.* Near the modern village of *Taksebt* are the ruins of the Roman city of *Rusubeser*, and a little to the W. the more important ruins of *Tigzirt*, including a small temple in a good state of preservation.

68½ m. *Cape Corbelin*, near which is *Azzefoun*, now called *Port-Gueydon*, after Admiral de Gueydon, a late Governor-General, a village built on land obtained by sequestration after the insurrection of 1871. This was formerly a Roman position, *Rusazus*. The ruins of an aqueduct and of several solidly constructed buildings may yet be traced.

103½ m. In about 10 hours after leaving Dellys the steamer passes *Cape Carbon*, or *El-Metkoub*, "the pierced," so called from a remarkable grotto or natural arch at its foot, through which a boat can pass in fine weather. Shaw mentions a tradition that it was a favourite resort of the celebrated anchorite Raymond Lully, who was subsequently stoned by the natives whom he hoped to convert, and who only survived long enough to reach his native Majorca. On the summit is a lighthouse of the first magnitude.

Beyond this is *Cape Noir*, and still farther, forming the eastern point of the Bay of Bougie, *Cape Bouac*, on which formerly existed a Turkish battery of 4 guns, whence the arrival of vessels was signalled to the town by the sound of an instrument called *bouc*, the sounder of which is in Arabic *bouac*. There is now a small lighthouse of the third order on the site of the old fort.

106 m. **Bougie** (Ar. *Boujaïa*), 5086 inhabitants.

Bougie is the natural seaport of Eastern Kabylia, a region very distinct from the Kabylia of Djurdjura, of which Dellys is the port. The town is built on the slope of a hill, and commands a glorious view of land and water, with Mounts Babor and Ta-babort as a background, 6455 ft. high, crowned with forests of cedar and pinsapo. The poet Campbell, who visited Bougie in 1834, thus records his impression: "Such is the grandeur of the surrounding mountain scenery that I drop my pen in despair of giving you any conception of it. Scotchman as I am, and much as I love my native land, I declare to you that I felt as if I had never before seen the full glory of mountain scenery. The African Highlands spring up to the sight not only with a sterner boldness than our own, but they borrow colours from the sun, unknown to our climate, and they are mantled in clouds of richer dye. The farthest off summits appeared in their snow like the turbans of gigantic Moors, whilst the nearest masses glowed in crimson and gold under the light of the morning."

All the races who have successively inhabited Bougie during 2000 years—Carthaginians, Romans, Vandals, Berbers, Arabs, Spaniards, and Turks—have left considerable traces of their domination. The Roman *enceinte* is still traceable in many places; it had a perimeter of 3000 yards, and was further strengthened by detached works and a sea-wall. The Saracenic lines were constructed about A.D. 1067, and various portions of them still remain, notably a large arch at the landing-place, and two walls flanked by towers running up the side of the hill behind the city.

A very high state of civilisation existed in the 11th century, and it is curious to read in an old Arabic MS. how, during the reign of El-Mansour, in A.D. 1068, the heliograph, which we are fain to think a modern discovery, was in common use here. This prince was on very friendly terms with the Pope, who sent him 1100 artisans, skilled in their different professions. These erected a stately tower, which was called *Chouf er-Riad,* "the Observatory of the Garden," on the summit of which was an apparatus consisting of mirrors, corresponding with similar ones established at different points, by the aid of which they could communicate rapidly from one end of the kingdom to the other. During the night the signals were made by fires disposed in a pre-arranged manner.

In 1508, owing to the piratical practices of its inhabitants, Ferdinand V. of Spain sent an army and 14 ships of war under Don Pedro Navarro, to take possession of it. He restored the *Kasba* or citadel in 1509, and the defensive works were further strengthened and restored by Charles V. in 1545, who himself took refuge at Bougie after his repulse at Algiers.

Leo Africanus, who published his "History of Africa" in 1526, says: "Wonderful is the architecture of its houses, its temples, colleges, and palaces." After the defeat of Charles V. at Algiers, the Algerians took advantage of the occasion, and marched with all their forces upon it. They stormed the castle on the harbour, and the citadel on the heights, so that Alonzo de Peralta, the Spanish governor, was fain to demand a capitulation. He was allowed to return with 400 men to Spain, where the monarch condemned him to lose his head. After this the city fell into decay, and when Algiers was taken by the French, Bougie had only a small garrison of Turks, commanded by a Kaid, and was not in a position to offer any serious resistance to General Trézel, who took possession of it on the 29th September 1833. The most interesting buildings at Bougie are the ancient forts: *Bordj el-Ahmer* (the red fort), of which the ruins are seen half way between the koubba of *Sidi-Fouati* and the *Gouraia,* was,

before its destruction by the Spaniards, the most ancient in Bougie, and here it was that Salah Raïs established himself when he took Bougie from them.

The fort of *Abd-el-Kader,* on the right hand of the harbour as the traveller lands, was built before the arrival of the Spaniards in 1509, probably with the remains of an older Roman building, and was much injured by the earthquake of August 1856.

The *Kasba,* on the opposite side of the town, is rectangular in shape, flanked by bastions and towers, some of which were destroyed in 1853. It was built by Don Pedro Navarro, on Roman foundations, and bears Latin inscriptions, of which the following are translations:—

"Ferdinand V., illustrious King of Spain, has taken this city by force of arms from the perfidious children of Hagar, in the year 1509"—and "This city has been furnished with walls and fortresses by the Emperor Charles V., the African, grandson and successor of Ferdinand. To God alone be honour and glory. The year 1545."

The fort *Barral* to the N.W. was also built by Pedro Navarro, and owes its present name to the fact of General Barral, who was killed in 1850, having been interred there. His remains have since been removed to the cemetery. This also is used as a prison.

On the top of *Mount Gouraia* is the fort of the same name; below it is a barrack occupied by military prisoners; lower down to the W. Fort *Clauzel,* and on the beach, near the *Oued Seghir,* the Blockhouse *Salomon de Musis,* called after a commandant supérieur, assassinated by the Kabyles in 1836.

A new line of works has been constructed round the town, consisting of a masonry loopholed wall strengthened by bastions.

Bougie, strictly speaking, had no port; it is situated in a deep bay well protected from the N.W. and S., but quite exposed to the E. The ancient Roman harbour of *Saldae* was that part of the bay between the *Kasba* and the forage park beyond; it was probably named after an older Phœnician harbour called *Saldou* or *the strong.* A new harbour is in course of construction, which will, when completed, contain an area of about 15 or 20 acres. The streets being built on the slope of the hill are very steep, and many of them are ascended by stairs. The gardens which formerly surrounded so many of the houses are disappearing before the inevitable modern improvements; still there are some beautiful walks and magnificent old olive trees in the immediate vicinity—notably beyond the *Fort Abd-el-Kader*. Below the gate of the *Grand Ravin* may be traced the remains of an amphitheatre, in the arena of which is the tomb of the commandant Salomon de Musis. Numerous Roman remains extend up the base of *Gouraïa*, and medals and inscriptions are constantly found wherever excavations are made.

It is said that this town gave its name to the French word for a candle, first made from wax exported hence.

There can be little doubt that Bougie is destined to become one of the most important cities on the littoral. Not only is it the natural port of Kabylia, but also of the rich plains of Setif and Aumale. Very little labour is required to make the harbour perfectly secure, and in a military point of view it is strong and capable of easy defence.

There are two short excursions from Bougie which the traveller should on no account miss if he can possibly make them. They are very grand in feature and variety, and if the walk is too much he can obtain a mule or horse for a few francs.

(1.) To the **Lighthouse on Cape Carbon**, distant about 6 kil. A very easy road leads from the town along the flank of the mountain east of Gouraïa, through the Valley of Monkeys, the southern slope of which is well wooded with kharoub, olive, and oak trees; it then traverses the mountain by means of a tunnel, and passes over the pointed crest of the isthmus connecting the peninsula of Cape Carbon with the mainland. The northern face of the mountain is much more sterile, but covered in many places with scrub, the only trees being Aleppo pine. Nothing can exceed the sublimity of the landscape from every point of view. In front is the open sea, to the W. the littoral richly festooned with bays, capes, and promontories, and to the E. the majestic mountains of Kabylia.

(2.) To the top of **Gouraïa**, from which a magnificent view is obtained; there is a good road up, and the ascent may be made on foot or by mule in an hour; the whole excursion need not occupy 3 hours. 4 f. are usually paid for mules for either excursion.

[There is direct railway communication between Bougie and Beni-Mansour, on the line of railway from Algiers to Constantine. The traveller can reach **Aumale** by this route.

From Bougie there is a route and a service of diligences to Setif, through the Chabet el-Akhira, every day. See p. 200.]

The steamer continues its course across the Gulf of Bougie to *Cape Cavallo*. About half way, at a place called *Ziama*, are the ruins of the fortified Roman town of that name. A short distance farther, seen on the right, is the rocky promontory of *Mansouria*, beyond which is Cape Cavallo. Near this is a mine of argentiferous lead ore, and the hills around are full of iron and carbonate of copper.

Between this and Djidjelly is a small island of a bright red colour, called by the Arabs *El-Afia*.

In front of the latter town is a line of rocks, on one of which stands the lighthouse.

140 m. **Djidjelly** (3021 inhab.) is situated in a little bay, the entrance to which faces the S.E., formed by a line of reefs which seems to have been placed there to serve as the foundation of a breakwater. It does not, however, shelter the anchorage from N.W. to N.E., as it has several openings, one of which forms a pass 100 mètres wide and 10 deep. At the extremity of this is Cape Bougiarone, which affords some shelter from the E.N.E.

This is the natural outlet of a country rich in vegetable and mineral productions, extending up the valley of the Oued el-Kebir as far as Mila. It occupies the site of the ancient Roman colony of Igilgilis, which was a place of considerable commercial importance. During the Vandal invasion it shared the fate of other towns in the country.

After the Khalifas of the East had subdued Northern Africa, it passed under the Arab rule as a dependency of Constantine, and Yahia ibn el-Aziz built a summer residence there. This, as well as the town, was destroyed by the Sicilians, commanded by Roger II. in 1143. The ruins of this château are still visible on the *Plateau Galbois*. In the 16th century it had extensive commercial relations with Marseilles, Genoa, Leghorn, and Venice. In 1514 it surrendered to Barbarossa, who made it a port of refuge and repair for his piratical expeditions. In 1664 Louis XIV., desiring to found there a military establishment for the purpose of holding the pirates in check, sent an expedition under the command of the Duc de Beaufort to take possession of it. The land forces, consisting of 5200 regular troops, including a battalion of the knights of Malta, were under the immediate command of the Comte de Gadagne; he was further reinforced by 200 volunteers and 20 companies of marines, in all about 6000 men. The fleet consisted of 15 frigates, 19 galleys, and 20 smaller vessels.

The army landed on the 22d July 1664, occupied the town, and began to construct Fort Duquesne, to defend it against the Kabyles. Soon, however, a Turkish force arrived from Algiers with a powerful artillery. The Duc de Beaufort, who was on bad terms with the military commander, had left for Tunis, and the position of the French became very critical, and eventually untenable. Comte de Gadagne, seeing his troops demoralised, ordered them to embark, leaving behind not only his sick but the corps detailed to cover his retreat. Many of the soldiers were massacred, and the remainder carried off to slavery at Algiers.

This disastrous affair cost the French 1400 men, 45 guns, and 50 mortars, some of which guns were actually used against them in the insurrection of 1871. The Duc de Beaufort was subsequently killed in June 1669, in an unsuccessful attempt to raise the siege of Candia by the Turks. He was blown up by the explosion of a powder magazine, and his body was never recovered.

In 1803 an Arab from Morocco, named Ben-Arach, made Djidjelly the headquarters of his piratical expeditions, and captured 6 French coral fishing-ships and 54 prisoners, who were led chained to the town. In revenge, the Dey of Algiers sent three ships against Ben-Arach, who was known by the name of "the Pirate of Djidjelly."

In 1839 the Kabyles took prisoners the crew of a brig named " L'Indépendant," wrecked near Djidjelly, and refused to give them up without ransom. In consequence of this the town was attacked and captured by Colonel de Salles in May of the same year. At that time all that remained of the mediæval town was a square tower and the wall which protected the isthmus; little or no Roman ruins were apparent.

The old town was built on the rocky peninsula forming the extreme W. point of the bay. On the night of the 21st and 22d August 1856, a violent shock of earthquake, accompanied by a subterranean sound like thunder, was felt, and immediately a great proportion of the houses fell to the ground. The mosques, the old Genoese tower, and many others were destroyed. The sea retreated a great distance, and suddenly returned with immense fury: these disturbances lasted 40 seconds. On the following day another and more violent shock took place, accompanied by detonations and deep fissures in the earth, and dense clouds of dust; when the shock terminated, not a house remained standing. During a whole year the shocks continued almost daily till they gradually ceased.

The old city was restored as a citadel, containing only public buildings. A new town has been built on the shore of the bay to the E., surrounded by a wall and ditch, which enabled its small garrison successfully to support a siege of several weeks in 1871.

A route has long been in course of construction between Djidjelly and Constantine, which will open out a vast field for colonisation in a district where the quality of the land, the abundance of water, and the proximity of forests and mines, cannot fail to secure the prosperity of the projected villages.

[Djidjelly is perhaps the best point from which to attempt the **Ascent of Babor** and **Ta-babort**. The journey has no physical difficulties, but it will be found hardly practicable without the co-operation of the local authorities. The author performed it in March 1878, but it ought not to be attempted before May, on account of the snow on the summit of the mountains, and the difficulty of passing the rivers which take their rise in it.

The first night he passed at the lead mines of Cape Cavallo; the distance from Djidjelly to this point is about 35 kil., and occupied 4½ hours on horseback. The second day he proceeded by a very difficult path along the coast, visiting the picturesque cave of *Oued Taza* and the ruins of *Ziama*, and sleeping at *Aïn-Bou M'raou*, the residence of the Kaid of Ta-babort. The journey took 9 hours. Thence, on the third day, after a ride of 8 hours, he reached the village of *Beni Bizaz*, beautifully situated in an elevated valley between the peaks of Babor and Ta-babort; the scenery throughout was extremely beautiful and interesting in many respects. On the summit of the mountains are forests of cedar and African pinsapo, which latter has been described as a distinct species under the name of *Abies baborensis* of Cosson, a near ally of the *A. pinsapo*, which is confined to the S.W. of Spain. If the traveller cannot ascend Babor, he will see both the Atlas and the Spanish varieties growing in juxtaposition in the plantation of *Djebel Ouache*, near Constantine (see p. 197). The most easy and the most picturesque route by which to return to Djidjelly is through the beautifully wooded country of the *Beni Foughal*, the only tribe in Eastern Kabylia which remained faithful to the French in 1871. During the author's visit the trees were not yet in leaf, but the whole country was carpeted with violets, periwinkle, and blue irises.]

Beyond Djidjelly the embouchure of the *Oued el-Kebir* is passed; this, higher up, is the *Roummel* of Constantine, the Roman *Ampsagas*, a river celebrated in the history of the ancient territorial demarcations of the country; and farther on is Cape Bougiarone (*Dj. Bou Garoun* or *Bou Koroun*, Mountain of Horns, or *Djebel Sebâa Ruoos*, Mountain of Seven Capes). There can be little doubt of the Arabic origin of the former name, and that Shaw was in error when he described it as a term of reproach on account of the brutal and inhuman qualities of its inhabitants. He says of them: "They dwell not, like the other Kabyles, in little thatched hovels under the shelter of some forest or mountain, but in the caves of the rocks, which they have either dug themselves or found ready made to their hands. Upon the approach of any vessel, either in the course of sailing or distress of weather, these inhospitable Kabyles immediately issue out of their holes, and, covering the cliffs of the sea-shore with their multitudes, throw out a thousand execrable wishes that God would deliver it into their hands."

This cape is the most northerly point of Algeria, and rises in the centre to a height of 3600 ft. above the sea level. It is the *Treton* of Strabo and Ptolemy, and the *Metagonium Prom.* of Pomponius Mela.

At *Bougiarone* there is a fixed white light of the first order on a masonry tower, visible from a distance of 20 m. There is another at *Cape Afia*, nearer to Djidjelly, which has a flashing light 138 ft. above the sea, and is seen 19 m. in clear weather.

The coast is bordered by masses of rock to the N. and N.W., but to the E. the cliffs are lower. Passing this, and also the point called *Ras-el-Kebir*, the *Bay of Collo* is reached, at the commencement of which is

188 m. **Collo** (1269 inhab.)

The bay which serves as the harbour of Collo is protected from all the most dangerous winds, and offers not only a safe refuge for vessels trading on the coast, but a tolerably convenient landing-place for merchandise.

Behind the promontory of *El-Hjerda* is another bay, called by the natives *Bahr en-Nissa*, the Sea of Women, so called from a spring named *Aïn-Doula*, Fountain of Wealth, believed by them to be valuable in cases of sterility.

An inscription found here, bearing the legend COLONIA MINERVÆ CHVLLV, proves beyond doubt that it was the *Kollops Magnus* of Ptolemy and the *Chulli Municipium* of the itinerary of Antonine. It was a city of considerable importance during the Roman epoch, and its harbour was a frequent station of the imperial galleys.

It was here that Peter III. of Arragon debarked in 1282 for the purpose of conducting in person an expedition for the conquest of Constantine; but when he heard of the death of his ally, Aboo-Bekr Ibn Wuzeer, governor of that city, he left for Sicily. From 1604 till 1685 the French Compagnie d'Afrique had an establishment here.

The place was occupied by General Baraguay d'Hilliers in April 1843.

The environs are very picturesque. Towards the S. is a fertile cultivated plain, in the centre of which rises a cone-shaped wooded mountain, called *Roumadia*.

The streams near Collo are the only ones in Algeria where trout are found; the species (see p. 72) is peculiar to the *Oued Z'hour* and its affluents.

From Collo there is a good horse-route joining the railway from Philippeville to Constantine at Robertville --57 kil. in length.

A lighthouse with an intermittent green light is placed on the promontory of *El-Hjerda;* and there is a fixed red light at the entrance of the port.

In about 3 hours' steaming after leaving Collo, the boat passes between the island of *Srigina*, on which stands a lighthouse, and the coast, distant about ½ m., and passes **Stora**, a small, prettily-situated village, the inhabitants of which are principally engaged in curing sardines. For many years this was the regular station of the coasting steamers, as a bend in the coast gave some shelter from the most dangerous winds, except in unusually heavy weather, when it was imprudent even to approach the coast.

206 m. **Philippeville.** Pop. 13,394.

A magnificent harbour was completed in 1882; it is formed by the projection in a W.N.W. direction from Cape Skikdah, immediately to the E. of the town, of a grand mole or breakwater, 1400 mètres long, and by the projection in a N. direction, from Chateau Vert, W. of the town, of a mole of *pierres perdues* about 400 mètres long; the width of the entrance will be about 200 mètres, and it will have a lighthouse at the head of the grand mole. The area thus protected is divided into an outer and inner basin; the former has now an area of 95 acres, to be subsequently reduced by recovery of land to 150; it varies in depth from 8 to 19 fathoms; the inner basin will be of 45 acres, with a depth varying from 22 to 50 ft.

It is contemplated to increase this harbour to a very great extent, and, if the proposed works are carried out, it will have a surface of upwards of 1200 acres, effectually sheltered from all winds. During the great storm of 26th and 27th January 1878, nearly the whole of the harbour works were carried away, and every vessel in the harbour was wrecked. The whole has been reconstructed, and the breakwater widened to 30 mètres at the water-line; it is crowned with a parapet 5 mètres thick, and 13 mètres above the level of the sea. Vessels are able to lie alongside the quays, which are all revetted with large blocks of white marble from the quarries of Filfila.

There is very little to be said about the modern town of Philippeville, which is picturesquely situated between two hills, and built and fortified according to the common type of Algerian cities. It owes its existence to the necessity which arose, after the taking of Constantine, of having a more direct means of communication with that city than by Bône. On the 7th October 1838 Marshal Valée encamped on the site of the ancient city of Rusicada, and purchased it from the Beni Meleh for 150 f.

The Roman city was built on the site of a more ancient Phœnician one, the *Tapsus* mentioned by Scylax in his Periplus, whence is derived the modern name *Safsaf*, applied to the river which here falls into the sea.

It soon attained a high state of prosperity, and, with Cirta, Collo, and Mila, formed one of the four colonies of the Cirtensians. No city of Numidia with so small an area has furnished such a mass of archæological treasures. Many of these have disappeared, but all that remain are now carefully preserved in the ancient theatre, itself the most interesting ruin in the place.

An amphitheatre in a very perfect state of preservation existed outside the present gate of Constantine when the

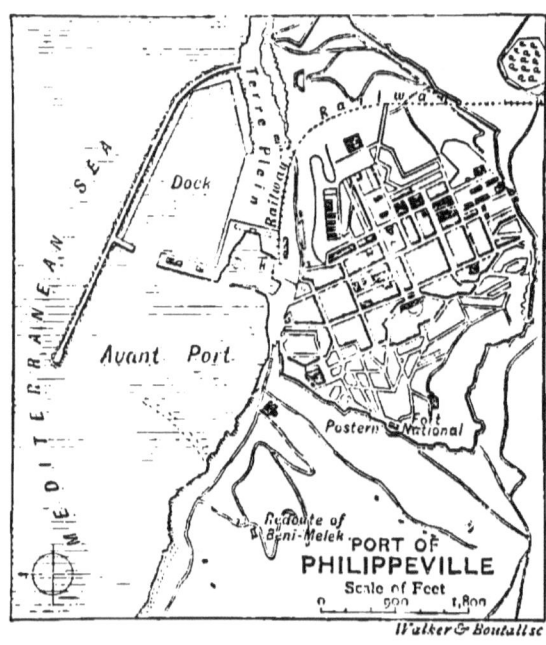

place was occupied, but its stones were taken away for building purposes, and the railway destroyed the last vestige of it.

On the plateau above are the ancient reservoirs, which were filled by a canal, bringing in the waters of the *Oued Beni Meleh*. These have been carefully restored, and still serve to supply the modern town.

The ancient baths were in the centre of the town, to the left of the Rue Nationale, and are still used as cellars to the military stores.

Rusicada was probably destroyed about the end of the 5th century, after which it disappeared from history, and its very name was forgotten. During the Middle Ages Stora seems to have usurped the place of Rusicada, as affording more shelter to the vessels trading with North Africa; but these, dreading the treacherous character of the coast, remained the shortest time possible, and preferred the greater security of Collo or Bougie to the W., or Bône to the E.

The traveller should visit the beautiful *villas and gardens of M. Landon*, at the Safsaf and on the road to Stora;

they are most hospitably left open for the public when he does not happen to be present.

A drive may be taken to STORA (4 kil.); the road is luxuriantly wooded with cistus, myrtle, arbutus, and heath, and commands splendid views of woods, rocks, and water.

Leaving Philippeville, the steamer directs her course towards the Cap de Fer, passing the small promontory of *Cap Filfila*, a continuation of the **Djebel Filfila**, where are *iron mines* on one side of the Oued Righa, and on the other the fine *marble quarries* belonging to M. Lesueur; they contain marble of a great variety of colours hardly yet developed, and an unlimited quantity of white, gray, and black. Specimens of these may be seen at M. Lesueur's atelier, behind the railway station at Philippeville, or on the kiosques at the Palais de Justice. The distance by road to the quarries is 25 kil. About 15 kil. E. of Filfila is BOU KSAIBA, where other deposits of marble, principally yellow, are found. Beyond this is the embouchure of the river *Sanadja*, and near it are the copper mines of *Ain-Barbar*, formerly belonging to an English company (see p. 126).

The *Cap de Fer* or *Ras el Hadid* is a jagged, rocky point, projecting so far into the sea as to have the appearance of an island when seen from Philippeville. The highest peak is 1500 ft. above the sea level. Its name has been given to it from its iron mines, which were formerly extensively worked. The N. side presents a wall of rock towards the sea. On it is a light of the third order, alternately flashing red and white every 30 seconds. Shortly after passing the point, the *Koubba of Sidi Akkach* is seen above a small bay. The next headland is called *Ras Takouch*, which affords a shelter for small vessels; it was frequented by the Italian merchants in the 14th century. A small rock, the *Ile Takouch*, stands out a mile from the shore. A small village, *Herbillon*, has been built here. From this the coast is steep and rock-bound as far as a conical rock called *la Voile Noire*, projecting ½ m. into the sea.

The *Cap de Garde*, like the Cap de Fer, appears from a distance almost as an island. It is a prolongation of the range of *Djebel Edough*, and is surmounted by a lighthouse, 469 feet above the sea, with a *fixed* and *flashing* white light eclipsed every minute, visible at a distance of 31 m. On the other side of the point is Fort Génois, after passing which the steamer anchors in the harbour of Bône.

264 m. **Bône.** Pop. 19,687. Seat of a Sous-préfecture, tribunal of premier instance, general commanding the subdivision, civil and military hospital, etc.

It is called by the Arabs *Annaba* (city of Jujube trees), and was founded by them after the destruction of Hippone.

The Kasba was erected by the Bey of Tunis in 1300; and from this time until the middle of the 15th century Bône was the resort of Italian and Spanish merchants, who carried on an extensive commerce with North Africa. In 1553 Kheir-ed-din, then Pacha of Algiers, sent a force to garrison the town; but they evacuated it after Charles V had taken possession of Tunis; for some time after it was constantly changing hands, the Genoese, Tunisians, and Turks all obtaining possession of it in turn.

In 1830, after the taking of Algiers, the inhabitants threw off the yoke of the Bey of Constantine, and at their request the place was occupied by a brigade of French troops, but soon after the change of government in France necessitated the concentration of all the available forces at Algiers, and Bône was evacuated. The French finally occupied it in 1832, when Captains Armandy and Youssef, with a few soldiers, entered the Kasba, and succeeded in defending it against heavy odds until succour arrived.

It is a cheerful, clean, and well-built town. Much of the old part has been destroyed, but some portion, including the Kasba, still remains. The streets are for the most part straight and wide, although some, such as the *Rues Friart*, *Philippe*, and *Suffren*, are very steep, owing to the town being built on uneven ground. The best

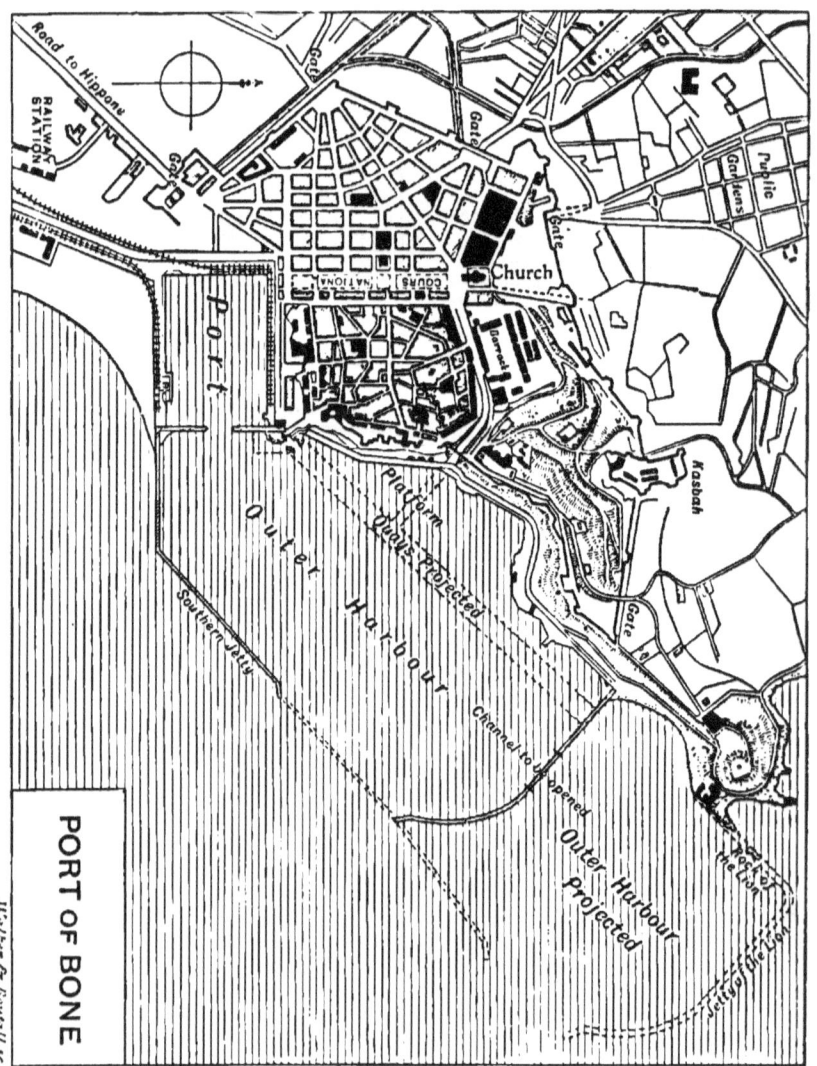

shops are in the *Rue Neuve St. Augustin*, and *Cours Nationale*. Amongst the principal squares is the *Place d'Armes*, which is planted with rows of trees, and has a garden with a fountain in the centre. The Grand Mosque occupies one side, and on the other there are houses and shops, all with arcades. The *Places du Commerce* and *Rovigo* are both ornamented with trees and fountains.

Through the centre of the town, from the cathedral to the harbour, runs the *Cours Nationale*, a delightful promenade, beautifully planted with trees and flowers. On each side are the principal buildings of the place, *Theatre*, banks, hotel, etc. At the end nearest the sea is a statue of M. Thiers, and at the opposite one is the Cathedral of St. Augustine, a building supposed to be in the Byzantine style of architecture, but much more resembling the case of a *Charlotte Russe*; fortunately only the façade is very conspicuous, and this is the least objectionable part of the structure.

The *Mosque, Djamâa-el-Bey*, in the Place d'Armes, has been constructed out of some of the ruins of Hippone. The exterior is in good taste; the interior is merely a repetition of all other mosques described.

The *Barracks*, capable of holding 3000 men, are two in number—one in the Rue d'Orléans, and the other near the Porte Damrémont. There is a large *Military Hospital* for 700 patients in the Rue d'Armandy, and a civil hospital capable of holding 350.

The town is plentifully supplied with good water from Djebel Edough. The climate was formerly exceedingly unhealthy, owing to the marshes at the embouchure of the two rivers Seybouse and Bou Djemâa, which enter the sea close together; now these have been drained by a chain of canals, and malaria has almost disappeared.

A short distance from the town is a *pépinière* belonging to Government, in which are deposited a fine marble sarcophagus and some other interesting Roman remains, worthy of a visit.

Formerly the anchorage in the bay was very insecure, but in 1868, after more than ten years' labour, the new harbour was finished, and is now as good as any in the colony, not excepting that of Algiers itself. It consists of an outer harbour, having an area of 150 acres, formed by two breakwaters, leaving between them an aperture of about 300 yards; within this is a basin containing 30 acres, surrounded with handsome quays, alongside which vessels can load in any weather. A still further extension of the harbour is being carried out (1889), which will best be seen by the dotted lines on the plan.

EXCURSIONS IN THE NEIGHBOURHOOD.

Naturally the first excursion that the traveller desires to make is to the spot hallowed by the labours and death of St. Augustine.

The ancient Carthaginian *Ubbo* or **Hippone** received from the Romans the name of Hippo Regius, not only to distinguish it from the Hippo Diarrhytus, but from being one of the Royal cities of the Numidian kings; it was created a colony of the Empire, and was one of the most opulent commercial centres of Roman Africa.

St. Augustine, who had been converted four years before, was ordained priest here A.D. 390; here he resided, a priest and bishop, for 35 years; and here also he wrote his "Confessions," and his "City of God."

In A.D. 428 the intrigues of the ambitious Count Boniface opened to the Vandals the door of the African continent, and Hippone was besieged by them for 14 months. St. Augustine died during this time, and in 431 the city fell, and its conquerors reduced it to ashes, all but the cathedral, which escaped, together with St. Augustine's library and MSS. The town, which was partially rebuilt under Belisarius, was again destroyed by the Arabs in the year 697.

St. Augustine was buried in the Basilica of Hippone. After the persecution of the Vandals had driven many of his disciples into exile, two of the last bishops are said to have carried off his relics with them and deposited them in the Basilica of Cagliari, where they remained for 223 years; they were then translated to Pavia, and there they repose at the present moment in a magnificent monument in the cathedral.

In 1842 the reliquary was opened, and the right arm of the saint abstracted for the purpose of being conveyed to Bône; it was taken over to Africa with great solemnity by a commission of seven bishops, twelve priests, and a number of monks and nuns, and deposited in the cathedral there.

An altar had been previously erected to his memory amongst the ruins of Hippone, surmounted by a bronze statue; this was at the same time solemnly consecrated, and a religious service has been celebrated there every year on the anniversary of his death. It is surrounded by an iron railing, but this has not protected it from the sacrilegious penknives of tourists, whose names cover every available spot in and around it.

Just below this is the only remnant of Hippone now existing, the cisterns and aqueduct which supplied the town with water from *Edough*. A large church has been built above the ruins, next to which is a hospital for old people kept by the *Petites Sœurs des Pauvres*.

Another pleasant drive is along the **Corniche Road** to **Fort Génois** (9 kil.) This fine new road was only made in 1885; it skirts the shore of the outer harbour, passes the Arab cemetery and the Plage Luquin, where are numerous villas and a bathing establishment, and here it joins the old road to the fort. There are beautiful views of land and water at every turn. Fort Génois was built by the Genoese after their occupation of Tabarca, to protect their ships when obliged to anchor in the bay. Three kilomètres farther off is the extremity of *Cap de Garde*.

Ascent of Djebel Edough.

By far the most interesting expedition in the neighbourhood of Bône is the excursion through the Forest of **Edough**. The road is quite practicable for carriages, but it is much more pleasant to do it on horseback.

This mountain is the celebrated Mons Papua, where took place some of the most celebrated events in the history of North Africa.

When the Vandal King Genseric laid siege to Hippone, during the year in which St. Augustine died, the inhabitants of this mountain witnessed from their natural fastnesses the extinction of Roman power in Africa. A century later Belisarius reconquered the country, and Gilimer, the last of the Vandal monarchs, fleeing before him, took refuge in these mountains, whence, before his surrender, he sent the well-known message to his conqueror, requesting that he might be supplied with a lyre, a loaf of bread, and a sponge. On being questioned as to the meaning of this strange request, the messenger replied that his master wished once more to taste the food of civilised people, from which he had been so long debarred, to sing to the accompaniment of the lyre an ode to his great misfortune, and with the sponge to wipe away his tears.

In the neighbouring port of Hippo was captured the great treasure of the Vandals: "Silver weighing many thousand talents, and a huge mass of royal furniture (Genseric having sacked the palace at Rome), amongst which were some monuments of the Jews brought to Rome by Titus after the destruction of Jerusalem. Subsequently, at the triumph of Belisarius in Constantinople, a Jew espying the same, standing by one of the emperor's familiar friends—'It is not good,' quoth he, 'to bring these monuments into the palace, for they cannot continue but where Solomon first put them. Hence it is that Genseric sacked the palace in Rome, and now Belisarius that of the Vandals.' The emperor, hearing this, sent them to the Christian church in Jerusalem."[1]

For several years after the French occupation of Bône, Edough maintained a sort of independence; its inhabitants

[1] Procop. "Wars of Vandals," trans. Sir H. Holcroft, book ii. c. 6.

avoided all intercourse with the conquerors, and abstained from all acts of aggression.

In 1841, however, a Marabout, who lived near the Cap de Fer, imagined that Providence had called him to become the liberator of his country, and, as then was always the case, the moment a fanatic began to preach the Jehad or holy war, he was surrounded by a host of followers as ignorant and fanatic as himself.

Several acts of hostility and brigandage were perpetrated, which could no longer be tolerated, and a force was sent to pacify Edough, under the command of General Baraguay d'Hilliers. Three columns ascended the mountain simultaneously, from Constantine, Philippeville, and Bône, and compelled the tribes to recognise the authority of the French. For a time, however, the Marabout Si Zerdoud continued at liberty, and urged his followers to resistance. The advancing columns drove the hostile Arabs on to a small promontory occupied by the Koubba of Sidi Akkach, between Cap de Fer and Ras Takouch, when, seeing that all further resistance was hopeless, they demanded *aman*. This was at once accorded, but while the negotiations were going on a shot from the thicket behind wounded an orderly of the General, who immediately gave the order for a general massacre. Many of the Arabs threw themselves into the sea and were drowned, the rest were slaughtered without pity.

Si Zerdoud escaped at the time, but was captured shortly afterwards, and immediately shot.

The road ascends the southern side of the mountain, which is at first rather bare, and covered with tufts of *diss* grass, but very soon cork oaks begin to appear, and long before reaching the culminating point the road traverses a thick forest of these trees and deciduous oak (*Quercus Mirbeckii*).

On the top of the hill, 3294 feet above the level of the sea, is the village of Bugeaud, created in 1843, and named after the well-known Maréchal. It is situated in a clearing, from which there is a magnificent panoramic view of the sea on one side, and of the bay and plain of Bône on the other, bounded by the mountains of the Beni Saleh.

The winter at Bugeaud is severe, but in summer it has quite an European climate, and is a favourite sanitarium for the good people of Bône, who cannot all manage to get away to France during the hottest months. A few villas have been built in the village and in its vicinity. After having traversed Algeria in every direction, the writer has seen no place to be compared with it as a summer residence.

About a mile farther on is the village of Edough, composed almost entirely of buildings connected with the cork establishment of Messrs. Lecoq and Berthon, who have a concession of 8000 hectares of forest land. There is a clean and comfortable *auberge* here, where an excellent breakfast can be obtained.

Instead of continuing along the high road, the traveller should turn off to the right, and follow a path, which has been made in connection with the aqueduct that conveys the waters of the Fontaine des Princes to Bône. At the head of the valley is a charming retreat, where the sirocco can never find its way; if we were inclined to disbelieve the people who said so, we have only to look at the trees themselves, covered with moss and polypodium, and to the great variety of ferns which line the roadside and peep out of mossy nooks and springs. Truly it is a princely spring, and deserves such a name on its own merits; but the Orleans princes once picnicked here before the days of the Second Empire, and the fact has been perpetuated in their honour.

An abundant and perennial stream flows down this valley, part of which has been diverted and carried in iron pipes for the supply of Bône. The ancient city of Hippo was supplied from the same source, and the Roman bridge still exists which carried the water across the ravine. It is covered with ferns and wild flowers, and a venerable oak tree grows from the very centre of it. The under-shrub here consists chiefly of tree-heath, myrtle, and are butus; the wild cherries almost attain the size of forest trees, while the ground is a perfect carpet of flowers and creepers.

At about 13 m. from Bône the forest has been much destroyed by fire. Fortunately many of the trees were only scorched and not entirely destroyed; they are beginning to sprout again, and the under-shrub will soon be as thick as ever. After passing this belt the character of the scenery changes, Aleppo pines begin to mingle with the oaks, the road takes a turn to the west, running parallel to the sea, and soon the burnt portion of the forest is shut out from view.

The first impression that naturally occurs to the traveller here is, that, though the whole country is an alternation of forest land and grassy slopes, there is not a sign of habitation; yet it is impossible to conceive a locality better suited for colonisation, especially for the growth of vines, which are destined, at no very distant period, to become the staple production of Algeria.

The mines of Aïn-Barbar are situated at about 25 m. from Bône. The right of working the mineral over an area of 1300 hectares was purchased by the Anglo-Algerian Mineral Company from the original concessionaires, but it has since been sold to a French company. The principal mineral is sulphide of copper, or copper pyrites, together with sulphide of zinc or blende. Small quantities of argentiferous lead ore have also been found. The work at these mines has been almost discontinued.

There is a bridle path by which a traveller can descend to the iron mines of Aïn-Mokra, and so by railway to Bône; but the road through the forest is so beautiful that he will generally be only too glad to return by the way he came. A few lions still remain in the neighbourhood, and have been seen within a mile or two of Bône; panthers are more common, but the numbers of both are decreasing very sensibly every year.

Excursion to the Iron Mine of Aïn-Mokra.

A railway, belonging to the mines, but open to the public, connects Bône with the iron mines of **Aïn-Mokra** or **Mockta el-Hadid**. The distance is 40 kil. and the time occupied about 2 hrs.

This mine was at one time simply a mountain of iron, which was blasted and carried off to Bône for shipment; now nearly all the mineral above the surface of the ground has been exhausted, and the veins, running in a slanting direction through the mica schist, are being worked by means of galleries. Farther to the W. it is still possible to find it *à ciel ouvert*, but the palmy days of the mine are over, and the company has transferred its activity in a great measure to Beni Saf. The ore contains 64 per cent of pure metal. 300,000 tons per annum might still be obtained if prices were sufficiently remunerative. It is observable here, as almost everywhere in Algeria, that the direction in which the deposits of iron ore run is from E. to W.

There are some fine plantations of eucalyptus along the railway, belonging to the Compagnie Algerienne.

To the S. may be seen the **Lake Fezara**, a large sheet of water about 12 m. square, frequented by numbers of wild fowl. A concession was made of the ground covered by this lake to the Company of Aïn-Mokra, on the condition that they drained it effectually, and planted a "sanitary cordon" of eucalyptus to the extent of 2000 hectares (5000 acres) around it. The work was commenced in 1877, a canal 15,729 mètres long was cut from the bottom of the lake to divert the water into the Meboudja, and thence to the Seybouse; the lake was really emptied on the 5th August 1880, but after every year of exceptional rain its basin becomes re-filled.

It was found impossible to grow eucalyptus, as the moment the roots of that tree touch earth impregnated with salt they die. So far, therefore, the drainage of the lake may be pronounced a failure.

[From Bône the traveller can proceed to Constantine, either by railway *viâ* Guelma, or by diligence to St. Charles, and thence by the railway running from Philippeville. The first part of the latter route is through a wild and hilly country; at 68 kil. from Bône and 91 from Philippeville it passes through **Jemmapes**, a flourishing village, near which, at *Oued Amimin*, are some celebrated hot sulphureous springs, much esteemed for the cure of rheumatic and cutaneous affections.]

Beyond Bône the coast curves round towards the N.E. to Cap Rosa, 52 miles E. of Cap de Garde. The rivers Seybouse and Boudjema both enter the sea close to Bône, and between them the small hill whereon stands Hippone may be seen. The shore hereabouts is very flat, and to the S. lies an immense plain, extending inland for many miles. About 30 kil. before reaching Cap Rosa, the river Mafrag discharges itself into the sea. Here the coast is more hilly, and is richly wooded.

Cap Rosa or *Ras Bou-Fhal* (288 m.) rises to an elevation of only about 300 ft. above the water, although the hills more inland have nearly four times that altitude. This was the *Ad Dianam* of the itinerary of Antoninus. It had a temple dedicated to that goddess, of which some vestiges were at one time visible. This has now been more usefully replaced by a lighthouse with a fixed white light, seen at a distance of 12 m. Beyond is a creek which communicates with the salt lake Guera-el-melah.

The ruins of the Bastion de France, where the French-African Company had its residence before removing to La Calle, are seen farther on, and after passing the small point of Cap Gros, the steamer arrives at La Calle.

298 m. **La Calle.** Pop. 3616.

The mail steamer stops on its way to Tunis when the weather permits, but the traveller should be careful to ascertain before starting whether the vessel will touch.

A small town, 15 kil. from the frontier of Tunis, the principal industry of which is the coral fishery; indeed, it is mentioned as being inhabited by coral merchants in the year 960. The sale of this article was regulated by officers appointed for the purpose. In 1520 the exclusive privilege of fishing the coral was granted to France by a treaty which was maintained until 1560, and was renewed shortly afterwards, and again dissolved in 1679. About this time a company was formed under the name of the "Compagnie d'Afrique," which obtained the sole right to the fishery. At first the French established themselves in a little bay to the W. of La Calle, which they named *Bastion de France;* but in 1677 they were obliged to abandon it and establish themselves at La Calle, then a flourishing town, called by the natives *Bordj el-Kala*. The Company was suppressed in 1798, when the Porte ordered the Barbary States to declare war against France. In 1807 the Dey of Algiers let the coral fishery to the English for a term of ten years, at an annual rent of 267,000 f. The French regained possession of it in 1817, at which time La Calle was burnt by the Arabs. In 1822 a M. Paret, of Marseilles, bought the fishery for eight years, and carried it on by means of 240 boats. In 1827 war broke out between Algiers and France, when La Calle was again destroyed.

Shortly after the capture of Bône the French determined to renew their commercial relations with the tribes around La Calle, and to provide once more a harbour of refuge for the boats engaged in the coral fishery. In the month of May 1836 Youssef, who had recently been named Bey of Constantine, made a reconnaissance of it, and on the 14th of July following Captain Berthier de Sauvigny took possession of it without resistance. It was found exactly in the condition in which it had been left after its destruction by fire on the 27th June 1827. A few houses were still habitable, or easily rendered so. That now occupied by the Commandant Supérieur has hardly undergone any change; the church is old, but has been restored.

An interesting picture of life at La Calle is given by the Abbé Poiret, who travelled in Barbary from 1785 to 1786.

When he landed, the country round was being devastated by the plague, and the *comptoir* of the French jealously barricaded its gates to prevent all communication with the interior. The Arabs, irritated and jealous at seeing the Christians exempt from a disease which was committing such cruel ravages amongst themselves, tried by every means in their power to introduce the contagion. They buried plague-stricken corpses at the gates of La Calle, they threw rags saturated with virus over the walls, and, independently of these secret attacks, a continued and open state of hostility seemed to prevail. La Calle was governed by an agent, having the title of governor, with about fifteen other officers under his direction. The Arabs were excluded from the place, with the exception of a few who were retained as hostages, or who were employed in manual labour. The inhabitants were from 300 to 400, mostly Corsicans and natives of Provence. Some were employed in the coral fishery; others, nominally soldiers, were occupied in

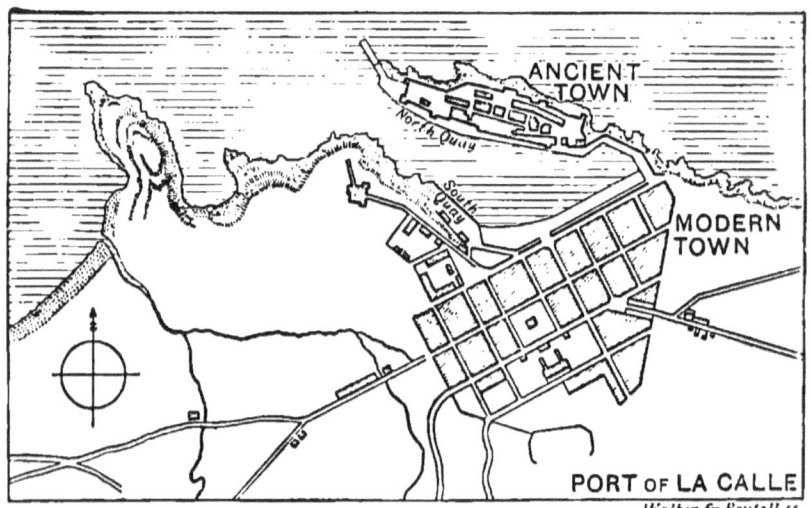

guarding the cattle when taken outside for pasture. Sometimes these same soldiers, in the guise of carters, were sent to the neighbouring forests to cut wood. Others, called *frégataires*, were occupied in loading vessels, transporting corn, cleaning the port, and similar works, and there was in addition a staff of bakers, blacksmiths, masons, and other artificers. All these employés were paid, fed, and lodged by the Company; but the fair sex was rigorously excluded. If sometimes the Governor was permitted to bring his wife, serious troubles were sure to result, and he was rarely able to keep her there for any length of time.

The climate was then exceedingly unhealthy. Violent fevers were of constant occurrence, which carried off their victims in four days, and the mortality amongst the employés was immense.

These were people of the worst character, as the Company received indiscriminately all applicants, without asking any questions. Most of them were convicts who had escaped from justice in France, men lost through libertinage and debauch, without principles of religion, or the least sentiment of probity.

At La Calle it was only the worst crimes of which any cognisance was taken; all others were allowed to go without punishment, as the Governor had only the shadow of authority, and it was necessary to humour this nest of ruffians always ripe for revolt. In addition to the heavy taxes paid directly to the State, the Company was subjected to indirect taxation to an enormous extent, and was subjected to the most humiliating restrictions. It was compelled to feed all the Arabs who chose to present themselves. If an Arab killed a Christian he was liable to a fine of 300 piastres as blood money, which was never paid; but in the event of a Christian killing an Arab, he was forced to pay 500 piastres, which sum was exacted to the last farthing. The Company was not permitted to appoint its own interpreters; these were always named by the State, and the only qualification that appeared to be required was sufficient sagacity to enable him to betray the Christian.

In 1807 Mr. Blanckley, the British Consul-General at Algiers, contracted with the Dey for the possession of Bône and La Calle,[1] which had been a century and a half in the hands of the French, whose contract had expired. 50,000 dollars, or £11,000, was the sum agreed on as an annual rent. This was actually paid for some years, without any result following, saving that of keeping out the French for a time.

The fishery was till lately almost entirely in the hands of Italian sailors, who came to fish on the coast, making La Calle their headquarters, and returned every year to their native country. There were as many as 230 boats engaged in the fishing. The banks are, however, becoming exhausted, and as there is no desire to encourage foreign enterprise in Algeria, an annual tax of 400 francs is levied on every Italian boat engaged, and one of 800 francs on boats of other nations. The consequence is that all foreign vessels are driven out of the market, and only about 60 small French boats are now engaged in the fishery; their crews are still mostly Italians.

[1] A facsimile of this document is given in "The Scourge of Christendom."

[*Algeria.*]

The ordinary mode of dredging is the same as that followed from the earliest times. A cross of wood, to each extremity of which small bags are attached, is lowered on to the bed of coral by means of a stone fastened to its centre. The line from the cross is attached to the boat, which is then rowed backwards and forwards in all directions, dragging the bags horizontally over the bed, which thus collect the fragments broken off by the stone. Some of the boats have begun to use the diving apparatus.

The old town of La Calle was contained within the present fortifications, on a ridge of rocks surrounded by the sea, excepting on the E. side, where an isthmus of sand connects it with the mainland. On this a new town has sprung up, which year by year is attaining greater importance. Extensive works for the preparation of sardines were established here, but the fish seem to have deserted the coast, and they are nearly all shut up. It was contemplated to create a new harbour of refuge in the bay of Bou Lilfa, a little farther to the W., the old port being too small to contain vessels of a greater burden than 100 tons. A beginning was even made, and more than 400,000 francs were expended without any tangible result; now that scheme has been abandoned, and it is proposed to shut up the present entrance to the harbour, which is exposed to the prevailing winds, and to open another on the E. side of the town.

In the vicinity are three large lakes, of which one, *Guerah el-Melah*, is situated south of the ruins of the Bastion de France; the second is *Guerah el-Oubeira*, a little to the west of the town; and the third is somewhat to the east of it, and is called *Guerah el-Hout*, or Lake of Fish; the last two contain fresh water.

Around them are extensive forests of cork trees, which furnish a large trade in that substance. Immediately surrounding the town, fruit trees tobacco, and especially vines, are grown with success.

[A pleasant excursion may be made

K

either by boat or on horseback (13 kil.) to the ruins of the **Bastion de France**, or *Veille Calle*, the first establishment formed by the French on the coast. On account of its insalubrity and the smallness of its harbour, it was abandoned in 1677, when the Compagnie d'Afrique transferred its establishment to La Calle. The ruins are still in a good state of preservation, and one can trace the outline of the fortified portion, the vaulted rooms and casements, the church, mill, and several other buildings.

About 12 kil. to the S.E. are the mines of **Kef oum-et-Teboul**, of argentiferous lead and zinc ores. An English firm takes the greater part of the ore for Swansea; in 1883 twenty steamers came here to load, and took upwards of 26,000 tons.]

306½ m. At 8½ m. beyond La Calle is the headland known as *Cape Roux*, the eastern extremity of the colony of Algeria. It is composed of rocks of a reddish colour, scarped on every side. A large cutting may be noticed in the rock, from the summit, descending to the sea. Formerly vessels anchored here, and the old Compagnie d'Afrique used thus to bring down the cereals purchased from the Arabs. The remains of the storehouse built by that Company may still be observed.

The French did not show their usual sagacity in fixing the boundaries of their colony; or, rather, a desire to avoid even the appearance of encroaching on their neighbours, and perhaps some pressure from other European powers, induced them to abandon much valuable territory, which, if the prescription of eighteen centuries deserves to be taken into account, undoubtedly belonged to Algeria.

After the fall of Jugurtha, B.C. 106, the country between the east coast of Tunis and the Atlantic was divided into three provinces, Africa proper, Numidia, and Mauritania. At subsequent periods these were further subdivided, but during all the political and geographical changes of North Africa, the river Tusca, or Oued el-Kebir, formed the eastern boundary of Numidia.

This continued, almost till the period of the French conquest, to limit the territory owning allegiance to the Dey of Algiers and the Bey of Constantine. When the present boundary question had to be settled, the French naturally claimed the line of the Tusca on the east; the Tunisians as stoutly contended that La Calle belonged to them; so a compromise was effected, fixing Cape Roux as the limit—about as unsatisfactory and undefined a frontier line as it is possible to conceive. The inconvenience of this was greatly felt so long as Tunis remained an independent State, but now that it is virtually French, the boundary question is of no importance.

315½ m. At about 9 m. E. of this cape is the Island of **Tabarca**, the history of which is most interesting. It lies close to the shore, the strait by which it is separated being about a quarter of a mile broad at the W. end, widening to nearly a mile at the eastern extremity. It has a small harbour, much frequented by coral boats when the weather is too rough to permit them to pursue their avocations at sea,' and vessels of a larger size sometimes come under the shelter of the island to the E.

In ancient times Thabraca, as it is usually called, or *Tabcrca*, the orthography found by the writer on a miliary column at Chemtou, was a Roman colony; and after the defeat of Gildon, under whose yoke Africa had ·groaned for twelve years, by his brother Mascezel, the former endeavoured to effect his escape by sea, but being driven by contrary winds into the harbour of Tabarca, he was taken prisoner, and put an end to his life by hanging himself in A.D. 398 (p. 29).

It was a very important city of the African Church; the names of several of its bishops are recorded, and in 1883 an inscription was discovered commencing with the words MEMORIA MARTVRVM, together with several fine mosaics of the Christian period.

Several Roman roads radiated from this place—one to the valley of the

Medjerda at Simitu, and others to Hippo Diarrhytus and Hippo Regia, which brought the produce of these rich districts to the sea for embarkation.

El-Edrisi (1154) speaks of it as a strong maritime place moderately peopled, and the environs of which are infested by miserable Arabs, who have no friends, and who protect none. It was even then a port of refuge much frequented by Spanish vessels engaged in the coral fishery.

In 1535 took place the celebrated expedition of Charles V. against Tunis. On the conclusion of peace the perpetual right of fishing for coral was conceded to the Spaniards.

About the same period Jean Doria, nephew of the celebrated Andrea Doria, captured on the coast of Corsica the no less celebrated Algerian corsair Draguth. On the partition of the spoil he fell to the share of one of the Lomellini family of Genoa, who exacted as the price of his ransom the cession of Tabarca. This was granted by Kheir-ed-din, and confirmed by the Porte.

The Lomellini came to an agreement with Charles V., who undertook the fortification and defence of the island, and built the citadel still existing, principally with the stones of the ancient city on the mainland. The Genoese agreed to pay 5 per cent on all the commerce which they made. Soon, however, the Spaniards neglected to keep up the works or pay the garrison, and the flag of Genoa was substituted for that of Spain; and though the governor was still named by the latter power, he was obliged to render his accounts to the Lomellini.

The inhabitants of the mainland owned allegiance neither to the Bey of Tunis nor to the Dey of Algiers.

Peyssonnel visited it in 1724, when it was occupied by the Genoese. He describes in detail the fortifications armed with bronze cannon bearing the arms of Lomellini, which, he says, "make the island strong and sure, and in a condition neither to fear the Turks nor the Arabs of Barbary." It was inhabited by Genoese, and had a garrison of 100 soldiers, 350 coral fishers, 50 porters with their families, making a total population of 1500 men.

In 1728 the Lomellini family ceded the full sovereignty of the island to one of its members, Jacques de Lomellini, for 200,000 livres, and a branch of coral every year, valued at 50 piastres.

In 1741, during the war which Monsieur Gautier, the Consul of France, brought about between his country and Tunis, the latter took possession of the island. A part of the inhabitants, about 500 in number, effected their escape to La Calle, and thence proceeded to the island of San Pietro, to the S.W. of Sardinia, then uninhabited, where their descendants exist to the present day, under the name of Tabarcini, and still pursue the coral fishery, as well as aid in loading vessels arriving at their port of Carloforte for minerals.

The Tunisian historian, Hadj Hamouda ben Abd el-Aziz, says that 900 men, women, and children, were taken as slaves to Tunis; their descendants still formed an intermediate population between the Christians from Europe and the native Mohammedans.

A portion of these were subsequently redeemed and sent to colonise the island called *Plana*, off Alicante, on the coast of Spain, to which they gave the name of Tabarca.

The island itself is 400 ft. high, and its western side is crowned by the ruins of the fort built by Charles V.

The traveller should not fail to take a boat and row round the island. The grandeur of the rock and the castle are best seen from the sea.

On the mainland the Roman town covered a large area, the whole slope of the hill. The remains of many Roman buildings are still visible, but these appear to have been purely constructional, the few moulded stones that have been brought to light being of coarse workmanship and exhibiting no signs of refinement. One building appears to have been a palace, or public baths; it is called *Keskes* by the Arabs, and still contains several large vaulted halls in good preservation. There is a ruined church and fortified position behind the hotel, with

ROUTE 1. ALGIERS TO PHILIPPEVILLE, ETC. *Algeria*

a necropolis attached. A rude mosaic, with the inscription *Pelagius in pa*[ce], was found here in 1882, and sent to the museum of the Louvre, but it was destroyed on the way.

On the hill above is the *Bordj Djidid*, or new fort, built by the Tunisians; around it have been erected temporary barracks and other subsidiary buildings, sufficient for a large garrison, now, however, entirely withdrawn.

Close to the island may be seen the hull of the "Auvergne," a large four-masted steamer belonging to the Talabot Company, which was driven ashore in 1878; the wreck was pillaged by the Khomair, and though none of the crew were actually killed, some of them were grossly ill-treated, and this was one of the indictments against them, which ended in the occupation of their country and of the whole regency by the French.

About 10 kil. to the E., at a place called *Ras er-Rajel* (man's head), and again nearly E. of Cape Negro, 35 kil. distant, there exist large and valuable deposits of iron and copper ore. These have been granted by the Government of Tunis to the powerful company which already owns the mines of Mokta el-Hadid near Bône, and Beni Saf near Oran. They have agreed to lay down a line of railway to the mines, and to make a harbour by blocking up the shallow channel between the southern end of the island and the shore, thus forming a port which will be open only to the N.E., and which will be sheltered from the prevailing N.W. winds by the island itself. It will be necessary to dig a new channel for the river, which flows into the site of the new harbour during the winter months, for in summer it does not reach the sea at all, thus creating a marsh, which is a perfect hotbed of malarious fever. The whole of the property in the neighbourhood now belonging to the Beylick has been granted to the company, including the island itself, a great part of which will be blasted down to supply materials for the harbour works. There is no appearance, however, of the work being commenced.

A practicable carriage road between Tabarca and La Calle, and another to Aïn-Draham, have been commenced, but it is not yet (1889) finished.

The river which falls into the sea opposite Tabarca is the *Oued el-Kebir*, the Great River, or the *Oued ez-Zan*, River of Oak Trees, the ancient *Tusca*, which formed the boundary between the Roman province of Africa and Numidia. It is also called in some maps the *Oued Barbar*, probably on the authority of Marmol; but this name is quite unknown to the people of the country.

Stretching along the coast from Tabarca, nearly as far as Cape Negro, is a tract of country, in some places 15 kil. broad, called by the Arabs *Belad er-Ramel*, Country of Sand, or *Ramel es-Safra*, the Yellow Sand. This has been engulfed by sea sand, which is advancing imperceptibly but irresistibly in a S.E. direction, blown by the prevailing N.W. winds from the beach. There is no uncertain line of demarcation between it and the rich forest land beyond; it ends abruptly in a high bank, sometimes rising like a cliff 30 ft. high, sometimes sloping gradually down a valley like a glacier, but always advancing and swallowing up vegetation in its course.

335½ m. Beyond this is Cap Negro, where the French founded a trading station before their settlement at the Bastion de France in 1609. It was subsequently taken by the Spaniards, and for a short time occupied by the English; but from 1686 till its destruction it belonged to the French. The principal trade consisted of cereals, wax, oil, and hides.

About 25 m. to the north is *Galita* island, the ancient *Calathe*, once a favourite resort of pirates, when they wished to careen their ships or lay in fresh water. It is easily recognised from its outline, the S.E. extremity is rugged and steep, and the sugar-loafed peak over it appears isolated when seen from the north or south; in a bay on its south side is temporary anchorage. Off the N.E. end are three islets—*Gallo*, the outermost and largest, is about a mile distant; *Pollastro* is the centre and smallest; and *Gallina*, the inner, is half a mile from the island. At 1½ m. S.W. of the S.W. end of *Galita* are two other larger islets, *Galitona* and *Agnglia*. At a distance of 14 m. W. by S. of the north end of Galitona are the *Sorelle Rocks*. In 1847 H.M.S. "Avenger" was lost on one of them. The crew consisted of 270 persons, all of whom were lost, with the exception of a lieutenant and 4 men. A little farther on, about 3 m. from the shore, are two high rocks, the *Fratelli*, the *Neptuni aræ* of the Romans, one of them exactly resembling a high-backed chair; passing these the bold promontory of C. Blanc is passed, easily identified by the white colour at its extreme point; then an indenture of the coast-line marks the site of

377½ m. **Bizerta** (*q.v.*), a place which may one day play an important part in history as a naval station.

Beyond Bizerta is *Ras ez-Zebib*, where are the tunny fisheries of Count Raffo, and *Ras Sidi Ali el-Mekhi*, where the Bay of Tunis commences. This is enclosed between the cape just mentioned, the ancient *Promontorium Apollinis*, and *Ras Addar*, or *Cape Bon*, the *Promontorium Mercurii*. The extreme width of the entrance is 41 m., and its length 27. Close to the former cape is *Kamela*, or *Ile Plane*, the *Corsura* of the ancients, a low island, pierced through in one part by a natural arched canal, while on the opposite side of the bay is the lofty island of *Zembra*, the *Djamores el-Kebir* of the Arabs, and the *Ægimurus* of the ancients, with the smaller one of *Zembretta* and *Tonnara*.

South of Ras Sidi Ali el-Mekhi is the *Ghar el-Melah*, or Lake of **Porto Farina** (409½ m.), into which flows the river Medjerda. This was at one time the most famous arsenal and the winter port of the Tunisian fleet, and here our own Blake gained one of his most celebrated victories.

A little to the S.W. is the wretched little village of *Bou Chater*, the site of the celebrated city of **Utica**, *The Ancient*, one of the first founded in Africa. When later Phœnician colonists founded Carthage, Utica still maintained its importance though it was obliged to submit to the supremacy of the younger city. In B.C. 300 it fell into the power of Agathocles, and it subsequently played an important part in all the Punic Wars, but it is especially famous as being the scene of the unnecessary self-sacrifice of Cato. It continued to exist till the Mohammedan invasion, when it lost not only its being but its name, and was thereafter known by that of Bou Chater. The ruins still existing of the ancient city are not very extensive or interesting. Soon Cape Carthage is doubled, with the Arab town of Sidi Bou Said, then the site of the great **Carthage** itself; while the eastern horizon is bounded by a picturesque chain of hills, the most conspicuous of which are *Hammam el-Enf*, *Bath of the Nose*, so called from a fancied resemblance it bears to that organ, and to the existence of a celebrated thermal spring at its base; *Djebel Ressas*, the *mountain of lead*, and *Zaghouan*, the ancient *Zeugis*, which gave its name to the district of Zeugitana.

Eventually the steamer anchors at the **Goletta** of Tunis (437 m.), where we will leave it for the present.

ROUTE 2.

Algiers to Cherchel and Tipasa.

This route may be done either by taking the railway to *El-Affroun* and thence proceeding to Cherchel by the omnibus, passing through Marengo, or a carriage may be hired from Blidah for 25 f. a day. It is generally cheaper to hire there than at Algiers.

50 kil. *Blidah* (see p. 166).
57 kil. *La Chiffa*.
62 kil. *Mouzaiaville*.
64 kil. *Bou Roumi*.
68 kil. *El-Affroun*.
73 kil. *Ameur el-Ain*.
80 kil. *Bourkika*, at the junction of the Milianah road. From this point

the kilometric distances are measured from 1 upwards as far as Cherchel, the route being a departmental one, and no longer the continuation of that to Milianah.

85 kil. *Marengo.* 1536 inhab.

This is a clean little town, placed in the midst of a richly cultivated country, with vineyards extending over an area of many hundred acres. The fountains and reservoirs are supplied by a canal, which brings the water from the barrage of the *Oued Meurad.*

[From Marengo, a road 12 kil. in length leads to the ruins of the Roman town of **Tipasa**, called by the Arabs *Tefaced*, signifying "ruined." The road leaves the village by the western avenue, and, passing the tortuous bed of the Oued Meurad, enters the forest of Sidi-Sliman. To this succeeds a very picturesque country, watered by several streams, which, uniting, form the Oued Nador. The road eventually passes through heaps of cut stones and ruins of buildings, and enters the village of Tipasa. Here is a small *auberge*, in which one can lodge indifferently. The harbour is small, but sheltered from the W. wind by a projecting headland, and has a fixed green light elevated 102 ft. above the sea. It is said to have been founded by the Emperor Claudius on the ruins of an older city, probably Carthaginian. It was from this place that Theodosius (father of the emperor of that name) started for the conquest of Anchorarius (*Ouarenscnis*) during the insurrection of Firmus. The former was shortly afterwards beheaded at Carthage, and his son nearly shared the same fate.

In A.D. 484 the Vandal king Huneric imposed upon the Catholic inhabitants of this city an Arian bishop, in order to compel them to embrace that heresy; a great proportion in consequence fled to Spain, and such of the remainder as refused to apostatise had their right hands cut off and tongues cut out. The principal ruins, which are of great extent, consist of a *Basilica*, now known under the name of the *Eglise de l'Est*: it consisted of a nave and aisles with an apse. Around it are innumerable stone coffins, which were buried only just below the surface of the ground. There are also the ruins of a semicircular fountain of the Ionic order; the enclosing wall and tanks are still in existence, as well as portions of the fluted shafts of white marble. It was supplied by the *Aqueduct* of the *Oued Nador*, of which the ruins extend to beyond Marengo, and which is quite capable of restoration. A number of very interesting antiquities are collected together in the garden of the principal proprietor, Monsieur Trémaux; amongst others an immense amphora, measuring nearly 5 mètres in circumference, and two white marble sarcophagi, beautifully sculptured and almost perfect, belonging to early Christian times, and not later than the 7th century. The subject of one of them is a representation of the Good Shepherd.

At Tipasa the sea has encroached upon the land; and through the clear water parts of the ancient walls and fragments of broken columns may be seen. The shore is strewn with similar remains, partly buried under the sand. The small modern village is in the midst of the ruins of the ancient city.

An excursion may be made on horseback from Tipasa to Cherchel by the *briche* quarries of Djebel Chennoua.]

18 kil. *Zurich* (240 inhab.) A small village situated on the banks of the *Oued el-Hachem.* It was founded, in 1848, on the ruins of a Roman villa. An Arab market is held here every Thursday. This village made a very gallant defence during the insurrection of 1871. A party of 30 militia and 40 military prisoners, nearly all of whom were prostrate from fever, strengthened a private house by a hastily constructed stockade, and successfully held it during many days against a strong force of the Beni-Manasser.

22 kil. On the left of the road is passed part of the aqueduct which led the waters of the *Oued el-Hachem* and the copious springs of *Djebel Chennoua* into Julia Cæsarea. It consisted of two converging branches following the contour of the hills as open channels, or

traversing projecting spurs by means of galleries. In only two places was it necessary to carry the water over valleys by means of arches. The first was at this spot, the second a few kilomètres farther on, at the junction of the two branches where the united waters were carried over the *Oued Billah* on a single series of arches, of which five remain.

At the former place the water was carried over a deep and narrow valley on a triple series of arches, most of which are still entire, with the exception of a gap in the centre. The lower and middle series consisted each of 7 arches, of which 5 are complete; the upper one had 16, of which 13 remain. The masonry is only of cut stone as far as the spring of the middle arches; the upper part is of rubble. All the superstructure above the bottom of the specus has disappeared, but at the south end there still remains a circular basin, intended to break the fall of the water and receive any stones or sand that might be washed down from the hills, leaving only the clear water to flow into the duct beyond.

From Tipasa a direct road to Cherchel is in course of construction, but is not yet (1889) completed.

32 kil. **Cherchel.** Pop. 2680.

Cherchel was originally the *Jol* of the Carthaginians, and was made the capital of Mauritania, by Juba II., under the name of *Julia Cæsarea*. After various vicissitudes it was destroyed by the Vandals, but regained somewhat of its splendour under the Byzantines. Ibn Khaldoun informs us that it fell into the hands of the Merinides in 1300. The Moors from Andalusia found shelter here at the end of the 15th century; Kheir-ed-din took it in 1520, and in the following year Doria burnt part of the Algerian fleet here, but on attempting to effect a landing he was repulsed and obliged to retreat. When it was visited by Shaw in 1730 it was in great reputation for making steel, earthen vessels, and such iron tools as were required in the neighbourhood; its ruins were still very magnificent, but it was entirely destroyed by an earthquake in 1738. In those days there was a tradition that the more ancient city also had been destroyed by an earthquake, and that the port, formerly large and commodious, was reduced to its present dimensions by the arsenal and other adjacent buildings having been thrown into it by the shock. It is pleasantly situated in a very picturesque plateau west of the Oued Billah, and between the mountains of the Beni-Manasser and the sea. Ruins of former magnificence exist in every direction, and wherever excavations are made, columns and fragments of architectural details are found in abundance; unfortunately little or no regard has been paid to the preservation of the numerous remains which existed even as late as the French conquest. Most of the portable objects of interest have been removed to museums elsewhere, and nearly all the monuments have been destroyed for the sake of their stones. The large amphitheatre outside the gate to the east still retains its outline, but the bottom is encumbered with 12 or 15 feet of débris, and is at present a ploughed field; the steps, excepting in one small corner, have disappeared, and every block of cut stone has been removed. The theatre or hippodrome, near the barracks, is now a mere depression in the ground, though in 1840 it was in a nearly perfect state of preservation, and had a portico supported by columns of granite and marble, to which access was obtained by a magnificent flight of steps. Here it is said that St. Arcadius suffered martyrdom by being cut in pieces. Splendid baths existed both in the vicinity of the amphitheatre, where is now the *Champs de Mars*, and on the opposite side of the town overlooking the port. Even as late as the author's first visit to Cherchel, a curious old fort existed on the public place, built, as an inscription in the museum testifies, by the Caïd Mahmoud bin Fares Ez-zaki, under the government and by order of *The Emir who executes the orders of God, who fights in the ways of God, Aroudj, the son of Yakoub, in the year of the Hejira* 924. This was built of older Roman materials found on the spot by the celebrated corsair Baba Aroudj, surnamed by Europeans Barbarossa.

Numerous columns of black diorite, and the breccia of Djebel Chennoua, lie scattered about the place, as well as magnificent fragments of what must once have been a white marble temple of singular beauty. In the museum a great variety of fragments are collected, many of which probably belonged to the same building, together with broken statues, tumulary and other inscriptions, capitals and bases of columns, amphoræ, etc.; and in one corner, amongst a heap of rubbish, are some precious specimens illustrating curious facts connected with the state of the industrial arts during the time of the Romans. For instance, a small section of a leaden pipe shows us that such implements were then made by rolling up a sheet of the metal, folding over the edges, and running molten lead along the joint. An ingot of the same metal exists, as perfect as when it left the foundry, with the maker's name in *basso relievo*. There is a boat's anchor much corroded, but still perfect in shape, a sun-dial of curious design, and, most interesting of all, the lower half of a seated Egyptian divinity, in black basalt, with a hieroglyphic inscription. This was found in the bed of the harbour, and may have been sent as a present to the fair Cleopatra Selene from her native land.

One of the most interesting buildings in the town is the military hospital, once a Mohammedan mosque, supported on 89 columns of diorite, surmounted by capitals brought from other buildings, without regard to size or style. The bases are embedded in the ground, it having been found necessary to raise the floor in order to protect the building from damp. The mosque, which was of immense size, has been divided by partition walls to make four separate wards.

From an antiquarian point of view, there is no place in the province of Algiers so interesting as Cherchel and its neighbourhood; and however reckless has been the destruction of the precious architectural treasures which it contained, abundance still remains to testify to the splendour of the capital of Mauritania Cæsariensis.

The ancient cisterns, capable of containing two million litres of water, support part of the barracks, and have been thoroughly repaired. They now supply Cherchel, as they did the ancient city.

Marshal Clauzel nominated Hadj-Omar as Bey of Cherchel in the year 1835; but he was unable to maintain his position, and the town was taken by Berkani, a caliph of Abd el-Kader. In consequence of an act of piracy, Cherchel was seized by Marshal Valée, in March 1840; and in August of the same year the neighbouring chiefs submitted to the French rule.

During the revolt of 1871 Cherchel was blockaded on the landward side for about a month. A party of the insurgents carried massacre and devastation throughout its environs, the aqueduct was cut off, and the inhabitants had no water, save what was contained in the ancient reservoirs.

[If the traveller has a carriage he may proceed from Cherchel to the **Tombeau de la Chrétienne**, and reach the railway station of El-Affroun in time for the evening train to Algiers (see Rte. 3). Carriage from Cherchel to El-Affroun 18 f.; or if he can spare an extra day, he may visit both the Tombeau and **Tipasa** without returning to El-Affroun. Let him proceed by carriage to Tipasa, *viâ* Marengo, but without entering that village. 3½ hours. Go on to Montebello, a delightful drive of 2 hours over an indifferent road, but through a wild and picturesque country. After having visited the Tombeau, he may return and sleep at Montebello, where he will find rough but clean accommodation at the *auberge* of Madame Kaufmann; or he can go on to Coleah, a drive of 2½ hours farther.]

[Excursion from **Cherchel** to **Tenes** on horseback.

7 kil. *Novi*, a small agricultural village.

15 kil. *Fontaine-du-Génie*, another small village.

17 kil. *Oued Messelmoun*, where is an iron mine worked for some years by an English company.

All along the course of the road are

ruins of Roman hamlets and farms; one of these is on the left bank of the *Oued Sebt*, about 800 yards from the sea; another is 4 kil. farther to the W., but the most important is on the plateau of Sidi Brahim, situated between two little bays, that to the W. especially being well sheltered from the wind. There are the remains of a fortified position, of an irregular polygonal form, the walls following the configuration of the promontory. This contains large cisterns, and a postern with staircase descending to the sea. Behind it are the remains of the town, and traces of an aqueduct.

30 kil. *Gouraya*, a village in the neighbourhood of which are important iron mines. Up to this point the road is good and fit for carriages; beyond, it is only practicable on horseback.

45 kil. *Oued Damous*, the most considerable stream in this part of the country, flowing through a rich and fertile district, but inhabited only by Arabs and Kabyles. There are numerous Roman ruins scattered about, and there is reason to suppose that the *Cartili* of the itinerary of Antonine was at the mouth of this river.

After passing the Oued Damous, the aspect of the country changes, the mountains become higher and more abrupt, cultivated land ceases, and there appears no possibility of tracing a road to Tenes.]

ROUTE 3.

Algiers to Coleah and the Tombeau de la Chrétienne.

This journey may be made by diligence twice a day to Coleah, and a carriage hired to the Tombeau, or by a private carriage from Algiers.

Algiers to Staouéli (see p. 108).

About 2 kil. beyond Staouéli, the road branches off to Sidi-Feruch; and, passing over the beds of several mountain torrents, arrives, 3 kil. farther, at 26 kil. *Zeralda*, a village about 2½ m. distant from the sea.

4 kil. beyond Zeralda, the river *Mazafran* (lit. saffron-coloured water) is crossed by an iron lattice bridge, 73 mètres long.

[From this a road branches off to Tipasa, passing the village of *Castiglione*, formerly called *Bou-Ismail*, a favourite bathing-place for the inhabitants of Blidah and the plain; it traverses *Saidia*, a beautiful property belonging to the Rev. Edwyn Arkwright.]

From this point the road ascends through country for the most part uncultivated, and covered with brambles, to the village of

33 kil. *Daouda* (pop. 308), situated at an elevation of 300 ft. above the sea; founded in 1843, and now flourishing and prosperous. The country adjoining is extremely fertile and well watered, and the village contains a church and schools, and is one of the prettiest of the Sahel. 5 kil. farther is

39 kil. **Coleah.** 2336 inhab.

Coleah enjoys a certain amount of renown, from the fact of the celebrated Marabout Sidi Ali Embarek having lived and performed many miracles in this place. He was originally the servant of a landowner named Bou-Ismail. It is said that he used always to sleep instead of doing his work, notwithstanding which his oxen would continue to plough the same as if he were driving them. This extraordinary circumstance was reported to Bou-Ismail, who one day hid himself near by, to ascertain the truth of the report, and saw Ali ben Embarek asleep as usual, whilst the oxen were at work. Bou-Ismail, astonished at the sight, fell upon his knees before Embarek, and, ever afterwards treated him with the most profound respect, and on dying (A.D. 1630) bequeathed to him all his wealth. Ali ben Embarek was buried between a cypress and a palm tree; and in the earthquake of 1825, when the whole town was nearly destroyed, it is said that his koubba was the only building left uninjured.

In 1832 General Brossard was despatched to seize the Agha Sidi Mohammed ben Embarek, on the charge of having been implicated in the insurrection; but not being able to find him, took prisoners two Marabouts of the same family, and fined the inhabitants 100,000 f., of which sum, however, they were only able to pay 10,000 f. Coleah was blockaded by Marshal Valée in March 1838; and it was finally occupied by the French in 1839. An ineffectual attempt was made to take possession of it by the Bey of Milianah in 1841.

Coleah is placed on a plateau at a height of 450 ft. above the sea, and commands a magnificent view of the Metidja Plain, and of the range of the Atlas.

The town has been entirely rebuilt since its destruction by the earthquake in 1825; and like most other French towns in Algeria, consists of a few straight regular streets with tiled houses, and courtyards planted with fruit trees.

One of the most striking objects in Coleah is the garden which has been made in the small ravine separating the civil town from the military quarter. It is entirely the work of the French soldiers, and is kept with great care.

The principal *mosque*, now used as the military hospital, is a tasteful building, composed of five arched naves, supported by stone columns. There is a *minaret* attached, which has a striking appearance from the town. The koubba of Sidi-Embarek is a few paces from the mosque.

The camp, which is situated on a small hill to the S.W. of the town, is of considerable size, the barracks being able to accommodate 1200 soldiers; in addition to which there are commodious storehouses, and other buildings.

The *Market* is held daily in the Rue Es-Souk. The Arab market is held at the same place every Friday.

The principal object of interest, however, in the neighbourhood of Coleah is the great sepulchre of the Mauritanian kings, variously styled **Tombeau de la Chrétienne**, Tombeau de la Reine, or in Arabic *Kubr-er-Roumia*, tomb of the Christian woman.

It is one of three somewhat similar edifices, one of which is found in each province of Algeria, the other two being the Medrassen, or tomb of the Numidian kings in Constantine, and El-Djedar in Oran.

This, however, is the only one mentioned by any ancient author. Pomponius Mela, in his work "De Situ Orbis," written about the middle of the first century, after the death of Juba II., but before the murder of his son Ptolemy, mentions both Cæsarea (*Cherchel*) and Icosium (*Algiers*); and states that beyond the former is the *monumentum commune regiæ gentis*. This at once decides the nature of the building, which, though intended to be seen far and near, is yet entirely concealed from view at Cherchel by the mountain of Chennoua, the presumption being that the king would not care to have constantly within sight of his royal residence the tomb which he had caused to be constructed for himself. The resemblance to the Medrassen, or Tomb of the Numidian kings, from whom Juba was descended, is another presumption that it was erected by him in imitation of his ancestral mausoleum.

Juba II. married Cleopatra Selene, daughter of the celebrated Egyptian queen by Marc Antony, and there is every probability that this monument served only as his tomb and that of his wife who died before him. It is hardly likely that the remains of his son Ptolemy, the last of his race, could have been transferred from Rome to Africa. His only other child was a daughter Drusilla, wife of Felix, Governor of Judea, who said to Paul, "Go thy way for this time, when I have a convenient season I will call for thee."

The tomb must have been violated at a very early period in search of hidden treasure. A careful examination of the accumulated earth and dust within revealed traces of successive races who had visited the place, some of whom had even made it a place of residence, but none whatever of the bodies for whose reception it had been erected.

It is called by the Arabs *Kubr-er-*

Roumia, Tomb of the Roman, or rather Christian woman, the word *Roumi* (fem. *Roumia*) being used commonly by Arabs all over the East to designate strangers of Christian origin. Various explanations are given of this name. Marmol mentions a tradition, that under it were interred the mortal remains of the beautiful daughter of Count Julian, over the story of whose misfortunes the muse of Southey has shed so strong an interest.

Shaw states that amongst the Turks it was known by the name *Maltapasy*, or Treasure of the Sugar Loaf; and the belief that it covered some great accumulation of riches has exposed it to attacks by which it has been much ruined, and before which a less solid structure would have altogether disappeared. Marmol adds:—

"In the year 1555 Solharraes (Salah Rais) attempted to pull it down, hoping to find some treasure in it; but when they lifted up the stones, there came a sort of black poisonous wasps from under them, which caused immediate death wherever they stinged, and upon that Barbarossa dropped his design."

The Tombeau de la Chrétienne is built on a hill forming part of the Sahel range, 756 ft. above the level of the sea, covered with a brushwood of lentisk and tree heath, situated nearly midway between Tipasa and Coleah, and to the west of Algiers.

It is a circular building, originally about 131 ft. in height; the actual height at present is 100 ft. 8 in., of which the cylindrical portion is 36 ft. 6 in., and the pyramid 64 ft. 2 in. The base is 198 ft. in diameter, and forms an encircling podium, or zone, of a decorative character, presenting a vertical wall, ornamented with 60 engaged Ionic columns, 2 ft. 5 in. in diameter, surmounted by a frieze or cornice of simple form. The capitals of the columns have entirely disappeared, but an accurate design of them has been preserved amongst the drawings of Bruce.

The colonnade has at the cardinal points four false doors, the four panels of which, producing what may have been taken to represent a cross, probably contributed to fix the appellation of Christian to it.

Above the cornice rise a series of 33 steps, which gradually decrease in circular area, giving the building the appearance of a truncated cone.

The whole monument is placed on a low platform 63 m. 90 c. square, the sides of which are tangents to the circular base.

During the Emperor Napoleon's last visit to Africa he charged the well-known Algerian scholars, M. Berbrugger and M. MacCarthy, the late and present directors of the library and museum, to explore this tomb, which had never been penetrated in modern times, notwithstanding the attempt of Salah Rais in 1555, and the efforts of Baba Mohammed in the end of the 18th century, to batter it down by means of artillery.

In May 1866 a hole was drilled by an Artesian sound, which gave indications of an interior cavity, and shortly afterwards an opening was made from the exterior to the interior passage. Entering by this, both the central chamber and the regular door were easily found.

Below the false door, to the E., is a smaller one, giving access to a vaulted chamber, to the right of which was the door of the principal gallery. Above this the figures of a lion and a lioness are rudely sculptured.

From this passage a large gallery, about 2 mètres in breadth, by 2 m. 42 c. in height, is entered by a flight of steps. Along it are niches in the wall, intended to hold lamps. Its total length is 149 mètres. This winds round in a spiral direction, gradually approaching the centre, where are two sepulchral vaulted chambers, one 4 m. 45 c. by 3 m. 45 c., and 3 m. 45 c. high, and the other 4 m. by 1 m. 50 c., and 2 m. 75 c. high, separated from each other by a short passage, and shut off from the winding passage by stone doors, consisting of a single slab capable of being moved up and down by levers like a portcullis. The lining of the passage and chambers is of the most beautiful cut stone masonry.

A more convenient way of visiting

the Tombeau from Algiers, if time be an object, is to telegraph or write beforehand to any of the hotels at Marengo to order a carriage to be in waiting at El-Affroun station on the arrival of the morning train from Algiers. The traveller will have ample time to drive to the Tombeau and back, so as to catch the evening train from Oran to Algiers. He ought to provide himself with provisions and a few candles. As the key of the Tombeau is kept at a farm on the opposite side, he may be compelled to enter the building by an opening in the side opposite the door, a proceeding which necessitates a slight scramble. From Coleah there is a service of omnibuses every day to Blidah.

ROUTE 4.

Algiers to Rovigo and the Baths of Hammam Melouan.

Omnibuses from Algiers to Rovigo every day. There is also an omnibus at the rly. stn. of Gué de Constantine, in correspondence with the morning train from Algiers, and the evening one to it; but the most convenient way is to drive from Algiers straight to the baths, which can now be reached by carriage; formerly mules were required from Rovigo.

Leaving Algiers the road passes Mustafa Inférieur, the Ruisseau and Koubba, whence it descends gradually into the Metidja.

12·7 kil. *Gué de Constantine*, rly. stn.; service of omnibuses to Rovigo.

14 kil. Road crosses Harrach by an iron bridge.

23 kil. *Sidi-Moussa* (250 inhab.) An agricultural village on the *Oued Djemâa*, an affluent of the *Harrach*, at the junction of the roads to Bou-Farik, Rovigo, and Aumale, created in 1851, made a commune in 1861.

24·5 kil. Road crosses Oued Djemâa by a wooden bridge.

Hitherto the road has been over a highly cultivated part of the Metidja. As it approaches Rovigo it passes amongst orangeries and orchards of fruit trees, for which this place is celebrated, owing to the abundant means of irrigation.

30 kil. *Rovigo* (350 inhab.) Named after the Duc de Rovigo, Governor-General of Algeria, founded 1849, made a commune 1861.

The village is situated at the foot of the first slopes of the Atlas, at the point where the Harrach enters into the plain.

The road winds along the valley of the Harrach, through most picturesque mountain scenery; the sides of the ravine are well wooded with pines, thuyas, olives, etc., and the bed of the river filled with oleanders.

37 kil. **Hammam Melouan** (the coloured bath). A small and by no means a comfortable inn is situated within a stone's throw of the baths; as it contains only three bedrooms, each with one small bed, accommodation should be secured beforehand.

The baths are situated in an open part of the valley, containing about 10 acres of park-like land, with fine old olive and lentisk trees, well adapted for camping out; in the season, from the middle of May till the end of June, and again in October, there are frequently as many as 70 tents pitched here, many of which belong to Europeans and Jews. The guardian is authorised to receive 5 centimes for each bath, and as this fee brings him in 700 f. a year, it follows that not less than 14,000 are taken annually.

There are two principal springs, one of which flows through a rude bath in the ancient Arab Koubba of Si Suliman; the other is in a similar piscine in a wooden hut behind the auberge; both are dirty and ill cared for, and being only about 7 ft. by 4, they do not afford adequate accommodation for the large number of visitors who frequent them. Were the water properly economised, and all the sources collected and led into well-constructed bathing-places, 600 baths a day might be available.

The water has a temperature of 103° Fahr., and contains nearly as much saline matter as that of Nauheim. The latter has 31·4 grammes of saline matter in every kilogramme of water, of which 27·3 are common salt. The Hammam

Melouan contains 29·1 and 26·3 respectively ; while the water of the Mediterranean has 30·2 grammes of salt per kil.

The springs of Hammam Melouan contain, moreover, a small quantity of iron, the red deposit of which gives rise to the name.

These thermal waters are deservedly held in high repute both amongst natives and Europeans, on account of their healing qualities in all rheumatic and cutaneous affections.

ROUTE 5.

Algiers to Teniet-el-Ahd.

By taking the early train from Algiers to Affreville, the journey can be done in one day. A diligence starts every day from the latter place on the arrival of the train, leaving Teniet on its return the following day at 9.30 A.M. The journey occupies 8 hours.

Time is usually allowed for breakfast at the buffet of Affreville, but there is not always time to dine there on returning.

Carriages for the journey may be obtained at Milianah. The road leaves Affreville by the suburb of Charleville, and then strikes across the plain of the *Chelif*. On reaching the S. side of the plain, it takes a side sweep to the E., following the windings of the *Oued Massin*. By this means the necessary elevation is attained without any sudden or steep ascent. It is well engineered throughout, and is in good condition.

After the first 20 kil. the scenery is pretty, and the hills agreeably wooded with tamarisk, broom, juniper, and lentisk. Presently, as the road ascends, oaks and pines are seen among the brushwood. Several small auberges are passed.

27 kil. *Caravanserai of the Oued Massin* or *Anseur el-Louza*, built on open ground, surrounded by splendid woods of oak and pine. Here the diligence changes horses, and drivers stop to rest. Travellers sometimes pass the night here. Excellent shooting in the vicinity.

35 kil. *La Camp des Chênes*, a small inn picturesquely situated, with a grove of evergreen oaks in front of it. This is a convenient mid-day halt if the traveller has a private carriage. A good breakfast may be obtained. Through the valley on the right a glimpse is obtained of the *Djebel Esh-Sham*, near *Taza*. After this the road ascends through a narrow gorge, finely wooded with Aleppo pine, and passes over a *Col*, close to a remarkable hill of conical shape, called "the Sugar Loaf," crowned by a pile of limestone rocks.

47 kil. *Auberge de la Rampe*, a small, clean inn.

57 kil. **Teniet-el-Ahd.** 1115 inhab. 3807 ft. above the sea.

Horses and mules for the excursion may be procured at the hotel ; the "Rond Point," to which, in order to save time, travellers should go first, may even be reached in a carriage, but the road is very rough and sometimes impracticable. They should take provisions with them, and start as early as possible. It takes 2 hours to ride to the Cedars, and as many back. It would probably require nearly an equal time to go on foot, as the horses must walk all the way.

The village of Teniet-el-Ahd, signifying *Pass of Sunday*, from the Arab market held there every Sunday, is situated in a small grassy plain, surrounded by high peaks, at 3810 ft. above the sea level, and has quite an Alpine appearance. It commands the pass through a remarkable break in the Atlas, by which easy communication is obtained between the Tell to the N., the *Ouaransenis*, the Plateau of *Sersou*, and the *Hauts Plateaux* to the S. It is a pleasant, prosperous village, of one long street, shaded with plane trees, and commanded by a fort on an eminence to the W., containing the barracks, the residence of the Commandant Supérieur, etc. The old Bureau Arabe is in a small fortified enclosure on a hill farther W.

The Cedar forest is on the range which extends W. for 25 to 30 kil., and then, after rising into a bold conical peak, 5811 ft., turns suddenly to the

S., and forms a succession of low hills. The forest begins at about 3 kil. from the village, but it is at least 13 km to the châlet, called "Le Rond Point des Cèdres," 4977 ft., where there is a beautiful lawn bounded by a semicircle of trees. Near this are the largest cedars, here also is the house of the Garde Forestier, and a small châlet.

The *Cedrus Atlantica* is usually found in about 36° of N. lat., at a height of 4000 to 7000 ft. above the sea. The young trees have a pyramidal form, but when one rises above its neighbours, and a blast of wind, lightning, or an insect destroys its leading shoots, the branches extend laterally, and the tree assumes an umbrella-like aspect, forming a shade impervious to the least ray of sun.

There are 9000 acres of forest in this part of the range alone, of which about four-fifths are cedars, and the rest oak of different species, evergreen and deciduous. It is sad to see how many of the cedars are dead, having been burnt by Arab incendiaries. The lower portions of the range are covered with evergreen oak ; the upper portions, on the N. side, with cedars, which descend the S. flank for only a short distance, the increased temperature not suiting them. The largest of the existing trees, "La Sultane," is nearly 100 ft. high, with a diameter of 9 ft. ; another, "Le Sultan," now fallen, was even larger. The wild flowers are very beautiful in spring, especially the *Tulipa fragrans* and the *Fritillaria oranensis*, which are not found in the lower region. It is quite impossible to exaggerate the beauty of the forest. The road, as it winds round the spurs of the range, gives views, that change continually, of the mountains and the trees, which, to appreciate them properly, must be seen from above as well as from below. It is worth while to mount to the top of the ridge (5643 ft.) above "La Sultane," a steep climb of about 30 min. On reaching the crest, which is singularly sharp and well defined, a bare spur of limestone is seen, projecting S., from which a view of singular beauty is obtained. In front is the grand mass of the Ouaransenis, "L'Œil du Monde," with its triple peaks, unobstructed by any object to diminish its height or its grandeur. In the foreground is the Plateau of Sersou, an upland region, richly cultivated, and well wooded, gradually sinking towards the E. into the barren plain of the *Hauts Plateaux*, bounded in the far S. E. horizon by the mountain called *Sebäa Rous* or Seven Heads, which forms so conspicuous an object in the view from Boghar. To the N. are the various spurs descending to the valley of the Chelif, the mountains that bound the rt. bank of that river, Milianah and Djebel Zakkar, and even Bou-Zarea above Algiers. Almost as fine a view is obtained from the extremity of the forest, called *Teniet-el-Guetran*, without the necessity of climbing so high. Near the "Rond Point" is a chalybeate spring, whose waters have been found very efficacious ; it yields 8000 litres per hour.

There is a very fine view of the forest range from Bou-Zhouar, 4593 ft., the conspicuous conical mountain N.W. of the fort, and an equally fine one of the valley of the Chelif from Bou-Sar, 4266 ft., the N. point of the range W. of Bou-Zhouar.

The road to Tiaret has been commenced, but never completed.

About 25 m. south of Teniet, at the point where the Tell ends and the High Plateaux commence, is a district called *Sersou*, rather uncertain in its extent, abounding in prehistoric remains, such as large flat blocks of stone, *enceintes*, and tumuli, which are found on the plain, on the slopes and summits of the hills and in the valleys between them. These are mentioned in no work of travels, as they are rather out of the beaten track, but a preliminary survey has been made of them by Messrs. Letourneux and MacCarthy, and it is to be hoped that a more careful examination may soon be undertaken. At *Aïn-Toukria*, an immense surface, about 700 acres, was entirely covered with *enceintes* formed of walls of rough stones and tumuli, and a considerable number of interesting objects were discovered belonging to the ancient races who had inhabited the country.

ROUTE 6.

Algiers to Tizi-Ouzou and Fort National.

The journey is done by railway as far as Tizi-Ouzou, and thence by carriage or public conveyance. The line was completed in June 1888. Algiers to Ménerville. See p. 155.

kil.		kil.
..	Ménerville	53
7.	Blad-Guitoun	46
11.	Les Issers	42
16.	Bordj Menaïel	37
28.	Haussonvillers	25
36.	Camp-du-Maréchal . . .	17
43.	Mirabeau	10
53.	Tizi-Ouzou	..

7 kil. (from Ménerville) *Blad-Guitoun*, the "land of tents," a thriving village on an elevated position; to the N. of the road below it is a fine communal plantation of eucalyptus and Australian acacias.

11 kil. *Les Issers.* This stream is one of the largest in Algeria, having a course of about 130 m. Close by is the *Souk el-Djemāa* or *Les Issers* (the Market of Friday), a large caravanserai on the right bank of the river. There is an Arab market every Friday, as the name implies.

[There is an excellent road hence to the important village of **Dra el-Mizan**, and an omnibus runs every day, passing through.

1½ kil. *Isserville*, situated on the brow of a hill, with a beautiful view of the plain in every direction.

13 kil. *Chabet el-Ameur.* Wayside inn. The pass from which the village derives its name is at a little distance to the E. The village itself is 1½ kil. to the W. of the road.

29 kil. *Tizi Reniff.*
35 kil. *Bou Faima.*
39 kil. **Dra el-Mizan.** See p. 157.]

16 kil. *Bordj Menaïel*, burnt by the insurgents in 1871; it is now a commune, with 575 inhabitants.

28 kil. **Haussonvillers**, formerly called *Azib-Zamoun.* Before the insurrection of 1871 there were only a caravanserai and a few scattered houses at this place; these were burnt and the caravanserai besieged for 23 days; thanks, however, to the loyal conduct of the Amin el-Omina, who himself assisted to defend it, the building, containing 32 Europeans, held out till relieved by General Lallemand.

Now a flourishing village has been created under the auspices of the *Société Protectrice Alsacienne Lorraine*, presided over by the Comte d'Haussonville, occupied partly by families from those provinces, and partly by discharged soldiers, natives of the same, who have finished their period of service in the engineers, artillery and military train, preference being given to such as are sons of farmers.

The situation of this village is exceptionally good; it is at the junction of the roads to Dellys and Tizi-Ouzou. There is an abundant water supply, and the soil is exceedingly fertile; 5510 hectares of land have been allotted to its inhabitants.

After passing this point the line enters the valley of the Sebaou, which is *par excellence* the river of Kabylia, and drains nearly the whole of the Djurdjura range. It is called by several names, according to the district through which it flows, as is customary all over Algeria. It has a bar at its mouth like nearly all Algerian rivers, and cannot be used either for navigation or for floating timber, as during the rainy season and the melting of the snows it is an impetuous torrent, and in summer a mere thread of water.

36 kil. *Camp-du-Maréchal*, a small village to the S. of road, where was formerly a Kabyle village called *Dra-ben-Kedda.*

On the opposite side of the river to the N. is *Bordj Sebaou*, the ruins of a Turkish fort.

43 kil. *Mirabeau*, formerly *Bou Guelfa*, a village created by M. Dolfus, the well-known manufacturer of Mulhouse, who removed all his establishment to France after the annexation of Alsace and Lorraine to Germany.

53 kil. **Tizi Ouzou** (the gorge of the broom plant), 843 ft. above the sea. It is the chief place of an arrondissement comprising the territories of

Dellys, Dra-el-Mizan and Fort National administered by a sous-Préfet. 924 inhab.

Tizi-Ouzou, which was a flourishing village of about 60 houses before the insurrection of 1871, was then entirely destroyed. It has been rebuilt on a much larger scale, and more than 100 concessions have been given to natives of Alsace and Lorraine and colonists from France.

At a distance of several kil. are the villages of Tamouda and Mekla, inhabited by the Oulad ou Kasai, an ancient family, which had supplied several Bach-Aghas for the circle of Tizi-Ouzou. The actual chief, Ali ou Mohammed ou Kasai, had exercised the functions of Kaid up to the moment when it had been suppressed to make room for the appointment of elected Amins. He then retired into private life, but his influence continued as great as ever over his tribe. It was he who took the lead in the insurrection in this part of Kabylia. He plundered and destroyed the village and all the neighbouring farms, cut off the supply of water, and blockaded the fort from the 17th of April till the 11th of May. He was joined by Ben Ali Cherif, who, though he did not take any active part in the siege, lent to it the prestige of his name. Eighteen of the defenders died during this time, and seventeen were wounded.

The Kabyle and French villages are still as they were, quite distinct; to the N. of the village stands the Bordj, or fort, originally built by the Turks on Roman foundations, and subsequently enlarged and occupied by the French in 1855.

For grandeur of scenery no part of Algeria can compare with Kabylia, and none of it is finer than the Kabylia of Djurdjura. The traveller is particularly struck with the picturesque situation of the villages which crown the heights of the sharp spurs branching from the main range. The white minaret of a mosque usually towers above a cluster of red-tiled cottages. These have neither chimneys nor windows, and are built of mud and stones. The shape of the village is generally long and narrow, necessarily following the configuration of the ground on which it is built; and partly owing to the necessity, before the French conquest, for easy defence, every village is a fortified position, with the mosque as a citadel. The amount of cultivable land in Kabylia, also, is hardly more than sufficient for the wants of its population, this is another temptation to build their villages on the barren crests of the hills, so as to utilise every spot available for cultivation.

The door, the only aperture capable of affording light or air, is so low as to compel a man of average height to stoop on entering, and is placed in the middle of one of the longest sides; the single room is divided into two unequal portions by a low parapet wall, part being the sleeping-room of the family, and the smaller portion being devoted to their cattle. The partition serves as a shelf on which to place jars of dried fruit, flour, etc., and above the stable is a loft for fodder. A small hole at the farthest corner serves as the family cooking-place.

Under these circumstances, it is wonderful that they can preserve life at all; the stench of the stable, the smoke of the kitchen, the want of a proper supply of air and light, are conditions which set all hygienic laws at defiance, and doubtless give rise to much avoidable sickness and death. In every village there is a building, the *Djemâa*, which supplies the place of a club in more civilised states of society. It is usually placed at the entrance, and consists of a large hall with stone benches round the sides; here the men come to take their siesta, to discuss the affairs of the village, the latest political news, or the scandal of the day. The villages are generally filthy in the extreme, and reeking with foul odours of every kind, accumulating from generation to generation. One never enters a Kabyle village without a feeling of regret that they cannot adopt the migratory habits of the Arabs, and remove sometimes to "fresh fields and pastures new."

The Kabyles are exceedingly industrious, and frequently amass considerable property. They are very jealous of their wives; and, if report lies not, the latter have been known to give occasion for the feeling.

[A road has been commenced from this place to Bougie; it bifurcates about 3 kil. from Tizi-Ouzou, and follows the right bank of the river Sebaou.
4 kil. The road crosses, by a bridge, the picturesque gorge of the Sebaou.
21 kil. *Tamda*, a new village of 25 houses built on land once the property of Oulad ou Kasai, sequestered after the insurrection.
23½ kil. The road to the new French village of Mekla turns off to the right and crosses the Sebaou by a large bridge. On the left bank of the river may be seen the ruins of the Kabyle village of Mekla, destroyed during the insurrection.
28 kil. *Tulet Mizeb*. Here, near a fountain and a clump of orange trees, the inhabitants of old Mekla were located when their village was destroyed. On the left of the road, at a distance of 2½ hours, in the hills, is the village of *Mira*, where one of the new Franco-Kabyle schools has been established.
37 kil. *Azazga*, a prosperous village of 30 homesteads, residence of the administrator of the district, in a country well adapted for vines, and abounding in olive trees. There is a small auberge where a traveller can sleep in tolerable comfort. The road to Bougie has not yet been completed much beyond this point.]

From Tizi-Ouzou the ascent must be made by carriage.
110 kil. from Algiers. The road crosses the *Oued Aisai*, an affluent of the Sebaou, and frequently impassable after heavy rains.
The distance from Tizi-Ouzou to Fort National is about 17 m. The military road between the two places was made by 30,000 French soldiers in a remarkably short space of time, and is one of the most beautiful in Algeria. It leads at first over green cultivated hills and valleys; but as Fort National is approached, and the Djurdjura range entered, the scenery becomes exceedingly grand and striking. Many spurs of the Djurdjura are crossed, as the road winds up the mountains; till, in about four hours after leaving Tizi-Ouzou, the Fort is reached, which was seen an hour previously as a white speck high up on the mountain side.
131 kil. **Fort National**, formerly called Fort Napoleon; in Arabic "Souk-el-Arba," meaning the market of Wednesday. 3153 ft. above the sea. 262 inhab.

This place is situated almost in the very centre of Kabylia, and is in reality a walled and fortified town, rather than a fort. The walls are about 14 ft. high, and entrance is gained by the gates of Tizi-Ouzou and of Djurdjura.

In the insurrection of 1871, the garrison supported with courage and endurance a siege of 63 days; it was finally relieved by General Lallemand about the middle of June.

The actual citadel is placed on the highest point, and commands the rest of the fort. It was built after the insurrection of 1871, and contains admirably built barracks, the arsenal and other subsidiary military establishments. Water is brought from some distance by means of an aqueduct, which fills a central reservoir, whence it is distributed to the various buildings. Fruit trees are much cultivated outside, and a kitchen garden for vegetables is kept up by the soldiers.

The fort was built by the French in the year 1857, after a long and sanguinary struggle with the tribes of the *Ait-Iraten*, who were the original inhabitants of this district. The first stone was laid by Marshal Randon on 14th June 1857, and five months afterwards it was completed.

There are very few villages in Kabylia situated at a greater elevation than Fort National; the highest of all is *Ait-bou-Yousuf*, 3876 ft. above the sea.

The view from Fort National is magnificent. Towards the S. is the splendid mass of the Djurdjura, frequently capped with snow; and in the opposite direction lies the valley of the

[*Algeria.*] L

Sebaou, beyond which are ranges of low wooded hills bounded in the distance by the sea.

The highest part of the Djurdjura chain is *Tamgout Lalla Khadidja*, the peak of the Lady Khadidja, 7542 ft. above the sea. It is usually covered with snow from November till May, when it is quite inaccessible, but during summer a laden mule can cross it without much difficulty. The crest is entirely barren, save here and there, where a group of cedars have been able to find soil enough in which to take root; but in the valleys and lower spurs fine rich pasturage springs up after the melting of the snow.

[*Excursions from Fort National.*

1. The villages of the **Beni Yenni.** This may be made on foot or by mule in a day, returning to sleep at Fort National. Follow the carriage road beyond the fort as far as kil. 7. There a steep path descends to the right, crossing the *Oued Djemäa*, and mounting to the villages of the Beni Yenni, which are situated along the crest of the mountains, and are conspicuous by the presence among them of one of the Franco-Kabyle schools. They are four in number—*Aït-el-Ahsan*, *Aït-el-Arbäa*, *Taourirt Maïmon*, and *Taourirt-el-Hadj*.

This tribe is celebrated for the manufacture of that Kabyle jewellery so much prized by strangers. It used invariably to be made of silver, but of late years base metal has been substituted. Kabyle jewellers have never worked in gold. Two descriptions are usually made, one enamelled and the other plain, or only ornamented by the admixture of small pieces of coral.

Another interesting Kabyle industry is the manufacture of pottery. This is always made by the women, and as such a thing as a potter's wheel is unknown, each separate piece is moulded by hand and in the most grotesque possible manner. Still great taste is sometimes shown, and the forms in daily use are no doubt the tradition of Roman and Punic art. Two colours only are used in decorating them—red ochre and black peroxide of manganese, which both retain their colours after baking. A vegetable varnish is then rubbed in to give lustre to the vessel. The intricacy and diversity of design are really astonishing, and each village has its distinctive type.

They also make arms of various kinds, and folding book-stands cut out of a single piece of wood, sometimes inlaid with tin, and tastefully carved.

2. The traveller should not fail to visit the village of **Icherridhen,** the road to which used to pass over the ridge of a scarped isthmus, beyond which was the village surrounded by gardens. This configuration of ground made it a formidable military position. During the first expedition against Kabylia, in June 1857, the Kabyles, who had covered the slopes of the hill with intrenchments, held it for several hours on the 24th against all the attacks of the French troops. The division of General de MacMahon tried in vain to take it by assault; Bourbaki was wounded there at the head of his Zouaves; and the issue of the affair was getting serious, when the 2d foreign regiment rushed up the steep slopes on the left of the Kabyle position with singular intrepidity, and took it in reverse.

During the insurrection of 1871, Generals Lallemand and Cerès, after having relieved Fort National, found the Kabyle forces intrenched at Icherridhen in a more formidable manner than before; but this time its defenders had to contend against the French chassepots and mitrailleuses, and being attacked on both flanks they had to disperse without being able to carry off their numerous dead, which they had laden on mules.

3. To the N. of Fort National an excursion may be made to **Djamäat-es-Saharidj.** The most picturesque road passes by *Tizi-Rached*, where there is one of the Franco-Kabyle schools, and thence to the French village of *Mekla*, where the traveller can sleep at a fairly comfortable auberge. The Kabyle village of *Djamäat-es-Saharidj*, or market

of Friday and of the reservoirs, derives its name from the weekly market held here, and from two old Roman reservoirs under a fine spring in the centre of the village. This was the Roman *Bida Colonia*, and vestiges of Roman masonry, pavements, columns, etc., are seen in every direction. It is an extremely salubrious and beautiful spot, recalling some of the finest villages of Mount Lebanon. For this reason it has been selected for one of the Franco-Kabyle schools, which are likely to produce much good in the mountains. There is also an establishment directed by the Père Blancs (see p. 110) and an English Protestant mission. The neighbouring village of Mekla may be reached by carriage from Tizi-Ouzou, from which it is 20 kil. distant.

4. In fine weather, and when there is no snow on Djurdjura, the traveller can cross from Fort National by the **Col de Tirourda** or the **Col de Chellata** to the Oued-es-Sahel. The latter route is described at pp. 244, 245. The former journey can be done in one day by driving along the high road as far as the *Maison Cantonière*, 29 kil., and there having mules in readiness to proceed to Maillot or Beni-Mansour.

The carriage road runs at a short distance from the summit of the largest counterfort of the Djurdjura range, which is everywhere dotted over with villages of the great tribe of *Zouaoua*, one of the most warlike in Kabylia, whence the modern French word *Zouave* is derived. The native militia in the service of Algiers, Tunis, and Tripoli, were called Zouaoua, as at first none but members of this warlike tribe of Kabyles were enrolled, subsequently their ranks were opened to all Kabyles and Arabs indiscriminately, and the French adopted a corrupted form of the same word for their celebrated African regiments.

On the right are the villages of *Taourirt Teïdili* (Mamelon de la Chienne), *Taourirt Amran*, and *Ayoumi-n-Tesellend* (the plateau of the ash tree), conspicuous by their square minarets; on the left is the great market of *Sebt Beni Yahia*, where General Randon stopped during the campaign of 1854. Also to the left, on a spur with scarped sides, is the village of *Koukou*, the ancient capital of a kingdom mentioned as a powerful one by Marmol in the 16th century, and of which a few unimportant ruins are all that now remain of its ancient splendour. Recently a number of cannon were found there, one of which is a breechloader.

At 21 kil. from the Fort is **Ain-el-Hammam**, the chief place of the Commune Mixte of Djurdjura, and the residence of the Administrator. This is one of the largest and richest communes in Algeria, and the only one without a single French village. It has a population of 65,000 inhabitants, and an annual budget of 200,000 f. There is a small auberge where food may be obtained.

The road reaches Djurdjura by the Col of *Tizi-n-Djama*, overhung by immense limestone rocks (*azerou*), and then rises to the turfy Col of *Tirourda*, through a valley where, in 1857, the female Marabout of *Soumeur, Lalla Fatimah*, took refuge. Her capture hastened the submission of Kabylia. The descent from the spot where the carriage is left to Maillot or *Beni-Mansour*, on the high road between Algiers and Constantine, occupies about 8 hours, the only village passed is the Kabyle one of *Ta-kerbooth*, where nothing is obtainable. The scenery is extremely grand throughout, especially in early summer, when the ground is carpeted with wild flowers.]

ROUTE 7.

Algiers to El-Aghouat, through the Gorge of the Chiffa, Medeah, and Boghari.

This is a most picturesque and interesting journey. Many of the views, such as that of the high peaks of the Atlas from Mt. Nador; of the valleys of Medeah and the Chelif from the Dakla; of the upper valley of the Isser, with Djurdjura in the distance, from Ben

Chicao; of the Hauts Plateaux from Boghar; of the Sahara from El-Aghouat, are hardly to be surpassed

Moreover, on no other route can the physical geography of Algeria be so well studied, or the relations of the Tell, the Hauts Plateaux, and the Sahara to each other be so well understood; while the oasis of El-Aghouat, and the glimpses of desert life and manners to be obtained in and near it, would alone amply repay the trouble and expense of the expedition. But it is far more fatiguing than the journey to Biskra, and should on no account be attempted by persons in weak health, or by those who are not well inured to laborious travelling. The amount of expense is excessive, the roads bad, the diligences dilapidated, inconvenient, badly horsed vehicles, and the accommodation rough, but the caravanserais are managed by obliging people; the beds are clean, and the food remarkably good and plentiful.

Two or more travellers who are not pressed for time would do well to take a carriage, which can be hired at Blidah or Medeah for from 400 f. to 500 f. for the journey to El-Aghouat and back. They will then be able to stop when and where they please, and to start at their own hour. By the diligence time is vexatiously wasted, and the endurance of the passengers taxed to no purpose.

We advise those who undertake this journey to divest themselves as far as possible of all preconceived notions about the desert, as otherwise they may be disappointed (see p. 17).

50 kil. **Blidah.** See Rte. 10. p. 166.

The road leaves Blidah by the gate Bab-es-Sebt, and runs parallel to the railway, through the plain of the Metidja, for about 4 miles, as far as the wide and almost waterless bed of the river Chiffa, which is here crossed by an iron bridge. The small village of *Chiffa*, seen on the right, was almost destroyed by an earthquake in 1867. The traveller may proceed so far by railway, and there meet the diligence. A short distance beyond the bridge the road divides, that to Milianah and Cherchel continuing straight on through the plain, while that to Medeah and El-Aghouat turns to the left, and 2 miles farther on reaches the

60 kil. **Gorge of the Chiffa,** a tremendous rent in the mountains extending for a distance of 10 m., through which flows the small river Chiffa. The peak seen on the right, before entering the Gorge, is Djebel Mouzaïa, 5350 ft. The view looking back over the plain and distant hills is extremely beautiful. The sides of the Gorge are completely clothed with luxuriant vegetation, reaching to the summit of the surrounding mountains, save where in places the road is overshadowed by sheer precipices many hundred ft. in height, down the faces of which numberless small streams fall in showers of spray. The road itself is a wonderful piece of engineering, being blasted out of the solid rock for almost the entire distance, in some places carried high up the face of the cliff, and in others built out in the actual bed of the stream. It was executed by French military engineers, and was only completed in 1855, previous to which there was no direct route between Blidah and Medeah. The traveller who expects to find scenery equalling that of Switzerland or Italy will probably be disappointed. The Gorge of the Chiffa can better be compared to the Scotch or Welsh passes than to those of Switzerland; as snow mountains and glaciers, the most striking features in Swiss scenery, are here entirely wanting. The scenery has been much destroyed by the work of the railway to Medeah, which passes through the Gorge.

64 kil. A small *Inn* at the *Ruisseau des Singes*, where the diligences stop for a short time, and where refreshment and beds may be procured. The Ruisseau des Singes is a picturesque stream tumbling down a steep gorge on the left bank of the Chiffa. Behind the inn a steep path leads up to a garden, where an abortive attempt was made to cultivate tea, coffee, cinchona, and other exotic plants of economic value. The vegetation is rich and beautiful, and ferns and lycopodiums grow in great profusion,

mingled with olive, bay, lentisk, juniper and tree-heath. Apes are frequently to be seen, sometimes in great numbers.

A few hundred yards lower down the valley, on the opposite side of the road, or rather in the face of the cliff which supports the road, is a beautiful stalactitic cave: the key of the door is kept at the auberge.

68 kil. The stream bends to W. close 'under Djebel Mouzaïa, the road crosses it, and follows the right bank.

69 kil. *Hôtel des Voyageurs*, or *Camp des Chênes*. Here the Gorge of the Chiffa may be said to end.

72 kil. The road again crosses to the left; here the stream divides, the road follows the right stream.

74 kil. Road to *Mouzaïa les Mines* (7 kil.) turns off.

76 kil. *Auberge du Nador*, or *la Concession*. From this, looking back, there is a fine view of *Dj. Mouzaïa*. Here the old road to Medeah, steep but short, turns off.

From this point the road is carried by a series of gradients up the northern flank of the sandstone ridge of *Nador*. At first it follows the course of a stream called the *Ruisseau des deux Ponts*. There is a good deal of cultivation, and the views of the upper course of the Chiffa are extremely beautiful.

81 kil. *Auberge des deux Ponts*.

87 kil. Arab village and cemetery, with a very fine view.

90 kil. **Medeah**.[1] 4857 inhab. 3018 ft. above the sea.

Medeah is supposed to stand on the site of the Roman town *Media* or *Ad medias*, so called because it is situated half way between *Berouagia* (*Tanaramusa Castra*) and *Amoura* (*Sufasar*). Under the Turkish Government it was the capital of the Beylick of Titeri, which comprised all territory under Turkish rule outside of Algiers.

The last Bey, Bou Mezrag, offered his services to the French immediately after the capture of Algiers; but shortly afterwards he betrayed his trust, and General Clauzel proceeded to Medeah to instal a new one of his own selection, Mustafa ben Omar; the old Bey was interred at Blidah. His son, however, obtained permission to rejoin the rest of the family, and immediately commenced to rally the most influential Arabs of the Beylick around him, and against the nominee of the French authorities. To support the latter, Gen. Berthezène proceeded to Medeah in June 1831, at the head of 4500 men. The son of Bou Mezrag fled southwards, and was pursued by the French as far as the plateau of *Aouarat*, burning the harvest and cutting down the trees on their route. On their return to Medeah, Ben Omar represented that after such conduct it would be impossible for him to remain without a military force for his protection. This the general refused to leave, and the Bey quitted the city with the French troops.

Medeah, thus left to itself, submitted, first to the Bey of Constantine, subsequently to Abd-el-Kader, and finally to the Duc d'Aumale in 1840, who shortly afterwards was appointed commandant of it.

Medeah, finely situated on a plateau 3070 ft. above the level of the sea, is surrounded by a wall pierced by five gates, which was rebuilt by the French after the siege. The town is entirely French in character, and has nothing of particular interest to attract the stranger.

The principal buildings are the *Barracks*, capable of accommodating 1500 men; the military *Hospital*, containing 500 beds; and the Christian and the Mohammedan *schools*. There were formerly six mosques in Medeah, but now only one remains for its original purpose. The finest of them has been turned into a Roman Catholic church. To the E. of the town is an ancient *Aqueduct*, consisting of two tiers of arches, of which the lower are partly filled up, while the upper ones are left open, built into the wall of the town by the French. The water was conveyed in it from Djebel Nador. The present supply is derived from the same hills, but from a source

---

[1] A railway from the main line at the Chiffa, to Medeah and Berouagia, is (1889) in course of construction, but as the works are of a very difficult nature, it will not be completed for several years.

farther W. The date of the aqueduct is unknown.

The climate of Medeah, owing to its great elevation, is temperate and healthy. The vegetation is rather European than African,—apples, pears, gooseberries, currants, etc., growing in great perfection.

[*Environs of Medeah.*

A pleasant walk is to the *Piton du Dakla*. The view is indescribably beautiful, the country green, and well cultivated. There are some curious piles of sandstone blocks on the spur of Nador, which overlooks the valley of Medeah; they are said to be Roman, but are probably later. Near them is the foundation of a circular structure of a different age.

Mouzaïa les Mines, now called *Ville les Mines*, after the late Monsieur Ville, Inspector-General of Mines, situated in the plain W. of *Dakla*, under the ridges of the last spur of *Dj. Mouzaïa*. The copper mines are in the mountain behind the village. There is a road from it to that passing up the Chiffa valley.

Lodi, through which the road to *Ville les Mines* passes, is a thriving village, much given to the cultivation of the vine; but the whole country is very rich and well cultivated.]

The road leaves Medeah W. and follows the mountains, which sweep in a grand curve in a S.E. direction, round the head of the valley into which the plateau of Medeah projects. These mountains are remarkable for the total absence of all trees or scrub, or indeed any vegetation except short grass.

100 kil. Glimpses of the valley of the *Oued Ouzera* (*Chiffa*).

108 kil. Auberge, called *Auberge du* 108 *kil.*

112 kil. *Ben Chicao*, 3354 ft. above the sea, large caravanserai, built 1858; also an *Auberge du roulage*, where the food is excellent and cheap. The diligence stops here on its return journey for breakfast.

For the next 7 kil. the road descends through fine woods of evergreen oak and cork trees, some of which are of great age and size, also juniper and Aleppo pines.

118 kil. Descend into the *Oued el-Hammam*, the upper valley of the *Isser*, which is richly cultivated with corn, and forms a striking contrast to the mountains just passed.

120 kil. Picturesque Arab village and cemetery on right.

In the middle of this valley is the thriving village of

121 kil. *Berouagia* (394 inhab.), created in 1860, and made a commune in 1869. At a few kil. to the E. are some thermal springs, acidulated and ferruginous. On the left of the road are the remains of the Roman station *Tanaramusa Castra*, on the road from Auzia (*Aumale*) to Rubrae (*Hadjar er-Roum*), near Tlemçen: it is here that the road to the first place still branches off; it is quite practicable for mules. About 1000 prisoners are located here; they used to be let out to colonists, but this was found inconvenient, and they are now utilised in planting vines; they inhabit the old smala, and 400 hectares of land are appropriated for the use of this establishment. After passing this village the road ascends the hills which separate the valley of the *Oued el-Hammam* from that of the *Chelif*.

133 kil. Inn of *Aïn-Maklouf;* lodging may be had; good food. Diligence stops for breakfast.

140 kil. The road descends by a series of rapid curves, and crosses the broken gullies that occupy the right bank of one of the affluents of the Chelif. The groups of Aleppo pines are splendid; cultivation plentiful where practicable.

145 kil. Inn of *Aïn-Moudjarar*, or *le Camp des Zouaves*, a detachment of which corps was formerly employed in making the road here.

155 kil. Road disengages itself finally from the hills, enters the green valley of the Chelif, bare of trees, and crosses

157 kil., the *Oued Hakoum*, by a bridge close to a substantial farm called *Oued Bouktena;* near the Oued Hakoum is **Aïn-Moudjebar**, a large smala where

Spahis were quartered before the insurrection of 1871.

After this the road passes along the right bank of the Chelif to

166 kil. **Boghari**, more correctly *Bokhari*, on right bank. 1020 inhab. The water here is impregnated with sulphate of magnesia, and is slightly purgative. The market held on Mondays is important.

The Arab town stands on a spur of the hill facing the S.W. ; below are the hotels, school, telegraph-office, pharmacy, gendarmerie, etc.

The view of the opposite heights of *Boghar* is extremely fine. Boghari is a grand *depôt* for articles of Arab manufacture, burnouses, embroidered leather, etc., and of the trade generally, between the Tell and the Sahara ; excellent *bain Maure*.

Between Boghari and **Boghar**, the military station, the valley is very narrow, but it soon expands towards the S., and is shut in by low ridges of limestone, furrowed deeply, as if by streams or heavy rains. The Chelif winds below it in a bed 50 ft. below the surface, worn through the sandy soil. Beyond the boundary hills is the first steppe of the High Plateaux, a vast level waste of a dull brown colour. It is bounded to the S. by a range of low mountains, amongst which 7 sugar-loafed peaks—*Sebàïa-Rous*, in Arabic—are prominent.

Boghar was chosen by Abd-el-Kader as a suitable place for a military establishment ; and Berkani, his Caliph, founded a large fort, which was destroyed in 1840 by the French, who definitely occupied the place in 1841. It stands at an elevation of 2940 ft. above the sea level, on the side of a mountain ; and is divided into two distinct parts, consisting of the Fort, which encloses all the military buildings, and the village, which is situated below the Fort, on the road to Boghari. There are some pretty gardens under the cliff, watered by numerous springs, which gush out from beneath the rocks. Outside the Fort is a forest of junipers and pines.

175 kil. *Aïn-Saba*. After leaving Boghari the road traverses the plain of the Chelif, and then engages itself amongst the hills that appear once to have formed a basin to that river, but through which it has broken. The road made in 1868 is excellent, metalled and kept in order by regular cantonniers.

184 kil. A very fine view of the first steppe of the High Plateaux lying spread out beneath. A gentle descent leads to

185 kil. *Bou-Ghazoul* (Father of Gazelles), caravanserai, excellent accommodation, situated in a plain of dry soil, with a few patches of grass among wide patches of sand. A good deal of corn is grown in favourable seasons. In spring the ground is beautifully carpeted with wild flowers. The traveller is pretty sure to see fine examples of mirage between Bou-Ghazoul and Aïn-Oussera.

After leaving Bou-Ghazoul the road is very bad in some places.

222 kil. Caravanserai of *Aïn-Oussera*, poor accommodation. It stands on a slight eminence, with a scanty spring close to it, and a few stunted trees. Beyond this the ground is covered with alfa as far as the eye can reach in all directions.

241 kil. *Bou-Cedraïa*, an assemblage of huts used for the collection of alpha.

262 kil. *Guelt-es-Stel*, a fairly comfortable caravanserai, built by Marshal Randon in 1853. No water save such as is stored in a cistern. Leaving this the road leads up the valley by a continuous ascent ; then, rounding the hills to the left, it enters a plain which may be said to form the second steppe of the High Plateaux. For the first few miles the road is very marshy ; to this succeeds a vast plain of sand, covered with scanty vegetation. Between this and the next caravanserai, the road passes between the two large shallow salt lakes called *Sebkha Zahrez*; the larger one, that to the E. of the road, is about 25 m. long by 10 broad. It is a curious fact, that some springs of perfectly fresh water rise within the circumference of these salt lakes.

288 kil. *El-Mesran*, caravanserai du

banc de sable. The water here is too much impregnated with magnesia for drinking purposes. It is close to one of the largest of the dunes on which there is a scanty vegetation of tamarisk and broom. Thence the road descends, passes a large Arab cemetery with two koubbas, fords the *Oued-Melah* (salt river), and ascends the opposite hill, on which is

302 kil. The caravanserai of the *Hadjar-el-Melah*, or *Rocher de Sel;* also a very nice inn lower down, in a garden of poplars, willows, canes, etc. At the former there are no conveniences for lodging or obtaining a meal. At the latter the diligence stops one hour for breakfast, so that by providing himself with food, and eating it in the carriage, the traveller can leave the vehicle at the rock, and take a hasty survey of it. The Rocher de Sel is a jagged bare mass of hills, without a trace of vegetation. The stream is perfectly sweet before reaching it, but soon becomes impregnated with salt. The diameter of the salt rocks is about half a mile ; they are covered with a *débris* of blue slaty clay fragments of limestone, and crystals of gypsum. The fragments of stone upon the mountain present a remarkable variety of colours, including red, yellow, orange, green, black, violet, etc. ; small particles of iron pyrites are also common. The percolation of water through this has formed deep circular holes, the sides of which are honeycombed, and lined with glittering stalactites of salt. The traveller should be cautious in ascending the rock, as the edges of the pits are generally steep, and the pits themselves often of considerable depth. The cliffs and pinnacles of salt are most picturesque when seen from the stream, but the structure of the mass is best seen on the opposite side, where it has been quarried by the Arabs. On all sides trickle forth small streams, the banks of which are covered with crystals, which sometimes even arch over the water. This is one of the five mountains of salt mentioned by Herodotus as existing in the interior of Lybia.

From this point the country alters ; as the road ascends the *Djebel Sen-el-lebba* the spurs of the mountain are covered with alfa, and there is little wood to be seen except on the heights, where there are oaks and pines.

318 kil. *Aïn-Ouerrou*, a small auberge, with a fountain and garden. Soon a large Government mill is passed on the left, to turn which the water is dammed. Hereabouts the sandstone rocks are a curious conglomeration of petrified straw, stalks of plants, and other vegetable productions.

329 kil. **Djelfa.** Hôtel de France and Hôtel du Sud ; good. The town, which is 3792 ft. above the sea level, stands under the highest Col of *Djebel Sen-el-lebba* (the lion's tooth), the woodcrowned ridges of which are seen high on the right. The town consists of two streets at right angles to each other, planted with trees, and has a very neat appearance. Many Roman remains have been found here. At about 6 kil. N. of the village, close to a mill called *Moulin Randon* or *Moulin Mein*, there is a very large necropolis of megalithic tombs. In the neighbourhood is the great forest of Tadmitz, where there is a post of Spahis. On account of the height and exposed position of Djelfa, it is subject to the greatest extremes of temperature, intense heat in summer and great cold in winter.

352 kil. *Oued Sedeur*. The traveller can spend the night very comfortably here and procure good food.

367½ kil. *Aïn-el-Ibel* (Fountain of the Camel). Caravanserai badly kept. The neighbouring Hôtel du Roulage excellent. Hereabouts was found the *rat à trompe*, a rat with long hind legs and a snout, of which Canon Tristram tells the amusing story : "When the species was first discovered, General Vaillant offered rewards to his soldiers for specimens, and was promptly supplied with other desert rats, to the end of whose noses pieces of their comrades' tails had been ingeniously affixed. Some of the specimens were actually sent to Paris before the trick was discovered." Horned vipers also are common amongst the tufts of alfa. Their bite is fatal.

This is the only venomous snake in Algeria.

The road beyond this lies across a plain of alluvial deposit, capable of growing an unlimited supply of cereals, but little cultivated.

387½ kil. A ruined inn close to where the *Mokta-el-Oust* is crossed by a stone bridge of two arches.

399 kil. Caravanserai of *Sidi Maklouf*, from which there is a very beautiful view; there are remarkable beach lines along the ridges to the left. The caravanserai is fairly good, and stands picturesquely on a bare shelf of rock, with a steep cliff to the S., beneath which is a well-cultivated garden. There is also a little inn farther down, where the horses are fed. Near the former is the koubba of Sidi Maklouf, with a group of palms near it. Thence the road crosses a bridge, and then winds over numerous ridges, and descends into the bed of many a dry watercourse. The road now lies to the left of *Djebel Zebecha*, at the foot of which is a lake, dry in summer.

424 kil. *Mellili*. A small and poor-looking caravanserai, with accommodation for six persons.

Presently an opening is seen in a range to the right, and beyond it an isolated hill of a remarkable shape, called *le Chapeau du Gendarme*. Thence, after traversing a plain of loose sand, a small auberge is reached. Soon vegetation begins to appear; the dark palms open out, beyond which some of the buildings of El-Aghouat become visible. The *vieux camp* is passed on the right, and then, passing down a long straight road between high mud walls, the city is entered by the Porte d'Alger.

441½ kil. **El-Aghouat**. Situated in latitude 33° 48′ N. Pop. 4304, exclusive of a garrison of 1500 men.

El-Aghouat was taken by storm 4th Dec. 1852, by General Pélissier, after a severe combat, in which more than 2000 of the natives perished. In this battle Generals Bouscarin and Morand were mortally wounded.

El-Aghouat is a very ancient city; it formerly belonged to Morocco, by whom it was ceded to the Turks about the end of the 17th century; it changed hands frequently, being sometimes governed by the Beys of Titeri, and sometimes by those of Oran, but the real power always remained in the hands of a Djemäa or council, presided over by one of the local Marabouts.

It is 2437 ft. above the sea level, and has, in consequence, a climate nearly as cold as Djelfa. In fact, it is always cold in winter, when it frequently rains, and sometimes snows. The summers are much less oppressive than at the lower oases, such as Biskra. The town lies between two summits of a limestone ridge, bending N.E. and S.W.; the height to the N.E. is crowned by a barrack and the koubba, that of Sidi Maklouf; the height to the S.W. by the koubba of Si el-Hadj Aissa, also the military hospital, powder magazine, etc.

The latter saint was distinguished alike for his virtues and for the gift of prophecy which he is said to have possessed. In the year 1714 he foretold that the French should take Algiers, that they should encamp under the walls of El-Aghouat, and that they should even extend their power as far as the Oued el-Ahmar. This document was actually in the hands of General Marey, and one of the descendants of the Marabout recited it to that General shortly after the siege. On a lower eminence between these two is the new mosque.

The palm gardens, containing 21,000 date trees, extend in a curved line from near the point where the supply of water begins, from the Oued Djidi (*la prise d'eau*), broadening as it goes up to the town, and again on the other side they stretch into the desert. At their S.E. corner is the Arab cemetery; there is another Arab cemetery, in a wild situation, on the S.E. of the town, in the desert, about half a mile from the gate; near this is the Catholic cemetery. The military establishments are outside the town to the N.W.; farther to the north is *le vieux camp*, which deserves a visit in detail; the whole was constructed at different times by the men themselves. The origin of the name *Rocher des Chiens* is as follows: When El-Aghouat was taken by the French, a considerable number of Arab houses were mined, and many of the inhabitants killed; their dogs, to the number of 200, took refuge on this hill, whence they descended at night on predatory excursions; finally, it was found necessary to have them destroyed by the soldiers.

In the centre of the town is the *Place Randoin*, where is the residence of the general, the military cercle, with a beautiful garden, the Bureau Arabe, post-office, etc. There is an excellent *bain Maure*. The modern French town, with its fortifications, has been constructed with reckless disregard of the Arab houses and gardens. There are several dependent oases near El-Aghouat; one of these is *El-Assafia*, 10 kil. N.E., the houses of which are built of stone, held together by mud. It has a stream rising suddenly out of the sand in a deep bed overhung by oleanders.

An excursion may be made to the *Col de Sable*, a pass over the mountains W. of El-Aghouat, about 1½ m. from the town. From it there is a fine view of the oasis; and on the other side of the valley between the two ranges, and part of *Djebel Amour*.

It is not within the scope of this work to give itineraries for the desert of Sahara; but it would be incomplete without a short notice of the country of the **M'zab**, which is now annexed to Algeria. It consists of five oases in close proximity to each other: GHARDAIA *Beni-Isguen*, *El-Ateuf*, *Melika*, and *Bou Noura*, and two isolated oases farther N., BERRIAN and GUERRARA; the population consists of 40,000 inhabitants, and they possess 200,000 date trees. Until 1882 they enjoyed perfect independence, though paying a certain tribute to France; but in virtue of a decree dated 28th December 1882, their country was annexed to the French possessions, and they became subject to the same laws as govern the other native races under military rule.

GHARDAIA, 180 kil. from El-Aghouat, is the capital of the confederation, and it is there that the military commandant resides. The town is picturesquely situated on the side of a hill, crowned by the mosque; from this point a fine view is obtained of the 8000 date trees which this oasis contains. Two walls divide the interior of the town into three quarters. The centre one is occupied by the *M'zabi* themselves, a proud, exclusive, but active race, entertaining only commercial relations with the occupants of the other quarters. The eastern portion contains about 300 *Jewish* families, and that to the west is occupied by the *Medabiah*, or Arabs from Djebel Amour. The gardens belong exclusively to the M'zabis. *Melika* is not more than a kil. distant; it is considered the *Royal* or Sacred City of the confederation, but is in a poor and neglected condition.

Beni-Isguen is 2 kil. from Ghardaia, and is the principal *entrepôt* for European goods. It is surrounded by a curious walled line of defence. The irrigational works are exceedingly interesting and worthy of examination.

A little farther on is *Bou Noura* (the luminous), a small village with hardly more than 500 inhabitants.

El-Ateuf contains about 3000 souls and 500 houses. It is the only one of the oases that can boast of two mosques.

BERRIAN is 36 kil. N. of Ghardaia; it is small but well built and abundantly watered; is surrounded with a wall flanked by towers, built of round water-worn stones embedded in mud; its gardens contain 30,000 date trees.

GUERRARA is 60 kil. from Ghardaia, and it is undoubtedly the most curious of all. Its streets present an air of comfort and even luxury, which one hardly expects to find in the Sahara. The inhabitants are exceedingly hospitable, and the presence of numerous caravans coming from and going to Ghardaia and other places, give it an air of prosperity and commercial activity.

ROUTE 8.

Algiers to Constantine by Railway.

Distance in Kil. from Algiers.	Names of Stations.	Distance in Kil. from Constantine.
..	Algiers	464
2	Agha	462
6	Hussein Dey . . .	458
11	Maison Carrée . . .	453
16	Oued Smar . . .	448
19	Maison Blanche . .	445
26	Rouiba	438
31	Réghaia	433
39	Alma	425
42	Corso	422
49	Belle-Fontaine . . .	415
54	Ménerville (junction)	410
61	Souk-el-Haad . . .	403
65	Beni-Amran . . .	399
77	Palaestro	387
88	Thiers	376
99	Omar-Dra el-Mizan .	365
123	Bouira (Buffet) . .	341
137	El-Esnam	327
150	El-Adjiba	314
162	Maillot	302
169	Beni-Mansour (junction).	295
186	Sidi Brahim . . .	278
201	Mzita	263
210	Mansoura	254
226	El-Achir	237
239	Bordj bou-Arreredj .	225
246	El-Anasser . . .	218
254	Chénia	210
263	Aïn-Tassera . . .	201
271	Tixter	193
283	El-Hammam . . .	181
296	Mesloug	168
308	Setif (Buffet) . . .	156
322	Ras el-Ma . . .	142
339	St. Arnaud . . .	125
352	Bir el-Arch . . .	112
367	St. Donat	97
384	Mechta el-Arbi . .	80
403	Telergma	61
427	El-Guerrah . . .	37
436	Oulad Rahmoun . .	28
448	Kroub	16
453	Oued Hamimim . .	11
460	Hippodrome . . .	4
464	Constantine . . .	..

2 kil. *L'Agha.*
6 kil. *Hussein Dey.*
11 kil. *La Maison Carrée* (see p. 110).
Bifurcation of the line to Oran.
16 kil. *Oued Smar.* To the north of the line is the property of the late M. Cordier, where there is a complete collection of all the species of eucalyptus and other Australian trees, which have been introduced into the colony.

19 kil. *Maison Blanche.* The nearest station for Fonduk and the Barrage of the Khamis (see p. 111).
26 kil. *Rouiba.* There is a Government School of Agriculture here. The road to *Aïn-Taya* branches off to the N.
31 kil. *La Réghaia.* The line now takes a north-easterly direction, and enters the forest of La Réghaia, yearly becoming more circumscribed in area; it then returns to its former course and approaches
39 kil. *L'Alma* or *Boudouaou.*
This village was the scene of a brilliant action fought on the 25th May 1839, in which 951 French troops repulsed 6000 Arabs. Here also, on the 20th April 1871, the Franc Tireurs, under the command of Colonel Fourchault, supported by a few *Mobilisés* and Zouaves, drove back the bands of Kabyles, who, after the affair of Palaestro, sought to invade the plains.
42 kil. *Oued Corso.* The boundary of Kabylia.
49 kil. *Belle-Fontaine.* A village built by the Government for the reception of families from Alsace and Lorraine. Before arriving at the village, on the left hand of the route, is the *Koubba* of *Mohammed ed-Dibbah* (the murderer). This individual was made Kaid of Sebaou in 1737, and Bey of Titeri in 1745. He was killed during an expedition against Kabylia in 1753.
54 kil. **Ménerville.** Junction for Tizi-Ouzou.
This village was formerly named *Col des Beni-Aicha*, but its present and official title was given out of compliment to Monsieur de Ménerville, Premier President of the Cour d'Appel at Algiers. This is a very important position, being the easiest and most frequented entrance into Kabylia. It was destroyed by the Kabyles in 1871; in consequence their land was confiscated and distributed amongst colonists from Alsace and Lorraine.
There is some iron ore between it and the sea, and on the coast there is a small harbour, *Mersa ed-Dejaj* (the port of the fowl), now silted up with sand, but at one time a Roman position of some importance; a space of 25 acres is more or less covered with ruins, prob-

ably those of *Rassubbicarri*. Roman ruins are also found at Cape *Djinet*, farther to the E., between the mouths of the Isser and the Sebaou.

The line here takes a bend due S., and follows the course of the river *Isser*, the waters of which are abundant even in summer; the country is very fertile, and fig and olive trees are numerous. A fine view is obtained of the Djurdjura range.

61 kil. *Souk-el-Haad*.
65 kil. *Beni-Amran*.

A few kil. farther on the line enters the **Gorge of the Isser**, or of *Ben Hinni*. The hills on each side are steep and often precipitous, confining the river within a very narrow bed, so as to form a beautiful landscape. The 72d kil. is about the narrowest part of the valley, the rocks on each side being not more than 90 metres apart. Numerous cascades falling into the main stream, curious grottoes on the face of the hill, Kabyle villages perched on the summit of the mountains, and luxuriant vegetation everywhere, give to this portion of the gorge a peculiarly bright and pleasant appearance. Unfortunately the line goes through so many tunnels that the scenery is not seen to advantage, and a subsequent visit on foot is advisable.

77 kil. **Palaestro**.

This village, 591 ft. above the sea, is situated on a platform bathed on three sides by the river Isser. It was peopled by Tyrolese, Italians, French, and Spaniards, connected for the most part with the enterprise of opening out the gorge of the Isser. When the insurrection of 1871 broke out, it was in a tolerably flourishing condition, considering its size and secluded position. The story of the terrible tragedy then enacted, being, as it was, the most deplorable of the many which then took place, deserves to be recorded.

The village contained about 112 inhabitants; its position was isolated, surrounded and commanded on every side by mountains, and on the border of two tribes, one Kabyle, the other Arab, both ripe for revolt. Still no serious fears were entertained till, on 18th April 1871, it was suddenly surrounded by hostile tribes before any means could be adopted for defence. The village being entirely unfortified, it was determined to distribute the inhabitants in the three houses best suited to resist attack,—the priest's house, the barrack of the gendarmerie, and the establishment of the *Ponts et Chaussées*. Captain Auger of the Engineers and the priest directed the defence of the first, the maire commanded the second, and the conductor of *Ponts et Chaussées* the third. In the last, which was the best of the three, the women and children were placed. Soon the attack began, the haystacks and buildings round about were set on fire, and such as could not get into the village in time were murdered.

The assailants now advanced in considerable numbers to attack the curé's house, led by the *Amin-el-Omina* of the *Beni-Khalfoun*. The door was soon driven in, but the defenders succeeded in escaping to the gendarmeria with a loss of four of their number. One woman remained behind; she was kept a prisoner for some time and then killed.

At this moment the conductor of the *Ponts et Chaussées* managed to escape to *Fonduk*, where he gave information of what was going on, leaving the house, however, in which he had been stationed, which contained all the women and children, without any one to direct the defence.

On the 22d the maire, M. Bassetti, Captain Auger, and the brigadier of gendarmerie, entered into negotiations with the insurgents, who offered to conduct them safely to Alma, permitting them to retain their arms. Everything appeared settled, and the colonists in the gendarmerie were on the point of quitting, when one of their number made an offensive movement with his gun. This was the signal for a general massacre, in which only Captain Auger and the son of the maire were spared at the special intercession of the Amin.

In this horrible carnage 41 Europeans were killed, and even their corpses were found to have been the object of the most brutal violence; some were thrown alive into the burning houses, and all were stripped of whatever valuables they had.

The house of the *Ponts et Chaussées* was next attacked. Its door, badly made, offered no resistance. The defenders retreated to the upper storey. Fire was applied to the ground-floor, and they were again compelled to retreat higher to the terrace.

It was mid-day in April. In a space of 12 metres, 45 persons were crowded together behind the parapet of the terrace, 40 centimetres high. If they allowed their bodies to appear they were shot. The heat of the roof, brick vaults supported by iron girders, was intense; even their clothes caught fire. Stones and bricks were thrown upon them from below, which grievously wounded some of their number. A burning sirocco was blowing, and they had not a drop of water to quench their thirst. Several died, and one in a moment of madness committed suicide. The women uttered the most heartrending cries, but it was not till 6 o'clock in the evening, when the roof was on the point of falling, that these heroic men consented to treat with their assailants.

The Amin agreed to conduct all the men, women, and children to Alma, on condition that they consented to abandon their arms. This was agreed upon. Ladders were brought to permit them to descend. They were then taken to the residence of the Amin-el-Omina, where they found Captain Auger and the young Bassetti. Two days after Colonel Fourchault arrived on the spot with a column from Algiers, to find only corpses and blackened ruins. He had to fight his way there and back to Alma amongst those who had taken part in the massacre.

The prisoners, 40 in number, amongst whom were 32 women and children, were kept in captivity for 22 days, and only released on the termination of the insurrection, when Mokrani was killed.

The remains of the victims repose under the shadow of the church, and a monument, in the worst style of art, has been erected to commemorate the event.

Now Palaestro has been rebuilt, and considerably enlarged. Thirty families from Alsace and Lorraine have been located here, and additional concessions have been given to the families of the survivors with no sparing hand. A fort has been constructed, and considerable plantations of the eucalyptus and other Australian trees have been made.

[There is a bridle path hence, passing through the beautiful scenery of Bou-Zigza to Fondnk, p. 111.]

88 kil. **Thiers**, formerly called *Ain Omm el-Alleug*.

99 kil. *Omar-Dra el-Mizan*. Station for the little village of Omar, distant 2 kil. from the line, and for the much more important one of **Dra el-Mizan**, 12 kil. to the N.E. An omnibus meets each train, and takes the traveller in 1½ hour and for 1 f. to Dra el-Mizan. This village is situated in a beautifully fertile basin surrounded by the mountain chains of *Djurdjura* and *Maulikain*. It is built outside the fort which proved so useful during the insurrection of 1871. On that occasion the Kabyles attacked and destroyed the village, but the inhabitants took refuge in the fort, which was strictly blockaded by the enemy from the 22d April until relieved by General Ceres on the 4th June. A market is held here every Thursday.

[Instead of returning by the same route, the traveller may do so by *Les Issers* (see p. 143), and there is a horse road to Fort National.]

Due east of Dra el-Mizan, on the road to Fort National, is *Bordj Boghni*, so called from an old Turkish fort, the most advanced which this people occupied in Kabylia. Near the bridge at the entrance to the village is a pyramidal monument to the memory of 148 men massacred by the Kabyles here in 1866. A great market is held every Sunday, which was the principal focus of sedition in the insurrection of 1871.

123 kil. **Bordj Bouira** (the fort of the small well).

It derives its name from an old

Turkish fort in the neighbourhood.
It is now a flourishing village.
This is one of the few districts in
the province of Algiers where lions are
still occasionally to be found.
It is a convenient place at which to
pass the night when going to Tunis, as
the traveller can thus start by a later
train.

[There is a diligence service to Aumale.]

After leaving Bouira the line follows
an easterly direction between the *Oued
Eddous* and the *O. Zaiam*, through a
very fertile plateau, to
137 kil. *El-Esnam*, or *Aïn el-Esnam*
(the spring of images or statues), from
which place also there is a carriage
road to Aumale.
3 kil. to the S.W. are the ruins of a
Roman barrage in the *Oued Benian*
(valley of building), an affluent of the
Oued Berdi, which itself falls into the
Oued Zaiam. A little beyond the caravanserai, on the right of the road, are
two remarkable conical hills called *El
Messen* (les deux Mamelles), which
form a landmark for miles around.
After this the country becomes poor,
and would be uninteresting but for the
magnificent view of Djurdjura, with its
snow-clad peaks, which the traveller
enjoys during the whole of the day's
journey.
150 kil. *El-Adjiba* (the wonderful).
A few kil. S.W. of El-Adjiba are
some curious caverns at *Ahl Ksar*,
said to have been a Roman mine, and
farther on is the village of *Sebkha*,
where there is a salt spring, utilised
by the natives for the manufacture of
salt. The water is received into open
basins, and evaporated by solar heat.
162 kil. *Maillot*. At the *Col des Pins*
the carriage road to Bougie turns off to
N.E., and crosses the *Oued es-Sahel* by
an iron bridge. 4 kil. from this spot,
on the opposite side of the valley, is
the village of Maillot, built in 1883. It
is situated on the lowest spurs of the
Djurdjura range, in a very healthy and
picturesque situation, amongst groves
of olive trees. There is a very good
inn.

169 kil. **Beni-Mansour**. Junction
for Bougie (see Rte. 1). At 7 kil.
beyond the station is the old *Bordj
Beni-Mansour*, 923 ft. above the sea, a
small fort built to dominate the head of
the Oued es-Sahel. This was besieged
by the Kabyles in 1871 for 41 days.
They even brought against it a curious
old piece of ordnance, which probably
formed part of the artillery of the Duc
de Beaufort, abandoned during his
disastrous expedition to Djidjelly in
1664. It bears the inscription,

ANNO DEI 1635
DEOS ME AIVET.

(Deus me adjuvet.)
The view from the terrace of the
Bordj is magnificent. The whole of
the N. horizon is bounded by the Djurdjura range, only a few miles distant; its
highest peak, *Tamgout Lalla Khadidja*,
being nearly opposite the fort. Its
summit is covered with snow for nine
months in the year, and near the top is
the shrine of the *Lady Khadidja*, a pilgrimage to which is considered by the
Kabyles as a hardly less meritorious
action than one to Mecca. At the foot
of it runs the gigantic bed of the *Oued
es-Sahel*, in which only a few threads of
water are visible, the remainder being
taken up by groves of olive trees of
great antiquity. It is said that some
of these were actually grafted in the
time of the Romans; that the art of
grafting them had been lost amongst
the Kabyles, and only reintroduced
after the French conquest.
South of this, and parallel to the
right bank of the river, is another lower
range of hills, on the tops of which are
perched the villages of the Beni-Mansour, *Oulad bou Ali, Iril, Tirilte*, and
Taourirte. To the east the horizon is
shut in by the hills bounding the Oued
es-Sahel, between which, at no great
distance, is the mamelon of *Akbou*, the
country of Ben Ali Cherif. One can
even observe a small eminence on the
base, which is the curious Roman mausoleum near the village of Akbou (see
p. 244). The valley running up from
this mamelon towards Djurdjura is
the boundary between Constantine and
Algiers.

At the foot of the mound on which the Bordj Beni-Mansour is built is a small Christian cemetery, the last resting-place of Lieutenant the Baron Aucapitaine, who has rendered such important services to archæology in Algeria. He and his bride of two months died within three days of each other of cholera in 1867.

The line now traverses an undulating plateau covered with Aleppo pine, juniper, and brushwood.

186 kil. *Sidi Bruhim*. Where it is possible to sleep. This is the station for the **Bibans**, or **Portes de Fer**, 3 kil. distant, which are well worth careful examination.

The above names have been given to two remarkable passes by which alone access is obtained to the highlands of Mansoura beyond, 1104 ft. above the level of the sea. The mountains here are of the greatest possible interest, from a geological point of view. They consist of strata of black rock, sometimes hard and compact, like trap; at others, soft and friable, like schist, alternating with a softer substance, generally indurated clay. On the upper and outer surfaces of these ridges the softer material has been washed away, leaving the harder strata remaining, like Cyclopean walls, which often assume the most fantastic forms. Sometimes they are in considerable numbers, and parallel to each other, like the side-scenes of a theatre; sometimes they fringe the crests of the mountains like delicate fretwork, and at others they assume the form of grotesque animals; chameleons standing out in bold relief against the sky, or gigantic pythons winding their sinuous forms along the sides of the mountains.

The Grande Porte is that through which the rly. passes, following the course of the river, here called *Oued el-Hammam*. Lower down it takes the name of *Oued Shebba*, and after its junction with the river flowing through the *Petite Porte* it is known as the *Oued Marcgh*. The peculiar stratification of the hills on each side is here seen to admirable advantage.

The rivers in this district are so highly charged with magnesia as to be quite unpotable; the only good drinking water for miles round is obtained from a small spring in the bed of the river at the entrance of the pass.

Beyond, on an eminence to the right of the road and on the left bank of the river, are some very curious hot sulphurous springs, called *El-Hammam* (the bath). The ground covered by their deposit is about half a mile long; the springs bubble up in small circular basins, exactly like miniature Geysers, with a raised margin and a deposit of sulphate of soda covered with a layer of pure sulphur. The water in the largest one is carefully conducted into a rude bath which is much in repute amongst the natives. There is also a pool of still hot water, like those in the neighbourhood of the Geysers; the temperature of the water is sufficient to boil an egg in a few minutes; it varies from 172 to 200° Fahr., and the water contains 22 centig. of sulphate of sodium per litre.

To visit the smaller pass, called *La Petite Porte*, it is necessary to leave the high road about 2 kil. before the entrance to the larger one, at a bridge crossing an affluent of the main stream called the *Oued bou Ketun*. This is the pass followed by the column of 3000 men under command of Marshal Valée and the Duc d'Orléans in 1839— the first French troops to pass this formidable barrier.

The road, if such it may be called, passes along the bed of the above-named stream, which is also saline, and is enclosed between stupendous rocks, in some places not more than 12 ft. apart, presenting the same stratified appearance as in the larger gate. Presently the path ascends the left bank of the stream, and, making a detour to the right, joins the main road just beyond the hot springs.

The country beyond is mountainous and sterile, only here and there a few patches of cultivation, until—

201 kil. *Mzita*.

210 kil. *Mansoura*, a small Kabyle town in the kaidat of Mzita, 2637 ft. above the level of the sea.

[A very interesting excursion may be

made from Mansonra to Boni and Gelāa (see Rte. 18). There is a fairly good bridle path, and the distance to Boni is not more than eight hours by mule; it would be quite feasible to proceed thence to Kharata in the Chabet el-Akhira in two days (Rte. 12), spending the night at *Beni-Ourtilan*.]

226 kil. *El-Achir*.
239 kil. **Bordj bou-Arreredj.** 1219 inhab. 3063 ft. above the sea level.

When the Duc d'Orléans, with the army commanded by Marshal Valée, penetrated into the Medjana to effect the passage of the Portes de Fer, the camp was pitched at the *Aïn bou-Arreredj*, near which rose abruptly from the plain a steep and almost conical hill, crowned with the ruins of a fort built by the Turks in the end of the 16th century, out of older Roman remains. This fort had been twice burnt by the *Mokranis* in revolt against the Turks, and had subsequently been abandoned by the latter; it now served as a watch-tower where robbers, embracing as they could the whole plain at a single glance, were constantly lying in wait for travellers and caravans.

After the occupation of Setif it became necessary to station a force there permanently, in order to support Mokrani in his endeavours to establish French influence and to oppose that of Abd-el-Kader, whose lieutenant had inspired such dread amongst the population of the Medjana that they had entirely deserted the plain and retreated to the mountain.

The *Bordj* was rebuilt, and under the protection of its ruler, the Medjana became rapidly peopled, and the soil, which had lain fallow for years, was brought under cultivation.

In 1871, when the insurrection broke out, Bordj contained 90 houses in the town and 30 in the vicinity of it, with a population of 300, owning 15,000 acres of arable land. For the third time the town was destroyed (*ante*, p. 60) by the Mokrani tribe.

The town has been rebuilt on a much larger scale, and its territory has been augmented by the sequestration of the insurgents' property. A monument, in the form of a marble obelisk, has been erected in the village to commemorate the heroic defence of the place, the honour of which was principally due to the *mobiles* from Aix and Marseilles; on it are inscribed the names of those who fell.

The ancient Bordj, which was destroyed with the rest of the town, has been well rebuilt, and the whole place has been surrounded by a strong bastioned wall of defence. The old fort, which now constitutes the citadel, is situated at the N.E. angle; this it was which successfully resisted all the efforts of the rebels to take it in 1871.

The whole of the magnificent and fertile plain of the Medjana became the property of the State by the defection of Mokrani; thus one of the finest portions of the country has been opened out to colonisation.

[For a route from this place to Fort National by the Oued es-Sahel, see Rte. 20.]

246 kil. *El-Anasser*. After passing this place the line takes a bend, and runs considerably S. of the old high road; which it does not again rejoin till the junction of both at Setif.
254 kil. *Chénia*.
263 kil. *Aïn-Tassera*.
271 kil. *Tixter* (view line of snow-capped mountains).
283 kil. *El-Hammam*.
296 kil. *Mesloug*.
308 kil. **Setif.** 5833 inhab. 3573 ft. above sea level.

Setif, the ancient *Sitifis Colonia* of the Romans, was one of the most important cities that that nation possessed in Africa, and was made the capital of the province of *Mauritania Sitifensis*. In 419 it was injured by an earthquake, and later on, ravaged by the Vandals and the Arabs; but even at the time of the French occupation, traces of the ancient fortifications were distinctly visible. In the Middle Ages, El-Bekri, an Arabian historian, wrote that, although the walls had been destroyed, the city was still flourishing and well populated, and contained numbers of bazaars.

In 1839 it was taken by the French under General Galbois.

On the S. face of the citadel at this period was a single venerable aspen tree, the only one visible as far as the eye could reach; below this was a spring, the water of which flowed down and irrigated a valley leading into the *Oued bou-Sellam*. These waters have now been carefully utilised for the supply of the town and the gardens round it.

The town of Setif, as it exists at present, is entirely modern; and although traces of the ancient walls and ramparts are still visible, most of the Roman ruins which remained at the time of the French occupation have disappeared. The wide streets are lined with substantial modern houses, and many of them are bordered with trees. The shops are numerous and well supplied. The town is entered by the *Gates of Bougie, Constantine, Alger*, and *Biskra*, the first-named of which is in the military quarter.

The *Modern Citadel* forms a military quarter to the N. of the rest of the town; it contains the general's residence, barracks for 3000 men, an hospital that can make up 1000 beds, besides officers' quarters, storehouses, and all other requisite military buildings. It was almost entirely constructed by the men of the garrison stationed here, and was finished in 1847.

The walls of the ancient Roman city, restored probably by the Byzantines, have been incorporated in the modern French ones; they are of great solidity, and flanked by 10 towers.

On the *Promenade d'Orléans*, a dreary, ill-kept enclosure outside the *Porte d'Alger*, a collection has been made of Roman antiquities, such as columns, capitals, tombstones, fragments of sculpture and inscriptions, some of which make mention of the ancient *Sitifis*. Two of the most interesting inscriptions found here are the epitaphs of the Bishop Novatus, mentioned in the acts of the Council of Carthage and by St. Augustine, and of the martyr, St. Laurentius.

Here also has been erected a column, surmounted by a bust of the Duc d'Orléans, in commemoration of his expedition to the *Portes de Fer*.

In the house of the Commandant de Génie is a fine *tesselated pavement*, representing a head of Neptune surrounded by Nereids mounted on seahorses, dolphins, etc., which was discovered at Kasr Temouchent, where it formed the principal ornament of the fountain there. A few good pieces of sculpture have also been built into the walls of his garden.

Setif being so high above the level of the sea, its climate greatly resembles and is quite as healthy as that of the centre of France, although considerably hotter in summer. It is admirably suited to the growth of all kinds of European fruits, and in the plain in which it is situated cereals grow in great abundance. Its geographical position cannot fail to secure for it a great future, being, as it is, the junction of many of the most important lines of communication in the colony, such as those with Algiers, Constantine, Bou-Saäda, the Medjana, the Hodna and Bougie.

Its market, held outside the city gates, is one of the most important in Algeria, and is the rendezvous where the Kabyle from the mountains, the Arabs from the plains, and even the Saharans meet to exchange their produce. Every Sunday during the months of August, September, and October it is attended by not less than 8000 or 10,000 natives. The Bou Taleb tribe, about a day's journey distant, are celebrated for the manufacture of carpets and haiks.

By a decree of the 26th April 1853 a concession of 50,000 acres was made to the Compagnie Génevoise for the purpose of hastening European colonisation in this district. This company created several villages, amongst others Aïn-Arnat, El-Ouricia, Bouhira, Mahouan, Messaoud and El-Hamelia; but the object of the concession has not hitherto been attained, and a great part of the land has been simply let to the Arabs.

The country may be divided into two regions, very distinct from each other — the mountainous part, inha-

[*Algeria.*]

bited by Kabyles, similar to other parts of Kabylia elsewhere described, and the regions occupied by Arabs.

The latter are immense plains, the average height of which is about 3000 ft. above the sea, which stretch from the Medjana to Tebessa, possessing abundant pasturage, rich in cattle and grain, carpeted with the most beautiful flowers in spring, cold and bleak in winter, hot, parched, and dusty in summer; without a tree as far as the eye can range, save in the vicinity of modern French villages.

They are occupied almost entirely by two tribes, the *Oulad Abd-en-Nour* and the *Eulma*, and may be divided into two very distinct zones, the *Tell* and the *Sebakh*. The former is the most fertile, and abounds with ruins of Roman agricultural establishments; the latter has a salter and more arid soil, and its climate is hotter and more feverish. Before the French occupation these tribes were entirely nomade, but since then they have become much more stationary, and Arab villages have sprung up in every direction, where a spring or a well renders it possible.

From Setif the beautiful road through the **Chabet-el-Akhira** descends to Bougie (see Rte. 12).

At 9 kil. E. of Setif, on the high road, is *Kasr Temouchent*, or *La Fontaine Romaine*, where was found the tesselated pavement now in the house of the Commandant de Génie.

322 kil. *Ras el-Ma*. To the S. of the line may be seen an isolated mamelon, *Djebel Sidi Brao*, where a number of Christians are said to have been massacred during the Mohammedan invasion on refusing to embrace the religion of El-Islam.

339 kil. St. Arnaud.
352 kil. *Bir el-Arch*.
367 kil. *St. Donat*. 5 or 6 kil. to the N.W., and beyond the high road, may be seen the tomb of *Sidi Yahia*, the founder of the tribe of *Oulad Abd-en-Nour*. M. Féraud translates the inscription on it

"O toi qui es arrêté devant notre tombe
Ne t'étonnes pas de notre état :
Hier nous étions comme toi ;
Demain tu seras comme nous."

This brings to our recollection the inscription not uncommon in old country churchyards in England, which, with occasional variations, runs—

"Travellers, as you pass by,
View the ground wherein we lie :
As you are now, so once were we ;
As we are now, so shall you be."

384 kil. *Mechta el-Arbi*.
403 kil. *Telergma*. At 8 or 9 kil. distance to the N.W., on the high road, and 40 kil. from Constantine, is the pleasantly situated village of **Oued Atmenia**. It was created in 1864.

At 2 kil. from the village, in the property of the Comte de Tourdonnet, there was discovered in 1878, at a depth of from 5 to 7 ft. below the surface, the remains of an extensive range of buildings, the mosaic flooring of which was in so perfect a condition that an architect, M. Martin, was able to make drawings of it; this was published by the Archaeological Society of Constantine, and justly rewarded with a gold medal at the Paris Exhibition of 1878. The proprietor of this establishment was Pompeianus, proconsul of Africa, in the reign of Honorius, described in an inscription found at *Calamo* as *Viro clarissimo amplissimoque*.

The mosaics in the baths are by far the finest and most interesting that have yet been found in Algeria. They consist of numerous tableaux,—one representing the owner's house, with park behind. There are hunting scenes in which every huntsman and dog is named ; views of the stables, each horse having its name attached ; garden scenes in which the lady of the house is spinning under a palm tree ; and numerous other objects not only of great interest, but which give us an idea of the style of domestic architecture in use in Africa in the first and second centuries, the probable date of the building.

In the stable are the following names of horses :

ALTVS VNVS ES | PVLLENTIANVS
VT MONS EXVLTAS | DELICATVS

VINCAS NON VINCAS | TITAS
TE AMAMVS POLIDOXE | SCHOLASTICVS

Another mosaic gives the names of the huntsmen: CRESCONIVS, CESONIVS, NEANTVS, POMPEIANVS. The attendants are named, DIAS and LIBER; and the dogs, FIDELIS and CASTVS.

At 1 kil. beyond the village is the thermal spring of *Hammam Grous* and the ruins of the *Zaouia* of *Sidi Hamana*, who, according to Arab tradition, caused the hot springs to appear in order to facilitate the winter ablutions of his followers.

427 kil. EL-GUERRAH. Junc. for Batna and Biskra.

The line now takes a turn to the north.

436 kil. *Oulad Rahmoun*. Junc. for Aïn-Beida. In the neighbourhood are many interesting megalithic remains (see p. 197).

In the spring of Bou Merzoug is found a very remarkable fish, the *Tellia apoda*, a cyprinodon destitute of ventral fins; it has no other known habitat, and never strays more than half a mile from the source.

448 kil. **Le Kroub** (junc. for Bône and Tunis), more correctly *El-Khroub* (the ruined), from the tradition that an important town once existed here. There is a market, held every Friday afternoon and Saturday morning. About 3 kil. to the E. is the beautiful Roman monument called **Es-Soumah**, erroneously styled by the people of the locality *The Tomb of Constantine* (see p. 197).

153 kil. *Oued Hamimim*.
460 kil. *Hippodrome*.
464 kil. **Constantine**. See p. 185.

ROUTE 9.

Algiers to Aumale and Bou Saâda.

Service of diligences as far as Aumale.
25 kil. *Sidi Moussa*.

Hence the road branches off in a S.E. direction, following the right bank of the Oued Djemaa, which is in winter a veritable torrent, causing much injury to the farms on its banks. Several proposals have been made to embank it, but the expense has hitherto prevented anything being done.

30 kil. *El-Arba*. 1116 inhab.

A prosperous village situated at the foot of the Atlas mountains, founded in 1849, made a commune 1856. It owes its name to the Arab market held here on Wednesday. Oranges are grown here in great abundance, and of excellent quality, the land is rich both in cereals and tobacco, the culture of which is assured by irrigation from the *Oued Djemaa*. The houses are well built, the public buildings satisfactory, and the streets planted with trees. 2 kil. S. of it is the ex-Imperial farm of *Haouch Bou-Kandoura*, directed till after the fall of the empire by Mr. Hardy, the creator of the *Jardin d'Essai* at Algiers. The road now ascends to

43 kil. *Melab-el-Koran*, an auberge situated at about 1639 ft. above the sea. The road between Arba and Sakamodi is very picturesque, and worthy of a visit; beyond it is very dreary.

52 kil. *Sakamodi*. The highest point on the road to Aumale, 3282 ft. above the sea. In one of the ravines here a detachment of soldiers of the military train was overtaken by snow in 1848 and perished. It has only a small auberge and a few colonists.

60 kil. *Aïn-Barid* (cool fountain). The route now descends rapidly to

71 kil. *Tablat*, the ancient Tablata, where the diligence stops for breakfast; a poor hamlet, where, notwithstanding the excellence of the climate, colonisation has hardly yet taken root. A large bordj has been built here.

75 kil. The road passes the confluence of the *Oued Melah* and the *Isser*. There is a large caravanserai called *Mesoubia*, where it is possible to put up.

100 kil. *Les Frênes*, or *El Bethom*, the Arabic name for the *Pistachia Atlantica*, which somewhat resembles the ash; an insignificant hamlet.

108 kil. *Bir Rebalou* (more correctly *Akbalou*). A small village created in 1858 in a rich and fertile district. The

numerous farms around are in a high state of prosperity.

116 kil. *Les Trembles*. A poor, neglected little village, though situated in a rich and very healthy country.

[At 7 kil. from Les Trembles and 21 from Aumale, on the road to Bouira, is the village of Aïn-Bessem, of recent construction. Near the village are the ruins of an important Roman fortress, *Castellum Auziense*, but the walls have been almost entirely destroyed to build the colonists' houses. The spring, which gives its name to the place, is almost in the centre of it.]

128 kil. **Aumale**. Hôtel de Roulage. Pop. of the arrondissement, 28,769.

The ancient *Auzia*, known to the Arabs as *Sour Ghozlan* (Rampart of Gazelles), 2790 ft. above the sea. Auzia was founded during the reign of Augustus, a few years before the Christian era, and the epoch of its greatest splendour was the end of the 2d century, shortly after which it disappeared from history. It played a considerable part in the struggle of Tacfarinas against the Proconsuls, and again, at the end of the empire, in the wars of Theodosius against the revolted Mauritanians. The Turks built a fort here, out of the ruins of the Roman city, but when the first French expedition visited it in 1843 nothing but a heap of ruins remained of either occupation.

It was not till 1846 that the Government of Algeria determined to build a permanent military post at *Sour Ghozlan*, which received the name of Aumale.

The modern town, which consists of little more than a solitary street, is surrounded by a crenelated wall with 4 gates, those of Algiers, Bou-Saâda, Setif, and Medeah.

Several interesting excursions may be made in the neighbourhood, especially on the Roman road between it and Boghar. At 12 kil. W. of Aumale is a small monument called *Kasr bintes-Sultan*, palace of the Sultan's daughter. Beyond is the *Ghorfa des Oulad Miriam*, an old Roman tower, and at 26 kil. from Aumale, *Sour Djouab* the *Rapidi*

of the Itinerary of Antoninus, and perhaps the *Lamida* of Ptolemy, the *enceinte* of which is still visible.

Another excursion may be made to the thermal springs of *Hammam Ksanna*, situated about 33 kil. in an easterly direction. The road to them crosses the ¡Oued Achebour, which, after its junction with the Oued Merdja, becomes the Oued Akkal; it then passes between two tumuli, which, to judge by the stones lying about, probably conceal Roman ruins; then turning somewhat to the N., and leaving the route to Bou-Saâda to the right, it follows that leading to Bordj Bou-Arreredj.

The small garrison of Aumale made a very gallant sortie during the insurrection of 1871, and drove off a greatly superior force of the enemy under the personal command of Bou Mezrag, who left 300 of his followers dead on the field.

The journey on to Bou-Saâda is not one that can be recommended to the general traveller, unless he is disposed to submit to a good deal of roughness and discomfort for the purpose of seeing a Saharan mud town, with quaint streets, on a picturesque water-course, amid date groves. It can be done by diligence or mail-cart in about 24 hours, including a night's rest on the road. The cold is sometimes very great in winter.

After leaving Aumale there are fine views of the Atlas on the distant right. The route descends continually, and reaches the plain after 3 hours' drive.

35 kil. *Caravanserai of Sidi Aissa*. Thence over a perfectly flat plain to

60 kil. *Aïn-Adgel*. There is rough but decent accommodation at this caravanserai. The next stage is over a plain diversified by occasional hills to

102 kil. *Aïn-Kerman*, a solitary caravanserai; a little bit of vegetation beneath is about the only green spot on the route. In the distance, on the left, the salt mountain of El-Outaïa may be seen. Above the caravanserai are the ruins of a fortified position, of a square form, containing apartments which seem to have served as habitations; it is built of square dressed stones, and is evidently of the same epoch as the tombs of Bou-Saâda. The

country beyond is yellow and stony, and farther on there are immense dunes of sand skirting the bed of the Oued Bou-Saäda the whole way to the town.
132 kil. **Bou-Saäda.** Pop. 5112. No good accommodation is obtainable, but there are several cabarets kept by Maltese. The altitude is 578 mètres above the sea.

The oasis of Bou-Saäda is situated on the southern limit of the Hodna, and on the northern one of the *Oulad Naïl*. The town is surrounded on the S., E., and N. by gardens containing about 8000 palm and abundance of other fruit trees. It contains about 1000 houses built of sun-dried bricks, disposed in quaint, narrow, and tortuous streets. It is divided into distinct quarters, which were frequently, before the French conquest, at war with each other. It has a large population of Jews, devoted entirely to commerce and to the manufacture of gold and silver ornaments.

Bou-Saäda is celebrated for its manufacture of woollen goods, such as carpets, burnouses, haiks, etc. These are usually made by the women, and command a high price in the Tell.

The Roman occupation of this district appears to have been purely military. Nevertheless, at the Oued Chellal, there are remains of barrages, which prove that agricultural establishments existed at that place, though by no means to such an extent as in the eastern part of the Hodna.

At *Aïn-el-Ghorab*, 35 kil. to the S., there is a fine summer climate, with abundance of good water. Aïn-Melah is 10 kil. still farther S.; there may be seen many salt and fresh springs in close contiguity, which mingle their waters as they flow out of the place.

There are great numbers of megalithic remains in the country round. In the region of the *Madid*, to the N. of the Hodna, is an immense necropolis of the stone age. The mountains near Bou-Saäda abound in similar tombs.

[From Bou-Saäda there is a carriage road to Djelfa, 120 kil., but not very good; the first halt is at 60 kil., at an Arab village, where there is a caravan-serai; also one to Bordj bou-Arreredj by M'sila; and a third to Biskra by M'doukal and El-Outaïa — the last takes 3 days on horseback, or 4 to 5 with a caravan.]

ROUTE 10.

Algiers to Oran by Railway.

Distance in Kil. from Algiers.	Names of Stations.	Distance in Kil. from Oran.
..	ALGIERS . . .	421
2	Agha . . .	420
6	Hussein Dey . .	415
11	Maison Carrée . .	411
15	Gué de Constantine .	406
20	Baba Ali (Arrêt) .	401
26	Bir-Touta . .	396
37	Boufarik . . .	384
45	Beni-Mered . .	377
51	BLIDAH . . .	371
58	La Chiffa . .	363
63	Mouzaïaville . .	359
69	EL-AFFROUN . .	353
78	Oued-Djer . .	344
91	Bou Medfa . .	331
98	Vesoul Benian . .	323
110	Adelia . . .	312
120	AFFREVILLE . .	302
124	Lavarande . .	297
146	Duperré . .	276
160	Oued Rouina . .	261
170	St. Cyprien des Attafs .	251
173	Les Attafs . .	249
183	Temoulga (Arrêt) .	239
186	Oued Fodda . .	235
195	Le Barrage (Arrêt) .	227
203	Pontéba . .	218
209	ORLÉANSVILLE .	213
224	Oued-Sly . .	198
232	Charron . .	189
243	Le Merdja . .	179
254	Oued Riou . .	168
263	Djidionia . .	159
283	Les Salines (Arrêt) .	138
296	RELIZANE . .	126
315	L'Hillil . . .	107
332	Oued Malah . .	90
346	Perrégaux . .	76
360	L'Habra (Arrêt) .	62
370	ST. DENIS DU SIG .	52
376	L'Ougasse (Arrêt) .	46
381	Mare d'eau (Arrêt) .	40
395	Ste. Barbe de Tlélat .	26
404	Arbal (Arrêt) .	18
411	Valmy . . .	10
416	La Senia (Arrêt) .	6
421	ORAN (Karguentah) .	..

The train starts from the station on the quay, and passing the Agha, follows the edge of the shore as far as

6 kil. *Hussein Dey*, so called from a fine building which belonged to the last Dey of Algiers. It is now incorporated in the large establishment for the purchase and sale of tobacco, on account of Government. The country round is richly cultivated as market gardens.

A little farther the line turns inland, and reaches

11 kil. *La Maison Carrée*.

Junction of line to Constantine.

Here the line, which has hitherto gone in an easterly direction, makes an abrupt turn to the S.W., and passing between the Harrach on the left and the foot of the Sahel on the right, enters the Metidja, a vast fertile plain, 100 kil. long and 25 broad, contained between the first slopes of the Atlas and the high land of the Sahel. The population of this plain is steadily increasing, and it now contains 25,000 Europeans, principally engaged in agriculture.

15 kil. *Gué de Constantine*.
20 kil. *Baba Ali*.
26 kil. *Bir-Touta*.
37 kil. **Boufarik**. 3290 inhab.

Boufarik, at the time of the French invasion, was a pestilential marsh, tenanted chiefly by wild beasts. In 1832 it was occupied by General d'Erlon, who established an intrenched camp there; but for many years the malaria killed off the settlers almost as fast as they came, and the camp before mentioned acquired the name of *Le Cimetière*.

Even as late as 1863, an English writer, whose observations are always accurate, thus speaks of it: "Not a single French settlement in all Algeria bears such a death-fraught name; nowhere throughout the land has civilisation gained a victory at such an enormous cost. Wasting ague or malignant fevers cut off both old and young. Under the hot autumnal sun the exhalations from a swampy soil become a virulent poison, which the strongest cannot withstand."

At the present time, however, Boufarik is a healthy, flourishing country town, with large, clean, densely-shaded streets and squares, through many of which flow streams of clear water.

The most important market in the colony is held here every Monday for the sale of cattle and agricultural produce; it is well worthy of a visit.

A bronze statue of Blandan (see below) has been erected here by public subscription.

A few kil. to the S. in the mountains are the iron-mines of Soumah, where the ore, an oxide of iron, is excavated in galleries, and not *à ciel ouvert*, as is usually the case in Algeria. This mine belongs to the same company as that of Aïn-Mokra, near Bône, and Beni Saf, on the coast between Oran and Nemours. They are not worked at present.

45 kil. *Beni-Méred*. 503 inhab.

This village had in 1839 a redoubt and blockhouse, where a small detachment of cavalry was stationed for the protection of the roads. In 1841 a village was created by the military engineers, destined to receive a body of military colonists, a part of whose duty was to guard the great barrier, or intrenchment, intended to restrain the incursion of the Arabs in the direction of Algiers. In 1845 the village was increased and peopled by civilians. In the public place is a fountain, surmounted by an obelisk, erected in memory of Sergeant Blandan and 20 French soldiers, who were attacked in April 1842 by about 300 mounted Arabs. They maintained their defence in the most heroic manner until succour arrived, but only 5 of them survived. Blandan himself was amongst the slain.

51 kil. **Blidah**. 8893 inhab.

The word *Blidah* is a corruption of *Boleida*, the Arabic diminutive of *Belad*, a city.

Under the Romans Blidah was a military station, and it was occupied as such by the Turks. It was entirely destroyed by an earthquake in 1825, but was very soon rebuilt on the same site. During the first year of the French occupation the inhabitants of Blidah frequently resisted the French army. On the 26th of July 1830 they attacked the expeditionary column under General de Bourmont; they had a severe engagement with Marshal Clauzel on the 19th of November following; they subsequently joined the coalition organised by the lieutenants of Abd-el-Kader, and were severely punished by the Duc de Rovigo in 1832, and by the Comte de Damrémont in 1837.

The treaty of the Tafna put an end to these wars. Blidah was ceded to France, and Marshal Valée took possession of it on the 3d of May 1838.

The growth of fruit trees, especially the orange tribe, is increasing in a remarkable manner, and large quantities of oranges are sold in the market of Algiers and exported to France.

The situation of Blidah is exceedingly beautiful, at the foot of the first slopes of the Atlas Mountains, whose summits overshadow the town; while on the other side the Metidja plain stretches as far as the Sahel hills and the coast.

It is a pleasant residence for a few days, especially about April, when the trees begin to put forth their leaves, and the air for miles round is perfumed with the scent of the orange blossoms. The water supply is so abundant, and has been regulated with such care, that the environs are a succession of gardens, the roads are well shaded with trees, and there are charming promenades in every direction. The climate is distinctly colder than Algiers in winter, cooler perhaps in spring, but much warmer than the heights of Mustafa in summer. It is a good centre from which to make expeditions, as the hours of departure of the trains are later and more convenient than at Algiers.

The *Place d'Armes* is the principal square in the town. This Place is surrounded by arcaded houses, and planted with two rows of trees. The gates are called—the Portes d'Alger, du Camp des Chasseurs, de Bizot, Bab Zaouia, Bab er-Rabah, and Bab es-Sebt. The military buildings at Blidah are on an extensive scale, the *Barracks* accommodating 3000 men, and there are also large cavalry quarters.

The *Cavalry Barracks and Stud* should be visited for the sake of seeing the stallions, which are frequently of the best Arab races. There is stabling for 300 horses.

The most interesting promenades in the vicinity are—the various orange gardens, the Jardin Bizot, outside the gate of that name, the *Bois sacré*, a group of magnificent olive trees in the public gardens to the W. of the city, and, at a distance of about 2 m. beyond the walls, in the ravine of the *Oued el-Kebir*, at the head of which are the *Koubbas* of *Sidi Ahmed el-Kebir* (who died in 1580), and his two sons. These are like most of the other koubbas of the Arab marabouts, but are well worth visiting, on account of the picturesque beauty of the ravine in which they are situated.

Interesting fêtes take place annually here on the Prophet's birthday (*Moulôd en-Nebi*), the 12th and 13th of *Rabia el-Ouel*.

A few yards beyond the cemetery is the *Fontaine fraîche* on the left bank, a perennial source of pure water, which, rising from the mountain-side, beneath a huge rock on which a vast karoub is growing, is carried in an underground aqueduct to Blidah; it passes twice beneath the bed of the river. The fountain is covered by an ugly brick building erected in 1866. Above this spot the valley divides; the branch to the right has a good road practicable for horses or mules, and is extremely picturesque, well wooded and cultivated. After about a mile it widens, and in the space thus afforded is the village of *Beni Salah*, half hidden by luxuriant plantations of orange and fig. The path continues through most picturesque scenery up to the very cedars of *Beni Salah*, and is well worthy of being explored.

Another interesting excursion is the ascent of the mountain of *Beni Salah*, 5379 ft. high, due south of Blidah, which can easily be done on mules in one day. Each mule costs 5 f., and a guide 3 f.

The farm called *La Glacière* is reached in 2 hrs.; it belongs to M. Laval, proprietor of the café on the S. side of the Place d'Armes at Blidah, who is always most courteous to travellers, and will permit them to pass the night in his house should they desire to do so. He is busied in reclaiming his concession, and has some thriving plantations of conifers and chestnuts, also sheep and cattle. But his chief occupation is the collection of snow in his glacière, for use in summer.

From this point a walk of 45 min. brings one to the summit, where two solitary cedars form a conspicuous landmark from Blidah; the largest measures 7½ ft. in girth.

Hence the traveller should walk along the ridge to the westward in order to enjoy the view from the various summits, and the beautiful lawns and gullies, studded with wild flowers, which divide one group from another. The view from the highest peak, about ? m. from where the ridge is first gained, is singularly beautiful; at this point the Atlas bends towards the S., affording a view of its S. flanks, wooded with cedars, and often confused, barren ridges, that are piled one above the other as far as the eye can see, with Djurdjura in the distance. To the N., the spurs and valleys that descend into the plain of the Metidja, with towns and villages, and again bounded by the Sahel; to the W., Chennoua, the Tombeau de la Chrétienne, Kolea, different points in the Sahel range; and in the extreme W. there is in clear weather a fine view of Ouaransenis.

It is quite easy walking along the highest part of the ridge so far, as it preserves a uniform breadth of about 100 mètres, and is generally carpeted with turf.

Pursuing the walk, in less than 3 hrs. the traveller arrives at the *Koubba* of *Sidi Abd-el-Kader El-Djilani*, a walk of exceeding beauty. This is one of the numerous koubbas erected in honour of the founder of the most ancient and popular religious confraternity in the country. *Sidi Abd-el Kader* was a native of Djilan, in Persia, and died at Baghdad about A.D. 1165. He was the patron of the poor and afflicted, who solicit without ceasing alms in his name. The superior (khalifa) of the sect resides at Baghdad, and has *Mokhaddems*, or *Cheikhs*, all over North Africa, as local representatives of the order. The celebrated namesake of this saint, the Amir Abd-el-Kader, made a pilgrimage to his tomb, with his father, Mahi-ed-Din, when about 19 years of age.

The cedars are not to be compared with those of *Teniet;* they are much smaller, but they have the form and character of the larger ones, and few will be found not to admire the forest after walking through it for half an hour.

From the *Koubba* the descent lies by some old glacières and a spring of pure water, and the tourist who went eastwards on leaving Blidah will return to it from the west, having passed entirely round the head waters of the *Oued-el-Kebir*.

Another excursion may be made to the Gorge of the Chiffa and the Ruisseau des Singes (see p. 148).

56 kil. The line crosses the Chiffa by an iron bridge.

58 kil. La Chiffa. Here the diligence for Medeah meets the train (see Rte. 7).

63 kil. *Mouzaïaville.* 810 inhab. This village was completely destroyed by the earthquake of January 1867, by which the adjoining village of La Chiffa was also thrown down. Of 75 houses not one remained entire, and 40 lives were lost.

7 kil. to the S., under the Pic de Mouzaia, is the stud farm of Mr. Smith, an American gentleman well known in the racing world.

About 500 mètres S.E. of the village, at a place called El-Hadjeb, were the remains of the Roman post *Tanaramusa Castra*, where were found, amongst other things, a statue of Bacchus, and a tumulary inscription of Bishop Donatus, killed in the war with the Mauritanians, and buried here in A.D. 493.

69 kil. El-Affroun, an agricultural colony was established in 1848. 870 inhab. This also suffered cruelly from the earthquake of 1867; one only of its 100 houses escaped destruction, and 12 people perished. It is an annexe of the commune of *Mouzaïaville*, and traversed by the *Oued Djer*, which unites with the *Chiffa* to form the *Mazafran* river. In the bed of the

Oued Djer, which the line traverses a kilomètre W. of the station, is a spring of alkaline and gaseous water not unlike that of St. Galmier.
78 kil. *Oued Djer.*
91 kil. *Bou Medfa.* 764 inhab.

[This is the station for the baths of **Hammam R'Irha** (more correctly Righa), 12 kil. An omnibus meets the mail trains from Algiers and takes travellers to the establishment, at a cost of 2 f. 50 c. each person, without luggage. For a carriage (15 f.) it is necessary to write beforehand. The road, after crossing the railway and the Oued Djer, follows its left bank as far as 4 kil., the iron bridge, over which the route to Milianah strikes left. The road continues to ascend the left bank of the river, now called Oued el-Hammam. At 5 kil. it branches off left from the Marengo road, and shortly begins the ascent by numerous zigzags to Hammam R'Irha, 1800 ft.

The thermal springs occupy the site of the ancient Roman station of *Aquæ Calidæ*. Nothing of any importance remains, but the fragments suffice to attest that it must have been a place of considerable importance.

The view from here is very beautiful. To the E. are seen the high peaks of Berouagia and Ben Chicao, and on a clear day some of the buildings of Medeah can even be distinguished. In front, on the opposite side of the valley, is the village of Vesoul Benian (see below), and to the right is the remarkable mountain of Zakkar, which rises above Milianah.

Hotels.—*The Grand Hôtel and Établissement des Bains* (pension, 12 to 14 f.), surrounded by a beautiful garden, together with the hot springs themselves, are the property of M. Alfonse Arlès-Dufour, to whom also belongs the *Bellevue*, a building about 100 yards lower down the hill. It comprises a *Civil Hospital*, as well as a second-class hotel (pension, 9 f.) *H. de France*, in the village, homely (pension, 5 f.)

The waters of Hammam R'Irha are of two kinds—1st, the hot saline springs, the heat of which is about 158° Fahr. at their source, used for the baths; and 2d, the gaseous and slightly ferruginous springs, which are used for drinking. The former contain chlorides of sodium and magnesium, as well as sulphates of soda, magnesia, and lime. One of the latter, called by the Arabs Aïn el-Karis, issues from a pavilion in the village, at an easy walk from the hotel. It constitutes a most refreshing drink, and mixes well with wine. The effect of these waters on persons suffering from rheumatic or gouty affections is most beneficial. It is the only place within moderate distance of Europe where patients can undergo a course of baths during the winter with safety. March, April, and November are considered the best months.

The **Baths** are of three grades:—

1st. Those in the basement of the Grand Hôtel, which are supplied direct from the source. They consist of two *Piscines*, 30 ft. × 15 ft. The water in the cool one is kept at a temperature of 90 Fahr., that in the hot one at 110 Fahr. They are open from 6 till 8 A.M. and 4 till 6 P.M. for men, and from 8 till 10 A.M. and 2 till 4 P.M. for women. Patients on leaving the baths, enveloped in blankets, recline for some minutes on couches in an adjoining chamber, and then usually return to their private rooms, where they are recommended to go to bed for 1 or 1½ hr. Tickets for these baths are supplied at the bureau for 1 f. 50 c. No one is permitted to take the baths without the advice of the resident doctor. There are no *private* baths at the Grand Hotel.

2d. Those in the *Bellevue* or Civil Hospital.—Public (1 f.), private (1 f. 50 c.) The temperature of these baths does not exceed 104 Fahr. They are somewhat devoid of comforts, and are not recommended for ladies or invalids.

3d. Those which are confined solely to the use of Arabs—situated below the Bellevue.

The *Military Hospital*, to W. of the Bellevue, was founded in 1841.

Many pleasant walks and excursions may be made in the neighbourhood:—

To the beautiful pine forest of **El-Chaiba**, which clothes the slopes of the neighbouring mountains, and in which there are numerous footpaths. It commences 2 kil. to W.

To the *Tombeau de la Chrétienne*, drive of 3½ hrs. (carriage about 30 f.) See Rte. 2.

To *Milianah*, drive of 4 hrs. or ride over the hills of 3 hrs. (carriage about 35 f.) See below.

To the summit of *Zakkar*, walk of

10 hrs. there and back: advisable to take a guide.

To the *Ravin du Voleur*, on the Marengo road. About 2 hrs'. drive to the Auberge Gaspard, where good coffee can be had.

For sportsmen there is abundance of small game, and even wild boar, so that a few days or weeks may be spent very pleasantly at this establishment.]

98 kil. *Vesoul Benian*. The village is situated at about 5 kil. to the S. of the line, on the top of a high hill, looking down into the Oued el-Hammam, and exactly facing the bathing establishment of Hammam R'Irha. It was founded by Maréchal Randon in 1853, on a spot called by the Arabs Aïn-Benian; it was peopled by 43 families sent over from Vesoul in the Haute-Saone, numbering 223 persons, and having at their disposal 270,000 f. to enable them to commence work. A concession of 30 acres was given to each, and now the village is in a high state of prosperity.

105 kil. *Oued Zeboudj*, a small village to the S. of the line, in a very feverish district.

110 kil. *Adelia*. The line passes through a tunnel 2200 metres in length, and there attains its maximum elevation, being 500 mètres above the level of the sea; after which it descends rapidly, passing another and shorter tunnel. There is a road hence to Milianah, by which the distance is shortened one-half. An omnibus meets each train.

120 kil. **Affreville.**

Named after Mgr. Affre, Archbishop of Paris, killed on the barricades of Paris, in June 1848, when endeavouring to stay the further effusion of blood. His last words were, "Pastor bonus dat vitam pro ovibus suis."

A diligence starts on the arrival of the train for Teniet-el-Ahd (see Rte. 5).

[The traveller can sleep at Affreville if necessary, but if his destination be Milianah he will prefer to go there at once by private carriage, ordered beforehand from the hotel, or by the omnibuses which come to meet every train.

Milianah, 8 kil. to the N. 3090 inhab. Beautifully situated on a plateau of the *Zakkār* mountain, the highest summits of which attain a height of about 5000 ft., and command splendid views over the plain of the Chelif.

The route from Affreville is extremely tortuous, following the course of the *Boutan*, a river descending from the Zakkār by numerous cascades, but it may be greatly abridged by foot passengers. The ascent takes nearly an hour and a half in a carriage. The drive is one of great beauty, amongst well-watered gardens, producing both the semi-tropical fruits common in Algeria and those of more northern countries, alternating with spots where the hand of man appears never to have interfered with the natural vegetation of the place.

The modern town is built on the site of the Roman *Malliana*, some traces of which now remain in fragments of columns and broken pieces of sculpture.

After the decline of Tlemçen, A.D. 1500, the inhabitants declared themselves free, but were placed by Baba Aroudj under the dominion of the Turks. In 1830 the Emperor of Morocco took possession of the town; and in 1834 Abd-el-Kader installed Ali Ben-Embarek as caliph.

The French first marched against Milianah in June 1840, and found it deserted by the Arabs, who had set it on fire. The garrison left by them was blockaded by Abd-el-Kader for a long time, and suffered severely from disease and famine. When it was relieved subsequently by General Changarnier, of its garrison of 1200 men 700 were dead, 400 in hospital, and the remainder were hardly able to carry their arms. Had the relief been delayed but a few days longer the place would have fallen for want of defenders.

The plateau of the mountain on which Milianah stands is about 2400 ft. above the sea level. The town is well built and clean. In the centre of the *Place* is an old Moorish minaret, now used as a clock-tower. The Arab town and houses have been entirely replaced by modern French streets, the principal of which are bordered with plane-trees, and have streams of water running down either side of the road. They are especially pleasant in summer and early spring, and the view of the plain of the Chelif from the walls is fine at all times.

Milianah is surrounded by a bastioned wall, in which are two gates, viz. the *Portes du Zakkar* and *d'Orléansville*.

There are *barracks* for both infantry and cavalry, and a military *hospital*, making up 500 beds.

The *Catholic Church* is a poor building in the Place de l'Eglise; and of the 25 mosques which formerly existed in Milianah, there now remains but one of any importance. The *Koubba of Sidi Mohammed ben-Yussef* is worth a visit.

A Normal School for European and native female teachers was instituted here in 1875.

The town is lighted by electricity, the dynamos being worked by water power.

The environs are very picturesque, especially to the S., where the road from Affreville passes through a ravine luxuriantly wooded. The *Avenue of Blidah* is the favourite promenade; and without the walls are many fertile gardens, watered by the streams which descend from the Zakkar mountain.

Just beyond the gate is a public garden, a favourite evening promenade in summer, which used to be well kept up under the Empire, but which has been greatly neglected since.]

After leaving Affreville, the line enters the plain of the Chelif (see p. 81). The traveller who passes through it in winter, and much more in spring, will see before him, as far as the eye can reach, a sheet of verdure diversified by masses of wild flowers of startling brilliancy. But in summer the aspect is very different; the whole country is burnt up as if by a prairie fire; not a blade of green is visible; the heat is intense; and even the earth appears to be baked to the consistency of stone, and reticulated all over with wide and gaping fissures.

124 kil. *Lavarande*, named after the general of that name killed before Sebastopol.

Between this and Duperré the road crosses the river Chelif by an iron bridge. The remains of a Roman one are visible about 100 yards lower down the stream on the right.

138 kil. *Les Aribs*, created in 1879.

146 kil. *Duperré*, the name of the admiral commanding the French fleet in 1830. 523 inhab. The creation of this village dates from 1859, when 50 families brought direct from France were established here. Near this have been discovered the remains of the ancient town of *Oppidum Novum*, to which succeeded the Arab town of *El-Khadera*, mentioned by *El-Bekri*.

The name of this city was identified by an inscription found by Commandant Boblaye in 1842, recording that a monument was erected to a local dignitary, Caius Ulpius, by public subscription, *a re conlato oppido novo*.

160 kil. *Oued Rouina*, a village built by the Société Générale Algérienne, on the west bank of the Oued Rouina, which river comes from the mountains of Teniet-el-Ahd and falls into the Chelif close to the station. Its waters, when preserved by a barrage, will irrigate 4300 acres of land in the valley of the Chelif. Near it are the ruins of a Roman town.

At 4 kil. from the station, on the left bank of the stream, is a considerable deposit of iron ore.

170 kil. *St. Cyprien des Attafs*. Not far from the station of Les Attafs is a village of Christian Arabs, *St. Cyprien*, founded by Cardinal Lavigerie, Archbishop of Algiers in 1874, and peopled with young Arabs rescued by him during the famine of 1867. It is exclusively an agricultural village under ecclesiastical control; it has a population of 203 inhabitants, a church, a mission-house, and an establishment of sisters. It is in a high state of prosperity. Labour is held in honour amongst the converts, and even the hours of commencing and finishing it are regulated by the sound of the church bell. The curé is also maire, and the sisters show the example of working in the fields to the Arab women, who gladly follow their example. This is one of the most interesting experiments that has been

made in Algeria, and shows what can be done with Arabs by means of religion. A little to the east of the village is the large and handsome Hospital of Ste. Elizabeth, also built by the Cardinal for the use of the Arab tribes in the plain of the Chelif. This was solemnly inaugurated by him on the 5th of February 1876, and named in compliment to Madame Wolff, wife of the general commanding the division. On the N. side of the line, a little farther to the E., is a small village, Ste. Monique, also occupied by Christian Arabs.

173 kil. *Les Attafs.* An Arab market every Wednesday. At a little distance on the left of the line are the ruins of *Djebel Temoulga*, a Roman camp, and on the right those of *Oued Taghia*, identified as the Roman station of *Tigauda Municipium*, consisting of a long aqueduct and the foundations of public buildings and ramparts. These are called by the Arabs *Kasr Bint-es-Sultan*, palace of the Sultan's daughter.

183 kil. *Temoulga*. A station constructed for the purpose of taking in the iron ore from the mines of Dj. Temoulga, situated 3 kil. to the S. In consequence, however, of the expense of transport the works have been suspended.

The *Oued Fodda* is here crossed by an iron bridge of one arch. The stream has a course of 100 kil. from its source in the highest peak of *Ouaransenis*, of which a beautiful view is here obtained.

This mountain is one of the highest in Algeria, the culminating point, *Kef Sidi Omar*, being 6500 ft. above the sea. The ascent is from the E. side of the mountain, through a rich and well-watered country and magnificent forests; a very extensive view is obtained from the summit.

186 kil. *Oued Fodda*. A village created by the military authorities, represented by General Wolff commanding the division of Algiers, in a portion of the plain, capable of abundant irrigation by the water of the Oued Fodda (silver stream). When the necessary dams are constructed this will probably become one of the principal centres of colonisation in the valley of the Chelif.

195 kil. *Le Barrage*. A station so called from a barrage or dam of the Chelif, a work of great importance. The preceding is a better station from which to visit it. This is hardly an excursion which we recommend to the general traveller. The road is difficult and bad (2 hrs. by light carriage), and during the greater part of the winter the whole masonry is under water—nothing but a lake and a cataract is visible. Still it is possible to do it in the intervals between the morning and evening trains to Orléansville.

From the confluence of the Oued Fodda and the Chelif, for a distance of 12 kil., the united rivers flow through a steep and rocky bed. A point has been chosen at about 4½ kil. from the junction, at which to establish a *barrage de dérivation* 85 mètres wide and 11·75 mètres high, intended to irrigate an area of 12,000 hectares, of which about 4000, situated on the left bank, include the town of Orléansville.

The right bank is watered by a canal crossing the Chelif a little above Ponteba. The entire length of the canals will be about 90 kil., of which 16½ will be the common stream, 23½ the Orléansville branch, and 50 the branch for the right bank of the river. It is calculated that the volume of water in the Chelif during the driest season of the year, from the 15th July to the 15th September, does not fall below 1½ mètre cube per second, and often attains 3 mètres. During the rest of the summer it varies from 3 to 5 mètres, and in winter it increases from 50 to 400 mètres per second. The canals have been calculated, however, to contain 3 cubic mètres per second. The waterfall has been utilised for supplying the motive power with which to furnish Orléansville with electric light.

203 kil. *Pontéba*, a small village close to the bank of the Chelif.

209 kil. **Orléansville.** Sous prefecture, with an area of 232,489 hectares. The city has a population of 2270 inhabitants.

Orléansville is a town of some importance; the area enclosed by its defences is very great, but a small portion only of it has been built over.

The streets are wide, and all bordered with trees. The *Barracks* are extensive, accommodating 3000 men and 1000 horses; and the *Military Hospital* can furnish 500 beds. An abundant supply of water from the *Tsighaoul*, 3 kil. S. of the town, has been brought into the town by two conduits; this is of a very bad quality, and is only useful for purposes of irrigation, washing, etc. Orléansville was for a long time without good water; fortunately in digging for a well in the communal nursery garden, an underground stream of excellent quality was discovered, which is raised by means of a steam engine into reservoirs, and now supplies the town and railway.

An important Arab market, held near the *Porte de Milianah* every Saturday and Sunday, is attended by more than 10,000 natives, who bring horses, cattle, and the produce of *Ouaransenis* for sale. The value of the goods exhibited at these markets is said sometimes to reach £12,000.

The situation of Orléansville, standing as it does in the extensive plain of the Chelif, cannot be called picturesque, although it is surrounded at a considerable distance by hills. It was formerly entirely destitute of trees, but the Forest Department has made large plantations of Aleppo pines and other trees around the town, which have succeeded very well, and now afford a grateful shade to the inhabitants. Between these and the walls the space has been planted with Australian trees, so that Orléansville is actually one of the most shady places in the country. This was much required, as the heat in summer is very great; the climate, however, is not unhealthy. The town has been founded on the site of the Roman *Castellum Tingitanum*, and is called by the Arabs *El-Esnam*, signifying "the Idols," in consequence of the numerous pieces of sculpture having been found in the locality. In 1843 a fine mosaic was discovered, executed in black, red, and white, ornamented by five inscriptions, one of which is the epitaph of St. Reparatus, who died in the year 436 of the Mauritanean era, and another refers to the foundation of the Basilica, of which this mosaic formed the floor in the year 862 of the same era, corresponding to A.D. 325. There are also two curious specimens of abracadabra on the words SANCTA ECLESIA (sic) and SATURNINUS SACERDOS, of which we give the former on the authority of M. Piesse:—

A I S E L C E C L E S I A
I S E L C E A E C L E S I
S E L C E A T A E C L E S
E L C E A T C T A E C L E
L C E A T C N C T A E C L
C E A T C N A N C T A E C
E A T C N A S A N C T A E
C E A T C N A N C T A E C
L C E A T C N C T A E C L
E L C E A T C T A E C L E
S E L C E A T A E C L E S
I S E L C E A E C L E S I
A I S E L C E C L E S I A

The mosaic was at once covered up to preserve it from destruction, and it so remains (1889) concealed from view. It is, however, proposed to make it the prominent feature in the Square in front of the covered market. In the inscription in question the word ECCLESIA is spelt with only one c. It commences with the letter s in the centre of the seventh line, whence the words proceed many times in every direction. The fifth inscription contains only the words SEMPER PAX.

There is another mosaic in the garden of the Military Hospital; it appears to have been the floor of a bath. It contains a representation of a hunting scene; in the upper portion two men are attacking a wild boar, and in the lower a panther is advancing towards an unarmed rider; it also bears the inscription:—

SILIQVA FREQVENS FOVEAS MEA
MEMBRA LAVACRO.

Orléansville was definitely occupied by the French in April 1843.

[An excursion may be made to **Ouaransenis**; the name is more correctly *Ouancherich*, probably a Berber corruption of the Latin *Iuchorarius*. This may be done in one day by carriage, and there is a Bordj occupied by the administrator of the district, at which a traveller could possibly obtain accommodation. The scenery is very fine.]

A short distance from Orléansville the line crosses the *Tighaout*, 209 kil.; the *Oued Lalla Ouda*, 210 kil.; the *Oued Arousa*, 215 kil.; the *Oued Si Sliman*, 216 kil.; and arrives at

224 kil. *Oued Sly*, a village created by the Société Générale Algérienne, on the river of the same name, an affluent of the Chelif. A barrage constructed here irrigates about 12,000 acres of land. This is on the boundary between the provinces of Algiers and Oran.

232 kil. *Bou Kadir* or *Charron*.

243 kil. *Merdja*. The land about here is marshy and extremely unhealthy. The marsh of Sidi Abid, from which it derives its name, abounds in antelope. Bustards also are occasionally found here.

254 kil. *Oued Riou*. The name of a stream descending from the Ouaransenis to the Chelif.

Near the station is the village of Inkerman, one of the most prosperous in the valley of the Chelif, and the residence of the administrator of the district.

It is well watered, has an important cattle and grain market, and quarries of excellent stone, similar to that obtained from Malta and Port Mahon in the Balearic Islands.

[An excursion well worth making from this place is to **Mazouna**, the capital of the Dahra, or the mountainous ridge which lies between the Chelif and the sea. There is a regular series of omnibuses from Inkerman to Renault, and the driver for a small extra gratuity will gladly take the traveller to Mazouna, either going to or returning from Renault.

A tolerably good road leads from the railway station, crossing the Chelif by a bridge at a place where Si El-Kahal bin Awal, brother of Si El-Arbi, Khalifa of the Chelif and the Mina, has a house. An important Arab market is held on the right bank every Friday.

A few kilomètres farther the road begins the ascent of the *Dahra*, a name which signifies *back* in Arabic. It describes well the appearance of these hills from the S.; on entrance they are found broken up into a multitude of ridges, the highest of which is about 600 mètres above the sea. The *Dahra*, both in respect to its physical conformation and its population, is a miniature Kabylia; but though it long maintained its independence, and even acted an important part in the early Moorish wars and revolutions, it was conquered by the Arabs in the 14th century and partly occupied by them. The language spoken is Arabic, with an infusion of Berber words.

In the communal douar of Ouarizane, at the foot of the mountain, there is a station of the remount. Five or six stallions from Mostaganem are usually kept here.

At 18 kil. from the station there is a wayside fountain, the only fresh water since leaving the Chelif, and at 21 kil. the road crosses the Oued Temda, an affluent of the Ouarizane, and enters a beautiful valley fertilised by copious springs and laid out in gardens and orchards. To the right is the village of Oulad Mizian, where the road to Mazouna branches off, and to the left, that of Oulad Sidi El-Akhdar; the route now skirts the west side of an undulating basin of excellent land, and soon reaches

29 kil. The village of *Renault*. This was founded in 1845, and called after a general of that name who had passed a great part of his service in Algeria, and had assisted at the campaign which resulted in the surrender of Kabylia. He subsequently fell at the siege of Paris.

The village is in a highly prosperous condition, and contains several *auberges*, all tolerably comfortable. It is built in a plain, 3 or 4 kil. in diameter, surrounded by a chain of low hills. A mamelon, crowned by a fort, divides it into two portions, each of which contains about 50 houses. There can be no doubt that this was a Roman station; a building of cut stone was discovered within the site of the present

Bordj, which was unfortunately destroyed to provide materials for building the church steeple. The writer saw on the spot a Roman jar, perfectly well preserved, 3 mètres in circumference; it was covered with stamps, one only of which was legible, it contained the letters INDEOω.

About 12 kil. to the N. may be seen the ruins of a Roman fortified position. On each side are posterns and staircases, cut in the solid rock, and numerous columns, cisterns, and remains of houses still exist.

From this village a good road of about 5 kil. long leads to Mazouna, but the traveller will generally find it more convenient to branch off from the village of Oulad Mizian, and after having visited Mazouna, go on to Renault to pass the night.

Coming close to *Mazouna*, a view bursts upon the traveller which would repay a long journey. The hills above are bare and barren, but over against *Mazouna*, and on the opposite side of the ravine of *Aïn-Tounda*, a dense forest of fruit trees rises high up the hill, and spreads far down towards the valley of the *Chelif*; and as the gardens composing it are watered, it is of the deepest green all through the summer. Probably nowhere else does native cultivation offer so pleasing an aspect. The trees cultivated are the apricot, pomegranate, plum, quince, lemon, almond, jujube, pear, with a few peach, olive, karoub, and fig, but this last produces the best fruit on unirrigated ground.

Mazouna, with the suburb of *Bou-Halloufa*, on the opposite side of the ravine, has a population of 2000; that of the whole tribe, which owns 60,000 acres, is 4500. The only European in the town is a French schoolmaster appointed by Government. Nothing is manufactured here except a few bricks and a little pottery, which is sometimes painted by the women, like the Kabyle vessels. It is said in Mazouna that one-half of the population is Turkish by descent, but the men have mostly Arab features. The young girls are pretty.

Descending through the town to the bottom of the ravine, the visitor will come to a small but picturesque cascade. The stream has worn for itself a deep channel, and falls into a pool below. The rocks around are hung with ferns and creeping plants, amongst which, and behind the waterfall, a bathing place has been screened off, by a dry stone wall, from public observation. In the market-place above, a well-grown aspen tree is pointed out, which was planted by the messengers who brought to Mazouna the news of the French landing at Algiers.

The Dahra has a pop. of 22,000, governed by Kaids. Those of Berber descent live in stone villages, the Arabs in tents; the latter are most numerous near the Chelif, the former in the mountains. The soil is fertile and the climate temperate, and it is hoped that in a few years there will be a considerable European population here.

From Inkerman there is a regular service of omnibuses to *Ammi Moussa*, a military station.

At 14 kil. from this town, on the left of the road leading to Orléansville, is the interesting Roman ruin called **Kaoua**. It was evidently a citadel built of large finely-cut stone, surrounded by a wall, all being in so perfect a condition that the minutest details of cisterns, stables, staircases, etc., are visible. On the keystone of the entrance gate is sculptured a crown, within which is the inscription SPES. IN. DEO. FERINI. AMEN. The name of Ferinus is unknown; he was probably some local magnate living about the 4th century. There are many other Roman remains in the district of Ammi Moussa.]

263 kil. *La Djidiouia* or *St. Aimé*, a village created in 1872, and named after Madame Osmond, wife of the general commanding the province.

The Oued Djidiouia is a little to the east of the town, and about 7 kil. farther up there is a barrage well worthy of a visit. The dyke or dam is built of cut stone and hydraulic cement. It is 50 mètres in length, 17 in height, above the foundations, which have a farther depth of 11 mètres; the breadth at the base is 11 mètres, and at the top 4 mètres. This contains a lake winding amongst the hills to a distance of 2½ kil., and containing 2,500,000 mètres of water. The canal runs along the S. and E. sides of an amphitheatre of hills, and traversing a tunnel 224 mètres in length, reaches Ste. Aimé, and passes on to another village farther to the W., called Hamadana, created in 1876. It is calculated that this water, besides supplying the villages, will irrigate about 3400 hectares. The great difficulty regarding these barrages is to prevent them filling up with sand washed down by the rain. When the writer visited this in April 1877, the building was not finished, nor the water let into the canal, and yet there were 3 mètres of mud at the barrage. Since then it has become almost entirely silted up. It was commenced in October 1874, and cost 480,000 f., including 150,000 for canalisation.

To the E. of Ste. Aimé, in an old bed of the Djidiouia, are the remains of what is called a Roman barrage; the construction is of large blocks of concrete, without any trace of cut stone, and neither in the style of masonry nor in its outline does it resemble the work of that great people. It is more probable that it was the work of the Tlemçen dynasty.

283 kil. *Les Salines*. So called from the salt lake of Sidi Bou Zain, to the right of the line, containing an area of 4000 acres.

296 kil. **Relizane**.

The country round is well irrigated, and the town is supplied with water from the Mina, which flows about 3 kil. to the W. At a place where the river left the flat alluvial land, and broke in rapids to a lower level, a barrage of derivation has been built. This is simply a dyke with sluices, which prevents the water from entering the rocky bed into which it formerly descended, and diverts it into two lateral canals, from which it is distributed to the E. and W. Near the town a force-pump sends it into a large filter for the supply of the inhabitants. This barrage is capable of irrigating 8000 hectares.

The name of the river is probably taken from that of the Roman town, the ruins of which are still traceable a mile or two to the S.

315 kil. *L'Hillil*. A small village forming an annexe of Relizane on the Oued Illil, an affluent of the Mina, on which there is a small barrage which irrigates the country round about.

[An interesting expedition from l'Hillil is to the remarkable and little-known Arab town **El-Kalâa** (the fortress).

The kaid assured the author, who visited it in May 1877, that he was the first Englishman who had ever been there, and that very few French, except those connected with the administration, ever found their way to it. Nevertheless, the expedition can be done between the arrival of the first train from Relizane in the morning and the departure of that to Oran at night. A good carriage-road has been constructed, and an omnibus runs every morning, returning in the afternoon. The traveller should take his breakfast with him. If he happens to occupy a prominent position of any kind, or is recommended to the kaid, he is sure to be hospitably entertained, but otherwise he runs the risk of starvation if he depends on the resources of the village.

El-Kalâa is a town of Berber origin 17 kil. S. of l'Hillil, and 36 kil. N.E. of Mascara, picturesquely situated on the S.W. slopes of Djebel Barber, which descends almost perpendicularly to the Oued Bou-Mendjil. It occupies the mountainous centre of that *massif* situated between the Mina and the Habra, which was at one time occupied by fractions of the great tribe of Houasa. The village is divided into several portions, each situated on a projecting spur of the mountain, and separated from the next by a deep ravine. The houses are of stone, but in a dilapidated condition. The place is celebrated for its carpets, which resemble those usually obtained from Smyrna; nearly 3000 are made every year, and they are everywhere held in high esteem; the cost of them on the spot is about 10 f. a square mètre. They are made by the women; the process is most curious, but it will be difficult for the male stranger to obtain access to a house where they are being made. At the bottom of the hill, along the banks of the river, are beautiful gardens of fruit trees, especially oranges and lemons. The population is about 300. The only European in the village is a schoolmaster, who, as at Mazouna, is sent to teach the children French. They are most apt pupils, and some of their exercises are quite astonishing.

It is uncertain whether this was ever a Roman station, but the remains of two cisterns still visible are wonderfully like the work of that people.

The place is said to have been built by a chief of the Houara tribe, Mohammed ben Ishak, about the middle of the 6th century of the Hedjira, and after the extinction of that tribe it fell into the hands of the Beni Rachid, a branch of the Zenati, from Djebel Amour. It eventually submitted to the sovereigns of Tlemçen.

About the end of the 15th century of the Christian era, on the decline of the Beni Zeian dynasty of Tlemçen, the Arab confederation, known by the name of Mehal, declared itself independent. They descended from the High Plateaux, and invaded the plains of the Chelif and the Mina, and established themselves firmly at Kalâa, Tenes, Mostaganem, and Mazouna.

The Spanish occupation of Oran commenced about the beginning of the 16th century, and the Beni Rachid became in turns their allies and their tributaries. This state of things continued till 1517, when Baba Aroudj, who had already taken Algiers, appeared at the head of a Turkish army. The Mehal, under one of their most celebrated chiefs, Hamid el-Abd, were defeated; Tenes and Kalâa fell into the hands of the Turks, and Tlemçen opened its gates to Aroudj and recognised him as its sovereign. The Sultan Abou Hammou, dispossessed of his country and put to flight by the corsair, sought the aid of the Spaniards, who, having all their commerce cut off by the Turks,

[Algeria.]

gladly sent a force to replace their old ally on his throne. It was commanded by Don Martin d'Argote, who eventually marched on Kalâa, which was defended by Ishak, elder brother of Aroudj, with 500 Turkish infantry. After a spirited resistance he agreed to capitulate, on condition of being allowed to leave with arms and baggage, but no sooner had the Turks surrendered the place than the Spaniards fell upon them and put them all to death. The Spaniards then continued their march to Tlemçen, took that town, and pursued Aroudj to the Rio Salado, where he and all his people were killed.

Kalâa became subsequently annexed to the regency of Algiers, and so continued till the French conquest. After the fall of the Turks, the people refusing to recognise the Emir Abd-el-Kader, he attacked the town, and after a siege of three days he took it and gave it up to pillage. It submitted to the French in 1842, joined the insurrection of Bou Maza in 1845, was retaken by the French with considerable loss, since when it has remained tolerably quiet. Kalâa was used by the Turks as a place of deportation for all their most turbulent soldiers, and at the present day there are two distinct sections of the population, the Kouloughlis or descendants of Turkish fathers, and the native race, a mixture of Berber and Arab.

There are three other similar villages in the neighbourhood. *Tiliouanet* on the banks of the stream bearing the same name, 4 kil. E. of El-Kalâa. The word signifies *coloured*, on account of the perpetual verdure of the place. *Debba*, 800 mètres S. of El-Kalâa, on the same river as that town, and *Mesrata*, 2 kil. S.W., on the lower part of the Oued Bou-Mendjil. It was at one time of considerable importance, but was greatly destroyed by landslips in 1845. The traveller will not fail to remark the great number of koubbas, or tombs, of local saints in every direction.]

332 kil. *Oued Malah*, situated on a river of that name. In the immediate vicinity is a village called *Romei*, and

near the station is a tract of brushwood called the Forest of Keronia.

346 kil. **Perrégaux.** 2136 inhab. Named after the well-known general who fell at the second siege of Constantine. Arab market every Thursday. This is the place where the railway from Arzeu to Saida crosses the main line.

At 9 kil. to the S. is the great barrage of the Oued Fergoug, constructed by M. Debrousse. It is situated at the junction of three streams—the Oued Fergoug, the Oued Terzoug, and the Habra. The total length of the dam, including the *diversoir*, is 440 mètres; its thickness at the base is 40 mètres, and at the top 4½ mètres; its depth below foundation 11 mètres. It forms an immense lake, containing when full 38 millions of cubic mètres of water.

On the 15th December 1881 it gave way under the pressure of exceptionally high floods, drowning upwards of 400 persons, besides losing all the water supply, and laying dry the system of irrigational canals in connection with it. It has now been completely repaired and is full of water.

The sufferers were mostly Arabs and Spaniards; in the town of Perrégaux there was a depth of 5 ft. of water in the houses and streets, and long stretches of embankments, both on the Oran and Algiers line and on that to Saida, were swept away.

This work, as well as the railway between Arzeu and Saida, is due to the enterprise of a private company, one may almost say to the unaided exertions of the late M. Debrousse. He received no guarantee of interest from the State, but a concession of 24,000 hectares of irrigable land in the plain of the Habra, between Perrégaux and the sea, and the privilege of collecting the alfa over a vast area of land on the High Plateaux [see Rte. 26, from Arzeu to Saida].

A milliary column was found here, and is now built into the wall of the Company's office. It contains the following inscription, being a dedication to Gordian III. The figures which should have followed the letters M. P., *Millia Passuum*, have never been engraved.

```
 .    .    .       N
D  O  M  I  N  O   R
IMP   *  CAES  *  Mᴼ
ATONINO    *    GOR
DIANO       *   INVIC
TO  *  PIO  *  FELICI
AVG  *  PωS̃  *  MAXI
MO  *  TRIB  *  POT  *  BIS
P  *  P  *  COS  *  PRᴼ  *  CON
SVLA   *   NEPOTI   *   DI
VORVM      *    GORDIA
NORVM        *     M. P.
```

360 kil. *L'Habra.*

370 kil. **St. Denis du Sig.** 6998 inhab. The town is built on the right bank of the *Sig*, about 500 yards from the railway station, in the middle of a large and fertile plain. The streets and squares are well shaded by trees, running water everywhere abounds, and there are numerous gardens both public and private in the environs; a handsome church has been built, principally by the munificence of two individuals, and there is a civil hospital capable of containing 300 beds.

This district owes its fertility entirely to artificial irrigation. The Turks erected a barrage about 3 kil. S. of the town, at a point where the river is contracted into a narrow channel as it enters the plain. An inundation destroyed this, and the Engineer department commenced a new one in 1853, which was completed and greatly enlarged by the *Ponts et Chausées* in 1858, and which was capable of collecting 3 millions cubic mètres of water, and of irrigating a surface of 2000 hectares of land in winter and 800 in summer. This was sufficient in ordinary times, but in years of drought when more water was required it frequently failed, so it was determined to build a much larger one, 10 kil. higher up the stream. This was successfully accomplished; it contained 18 millions cubic mètres of water, and was filled for the first time during the winter of 1884-85. Some idea may be formed of the volume of water thus stored up, by imagining an acre of land piled up

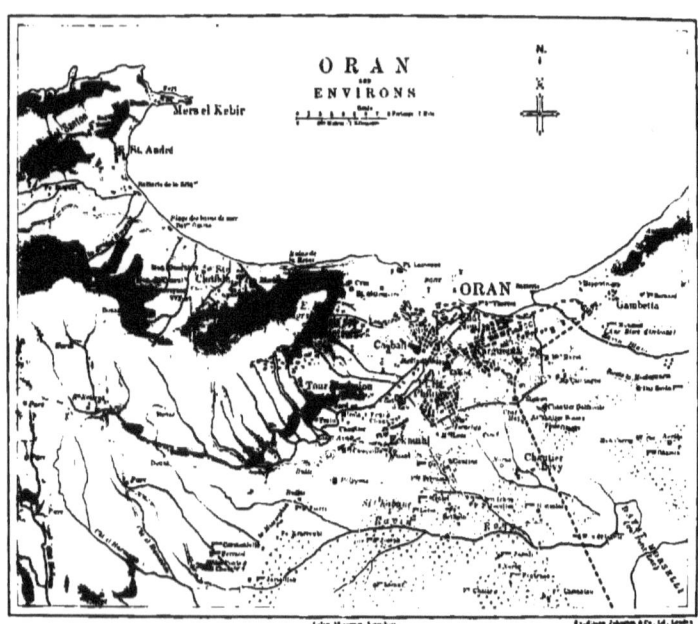

with water to the height of Mont Blanc! The writer was standing on the lower barrage on the 8th February 1885, at 5 P.M., when the upper one gave way; in a wonderfully short time the whole country was submerged; the smaller barrage went also; the water stood to a depth of 2½ mètres in some parts of the town of Sig. All bridges were destroyed, and the rich and flourishing gardens and farms in the vicinity were almost obliterated. Had this happened during the night, as was the case at Perrégaux two years previously, the loss of life must have been terrible; as it was, people were warned in time and not more than seven lives were lost. This also has been restored. The Union du Sig, at about 2 m. from St. Denis, is an agricultural association, of which, however, one of the principal objects has not been realised—the association of capital and labour. It is worked by a company having its seat at Paris.

The Habra and the Sig unite to the N. of this place in a marsh, and subsequently reach the sea under the name of Oued Macta, at a little bay between Arzeu and Mostaganem (see Rte. 26).

376 kil. *L'Ongasse.*

381 kil. *La Mare d'eau.* These are two small villages, the latter near the forest of *Moulaï Ismaïl*, where Don Alvarez de Bezan was signally defeated in 1701, and where six years later the Moroccan chief, Moulaï Ismaïl, had his army almost entirely destroyed.

395 kil. *Sainte-Barbe de Tlélat.* 1170 inhab. A village on the bank of the stream called *Le Tlélat*, at the extremity of the plain of the same name. The country round is watered to a certain extent by a small barrage on the Tlélat. This is the terminus of the "Ouest Algérien" Railway (see Rte. 25).

404 kil. *L'Arbal*, more correctly *Ghabal*, a village situated about 7 m. from the station which bears its name. Numerous Roman ruins in the vicinity. It was probably the Roman *ad Regias.*

411 kil. *Valmy.* Created in 1848. 640 inhab.

416 kil. *La Senia*, a pretty village of 484 inhab. Junction of line to Aïn-Temouchent.

421 kil. KARGUENTAH (ORAN).

CITY OF ORAN.

Capital of the province, residence of General Commandant, and of the General commanding subdivision, Intendance Divisionnaire, Préfet and Bishop.] Population of the city and suburbs:—

French . . . 18,247
Jews . . . 3,617
Mohammedans . 9,084
Spaniards . . 22,172
Other nationalities . 6,257

Total   59,377

Oran is not one of the Algerian towns which can claim a high antiquity; for although some writers attempt to identify it with the Portus Magnus or Quiza of the Romans, the evidence is but vague; and no traces of that nation's occupation have been found here, with the exception of a few coins.

It appears to have been founded in the beginning of the 10th century by two Arab merchants from Spain, who, frequenting this coast for purposes of commerce, obtained leave from the dominant tribe to form a small settlement there. They called it "Wahran," meaning "a ravine"; and it remained, until the date of the Spanish conquest, merely a village beside the stream, with a small harbour, and a fortification on the shore. The little town soon became, however, of some importance on account of its exports, and frequently changed masters. The original founders were driven out in 909, after holding it for seven years in the name of the caliphs of Spain; and after being several times burnt and rebuilt by the contending tribes, the town fell into the hands of the Almoahides, in the middle of the 12th century. These held it until their overthrow in the year 1270, by the tribe of the Ben-Zian, or Zianides, after which Oran became a part of the new kingdom of Tlemçen. It maintained, however, a considerable independence, deriving power from the importance of its commerce with Italy; and appointed its own governor, simply paying customs to Tlemçen.

Being one of the nearest ports to Spain, Oran had always an intimate connection with the Moors in that country; and received fresh inhabitants as the Mohammedans retreated before the conquests of the Christians. About this period Moulaï ben-Hassan, one of the last Moorish kings of Granada, took refuge here for a time, when driven from his kingdom by dissensions with his son and reverses in the wars with Castile; and in A.D. 1500, on the final triumph of the Cross over the Crescent in the Peninsula, the expelled Moors, although at first received with but little hospitality, settled here in great numbers; and under their influence the export trade of the town gave place almost entirely to the pursuit of piracy.

The exiles did not remain long unmolested in their new home. Ferdinand the Catholic turned his thoughts to the extirpation of these dangerous neighbours; and in the year 1505, through the persuasions of Cardinal Ximenes, despatched a force, under the command of Don Diego de Cordoba, against Mersa-el-Kebir. The king himself lacked funds for the enterprise, but these were supplied by the Cardinal; and the expedition, in consequence, gained the name of the "Crusade of Ximenes de Cisneros," and was regarded as a holy war, all who fought in it having indulgence from certain fast-days for the remainder of their lives. The port was soon overcome; and in 1509 another fleet sailed from Carthagena led by the Cardinal himself, and, assisted by land forces from Mersa-el-Kebir, took possession of Oran.

The Spaniards had now a firm footing in Africa; but they did not extend their advantages, contenting themselves with fortifying Oran, converting its mosques into churches, and appropriating its treasure to Christian uses: besides massacring its inhabitants and introducing the Holy Inquisition.

In the year 1519 the Turks, led by the pirate Barbarossa, attempted to take possession of the town; but they were defeated by the governor, the Marquis of Gomarez, with great loss. The Spaniards found their settlement at Oran a barren and expensive honour, and at one time, before the battle of Lepanto in 1574, thought of abandoning it, when a change of fortune in Europe enabled them to give more attention to Africa. They could not, however, resist the increasing conquests of the Turks, who, having overthrown the native kingdom of Tlemçen, consolidated their power throughout the Barbary states, and deprived Spain of the tribute it had received from the neighbouring tribes. During the next century they watched the Christians jealously; and having driven them from all the small places over which they had obtained sway, waited until an opportunity should offer to take possession of Oran itself.

In the year 1700 Philip V succeeded to the throne of Spain; and the civil war which ensued between him and the Archduke Charles prevented him from sending succour to Oran when it was attacked in 1708, by the Bey of the province, under orders from Algiers. After a brave but hopeless defence, the garrison was obliged to capitulate, and Oran became the chief town of the Beylick.

Spain could not quietly acquiesce in this disgrace; and after tranquillity was restored in Europe by the Peace of Utrecht, Philip despatched a fleet, which, in 1732, regained possession of the town. The garrison, being now more than ever subjected to attacks from the Turks, was considerably increased, and succeeded in holding their difficult and somewhat useless position until 1790, when a fearful earthquake, which continued for several days, almost annihilated the place; and while it was yet suffering from the loss of fortifications, munitions of war, and a third part of its garrison, it was attacked by the Bey of Mascara. Nevertheless, with reinforcements from Spain the Christians succeeded in defending it until the middle of 1791, at which time a treaty of commerce between the regency of Algiers and the Spanish government was entered into and enabled Oran to make an honourable capitulation. In March 1792 the Spaniards finally quitted Africa, carrying with them their arms, but leaving standing such of the fortifications as the earthquake had spared.

For the next forty years Oran was merely an unimportant town of the Beylick of that name, and was rebuilt and repopulated chiefly by Jews and Arabs; but the government was not such as to encourage either commerce or industry. The Beys followed each other in quick succession, generally meeting with violent deaths; they perished by poison or pestilence, or died upon the field of battle while levying tribute from rebellious tribes; and some were executed by their masters at Algiers for misappropriation of the levied tribute. They indulged in every form of tyranny and vicious pleasure; and when the French took possession of Algiers in 1830, Hassan, the last Bey of Oran, immediately offered them his submission, and was speedily shipped off to Syria.

For a short time the Beylick was given by Marshal Clauzel to Sidi Ahmed, a prince of Tunis; but the Marshal's policy not being approved by the Home Government, Oran was occupied in 1831; and since that time the French have remained undisturbed masters of the town, although the desultory war with the neighbouring tribes, and especially with Abd-el-Kader, was continued until the year 1847.

The town of Oran is situated at the head of the gulf of the same name, about 600 m. S. of Marseilles, and 220 m. E. of Gibraltar. Like Algiers, it is triangular in form, and presents a striking aspect from the sea, rising on the steep slope of the *Djebel Murdjadjo*.

High above the town, on the summit of this ridge, stands the *Fort of Santa Cruz*; and a little lower down that of *St. Grégoire*. The coast, from Cape Falcon on the W., is partly flat and partly rocky. Cape Ferrat on the E. is rocky and precipitous, the cliffs around the last-named headland rising more than 1000 ft. above the water; and the bay is fully exposed towards the N.; but the small fortified promontory of *Mersa-el-Kebir*, jutting out into the sea about 2 m. to the W., forms at all times a secure and excellent harbour. At the extremity of the point is a lighthouse.

Oran has two harbours: the old or inner one is small but commodious, with an area of 10 acres; the new or outer one has 60 acres, with 1200 yds. of breakwater, and 328 yds. of quays; they are capable of containing a considerable number of vessels of the largest size.

A considerable trade is carried on between Oran and England in alfa fibre and cereals, wine and marbles. The exports from Oran are about on a par with those from Algiers.

In 1792 Spanish Oran was almost destroyed by an earthquake, and the modern city is entirely French in character. It has undergone an entire transformation of late. The old portion, built low down in the ravines, and around the harbour, still remains unchanged, but an entirely new quarter has arisen on the breezy heights towards the E. This was rendered possible by the destruction of the old ramparts, and the construction of new defensive works at a much greater distance from the town. The highest part is the *Place d'Armes*, a handsome square with a garden in the centre, and an immense *Mairie* occupying the entire eastern side; this is very ornate, but it would have been finer had a scarcity of funds not compelled the municipality to suppress the upper story. From the E. runs the *Boulevard Nationale*, in the direction of the *Porte de Mascara*; in it is situated a new and imposing *Jewish Synagogue*. The pleasantly-shaded Promenade de l'Étang is the most popular place of resort. It has a splendid view of the sea, port and gulf. The military band of the garrison sometimes plays here.

Churches and Mosques. These are not very remarkable. The most important is the *Cathedral of St. Louis*, in the Place de l'Église. This was formerly a chapel belonging to a convent of monks of the order of St. Bernard; and afterwards, about 1710, was turned into a synagogue, and was used as such for more than twenty years. The present building was erected in 1839, under M. Dupont as architect. A stone, on which the arms of Cardinal Ximenes are carved, was found in the débris of the old Spanish church, and now forms the keystone of the arch in front of the choir. On the vaulted roof of the latter is a fresco of the landing of St. Louis at Tunis, painted by M. St. Pierre. The site of the ancient chapel is at the back of the choir; and a small portion of the walls of the original building are incorporated in those of the modern church.

The *Church of St. André*, in the Place des Carrières, is a small edifice, formerly a mosque, possessing nothing worthy of particular notice.

The *Église de la Mosquée* is in Karaguentah, of which it is the parish church.

The old Jesuit school and chapel has been appropriated by the municipality, and will be turned into a secular school for girls; a large Lycée is being built for boys, and there is an excellent girls' school kept by the *Sœurs Trinitaires*.

The *Grand Mosque*, in the Rue Philippe, is entered by a porch decorated and restored by M. de Sorbier. At the entrance of the mosque itself stands a white marble fountain said to have been originally brought from Spain, at a cost of 5000 f. The interior consists of a large dome, supported on low columns, and destitute of ornament or decoration. This mosque was founded to commemorate the expulsion of the Spaniards from Oran, with the money procured from the ransom of the Christian slaves. There is a pretty octagonal minaret attached to this building.

The only other mosque of any importance is that of *Sidi el-Houari*, below the Kasba; it is held in great veneration by the Arabs; part of it has been taken by the French as a military store.

The *Theatre*, situated near the Promenade de l'Étang, is very small, although commodiously arranged. It can accommodate only about 700 persons. A French company plays during the winter months, and in summer performances in Spanish are generally given by a company from Carthagena or elsewhere.

A *Museum* has been formed under the auspices of the *Société de Géographie et d'Archéologie*, which is temporarily placed in one of the wards of the old civil hospital; it is particularly intended to collect there all the antiquities found in the department. An excellent beginning has been made, the most interesting objects being the fine mosaics from St. Leu, which gave a clue to the re-discovery of the lost Numidian marbles.

The *Château Neuf*, built by the Spaniards, is the citadel. It is the residence of the general commanding the division, who occupies that portion of the building which was in former times the palace of the Beys. The other part of it is used as a barrack.

The *Château Vieux*, or *Kasba*, was the ancient citadel of Oran, and was several times surrendered to foreign troops; in 1509, to the army of Ximenes; in 1708, to Mustafa ben-Youssef; and again, in 1732, to the troops of the Duc de Montemar. Like the Château Neuf, it consisted of two parts, the higher being the residence of the Spanish Commanders, and comprising a chapel, among many other buildings; and the lower containing the arsenal and barracks. The upper part of the Kasba was entirely destroyed by the earthquake of 1790; but the lower part is still used as a barrack and military prison; the civil prison is at Karaguentah, and capable of containing 300 persons.

Oran is strongly fortified. The *Fort de la Moune* is at the western extremity of the harbour. *Fort St. André*, in the centre of the town, formerly mounted 36 guns. Beyond Fort St. André is *Fort St. Philippe*, built to replace the old Castle of the Saints, called in Spanish "*Castillo de los Santos*"; and above, on the heights of the *Pic d'Aidour*, more than 1000 ft. above the sea, stands the *Fort Santa Cruz*. The view from this fort is magnificent. A little chapel has been erected just below, to commemorate the cholera year of 1849; this subsequently had a tower added, surmounted by a colossal statue of the Virgin, a replica of that of Notre Dame de la Garde at Marseilles; it is styled *Nôtre Dame de la Salut de Santa Cruz*. On the height above *Mers-el-Kebir* is a fort armed with two 14-ton guns, which commands the coast on both sides, and crosses fire with a similar work at the *Point du Ravin blanc*, to the E. of the town. Notwithstanding its apparently impregnable position it was taken by assault in 1708.

There is a subterranean communication between all the forts, the galleries passing underneath the town, mounting and descending the various hills. Permission can be obtained to visit these by application to the Colonel of Engineers.

The walls which surround the city contain 9 gates, viz.—

Porte de Mers-el-Kebir; Porte de Santon; Porte du Ravin; Porte de Tlemçen; Porte Sidi Charmi; Porte du Cimetière; Porte de Mascara; Porte de Mostaganem, and *Porte de l'Abattoir*.

Among the public buildings not yet enumerated should be mentioned the new *Military Hospital*, adjoining the Cathedral of St. Louis, an imposing edifice, capable of accommodating 1400 men.

The Civil Hospital is on the high ground at Karaguentah, holding 600 patients.

In the Place de l'Hôpital, just opposite the tunnel communicating with the Rue de l'Arsenal, is a house now used as military quarters, once the *Inquisition*; an inscription let into the wall states that it was built at the expense of the State in 1772.

A visit should be paid to the negro quarter, peopled by nearly 3000 of that race, and Arabs.

Oran is well supplied with water. The stream *Ras-el-Aïn*, which rises about a kil. beyond the walls, is brought by means of an underground tunnel into the town. A further supply has been brought from the fine spring at Brédéah, at 25 kil. on the road from Oran to Temouchent.

ENVIRONS OF ORAN.

7 kil. **La Senia**, a small village, the inhabitants of which are all employed in agriculture, and in the cultivation of vegetables and fruit, which are sent to Oran, and thence shipped to various foreign ports. It is approached through an avenue of mulberry-trees, and is worth visiting, although it contains nothing of special interest. The population is 484.

8 kil. **Mers-el-Kebir**. A road, cut out of the solid rock for a great part of its length, in one place passing through a tunnel 50 yards long, connects this port with Oran.

2 kil. Underneath the road at this point is a curious cave, into which a boat can enter in smooth weather; it is frequented by seals, and is called *la Grotte des Veaux Marins*.

3 kil. from Oran is a small bathing-establishment called **Les Bains de la Reine**, erected at the source of a warm mineral spring. It is so called after Isabella the Catholic, who in the 16th century brought her infant daughter to this place for the sake of these waters. The spring rises in a cavern or narrow cleft in the rock, about 20 ft. in length by 10 ft. in height. The temperature is about 85 Fahr., and the water contains large quantities of salt and magnesia. There are several separate baths, as well as the "Piscine," or bathing-place for the poorer classes. They are said to be peculiarly efficacious in cases of rheumatism. There is a restaurant attached to the establishment, where bedrooms also may be obtained.

A short distance beyond the Bains de la Reine, the road crosses a ravine called the *Salto del Cavallo*, and farther passes the villages of *Saint André*, chiefly inhabited by fishermen and sailors ; *Sainte Clotilde*, 200 inhab., principally occupied in the cultivation of vines ; and *Saint Gérome*, an agricultural village. Beyond is **Mers-el-Kebir.**

The fort, said to occupy the site of one built by the Romans, was taken by the Spaniards under Don Diego de Cordoba in 1505. Previous to this it had been one of the strongholds of the pirates who infested this coast, and were the terror of the neighbouring countries. In 1708 the Turks carried it by assault, and massacred the garrison to the number of 300. They in their turn had to surrender to the Count de Montemar in July 1732, after a sanguinary struggle, a few days after the fall of Oran. In 1791 the Turks, for the second time, became masters of Mers-el-Kebir; and at length, after various vicissitudes, it fell into the hands of the French. It occupies the extremity of the rocky promontory before described as forming a safe harbour in the most tempestuous weather. The fountain at the entrance is surmounted by the arms of Ferdinand of Arragon. It now contains the convict establishment. On the extremity of the point is a lighthouse with a fixed white light, visible at a distance of 8 m.

A new fort, intended to command the harbour and existing fort, has been constructed on the summit of the hill above.

The *Village* is unimportant, but picturesquely situated on the western side of the fort.

Aïn-et-Turk, 8 kil. beyond Mers-el-Kebir, is a pretty village, consisting principally of two long streets sloping down to the sea, and bordered by houses, nearly all of which stand in gardens. The inhabitants are occupied in agriculture, and in raising cattle. Vines are grown to a considerable extent around this place. Pop. 593.

Bou-Sfer, 6 kil. from Aïn-et-Turk, is another village on the margin of the plain "*des Andalouses.*" As at Aïn-et-Turk, agriculture gives employment to nearly all the population, which amounts to 851.

At 25 kil. E. of Oran is the Arab village of **Kristel,** under the Mountain of Lions, where there are some interesting caves. There is no carriage-road, but a mule-path, and one can go by a fishing-boat.

Kristel has abundance of water, and it is probable that one day Arzeu may be supplied thence. This will be a necessity if it is ever to rival Oran as a commercial depôt.

ROUTE 11.

Philippeville to Constantine by Railway.

Kil.		Kil.
..	Philippeville, Port, to	87
2	Philippeville, Goods Stat.	85
10	Saf-saf	77
19	St. Charles	66
29	Robertville	58
37	El-Arrouch	50
46	Col des Oliviers	41
60	Condé Smendou	27
73	Bizot	14
80	Hamma	7
87	Constantine	..

This line, belonging to the P.L.M. Company, is a triumph of engineering, having to ascend from the sea to the height of 2093 ft. (level of Constantine), and to cross a chain of mountains still higher, presenting difficulties that appeared almost insurmountable to the construction even of a road.

On leaving the station the railway enters a tunnel beneath the Djebel Abdouna, on the flanks of which are the barracks, etc., and then ascends the wide, richly-cultivated valley of the Oued Saf-saf.

2 kil. *Philippeville.* Goods stat.

10 kil. *Saf-saf.*

19 kil. *Saint Charles.* Here the road to Jemmapes and Bône diverges from that to Constantine. Diligences call at the station. The village (147 inhab.) is situated in a fertile district.

29 kil. *Robertville.* 579 inhabit.

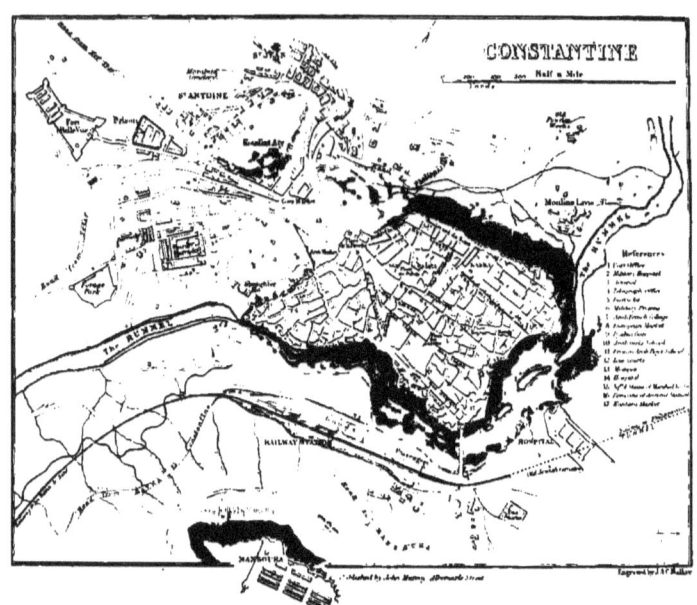

The corn-lands are extensive and rich. They gradually become scantier as the railway ascends to

46 kil. *Col des Oliviers.* Here the train waits 15 min. It is a narrow col between the valley of the *Oued el-Khamza* on the W., and that of *El-Arrouch* on the E., across which one sees the twin peaks of *Djebel Toumiet*, "Les deux Mamelles" (2931 ft.) After leaving the station the railway ascends the mountain of *El-Kantour* by a series of curves, following to a great extent the old post road. The views looking back are very striking. The previous course of the line is seen far below, and the beautiful valley of *El-Arrouch* is spread out towards the N. till the highest point is passed, after which the railway descends to

60 kil. *Condé Smendou.* 1570 inhab. After passing through a tunnel under the village, the valley of the *Oued Smendou* is followed as far as *Aioun Saad*, where it is quitted for one of its affluents. This is followed to the top of a col, after passing which an affluent of the Roummel is followed to

73 kil. *Bizot.* 237 inhab. A village named after an engineer officer killed at Sebastopol. It is built on a spot called *El-Hadjar*, "The Stones." Water is scarce, and attempts to sink an Artesian well having failed, it has been brought from a distance by an aqueduct. The land, however, is fertile, and vines and fruit-trees flourish. On leaving it the railway sweeps round the valley, and the beautiful oasis, for such it is, of *El-Hamma* comes into view. Several hot springs here burst from the limestone strata, producing the most luxuriant vegetation, whose varied colours contrast most strikingly with the gray of the limestone and the uniform green of the corn-lands. Every kind of tree grows luxuriantly; among them the date-palm, the fig, and the pomegranate. From an inscription, found here in 1857, we learn that in the time of the Romans it bore the name of Azimacia.

80 kil. *El-Hamma* stat.

In a few minutes Constantine comes into view; but unfortunately the full grandeur of its site can scarcely be appreciated from the railway, which is carried of necessity along the limestone ridge above the city; so that the marvellous beauty of its position, enthroned on an isolated pedestal of rock, can hardly be realised.

A tunnel under Djebel Meçid, N. of the city, is passed, and the station, on a plateau at the foot of Mansoura, is reached.

87 kil. **Constantine.** 31,726 inhab. Capital of the province; residence of general commanding, of préfet, bishop, and other high functionaries.

The remarkable situation of this city has pointed it out from the earliest times as an important fortress, and as one of the natural capitals of a country which has been the scene of perpetual wars and revolutions. Its ancient name was *Kerth* or *Cirta*, and it was the seat of the Massessylian kings, partaking of the fortune of its neighbour, Carthage.

Narva, whose wife was sister to Hannibal, was king in B.C. 230. He was succeeded by Syphax, who had obtained the hand of Sophonisba, daughter of Hasdrubal; but Massinissa, king of the Massylians, who was also in love with her, took advantage of the breaking out of the Second Punic War to ally himself to Scipio Africanus, and by his help deposed Syphax, and obtained possession of Cirta and of Sophonisba, B.C. 202. Scipio having demanded her as a prisoner of the Roman senate, Massinissa sent her a dose of poison, which she instantly drank, merely remarking that she would have died with more honour had she not wedded at her funeral.

Massinissa reigned at Cirta until the breaking out of the Third Punic War, which his secret alliance with Rome had done much to foment; and died B.C. 148, leaving his throne to his son Micipsa.

In his division of the kingdom, Micipsa left Cirta to his son Adherbal, who was besieged and killed there by Jugurtha, B.C. 112.

This was the commencement of the Jugurthine War, during the beginning of which the Numidian prince held his capital against the Romans, until in B.C. 109 Metullus and Marius took the command in Africa, and he was obliged to fly to more distant parts of his kingdom. The Romans then occupied Cirta, and from that stronghold carried on the war, until Jugurtha was betrayed to them, B.C. 106. The kingdom was shortly after given to Juba, who took the side of Pompey in his struggles with Julius Cæsar; and in B.C. 49 was able to defeat a Roman army.

In B.C. 46, on the fall of the party of Pompey, after the death of Cato, Juba surrendered Cirta to the allies of Cæsar; and after it had been much beautified and honoured with the name of "Cirta Julia," it remained the seat of a Roman colony until A.D. 304.

At that time Alexander, the Numidian peasant, raised a revolt against the Empire, and holding Cirta against the Romans, it was taken by them and destroyed after a siege; but being once more restored in the year 313, it then changed its ancient name for that of Constantina.

Cirta was no less celebrated in ecclesiastical than in profane history. In 257 St. Cyprian was exiled here; in 305 Secundus, primate of Numidia, caused a council to assemble within its walls to examine into the case of the *traitors*, or those who surrendered their church ornaments and sacred books during his persecution, and this assembly was the indirect cause of the Donatist schism. Sylvain, primate of Africa, held a second council here in 412, at which St. Augustine assisted. The acts were lost.

In the time of St. Augustine the bishop of this place was a Donatist; and to this fact, as well as to its natural strength, it is perhaps owing that when Genseric and his Vandals overran the country, the city escaped destruction; and Belisarius, after he had driven out the barbarians, found the Roman buildings still intact. Additional works seem to have been undertaken at this time, as the aqueduct, part of which still remains, is said to date from the time of Justinian.

Constantina was not, however, at any time as large and flourishing as Cirta had been, whose palmiest-days were in the peaceful reign of Micipsa; and now with the Arab invasion, in the middle of the 7th century, we come to its darkest period. It became a prey to the various Arab dynasties which disputed the government of the country; and in successive sieges its ancient monuments were destroyed, although not effaced, as scattered Roman ruins covered the ground at the time of the French occupation, and have only disappeared in consequence of their improvements.

The city preserved its Latin name, and was at times the capital of the Arabs; but it seems to have been of little importance to them, and for a hundred years, until the end of the 15th century, governed itself as a Republic.

It was entirely fallen from its ancient grandeur when the Turks became masters of the country; but its inhabitants did not submit tamely to their rule; and after conquering and losing it several times, they built a fort adjoining the city in 1629, and in 1640 appointed a Bey for the province, who had his headquarters at Constantine.

Entirely subject to the Dey of Algiers, and called to give an account to him every four months, the government of those Beys was very insecure; and only one name among them especially stands forth, that of Salah Bey, who came into power about 1771, and was distinguished for his wise government for more than twenty years. To him are attributed most of the Mohammedan buildings, and especially the restoration of "El-Kantara," the bridge which brought the road and the aqueduct into the city.

This ambitious work raised suspicions in Algiers that he intended to make himself independent; and the Dey sent another governor to replace him, who besieged the place and forced Salah Bey to submit. He consented to come forth on condition that he might pass through the besiegers holding the burnous of one of the Arab chiefs, a recognised sign of safe-conduct; but no sooner had they reached the street than the Arab wrenched away his cloak, and Salah was surrounded by the soldiers and strangled.

To him succeeded a list of nearly twenty Beys in a little over thirty years, their short, stormy administrations being finished generally by the bow-string, poison, or the sword. But in 1826 there arose a rival to the Algerine power in Hadj-Ahmed, who, after the fall of Algiers, maintained himself independently in Constantine.

He led his troops against the French in 1830, and fought bravely at Algiers, retiring before the capitulation was signed. The French decreed his deposition in December of the same year, but quite ineffectually, as Ahmed took the title of Pacha, which was ratified by the Porte; and he retained the sovereignty of Constantine until 1837.

His reign was marked by cruelties and extortions of every kind; but his people rallied round him against the French, and made a desperate defence of their city. He was assisted in the government by a Kabyle named Ben-Aïssa, a man of low origin, but of great power; and during the French sieges Hadj-Ahmed remained outside the town with his desert troops, while Ben Aïssa took command within the walls.

The first French expedition against Constantine was made in November 1836, under Marshal Clauzel, an officer of great ability, but who, on this occasion, committed the grievous fault of underrating his enemy, and trusting too much to the assurance that had been made to him that no serious resistance would be offered.

The Marshal was accompanied by H.R.H. the Duc de Nemours, to whom was attached as A.D.C. a young captain of tat-Major, now Marshal de MacMahon. The commandant, subsequently General Youssef, who had rather prematurely been named Bey of Constantine, was also of the party. The army, consisting of 8776 men, left Bône on the 13th November and arrived before Constantine on the 21st, without having encountered any opposition, but much exhausted by fatigue and privation. The assault was made on the night of the 23d by the bridge of El-Kantara, but was repulsed on all sides with frightful loss; and the Marshal, owing to the inclemency of the season and the impossibility of revictualling his army, was compelled to retreat to Bône, where he arrived on the 1st of December, the whole army being in the last stage of exhaustion. The corps under his command was dissolved, and the Marshal himself relieved of command, and recalled to Paris.

In the following year a second expedition was organised, consisting of 10,000 men, under command of the new Governor-General Damrémont. It was organised in four brigades, the first of which was commanded by the Duc de Nemours, and arrived before Constantine on the 6th of October 1837. Shortly after fire was opened General Damrémont was killed when examining the breach; the command was taken by General Valée, the commandant of artillery, and on the following day the assault took place. Great losses were sustained on both sides, and many of the inhabitants, in attempting to escape by means of cords into the ravines around, were dashed to pieces.

No traveller can fail to be deeply impressed by the magnificence of the situation of Constantine, whose grandeur and picturesque beauty are probably unsurpassed by that of any city in the world; and it can be truly said to deserve all the praise that has been so lavishly bestowed on it by writers on Algeria.

Nature seems to have constructed it entirely with a view to defence and picturesque effect. It occupies the summit of a plateau of rock, nearly quadrilateral in shape, the faces corresponding to the cardinal points, and its surface sloping from N. to S. Its sides rise perpendicularly nearly 1000 ft. from the bed of the river Roummel,[1] which surrounds it on the

[1] The Roummel below Constantine becomes the *Oued el-Kebir*, the ancient *Ampsaga* or *Ampsagas* which formed the boundary between the kingdoms of the Massessylians to the W.

N. and E., and it is connected on the W. side only by an isthmus with the mainland. The deep ravine, through which the Roummel flows, varies in breadth from about 200 ft. on the S.E. side, to nearly double that distance opposite the Kasba; and is spanned on the N.E. by four natural arches of rock, about 200 ft. above the stream, one of which serves as the foundation for the bridge of *El-Kantara*.

On the N.W. side the precipices are the highest; and it is looking towards this point from the plain of the *Hamma* that the most splendid view of the city is obtained. To the N.E. and S.E. the heights of *Mansoura* and *Sidi M'cid* command the city. On the last-named hill stood a ruined koubba of the saint whose name it bears. The isthmus before mentioned connects Constantine with the hill of *Koudiat-Ati*.

The situation of Constantine, however, cannot be thoroughly appreciated unless a walk be taken round the outside of the city, and we would advise the traveller to postpone his exploration of the streets until this has been done.

We will suppose him to leave the city by the Place de la Brèche, where formerly stood the Porte Valée, occupying nearly the same place as the older Bab el-Oued. In front was the hill of Koudiat-Ati, where the French storming batteries were erected Oct. 1837. The ground is now (1889) being levelled, the hill cut away, and a large plateau in course of construction, which will become the site of a new faubourg. Here is the corn-market, between the suburbs of St. Jean to the W. and St. Antoine to the E. In front of it are two squares planted with trees. That on the left is a garden, in the centre of which is a bronze statue of Marshal Valée; that to the right contains fragments of Roman antiquities—columns, capitals, inscriptions, too bulky to be placed in the Museum.

and the Massylians to the E. At the sources of the Bou Merzoug, one of its affluents S. of Constantine, M. Cherbonneau found an inscription containing the words CAPVT AMSAGÆ.

A path to the left, close under the wall, descends through a camp of Arabs, busily engaged in various trades, to the gate *Bab-el-Djabia* (Gate of the Reservoir), so called because in former days there was a reservoir here, fed by the aqueduct of Koudiat-Ati. It is a very curious Arab structure, set at right angles to the wall, which here is built of large blocks of stone without mortar, probably Roman, and the gate is itself, in its lower part at least, of the same period.

At the right of it is a curious inscription in Greek and Latin, as follows:—

Π ʻΙΟΥΛΙωΙ ʻΓΕΜΙΝΙωΙ

ΜΑΡΚΙΑΝωΙ ʻΠΡΕϹΒΕΥΤΗΙ ʻ

ϹΕΒΑϹΤωΝ ʻΑΝΤΙϹΤΡΑΤΗΓωΙ

ΥΠΑΤωΙ ʻΑΔΡΗΝωΝ ʻΠΟΛΙϹ ʻΗ

ΤΗϹ ʻΑΡΑΒΙΑϹ ʻΔΙΑ ʻΔΑΜΑϹΕΟΥϹ

ΚΟΙΑΦΟΥ ʻΠΡΕϹΒΕΥΤΗ ꞉ ʻ
+
ΑΔΡΑΗΝωΝ ʻΕΠΑΡΧΕΙΑϹ

ΑΡΑΒΙΑϹ

TRANSLATA AB VRBE SECVN
DVM VOLVNTATEM MARCIA
NI TESTAMENTO SIGNIFICAT
D   D

The translation of the Greek inscription is as follows:—

"To Publius Julius Geminius Marcianus, chief officer of the Augustan (legionaries), propractor, (pro)-consul, the township of the Adreni of Arabia (erected this memorial) by the hands of Damases Koiaphas, (as being) chief of the Adraëni in the province of Arabia."

Another inscription mentioning the same offices is let into the wall of the Kasba (*q.v.*)

Above the block containing this inscription is a cipus bearing a Latin inscription, which forms the impost of the arch.

A steep path descends from the gate to the Roummel, passing by some masses of Roman rubble, of which the use has now been forgotten. Roman masonry is seen at intervals in the city walls. There was once a gate here, *Bab-Heminccha* (Gate of the Tunnel), so called because it opened a covered way leading down to the river, so that the inhabitants might get water without danger from assailants. On the left bank of the Roummel, close to the cliff, is the *slaughter-house*; a little higher up, on the same side, the *Bardo*, a large ugly building formerly used as barracks for the Turkish cavalry, and now for the Spahis. About a mile higher up the stream, on the Oued Merzoug, just above its junction with the Roummel, are the remains of the Roman aqueduct which spanned the valley between Djebel Guerioun and Koudiat-Ati. Five arches remain, about 60 ft. high. They are built of huge blocks of limestone without mortar; and to ensure additional security, the bases of the piers are considerably broader than the piers themselves, narrowing gradually as they ascend. There is a tradition that the aqueduct was constructed by Justinian.

Returning to the *Abattoir*, a bridge crosses the Roummel under the rock called *Sidi Rached*, the most southern point of the cliff on which Constantine is built. It is said that the Turks used to throw suspected or faithless wives from the top of this rock. There are the remains of a fine Roman tower on its top. Here is the beginning of the grand gorge which extends round the E. and N. sides of the city. The cliffs are scarcely more than 15 ft. apart in this place.

After crossing the bridge a short tunnel is traversed, and a warm spring reached. The water is collected into cisterns and used for washing. A few yards farther on, beyond a quarry, is the place assigned by tradition to the martyrdom of SS. Marius and Jacobus, who perished here in A.D. 289. The inscription recording the event is rudely carved on the face of the rock, and was apparently the composition of an illiterate person; but it has been so much damaged by time and neglect that it will soon be quite illegible. It ran as follows:—

    IHI . NON SEPT . PASSIONE MARTYR
    ORVM HORTENSIVM MARIANI ET
    IACOBI ATI IAPINRVSTICI CRISPI
    TAT | MELTVNI DICTOR I SILBANI EGIP
    TII SCI DI MEMORAMINI IN CONSPECTV ANI
    CVORVM NOMINA SCITIS QVI FECIT IN XV.
    ✠

This has been thought to mean—

"Quarto nonas Septembres passione martyrorum hortensium Mariani et Jacobi, Dati, Japini, Rustici, Crispi, Tati, Meltuni, Victoris, Silvani, Egiptii, Sancti diei (?). Memoramini in conspectu Domini. Quorum nomina scitis qui fecit indictione quinta decimâ."

Hence the path ascends to the hill *Mansoura*, whence a most interesting view is obtained, as the traveller walks northward, of the Arab quarter and its tanneries, which are built in the most perilous positions, on the very edge of the precipice. The steep cliffs afford nesting places to numbers of jackdaws, hawks, and falcons; while storks build upon the housetops. Remains of two Roman bridges are to be seen low down in the ravine. They probably afforded a means of access to the suburb which undoubtedly covered the plateau of Mansoura at that time. A splendid *Triumphal Arch* was still standing here in 1724; it perhaps formed a part of the decorations of the *Hippodrome*, whose remains were discovered and destroyed when the railway station was built. Shaw, who saw it in the year above mentioned, says: "Among the ruins to the S.W. of the bridge we have the greatest part of a triumphal arch called Cassir Goulah, or the *Castle* (as they interpret it) *of the Giant*, consisting of three arches, the middlemost whereof, as usual, is the most spacious. All the mouldings and friezes are curiously embellished with the figures of flowers, battle-axes, and other ornaments. The Corinthian pilasters erected on each side of the grand arch are panelled like the gates of the city, in a style and fashion peculiar to Cirta."

The barracks on the summit of Mansoura are occupied by the Chasseurs d'Afrique; lower down just above the railway station, is the École Normale.

At the N.E. angle of the city was the bridge of El-Kantara. It would appear from the Arab chronicles that the other bridges were destroyed in 1304, when Ben-el-Emir, Kaid of Constantine, revolted against the Emir

Khaled. Enough remains of the Roman works at El-Kantara to merit a detailed description.

Advantage has been taken of one of the natural arches over the Roummel for the foundation of the bridge. Looking at the ruin from the S. side, it will be seen that there were originally three piers, of nearly the same size, and equidistant.

Between the first and second of these, counting from the E., a perfect arch remains. It was double, with a considerable space between the vaults, of which the upper one, built of massive blocks, carried the roadway; the lower one, carefully finished, was merely ornamental. This was evidently the only arch beneath which water passed, as the stream must always have been scanty, and the rocks have no appearance of being waterworn elsewhere. The interval between the second and third piers is walled up. This would seem to have been done nearly at the time of the original construction, for the stones are precisely the same as those used in the piers, and worked in the same way; but the lines of masonry do not exactly correspond. Between the third pier and the rocks there was a half arch, which apparently was filled in like the others, though on the S. side the wall has fallen away completely. A similar half-arch appears to have existed between the first pier and the rocks; but these abut on the pier so closely that it is not easy to make out the construction in this part. Some years ago the writer was still able to trace on the S. side the bas-relief so quaintly described and figured by Shaw "of a lady treading upon two elephants, with a large escallop shell for her canopy. The elephants having their faces turned towards each other, twist their trunks together, and the lady, who appears dressed in her hair, with a close-bodied garment, like the riding-habit of our times, raiseth up her petticoats with her right hand, and looks scornfully upon the city." On a subsequent visit he was unable to find it.

This system of piers and arches supports a level roadway; above which was a second stage, consisting, it is said, of six arches. Of these one pier remains on the E. side, with the arch and half pier between it and the cliff, and a corresponding half pier on the W. The height of the whole structure was nearly 220 ft. above the soil on which its foundations rested, which are themselves 184 ft. above the river; so that the whole was not less than 404 ft. in height.

An excellent description of this arch has been left by El-Bekri, the Arab geographer of the 11th century, who says: "This bridge is of a remarkable structure, its height above the level of the water being about 100 cubits; it is one of the remains of Roman architecture; it is composed of five upper and lower arches which span the valley. Three of these, namely, those to the W., have two stories, as we have said; they are intended for the passage of water, while the upper ones form a communication between the two sides of the ravine. Regarding the others, they abut against the mountain. These arches are supported by piers, which break the violence of the torrent, and are pierced at their summit by small openings. When there are extraordinary floods, which sometimes take place, the water which rises above the top of the piers escapes by means of these orifices. This is, we repeat, one of the most remarkable buildings ever seen."

Peyssonnel, who visited it in 1724, describes it as "a very fine structure, with three rows of arcades, and a height of about 250 ft., but rather narrow, having fallen."

Shaw saw it in 1740; he says it was "indeed a masterpiece of its kind, the gallery and the columns of the arches being adorned with cornices and festoons, ox-heads and garlands. The keystones also of the arches are charged with caducei and other figures."

Bruce also visited it in 1765, and has left two drawings of its actual condition at that period.[1]

Subsequently it was thoroughly restored by Don Bartolommeo, an architect of Menorca, in 1793, during the

[1] "Footsteps of Bruce," p. 49, Pl. IV.

reign of Salah Bey, with materials chiefly obtained from the destruction of other Roman edifices. It stood as he left it till 7 A.M. on 18th March 1857, when the pier of the upper stage nearest to the town suddenly gave way, with the two arches resting upon it. It was found impossible to restore it; the bridge was in consequence battered down with heavy artillery on the 30th of the same month. The substantial modern iron structure was built in 1863; the aqueduct beneath it in 1857.

It was this bridge and gate which were attacked by the French in 1836, under General Clauzel, when they made their first disastrous attempt upon Constantine.

From the E. end of the bridge there is a beautiful view W. through the ravine; at the beginning of which may be seen the remains of the road that afforded access to the city after the destruction of the old bridge. It descended close under Djebel Meçid; then crossed the ravine, and reached the gate close to the W. end of the bridge.

A new road and tunnel have been made (1889) along the right bank of the Roummel, from which superb views are obtained of the ravine, the natural bridges of rock, and the opposite cliff, on which the Kasba stands.

Returning to the bridge of El-Kantara, the traveller should now cross the railway, and ascend Djebel Meçid to the large unfinished building intended for an Arab college, now occupied as a civil hospital, passing on the right the Jewish cemetery. The tombstones are solid blocks, a foot thick, laid upon the ground without fence or distinction of any kind. Leaving the hospital on the left, a path descends the precipitous cliff to the valley of the Roummel. Before doing this, the traveller should, if possible, ascend Djebel Meçid to his right, for the sake of the fine view it affords over Constantine and its neighbourhood. There is a good view also from the rock beyond the hospital, immediately opposite the Kasba. This is reached by a path through the pine plantation.

As the traveller descends into the valley of the Roummel he has before him a most beautiful view over the Hamma and the corn-lands beyond, with high mountains in the distance.

At the bottom of the precipice are the warm baths of Sidi Meçid, much frequented by both Arabs and French. They are beautifully situated in a luxuriant garden. There is one immense semicircular piscine built by the men of the 63d Reg., two smaller ones, and three private bathing-places in the sides of the rock, shut in by doors. The water is beautifully clear, and has a temperature of 86° Fahr. Numerous Roman inscriptions have been found in the vicinity, showing that it was a common custom to have country-houses and gardens here. Two identical ones, 100 paces apart, which have often been quoted, but which the writer has never been able to find, are exceptionally interesting; they are said to be carved in bold letters on the polished surface of the rock, and to contain the words:

LIMIS FVNDI SALLVSTIANI.

Did this actually indicate the limit of the property of Sallust, the great historian and pro-consul, where he was wont to come in his hours of leisure to combine the charms of philosophy with the more material pleasures of this life? He had abundant means of acquiring property during his pro-consulate, and his magnificent house on the Quirinal was enriched with the plunder of Hippo, Kalama, Tagaste, and Cirta.

From the baths of Sidi Meçid a path winds under the cliff, and comes suddenly upon the bed of the Roummel, at a point where the river falls over several ledges of rock in a series of picturesque cascades. Opposite is the perpendicular cliff of the Kasba the Tarpeian rock of the Turkish city 500 ft. above the river. It was over this cliff that upwards of 300 of the inhabitants let themselves down by ropes, to escape the French. Most of them perished miserably. The stream can here be crossed dryshod, when not swollen by rains. A path up its left bank, close to the race that carries water to the flour mills, should be followed for a short distance, for the sake of the view of the natural bridges.

Returning to the mouth of the gorge, a good road winds past the Moulin Lavie, and up the hill to the Place Valée; on the left, close under the cliff called Bordj el-Açous, are the neglected ruins of the **Tomb of the Silversmith** Praecilius, discovered in 1855. It had two stories, both paved with mosaics, and was formerly about 19 ft. long by 10 ft. wide. The exterior had a pavement of mosaic, extending along the length of the façade. In the interior of the lower tomb are niches in the walls for receiving the sarcophagi. One of these, which was removed and opened, was found to contain a perfect skeleton; and on its stone side was a long, but very inaccurate Latin inscription relating to Praecilius, who was a goldsmith or jeweller of Cirta, and died at the age of more than 100 years, after a prosperous and enjoyable life.

The original inscription has been thus translated by Mr. Alexander Graham:—

"Here silently I lie, describing my life in verse. I have enjoyed a good reputation and the greatest of prosperity. Praecilius is my name, a native of Cirta, following the art of a goldsmith. My honesty was extraordinary, and I always stuck to the truth. I was courteous to every one, and never refused to sympathise with others. I was merry and always enjoyed pleasure with my dear friends. After the death of the virtuous Lady Valeria I found life different. As long as I could, I passed an agreeable and holy life. I have becomingly celebrated 100 happy birthdays. But the last day came when I must throw off this mortal coil. While I was alive I made preparation for my death. Fortune, which has smiled upon me, never deserted me one single instant. May she accompany you through life, and may you arrive at the same state as myself. Here I await you. Come!"

Much of the mosaic work has been destroyed, but some of the devices may still be traced. The lower story is built in the rock, but part of the walls and all the roof have disappeared, and the whole place is now in such a filthy condition that it requires a considerable amount of courage to venture on an examination of it.

Beneath the tomb of Praecilius is the **Esplanade de la Brèche**, used as a market-place for the natives.

This walk finished, the traveller would do well to hire a carriage, and drive round the environs. Leaving always by the Place Valée, he should descend to the garden of the **Poudrerie**, an order to see which will be readily granted by the officer commanding the artillery in the Kasba. From this place the best view of the cascade of the Roummel is obtained, and this is perhaps the finest of all the views around Constantine.

Regaining the main road, and following it nearly as far as the Pont d'Aumale, the traveller should take the road to El-Mila, which passes over a smaller iron bridge to the left, and mounts the hills on the left bank of the river. The view looking back to Constantine, with the fertile valley of the Roummel in the foreground, brilliant with every shade of green, is more beautiful than words can describe. 2½ kil. from the junction of the roads is the small oasis of **Salah Bey**.

Even in the times of the Romans this was a favourite summer residence of the inhabitants, and some traces of their villas are still visible amongst the cornfields.

Towards the close of last century Salah Bey conceived the idea of building a palace here. He repaired the cistern containing one of the hot springs which irrigate the place, planted trees and commenced to build a house. Unfortunately he incurred the displeasure of the populace by decapitating a much venerated saint, Si-Mohammed, who attempted to overturn his authority.

M. Cherbonneau relates the legend that the body of the saint was transformed into a crow, which, after much sorrowful croaking, flew at once to the country palace, which it cursed, and then disappeared. The Bey, frightened at the curse, erected a koubba to the memory of the marabout, which he called *Sidi Mohammed el-Ghorab*, signifying "My Lord Mohammed, the Crow."

This koubba still exists, and in an adjacent building are the tombs of some of Salah Bey's family, but the palace was despoiled by Ahmed Bey, and all its ornamental work carried off for the construction of his palace in Constantine.

The traveller should now return to the Place Valée whence he set out; but instead of entering the city he should turn off to the right, descend the hill past the Government Forage Park, cross the Roummel by an iron bridge, visit the Pepinière a little beyond, advance still farther, and, turning to the left, cross the wide sterile plateau of Mansoura, on the top of which is a fortified position containing the cavalry barracks. The view of the city from this point is particularly fine. It is pleasant to observe how successfully this barren hill has been laid out with Aleppo pines; the writer saw it before a single tree was planted, and now it affords a delightfully shady retreat for the inhabitants of the city. The road now descends the hill of Mansoura, and, crossing behind the railway station, enters the city by the bridge of El-Kantara.

From Mansoura a good view is obtained of the highest peak of Djebel Meçid, which commands the city, and which, on that account, has been occupied by a defensive work. The ruins of a Roman fort were found on excavating the foundations; it had 3 distinct *enceintes*, but no cisterns were discovered.

Constantine itself hardly bears out the expectations which will be formed of it when seen from a distance. The town is, as usual in Algeria, a mixture, partly Arab and partly French; and hardly any traces now remain of the splendid city of Cirta, of which it is the successor.

The Arab quarter is quite as curious as that of Algiers; and appears to have been left even more thoroughly unchanged, though becoming every year more circumscribed in extent by French improvements.

The north margin of the plateau is lined by the *Boulevards*, excepting at the northern corner, which is occupied by the Kasba.

Near this point has been erected a new Prefecture, from which there is a very extensive view of the plain below.

The lower part of the town is still

[*Algeria.*]

entirely native, but it is contemplated soon to drive a wide European street through the centre of it. The Janissaries' barracks, near the Hotel d'Orient, were demolished in 1874, and a covered market and theatre have been erected on the site.

The *Place du Palais*, bordered by rows of acacia-trees, is the most important of all the Places; and in it is the church of Nôtre Dame, the Cercle Militaire, and the best cafés; while its N. side is formed by the palace of Ahmed Bey, from which it takes its name.

The *Place Négrier*, at the northern end of the Rue de France, is named after General Négrier, who was at one time commandant of the province. It is triangular in form, is planted with trees, has a fountain in the centre, and is bounded on the N.W. side by the mosque of Salah Bey.

The *Place des Galettes*, or *Rahbti es-Souf*, between the Rue Combes and the Rue Vieux, is occupied by a vegetable market, and being in the native quarter is exceedingly picturesque.

Churches and Mosques.— The **Cathedral** of *Nôtre Dame des Sept Douleurs*, in the Place du Palais, formerly the mosque of *Souk-el-Ghazel*, was built by Abbas ben Alloul, in the year 1730. The ancient "mimbar" or pulpit, which is richly ornamented, still remains, as do also some gems of Moorish ornamentation in coloured plaster and ancient tiles which decorated the original mosque; but the aspect of the whole is mixed and incongruous, and the frescoes in the sacrarium are hideous.

The **Djamäa el Kebir**, or *Grand Mosque*, in the Rue Nationale, is built on the ruins of a Roman temple, which, according to M. Cherbonneau, was formerly a pantheon, as two inscriptions, one to the Goddess of Concord and another to Venus, have been discovered. On a pedestal, which formerly supported

o

a statue, close to the minaret, there was an inscription in Latin, recording the name of the Roman Quæstor who erected it; and near the western gallery one in Arabic to commemorate the death of Mohammed Ibrahim, which took place in the year 1221.

This mosque formerly stood in the Place Betha, but the construction of the Rue Nationale caused that square to disappear, together with the minaret and part of the court of the mosque. A new façade has been built in the street; above the door is an Arabic inscription in honour of Napoleon III, which did not share the fate of similar inscriptions at the revolution.

Djamäa Sidi el-Kettani, known as the mosque of Salah Bey, in the Place Négrier, of which it forms the western side, is the finest of all the mosques of Constantine. It was erected by Salah Bey, who also built the adjoining *Medresa*, or Ecclesiastical College, and the *Harem*.

This mosque is entered by a large, arched, iron-bound door, beyond which is a flight of marble steps, partly black and partly white, leading into a marble-paved court, around which runs a circular gallery, and the interior is entered from this court by two carved doors. It is of a rectangular shape, and divided into naves by columns of white marble. The ceiling is of red and green planks placed alternately, on which are painted various designs. The whole is surmounted by two cupolas. The "mihrab," corresponding to the Christian sacrarium, is a recess, the roof of which is supported by four columns, and decorated with arabesques; and the walls are covered with variously-coloured tiles. The "mimbar," or pulpit, is beautifully ornamented with marble, agate, and other kinds of stone; it was brought from Italy. The façade and the minaret of this mosque were reconstructed by the same architect who patched up the Grand Mosque.

At the end of the Court of the Medresa are the *Tombs* of Salah Bey and his family, surrounded by a railing, and surmounted by a dome.

The *Harem* of Salah Bey, near the Medresa, is now converted into a school.

Djamäa Sidi el-Akhdar, in the Rue Combes, which is used by the "Hanefi" sect, is decorated internally, something in the same manner as that last described, but in worse taste. The tombstones in the place of burial bear the names of many celebrated personages. The *minaret*, nearly 80 ft. in height, is of great beauty. It is of octagonal shape with a projecting covered gallery round the top.

There are several other mosques in the city; but those above described are the best worth inspecting.

The *Tomb* of a famous saint of Morocco, which is constructed partly out of Roman remains, is in the Rue Combes. Entrance is obtained by means of some stone steps, leading to a vine-covered terrace, on to which the tomb opens.

The **Palace of Constantine** is an interesting building; it is by no means venerable in point of age, being the work of El-Hadj Ahmed, the last Bey, but it is an excellent type of Moorish architecture, and it is constructed out of materials of a much older date.

At the farther end of the Place du Palais is seen a heavy and inelegant mass of masonry, the appearance of which is by no means improved by being pierced with several modern doors and windows, but on passing the principal entrance this impression is instantly dispelled. The central space is occupied by a garden, round which are cloistered walks and porticos giving entrance to the various apartments.

The site used to be a mass of filthy lanes and crumbling houses. In 1826 El-Hadj Ahmed was named Bey, and he immediately conceived the idea of building a palace worthy of the rulers of Constantine. He commenced, by fair means or foul, to obtain possession of the ground necessary for his purpose. A Genoese of the name of Schiaffino, engaged in the exportation of grain at Bône, was charged to procure from

Italy the marble necessary for the work, which was laboriously brought, ready sculptured, on mules from the coast. Complaints of his extortion to the Dey of Algiers caused the work to be suspended for a time; but in 1830, becoming, by the fall of the Dey, absolute master of the province, he resumed it with renewed vigour. He collected his workmen; without the least scruple he commenced to demolish the houses which stood in his way; all the principal mansions of Constantine were despoiled of their choicest works of art, old encaustic tiles, marble columns, carved woodwork; the summer palace of Salah Bey was entirely destroyed in this manner. And so the palace, which under ordinary circumstances would have been the work of generations, rose as if by enchantment in the short space of six years. It is of an oblong shape, with an area of 5609 square mètres. It contains three principal buildings of two stories, consisting of numerous small rooms opening into wide galleries supported by columns.

Between two gardens is the Bey's pavilion, now the private office of the general, joined to the rest of the building by a cloister supported by a triple range of columns. Throughout the whole building the different styles of these pillars indicate the diversity of sources from which they were obtained; some are slender and elegant, others heavy and massive, with every variety of form, round, square, octagonal and twisted; their capitals are equally heterogeneous, but the effect of all, surmounted by the elegant Moorish arch, is good, though marred by the dead black colour of the arches and the ungainly draperies depicted above them.

The main walls for a height of several feet are covered with beautiful old tiles, while above them are ridiculous frescoes representing flowers, fruit, grotesque views of cities, forts, and vessels, said to be the work of Christian prisoners.

In some of the upper rooms are most exquisite specimens of Arab carpentry in old oak and cedar.

Space does not admit a detailed description of this palace; the visitor will be shown the chamber where the Emperor slept, the hall of arms, trophies of the various campaigns made in the province, the Bey's throne, and other interesting objects; but nothing will please him more than a walk round the lower cloisters which surround the gardens.

The palace is now the residence of the general commanding the division, and contains various public offices connected with his command, such as the direction of Engineers, Artillery, etc.

The **Kasbah**, or Citadel, at the N. corner of the town, has been entirely modernised by the French, who have built in it three separate *Barracks*, capable of containing together 3000 men; exceedingly comfortable, no doubt, for the soldiers, but a blot in the magnificence of the landscape. The original building was erected by the Romans, who also constructed the *Cisterns*, which were discovered while making the necessary excavations for the new works. They are of great extent. Shaw says that in his time they were 20 in number, having an area of 50 yards square. The large Roman magazine for storing corn has been discovered more recently. The French have erected within the walls a fine *Hospital* for 1500 persons, which is nursed by the sisters of St. Vincent de Paul. At the time of the French siege the Kasbah was the last stronghold of the Arabs, who there made a desperate defence against General Rulhieres; and finally, sooner than fall into the hands of the invaders, hundreds of the besieged — men, women, and children attempted to lower themselves into the gorge by means of ropes. Through being overloaded many of these broke; and the bed of the ravine soon presented a frightful spectacle of heaps of mangled bodies of the dead and dying.

Numerous Roman remains have been and are still being discovered at this spot; and the walls of the Kasbah are decorated with many inscriptions which have been let into them, both inside and out. One of these, on a split stone, mentions the same officer to whom the stone at the Bab el-Djabia was dedicated. It runs :—

ΠꞋΙΟΥΛΙΟΙΝꞋꞋΕΜΙΝΙΟΝ
ΜΑΡΚΙ Α ΝΟΝι
ΠΡΕϹΒΕΥΤΗ ΝꞋϹΕΒΑϹꞋꞋ
ΤωΝꞋΑΝΤΙ ϹΤ ΡΑΤΗΓΟΝ
ΥΠΑΤΟΝꞋΙΙ ΔΥΛΗ ΚΑΙΟ
ΔΗΜΟϹꞋΑΔ ΡΗ ΝϾωΝꞋ ΠΕΤΡΑ
ωΝꞋΜΠΤΡΟΠϾ ΑϹωϹꞋΤΗϹꞋΛ
ΡΑΒΙΛϹꞋΑΜ ΑΥΔΙΟΥ ΑΙΝϾ
ΟΥꞋ ΠΡΕϹΒΕΙꞋΤΡΥꞋΕΥΕΡΓΕΤΗꞋꞋ
ϾϾΚΤϾϾ ꞋΥΜΒΔΥꞋΑΝϾΘϾ
ϹꞋꞋꞋΙ

It appears to commemorate a statue raised to Marcianus by the district that had benefited by his rule.

The officers and soldiers who fell in the sieges of 1836-37 are buried within the fort, under a monument recording their names, which include those of Generals Damrémont, Perrégaux, Combes, Vieux, and Serigny.

The traveller should not fail to visit the **Garden of the Artillery**, in the Kasbah, from which a magnificent view, looking down into the ravine of the Roummel, is obtained.

The **Palais de Justice**, in the Rue Potier, is a rather handsome building.

The **Museum** is in one of the rooms of the Mairie. It contains a collection of antiquities, some of which are exceedingly interesting, especially a bronze statuette of the winged figure of *Victory*, which was discovered beneath the Kasbah, and presented to the Museum by Col. Ribot. This is one of the most exquisite objects of art ever found in Algeria. A fine model of the Medrassen is also deposited there. Opposite the public garden is a collection of larger objects, such as statues, columns, tombstones, friezes, etc. It is curious to remark that the monumental inscriptions appear to indicate that the inhabitants of Constantine were celebrated for longevity, many of them exceeding the age of 100 years! M. Cherbonneau gives a list of 15 tombstones observed by him at Constantine recording ages from 100 to 131 years.

There are very remarkable subterranean passages under the city, the entrances to which are now bricked up. An eye-witness thus describes us:— "In 1858, visiting in company with my learned friend, M. Cherbonneau, the courtyard of Ben Zaghbib's house, now occupied by Dr. V——, we were shown a gate, by which we descended into a subterranean passage, high, spacious, and solidly built, like that in the Tombeau de la Chrétienne. Here the inhabitants took refuge during the siege of Constantine by the French in 1837. We dared not penetrate far, as there was a perfect labyrinth of passages, blocked up by square stones, earth, and the filth of ages. But what we saw sufficiently confirmed the native tradition that Constantine is built on vaults, intended not merely to sustain the superstructure, but probably to serve as storehouses for provisions, material of war, etc., and that one can walk all round the city underground. The insular position of the city, which rendered all extension of its area impossible, may have caused the construction of these underground passages and vaults as storehouses in time of peace, and places of refuge during sieges.

"We saw another door leading into them a few steps in front of the great mosque, but the Arabs declare that there are two principal orifices besides, one in the Kasbah, and one near the Porte de la Brèche."

Water is supplied to Constantine by means of an aqueduct, which brings a copious stream from Aïn-Fesgiah, 60 kil. on the road to Batna, into the city. The Roman cisterns, containing 12,000 cubic mètres, have been repaired, and are supplied from *Djebel Ouache*, by another aqueduct which crosses the ravine by the bridge El-Kantara. This supply is now used only for the Kasbah, and as a reserve in case of drought or siege.

The *Stone Pyramid*, erected to commemorate the death of Governor-General Comte de Damrémont, stands outside the city, near the junction of the roads from Setif and Batna. An inscription in French records his death, which took place on 12th October 1837, while visiting the batteries. The same inscription in Arabic is on the S. side of the pyramid. He was killed by a bullet almost at the same time that General Perrégaux was mortally wounded. Constantine was taken by assault on the following day, General Valée having assumed the chief command.

Markets and Manufactures.—There are several large markets at Constantine, among which may be mentioned the corn market, held outside the Place Valée, which is the most important in Algeria. The municipal duty charged for weighing grain there, produced in 1873 nearly half a million francs. The vegetable, fruit, and fish market is next to the Hôtel d'Orient.

The chief manufactures of Constantine are leather goods, such as shoes, saddles and harness, and articles of embroidered leather, some of which are of great beauty, and woollen fabrics, especially *Haiks* and *Burnouses*. It is estimated that nearly 100,000 of these garments are woven yearly in Constantine. The finest and most expensive kind, called *Gandouras*, are made partly of wool and partly of silk, and are beautifully soft and fine. *Tlellis*, or tent cloth, is also extensively woven. The chief commerce is in cereals and wool.

EXCURSIONS IN THE NEIGHBOURHOOD.

Bou Merzoug.O—An interesting expedition to the student of prehistoric remains is to the source of the *Bou Merzoug*, which formerly supplied Constantine with water. Here, over an immense extent of hill and valley, not less than 12 kil. in length, are found almost every known type of megalithic monuments. These were first explored by Mr. Christy and M. Féraud in 1863, who examined more than a thousand during the three days of their stay there. This fountain is the only known habitat of a curious little fish, the *Tellia apoda* (see p. 72).

Djebel Ouache.—A pleasant drive of 6 kil. is to *Dj. Ouache*, more correctly *W'ehash* (wild or savage mountain). Here are situated the reservoirs constructed for supplying Constantine with water, and on which it was dependent before those of Aïn-Fesgiah were conveyed to the town. The basins are now used principally for the supply of the Kasba, and the plateau of Mansoura. Beautiful plantations have been made here, and what will particularly interest the traveller, a considerable number of the rare African pinsapos (see p. 118), growing side by side with the better known variety of Spain.

Es-Soumah and **Mahadjiba.**O This excursion is best made on horseback, in two days, spending the night at the village of El-Aria, but there is a good carriage-road all the way. The travellers will have to diverge a little from the high road to reach the Roman ruins described.

Es-Soumah may easily be reached on foot from Le-Khroub, a station on the railway, which is only 3 kil. from it. It is called by the Arabs Es-Soumah, the minaret, a term which they habitually employ to designate any ancient mausoleum or tower-like monument. Europeans generally, but erroneously, call it the "Tomb of Constantine."

The ruins of this once beautiful edifice, the history of which is quite unknown, are in the purest Doric style, and probably date from the 1st cent. It is built on a mound near the eastern boundary of the territory of Cirta, as has been proved by the discovery of a stone bearing the inscription A.P.C. (*ager publicus Cirtensium*), and close to the high road between that city and Kalama on the one hand and Lambessa on the other. Its object was either to serve as the mausoleum of some distinguished person, or to commemorate a great victory.

The building, as it now exists, is composed of three principal parts, a square base, of nearly 3 mètres high, surmounted by three gradients, each 0·54 mètre in height. Above these gradients rises a plinth of 1·10 mètre, crowned by a splendid cornice, of a bold and firm, yet refined character, measuring 0·76 mètre in height. At this level a course of stones 0·54 mètre high, retired from the cornice by 0·30 mètre on all sides, extends like a pavement over the upper surface of the monument, and serves as a footing to four square pillars that occupy each angle, leaving a distance outside of nearly a yard on the two exterior faces. The courses of stone in the pillars are 0·61 mètre high, and 1·74 mètre on each side. Prominent round bucklers decorate the outward faces of each of these pillars.

Unfortunately at this point the monument has been thrown to the ground, and it is amongst the ruins that a search must be made for the completion and restoration of the buildings. No doubt earthquakes contributed greatly to its destruction, but there is abundant evidence that the hand of man was not foreign to the work. Part of the material is scattered in every direction, but it is principally on the N. side that it lies heaped up to the level of the floor.

About 10 m. farther, on the old road between Constantine and Guelma, are the ruins of **Mahadjiba,**Ɵ or Kasr-el-Mahdjouba, the *Castle of the Female Recluse* and the Seniore of the Itinerary of Antoninus.

The position of this city or stronghold was admirably chosen from a strategic point of view, being built on an isolated hill, the top of which is a rough triangle rising abruptly from the plain, and sloping backwards towards its base in a series of terraces.

In front of it is an extensive stretch of rich corn and pasture land, reaching as far as Constantine, while behind it on the south is a narrow pass in the Fedj-bou-Ghareb, a remarkable scarped hill of compact limestone, giving access to the plain of the Amer Cheraga and Oued Zenati, in which are situated 83,000 out of the 100,000 hectares of land so lavishly granted to the Société Générale Algérienne by the late Emperor.

Thus this position completely commanded the ancient highway between Cirta and Kalama, as it now commands the Arab road between Constantine and Guelma.

The whole hill is covered with the remains of buildings constructed of huge blocks of cut stone; some of the walls are entire to above the level of the first floor, the holes for the reception of the joists being distinctly visible. The principal and best preserved edifice is the tower, from which the ruins derive their Arab name, an elegant and massive building, which perhaps formed the citadel of the place. At the base of the hill below the citadel is an arch of cut stone, giving access to a subterranean passage, whence flowed a stream of water. This is now choked up, and the water has forced itself a passage through the *debris* about a hundred yards farther down, where it has created a little oasis of trees, the only ones as far as the eye can reach.

On the opposite side of the valley is El-Aria, a village founded in 1875, where the traveller will be able to find accommodation for the night, and he can return to Constantine on the following morning either by the high road or by a shorter bridle-path over the hills.

El-Kheneg.Ɵ—A very interesting excursion, which, however, must be made on horseback, is to the ruins of *El-Kheneg*, erroneously called by the Arabs *Kosentina-Kedima*, or old Constantine,—in reality the ancient Roman *Respublica Tidditanorum*. It is situated about 23 kil. N.W. of Constantine, on the same river which flows past the capital, and the general character of the ground on which the two cities are situated is very similar. There are very well preserved remains of a Roman road, a Roman citadel restored by the Byzantines, many other ruins of the same character, and numerous dolmens. About 4 kil. E. of it, and the same distance from the confluence of the Oued Smendou and the Oued El-Kebir, by which name the Roummel is here called, is the **Tomb of Lollius.** It is of a cylindrical shape, 20·30 mètres in diameter and 5·50 mètres high, raised on a base. It appears to have been a cenotaph raised by Marcus Lollius to five members of his family. It bore the following inscription:—

```
M . LOLLIO . SENECIONI . PATRI
GRANIAE . HONORATAE . MATRI
L . LOLLIO . SENECIONI . FRATRI
M . LOLLIO . HONORATO . FRATRI
P . GRANIO . PAVLO . AVONCVLO
Q . LOLLIVS . VREICVS . PRAEF . VRBIS .
```

The last name, the founder of the monument, is the same person before whom Apuleius, author of the "Golden Ass," so eloquently pleaded his cause when summoned to the tribunal of the pro-consul Claudius Maximus on a charge of fraud and sorcery. The family of Granius, mentioned in the previous lines, were the plaintiffs in the case. This monument, therefore, is one possessing the deepest historical interest.

The epitaph of Lollius himself was found at Kheneg, and was as follows:—

```
Q . LOLLIO . M . FILIO .
QVIR . VIRICO . COS .
LEG . AVG . PROVINC . GERM .
INFERIORIS . FETIALI . LEGATO .
IMP . HADRIANI . IN . EXPEDION
IVDAICA . QVA . DONATVS . EST
HASTA . PVRA . CORONA . AVREA . LEO .
LEG . X . GEMINAE . PRAEF . CANDIDAT .
PROCOS . ASIAE . QVEST . VRBIS . TRIB
LATICLAVIO . LEG . XXII . PRIMIGENIAE .
IIII VIRO . VIARVM . CVRAND .
D.D.                PATRONO                P.P.
```

To Quintus Lollius, son of Marcus (of the tribe of) Quirina (surnamed) Urbicus; Consul, Legate of the Emperor in the province of Lower Germany; Fetial, Legate of the Emperor Hadrian in the expedition to Judea, where he was presented with a pure lance (or without an iron head), a crown of gold; Legate of the Xth Legion Gemina, Praetor Candidate of Caesar, Tribune of the People, Candidate of Caesar, Legate of his Pro-Consul of Asia, Quaestor of the City; Tribune laticlave of the XXII. Legion Primigenia, one of the Four Inspectors of Roads; Patron. By the decree of the decurions, and at the public expense.

Dolmens of Kheneg.O—On the S.W. declivity of the rocky crest of Kef-oum-Hadidan, at 500 mètres from the remains of the Roman citadel, are 3 dolmens close together; the flat slabs are 2·30 to 2·50, and the upright ones 1·50 in height. Enclosures of rough blocks, of irregular shape, surround them, leaving only a narrow passage between them and the dolmen. They

are called by the natives El-Haounet, the shops. A few steps farther down are the remains of several more, and amongst them some of a circular form.

ROUTE 12.

Constantine to Algiers, by the Chabet el-Akhira.

From Constantine to Setif there are two trains daily. From Setif to Bougie there is a service of diligences daily, starting at a very early hour in the morning, and taking about 14 hours; but it is best to hire a carriage and make the journey in two days, spending the night at Kharata.

For several reasons it is more advisable to make the journey from Setif to Bougie than from Bougie to Setif: it is always easier to descend a hill than to mount one; the scenery is far grander looking down than looking up; and it is better to pass through the tamer scenery first, and thus prevent the grandeur of the Chabet from dwarfing what, under any other circumstances, would be considered a very beautiful landscape. The diligence is much cheaper and not at all bad when descending, but the traveller should avoid it when ascending, as it starts so early that owing to darkness he misses some of the finest scenery, which is not the case when leaving Setif.

Almost any amount of inconvenience will be repaid by the magnificence of the scenery between Kharata and Cap Okas, which is hardly to be surpassed in any part of the world. There is certainly nothing to equal it within easy range of the basin of the Mediterranean, except perhaps in Corsica.

It was the Commandant Capdepont who made the first reconnaissance of the *Chabet-el-Akhira*, and suggested it as a route between Setif and the sea. M. L'Epinay was the engineer who first reduced this idea to a practical form: the route was traced by the military engineers, and subsequently completed by the department of the *Ponts et*

Chaussées, under M. de Lannoy, in 1873.

It offers the double advantage of being shorter than any other route, as it reduces the distance between Setif and the sea to 102 kil., and it traverses for a shorter distance the region where snows may impede circulation in winter.

Many travellers who do not intend visiting Constantine may content themselves with a journey from Bougie to Kharata and back (see p. 114).

Setif. (See p. 160.)

The road leaves *Setif* by the *Porte de Bougie*, and crossing the parade-ground descends the valley of *Fermatou*, crosses the head of the river *Bou Selam*, and arrives at

4 kil. *Fermatou*. A small village on the left of the road.

At 4 kil. N.E. are the Roman ruins of *Aïn-el-Hadjar* (Spring of the Stone).

The road then crosses the *Oued Goussimet*, near which branches off another horse-path to the W., which, making a considerable circuit, rejoins the new road beyond Ta Kitount.

The road now pursues a northerly direction, through a series of richly cultivated valleys belonging to the Compagnie Génevoise.

11 kil. *El-Ouiricia*. A small village belonging to the same company. It was entirely destroyed during the insurrection, and one of the colonists who refused to leave his property was murdered, but it has been rebuilt since then. Here a road branches off to the right, leading to a farm of the Geneva Company.

14 kil. Road crosses a long chain of hills running E. and W., the eastern peak of which is *Djebel Assel*, and *Mount Babor* bursts into view.

15 kil. Bordj of *Kaïd Mansour* on left of road. Lower down numerous Kabyle villages and gardens along the *Oued Faïd*.

21 kil. *Aïn-Maghramma*. Relay.

22 kil. The road here takes a N.W. direction, following the course of an affluent of the *Oued bou-Tafsa* to

28 kil. *Les Ammoucha*.

32 kil. *Col de Ta Kitount*, where is a small roadside auberge. Shortly before reaching it, on the left-hand side, is a spring of ferruginous aerated water, very agreeable to drink, and which is bottled off and sent all over the country. From the *Col* is seen the fort of *Ta Kitount*, perched on an elevation to the left. It resisted all the attempts of the Kabyles to take it in 1871. It is situated 3448 ft. above the sea, and commands a splendid view of the country round. The present fort is built on the site of a Roman work, as is proved by the numerous fragments of sculpture, coins, etc., which have from time to time been found here.

47 kil. After a rapid descent to the bed of the *Oued Berd*, the road turns to the left and crosses an affluent of that river, the *Oued Allaba*, by a lattice bridge.

Not far from this spot is the hot alkaline spring of *Hammam Gergour*.

Beyond this a bridge crosses the *Oued Berd*, carrying the road to the right bank of that river. It now crosses several streams, one of which, the *Oued Tamala*, is salt, and reaches

53 kil. **Kharata**, where is a fairly good hotel.

Up to this point the scenery is very fine, but it is at Kharata that the gorge of the **Chabet-el-Akhira** commences.

Kharata is 1280 ft. above the level of the sea, and possesses a fine summer climate. The gorge acts as a huge windsail, so that even during the hottest days of summer there is always a fresh breeze blowing through it from the sea.

[From *Kharata* an excursion might be made to the top of *Mount Babor*.

The ascent is by no means a difficult one, and may be made nearly to the summit on mules. It would be as well to take a tent and camp for two nights at the village of *Oulad Scad*, or any other near the top, and devote the intervening day to an exploration of the summit. Guides and mules can easily be procured at Kharata, and the hospitality of the Kabyles to travellers is proverbial. (See also p. 118.)

Babor is 6447 ft. above the level of the sea; the summit, which is covered with snow during a great portion of the winter and spring, is crowned with a forest of cedars and pinsapos. The latter is a variety of the Spanish species *Picea Pinsapo*, and is found only on two peaks of the Atlas, *Babor* and *Ta-Babort*, where it was discovered in 1861. It is remarkable for the pyramidal form of its trunk and top, and for the hardness and compactness of its timber.

The forests on the two peaks have an area of 9000 acres, but for all practical purposes they are unapproachable.

The view from the peaks is exceedingly grand. Care, however, should be taken not to attempt the ascent save in very settled weather. May and November are the best months, the former especially, as then the country is clad in its vernal tints.]

Immediately beyond Kharata commences the entrance to the gorge, and the first idea that crosses the traveller's mind is the powerlessness of words to depict scenery so grand.

A huge defile, 7 kil. in length, winds in a tortuous manner between two mountains, from 5000 ft. to 6000 ft. high. At the bottom, an impetuous torrent has worn itself a deep and narrow channel, from either side of which the rocks arise sometimes almost perpendicularly, sometimes actually overhanging the bed of the river, to a height of nearly 1000 ft. So narrow is this gorge, that although the road is cut in the side, at from 100 to 400 ft. from the bottom, there is hardly any spot where a stone could not be thrown from one bank to another, and so steep is it, that before the first trace of the road was made by the French an Arab could not pass along it on foot! The only means of approaching it was by descending and ascending the lateral valleys, and exploring a small portion of the main ravine on each side of them.

For about half its length the road passes along the right bank; it then crosses to the left side by a curved bridge of seven arches, which side it subsequently follows during its whole course. There are numerous lateral valleys, each adding its tribute of water to the main stream, frequently by the most beautiful cascades.

The peculiar vertical stratification to be seen here is in some places not unlike that of the *Portes-de-Fer*, but the substance being harder, it does not form itself into such grotesque shapes. Wherever there is a slope sufficient to retain a little earth, it is covered with luxuriant vegetation; and as the road approaches the end, trees become more abundant, and finally the slopes are clothed with a forest of cork and other oak trees.

On a stone, about the middle, is engraved the legend—" *Les premiers soldats qui passèrent sur ces rives furent des Tirailleurs, commandés par MM. Desmaisons, etc., 7 Avril, 1861.*"

Troops of monkeys are often met here, and the holes and caves in the rocks afford shelter to great coveys of pigeons, themselves the objects of attraction to the eagles seen soaring above.

61 kil. The gorge ends; on a rock to the left is carved the inscription:

PONTS ET CHAUSSÉES
SETIF.
CHABET-EL-AKHIRA
TRAVAUX EXÉCUTÉS
1863-70.

The bordj of *Kaid Hassen* is some little distance off, amongst the hills; this is in the country of the *Beni Ismail*, and it is here that the short cut from *Cap Okas* joins the high road.

The scenery from this point, though of a different character, is hardly less beautiful than the Chabet. The river here takes the name of *Oued Agrioun*, and the hills on each side widening out, it flows along a much wider bed in the most beautiful tortuous manner, through thickets of oleanders.

This region is finely wooded; the summits of the hills are covered with pines and cedars, and their slopes, furrowed in every direction with perennial streams, are clothed with forests of cork and other varieties of oak, the finest of which is the *Chêne Zain* (*Quercus*

Mirbeckii), while the ground amongst them is brilliant with bracken, heath (*Erica arborea*), myrtle, and a thousand wild flowers of every tint and hue.

The mineral wealth of these hills is also great, though hardly at all developed ; rich mines of iron, copper, and argentiferous lead ore have been discovered, and only await means of conveyance to the coast to enable them to be worked with advantage.

77 kil. The road now leaves the *Oued Agrioun*, and turning westwards, passes along a plain covered with brushwood and some fine trees. Here, and all along the route to Bougie, are noble specimens of the Atlas ash (*Fraxinus Australis*), which, in its spring foliage, is most beautiful. Grand old olives mixed with them afford, by their more sombre green, a grateful contrast to the lighter tints of the other.

85 kil. *Sidi Rchour*, a small inn, "Rendezvous de Chasse," affords sleeping accommodation if necessary.

87 kil. Here commences the ascent of Cap Okas.

This is a bold and bluff promontory jutting out into the sea, on the vertical cliff of which a road has been rather excavated than built, at a height of 100 ft. above the sea, like the stern gallery of an old ship of the line. The view both E. and W. is most beautiful ; on one side is a long stretch of beach fringed with green, behind which rise the hills whence the traveller has just emerged, and beyond these the more distant blue mountains culminating in the snow-clad peak of Babor. On the other is the Gulf of Bougie, a vast amphitheatre of water bounded by the most picturesque mountains.

Near Cap Okas is the tomb of a venerated saint, *Si - Mohammed bin Nasir*, a man of such holiness that, though living in absolute solitude, whenever he began to pray the Marabouts of all other countries flocked to him in the form of birds to hear but the sound of his voice !

95 kil. *Tichy*, a small wayside post-office.

The road now crosses the *Oued Djemäa*, and traverses the plain of Bougie between well-wooded mountains and the sea.

This plain is to a great extent overgrown with brushwood and bracken, but it is fertile and well watered, and was highly cultivated by the Romans, as the remains of farms and hydraulic works testify. During the first years after the conquest it was the scene of constant combats, and even in 1871 it was occupied by the Kabyles, and all the European buildings on it destroyed.

At first it was a hot-bed of malaria, but as soon as it was possible for the French troops to commence works of drainage, the malaria disappeared.

105 kil. The *Oued Soumam*, the name here given to the *Oued es-Sahel*, is crossed by an iron lattice bridge ; the road subsequently passes over several other streams and reaches

112 kil. **Bougie**. (See Rte. 1.)

ROUTE 13.

From Bougie to Beni-Mansour and on to Algiers by Railway.

Kil.		Kil.
..	Bougie	89
12.	La Réunion	77
24.	El-Kseur	65
32.	El-Maten	57
42.	Sidi-Aich	47
47.	Takriets	42
54.	Ighzer-Amokran . .	35
58.	Azib-ben-Ali-Chérif . .	31
65.	Akbou	24
76.	Allaghan	13
81.	Tazmalt	8
89.	Beni-Mansour	..

This line ascends the *Oued es-Sahel*, which commences near Aumale, and terminates in the Gulf of Bougie, at 4 kil. E. of that city. This river, known to the ancient geographers by the name of *Nasava*, *Nasoua*, or *Nasabeth*, like most of the rivers of Algeria, changes its name according to the territory it traverses. Thus it is successively called *Oued Akbou*, *Oued Soumam*, *O. Beni Mesaoud*, and *Oued el-Kebir*, the great river. Its mean breadth is 40 mètres, but in some places it is as much as 200 mètres wide, and its depth is equally variable. Its principal affluents are, on the right bank, the *Oued bou-Sellam*, coming from near Setif, and the *Oued Amazin*, which descends from *Guifsar*. The only important one on the left bank is the *Oued Gheir*. In summer the water decreases greatly, and more than half its bed is dry; but in winter it swells with every fall of rain, and becomes a formidable torrent.

In 1847 Marshal Bugeaud descended it to Bougie, where he met the column of General Bedeau from Constantine, which had come by Setif; these were the first French troops who made a reconnaissance of this part of Kabylia. Many of the tribes tendered their submission to these officers, and later, in 1849, Generals de Salles and Saint Arnaud, after a severe struggle, conquered the Beni Seliman, and again visited the tribes who had before submitted.

This valley has always been ready to rise on the slightest provocation. It was the scene of the insurrection of Bou Baghla, and it was from Seddonk, the residence of the Haddad family, that the *mot d'ordre* was given which spread the flames of revolt over Kabylia in 1871 (see p. 60).

The principal riches of the district are olive oil, honey, wax, and grapes; the last are rarely made into wine, but sent to the market at Algiers, where they arrive after all the others are over, and command a high price. They are also made into raisins.

12 kil. *La Réunion*, a village near the Oued Gheir, created in 1872.

After passing this village is the *Tombeau de la Niege*, a monument erected in honour of a company of French soldiers lost in a snowstorm.

24 kil. *El-Kseur*. On the S. of the line are the ruins of El-Kseur.

The name "The Palace" has been given on account of the ruin of an entrenched camp, built in *bétou*, by Abou Tachefin, Sultan of Tlemçen, about A.D. 1327, during his futile attempt to take the city of Bougie. He retired in the following year, leaving, however, troops stationed along the Oued es-Sahel.

About 4 kil. from it are the ruins of *Tiklat*, O the ancient Tubusuptus. A very fine cistern still remains, capable of containing 12,000 cubic mètres of water.

From this place there will branch off a road to *Tizi-Ouzou*, which is rapidly approaching completion.

On the opposite bank of the river is *Oued Amisour*. It is situated about 3 kil. from the right bank, and 26 kil. from Bougie. A road will eventually connect it with Bougie by the right bank of the river.

32 kil. *El-Maten*, a small village near the Oued Tifera; north of the line, on the hill above is a Kabyle village of the same name.

42 kil. *Sidi-Aich*, an important village where a market is held every Wednesday. The land is well suited for the growth of figs, olives and other fruit. The administrator of the district resides here. Numerous Kabyle villages may be seen perched on the hillsides in every direction.

The line now crosses the valley by a fine viaduct.

47 kil. *Takriets*, a road to the S. conducts to Seddonk, the country of the famous Haddad family, whose chief, Sheikh Mohammed Amzian ben Ali El-Haddad, Mokaddem of the great religious confraternity of *Sidi Moh ummed bou Kuberain*, from his cell at *Seddonk*, which he had not quitted for many years, in one day set the whole of Kabylia in flames. Without his order the insurrection of 1871 could never have extended to Kabylia. He died in Constantine a few days after his condemnation; his body was embalmed, and will no doubt one day be transported to Kabylia, hereafter to become an object of veneration for future generations, if permitted by the French. His sons were also sentenced to perpetual imprisonment in New Caledonia, but escaped.

54 kil. *Ighzer-Amokran*.

58 kil. *Azib-ben-Ali-Cherif*, the charming residence of the well-known person whose name it bears.

Si Mohammed Said ben Ali Cherif is descended from a Moroccan Cherif, Moulaï Abd-es-Selam ben Machiche, who settled there in the 18th century.

He married the daughter of the Marabout of *Illoula*, and their descendants have ever since been at the head of the *Zaouia* of *Chellata*. This family has produced many writers of celebrity, and, though it remained on amicable terms with the Turks, it never submitted to their authority. The present head of the family rendered great services to the French at the period of the conquest, was especially honoured by the late Emperor, and was created Bach-Agha of Chellata. Having unfortunately allowed himself to be drawn into the insurrection of 1871, he was tried and convicted at Constantine, but subsequently received a free pardon from Marshal de MacMahon, President of the Republic, who better than any man living knew the value of his former services.

Here the traveller, well recommended, is sure of receiving princely hospitality. It is a spacious building, and in the ravine below, on the banks of a considerable stream, is a beautiful garden of flowers and fruit trees, in which is a pavilion shaded from every ray of sun, and furnished in the most luxurious manner. He is one of the few Arabs who take any interest in horticulture, or seem to care for the cultivation of fruit. He has a European gardener in his service, and there are not many gardens, even at Algiers, so beautifully kept, and none so plentifully irrigated. In addition to this, he has been most successful in introducing a better system of cultivation on his estate, and has constructed a European olive oil mill, which is most remunerative.

65 kil. **Akbou.** An important village to which a vain attempt was made to attach the name of *Metz*. It is admirably situated on an elevated mound to the north of the high road, with a charming view looking both up and down the valley; the land allotted to the colonists is of an unusually good quality.

Close to it is the old Bordj of Ben Ali Cherif, purchased by the State before the insurrection.

On the opposite side of the river is a ridge of steep hills close to its right bank, called Geldaman, the western point of which has been separated from the rest by the river, and now forms an isolated *mamelon* in the middle of the plain called the *Piton d'Akbou*, which is seen from a great distance on both sides. On a small platform at the west side of this hill, and about 100 ft. above its base, is a remarkable Roman mausoleum, still in a good state of preservation. The general shape is that of a pyramid surmounting a cubical base, three of the sides being decorated with false windows, while the fourth contained the door. Above the latter was an inscription in white marble, no trace of which now remains. The execution of the monument is admirable, but the style is debased. It can be seen from the train.

[From Akbou the ascent of the Djurjura range, by the pass of Chellata, may be made. See Route 20.]

76 kil. *Allaghan.*
81 kil. *Tazmalt.*
The richest village in the valley: it takes its name from the Bordj of the same name, on the opposite side of the valley, destroyed in the insurrection of 1871.

89 kil. **Beni-Mansour** (see p. 158). Here the railway joins the main line between Algiers and Tunis.

ROUTE 14.

Constantine to Batna and Biskra.

CONSTANTINE.

Kil.			Kil.
..	El-Guerrah	. .	202
13	Ain-Melila	. .	189
31	Les Lacs	. .	171
47	Ain-Yagout	. .	155
56	Fontaine Chaude	. .	146
64	El-Maader	. .	138
70	Fesdis	. .	132
81	BATNA (Buffet)	. .	121
92	El-Biar	. .	110
114	Ain-Touta	. .	88
122	Les Tamarins	. .	80
146	El-Kantara	. .	56
165	Fontaine des Gazelles	. .	37
174	El-Outaïa	. .	28
184	Ferme-Dufour	. .	18
202	BISKRA	. .	..

37 kil. Constantine to El-Guerrah,

see Route 8. This is the junction of the line from Algiers to Constantine.

13 kil. *Aïn-Mclila*.
31 kil. *Les Lacs*. There are two salt marshes called *Tinsill* and *Mzouri*, partly covered with long grass, and the haunt of flamingoes and other wild fowl of all kinds. A few Europeans engaged in the manufacture of salt live here, but otherwise the country is only occupied by Arabs, whose flocks and herds may be seen all round.

47 kil. *Aïn-Yagout*. The station is about 1500 mètres from the village. This is the nearest station to the **Medrassen**, and mules and even a carriage can be obtained for that purpose. The best plan for making the excursion is to stop here by the train from El-Guerrah, and continue the journey to Batna in the evening. The interval, nearly 8 hours, is amply sufficient to ride to the Medrassen. The distance is less than 10 kil. Or it may be done from Batna by taking the morning train and returning in the evening. It can be seen very distinctly from the train, a little before it reaches the *prise d'eau* of Fontaine Chaude.

This remarkable monument, very similar to the Tombeau de la Chrétienne near Algiers, was situated on the high road between Theveste and Diana Veteranorum. The form is that of a truncated cone, placed on a cylindrical base, 58·80 mètres in diameter; the total height is 18·30 mètres. The lower portion, which forms a vertical encircling zone or ring, is ornamented by 60 engaged columns, of which not one-half are now perfect. The upper part, or roof, gradually diminishes by a series of steps, each 57 cent. in height, and 92 in breadth. The columns are stunted, much broader at the base than at the top, the height being about four times the lower diameter. They rest on three steps, which serve as base both to the monument and to the columns. The capitals are Doric, and above them is an entablature with a large, bold cavetto, as if of Egyptian origin. Commandant Foy, probably following the description of Shaw, calls them of the Tuscan order; Colonel Brunon, criticising the former, remarks that the capitals belong rather to the *genre Egyptien* than to the Tuscan order, the truth being that they are neither one nor the other, but purely Greek. Greece and Egypt seem to have inspired the ornamentation, while the *tumulus* suggested the monument itself, as it did the Tombeau de la Chretienne, Etruscan tombs, and the Pyramids of Egypt. The actual conical part has lost its apex, if it ever had one. The exterior masonry is remarkably fine, the stones being of great size, well cut, the joints not more in some places than the thickness of a knife, and each stone joined to its neighbour by a massive clamp, probably of lead, the search for which has greatly contributed to the destruction of the building. Unfortunately the interior masonry was of a much inferior kind, and an extensive subsidence of it has caused a dislocation of the outer coating.

Various attempts had been made to penetrate it, but for a long time without success. Salah Bey endeavoured to force an entrance by means of artillery. General Carbuccia commenced to explore it in 1849 and discovered the passage leading to the sepulchral chamber; but owing to the roof having fallen in he was unable to penetrate farther. Commandant Foy resumed its exploration with no better success; Monsieur le Garde du Génie Bauchetet failed likewise in 1866; but being again sent in 1873, with more ample means, he succeeded in clearing away the *débris* and penetrating to the central chamber, which he ascertained to be 3·13 mètres long by 1·40 mètres broad. Nothing of any interest was found inside, but clear evidence was obtained that it had been opened at some former period, and that an attempt had been made to destroy the building by means of fire. Great quantities of charcoal and lime — the latter the calcined stone of which it is built — were discovered, and the fire having communicated to the woodwork which supported the roof of the passage, the superincumbent masonry had fallen in and obstructed the entrance. The masonry in the passage and chamber is very inferior to that of the Tombeau de la Chrétienne, and it differs from the latter by the passage going straight to the centre instead of in a spiral direction.

Numerous tumuli, also of a circular form, were discovered around, together with the traces of a bastioned enclosure, proving the place to have been an immense necropolis, subsequently used as a fortress, of which the Medrassen was simply the principal tomb.

There have been many speculations as to the meaning of the word and the destination of the building, which is not mentioned by any classical author. There can, however, be little doubt that the word *Medrassen*, as it is usually written, or *Madghassen*, which is the more correct orthography, is the plural of the Berber word *Madghes*, the patronymic designation of an ancient family from which Masinissa was descended. Ibn Khaldoun says that Madghes was the son of Berr Ibn Kais; he bore the name of El-Abter, and was the father of the Berbers-Botr. The name still exists in that of the tribe inhabiting the vicinity, the Haracta-*Maader*, and in that of a stream, the Oued *Maader*.

It is much more probable that this was the tomb of the Numidian kings —perhaps of Masinissa—than that of Syphax, to whom it has been referred, whose capital was at Siga, near the Tafna, and who only occupied Cirta for a short period. This would lead us to assign the date of B.C. 150 as about that of its construction, a supposition amply supported by the style of the architecture.

64 kil. *El-Maader*, see above.

70 kil. *Fesdis*, a small village on the Oued Batna. The arid plateau, over which the line has hitherto been carried, here gives place to a partially wooded valley, which forms an agreeable contrast to the plains.

81 kil. **Batna** (the Arabic word *Batna* means *we have spent the night*, or bivouac).

2548 inhab.; 3350 ft. above the level of the sea. Headquarters of a military subdivision.

The streets are wide, built at right angles, and lined with low tiled houses, the whole town being enclosed by a wall. The principal building is the *Barracks*, which can hold 4000 men. There is a *Church* and a *Mosque*, and in the neighbourhood a curious negro village of sun-dried bricks.

Batna was occupied shortly after the expedition of the Duc d'Aumale to Biskra in 1884, to command the passage by which the Nomads of the Sahara periodically enter the Tell; in this sense it is of great importance, but to the traveller it is of no interest whatever, save as being a convenient halt between Constantine and Biskra, and the starting-point of excursions to Lambessa, Timegad, the Cedar forest, and the Aurès mountains.

EXCURSIONS IN THE NEIGHBOURHOOD OF BATNA.

Lambessa, 10 kil. E. of Batna; although on the road to Timegad daylight will not admit of both being visited on the same day. The traveller will find it most convenient to drive here on the day of his arrival from Biskra or Constantine, and to devote the whole of the following one to Timegad.

The modern village is close to the Roman ruins; the principal building in it is the prison once occupied by political offenders, mostly victims of the *Coup d'État;* but now it is an ordinary convict establishment for Europeans and natives.

Lambæsis was a purely military town, built in or about A.D. 169, as the headquarters of the Third Augustan Legion; around it the families of the soldiers, and the merchants who gained a living by them, grouped themselves, till it ultimately became an important city of about 60,000 inhabitants.

The camp itself was a rectangle of 500 mètres long by 420 broad, exactly facing the N. Little of its ramparts remain, but recent excavations clearly show its size and form. Part of the prison and its gardens occupy the S.W. corner of the position. It was entered by four gates, of which only those on the N. and E. faces still remain. The former was the principal one; it had two openings, and was defended by towers engaged in the wall. From this point two roads proceeded, one to Tebessa, and the other to Constantine and Setif. It was the custom of the Romans to place the tombs and monuments of the dead on each side of the high roads; those just mentioned have many in the vicinity of the place.

Two streets traversed the camp from N. to S. and from E. to W.; at their intersection stands the principal ruin of the place, the **Prætorium.**

It is a large rectangular edifice, 28 mètres long, 20 mètres broad and 15 high. The principal façade, to the S., had a splendid peristyle, having massive columns in front, which corresponded with Corinthian pilasters engaged in the walls. This extended only to half the height of the wall, leaving a second story externally, but there is no trace of this in the inside, which is undivided in height. The other sides also are decorated with detached columns, corresponding to the pilasters of the lower story, the cornice turning round and forming the entablature. On the N. side there are three detached columns on each side of the principal entrance, between which and the smaller doors is a niche to contain statuary. All the keystones are sculptured, but not very artistically. That over the principal gate bears a basso-relievo of a standard, with the inscription "Legio tertia Augusta." The interior forms a vast hall; on each side there is one large and two smaller doors, and above the central and larger ones another arched opening, used probably as a window. The walls are strengthened internally with pilasters, on which are engaged columns; still it appears doubtful whether the building ever was covered otherwise than by a velarium.

The interior has now been converted into a museum, wherein are collected various objects of antiquity which have been discovered in the vicinity; the best of these, however, have been sent to the museum of the Louvre at Paris.

To the S.E. of the Prætorium, still within the military camp, are the ruins of **Thermæ,** in which some fine Mosaics were found—other Mosaics still exist *in situ* within the gardens of the prison.

If we now leave the camp and proceed towards the E., we come to what is called the **Arch of Commodus**; it is tolerably entire, but of an exceedingly depraved style of art; there are two niches on each side, but without any archivolts. Through this passed the road leading to *Verecunda, Thamugas, Mascula* and *Thersaste.* On the opposite side of the road may be traced an **Amphitheatre,** nearly circular in shape: it must have been large enough to accommodate 12,000 spectators. It is now almost entirely destroyed, but there are people still alive who remember it in an excellent state of preservation.

About a kilomètre to the S.E. of the Prætorium is the **Arch of Septimius Severus,** the public **Latrinæ,** the so-called **Palace of the Legate,** and still farther to the S. the **Forum.** Near it is the **Temple of Æsculapius,** constructed by Marcus Aurelius, of which only one column is now standing. It was a remarkably fine building, and, like the amphitheatre, not many years since its façade was entire. W. of the Forum is the octostyle **Temple of Jupiter,** a most interesting building which has lately been cleared of *débris.*

An *aqueduct* led from the spring called Aïn-Boubenana to the southern gate of the camp. The principal *Necropolis* was to the E. of the city, between the Oued Necheb and the Oued Marcouna, and covered an area of more than 15 hectares.

About 3 kil. to the N. of the Prætorium is the **Tomb of T. Flavius Maximus,** commander of the Third Legion, which has been carefully restored by the French. It is a square, terminating in a pyramid, about 6 mètres in height. According to an inscription it was erected to carry out the will of Maximus, who left 12,000 sesterces for that purpose, by Julius Secundus, a centurion of the Third Legion, of which Flavius Maximus was prefect. When the remains of the Roman general were replaced in the tomb by the French after its restoration, the garrison of

Batna marched past and fired a salute in his honour.

At 3 kil. S. of Lambessa are the ruins of **Markouna** the ancient *Verecunda*. This was probably a suburb of the former city. There still exist two triumphal arches, on one of which occurs the name Verecunda.

About 3 kil. beyond Markouna, the student of pre-historic remains will find a very remarkable megalithic monument, called by the natives *Mza-Sedira*, tomb of Sedira. It is a trilithon, 3 mètres high, the uprights of which rest on a base of two courses of rough stones. It appears to have been surrounded by a parallelogram of stones arranged in parallel lines.

The excursion to **Timegad** will occupy a whole day. The distance from Batna is 36 kil. and the road excellent for a great part of the way and quite practicable throughout for a light carriage; the drive there and back will occupy 10 hours, so that but a short time will remain for an inspection of the ruins. A small house has lately been built by the officials charged with excavating the ruins, but it is rarely open; attached to it is another for the use of the Arab guardian, in which a traveller, who is not very particular, may pass the night, or he may sleep at the Bordj of the Oued Taga, but ordinarily the entire excursion should be made in a single day.

These ruins are certainly the most remarkable in the colony; they have lately been entirely excavated, and are hardly less interesting than Pompeii. They were visited by the author in 1875, and described in his "Footsteps of Bruce." Shortly after an excellent report on them was written by Professor Masqueray; in 1880-83, they were carefully examined and excavated by the Government engineers, under the supervision of M. Duthoit, architect-in-chief of historical monuments in Algeria, whose admirable plans of Timegad and Lambessa have been published in the proceedings of the Archæological Society of Constantine for 1883-

84; and lastly, they were described and illustrated by Mr. Alexander Graham, in an article on the Remains of the Roman Occupation of North Africa, published in the "Transactions of the Royal Institute of British Architects," vol. i., New Series, 1885.

Thamugas was situated at the intersection of six Roman roads; two went through Lambæsis, in the direction of Setif; a third to Diana Veteranorum (*Zana*); two more to Theveste by Mascula (*Khenchla*), and a sixth northwards to Constantine. It appears to have been of as great importance as Lambessa, to judge by the size of its public buildings, especially the theatre, and the area covered by its remains, while its architecture is undoubtedly older and purer. There is nothing at Lambessa to equal the triumphal arch here.

It is mentioned by Ptolemy under the name of Thamutuda; in the Itinerary of Antoninus as Tamugada, and it occurs in various inscriptions as Thamugas. It is elsewhere described as *Colonia Marciana Trajana Thamugas*, and *Colonia Ulpia Thamugus;* and on an inscription, still in perfect preservation near the Forum, there is an allusion to the thirtieth *Legion Ulpia*, and a celebration of the victories of Trajan over the Parthians. From this M. Leon Renier concludes that the Emperor, wishing to recompense the veterans of the 30th legion, *Ulpia Victrix*, for their participation in the war against the Parthians, established them at Timegad, not only as being a vast and fertile country, but a position of great military importance, from which they might be able to suppress the turbulence of the neighbouring mountaineers.

The inscription above mentioned exists in duplicate on two fine pedestals of white marble, of octagonal shape, the height being 1½ mètre, and the width of the faces from 50 to 30 centimètres.

VICTORIAE
PARTHICAE
AVG. SACR.
EX · TESTAMENTO
M. ANNI · M. F. QVR.
MARTIALIS · MIL.

```
[LEG III      AVG.       DVPLC
ALAE.     PANN.     DEC.     AL
EIVSDEM.    >    LEG III  ·  AVG
ET.   XXX.   VI.PLAE   VICTIC
MISSI.      ·       HONESTA
MISSIONE    '   AB   '   IMP  .
TRAIANO           '          OPTIMO
AVG.      GER      DAC.      PARTH
SING.   HS.   VIII.   XX.   PR.   ✕
ANNII  .   M.   LIB.   PROTVS
HILARVS           ·           EROS
ADIECTIS   '   A.   SE.   HS.   III.
PONEND.               CVRAVER
IDEM        Q.        DEDICAVER
          D.   D.
```

Thamugas is mentioned in the Acts of Saint Mammarius and in the Theodosian Code. It subsequently became the great focus of religious agitation during the 4th century. In 398 its bishop, Optatus, sided with the Count Gildon in his revolt against Honorius, and was regarded as the recognised head of the Donatists. St. Augustine, who often alluded to him, says that during ten years Africa trembled under his yoke. Amongst other bishops of Thamugas are Novatus, who assisted at the Council of Carthage in 255; Sextus, who died in 320; Faustinus, who was present at the conference of Carthage in 411; and Secundus, who was exiled by Hunerie in 484.

When Solomon arrived for the first time in the Aurès, in 535, he found the city ruined. It had been destroyed by the inhabitants of the Aurès mountains so as not to become a source of danger to them should the Byzantines take it. He restored the citadel at least, in the same style as the other fortresses throughout the country. The proof of this is evident; but the other public buildings bear no trace of a restoration posterior to their original construction.

At the time of the Arab invasion it was a Christian city, as in 646, under the government of Gregory, a Christian church was built, the ruins of which still exist. It is a square building, with a circular apse at the east end, divided into a nave and two aisles by columns, three on each side, of rose-coloured marble, the centre one on each side only being free; the others are engaged in the walls, right and left of the apse and of the entrance. On the lintel of the door was inscribed on white marble:—

In temporibus Constantini Imperatoris
Fl. Gregorio Patricio Joannes dux
de Tigisi offeret donum Dei+Armenus.

The ruins occupy a large undulating plain, cut into two portions by a watercourse, which was either entirely covered over, so as to admit of easy communication, or only embanked with masonry, and bridged at intervals. This runs S. and N. On the W. side are extensive ruins of buildings; but the only one of importance is the small Christian church just described.

The principal buildings are situated on the right or E. bank of the ravine; they consist of a Byzantine fortress, theatre, forum, triumphal arch, a huge temple, public latrine, and innumerable other buildings, too much ruined to admit of absolute identification.

The first of these was originally of Roman construction; the regular and careful masonry of that people can be recognised in some few places; a posterior restoration by the Byzantines can also be easily identified, as they invariably employed the cut stones of the former buildings, without much regard to perfect adaptation, using also tombstones and any other material that came most easily to hand. The third restoration is of a very inferior character, the stones being small, irregular, and very loosely put together.

The general plan of the *enceinte* and a great part of the walls are still entire. It is a large quadrangle, about 110 metres by 90, flanked on each side by salient towers, 3 in number. That on the eastern side is not in the middle, and is much more salient than those at the angles. In the part of this tower facing the interior may be seen the remains of a circular brick dome, the crown of which has disappeared, and in its place there is a rude attempt to complete it by means of loosely piled stones. Some remains of columns are seen in the interior court belonging to a small building, perhaps a church.

The **Theatre** was cut in the abrupt northern flank of a hill, the opposite side of which gradually sloped towards the S. This monument was of considerable dimensions, and intended for the accommodation of a considerable population. The building was executed in a substantial manner, the walls being generally of solid rubble masonry, faced with cut stone of considerable dimensions.

In the interior, where the masonry may have been covered with cement or other materials, the angles were made sharp by brickwork. Although the columns actually found on the spot are all in stone of an inferior description, they were numerous. On the stage may be counted the remains of 14.

The **Forum** has lately been unearthed. The N. façade had a colonnade in its entire length, from which the inhabitants must have enjoyed one of the most charming views it was possible to imagine. "In the middle of it was a gateway of a monumental character, having an order larger than that of the colonnade. A flight of 10 steps within this gateway formed the principal approach to the Forum, which measures 49·30 mètres by 44·30 mètres, entirely paved, and surrounded by a broad colonnade of the Corinthian order, raised 2 steps above the general area. On the E. side was the Basilica, and on the S. the Theatre, to which it had probably access" (*Graham*).

Great numbers of inscriptions and pedestals lie scattered about in this neighbourhood. One, still very perfect, is in a character resembling the Gothic. It runs as follows :—

Vocontio
P. Fl. Pudenti Pomponiano
C(*larissimo*) v(*iro*) erga civeis
Patriamque prolixe cultori exercitus
Militaribus effecto multifariam
loquentes litteras amplianti Atticans
facundiam ad aequanti Romano
nitori
ordo incola patrono oris uberis
et fluentis nostr(*i*) alteri fonti.

Towards the N.W. of the town, nearly in the axis of the colonnade of the Forum, from which, at all events, it formed a striking view, exists a **Triumphal Arch**, one of the most important monuments of the kind in Algeria. It consists of three openings, the central one 3·26 mètres wide, and the side ones 2·19 mètres ; above the latter are square niches for statues. The monument is of the Corinthian order ; each front is decorated by four fluted columns 5·96 mètres high, occupying the angles and the spaces between the arches. To each column corresponds a pilaster, both raised on a common pedestal.

The entablature connects all the columns and pilasters together, and was itself surmounted by an attic, with an entablature, a portion of the architrave of which now alone remains. Over the two lateral arches and the square niches, and supported by the two columns, are two curved pediments, the cornices of which (as also the main cornice profile round) are set back over the columns, an arrangement not unfrequent in the colonies of the empire. The attic, intended no doubt to receive the dedicatory inscription, and perhaps also to support sculpture, appears to have extended over the whole top of the building. None of the original inscription remains in place, but fragments have been found below and near the Forum, from which M. Leon Renier restores it as follows :—

Imperator Caesar diri
Nervae filius Nervae Trajanus
Augustus Germanicus Pontifex maximus
Imperator III. tribunicia Potestate IIII.
consul III. Pater patriae coloniam
Marcianam Trajanam Tha-
mugadi per legionem tertiam Augustam
fecit . . . unatim . . . Gallus legatus
Augusti pro praetore
Dedicavit.

The two façades are identical in feature, and each is in itself perfectly symmetrical, except that the capitals of the two middle columns on the southern façade, instead of having the angle of the abacus supported by volutes, have eagles in their place. The square niches have had each their separate entablature, and columns supported by sculptured brackets ; all the arches have archivoltes.

The mass of the monument is of sandstone, but the columns, capitals and bases of the pilasters, brackets and entablature, are entirely of white marble, as was also the crowning of the attic ; the sides of the attics were certainly covered by slabs, most probably of the same material.

M. Masqueray found amongst the ruins of the Byzantine Citadel, an inscription from which he concludes that this building was called the arch of the Gods, ARCVM PANTHEVM, but this, according to Mr. Graham, does not adapt itself to the shape of the attic. It was probably surrounded with statues and dedicatory pedestals, forming a group of which any city might justly have been proud.

The next important building has been supposed to be a **Temple to Jupiter Capitolinus**. The ruins show that it must have been a very splendid edifice.

A large court probably existed before the entrance, as the vestiges of a colonnade are still visible parallel to the principal façade. This was most powerfully constructed ; a transverse wall, which may have corresponded to the entrance of the cella, measures nearly 2 mètres in thickness, the stones varying from 1 to 1¼ mètre in length, and from 65 centimètres to a mètre in breadth, and 50 centimètres in height. An attic base in blue limestone lying on the spot, measures 1·97 mètre in breadth at its plinth. The most massive parts were built according to the Roman system of rubble, cased in cut stone masonry, composed of blocks of great size. The columns were fluted, of the Corinthian order, their diameter is 1·30 mètre. The capitals were in two stones on account of their great size.

An inscription was here found on four stones, surrounded by a moulding, of which the following is a copy :—

Pro magnificentia saeculi dominorum nostrorum Valentiniani et Valentis semper Augustorum et perpetuorum, porticus capitolii, serie vetustatis absumptus et usque ad ima fundamenta conlapsus, novo opere perfectas exornatasque dedicavit Publilius Caeionius Caecina Albinus, Vir clarissimus, consularis, curantibus Aelio Juliano, iterum rei publicae curatore, Flavio Aquilino, flamine perpetuo Antonio Petroniano flamine perpetuo Antonio Ianuiariano flamine perpetuo.

The traveller should not miss a visit to the **Cedar Forest** situated in *Djebel Tuggurt*, the mountain to the N.W. of Batna.

In fine weather a carriage can drive about 2½ kil. beyond the Garde Forestier's house, which is at 15 kil. from Batna, but the excursion is far better made on horseback ; it will occupy a full day. It is well for the traveller to know that after crossing the bridge over the stream he should keep to the right : an ascent of ¾ of an hour will bring him to one of the best views, *Col de Boujat*.

The trees are not so fine as those of Teniet, and they have been very injudiciously cut down during the last 20 years, but the forest is very extensive, the views magnificent, and one cannot help being gratified to find, what is wanting at Teniet, a considerable growth of young trees with which the spaces left vacant by the old ones are covered. On the upper parts of the mountains and on their southern slopes there are many fine oaks, junipers and pines. The cedars do not flourish exposed to the sirocco.

From Batna a light waggonette runs to **Aïn-Khenchla**, doing the journey in 12 hours. There is also a horse road to Setif ; the total distance is about 120 kil., and there are two Kaids' houses and one or two farms on the way, at which a traveller can sleep.

[*Excursion in the* **Aurès Mountains**.

The foregoing are excursions which every tourist can do with ease during the time he is likely to be detained at Batna, but for the more enterprising traveller, who is prepared to travel on mules, and to spend a week or two in tents or in such accommodation as he may find available, and who does not shrink from an absence of every kind of European comfort and the presence of a very considerable amount of native discomfort in the shape of fleas, the author would strongly advise a tour in the Aurès Mountains. This may be made in almost any direction, as the country is thickly populated and villages are numerous. Mules will cost from 4 to 5 f. per diem, and no doubt a guide can be procured through the aid of the authorities at Batna, without whose concurrence the journey should not be attempted.

The geographical term *Aurès*, corresponding to the *Audon* of Ptolemy and the *Mons Aurasius* of other geographers, comprises at the present day that mass of mountains stretching between the route from Batna to Biskra on the W. and the *Oued el-Arab* on the E. It does not extend farther N. than Batna or as far S. as Biskra. Its greatest length from E. to W. is 120 kil., and from N. to S. 70 kil., the whole area being about 800 square kilomètres.

Its inhabitants, the *Chawia*, are a branch of that great Berber race which has occupied the N. of Africa from Egypt to the Atlantic from prehistoric times. The Kabyles form another branch; both speak slightly different dialects of the same language, but the former shut up in their mountain fastnesses, hardly yet known to the world beyond, have remained far less mixed with foreign elements than the latter, at least since the time of the Arab conquest.

The *débris* of the Roman, Byzantine and Vandal colonies no doubt found refuge here when driven from the surrounding plains by one set of conquerors after another, or under the influence of religious persecution, and as a consequence, both the features, language, and customs of the people bear unmistakable testimony to their classic origin.

All the old writers who have visited the country describe in glowing terms the beauty of its women. Morgan, who wrote in 1728, and whose interesting "History of Algeria" is too little studied, remarks, "What numbers have I seen, particularly females, who, for well-featured countenances, fair curling locks and wholesome ruddy looks, might not vie with or even be envied by the proudest European dames." Shaw and Bruce bear testimony to the same fact, and the writer can honestly assert his conviction that in no country is the average of female beauty higher than in the Aurès mountains. It is true that hard labour from earliest youth soon causes this to fade, but nothing can mar the classical regularity of features which mark their European rather than their African origin.

Their language is full of Latin words, and in their daily life they retain customs undoubtedly derived from their Christian ancestry. They observe the 25th of December as a feast, under the name of *Moolid* (the birth), and keep three days' festival both at springtime and harvest. They use the solar instead of the Mohammedan lunar year, and the names of the months are the same as our own. They are emphatically shepherds as well as agriculturists, having few or no cattle, but immense flocks of sheep and goats. The great difference between them and the Arabs in this respect is that the latter are nomades, while the former rarely ever leave their native valleys. The word *Zenati* is also used as a synonym for *Chawi*.

These remarks must be taken to apply principally to the *Chawi* of the Aurès; the race itself has a far wider geographical distribution, but beyond these inaccessible mountains it has got more or less mixed with other elements.

The following was the author's route but, as before remarked, it may be varied to almost any extent, and much longer stages can be made—

1st day.	Batna to El-Arbäa	8	hours.
2d ,,	,, to El-Manäa	5	,,
3d ,,	to Mines of Taghit	4	,,
4th ,,	to El-Bali	4	,,
5th ,,	to Oued Taga	4	,,
6th ,,	to Timegad	3	,,
7th ,,	to Omm el-Ashera	3	,,
8th ,,	to El-Wadhaha	2½	,,
9th ,,	to Bou Hammama	6¼	,,
	(including ascent of Chellia).		
10th ,,	Aïn-Meimoun	5¼	,,
11th ,,	Aïn-Khenchla	5	,,

Space will not admit of a detailed description of this interesting expedition; the author unwillingly limits himself to a very few remarks regarding each stage.

El-Arbäa.—Probably the most picturesque and characteristic Chawi village in the Aurès. Situated high upon the face of a hill, the base of which is washed by a beautiful stream, and the crest of which is cut and serrated in the most fantastic manner.

El Manâa.—The principal residence of the Kaïd of the Aurès, Si Abbas, renowned for his hospitality, and who always keeps a comfortable guest chamber ready for the use of travellers.

The town is beautifully situated at the confluence of the *Oued Abdi* and the *Oued Bou Zaina.*

Mines of Taghit.—Here are mercury mines, which belonged to the late Mr. Wellington Vallance.

El-Bali.—A village on the left bank of the Oued Abdi, just under *Dj. Mahmel*, the second highest peak in Algeria.

Oued Taga.—Here is a comfortable bordj, formerly belonging to Si Abbas, Kaïd of the Aurès, now the property of the State, where the traveller will certainly be able to lodge. Batna may be reached in four hours from this point.

Omm el-Ashera.—A small village near the plain of *Firis*, near which, on *Djebel Kharouba* and *Djebel Bou Driecen*, are great numbers of highly curious megalithic remains, consisting not only of the ordinary type of Dolmen, but of circular tombs of a much more unusual construction.

Timegad, see p. 208.

El-Wadhaha.—This is merely a convenient halting-place prior to the ascent of Chellia; there is no village or habitations, and if the traveller is unprovided with a tent; he must select some other place in which to pass the night.

The ascent of Chellia is quite easy, and can be made from this point in 2½ hours; the traveller can ride to within a few hundred yards of the top. Chellia is the highest point in Algeria, 7611 ft. above the sea, 23 ft. higher than Dj. Mahmel, and 69 higher than Djurdjura. The view from the summit is one of exceeding grandeur. The descent may be made by the opposite side of the mountain, and the night's halt at

Bou Hammama, a small village on the edge of the plain of Melagou.

Ain-Mimoun is a lovely spot in an extensive cedar forest. There are both civil and military establishments for sawing timber, and the traveller will have no difficulty in obtaining rough shelter for the night.

Ain-Khenchla, the *Mascula* of the Romans, a large and thriving village, where the traveller will again find himself in a settled part of the country; it possesses a good inn, and there is communication by diligence with Ain-Beida and Batna.[1]]

92 kil. *El-Biar.*
114 kil. *Ain-Touta.*
122 kil. *Les Tamarins.*

The line now passes into the valley of the *Oued Fedala.* On the left is *Djebel Mellili*, rising above the lower hills; on the right a grand mass of limestone, with upheaved strata, dipping to the S. On the isthmus between the Oued Ksour which presently joins the Oued Fedala, right — and the O. Fedala are the ruins of a Roman town, "Ad duo Flumina."

146 kil. **El-Kantara.** The station is 800 mètres from the remarkable gorge in Djebel Metlili, in which the hotel is situated. Owing to a tunnel the railway traveller misses the first striking view of the oasis beyond. If he is not pressed for time it is well worth passing a day in this beautiful spot, where alpine scenery and tropical vegetation are met with together in such a wonderful combination.

El-Kantara was the *Calceus Herculis* of the Romans; and numerous fragments of Roman work and inscriptions have been found. Among others the following, showing that a part of the famous Third Augustan Legion was quartered here:—

MI IO V RI O
I T HO IO V I I
I J M AU TI
O B A V I T
I N L I N
R V F V S
L E G. III. AVG.

[1] For fuller information regarding the Aurès Mountains, see "Footsteps of Bruce," p. 61.

The Roman bridge is at the N. entrance of the defile. It consists of one massive semicircular arch resting upon the rock at either side. It was "restored" in 1862, and all appearance of antiquity removed. The ancient bridge is not now used, the route following the left bank of the stream, instead of the right one adopted by the Romans.

The commencement of the gorge is not more than 200 mètres beyond the hotel. It is a rent in the limestone range, just 40 mètres wide at its narrowest part, and about 300 mètres long. The cliffs that bound it are broken into pinnacles, and the river roars below in a deep bed over rounded boulders. It widens at its S. end; and as the traveller passes out of it a wonderful view is displayed before him. The river emerging from its narrow bed, widens into a goodly stream, and right and left of it is a forest of 15,000 date-palms (of which this is the N. limit), interspersed with oranges, mulberries, apricots and apples. Quaint Arab houses emerge from the green sea of foliage, and beyond, over a valley that in spring is green with corn, are some castellated red cliffs, backed by a limestone range.

There are three villages in the oasis: Dahraouia on the right bank, Khekar and Kbour-el-Abbas on the left. They are well built and clean. The houses are usually of one story, with a terrace, on which a tent is often pitched. The woodwork of the doors and roofs is of palm wood. The square towers so frequent in the oasis are for watchers, to guard the fruit when ripe. The inhabitants seem a kindly, unsophisticated race, mostly dark, but some are fair and blue-eyed. They are very industrious. The men work in the gardens, till the fields, or follow a trade. The women weave. They are unveiled, and may be seen washing clothes at the fountain, as unrestrained as if they were in France or England.

The Djebel Metlili dips to the S. Its limestone cliffs are highly charged with quartz. Some of the beds on its S. face are full of fossil shells, as are also the beds of black marl on the right bank of the stream to the N. Bands of gypsum are frequent, especially in the range S. of the Djebel Metlili, which, unlike it, dips to the N. .

There are numerous Roman remains, but none of great consequence, near El-Kantara, one of these, at 7 kil. distance, is called by the natives Kherbel-el-Bordj, the ancient Burgum Speculatorium, built in the reign of Caracalla (217 to 221), by order of Marcus Valerius Senecio, Imperial Legate in Numidia, and under the direction of a prefect of the III. Legion, for the protection of the *speculatores* or outposts of that Legion. An inscription recording this fact was discovered by M. Renier in 1851.

After about 10 kil. the ranges N. and S. approach one another, turning abruptly towards the stream. This is the S. end of the plain of El-Kantara. The S. range terminates in a fine cliff, about 30 mètres high, crowned by a disused semaphore. To the N. is a spur of conglomerate.

165 kil. *Fontaine des Gazelles*, a solitary farm close under a range of low sandhills. A copious warm spring, slightly saline, bursts out of the sand with a temperature of 76° Fahr. at its origin. Its overflow makes a luxuriant marsh, which has formed a small oasis. This is the ancient *Aquas Herculis*. About 2 kil. to the E. is a small hot lake, very pleasant for a bath. Near the spring may be seen a bed of enormous subfossil oysters, some of which are 18 in. in length. These have been drifted here from the bed which lies under the range of hills to the E.

174 kil. *El-Outaïa*. The Arab village is on a low hill to the S., built probably on a Roman site, and of Roman materials. The mud walls rest in places on Roman blocks.

[The *Montagne de Sel* can be conveniently visited from here. An Arab with a mule costs 4 f. It takes about ¾ hr. to reach the base of the mountain. A few hundred yards from the left bank of the stream are some insignificant Roman ruins. A few rectangular plinths, with the bases of columns hewn out of the same block, remain in position. The mountain, which is one of the five mentioned by Herodotus, is a mass of bluish-grey rock salt, at the S.W. end of a limestone range, dipping, like the last, N. That it has been forced up from below is evident when any point is reached sufficiently high to see the way in which masses of sand have been torn up out of the plain, and elevated upon pinnacles and mamelons of salt. The strata are a good deal contorted at the point where the eruption took place, and beyond it they have the appearance of having been forced forwards and upwards, and piled together in confusion. The Arabs have used the salt for ages; but it is not quarried regularly.]

The line now strikes S.E. across the plain. To the N. is the fine valley of the Aurès, down which the Oued Abdi flows into the Oued Kantara. The united streams are called the Oued Biskra.

Beyond this cultivation is scanty, and sand predominates. There are usually a good many Arab encampments. Its S. boundary, the Djebel bou-Ghazal, is a limestone range of no great height. In the foreground are bare hills of sand, then a second limestone range, lower than the first; and beyond, the vast plain, stretching with no visible elevation to the horizon, and dotted with dark spots, the largest of which is the oasis of Biskra, 8 kil. distant.

202 kil. **Biskra**, is situated lat. 34° 51', at a height of 360 ft. above the sea-level. The name does not denote a single town, but a union of five villages scattered through the oasis, which is a strip of cultivated ground on the right bank of the stream, about 3 m. in length, and from a ¼ m. to ¾ m. in breadth. The two oases of *Gaddecha* and *Filiah*, opposite to Biskra, on the left bank, are also considered to belong to it. These villages are all of the ordinary Arab type, houses built of hardened mud, with doors and roof of palm wood. Among the ruins of what the French term "**Le vieux Biskra**," where, before the new fort was built, they fortified the Kasba of the federation existing before their arrival, may be seen a few blocks of Roman work, and one or two Roman columns. This is all that remains of the outpost of *Ad Piscinam*. The French settlement is confined to the N. end of the oasis, close to the spot where the canal for irrigation, termed "La Prise d'Eau," is diverted from the river.

The Fort St. Germain, so called from an officer who was killed at Seriana during the insurrection of the Zaatcha in 1849, is an extensive work, capable of resisting any attack likely to be made against it by Arabs, and of sheltering the civil population, if necessary. It contains barracks, an hospital, and all the other buildings necessary for the use of the garrison, which, however, is not now a large one. In front of the principal entrance is the *Jardin Public*, an agreeable and shady walk, with the *Church* in the centre. The *Market-place* is worth a visit for the curious nature of the wares exposed for sale, and the picturesqueness of the vendors and buyers.

The climate of Biskra is delightful during 6 months in the year. Nowhere in Algeria can one find a more genial temperature, a clearer sky, or more beautiful vegetation; but in summer the thermometer frequently stands at 110° Fahr. in the shade, and from 80 to 90° at night. The mean temperature of the year, on an average of 10 years, is 73°, the maximum and minimum 124° and 36° during the same time. It is practically rainless, the only drawback is the prevalence of high winds.

An experimental Government garden was created at Biskra, but owing to the absence of good management, and from insufficiency of funds, it did not prove a success, and has now been abandoned. This is hardly to be regretted, as the intelligent enterprise of a private individual has successfully carried out what the efforts of the State had failed to accomplish. M. Landon, a French gentleman of fortune and education, after having devoted several years to foreign travel, has fixed his winter residence at Biskra, where he has created a charming retreat, and devotes himself to the cultivation of his property, in which he has successfully acclimatised many precious tropical fruit trees and other plants. These gardens can be visited on presentation of an address card.

The oasis of Biskra contains 100,000 date palms, besides several thousand fruit trees of other sorts. The palms are not enclosed within high walls, as at El-Aghouat and El-Kantara, but are planted in detached groups, or as hedges to the extensive fields of barley and luxuriant gardens of vegetables. The trees are not quite so large as those of El-Aghouat, but the way in which they are planted renders them far more picturesque, and delightful walks or rides may be taken in all directions through and round the oasis.

The supply of water from the Oued Biskra is very copious throughout winter and early spring, nor does it fail entirely even in summer, except in very dry seasons. It has been supplemented by the energy of the French, who have caused Artesian wells to be dug here and in some of the neighbouring oases, so that the most may be made of the ground that is capable of bearing corn.

We would advise travellers to be in no hurry to quit Biskra, as there is a great deal to see in the neighbourhood.

About 6 kil. N.W., under the Djebel bou-Ghazal, is the **Fontaine Chaude** —Ar. *Hammam Salahin*—i.e. "Bath of the Saints." It bursts out with great violence and volume, giving, it is said, 40 litres per second. Its temperature at its source is 112° Fahr. Baths have been erected round it, much frequented by French and natives. One is specially reserved for officers, but permission to bathe in it, and the key, can easily be obtained. All, however, are very bad. The surplus water is first collected in a reservoir outside, where poor Arabs bathe, and thence flows down the hill into a marsh, turning 2 or 3 Arab mills as it goes. In the stream, close to the marsh, are quantities of small fish, *Cyprinodon calaritanus*, identical with those found in the hot springs of the oasis of Jupiter-Ammon in Egypt. The temperature of the water in which they live is about 96° Fahr. It is proposed to convey the water of this spring to Biskra, and to form a bathing establishment close to the railway station. There are 2 small lakes of warm water near the *Fontaine*, and just behind it is a low hill of a formation that appears to be volcanic. At 5 kil. to the S.E. is a remarkable *megalithic enceinte*, with salient portions in the form of redans, and several rude staircases have been cut in the rocky slope. Two or three larger stones on the summit appear to have formed a sort of monument. The summit of the mound is too small to have contained a garrison; most probably it was a temple or sacred place of some kind.

Biskra is the capital of the *Ziban*, (plural of *Zab*), whose prosperous villages, buried in groves of palm and fruit trees, and surrounded by barley fields, are dotted over the vast plain extending from the foot of the Aurès to the *Chott Melghigh*.

Excursions may be made in various directions to the different oases, one of which at least should be visited. We proceed to describe that of **Sidi Okba**, 20 kil. S.E. The road is practicable for a light carriage, and the drive occupies 2 hrs. Crossing the Oued Biskra, here a stony tract, a quarter of a mile broad, with a deep stream flowing in the centre, the small oasis of Filiah is passed on the right, and the plain, here sparingly cultivated, is entered. In the distance is seen the long low line of the palms in the oasis of Sidi Okba. To the left are fine views of the Aurès, with the oases lying at the feet of their spurs. These occur in the following order from Biskra:—Chetma, 8 kil.; Droh, 13 kil.; Sidi-Khelil, 14 kil.; Seriana, 17 kil.; Garta, 21 kil. After a drive of 2 hrs. the village of Sidi Okba is reached, composed, like all others, of houses of one story, built of dried mud. The market-place and the small shops are extremely quaint and curious. But the chief interest of the place is centred in the mosque, probably the most ancient Mohammedan building in

Africa. It is square, each side about 35 mètres long, with a flat roof supported on a number of rude columns, one of which, with a spiral ornament round it, may possibly have been brought from a Roman building. The rest are extremely rude imitations, in clay, of stone pillars. At the N.W. corner is the shrine of Sidi Okba, in a sort of chantry screened off from the mosque. It is a tomb of the ordinary Marabout type, hung round with silk, ostrich eggs and other pieces of tawdry furniture, among which a large gilt mirror frame is conspicuous. On the S. side of the mosque is the pulpit. The minaret should be ascended for the sake of the view, which alone repays the trouble of the journey. There is an Arab legend that this minaret will tremble visibly when Sidi Okba is invoked according to a prescribed form of words. There is a carved wooden door on the E. side of the mosque of admirable workmanship, and on one of the pillars a rude inscription in early Cufic characters, perhaps the oldest Arabic inscription in the world, and very grand in its simplicity —*This is the tomb of Okba, son of Nafa. May God have mercy upon him.*

Sidi Okba is the religious, as Biskra may be styled the political, capital of the Ziban. It derives its name from the illustrious warrior who, at the head of a small body of Arab horsemen, went forth at the bidding of the Khalifa Moaouia to conquer Africa in the 60th year of the Hedjira. What Rome had taken centuries to effect Okba accomplished in a marvellously short time; and when he had extended his conquest from Egypt to Tangier he spurred his horse into the Atlantic and declared that only such a barrier could prevent him from forcing every nation beyond it who knew not God to worship Him only or die. Many revolts took place before the power of the conqueror was consolidated, and in one of them—at Tehouda, about 700 mètres from the oasis of Sidi Okba, in A.D. 682 (A.H. 63)—he, with about 300 of his followers was massacred by a Berber chief of the name of Koceila, whom he had subjected to great indignity. When later the Arabs had reconquered the country in which Biskra now stands, they buried their leader at the place which bears his name.

A visit to the oasis of **Oumach** gives the traveller an opportunity of seeing a specimen of the *dunes* of sand, so characteristic of the desert.

Chetma is within a drive of 1 hr. and is worthy of a visit. The houses are on a somewhat larger scale than those at Sidi Okba or Biskra.

ROUTE 15.

Biskra to Tuggurt.[1]

As we observed when concluding the route to El-Aghouat, it is hardly within the scope of this work to describe the routes between the various oases in the Sahara. Still, as Englishmen, and Englishwomen also, are becoming year by year more adventurous, we give one of the most interesting routes as a specimen of desert travel.

None, however, who are not in robust health and capable of undergoing considerable fatigue and privation should attempt it.

The best means of performing the journey is on horseback, and before starting the traveller would do well to take the advice of the authorities as to the hiring of transport and guides; especial care being taken that some of the party should understand both the French and Arabic languages. A guide can always be obtained at the hotel.

A light waggonette may be hired at Biskra for the trip, and with 3 hors s ought not to cost more than 400 or 450 f.

The traveller should provide himself with such provisions and wine as he may require for the journey, and abstain from drinking too much desert water.

Bedding ought also to be taken, as

[1] The distances here given must only be taken as an approximation to the truth.

the caravanserais are quite unprovided in this respect. A diligence runs every second day and makes the journey in three days. It is a wretched conveyance.

The best time for this journey is autumn or early spring; by the beginning of May the heat is already too great for desert travelling.

1st day. After leaving the hotel the road leads for about an hour through the palm groves of Biskra, and then emerges into a slightly undulating plain covered with a thick scrub of terebinth, as high as the heads of the goats which browse amongst it.

36 kil. The track crosses the *Oued Biskra* twice. After rains this river is very deep, with so much mud at the bottom as to be fordable only with great difficulty by carriages.

38 kil. *Saada.* The character of the country does not change before reaching this place, which is a fortified caravanserai, with rooms for travellers, but no furniture of any kind, neither are provisions procurable.

61 kil. *Ain-Chegga*, a caravanserai like the last, offering only the protection of its roof to travellers. It is situated on comparatively low ground, in the centre of a vast, shallow, treeless basin. Gerboa rats abound here, and afford a by no means unpalatable meal *faut de mieux*.

2d day. After leaving Chegga, the country is bare and uninteresting, closely covered with short scrub, interspersed with patches of brushwood. The road gradually ascends from the basin where Chegga stands until a plain or table-land of no great elevation is attained.

76 kil. The table-land here suddenly ceases, and a view is obtained of a great plain, that of the *Oued Gheir*, stretching far away to the S. and also (a little to the left or S.E.) the great lake called the *Chott Melghigh*, 300 kil. long. From the edge of this plateau, looking back, the last dim view is obtained of the bold and beautifully coloured mountains of Biskra.

The route now follows the course of the Oued Gheir, whose length is about 100 kil., and along which is a chain of smaller chotts, which it connects with the Chott Melghigh.

After the next 16 kil. palm oases are more or less frequently met with. The road, on leaving the table-land, descends by a steep sand-hill, and the station for the mid-day halt is 2 kil. farther on, at *Kef el-akhdar*, where there is an Artesian well of brackish water, surrounded by a wall 8 or 9 ft. high, which gives the only shade or shelter to be found.

At *Selil*, 7 kil. before this place, there is a well of better water, unmarked or unprotected by a wall, but this is not recommended as a halting-place, as it breaks the day's journey too unequally.

The road now runs parallel to the western shore of the Chott, at a distance of about 4 kil., and the heat is not unfrequently tempered by cool and welcome breezes passing over its waters. The country, though gradually ascending, is devoid of hills, the soil becomes more sandy, and the road heavier; but the brushwood is so thick that the track has to wind in and out amongst it.

110 kil. Here, about two hours before reaching the halt, the traveller comes upon the first *dune* of true desert sand.

112 kil. *Meroman*, the first oasis of the Oued Gheir, is passed on the left. Beyond this, a thin dark line on the horizon ahead indicates the oasis of *Maghaier*, where the traveller must pass the night.

A shorter and more pleasant route for horses passes between these two oases, much nearer to the Chott Melghigh.

123 kil. *Maghaier*, a village of sun-dried bricks, surrounded by a mud wall, situate at one side of a large oasis containing 50,000 date palms. After passing the gate the traveller will probably be conducted to the house of the Sheikh, where he is sure of such hospitality as the place affords. On leaving, a present will be expected, though never demanded.

A caravanserai, very good and clean, has been built at about a quarter of an hour's walk from the Sheikh's house.

3d day. On leaving Maghaier the

road passes a succession of oases, decidedly the most pleasant section of the route. The road itself, however, is sandy and heavy.

133 kil. Here, about 1½ hr. from Maghaier, is a spring of good water, surrounded by two or three palm-trees.

After passing this spring, and at 5 kil. to the right of the road, is the oasis of Sidi Rahel, where an Artesian well was sunk in 1874.

155 kil. Halt for breakfast at the Artesian well of *Meza Berzig*, where are a few young palms, replacing those destroyed during the insurrection of 1871. Two hours after leaving this is a pond of tolerably good water, thickly fringed with rushes and other aquatic plants—a veritable "diamond in the desert." Beyond it the track is long, sandy, and very heavy, skirting three or four oases, amongst them *Ourlana*, with its famous Artesian well. There is a caravanserai here, but it is in a very dilapidated condition; the traveller would do well to ask hospitality at the Sheikh's house. The next oasis is that of

183 kil. *Tamerna*, a village apparently of greater importance than Maghaier, built, like it, of mud; but on a conspicuous mound within it stands the ruin of a building of cut stone, circular in plan, composed of a continuous arcade of horse-shoe arches.

On the outskirts of the village is a caravanserai, worse even than the others. The Sheikh's house is 15 or 20 minutes' walk distant, within the village.

4th day. The road this day passes through fewer oases than on the previous one, and is very trying for the horses. The sand becomes finer in grain as one approaches Tuggurt, which is surrounded on every side by the true desert sand. About three hours after starting, the road skirts the fine oasis of *Sidi Rachid*, which is often selected as a halting-place. Thence it lies over gently undulating plains, varied by low hills of sand.

203 kil. The most convenient halting-place is at *Gamrha*, a large oasis on the right of the road, four hours from Tamerna. Here is a clear and rapid stream of nearly sweet water. Soon after leaving this place one gets a glimpse of Tuggurt, on a distant hill; between the two places, however, one passes neither oasis nor water, nothing but sand the whole way. It is sometimes disposed in steep ridges about 20 feet high, so loose that it has to be passed with the greatest care, to avoid the burial, more or less complete, of carriage and horses.

Along one part of the route is seen a succession of round pillars of rubble masonry, 12 ft. high, to mark the track, which is apt to be effaced by sand-drifts.

223 kil. **Tuggurt** stands out an imposing and conspicuous object on the brow of a hill, with its domes and towers in bright relief against the magnificent mass of palm-trees behind them.

The approach of strangers is a rare event; and, in the crowds which gather round the gate, in their freedom and vivacity of gesture, in the brightness of their costume and the deeper hue of their faces, the traveller will obtain a most interesting picture of Oued Gheir society.

On passing the gate, the traveller sees an irregular market-place situated on an ascent. On the right is a long line of arcades, on the left is the wall of the Kasba, which is surrounded by a large dome; in front is the chief mosque, with its dome and minaret; near it is another minaret of a ruined mosque.

Tuggurt covers a space, whose longest diameter is 400 mètres, on a slope inclining to the S.E. It was once surrounded by a ditch or moat, which is now filled up. The houses nearest the line of the old moat all join each other, and, after the manner of the Oued Gheir villages, form a continuous fence or wall, interrupted only by the town gates, of which there are two.

The town is divided into quarters, respectively occupied by the citizens proper, the Beni Manseur, the Jew converts to Islam, the negroes, and the foreigners. Besides these there are other divisions.

The houses are, for the most part, built of sun-dried bricks, but are sometimes decorated with burnt bricks, disposed in a manner to resemble tracery. They rarely rise a story above the ground floor. The streets are narrow and winding.

There are in all 20 mosques. Of these the two already mentioned are of much more importance than the rest. One of the two is now used as a carpenter's shop. The other, whose cupola dominates the market-place, is in bad repair, but possesses some very fine plaster arabesque work, the design of a Tunisian architect. From the minaret of the first mentioned of the two mosques a very fine panoramic view of the surrounding desert and oasis, including that of Temacin with its mosque, may be obtained.

On entering Tuggurt by the Biskra gate, the traveller, to reach the entrance of the Kasbah, has to pass the entire length of its wall, already mentioned as bounding the market-place on the left. The Kasbah consists of many courts. Its outermost court is nearly as large as the market-place, and, like it, is furnished with arcades on one side. The commandant's residence, the barracks, and the hospital, are all within the *enceinte* of the Kasbah. It is built of dressed stone—a rare distinction in the Oued Gheir—and contains some rooms of fair dimensions. In one of its inner courts is a delightful garden, through which runs a stream of water from an Artesian well within it. There are three such wells in Tuggurt.

There are hardly any French residents. The garrison is entirely native, and the population is about 7000.

The oasis of Tuggurt contains 190,000 palm trees. Shady lanes, beside streams of water, lead through the groves. Under the palms are gardens in which grow luxuriantly fruit trees, corn and vegetables.

Marshes and salt lakes cover a large area near Tuggurt. The abundance of water here and throughout the Oued Gheir is the cause of a malignant fever at the end of April, and again early in the autumn, frequently fatal to Europeans, whilst the purgative nature of the water is a fertile source of diarrhœa and other similar complaints.

After the insurrection of 1871 the Government established a regular military post at Tuggurt, but after the capture of Bou Choucha, in 1874, this was abolished, and part of the surrounding tribes were placed in the circle of Biskra, and part in that of El-Aghouat.

Tuggurt has two suburbs, one to the S. among the marshes, and one to the N.E. on a hill. The *Compagnie de l'Oued Rirh* possesses a house and a small piece of land here.

From Tuggurt an excursion may be made to **Temacin**, an oasis about 20 kil. to the S.W. About half-way, but a little to the left of the direct road, is a lake of salt water, the margin of which is thickly fringed with tamarisks, rushes, etc.; it abounds with waterfowl. Nearer Temacin is another and larger one, connected with the stagnant moats surrounding the walls of the town. In these occur great quantities of *Chromidæ*, the only true African fish found in Algeria, and which are found as far as the E. coast of the continent.

Temacin is a large town, forlorn, neglected and ruinous, covering a gently rising mound, and surrounded by a wall and stagnant moat. This, with its rude bridge, the arched gateway, the successive tiers of houses, as they rise in terraced ruin to the crest of the mound, combine to give to it a strange and weird dignity, in good keeping with its position as outpost at the desert end of the Oued Gheir. After passing through the winding and narrow streets of the town a central square or place is reached, in which is the Kaid's house. Like all its neighbours it is of sun-dried brick, and of the heaviest and rudest construction.

At about 2 kil. to the S.E. is another village, containing the Zaouia of a celebrated Marabout, whose descendant still lives here. The streets are comparatively clean and well kept, affording a marked contrast to those of Temacin. The tomb-mosque adjoins the house of the Marabout. The part containing the tomb, though erected only 10 or 12 years ago by a builder from Tunis, has already the appearance of antiquity. The arabesque work on the interior of the dome is good, but inferior to that at Tuggurt. Iron and glass gates of rude design, but highly prized here, separate the shrine from the main body of the mosque devoted to ordinary religious service.

We cannot leave the desert without a few words on the immense benefits which the French have conferred upon it by the sinking of Artesian wells. In 1856 many of the oases in the desert had become uninhabitable by the filling up of existing wells, the number of gardens diminished daily, and the population began to emigrate to less desolate parts of the country. Government wisely determined not to clear out existing wells, always a difficult and even dangerous operation, but rather to dig new ones by means of Artesian boring apparatus.

The first attempt was made at Tuggurt in 1856; after five weeks of labour the waterfield was tapped at a depth of 60 mètres from the surface, and almost immediately afterwards a river rushed forth yielding 4000 litres a minute, double the quantity afforded by the well of Grenelle at Paris. The joy and gratitude of the inhabitants can well be understood, and manifested itself by singing, dancing and *fantasias* of every description.

Ever since similar scenes have been taking place, not perhaps with the same amount of astonishment, but with no less rejoicing.

ROUTE 16.
To Tebessa.

Distance in kil. from S.A.	Names of Stations.	Distance in kil. from Tebessa.
	Souk-Ahras . . .	128
11	Oued Chouk . . .	111
28	Dréa . . .	100
36	Mdaouronch . . .	92
68	Aouinet-ed-Dieb . .	60
96	Morsott . . .	32
128	Tebessa . . .	..

Until 1889 it was only possible to visit this interesting place by a long and fatiguing route, but now a branch railway has been constructed which leaves the main line from Bone to Tunis at Souk-Ahras, and the journey can be made thence in 7 hrs.

After leaving Souk-Ahras the line follows the course of the Medjerda for a distance of 7 kil. till the junction of that river with the *Oued Mauepub*; it crosses the latter by a viaduct, and runs through a picturesque and wooded valley as far as 11 kil., *Oued Chouk*, the valley of spines or thistles; this is a watering station.

28 kil. *Dréa*. The station is badly named, being remote from the locality whose name it bears; it is better known to the Arabs as *Sidi Brahim*, from a Marabout close to the station. On the high table-land to the E. is the prosperous village of *Zarouria*, 12 kil. in a direct line from Souk-Ahras.

36 kil. *Mdaouronch*. An important depôt for Alfa. 12 kil. to the W. are the ruins of the ancient *Medaura*, where St. Augustine commenced his studies, and the birthplace of Apuleius. (See p. 230.)

58 kil. The line passes close to an isolated mountain, *Djebel Ouenza*, near the top of which is a curious perforation. This is said to have been made by Sidi Okba with his spear, on purpose that he might have some place to which to tie his horse!

63 kil. The line crosses the *Oued Mellegue*, up the valley of which it has been running (p. 230).

63 kil. *Aouinet-ed-Dieb*, another depôt for Alfa. See p. 230.)

74 kil. Junction of the *Oued Mellegue* and the *Meskiana*. Before this the former river is named *Oued Chabro*. The ground being full of magnesia the water is quite bitter.

96 kil. *Morsott*. Numerous Roman remains in the neighbourhood; one tower may be seen to the left close to the station.

118 kil. On the left is a hill, abrupt towards one side and sloping on the other, called by the Arabs *Bel Kef*, and by Europeans "the Gendarme's cap."

128 kil. **Tebessa.** 1878 inhab. 2950 feet above the sea.

We have no certain information as to the date of the first foundation of Tebessa; neither Strabo nor Pliny make mention of it, and its name appears for the first time in Ptolemy. It is not probable, therefore, that its existence as a Roman station could have preceded the reign of Vespasian (70-79). Situated on the high plateaux which command both the Sahara and the Tell, its position, from a strategic point of view, was the most advantageous which it is possible to conceive. In the reign of Hadrian (123) the imperial government thought it advisable to connect it with Carthage by a great highway, which work was carried out by the III. Legion Augusta, under the direction of Metilius Secundus, lieutenant of the emperor; the record of this work still exists :—

IMP. CAESAR
DIVI. NERVAE. NEPOS
DIVI. TRAIANI. PARTHICI. F.
TRAIANVS. HADRIANVS
AVG. PONT. MAX. TRIB.
POT. VII COS. III
VIAM. A. CARTHAGINE
THEVESTEN. STRAVIT.
PER. LEG. III. AVG.
P. METILIO. SECVNDO
LEG. AVG. PR. PR.

Another inscription gives the exact distance, 191 miles 700 paces. It formed also the junction of the roads to Cirta, Hippone, Lambessa and Tacape (mod. Gabes). It was probably also an entrepôt for the commerce of Central Africa as well as for the produce of the country.

Christianity was introduced into Carthage about A.D. 150, and Theveste was probably one of the first places to follow the example of the African metropolis. Four bishops are recorded as having ruled over the church here, of whom the first assisted at the council of Carthage, presided over by St. Cyprian. Their names are :—

Lucius	. .	A.D. 255
Romulus	. .	,, 349
Urbicus	. .	,, 411
Felix	. .	,, 484

St. Maximilian and St. Crispin suffered martyrdom here, the former under the proconsulate of Dion, the latter under Diocletian. St. Optat records that a Donatist council assembled at Theveste in A.D. 350.

In 428 and 429 Hippone was besieged by the Vandals, and it was during this period that St. Augustine died. The Count Boniface subsequently signed a treaty abandoning to the Vandals the three Mauritanias and Numidia W. of the Ampsagas (mod. Oued el-Kebir). In 443 a second treaty was concluded at Carthage between Genseric and Valentinian, by which the Vandal king restored to the Emperor of the West the three Mauritanias and Western Numidia in exchange for Eastern Numidia and other provinces, and from this moment Theveste became part of the Vandal kingdom.

It soon fell into insignificance and disappeared from history until restored by the Byzantine armies. Solomon, successor of Belisarius, was the second founder of Theveste, which he fortified, as he did other cities in Mons Aurasius (Aurès) and elsewhere, and enclosed it within ramparts and towers, the tracing of which exists to the present day; the citadel, containing the modern town, is as imposing in appearance as when built thirteen centuries ago.

A very interesting inscription in one of the openings of the triumphal arch records this fact, and is the only one hitherto found in Algeria making any allusion to the Vandals—

✝ Nuto divino felicissimis temporibus
piissimorum dominorum
nostrorum Justiniani et Theodorae
Augustorum post abscisos ex Africa
Vandalos extinctamque par Solomonem
gloriosissimo magistro militum ex
consulte Praefecto Libyae ac patricio
universam Maurusiam gentem
providentia ejusdem aemineutissimi
viri Theveste civitas a fundamentis
aedificata est.

Belisarius had hardly quitted Africa when insurrection broke out in the south. Solomon resisted bravely for 4 years, but was killed before the walls of Tebessa in 543 A.D., after which the history of the place is enveloped in obscurity during the time that it formed part of the Eastern empire.

Then came the Arab invasion under Okba ben Nafa, and Abdulla ben Djaffer, which destroyed the last trace of Greek supremacy, and converted Mauritania and Numidia to the religion of El-Islam. During the Mohammedan domination Tebessa partook of the vicissitudes of the dynasties which at various times held the district, and finally submitted to a French column under General Randon in 1842, although it was not until 1851 that it was permanently occupied.

Tebessa is situated at about 18 kil. from the Tunisian frontier, north of the mountains of Bou Rouman, which enclose the basin of the Oued Chabro, an affluent of the Oued Meskiana. It has an abundant water supply, and is surrounded by beautiful gardens. In front is an extensive plain watered by numerous streams flowing into the Oued Chabro, which winds along the bottom of the valley.

The modern town is contained within the walls of the ancient Byzantine citadel, which, however, occupies but a small portion of the ancient city. Its high walls flanked with towers are still in a tolerably good state of preservation, and are evidently built of still older materials.

It is almost square in form, the perimeter being about 1070 mètres in extent. The walls are built of large cut stones, and it is strengthened by 14 square towers, of which 4 are at the angles, and the rest irregularly distributed between them. The height of the wall varies from 5 to 10 mètres; that of the towers from 10 to 12, and the thickness of the masonry from 2 to 2·50. It has three gates, the *Bab el-Kedim*, or old gate, the *Bab el-Djedid*, or new gate, and the *Bab el-Kasba*, or gate of the citadel, which forms the entrance to the new quarter occupied by the troops. The first of these is also called the gate of Solomon; the second is formed by the arch of Caracalla.

The whole country round is covered with Roman remains, proving not only the great extent of Roman colonisation, but the high state of civilisation that prevailed under their rule, neither of which are at all likely to be approached in modern days. Amongst the ancient monuments in and around the town itself are—

The tetrastyle **Temple of Jupiter** usually but erroneously called Temple of Minerva, owing to the eagles on the entablature being mistaken for owls. It is situated within the present *enceinte*, and is of the Corinthian order, 11 mètres long, including the pronaos, by 8 mètres broad. The material of the main building is compact limestone. Each side is strengthened by four pilasters, and in front is the portico supported by six monolithic columns of cippolino, four of which are in front. It is raised on a basement or podium 3·66 mètres high, in which are three vaults now filled up, and access to the temple is attained by a handsome flight of cut stone steps.

This portico is preserved by a multiplicity of iron tie rods and straps that are anything but picturesque. One-half the ingenuity and labour used in this would have sufficed to reconstruct the portico, stone by stone, in a vertical position.

The entablature is not of a regular form, the architrave and frieze forming one height; over the columns and pilasters are panels ornamented by *bucranes* or ox skulls. The intermediate spaces are occupied by panels highly sculptured. This is immediately crowned by the cornice, above which is a highly ornamented attic, now about equal in height to the entablature. No doubt it had a cornice, which has disappeared. In the panels between the *bucranes* are eagles holding thunderbolts, on either side of which are serpents and branches with trilobate leaves. On the attic, the vertical panels over the columns and pilasters have trophies of armour, and the oblong ones alternately garlands and double horns of plenty.

The attic on the front has no sculpture, and this was doubtless intended to receive marble slabs with a dedicatory inscription. The soffits between the columns are everywhere richly decorated, and between the two central columns is the head of Jupiter Tonans. It was originally surrounded by an enclosure wall, the gate of which now actually serves as the front door of the mosque opposite.

This building has been put to many uses since the French occupation; at first it was a soap manufactory, then the *Bureau du Génie*, subsequently a prison, and a canteen; and lastly it was converted into the parish church, with ecclesiastical fittings in the worst style of the *génie militaire*. It is greatly to be desired that the hideous modern additions may be removed, and the temple restored to its original beauty. At the present time it is used by M. Delapart, the Curé of Tebessa, a most enthusiastic antiquary, and beloved by all classes of the community, as a depôt for many valuable antiquities which he has collected in the Basilica and elsewhere, this is well worthy of a visit.

The triumphal **Arch of Caracalla** is a really magnificent monument of the description called *quadrifrons*, each face representing an ordinary single arch of triumph. The only other known specimens of the kind are the arch of Janus Quadrifons, at Rome, much inferior to this both in size and beauty, and the great arch at Tripoli in Africa, which is a much finer building. There is also an imperial medal in existence containing a similar arch, dedicated to Domitian. This monument is built of large blocks of cut stone. A pair of Corinthian monolithic disengaged columns flank each arch, behind which are pilasters. Each column stands upon its own pedestal, and not, as is usually the case in African monuments, upon one common to each pair of columns.

The soffits supported by these, and also the central ceiling, were richly decorated. The entablature is composed of a highly ornate architrave, with rounded leaves at the angles, above which is a cornice. There is also a lofty frieze, as though for the reception of an inscription, and this also is surmounted by a cornice.

Above the N. façade is a small building, intended as a niche to contain a bust or statue; the semicircular base is still in place. It is fronted by two isolated columns, with corresponding pilasters on the right and left of the niche. The whole is covered with a flat roof, with a plain architrave and cornice on the outside. Another was probably built on the S. side; indeed, but for the inscription on the inside, one would be tempted to believe that there must have been one above each façade. The head of a bust, evidently belonging to this niche, and supposed to be that of Septimius Severus, was found in the neighbourhood, and was taken to the Engineers' office in the Palace at Constantine.

From the inscriptions on the interior we learn the history of the building. There was a rich family of Tebessa represented by three brothers, Cornelius Fortunatus, Cornelius Quintus, and Cornelius Egrilianus. The last of these commanded the 14th legion, Gemina, and died leaving all his property to his two brothers on certain conditions. The first was that they should erect a triumphal arch surmounted by two tetrastyles, enclosing statues of the two Augusti. In the Forum also were to be placed statues of the divine Severus and of the goddess Minerva. 250,000 sesterces were to be expended on these works. A further sum of 250,000 sesterces was to be devoted to affording gratuitous baths to the inhabitants in the public *thermæ*, and lastly 170 lbs. of silver and 14 lbs. of gold were to be deposited in the Capitol for a purpose which is not clear from the inscription. The days available for public baths are recorded in another inscription, on the opposite side of the arch.

On each façade, above the arch, was a tablet containing a dedicatory inscription. The western one was in honour of Julia Domna, wife of the Emperor Septimius Severus, and mother of the two Emperors Caracalla and Geta.

The key of the arch below is decorated with an eagle holding thunderbolts, supporting a medallion, out of which rises a female bust, wearing a high mural crown, typical, perhaps, of Julia Domna herself or of Rome.

Septimius Severus died in A.D. 211, and the two Augusti mentioned in the Testament were evidently Caracalla and Geta. Caracalla murdered his brother in 212, consequently the date of the Testament is fixed between those two years, though the execution of the work may have been a little later. The east façade bears a dedication to Septimius Severus himself. It has a medallion similar to that on the W. front, of a warrior in armour, resting on a head of the Medusa, representing probably Septimius Severus himself, and the terror which his countenance was supposed to inspire. It runs as follows:—

DIVO . PIO . SEVERO . PATRI
IMP. CAES. M. AVRELI . SEVERI . ANTONINI .
PII. FELICIS . AVO. ARAB. ADIAB. PARTH. MAX.
BRIT.
MAX. GERM. MAX. PONT. MAX. TRIB. POT XVII.
IMP. II.
COS. IIII. PROCOS. P.P.

The southern inscription is illegible; it is believed to have been in honour of Caracalla; and the northern one is wanting, and, if ever executed at all, was probably in honour of Geta to complete the series. The two other medallions are obliterated.

The partial destruction of this arch may date from the fifth century, when the city was deserted by its inhabitants and sacked by the Numidians; but its preservation at all was undoubtedly due to Solomon having so traced the walls of the citadel as to adopt it as the principal entrance gate.

One of the most interesting ruins in Algeria is that of the great **Basilica** of Theveste. It is situated about 600 mètres N.E. of the modern town, and consists of a vast edifice, 65 mètres long by 22 broad, enclosed within a wall 180 mètres long by 39 broad, strengthened at intervals by square towers, only two of which remain.

The principal entrance to the enclosure is to the S.W. The arch is quite entire, but the numerous subsidiary buildings in the court are razed to the ground, except where they seem to form actually part of the main structure.

The masonry throughout is of immense blocks of stone, carefully cut and adjusted, almost without the use of mortar; nevertheless, it bears unmistakable evidence of having been constructed at various epochs. The original building, however, was evidently the

[*Algeria.*]

Roman basilica, pretty exactly as Vitruvius describes it, with a nave and two aisles, the farther end being furnished with a semicircular apse.

The reader need hardly be reminded that the ancient Basilica was a court of justice; the praetor or principal judge was seated in the apse, with assessors on either side. A railing separated this from the nave; and, according to Vitruvius, the lateral aisles were surmounted by galleries looking into the nave. This peculiar form was so perfectly adapted for Christian worship that it was at once adopted by the Western Church. The bishop took the place of the praetor *in cathedrâ*, and his subordinates in the hierarchy those of the assessors. The altar, like the pedestal and statue of the god among the ancients, was situated before him, separating him from the congregation collected in the nave and aisles; the gallery above the latter became the clerestory, and the open court in front the narthex, in which the unbaptized remained during the performance of religious ceremonies.

The access to this building is by a flight of thirteen steps of unequal width, the greater number of which are destroyed, leading into the peristyle by three doors, a large one in the middle and a smaller one on each side. This court must have been most imposing. It was surrounded by an arcade, each side supported by four columns, between which were pedestals, probably destined for statues; the central portion was open to the sky, and in it was an elevated basin or fountain, the whole resembling very much in design the court of a Moorish house of the present day.

From the right or east wall of this were doors leading into two small chambers, one of which was the baptistery, the font being still tolerably perfect in the centre of the floor. The other chamber is of irregular shape, having been added at a subsequent period.

Beyond this comes the main body of the building, entered by three doors. It consisted of a nave with apsidal end and two aisles. The nave and aisles were separated by piers and engaged shafts in two superimposed orders, the whole being arcaded, and the aisles having a gallery. The walls were built of fine white limestone; the columns are of gray granite, white marble, and blue cippolino, the first and last probably of Greek origin. Many of the columns are broken; the bases are all in their original position.

It is easy to recognise the period of the Pagan Emperors; a later epoch, with a certain amount of Christian art; and ultimately a period of absolute decadence, probably the last time that Christians worked in this country. The first is marked by Corinthian columns, the capitals of which are in the most correct form, and the shafts of polished marble and granite, and of a beauty which would only have been marred by fluting. The second is represented by fragments of fluted and spiral columns, the capitals of which were richly decorated with foliage; and lastly, there are rough productions in stone, out of all keeping with the rest of the building, the capitals of which bear grotesque representations of fishes, perhaps used as the symbol of Christ.

Most of these last have now been removed to the museum and church.

The apse is raised above the level of the nave, with three steps on which to mount to it. On either side is a square chamber, corresponding to the termination of the aisles. From the first to the fourth pillars on each side, and again across from the fourth on one side to the fourth on the other, are grooves to receive a railing, showing that this part was divided off with the apse to form, perhaps, at first the prætor's court, and subsequently the sacrarium; in the centre of this space is an oblong vault or cavity. The whole of the floor is covered with tesselated pavements of very elegant designs and admirable execution. These are almost perfect in condition, and have been judiciously covered over with a layer of earth to protect them from injury.

Descending from the east side aisle by a flight of about thirteen steps is a chapel of the form of a trefoil inscribed within a square.

From the north and south apses are communications with small lateral chambers right and left, and from the south one there is access through a small anteroom to a sepulchral chamber beyond; the front of each apse was arched, the arches supported on each side by columns of green cippolino.

In the centre of the square contained between them was what appears to be the foundation of an altar; the walls were covered, for a part at least of their height, with a mosaic of the richest marbles, porphyry, and serpentine, so disposed as to form either pictorial designs or geometric patterns, while the ceiling was a mosaic of glass, quantities of tesseræ, both coloured and gilt, having been found amongst the *débris*. The floor also was mosaic.

This building was probably an addition, subsequent to the erection of the main body of the basilica. It is also certain that it must have replaced a still older structure, as traces of tesselated pavement were found 4 ft. below the actual floor.

A large sarcophagus of marble, with Christian figures rudely sculptured, was found at the bottom of the stairs.

In the sepulchral chamber above mentioned was found a tesselated pavement, containing four inscriptions recording the interment of individuals beneath them. One is that of Palladius, Bishop of Idicra, near Cirta (Constantine), who died here on his return from the Council of Carthage, under Huneric, in 484. This inscription was headed by a cross, having in the lower right hand angle the letter *Omega*. It is curious to observe that the corresponding one on the left hand does not contain the *Alpha*, as is usually the case. It has been said that this was owing to the fact of the bishop having died out of his own diocese. The tomb was opened, thus destroying the inscription, but the bishop's skeleton was found perfectly preserved after fourteen centuries. It rested on a bed of laurel leaves, and its brown hair was undecayed. These venerable remains are preserved in the church of Tebessa.

Another tomb was opened, that of Marcella, and in it were found perfectly-preserved bones and light hair. The inscription was also necessarily destroyed, but the others (three in number) were allowed to remain intact.

There were various buildings, probably cells or shops, outside and against the main structure, and the whole was surrounded by a strong wall, flanked at intervals with towers, like a vast fortified convent. This it doubtless was during the later years of its existence, but unfortunately its history is entirely unknown, and its original destination, or at least the destination of the older portion of it, must remain a matter of conjecture.

From a careful study of the architecture of this building, however, the grand simplicity of its design, and the richness of its materials, it is difficult to believe that the earlier portions of it could have been built after the introduction of Christianity into Teveste, when art was already in its decadence. The presumption is strong that it could not have been commenced later than the end of the 1st or beginning of the 2d century; this would make it older than almost any of the Roman monuments of Algeria, as it certainly was superior to most of them in elegance and simplicity, though less florid in decoration.

A new *Church* has been built by the good Curé Delapart, which is itself quite a museum. All the fragments of Christian architecture which he could collect have been worked up into the building. One of them is of exceptional interest, being a small panel of glass Mosaic, supposed to be that made to record the consecration of the Basilica. The altar even has been brought from that building.

Some fine **Mosaics**, probably belonging to public baths, were discovered in 1886 in the cavalry quarters. They are now enclosed in a building erected for their preservation, the key of which is in charge of the Curé. One of the subjects represents Amphytrite surrounded by Nereids; another represents a vessel laden with large amphorae, and the inscription *Fortuna redux*. The most curious is a sort of game—the ground is covered with compartments in which are represented animals such as a bull, an ostrich, a gazelle, and a wild boar, each having numbers attached, as in the cups of a bagatelle board; probably leaden quoits or some such things were thrown into these. This is called the hall of Marcellus, as it contains the figure of a person so named.

Roman Aqueduct of Ain-el-Bled. The spring of *Ain-el-Bled*, which affords 2000 litres of water per minute, furnishes the town with water, and irrigates the gardens to the N. and E. It is brought to the town in a massive Roman aqueduct, 900 mètres long, passing over a bridge of the same period. There is a second Roman aqueduct, that of *Ain-Chola*.

Within the town is a Roman house still used as a habitation. It is of great size, and was probably the palace of some important personage. Half of it is buried under the soil, and the absence of all exterior openings of the same date as its erection, except the entrance, now bricked up, induces the belief that it had an interior court.

Outside the gate of Solomon, on the verge of the ravine which divided ancient Theveste into two equal parts, are the remains of a theatre, now entirely overgrown with grass, and of no particular interest. It was about 52 mètres in diameter, and nearly circular in form.

Of the forum no trace now remains. It occupied the site of the present esplanade planted with trees, in front of the modern citadel.

What cannot fail to strike the traveller with astonishment is the enormous amount of beautifully cut stones, of great size, lying about in every direction; not only are the Byzantine fortifications, the modern French Kasbah, and half the houses in the town, built of them, but even the garden enclosures around, and the ground is full of them wherever excavations are made.

About 600 mètres to the south of the town is the Marabout or Zaouia of Sidi-Abd-er-Rahman, who is supposed to have founded it.

There are many other Roman ruins of interest in the circle of Tebessa, and on Djebel Mistiri, west of the town, and extending as far as Djebel Youkous, are a number of megalithic tombs of a circular form. They are about 100 in number, situated in a single line, the right of which rests on the ruins of a Byzantine tower. The largest is about 2·43 mètres high, and from 3½ to 9 mètres in diameter. They differ from those of Foum Kosentina by being built in successive and gradually decreasing courses, without any single covering stone; they rather resemble the Medrassen and the tombs in its vicinity.

[Excursions may be made from Tebessa to the following places:—

1. *Soumat-el-Kheneg*, O, situated about 9 kil. S. of Berzegan, on the ancient Roman road between Theveste and Capsa. This is the mausoleum of C. Julius Dexter, a standard-bearer, who lived in a farm near Teriana.
2. *Souma bint-el-Abri*, O, the minaret of the chief's daughter, 60 kilomètres from Tebessa, on the last northern slopes of Djebel Foua. This is a very interesting monument, in a good state of preservation, and though it contains no inscription, it is believed by the Arabs to be the resting-place of the celebrated Kahina, chieftainess of the Aurès, the legend regarding whom is given at p. 321. It is certainly a Roman mausoleum of a very ordinary type, and of a date much anterior to that of Kahina.
3. *Feidjet el-Ghousa*, Θ.—Situated at 50 kil. S. of Tebessa, in the plain of Bou-Djebel. This is a tumulary monument, surmounted by a double inscription, showing that it was erected by two brothers to the memory of their father and mother.
4. But by far the most interesting excursion is one across the Tunisian frontier to **Hydra**, the ancient Ammædara, where still exists one of the most important triumphal arches in North Africa. The distance is about 36 kil.; the traveller will require to take everything he may require in the shape of food with him, as no provisions are procurable. There is a house belonging to the Tunisian Customs department at which it may be possible to sleep if the traveller takes his own bedding.

The arch in question is a very handsome one, the peculiar feature of which is the unusual height of its entablature, which is half of the columns. On the frieze is the following inscription:—

IMP. CAES, L. SEPTIMIO, SEVERO, PERTINACI
AVG. P.M. TRIB. POT. III. IMP. V. COS. II. PP.
PARTHICO . ARABICO . ET PARTHICO
AZIABENICO . DD. PP.]

ROUTE 17.

Tebessa to Souk-Ahras, by Khamisa.

This is a journey which we do not recommend to the general traveller. Any one undertaking it must be content to put up with a little rough life, to take his provisions with him, and carry his own tent. Most travellers will be content to proceed to Tebessa by the railway, which has been constructed since this route was written, see p. 221.

Still, if one is able to dispense with the comforts of civilisation for a few days, he will find the journey a most interesting one from an archæological point of view.

After leaving Tebessa, the road goes nearly N., crossing the plain of Tebessa.

5 kil. The Roman, or perhaps Byzantine ruins of *Khooshada*, a considerable post.

8 kil. At the foot of the mountain the spring and ruins of *El-Kissa*, Θ. Numerous tombstones have been found here, and amongst them a large proportion belonging to centenarians. Several hundred yards from the ruins is a handsome monumental tomb, in a very good state of preservation.

The road now passes over picturesque but desolate mountains of limestone. At

13 kil. *Aïn-Azouagha*, there is a beautiful spring of clear water, and fine scenery.

26 kil. *Bordj Kaid El-Akhdar*, the residence of the Kaid of that name, a large stone building like a caravanserai, where there is a little cultivation, and where the traveller can lodge

in a case of necessity. The road now emerges into a long dreary plain, covered with artemisia and rosemary, and follows the Tunisian frontier at a distance of a few miles.

32 kil. *Birket-el Faras* (Lake of the Mare), an extensive swamp, very deep in the centre. Ruins of Roman posts every few miles along the route.

40 kil. *Djebel bou-Jugar* or *bou-Djabar*, an isolated hill through which the frontier passes. E. of it is a very remarkable flat hill called El-Kaläa or Kaläat es-Sanan, which from this point exactly resembles a gigantic martello tower perched on the top of a mountain. In a depression on the summit is a Tunisian town, the ancient capital of the Harars. The road to El-Kaläa is by a narrow path in the rock, accessible only on foot. El-Meridj is the best starting-point, distance 15 kil.

The name Kaläat es-Sanan is derived from that of the first Mohammedan chief who governed the country, Hannach bin Abdulla es-Sanani, a native of Sanäa in Arabia Felix. This mountain is said to contain iron ore, but it has not been explored.

52 kil. **El-Meridj.** A smala of Spahis, 2300 ft. above the sea, and first of a chain of frontier stations which extend to the sea E. of La Calle. It is an immense fortified enclosure, with quarters for the European commissioned and non-commissioned officers, together with stables for the Spahis's horses. The Spahis themselves live outside in tents, and cultivate the land allotted to them. There are about 70 Spahis and 5 European officers. It has an abundant water supply and an excellent garden, but the climate is exceedingly unhealthy in summer, and during two or three months every year the garrison has to be removed to Tebessa. There is a canteen in the fort, at which provisions can be obtained, but travellers properly recommended by the Commandant of Tebessa are sure to meet with a cordial reception from the officers stationed here.

From *El-Meridj* the direct road to Souk-Ahras is by *Aïn-Guettar*, continuing along the frontier, but with the exception of that fort there is not much to interest the traveller here. Aïn-Guettar, like El-Meridj, is a smala of Spahis, 20 kil. S.E. of Souk-Ahras, celebrated as being the place where the first act in the insurrection of 1871 took place.

On the 22d of January 1871 the Commandant detailed several of his men for service in France. They murmured, refused to obey, and on the 23d, after a council, 93 of them struck their tents and left. Subsequently they murdered one of their European non-commissioned officers, and joined the Arabs in attacking Souk-Ahras.

Near it is *Taoura*, O, the ancient Tagura, where are numerous interesting Roman remains; as, indeed, there are all over the country. In no part of Algeria had the Roman sway taken so deep a root as in this province.

Instead of taking the direct road, we advise the traveller to make a détour to the N.W. for the purpose of visiting the interesting ruins of *Mdaourouch*, *Tifesh*, and *Khamisa*. But to do this he ought to provide himself with a tent, unless he is assured beforehand that there will be Arab encampments in which he can pass the night.

Starting from *El-Meridj* the track—for road there is none—passes over a plain swarming with game and wild animals—hares, hyenas, jackals, wild boar, partridges, *poules de Carthage* (smaller bustard), quails, etc., while in the more distant hills are red deer in considerable numbers, though extremely wild.

In front are seen four or five isolated peaks, *Djebel Abou Khadera*, *Djebel Kalb*, *Djebel Maadther*, and *Djebel Makheirega*, etc.; while to the right is *Djebel Ouenza*, where are many interesting Roman remains, O, amongst others 40 or 50 deep excavations in the rock, probably for the purpose of storing corn.

69 kil. *Aïn-Esh-Shania*, O. Here a beautiful and abundant spring issues from the midst of a thick grove of fig trees at the foot of a Roman or Byzantine tower, built probably to protect what must have been an important

road between Carthage and Mascula (*Aïn - Khenchla*). This is manifest from the numerous foundations of farms, or wayside establishments, everywhere seen along the route. A similar tower, the *Kasr el Ahmer*, exists about 6 miles from the smala of Aïn-Guettar, the distance between each being one day's march. The fortification is about 9·14 mètres square, the walls being nearly 1·50 mètres thick, 50 cent. on each side, of solid blocks of cut stone, the interstices being filled up with rubble masonry. There appears to have been only one opening, with the exception of loopholes, a door, only the arch of which is now visible; the interior and exterior, as far as the spring of the arch, being filled up with the *débris* of the building. The tower must have been of great height, as 15·50 mètres of the wall is still standing on one side. This is a charming spot for a halt of an hour or two.

On leaving this the road passes through a defile separating *Djebel Kulb* (Mountain of the Heart) from *Djebel Maadther*, a part of which is through a forest of Aleppo pines, and emerging from the wooded country enters a plain in which flows the salt river of *Oued Melleguc*.

79 kil. *Aïuenat-ed-Diab* (more correctly *Aïoun-ed-Diab*, the Springs of the Jackals), 2390 ft. above the sea, a convenient camping place on the right bank of the *Oued Melleguc*, where is a fountain of sweet water, the only one for miles around.

On the opposite side of the river is seen the conical isolated peak of *Kef-er-rakhm*, and to the right of it Djebel *Makheireya*, which was visible from El-Meridj; on the top is a curious perforation like a natural arch.

After crossing the river the plain is sterile, affording but indifferent pasturage, till

91 kil. *Anchir Damous*, ☉, the ruins of a considerable Roman town. After passing this the country becomes more undulating and fertile. Shortly before reaching Mdaourouch, on the right side of the road, a few dolmens are passed.

115 kil. **Mdaourouch**, 3070 ft. above the sea, the site of Medaura, one of the most ancient Roman colonies of Algeria, is admirably situated in a wide extent of fertile land, well watered, and on the S. side bounded by wooded mountains. It is the residence of *Hamama bin El-Howshat*, Kaid of the *Mahátala*, who has a well-built bordj amongst the ruins, and is extremely hospitable to strangers. His official residence is at *Tifesh*.

The site of the ancient city is well marked by ruins covering an immense extent of ground, for the most part only foundations of houses built as usual of large cut stones. To the east of the Kaid's house is a square tomb, with pent roof almost complete. It consists of two stories, the upper one having an arch in the middle and one end open, as if half of the roof of the lower story had been used as a terrace for the upper room.

At the extreme W. is another important building, perhaps a basilica, which cannot well be traced as it is buried nearly as deep as the crown of the lower arches.

But the most important of all is the Byzantine fortress or palace, consisting of a central keep, a tower on each side connected with it by curtains, the inner sides of which were probably cloistered, and an enclosure behind completing the *enceinte*.

The building is constructed of much older Roman materials; amongst which one sees bases and capitals of Corinthian columns; one very perfect bas-relief of a Roman in his toga, on the upper tier of masonry in the southern tower; and numerous fragments of sculpture and tombstones.

This building is said to have been originally erected by the prefects Gabinius and Sabinius. From a bilingual inscription in Greek and Latin over the main entrance, unfortunately very much defaced, we have no difficulty in concluding that, like many other similar monuments, it was restored by the Byzantine general, Solomon.

The inscription has thus been restored by M. Leon Renier:—

✚ CVM [. . . . . . A] EDIFICATA EST TEMPORI-
BVS [PIISSIM] ORVM DOMINORVM NO[STRORVM]
JUSTINI[ANI] ET THEOD[ORAE PROVIDENTIA
S]OLOMONIS GLORIO[SI] EX CONSV[LE MAGIS-
TRI MILITII] IS ET PRAEFECTI AFRI[C A]E✚

Many tombs lie scattered about, one distinctly Christian bears, within a circle, the following inscription :—

℞
α|ω

MVNIVS IVLIVS
BARGEVS NEPOS VIR BONE
STVS VIXIT IN PACE FIDELIS
ANIS XXX III MINCS . ES XIII
DEPOSITVS EST V IDVS SEP
TEMBRES HIC SEC.

Medaura was the birthplace of Apuleius, a philosopher and romancer. The most famous of his works extant is the "Golden Ass," an allegorical work in eleven books, which contains the beautiful story of Cupid and Psyche. He was born A.D. 114, and was the first great original thinker produced by Numidia, if we except Juba II. who was educated at Rome. He subsequently settled at Œa, the modern Tripoli, the country of his wife.

St. Augustine pursued his studies here till the age of 16, when he went to attend a course of rhetoric at Carthage.

The road, after leaving *Mdaourouch*, passes over a series of low hills, all well cultivated ; but on reaching the culminating point one is quite unprepared for the magnificent panorama which bursts into view. As far as the eye can reach, E. and W., and about 4 m. across, extends the magnificent valley of *Tifesh*, one continuous cornfield, without a break, and without the apparent delineation of a field, or an acre of untilled land. Through it winds the *Oued Tifesh*, which flows in a westerly direction, and, after receiving numerous tributaries, eventually becomes the Seybouse and falls into the sea at Bône. There appears to be no limit to the amount of grain which can be produced here, and only the iron horse is wanting to carry the locked-up produce to an advantageous market. On the northern side of the plain runs a line of mountains parallel to that which the traveller has just crossed, and on the southern slope of it are the ruins of

133 kil. **Tifesh**, the ancient *Tipasa*, 3140 ft. above the sea. El-Bekri remarked that Tifesh was a city of great antiquity, remarkable for the height of its buildings and for the extent of its ancient ruins.

When the first Arabs, successors of Mohammed, invaded Africa, Tipasa resisted them for a long time. It was subsequently taken and pillaged, but soon sprang up again from its ashes. It was destroyed a second time by Mousa En-Nasser, and yet once more by Moulaï Nasser, son of the sovereign of Tunis in 1057.

Although one cannot conceive a finer position, the remains of the ancient city are by no means so extensive as at either Mdaourouch or Khamisa. The only remarkable ruin is that of the ancient fortress, built probably by the Romans, certainly restored by the Byzantines, as several Roman tombstones are embedded in its walls. It is built on a spur gently ascending from the plain, but separated from the main range by a remarkable ravine, which cuts it off like a gigantic natural ditch. Advantage has been taken of this conformation to construct a fortified position of considerable extent, occupying the whole of the sloping face of the hill. The interior is built up in massive terraces, the top of all being crowned by a citadel. The walls are about 9 ft. thick, of huge blocks of cut stone, and flanked at intervals by square towers. The tracing of the whole is perfectly visible, though only little remains of the walls.

Besides this, the only other important building remaining is one of which the character cannot be surmised. It has one very large arch, but all the cut stone facing has disappeared, with the exception of a fragment of the soffit of the interior, and two gigantic stones forming a cornice on the exterior ; the rest are lying around.

The Kaïd of *Mdaourouch* has a bordj a short distance to the W., and the tents of the Sheikh of the district, Mohammed ben Ahmed, of the *Oulad*

Si Moussa, are usually in the neighbourhood.

It is said that at *Ouarce*, about 4 kil. to the S.E., there are numerous dolmens.

Leaving Tifesh, the road turns to the right, going through the range of hills by a narrow and tortuous defile. Here are many remains of the ancient Roman road leading to

145 kil. **Khamisa**, ancient *Thubursicum Numidarum*, 3084 ft. above the sea.

The ruins of the ancient city cover a vast extent of ground, including several hills and the intervening valleys on the northern slope of the range separating it from Tipasa. It rose in terraces of various widths, the whole forming an irregular amphitheatre. Gardens no doubt surrounded it in all directions, as is manifest from the ruins of detached villas, and wells in which the marks of ropes rubbing against the stone facings are still traceable, and hydraulic works of every variety, such as cisterns and aqueducts.

The city must have been one of great importance in point of magnitude, though one sees nothing of the exquisite architecture for which Tebessa is so distinguished.

The principal buildings are:—A *triumphal arch*, quite perfect as far as the keystone, through which the road from Tipasa entered. It is constructed of comparatively small stones, and is not particularly elegant.

N.E. of it, and on the slope of the highest part of the hill, is the *Basilica*, which must have been an immense structure built on various levels. It is in a very imperfect condition, but enough remains to show that its length must have been more than 66 mètres. Several fragments of huge columns are lying close to it. It is now the site of an Arab encampment, and the yelping and savage attacks of a hundred Arab dogs make a visit to it by no means a pleasant operation.

To the N.W. of this, nearer to the head of the main valley, are what appear to be the remains of an immense *Palace;* and here it was that an inscription was found containing the name of the city, thus fixing a site which before was doubtful. It ran as follows:—

IMP . CAES . M . AVRELIO . CLAVDIO . PIO . FELICI . AVG . P.M . GOTHICO.M . PARTHICO . M . TRIB . P . III . COS . II . P.P.
PRO COS . RESPVB . COLONIAE
THVBVRS . NVMIDARVM .

Imperatori Caesari Marco Aurelio Claudio Pio Felici Augusto Pontifici Maximo Gothico Maximo Parthico Maximo tribunitia Potestate III. Consuli II. Patri patriæ Proconsuli Respublica coloniae Thubursicensium Numidarum.

This inscription is further interesting as settling an obscure point of history regarding the 2d Consulship of Claudius.

In it were discovered marble sculptures of various colours and great beauty. Access to the building was by a triple arch, now buried in *débris* as far as the spring.

Lower down, at the base of one of the hills, is the *Theatre*, the ground-plan of which, and a considerable portion of the superstructure, are entire; the stones of the remainder are all lying about, and it would neither be a difficult nor a costly task to reconstruct the building exactly as it existed.

The seats for the spectators are to a great extent entire, and not even covered with vegetation. Facing this is the stage, which, instead of being a straight line, is formed by three semicircles which do not actually intersect each other, but are separated by small spaces. These were probably intended to contribute towards the scenic effect of the stage. The façade of the building was drawn as a tangent to these circles, and from each of them there was a door leading out of the building. The length of the façade is 53·33 mètres, and the interior width of the building 59·43 mètres.

Between the curved parts of the stage and the façade were four small chambers opening outwardly. They have no openings save the doors. On each side of the proscenium are two entrances, through one of which passes a water conduit. There are also several small chambers, used doubtless for theatrical purposes.

A short distance from this are the ruins of what probably were either the public *Baths*, or the water source of the lower town. A spring of very brackish water issues from it, now called *Aïn-el-Yahoodie* (Spring of the Jew), which tradition says was once thermal. The water is now quite cool, but unpotable.

All around are numberless foundations of houses, some of them with a few feet of the superstructure remaining, sufficient to show that the Roman house of that period was very similar to the modern Moorish one—an open central court surrounded by the family apartments.

There are also numerous *Tombs* in every direction in a very perfect condition. Many carefully record the age of the person buried beneath, but none the date when he died. Some have sculptures as well as inscriptions, and others sculptures only. Most of them are headstones marking the vaulted tomb below. Some, however, are handsome monumental structures of one or two stories. The best of the headstones is on the hill E. of the theatre. It represents husband and wife joining hands before an altar, below whom are two Cupids with reversed flambeaux.

Another close to it represents a man riding on horseback, with the inscription :—

Q . POMPEIVS
Q . F . QVIR
SATVRNI
NVS . PIVS
VIX . AN . LXXXI
H . S . E .

It is very remarkable to note the great age recorded on these tombstones. It is by no means rare to find the age upwards of a century.

These ruins have been very little explored, and offer a vast field for antiquarian research.

It is probable that this city had to suffer the fate of most others in Africa, frequent destruction and rebuilding, as wherever excavations are made the ruins of older structures are found below existing foundations.

After the destruction of Carthage, B.C. 146, Rome took possession of the Punic colonies along the coast, and made the neighbouring districts into a Roman province. It is possible that Thubursicum was founded about this period. At all events an inscription proves that it was rebuilt for the third time by Caius Gracchus at the same time that he attempted to form a Roman colony at Carthage.

The Arab legend regarding the destruction of Khamisa is as follows :—A Christian princess of rare beauty, named Khamisa, governed the city. Her husband, Mdaouroueh, king of Medaura, had repudiated and waged bitter war against her. Khamisa, unable to withstand him, learning that the Mohammedans had already conquered Hydra, Tebessa, and Gastal, sent a deputation to implore their assistance. Okba listened favourably to her petition, took Medaura, killed her husband, converted her subjects, and made her his favourite wife. But not trusting too implicitly to the good faith of his new converts, he took the precaution to demolish the fortifications of Khamisa before proceeding on one of his expeditions. It rebelled notwithstanding, whereupon he destroyed the entire city to its foundations.

The more probable derivation of the name Khamisa is from the fact of a great market having been held on the spot every Thursday, from the earliest times. Nothing is more common than for places in Algeria to be named after the markets. Thus the site of Thubursicum became *Souk-el-Khamis* (the market of Thursday) or *Khamisa*.

Nevertheless, the ancient name survived the city 8 centuries. *Ibn Chemau*, a Tunisian writer of the 15th century, recounts in his chronicle that during the reign of Abou Faris in 1337, a war broke out between that prince and the Amir of Bône, when the former pursued his enemy *as far as Teboursouk, which is situated in the country of the Hanencha at the source of the Medjerda*.

In front of the ruined city, which had a northern aspect, is an amphitheatre of hills, the open side of which is to the E. In this rises the famous river *Medjerda* (Begradas of the ancients), here a mere thread of water. It flows south of *Souk-Ahras*, enters the regency of Tunis, and falls into the sea near Utica.

Through the fertile and picturesque valley of the Medjerda, the hills enclosing which commence to slope upwards almost from the river's bank, lies the way to Souk-Ahras, which is 29 kil. N.E. of Khamisa (see p. 300).

ROUTE 18.

To Aïn-Beida.

A railway is in course of construction (1889) from the main line at *Oulad Rahmoun* (p. 163), but until that is finished, the traveller must either go by diligence from *Oued Zenati* (p. 237) or follow the longer road, which is pretty much the same as that which will be adopted by the railway. This we give, but the distances are measured from Constantine.

38 kil. Ruins of *Sigus*, an ancient and celebrated city, memorable as the residence, during various epochs, of several Numidian kings. The destruction of this place appears to have been very violent, and little remains save the foundations of a few buildings and a considerable necropolis. On the rocky plateau, opposite and S.W. of the latter, are many so-called megalithic remains, dolmens, cromlechs, menhirs, etc. Almost everywhere in Algeria these are found in the vicinity of important Roman positions, and here one was opened by M. Thomas in 1876, and found to contain amongst other things a bronze coin of the reign of Domitian; this proves beyond all doubt that whatever the age of other *prehistoric* monuments may be, this one at least is well within the *historic* era. Sigus was one of the 30 free cities mentioned by Procopius.

At about 14 kil. N.E., on a detached mamelon, are the remains of a Roman or Byzantine fortress at *Aïn-el-Bordj* (Well of the Fort). The walls and citadel are very perfect. (? Turris Caesaris.)

39 kil. *Bordj Zikri*. Maison de commandement, occupied by the Kaïd of *Segnia*. Here for 3 months in the year the stallions of the remount are stationed. There is a poor wayside *auberge*.

After leaving this the road enters the plain of *Bahira-et-Towila* (the long plain); long, as its name implies, level, and richly cultivated.

59 kil. *Aïn-Fakroun*. A large caravanserai where the traveller can lodge and sleep in tolerable comfort. 2600 ft. above the sea. A small village was created here in 1879.

The road still continues over extensive treeless plains, devoid of all permanent habitations, though Arab tents begin to be numerous.

71 kil. *Aïn-Moulaber*. Auberge and farm where the diligence stops for breakfast. There is an abundant water supply, which has enabled the proprietor to create a little oasis of trees. Roman ruins in the neighbourhood.

89 kil. *Omm-el-Boaghi*. Government caravanserai, on the slope of a hill which forms the N.E. boundary of the valley. Here one can lodge if necessary. There is a small fort built of Roman materials above the caravanserai; the only other classical association connected with the place is that of the Augean stable, which it closely resembles.

95 kil. The ruins of a Roman station.

101 kil. *Bir Rogüa*. An isolated well surmounted by a masonry superstructure. Near it is a dolmen consisting of two flat stones, each 3 mètres long, 1 mètre broad and 25 cent. thick, supported at the angles by four vertical stones 50 cent. square. About 65 mètres to the E. three upright stones indicate the position of another, now destroyed.

115 kil. **Aïn-Beida**. 3036 ft. above the sea. 2445 inhabitants. The name of the place means *white fountain*, from a source which yields 400 litres of water per minute. There is a fairly comfortable inn here.

Chief town of the *Haracta* tribe. The country round produces grain in immense quantities. The cattle and wool of the Haracta are also celebrated.

At *Djebel Righis*, 40 kil. W. of Aïn-Beida, are some ancient copper mines worked by the Romans, both *à ciel ouvert* and by means of galleries. The ore yields 14 per cent of pure metal.

At *Djebel Hamimat*, 42 kil. W.N.W. of Aïn-Beida, is a mine of oxide of antimony, one of the only two places in the world where this mineral has been found. It is usually met with as a sulphide.

At *Djebel Garca*, 48 kil., a mine of argentiferous lead ore exists; and at Djebel Tafrent, 49 kil. to the S., is found sulphate of iron.

Before the troubles of 1852 the only buildings at Aïn-Beida were the three Bordjes, now occupied by the Administrator, the garrison, and the remount. The Haractas were then the most insubordinate tribe in the country, and besieged the forts, which were in a precarious position, when they were relieved by a few hundred horsemen under *Ali bil Arabi*, who was rewarded for his devotion by being made Kaid, which office he still holds. Houses began gradually to surround the forts, the Jews scattered amongst the tribes settled under its walls, and soon a prosperous town sprang up.

The Arabs in this circle are much more superstitious than religious. They know hardly anything of their religion except a few outward observances which they have learnt by tradition. On the other hand, great numbers of them are affiliated to the various religious confraternities or khouans, especially to that of Sidi Mohammed ben Abd-er-Rahman bou Koberain. The writer had a curious instance of the indifference of the Kaid of Aïn-Beida to one of the most rigidly observed Mohammedan customs, the seclusion of women. At an entertainment given to him and his family, the married and unmarried daughters of the Kaid were present, and sat with him as in European society.

This may be explained by the large admixture of Berber blood amongst them, their *patois*—the *Chaouia*—being unmistakably a dialect of that language.

The circle of Aïn-Beida is full of Roman remains, O. In the town are many vaults, which probably served as *Silos* for storing grain; one in the Curé's house is still perfect, and has its stone door in working order.

[From Aïn-Beida there is a service of diligences to **Aïn-Khenchla**, distant 108 kil. and 95 kil. from Batna.

The road passes close to the ruins of **Kasr Baghai**, O, the ancient Bagaia, a city which had already attained considerable importance during the Imperial era, as is proved by numerous inscriptions. During the time of St. Augustine it was one of the African cities in which Christianity had attained the most progress. Several councils were held here; but religious dissensions soon began to produce their destructive effect; the Donatists burnt the Basilica and committed the sacred books to the flames. Solomon was charged by Justinian to re-establish order in Africa. One of his captains, Gantharis, sent to operate in Mount Aurès, established his camp at Bagaia; Procopius says that it was then in ruins. It is probable that the Byzantines then built or restored the immense fortification, the trace of which is still entire. It consists of an irregular quadrilateral figure, the sides varying in length from 770 to 1227 feet, with round towers at three of the angles, and a square one at the fourth. The wall is further strengthened at irregular distances by square salient towers. On the N.W. side is a second enclosure or citadel; near the W. angle are the remains of a Mohammedan mosque, decorated with ancient columns still standing.

The identity of Aïn-Khenchla with the ancient Mascula admits of no doubt; its distance from known points would prove the fact, even had not an inscription been found recording that, about A.D. 370, Publius Caecina Albinus rebuilt the town which before had been destroyed.

This interesting inscription has thus been restored :—

Pro splendore felicium sæculorum dominorum nostrorum Valentiniani et Valentis semper Augustorum ... atæ ... ve ... omni Masculæ ... a fundamentis construxit (atque dedicavit) Publilius Cæcionius Cæcina Albinus vir clarissimus consularis sexfasculis provinciæ Numidiæ Constantine.

Mascula is more famous in ecclesiastical than in profane history. Several of its inhabitants are celebrated in Roman martyrology, especially Archinimus, who was condemned to death by Genseric. Its bishop, Clarus, attended the Council of Carthage in A.D. 255. Another, Donatus, ceded to the persecutions of Florus, proconsul of the district, and revealed the place where the holy books had been concealed. He was the first of the recreant bishops who was interrogated by Secundus Tigisitanus on the subject, before the Council of Cirta in 305. Another bishop, Januarius, was exiled by Hunneric in 494, and a second of the same name assisted at the Council of Carthage in 525.

The value of Mascula as a strategic position, situated, as it is, in a wide and fertile plain just beyond the northern slopes of the Aurès mountains, has always been recognised. It was probably here that Solomon placed his camp during his second expedition, and there is reason to believe that it is the *Malich*, the scene of one of the battles of Sidi Okba.

After the first Arab invasion it was still inhabited. El-Adouani thus alludes to it:—" At the foot of the mountains of Amanora there are three cities, Baghaï, Khenchla, and Guessas, inhabited by Christians, each one surrounded by vast gardens, irrigated by the waters descending from Dj. Mahmel."

Khenchla has now been created an European centre of colonisation and hief place of a circle. Colonists have been attracted to the spot not only by its fine climate, resembling very much that of Provence, but by concessions of from 25 to 40 hectares of land given by the State. The great fertility of the soil, its proximity to vast forests, and the mineral riches of its mountains,

ought to secure the prosperity of this line though distant settlement.

To these advantages may be added its position, midway between Batna and Tebessa, and in close proximity to the openings of the various valleys which traverse the Aurès. It was made the centre for supplying the armies of General Herbillon in 1847, and of Gener-al St. Arnaud in 1850, in their expeditions against the Nememchas.]

ROUTE 19.

Constantine to Bône by Railway.

This line, from Khroub onwards, belongs to the *Compagnie des Chemins de Fer de Bône à Guelma et Prolongement;* between Constantine and Khroub, to the *Compagnie de l'est Algerien.*

Constantine to Khroub, see p. 163.

Distance from Khroub.	Names of Stations.	Distance from Bône.
..	Khroub	203
15	Bou-Nouara	193
27	Aïn-Abid	185
42	Aïn-Regada	180
53	Oued Zenati	174
69	Bordj Sabath	162
80	Thaya	156
95	H. Meskoutin	148
101	Medjez Amar	135
115	Guelma	123
119	Millésimo	119
123	Petit	115
135	Nador	101
148	Duvivier, bif. S. Ahras.	95
156	O. Frarah	80
162	Saint-Joseph	69
174	Barral	53
180	Mondovi	42
185	Randon	27
193	Duzerville	15
203	Bône	..

15 kil. *Bou-Nouara.* A small village constructed by the *Compagnie Général Algérienne* (see p. 108). On the S.W. slopes of *Djebel Mazala,* about 2 kil. N. of the village, is a megalithic

necropolis, containing monuments of many varieties; the general type is a dolmen composed of four vertical blocks and a table, forming a rectangular chamber, the whole surrounded by a circle of stones.

27 kil. *Aïn-Abid.* Another of the same society's villages.

42 kil. *Aïn-Regada.* A third village belonging to the same society, in a very unhealthy situation. The line henceforth follows the course of the *Oued Zenati*, which, after its junction with the *Oued Cherf*, becomes the *Seybouse*.

53 kil. OUED ZENATI. A rather important village. In this district are situated 83,000 of the 100,000 hectares of land so lavishly granted by the Empire to the *Société* (now *Compagnie*) *Général Algérienne*.

There is a service of diligences daily to Aïn-Beida.

69 kil. *Bordj Sabath.* A very unhealthy district ; no village.

80 kil. *Thaya.* A most interesting excursion may be made from this place to the great **Cave of Djebel Thaya.** It may easily be done from Hammam Meskoutin in a single day. Take the 6.24 A.M. train, which arrives at Thaya at 7.10 A.M. Arrangements should previously have been made at the buffet for mules ; the distance from the station is only 6 kil. The traveller should not fail to take food with him, and above all a supply of blue and red lights with which to illuminate the cave. He can return to Hammam Meskoutin by the train passing Thaya at 7.25 P.M.

All the necessary arrangements can be made by the proprietor of the hotel.

The opening of the cave is on the N.W. side of the mountain, which is composed of a compact limestone. The entrance-passage is spacious, being in no place less than 3 mètres in height. The exterior portion opens out like a hall, well lighted, dry, and adorned with beautiful tufts of ivy-leaved and other ferns. On the sides are carved numerous Roman inscriptions, so much effaced by time as to be hardly legible. M. Bourguignat, who was one of the first to explore this cave, has published an elaborate but rather fanciful description of it. He counted 53 inscriptions on the left, 8 on the right, and 3 on the roof. Nearly all begin with the letters B.A.S. ; one, better preserved than the others, has the words BACACI. AVG. SAC., from which it is inferred that this cavern was dedicated to the god Bacax ; it is further gathered from the inscriptions, that every year the magistrates of *Tibilis* (Announa) came, with much ceremony, on a pilgrimage to Thaya, to offer a sacrifice to the god of the cavern. The inscriptions contain the names of consuls who were elected under the Emperors Caracalla and Geta, A.D. 211, and from this date they are mentioned up to A.D. 268. The following is one of them :—

BACCACI . AVG . SAC .
GENTIANO . ET . BASS
O . COS . VII . Id . MAIAS
C . IVLIVS . FRONTO
NIANVS . ET . Modes
tinvs . purdes
MAgg . Thib.

which may thus be rendered :—"In the year of the Consuls Gentianus and Bassus (A.D. 211), the 7th of the Ides of May, Caius Julius Frontinianus and Modestinus, Magistrates of Thibilis, offered sacrifice to the august Bacax." One is commemorative of two brothers who strayed into the cavern and were lost there—an accident which might very easily happen at the present day, and which probably would happen to any one entering without experienced Arab guides. The god Bacax is unknown to history ; probably he was one of the local deities adopted by the Romans.

On leaving the passage containing the inscriptions the cave descends at an angle of not less than 45 degrees ; the ground is covered with a thick layer of loose stones, which roll down with alarming velocity at almost every step made in advance. Great care should be taken to keep well to the right hand, as on the left there is an abyss which has never been explored, but which must be of great depth, and nearly vertical.

From the foot of this ramp the cave extends, with many accidents of level, to nearly three-quarters of a mile in length and a thousand feet in vertical depth. The descent is difficult, and even dangerous throughout, as deep holes occur at numerous places, in which an unwary explorer might easily be engulfed. Sometimes he has to drop down steep precipices, by the aid of projecting stalagmites, at others to slide down muddy gradients, now to creep through small holes and narrow passages, and again to wade through pools of liquid mud. He has to traverse vast halls, intricate labyrinths, passages and chambers of every size and form. Groves of stalactites and stalagmites adorn the sides, while the lofty vaults are hung with the most exquisite fretwork, like the roof of a Gothic cathedral. The finest of all is the great domed chamber, at the bottom, which gives to the cave its Arab name, *Ghar el-Djamâa* (Cave of the Mosque); it is an immense, nearly circular cavity, with domed roof; from the ground rise magnificent stalagmites, like the trunks of palm trees, and in the centre is a huge block of stone, which M. Bourguignat imagines to have been an altar to Bacax.

In visiting this cave a few precautions are absolutely necessary.

1. The traveller should never attempt to penetrate without Arab guides.
2. He should have an abundant supply of candles, matches and blue lights, or magnesium wire.
3. He should have canvas shoes with hempen soles to prevent himself from slipping, and he should only wear such clothes as he is content to abandon afterwards.

95 kil. **Hammam Meskoutin.**

This is a place at which no traveller in Algeria, who can spare the time, should fail to spend a few days, as, in addition to the wonderful natural phenomena of the place itself, there are several most interesting excursions to be made.

Hammam Meskoutin, or the *Accursed Baths*, were known to the Romans under the name of *Aquæ Tibilitinæ*, so called from the neighbouring town of Tibilis, afterwards Announa. Some of the Roman baths cut out of the rock are still used by the hospital patients; but the largest one is higher up the stream, which has since changed its course, owing to the mass of deposit having gradually raised the surface of the rock over which it then flowed. The temperature of the water is no less than 203° Fahr.! which, taking into consideration the height of the source above the sea-level, is just about boiling-water heat; and is only surpassed by the Geysers in Iceland and Las Trincheras in South America, the former of which rises at 208°, and the latter at 206° temperature.

The whole scene is most extraordinary, and the mass of still waterfall is a sight never to be forgotten. The surface of the rock where the waters rise is everywhere thickly encrusted with carbonate of lime as white as marble. On issuing from the earth they fall in a succession of little cascades into a richly wooded glen, shut in by hills, and by the stream below the natives may be seen cooking their provisions and washing their clothes in the hot water. Above the cascades are numerous little natural basins of a creamy-white colour, bubbling over with boiling water. The rock over which the water falls is rough and uneven, owing to the thick calcareous deposit, and presents the appearance of a petrified rapid.

Above and below the sources are some enormous cones, the largest of which is about 11 mètres high and 12 in circumference. These were evidently deposited by the action of the waters overflowing the edges of the basins wherein they rose, which were thus gradually raised higher and higher, until the spring had no longer force sufficient to run over, but was obliged to find another outlet.

Earth has gradually collected on some of them, in which shrubs and flowers have sown themselves, giving the whole the appearance of huge flower-pots. Many of them have been split as if by earthquakes.

Clouds of dense steam rise from the falls and from the earth in all directions.

The *best view* is from below, where, looking up at the white shining rock and steaming water, the scene is very strange, and almost unearthly.

These springs are extremely efficacious in cases of rheumatism and nervous or cutaneous diseases, and for healing wounds. The volume is very large, being, from the two principal, 18,000 gal. per hour. The carbonate of lime becomes nearly all precipitated as the water cools, and when quite cold it is used for drinking purposes.

About ¾ m. from the hospital are some other springs, which are ferruginous and sulphureous. Their temperature is about 170° Fahr. The usual mode of application is by means of ordinary baths; but douches and vapour baths are also employed.

The convenience of being able to make use of both saline and ferruginous springs close together, ought to make Hammam Meskoutin become an important watering-place; and certainly, should this be the case, it will be able to vie in beauty of situation with any of the most celebrated baths of Germany or France.

The only drawback to them is that during the summer months, from July to October, the climate is somewhat feverish; at other times the traveller runs no risk whatever.

M. Piesse thus quotes the Arab legend which gives its name to the springs:—

"An Arab, rich and powerful, had a sister, but finding her too beautiful to be married to any save himself, he determined to espouse her, spite of the prohibition of the Mohammedan law and the remonstrances of the elders of his tribe, whose heads he cut off in front of his tent. Then commenced the usual marriage festivities, and as the accursed couple were about to retire, the elements were set in commotion; fire came out of the earth, the water left its bed, and the thunder pealed forth in a fearful manner. When tranquillity returned, the Arab and his sister and every one connected with the feast were found petrified, the cones still representing the actors in this drama."

At a distance of about 1500 mètres from the hotel is a curious *cave*, containing a *small lake of water*. In July 1879, after a storm and heavy rain, a subsidence of the soil took place, which exposed to view an opening, giving access by an easy slope to a cave, at the bottom of which is a considerable body of the purest and most limpid water. As it takes a sudden turn to the right and becomes lost to view, it is impossible without a boat or a raft to ascertain its extent; the depth close to the edge is from 15 to 20 mètres. The formation of the rock in which the cave exists is very similar to that near the hot spring, evidently a calcareous deposit, tinged with rose colour by oxide of iron. The water is quite cool, though sometimes a slight amount of warm vapour exists in the cave. The traveller should take candles and some blue lights with him to illuminate the grotto.

[*Excursions in the Neighbourhood*.

1. To **Roknia**, O. About 12 kil. N. of the station is the Megalithic Necropolis of Roknia, covering a space of 5 or 6 kil. in extent. The monuments have been much destroyed by indiscreet investigators, but a vast number still remain entire. They are small in size and very close together. The dolmens are usually composed of 5 stones; 4 uprights and 1 horizontal slab; these are usually placed 4 or 5 together in one general enclosure.

2. To **Announa**. There is a bridle path over the hills which greatly shortens the distance, but should the traveller prefer to go by carriage he should proceed to the high road from Guelma to Constantine. At the 84th kil. he will pass the small hamlet of *St. Charles*, and at 86 kil. that of *Ain-Amara*.

Just after passing the 87th kilometric stone, a narrow path to the left descends a steep ravine, in which flows the Oued Announa, and mounts to the plateau on which stood the Roman city of Tibilis. The distance in a direct line is not more than three-quarters of a mile from Ain-Amara—by the road it is about a mile and a half.

The ruins stand on an open platform scarped on all sides except the S.W., where it joins the lower counterforts of

Ras el-Akba. The view in the opposite direction, looking eastward towards Guelma, is extremely fine, and these two considerations, capability of defence and a picturesque situation, appear here, as everywhere else in Algeria, to have determined the selection of the site. The ruins are worthy of a visit, though by no means in the best style of Roman art. They consist of a triumphal arch of the Corinthian order, with a single opening; on each side are two pilasters, the capital of one only exists; in front of these were disengaged columns, which have entirely disappeared, as also the whole of the entablature.

There are the remains also of what appears to have been another triumphal arch or one of the city gates, with two openings of equal size. The piers, which supported the arches, had a double Corinthian fluted pilaster embracing each angle, or eight pilasters to each pier. There is a Christian basilica, probably of the Byzantine period, and several other buildings of greater or less importance, fragments of the city walls, and frusta of columns lying about in every direction.]

101 kil. *Medjez Amar*, now a farm, formerly a fortified camp built by General Damrémont. After the failure of the first expedition against Constantine, Ahmed Bey, hoping to surprise the French, attacked it at the head of 10,000 men on the 10th September 1837. He was repulsed with great loss; and the army starting thence on the 1st of October arrived before Constantine on the 6th, and took that city on the 13th.

Here is the junction of the *Oued Zenati*, afterwards *O. Bou-Hamdan*, with the *O. Cherf*; their united waters form the *Seybouse*.

115 kil. **Guelma.** A modern French city of 4025 inhab. 1203 ft. above the sea. It is built on the ruins of the Roman *Kalama*, 2 kil. S. of the right bank of the Seybouse. It is a fortified place with a citadel, in which are extensive barracks, hospital and other military buildings. It is beautifully situated, the streets well planted with trees, and charming shady walks outside the walls.

Kalama is named for the first time in history by St. Augustine; its bishop then was Possidius, for 40 years the intimate friend of the saint, and subsequently his biographer. When the French took possession of it in 1836, the ruins of the ancient *enceinte* and many of the principal buildings were, if not entire, at least traceable. The French city has been built principally out of the ancient ruins, and all that now remains to testify to its ancient splendour are the remains of the theatre, fragments of the baths, and a number of inscriptions and sculptured stones in the public garden.

Amongst these is a remarkably interesting monument, the tombstone of a young man 29 years of age, who too confidently hoped that his wife would have rested beside him. The work is rude in point of art, but extremely beautiful in conception. It is a monolith of rose-coloured marble, square in plan, consisting of a pedestal with cornice, plinth and base, supporting a crowning part rising on the same plan, terminating in an architectural feature which has now disappeared. On the principal façade the top piece bears a circular wreath enclosing two portrait busts in relief, that of the man only being completed, the features of the woman are not chiselled. The plinth has a garland suspended from the cornice, below which the surface is divided vertically for two inscriptions; that of the man only is filled up.

Diis Manibus Sacrum.
Fl. Nævilla Vixit Annis viginti novem diebus quindecim.

On the left side of the plinth is a folding door just shutting, symbolical of the terrestrial home which is being closed for ever. Above the cornice on the same side is another one opening, representing the life to come. This is confirmed by the opposite side, which bears on the plinth the figure of a winged child with reversed flambeau, while above it is a cock crowing, to represent the opening day. The cock is standing on a figure resembling a loop; it may possibly be intended for a serpent, the emblem of immortality.

The theatre is close to the grain market: the steps are still tolerably perfect, as is the wall of the building around them, and the entrances at each side; but all in front of this semicircle, including the proscenium, has disappeared. It was of considerable size, and the spectators were able to enjoy a beautiful view of the mountains bounding the valley of the Seybouse.

The ruins of the baths are in the modern citadel: two large arches are still entire, and the springs of vaults on each side show that the walls in which they are pierced were united into a vast hall from which the other chambers had entrance. The masonry is not to be compared in quality to that of *Khamisa*, or other ancient cities; it is of rubble, partly of stones and partly of bricks, with only the arches, corners, and bearings of the vaults of cut stone. Above each side of the arches appear to have been square turrets, the object of which is not apparent. Close to them were discovered 4 or 5 large cisterns in a perfect state of preservation, and near them an abundant spring of fresh water; this has been led into the cisterns, and they now serve to supply the citadel.

The ruins of a circular temple were discovered in the Rue Mogador, with an inscription bearing the name of Marcus Aurelius (Septimius Severus). This has been entirely broken up, and the bases and capitals of the columns removed to the public garden above alluded to.

There is an important grain and cattle market held here every Monday.

[At 7 kil. on the old road leading to Bône is *Hammam-Berda*. A thermal spring gushing out close to the road, yielding 80 litres of water per second. The water is quite sweet, and irrigates all the valley through which it flows. This was evidently a favourite spot with the Romans, as there are ruins of baths and other buildings still remaining.

Another excursion may be made to the top of *El-Maouna*, the highest peak

[*Algeria.*]

in the neighbourhood, about 1000 ft. high, and distant 15 kil. The ascent may be made on horseback. The scenery is very beautiful, the road passes through forests of oak, and on the summit there is a depression shaped like an Arab saddle, in which is a lake about 1 kil. in diameter. There is a quarry of fine rose-coloured marble here, which was much used by the Romans of Kalama, and is still worked.]

On leaving Guelma the line descends the valley of the Seybouse; the country is exceedingly picturesque and fertile, woods of olive and other trees alternating with cultivation and pasture-land. The telegraph poles between Khroub and Guelma are all of eucalyptus wood, the first used in the colony; they were grown in the neighbourhood of Aïn-Mokra, and were from 7 to 9 years old.

119 kil. *Millésimo.* A small village to the N. of the line, between it and the Seybouse.

123 kil. *Petit.* A small village to the S. of the line.

135 kil. *Nador.* Is one of the zinc mines belonging to the well-known company of *La Vielle Montagne*, but it is not a very important establishment, and was only purchased to avoid competition.

148 kil. DUVIVIER. A dirty but pleasantly situated village, whose single street is well shaded with ash and beech trees. It was created in 1857, and named after a general; it was erected into a commune in 1871. It has a market every Sunday, where a considerable trade is carried on in wool and cereals.

156 kil. *Oued Frarah.*

162 kil. *St. Joseph.*

174 kil. *Barral.* So called after the general killed near Bougie in 1850. This village was made an agricultural colony in 1841 and a village in 1851.

An antique marble column, with an unsightly vase-shaped base, has been erected "Au brave Capitaine Mesnu, mort pour la défense de Barral, 15 Juin 1852." This brave soldier reposes under a more suitable monument, a plain iron cross, outside the village

R

gate. He was killed in heading a sortie of Spahis when the village was surrounded by the insurgents of 1852.

180 kil. *Moudori*. Close to it is the property of *Guebar bou Aoun*, once the property of M. Nicolas. It was here that the Irish labourers got out by Marshal de MacMahon in 1869 were located. The experiment proved a complete failure ; none of them understood a word of French, they could not work out of doors during the heat of summer ; some died, many were sent home. The last batch of them took passage in a vessel which was run down by another on entering the harbour of Bordeaux, and were drowned. At 10 kil. to the E. is the village of *Oued Besbes*, belonging to the *Société Général Algérienne*.

185 kil. *Raudon*. The village is 7 kil. to the E. It was created a commune in 1868.

193 kil. *Duzerville*. Named after General Monk d'Uzer.

The line finally crosses the *Oued Bou Djemāa*, not far from the ancient Roman bridge, and arrives at 203 kil. **Bône** (see p. 121).

ROUTE 20.

Excursion through the Kabylia of Djurdjura from Bordj bou-Arreredj to the Oued es-Sahel and Fort National.

Bordj bou-Arreredj.

	Kil.		Miles.
Bordj Medjana	12	=	7½
Bordj Boni	16	=	10
Gelaa	6	=	3¾
Ighil Ali	13	=	8¼
Akbou	21	=	13¼
Ti-lilkouth	16	=	10
Fort National	22	=	13¾

The above are the distances *on the map*; they by no means represent the amount of ground to be gone over.

By taking the ordinary railway route to Fort National (p. 143), the traveller obtains a splendid glimpse of Kabylia ; but thoroughly to explore the country, and to see beyond all doubt the finest mountain scenery in Algeria, he would do well to find his way either from Constantine or Algiers to *Bordj bou-Arreredj* (p. 160), and commence his excursion from that point. He must not shrink from a slight amount of inconvenience ; he must be content to do without *auberges*, and to make the journey either on horse or on mule back. The authorities at Bordj will gladly assist him in obtaining the necessary animals and guides ; the writer paid 5 f. a day for his mules. Tents would greatly conduce to the comfort of the expedition, especially if it contain ladies ; but the traveller will always find some place in which to pass the night, without any very serious inconvenience, provided he carries his own bedding.

The first stage of his tour is to Bordj Medjana, a flourishing village built on the site of the *Castellum Medianum* of the Romans, and the ancestral residence of the celebrated Bach Agha El-Mokrani, leader of the insurrection of 1871 (see p. 59). The Bordj, which was built by the Bach Agha, under the direction of French engineers, was completely dismantled after the confiscation of his lands, the outer walls only being retained ; it contains the church, school, and other communal buildings, and constitutes a place of refuge to which the inhabitants of the village may retreat in case of attack. A beautiful spring issues from some Roman remains below the fort, and forms the only water supply of the village.

From this place a ride of 4 hours takes the traveller to the fort or blockhouse called Bordj Boni, which contains a suite of rooms and stabling, in which shelter, if nothing more, can be obtained ; it was built after the last insurrection, principally for the convenience of Government officials visiting the district. There is an excellent spring at the foot of the mound on which the fort is built, and from the platform around it magnificent views of the Djurdjura range are obtained.

From this to Gelaa is a ride of not more than an hour and a half, through the most magnificent mountain scenery. The road winds up and down steep hills in a most tortuous manner, sometimes passing over the intervening ridges, and at others encircling their sides. On the right hand is a deep abyss, beyond which is a mass of hills and valleys, clothed to their summits with verdure, resembling a tempestuous sea suddenly arrested and turned into rock. On the left the view is more extensive ; the foreground is as wild, while range after range of mountains succeed each other in ever-changing variety of form and colour, till the extreme distance is shut in by the majestic snow-capped ridge of Djurdjura. No other peak can ever depose this from its place as the monarch of Algerian mountains. Chellia and Mahmel, in the Aurès, may be higher, but they rise from more elevated ground, and thus lose much of their grandeur ; while for beauty of outline and richness of tints, the Djurdjura range, seen from the south, with the Oued es-Sahel at its foot, is superior to them both.

Kalâa — or Gelâa, as it is here pronounced, meaning a fortress in Arabic — is one of the most picturesquely situated villages in Kabylia. It is built on the extreme end of a mountain, more than 3000 ft. above the sea, surrounded on three sides by precipitous ravines, through one of which flows a tributary of the Oued Sellam. The cliffs descend in a succession of perpendicular scarps, separated from each other by narrow terraces, so as to be quite inaccessible. The fourth side, where the hill rises behind the village, can only be reached by a narrow winding path, which a few resolute men might defend against an army.

In former times this was a city of refuge for such as wished to escape the justice or vengeance of the Turks, who never succeeded in reducing its inhabitants to their sway. Its proximity to the *Biban*, or Portes de Fer, itself a strong position, enabled the Beni Abbas to command that pass, and consequently the route between Algiers and Constantine, and they were in a position to exact a tribute from the Turks as the price of keeping open this communication.

The village of Gelâa is divided into two portions, each ruled over by a Sheikh independent of the other. The lower portion belongs to the Oulad Aissa, and the upper to the Oulad Hamadoosh. It is the principal place of the Beni Abbas, a once powerful confederation, extending N. and S. from beyond the Oued es-Sahel to Boni, and E. and W. from the river of Gelâa to the Oued Maghir. The villages in this district are well built, of stone, roofed with tiles, and very often they have small enclosures or gardens attached, while the interiors are finished off with great neatness, and even some rude idea of decorative art.

The inhabitants of Gelâa have little or no arable land, but they are famous for the manufacture of bernouses. They make a considerable quantity of olive oil, and are renowned merchants, purchasing the carpets and haiks of the S., and selling them at the markets of Constantine and other great towns. Between the two villages are a number of small springs, quite dry in summer, so that for several months in the year the water supply of each village has to be brought from the valley below. In the upper village is an ancient mosque, with some wood carving over the door ; in the cemetery attached is buried the Bach Agha el-Mokrani. His body was brought here after the battle of Oued Souflat, where he was killed. It is much to be regretted that his tomb should be quite unmarked. The Commandant Supérieur of Aumale, Colonel Trumelet, had the happy idea of marking the spot where he fell by a stone bearing this inscription, "Ici tomba mortellement, frappé par les balles du 4ème de Zouaves, le 5 Mai 1871, le Bach Agha de la Medjana, El-Hadj Mohammed ben el-Hadj Ahmed el-Mokrani, chef de l'insurrection."

The connection of the Mokrani family with Gelâa dates from the 16th century, when one of the ancestors, Ben Abd-er-Rahman, established a little principality here after the expulsion of the Spaniards from Bougie. The last of these princes was murdered by his subjects in A.D. 1600. Mokrani owned several houses in Gelâa, and his brother was at one time Kaid of the Beni Abbas. There is a large guest chamber in the upper village, and the traveller will be sure of hospitable treatment from the Kaïds of either portion, who are admirable specimens of Kabyle gentlemen.

One of the most interesting sights of Geläa is the extraordinary method employed for storing grain—in enormous baskets of alfa grass, 4 to 4½ mètres high and 3 in diameter at the thickest parts, resembling gigantic bottles with the necks knocked off. These are raised about a foot off the ground, and four or five of them are placed side by side in a room. In these vessels, called *Zaräa*, a reserve supply of corn has been known to keep good for fifty years.

There is a direct route from this village to Akbou, but the traveller would do well to make a détour in order to see **Ighil Ali**, the most considerable village in the Beni Abbas territory.

After passing through the village the traveller has to descend a path so steep and difficult as hardly to be practicable for mules. On reaching the bottom of the hill, however, it improves, and soon the high road between Bordj bou-Arreredj and the Oued es-Sahel is reached. The scenery is still remarkably grand, but less green than before reaching Geläa. The ground is poor, schistose, and only adapted for the cultivation of fig and olive trees, which constitute the principal riches of the country.

After about four hours' riding Ighil Ali is reached; in fact, there are three villages placed so close together as to form but one—Ighil Ali, Tizairt and Azrou.

The last crowns the hill to the west, while the two others at its foot are separated by an inclined plane, in which is situated the Medressa. It was one of the favourite ideas of Napoleon III. to educate the Arab and Kabyle races in the French language and ideas. Numerous educational establishments were organised with this view at Algiers, Constantine, Fort National, and elsewhere, nearly all of which collapsed with the Empire. Amongst others, a college was established here at which Kabyle youths were taught both Arabic and French. These villages are much better built and more picturesque than most others in Kabylia; many of the houses have two stories, some even three; the walls are decorated with arches and quaint holes for ventilation, and not a few have arched colonnades.

The general appearance of the whole, sloping upwards in a pyramidal form, is not at all unlike many Italian villages. They used to be celebrated for the manufacture of arms, but as that is now a forbidden industry, they have extended their manufacture of bernouses, silver ornaments, etc.; and one of them, Tizairt, is celebrated for its wood-carving. The objects most usually manufactured are maces, not unlike those of Gog and Magog, and spoons and trinkets connected by chains cut out of a single piece of wood.

After leaving Tizairt the road descends rapidly, passing numerous picturesquely-situated Kabyle villages, and enters the Oued es-Sahel, a little below the ruins of Bordj Tazmalt, a fort destroyed during the last insurrection.

At this point the road enters the great valley called Oued es-Sahel, or *river of the coast*.

The new village, which bears the old name, is on the opposite side of the river.

After traversing the rich plains of the Beni Melekeuch, the road passes to the north of the celebrated mound of *Akbou*, and soon reaches the village itself.

Akbou is the ancient *Ausum*, and is the country of the well-known Bin Ali Cherif (see Rte. 13).

From this place the ascent of the Djurdjura range commences, through a rich and highly cultivated country, abounding in fig, olive, and ash trees. The two first are the riches of the country; the last (*Fraxinus Australis*) is also of great utility, as its leaves afford excellent food for sheep and goats in summer and autumn when the grass fails.

At two hours' distance is the village of **Chellata**, the chief place in the country of Illoula, and the ancestral home of Ben Ali Cherif. There is a large Zaouia here for the education of Kabyle youth—one of the most renowned in North Africa—kept up at his expense; and in the enclosure in front of it are interred the members of his family. To visit such a holy place as this in Tunis or Morocco would be impossible; in Algeria the Mohammedans no longer dare to exclude Christians from their mosques; but it requires very little penetration to see that their presence is most distasteful to them. Beyond this the place is of no interest, and, like all other villages in the Kabylia of Djurdjura, it is extremely filthy, a marked contrast to the scrupulous cleanliness of those on the other side of the Oued es-Sahel. The writer and his party pitched their tents on a grassy slope, well clear of the village and its evil odours, and were on their mules before daybreak on the following morning, hoping to see the sun rise from the summit. It took an hour to reach the *Col de Chellata*, one of the passes leading from the Oued es-Sahel, across the Djurdjura range, between the peaks of Tili-jouen on the left, and Tizi-bart (5670 ft.) on the right. From the top of the former there is an unequalled view, in some respects finer than that from Chellia, inasmuch as the foreground possesses greater boldness and variety of outline.

Commencing from the west there is a splendid view of the whole crest of the Djurdjura range, with its two most conspicuous peaks, *Azrou-n-Tchour* (5980 ft.) and *Tamgout Lalla Khadidja* (7543). These are crowned by *Welis* or Saints' tombs, favourite places of pilgrimage with the Kabyles: beyond these, to the north, is the country of the Beni Illilten, Fort National, and the sea in the extreme distance. More than 50 villages can be counted in this direction. On the opposite side of the pass are the mountains of Babor and Ta-Babort, crowned with their forests of Cedar and Pinsapo; that of the Beni Abbas completes the panorama; while the ever-present Mamelon of Akbou, surrounded by a great stretch of level land, thickly covered with olive groves, occupies the foreground to the south. The effects of light and shade seen here at sunrise will never be forgotten, and probably, with the exception of the short ride from Boni to Gelaa, there is no view to equal it in the whole colony of Algeria or Regency of Tunis.

After passing through this defile the road descends rapidly towards the *Ti-filkouth* or river of the *Beni Illilten*, by a steep and difficult road, but one of exquisite beauty. The whole country is cultivated with as much care as a garden. The road is completely overshadowed by magnificent ash trees, while the banks on either side are covered with ferns, broom, wild roses, and flowers of every colour, and a clear cold stream flows at the bottom, fringed with magnificent wild cherry trees.

After ascending the opposite bank the road passes through the village of Ti-filkouth, and winds through the most delightful shady lanes and orchards, mounting and descending almost perpendicular precipices, crossing rapid streams, but always passing from one scene of loveliness to another, till, after a ride of about two hours from the stream at the bottom of the valley, the village of *Soumar* is reached. Here the writer passed the night, and was entertained by the *Amin el-Omina* with true Berber hospitality.

Leaving this, a ride of fifteen minutes brings the traveller to the high road from Fort National to the Oued es-Sahel by the Col de Tirourda, and close to a house which has been erected by the Engineer Department for its employés. The distance hence to the fort is 30 kil.

The scenery now changes somewhat —it never ceases to be exceedingly grand—and the view of the Djurdjura range improves as it is seen in full front, instead of foreshortened from one end. The admirably engineered, but bare and shadeless road, with its regular curves and gentle gradients, becomes intolerable after the wild, shady lanes and natural scenery through which the traveller has just passed; and it is not without a feeling of relief that he reaches Fort National (see p. 145), thence to proceed by the prosaic but convenient diligence to Tizi-Ouzou and so to Algiers.

ROUTE 21.

Algiers to Ténès by Orléansville.

Algiers to Orléansville by railway. Diligences to Ténès, in connection with the trains.

Leaving Orléansville by the Porte de Ténès the Chelif is crossed by a light bridge 200 mètres in length. Just beyond, on the right bank of the river, is *La Ferme*, once a military agricultural establishment of 50 acres in extent, now an annexe of the commune of Orléansville.

From this the route passes over dreary country, with very scanty vegetation. Looking back upon Orléansville, the trees planted in and around that town are the only ones in sight, the rest of the plain being sandy and bare, here and there varied by patches of scrubby brushwood.

220 kil. *Aïn-Beida* (the white fountain). A small isolated colony of a few houses. A little farther may be seen to the right of the road a koubba, dedicated to *Sidi Abd-el-Kader;* and to the left that of *Sidi Mammar ben-Mokhala*, and a village called *Warnier*, after a well-known deputy for Algiers, who died in 1879.

229 kil. *Les Cinq Palmiers*, where there is a small but good inn. The diligence stops here for dinner going to Ténès, and for breakfast on returning.

238 kil. *Les Trois Palmiers*.

241 kil. *Kirba*. From this point the aspect of the country becomes more varied, the road running for some distance parallel to the river Allala, which flows through some pretty valleys and glens.

On the right of the road are the ruins of a Roman fort, but the stones have mostly been made use of by the *génie* for building bridges, etc.

Several ruins of Roman forts exist along this road. The mountainous country through which it passes appears never to have been thoroughly Romanised, and the population is to this day in great part Berber.

256 kil. *Montenotte*, a prosperous agricultural village.

At 11 kil. from Montenotte, in the valley of Oued Allala, and at 7 kil. from the high road, is the village of Cavaignac, created in 1879. The copper mines of *Oued Allala* to the E. are no longer worked, but another copper mine was opened in the spring of 1874 on the hill to the W. The road hence to old Ténès passes through a wild and beautiful mountain gorge.

Following the works which convey the water supply of Ténès from the Oued Allala, not far from old Ténès the remains of the Roman water-works can be traced for a few yards, but their barrage was placed lower down in the water-course than the modern one.

Large tracts of forest which covered the mountains on both sides of the road were burnt by the Arabs in the summer of 1873.

260 kil. *Old Ténès*. This town, inhabited entirely by Arabs, is surrounded on three sides by a deep ravine, at the bottom of which flows the Allala, and is often called Little Constantine. It was once a noted pirates' nest.

There are still to be seen in the rocks on which this town is built large iron bolts to which the inhabitants used to fasten their galleys after having drawn them up the river. To the E. of the town may be seen the remains of the old Roman road, which did not follow the aqueduct, but ran behind the hill on the right bank of the river. Two arches of the bridge which crossed the O. Allala are still in a good state of preservation.

The town itself is surrounded by a *Pisé* wall flanked at the corner by large square towers, probably the work of the Spaniards, now in a very ruinous condition.

261 kil. **Ténès**. Population, 2364.

Modern Ténès, founded 1847, is situated on the site of the Phœnician town, afterwards the Roman colony of Cartenna. We learn from Pliny that it was *Colonia Augusti*, a colony of the soldiers of the Second Legion. This latter fact appears to indicate a warlike character in the neighbouring native tribes, and from an inscription found here and preserved in the Museum of Algiers, we gather that these were the Bakoyta mentioned by Ptolemy.

The "Itinerary" of Antoninus says that Cartenna is 63 m. from Cæsarea (Cherchel), but there does not appear to have been a Roman highway along the coast. The great road between the E. and W., and for the most part Roman colonisation, kept in this part of Africa to the great plains. Cartenna was deserted for old Ténès by the Berbers at an unknown but early period—tradition says on account of the bleakness of its situation. Before the railway from Algiers to Oran was made, Ténès was the port of the central Chelif plain, and had a large export trade, but it is now a declining town. The harbour, about a mile distant, is an artificial one, similar to that at Algiers, but is open to the west wind. Outside the town, on the western side, is a public garden where several Roman tombs with inscriptions may be seen; one is that of a soldier of the 24th Legion.

In the neighbourhood are the remains of several Roman and two Phœnician wells of considerable size, near which a number of coins of both nations were found, also a Punic inscription, now in the Museum at Algiers.

ROUTE 22.

Mostaganem to Tiaret by Railway.

Distance in kil. from Mostag.	Names of Stations.	Distance in kil. from Tiaret.
..	Mostaganem . . .	197
6	Pélissier . . .	191
21	Aïn-Tédelès . . .	176
32	Oued el-Kheir . . .	165
47	Mekalia	150
55	Sidi-Kheltab (1) . .	142
64	Bel-Hacel . . .	133
76	Relizane . . .	121
85	Oued Khellong . .	112
95	Sidi-Moham. ben Aouda	102
119	Fortassa . . .	78
134	Djilali-ben-Amar . .	63
163	Mechéra-Sfa . .	34
173	Sidi-Ali-ben-Amar .	24
187	Tagdempt . . .	10
197	Tiaret . . .	..

The line from Mostaganem to Tiaret was completed in 1889; it is divided into nearly equal sections by the main line from Algiers to Oran at Relizane. The ordinary traveller will hardly care to make the first half of this journey: the whole interest of the route, and it is considerable, is contained in the southern section.

Mostaganem. 11,312 inhabitants. There was a maritime town here in Roman times, whose harbour disappeared during a terrible earthquake, in the reign of the emperor Gallien. Under the Moors it was a town of but little importance, but in 1516 it was taken from the Sultan of Tlemçen by Aroudj, and was fortified and made a provincial capital by his brother, Kheir-ed-din, shortly afterwards.

In 1558 it was attacked in vain by the Spaniards. The 16th century was the period of its greatest prosperity. It had then a population of about 40,000, with considerable commerce, and the rich country round it was highly cultivated. Exposed to the attacks of Spaniards and Arabs, and impoverished by misrule, this prosperity was of short duration, and had long disappeared when the French took possession of it in 1833.

It is now the centre of an important agricultural district, with 17 European villages, and of a superior native population living in stone houses. The roads are excellent, the soil is fertile, and though the rainfall is small, springs and wells abound, and water large gardens filled with fruit trees, such as pomegranate, orange, apricot, etc. The fig is, however, almost the only tree in the district on unirrigated ground. The inhabitants say the climate is superior to that of Algiers, and it is at least much drier, but it lies on a tableland 300 ft. above the sea, with very little shelter from the winds.

A picturesque and curious Arab town, called *Tijdit*, sweeps round Mostaganem to the E. in a semicircle, separated from it by a fortified wall and the cliffs of the ravine of the *Aïn Sucfra*, whose bottom is occupied by irrigated gardens, from which the white Moorish houses rise in irregular steps.

The most interesting drive within easy distance is to *Aïn-Bou-Dinar*, 13 kil., a French village, which lies on a ridge above the valley of the Chelif, a few miles from its mouth. Walking to the slopes just beyond the village, an extraordinary view opens suddenly. The river is seen some 500 ft. below, winding through the rich valley to the sea. The Turkish bridge and French village of *Pont de Chelif* are visible higher up the stream. Under the hills beyond the Chelif are Arab tents and gardens, surrounded by the prickly pear. Numerous koubbas and Berber houses stand out on the opposite mountains of the Dahra, of which the most conspicuous is *Montagne Rouge*, so called from its red soil and cliffs of a yet deeper tint.

[A route has been made through the Dahra, passing *Cassaigne* and *Renault*. At 1 kil. from the house of the Agha of *Nekmaria* on this road are the caves of the *Oulad Riah*, where took place a tragedy which created a great sensation in Europe at the time.

In April 1845 commenced the insurrection of the Dahra, instigated by Bou Maza, to quell which a column was sent under the command of Colonel (afterwards Marshal) Pélissier.

In June he pursued a body of the *Oulad Riah*, who took refuge in some immense caves, situated in a deep ravine between two isolated hills.

We feel that only an eye-witness should narrate what followed. A Spanish officer[1] in the French service, writing to the *Heraldo*, states:—

"On the 18th, the column of Colonel Pélissier left early to besiege the famous grotto or cavern which we had observed the day before, situated on the bank of the *Oued Frechih*.

"After having sent chasseurs in front of the most accessible openings of *El-Kantara* (the ravine above mentioned), the troops commenced to cut wood and to collect straw to light a fire on the west side, and thus oblige the

[1] "L'Afrique Française," p. 440. P. Christian. Paris, 1846.

Arabs to surrender, as any other means of attack would have been most sanguinary, and probably fruitless.

"At 10 A.M. they commenced to throw the faggots from the counterfort of El-Kantara, but the fire did not declare itself before noon. During the evening our tirailleurs approached nearer, and shut in the openings of the cave. Nevertheless, one of the Arabs succeeded in escaping from the east side, and seven others gained the banks of the stream, where they obtained a supply of water in their leathern vessels.

"At 1 P.M. the soldiers commenced to throw faggots at the eastern opening, which this time took fire before the two openings of the other side, and by a singular circumstance the wind blew both the flames and the smoke into the interior without almost any escaping outside, so that the soldiers were able to push the faggots into the openings of the cavern *as into a furnace.*

"It is impossible to describe the violence of the fire; the flame rose above the top of El-Kantara (more than 60 mètres), and dense masses of smoke swept like a whirlwind before the entrance of the cavern. They continued to supply the fire all night, and only ceased at daybreak. But then *the problem was solved;* no further noise was heard.

"At 4½ A.M. I went towards the cave, with two officers of engineers, an officer of artillery, and a detachment of 50 or 60 men of these corps. At the entrance were found dead animals, already in a state of putrefaction; the door was reached through a mass of cinders and dust a foot in depth, and then we penetrated into a great cavity of about 80 paces in length. Nothing can give an idea of the horrible spectacle which presented itself in the cavern. All the bodies were naked, in positions which indicated the convulsions which they had suffered before death. What caused most horror was to see infants at the breast lying amongst the *debris* of sheep, sacks of beans, etc.

"The number of corpses amounted

to 800 or 1000. The Colonel would not believe our report, and sent other soldiers to count the dead. They took about 600 out of the cave, without counting those *entassés les uns sur les autres comme une sorte de bouillie humaine*, and the infants at the breast, who were nearly all concealed below the clothes of their mothers. The Colonel testified all the horror which he felt at this frightful spectacle, and principally dreaded the attacks of the journals, which could not fail to criticise so deplorable an act."

It is not fair to quote this, without quoting also the justification of the act which appeared in the *Akhbar*.

"In order that the public may be able to appreciate these sad events, it ought to understand how important it was *pour la politique et pour l'humanité* to destroy the confidence which the population of the Dahra and of many other places had in the caves. . . . . Colonel Pélissier invested them, an operation which cost several lives, Arabs and French. When the investment was complete, he tried to parley with them by means of the Arabs in his camp: they fired on his *parlementaires*, and one of them was killed. Nevertheless, by persistence, he succeeded in opening negotiations, which lasted all day, without result. The Oulad Riah always replied, ' Let the French camp retire ; we shall come out and submit ourselves.' It was in vain that repeated promises were made to respect their persons and property, to consider none prisoners of war, but only to disarm them. From time to time they were informed that combustibles were collected, and that they should be warned if they did not finish. Delay succeeded delay till the night arrived." After passing in review the probable consequences of retiring from the attack, the narrative continues : " He decided on employing the means which had been recommended to him by the Governor-General ;" with what success we have already seen.

The caves are still exactly in the condition in which they were then left, and no Arab can be induced to enter them.]

About 3 kil. from Mostaganem is Mazagran.

Mazagran, celebrated as the place first attacked by Abd-el-Kader, after the rupture of the treaty of the Tafna of 1837. But Mazagran is most famed for its having in 1840, with a garrison of no more than 123 men, under Captain Lelièvre, repulsed the prolonged assault of a great body of Arabs under Mustapha ben-Tami, caliph of Mascara. A column has been erected to commemorate this feat, which is recorded by an inscription. The church was also built in commemoration of the same event.

6 kil. Pélissier.
21 kil. Ain-Tédelès.

Two uninteresting French villages. 4 kil. to the E. is *Bellevue*, formerly called *Souk el-Mitou*, and beyond there is no European colonisation whatever in the country till we reach Relizane ; the line passes over red sandy ground, low hills covered with a forest of thuya, and subsequently the wide plains of the Mina. The various stations are :—

32 kil. *Oued el-Kheir*.
47 kil. *Mekalia*.
55 kil. *Sidi-Kheltab*.
64 kil. *Bel-Hacel*.
76 kil. *Relizane*, see p. 176.

Beyond this, after passing the cultivated land of Relizane, the line enters the valley of the Mina, one of the most considerable of Algerian rivers, taking its rise in the district S. of Tiaret. It is very sinuous in its course, and generally flows in a deep bed ; water-courses, dry for the most part of the year, cut up the valley deeply on each side, and furnish their tribute to the main stream during rainy weather.

85 kil. *Oued Khellouq*.
95 kil. *Sidi-Mohammed ben Aouda* ; the tomb of this local saint is in an Arab village. On a remarkable peak behind it is a koubba in honour of Sidi Abd-el-Kader el-Djailani, one of many which are seen all over the country, generally in the most prominent positions. Up to this point the ground has been very arid ; beyond, richer vegetation and Arab cultivation is seen, and when the writer passed (in March) the whole country was covered with

what seemed the richest mosaic of wild flowers of ever-changing colour.

119 kil. *Fortassa*. A European village 2 kil. to the W., on the road to Mascara. Roman ruins to the E. of line.

134 kil. *Djilali-ben-Amar*.

146 kil. Note here the peculiar conformation of the rock, which explains how so many huge slabs were used in monuments similar to those of Méchéra-Sfa. It is disposed in strata, broken up into more or less isolated masses, and the strata frequently separated from each other by layers of earth. It is sometimes difficult to decide, on a cursory examination, whether these are natural masses of slabs piled one on the other, or megalithic constructions.

163 kil. *Méchéra-Sfa*. This is the station for the wonderful megalithic monuments called *Souama* (the minarets) by the Arabs. The best way to see them is to make a picnic from Tiaret, come here by the morning train, and return by the evening one. It will be easy to hire horses or mules at the station, especially if the traveller orders them on going to Tiaret.

They are distant about 7 kil. from the station, on the left bank of the Mina, which has dug itself a deep rocky bed, and here encloses a peninsula, surrounded on three sides by the river, with steep and sometimes precipitous cliffs.

The name Méchéra-Sfa signifies *Ford of the flat Stones*. The whole promontory is of the construction which we have mentioned above ; huge layers of stone of varying thicknesses, natural monoliths squared and dressed by nature, ready to serve as roofs for chambers dug out in the softer strata below them, or to be transported for use elsewhere.

Immediately on crossing the ford of the Mina we come upon what was undoubtedly a cemetery, but one which probably served from very early Numidian till quite late Christian times. The tombs are generally buildings made of large naturally squared stones roofed in with immense monoliths, and now open towards the river. They probably were at one time completely enclosed, but the stones forming the front walls have either been washed down the hillside by rains, or thrown down by excavators in search of treasure or antiquities. One of them is still tolerably entire. It has a front wall of large squared stones in which is a small entrance ; the roof is supported by a rough pillar. On the walls are three rude sculptures in relief, which have been thought to represent the Christian symbols of a fish, a dove, and a lamp.

Sometimes advantage has been taken of the rock itself to form one or more sides or even the roof of the building, and in nearly every instance the floor has been excavated in the soil.

There are several tombstones undoubtedly of Roman origin ; one bears a Latin inscription between two rose-like ornaments. It begins with the usual formula, D.M.S., but this is no proof that it was pre-Christian. The Christians, not to offend too much the prejudices of the pagans, adopted this commencement, only instead of understanding by it " Diis manibus sacrum," they understood it to mean " Deo magno sacrum."

Beyond this necropolis the entire summit of the hill has been converted into a stronghold divided off into three portions by cross walls, all of large but not gigantic stones, which bear no appearance of having been even hammer dressed. There are here and there a number of drinking troughs hollowed out of single blocks, but with this exception there is no trace of cutting. The whole interior of the place is covered with ruins of houses of the same rude construction—no trace of architecture or luxury of any kind. M. de la Blanchère considers that this must have been a Christian city, and speculates as to what was the name of its bishop.

It may have been so, or perhaps only a fortified position or *oppidum* destined to receive the inhabitants of the neighbouring districts in time of war or danger. The megalithic tombs below were probably those of important personages ; they are not numerous enough to indicate that they were the ordinary sepulchres of a city. On the plateau opposite, above the right bank of the river, there are also a number of megalithic tombs, of the dolmen type, which were crowned by tumuli of earth.

187 kil. *Tagdempt*, or *Takdemt*.
Best known as the headquarters and arsenal of Abd-el-Kader in the days of his power. It was destroyed in 1841. The hillside to the E. is covered with ruins of rough stone buildings; on a mamelon to the W. is the ruined house which . the Emir himself occupied. Takdemt was at one time a Roman station of some importance, perhaps *Gadaum*, and here Abd-er-Rahman founded the Capital of the Ibadite empire in A.D. 761.

197 kil. **Tiaret.** 3552 ft. above the sea. This is supposed to occupy the site of the Roman station *Tingurtia*. Ibn Khaldoun mentions it under the name of Tahert, and records that it was one of the places which offered a formidable resistance to Sidi Okba on his march to Tangier. An Arab town followed, and the present one was built by General Lamoricière in 1842. It was originally all contained within a fort, built on the lower slopes of *Djebel Guezzoul*; but as this left no room for extension, a new town has sprung up in the valley below, and on the slope of the opposite hill, which is crowned by a negro village. In the former are the troops, the merchants more especially depending upon them, and the Commandant Supérieur, who governs the Military Commune of *Aflou* in the south; while in the latter one are the civil establishments and inhabitants presided over by the *Administrateur* of the *Commune Mixte*, and the *Maire* of the town.

There is a Government stud-farm and a Smala of Spahis near the town, to the E. The whole country round is covered with Roman ruins. The traveller must not, however, expect stately buildings like the triumphal arch and Forum of Timegad, or the quadrifrontal arch, temple, and Basilica of Tebessa— all the ruins here are devoid of architectural merit: he will not even find cut stones, marble ornaments, or other objects which distinguished the Roman style. Nothing has been overthrown and destroyed by the hand of man; here buildings have fallen down by the action of time and weather; but their very number and extent prove how complete was the Roman occupation of the country, and how highly the land must have been cultivated by them, and no doubt also by the native Numidian. Roman influence here had little to do with luxury or art, but was eminently favourable to agriculture.

Nothing is more surprising when passing through the rich valley traversed by the railway than to note the utter disproportion between the extent of cultivable land and the present number of inhabitants it supports. Owing to the lazy and unthrifty habits of the Arab, who will always plough round a thistle rather than root it up, it takes a greater extent of land to maintain him in misery than it would do to make an European family rich and prosperous. So far there is little appearance of any European colonisation in the country, but the powerful humanising agency of the railway will no doubt effect a transformation before many years have elapsed. The ruins of the past prove what this may become in the future; the Commune Mixte of Tiaret alone contains nearly one hundred places corresponding to Roman cities and villages sufficiently important to leave their vestiges apparent at the present day.

The chief object of the traveller in coming to Tiaret will doubtless be to visit the extraordinary monuments called the **Djedars** (walls or buildings in Arabic). This can be done in one long day. Take a carriage and drive about 35 kil. on the road to Frenda, and when opposite the first or most eastern of the Djedars, which is clearly seen from the road, turn into the fields and drive straight to the foot of the isolated peak on which it is situated. As there is no water here send the carriage on to a spring called *Aïn-Ghorab*, and having inspected the first three Djedars rejoin it on foot, and so return to Tiaret. The traveller will have only about 3 kil. to walk. Should he not be satisfied with this group and desire to visit the other as well, it can best be done

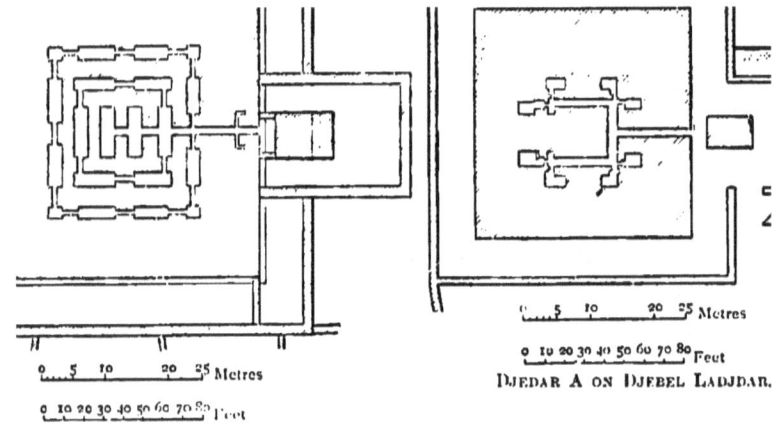

DJEDAR F AT TERNATEN.

DJEDAR A ON DJEBEL LADJDAR.

RESTORATION OF A.

by sending a horse on the day before and riding to it.

The Djedars are built in two distinct groups between Tiaret and Frenda. The first consists of three monuments on three separate but contiguous peaks of *Djebel-Ladjdar* (hill of the Djedars) : the second is at some distance to the W., at *Ternaten*, at a place called *Koudiat Heraoui*, O ; each is distinctly seen from the other.

The general form of all three monuments is the same—a rectangular or square podium surmounted by a pyramid. In this respect they differ from the older and finer buildings of the same kind, the Tombeau de la Chrétienne and the Medrassen, which have a round base crowned by a cone.

Some are in a good state of preservation, others are in a more or less ruinous condition ; two of the first group and one of the second can be easily entered (candle required).

The disposition of the passages and sepulchral chambers will be best understood by the woodcuts, which we have borrowed from M. de la Blanchère's Memoir. A is the first of those on Dj. Ladjdar ; F, the largest, but the least carefully constructed, is one of those at Ternaten. They are built of finely-cut stone ; that marked A is the most instructive of all ; it is situated most conspicuously on an isolated conical hill ; it is 34·60 mètres square, the podium is 3·50 mètres high, but it is not easy to determine the original height of the pyramid above it. The two portions are separated by a single string course, which is in fact the first and projecting step of the pyramid. This was of cut stone steps, filled in with a mass of rubble masonry.

The monument was surrounded at a distance of 8 mètres by a wall, forming a sort of sacred enclosure, probably planted as a garden ; it also was of cut stone, in some places as much as 6 mètres high. The courses of masonry receded about 10 centimètres from each other, which produced a very pleasing effect. In front of the east side was an isolated platform, ascended by a flight of steps, and probably connected with the main building by means of a drawbridge. The door of the pyramid was here, above the podium. It is probable that this platform was designed for some sort of religious ceremony.

The whole was surrounded by an outer wall of irregular shape of which only traces remain.

The chambers are roofed with enormous flat slabs of stone, and both they and the passages are sufficiently high to admit of a person standing erect. They were generally shut off from each other by stone doors, which sometimes descended from above, sometimes opened like an ordinary door, and sometimes slipped into lateral grooves.

These monuments are mentioned only by one author, Ibn-er-Rakik, a historian of the 10th century. Ibn Khaldoun, quoting from him, says that an inscription existed on one of them, "I am Soleiman the Serdeghos (Stratego). The inhabitants of this city having revolted, the king sent me against them. God having permitted me to conquer them I have caused this monument to be erected to perpetuate my memory."

The late General Dastugue found an inscription here which he sent to Baron de Slane, the learned translator of Ibn Khaldoun, who thought he traced in it the words *Soleiman* and *Strategos*, thus identifying it with that quoted by his author. This has been much disputed, and no one since has ever been able to find the inscription in question.

It is hardly possible that the celebrated Byzantine general, the successor of Belisarius, actually constructed any of these monuments. They are manifestly tombs, and the only question is that of the date of their construction. Numerous fragments of rude sculpture exist in them ; the monogram of Christ, a lamp, fishes, pigeons—all funereal emblems ; many short inscriptions, one commencing with the letters IN DEO X (Christo) ; another, portion of a dedication to Caracalla, taken from some other building.

M. de la Blanchère concludes that they vary from the 5th to the 7th century ; that they were the sepulchres of a native dynasty catholic in religion, which may have been at one time a vassal of the Romans before the Vandal invasion, subsequently allied to the Byzantines, and that it lasted as late as the Arab invasion, when probably it was swept away. The princes mentioned by Procopius were possibly of this family, Mephanias and his son Massonas.

[There is a route from Tiaret to **Frenda**, 56 kil., and thence to **Mascara**, 105 kil. The writer has done the journey, and he can conscientiously advise future travellers to leave it undone. The only thing of interest is the ruined fortress of *Tayramaret*, O, half way between Frenda and Mascara. The vicinity is covered with the foundations of Roman farms, each with its cistern; the fortress is rectangular, protected at the angles by bastions and with gates defended in the same manner. To see this, however, it will be necessary to stay a day here, and the only place where a traveller can put up is at the house of a well-known and very hospitable kaid, Abd-el-Kadir Boukors.

Between Tiaret and Tenict-el-Ahd there is no road, but the country is practicable on horseback, it is full of Roman remains, O, and is well worthy of being explored.[1]]

ROUTE 23.

Oran to Tlemçen.[2]

The first part of the road is by train.

Kil.		Kil.
..	Oran	70
6	La Sénia . . .	64
20	Misserghine . .	50
31	Brédéah . . .	39
36	Bou-Tlelis . . .	34
47	Lourmel . . .	23
56	Er-Rahel . . .	14
64	Rio Salado . . .	6
70	Aïn-Temouchent .	..

The train runs for the first 6 kil. along the Algiers-Oran line, as far as

[1] See "Une Reconnaissance Archéologique entre Tenict-el-Ahd et Tiaret," par Victor Waille.—Bull. de la Corres. Afr. 1848, Nos. V., VI.
[2] It will ordinarily be found more convenient to go to Tlemçen by Sidi Bel Abbes (see pp. 268, 269, 270), and to return by this route.

La Sénia, where that to Aïn-Temouchent branches off to the S.W., following the course of the old Route Nationale.

20 kil. *Misserghine*. Population, 1370.

About 2 kil. from the *Sebkha* of Oran, a marshy lake 38 kil. long by 8 broad, the waters of which are impregnated with salt.

Misserghine is one of the prettiest villages of the department, and the traveller, if he has time, will be glad to inspect the orphanage, founded by Père Abram, and conducted by the brothers of Nôtre Dame de l'Assomption. It contains about 130 boys and 90 old men, for whom the brothers receive a small allowance from the Department. The property is highly cultivated, and produces not only everything required by the establishment, but serves as a nursery garden for the country round. The fruit, vegetables, wine, and especially their celebrated Mandarine liqueur, are sent for sale to Oran. Near it is a female orphanage conducted by the Sœurs Trinitaires, containing young girls and old women.

Mounting a ravine, to the right of the village, where the road in spring-time reminds one of an English country lane, after going about 2 kil. one arrives at the only ostrich farm in this province; it has been pretty successful, but the space is too confined for further extension.

31 kil. *Brédéah*. Here is a copious spring from which Oran is supplied with water; the pumping engine was erected in 1880, and furnishes 100,000 cubic mètres of water *per diem*.

36 kil. *Bou-Tlelis;* a prosperous little town to the W. of the line.

47 kil. *Lourmel;* so called after a general of that name killed at Sebastopol; many fine gardens.

56 kil. *Er-Rahel*. From this village there is a road to *Hammam bou Hadjar;* see farther on. The Sebkha or salt lake finishes here.

64 kil. The line crosses a salt stream, the *Rio Salado*, the *Flumen Salum* of the ancients, and the *Oued Malah* of the Arabs, which falls into the Medi-

terranean between Cape Figalo and Camnerata.

70 kil. Aïn-Temouchent. Pop. 5496.

The land here is watered by two streams, the Oued Temouchent and Oued Senan, which are also utilised as motive power for mills.

The village was built in 1851 on the ruins of a Roman town, called by Pliny *Oppidum Timici*, from the excavations of which many interesting relics have been obtained; amongst others a bas-relief of the death of Cleopatra, now at Oran.

A monumental mairie has recently been constructed; the façade is of cut stone, with columns and arches of gray marble obtained in the neighbourhood.

[On the road between this village and Aïn-el-Arbaa, and 7 kil. from the latter, are the thermal springs of **Hammam bou Hadjar** (Bath of the Rock), which are much esteemed by the Arabs, and were used by the Romans, as ruins there attest. They have not been much used hitherto by Europeans owing to the want of accommodation. The water resembles that of Vichy; it gushes out of the ground in a column 1 mètre high, and 15 centimètres in diameter; its temperature is 80° Cent., 176° Fahr. At a short distance from it is a cold gaseous spring.]

A hotel was opened here in the summer of 1889.

An excursion may be made from this point to **Beni Saf**, see Rte. 24.

There are diligences between Aïn-Temouchent and Tlemçen, and *vice versâ*, in correspondence with each train. The journey occupies 8 hours.

14 kil. *Aïn Khial*.

23 kil. *Aïn Tekbalet*.

The small village of this name is about a mile from the road. By the roadside there is a small house and a fountain, and close to them are quarries of the beautiful alabaster known as **Algerian onyx**.

The discovery was made in 1849 by Signor Delmonte, of Oran, owner of the more famous quarries of Numidian marble near Kleber (p. 273). They are interesting not only on account of the beauty and value of the stone but geologically, as such deposits are not usually found in large masses, but generally only in grottos as stalagmite. This onyx was at one time much in demand, and may again become so, now that railway communication has considerably lessened the cost of transport. It was known to the ancients, and pieces of it may occasionally be picked up in the gardens at Rome. Columns of it, found in excavations in the mosque at Mansoura, may be seen in the mosques and museum at Tlemçen, 2·50 mètres in height, and 1·49 mètre in circumference.

The scenery around now begins to be of a more pleasing character, as the road ascends through wild hilly country to the plateau above the *Isser*. From this point a fine panorama opens out, comprising in the foreground the picturesque towers and walls of Tlemçen, and bounded in the distance by the range of the *Djebel Nador*.

44 kil. *Le Pont d'Isser*. 184 inhab. This village, situated in a fertile valley, makes little or no progress, owing to its unhealthiness. Great natural advantages in Algeria are frequently counterbalanced by the insalubrity of climate, so that the most fertile districts are often not the most prosperous.

At 7 kil. E. of this bridge, on the left bank of the Isser, is the alkaline spring of Hammam Sidi Abdeli; it springs out of a natural basin, near which are traces of Roman construction, and yields 150,000 litres per hour.

52 kil. *Negrier*. A small village of 184 inhab., founded in 1849, and named after a French general.

Crossing the *Saf-Saf*, and passing through highly cultivated country, the road ascends to the plateau on which Tlemçen is situated.

66 kil. **Tlemçen**. Pop. 17,123.

Every one has heard of Granada and its Moorish antiquities. The name of Tlemçen is known to comparatively few, yet it was a contemporary city not less illustrious, with a population of 100,000 or 150,000, renowned for its philosophers and its artists, the seat, equally with the Moorish cities in Spain, of civilisation and refinement, of commerce and wealth, the centre of an extensive trade, the capital of a powerful nation; and even now it is hardly inferior to it in beauty of situation and in architectural interest. It has no one grand monument like the Alhambra, but it possesses many religious edifices, which, if smaller, are hardly less beautiful.

Tlemçen lies about 2500 ft. above the sea, on the northern slope of a mountain called *Lella Setta*, and its climate, vegetation, and scenery resemble those of Central Italy. Frost, though never severe, is not uncommon, and snow occasionally lies on the ground for a fortnight at a time. Changes of temperature are also both sudden and frequent.

The neighbourhood, irrigated by numerous springs and streams of water, is highly cultivated, and the luxuriance and abundance of apple, pear, cherry, almond, peach, and still more of fig and olive trees, explain the name of Pomaria given to the original Tlemçen by the Romans; but the winters are too cold for the orange or lemon to flourish, except in the most sheltered situations. The olive trees are remarkably fine and very productive; the oil made from them is equal to that of the S. of France. Each olive tree is said to be worth 15 f. a year, and the number of young trees planted by the colonists shows that the cultivation must pay them well.

Pomaria was not an important town, and seems to have been so utterly ruined in the disastrous period which followed the Vandal invasion, that its very name was forgotten, when A.D. 790, or 174 of the Hegira, Idris ben Idris ben Abd-Allah, an able and enterprising monarch, obtained possession of the site from the Berber nation of the Zenata, and established his brother in possession after he had commenced building a great mosque. The Idrissides held Aghadir, as Tlemçen was then called, 140 years. The Fatimites next possessed it 24 years, and it then fell into the power of the Ifrenides for 125 years. During the succeeding dynasty of the Almoravides, who conquered Aghadir A.D. 1080, it grew greatly in importance. A new town called Tagrart rose on the site of the present town, and to W. of Aghadir, separated from it by a stone's throw, and with distinct fortifications. The name of Tlemçen was eventually given to the two united towns. Aghadir remained for many years the royal city and "the city of soldiers," among whom was a guard of several thousand Christians. Tagrart became the city of commerce. Foreigners, Jews, and Christians received full protection, and the latter possessed a church. The present barracks of the Spahis was the Kissaria, or the Bazaar of the Frank, made over to the Catalan, French, Genoese, Pisan and Venetian merchants, with its wall and its gates closed at sunset, under the exclusive government of the consuls. It is supposed there were at one time 5000 Christians in Tlemçen, governed by their own representatives.

The greatness of Tlemçen, which commenced under the Almoravides,[1] culminated under the Almoahides, who succeeded them A.D. 1145, and a new wall surrounding the double town was commenced A.D. 1161.

Under the two dynasties of the Almoravides and the Almoahides Tlemçen was one of the chief cities of the great Mohammedan empire of the West; but (1212) the battle of Nova Tolosa dealt a fatal blow to the power of the latter, and Tlemçen was taken from them A.D. 1248 by Ghamarasan, chief of the Zenata tribe of Abdel-Ouad,[2] and became under him and his successors the capital of a kingdom embracing the present provinces of Oran and Algiers. The most notable events under the early Abd-el-Ouadites were the two long sieges to which the ambition of the Merenides, the dynasty then ruling in Fez, subjected Tlemçen, the immediate cause of both being the refusal of the Sultan of Tlemçen to give

[1] The word *Almoravides* is a corruption of *El-Morabetin*, pl. of *Morabet*, a religious person. *El-Moahides* is correctly *El-Mouhedoun*, or affirmers of the unity of God.
[2] We adopt the ordinary orthography instead of the more accurate one of Abd-el-Wahid, etc.

up fugitives. The first siege was raised A.D. 1308 in consequence of the murder of Abou Yakoub, Sultan of Fez, after lasting over eight years, during part of which Tlemçen was closely invested and the besiegers' camp was surrounded with a wall, of which a portion still remains at Mansoura. The second siege commenced in 1335. The wall of Abou Yakoub was again employed by his successor, Abou el-Hassan Ali, known as the Black Sultan, and the investing force secured against a sudden attack from behind by a line of towers. The city fell into his hands in 1337; but the Merenides lost it again ten years after the death of Abou el-Hassan in 1348-49.

Abou Hammon Mousa, another Berber of the tribe of Abd-el-Ouad, succeeded in expelling them in 1359, and the Abd-el-Ouadites held it till 1553, though during a great part of this period their power did not extend beyond Ténès, while for the last forty years they were vassals of the Spanish sovereigns who are said to have garrisoned the Mechouar and to have built that part of the existing wall which faces the town.

In 1553 Tlemçen was captured by the Turks under Salah Raïs, Pacha of Algiers. The fall of the town was not less complete than that of its royal family; and the Arab proverb was verified, that "where the hoof of the Turkish horse has trod the grass refuses to grow." Science, literature, and art, which had been long decaying, became extinct; agriculture declined, manufactures and commerce almost ceased; at such a distance from the sea it had not the resource of piracy, the only trade which flourished. The palaces have long vanished; not a Moorish villa is to be seen in the neighbourhood. Even the olive trees either appear to be centuries old, or else to have been planted since the French occupation.

From 1830 to 1834 the possession of the town was disputed between Abd-er-Rahman, Emperor of Morocco, and the Turkish troops, who, during the latter part of these four years, were in the pay of France and held the Mechouar.

Abd-el-Kader appeared before the walls in 1834, when the Moors evacuated the town. Gen. Clauzel entered Tlemçen in Jan. 1836; and after imposing a fine of 150,000 f. on the inhabitants, left Captain Cavaignac in command of a small garrison in the Mechouar, or citadel. The town was then again besieged by Abd-el-Kader; but Cavaignac, with his garrison of 275 men, succeeded in holding it against the whole army of the Emir until the following June, when he was at length relieved by Gen. Bugeaud.

In 1839, by the treaty of the Tafna, Tlemçen was ceded to Abd-el-Kader, who made it his capital; but his troops were perpetually quarrelling with the inhabitants, and the ruined condition of a great part of the town dates from this period. Before long, war was renewed, and in 1842 the town was occupied by the French.

It is now extremely prosperous; the neighbourhood is fertile and singularly well supplied with water, and it is the chief town of an extensive district which exports annually large quantities of olive oil, olives, dried figs, wool, sheep, horned cattle, corn and flour, besides cloths, carpets, and leathern articles of native manufacture. Alfa is brought here from Sebdou, 43 kil., to the S., and prepared for exportation. The special manufactures of the place are brightly coloured blankets, and the red shawls called *tahlila*, worn by the Jewish women.

Amongst the remains of Moorish architecture within the walls of Tlemçen, the following are the best worth visiting.

The chief mosque, **Djamāa-el-Kebir**, in the Place d'Alger, has 72 columns, all square except 2. The arches are horseshoe, and for the most part round and plain, but some few are pointed, and others decorated on their interior side with plaster-work. The ceilings are of wood, and plain. The mihrab, which is on the S. side of the mosque, is finely ornamented with arabesques, lighted from above; and its round horseshoe arch is very beautiful. On it is the date A.H. 530, corresponding to A.D. 1136, which

[*Algeria.*]   s

shows that the mosque was built under the Almoravides. The present building, however, is the successor of a much more ancient one, founded, according to Ibn Khaldoun, in A.D. 790. The large chandelier, with a diameter of 2·44 mètres, was the gift of Ghamarasan, the first of the Abd-el-Ouadite Sultans, A.D. 1248 to A.D. 1283, who himself was buried here. The courtyard is partly paved with Algerian onyx, and the basin of the fountain is of the same material. The minaret, which is of brick, and about 34 mètres high, was built by Ghamarasan.

The **Mosque of Sidi Ahmed Bel Hassan el-Ghomari**, now an Arab school, and situated in the same Place d'Alger, has been restored by the French and offensively decorated on the exterior with modern tiles. The interior, however, contains some exquisite productions of Moorish art, especially the arabesques round the mihrab; their variety, richness, and refinement is probably unsurpassed anywhere. The date of this work, A.H. 696, or A.D. 1296-97, is inscribed here, and in the centre of the third arch. The mosque is supported by six columns of Algerian onyx. Nearly all the walls and arches have been covered with arabesque decoration, and the greater part remains.

On the opposite side of the square next to the mairie was the Medressa or college, now destroyed, where Ibn Khaldoun taught.

The **Mosque of Sidi Abrahim** is worth a visit, and in the tomb of the saint, which is contained in a separate building, there are some remarkably fine arabesques.

The above is almost all that remains of ancient Tlemçen within the walls worthy of particular notice; nor have the walls themselves fared better—they have been replaced by modern defences.

The destruction of the **Mechouar**, or citadel, has been most complete. Built in 1145 as the residence of the governor, it became the palace of the Abd-el-Ouadites. The Arab writers often make mention of its splendour and of the brilliancy of the court held there; but the Turks and time, and the Génie militaire, have spared nothing except the minaret of the mosque and the outer walls.

The **Museum**, or rather the want of one, is a disgrace to the city; many precious relics are stowed away, without care or order, in some of the lower rooms of the mairie. These consist of tumulary inscriptions; fragments of tile mosaics; arabesque work; columns of Algerian onyx excavated from the ruins of the mosque at Mansoura; and catapult balls, some weighing about 250 lbs., supposed to have been used during the two great sieges in the beginning of the 14th century.

The most interesting objects are— first, the standard cubit measure of the *Kissaria*; it is in marble, and bears in Arabic the inscription, "Praise and thanks be to God, this is the cubit measure of the Kissaria, which may God establish. In the month of Rabeea Eth-Thani, in the year 728," corresponding to March 1328. The length of this cubit is 47 centimètres, or 18½ inches. And secondly, built into a wall, an onyx slab with a long Arabic inscription, THE TOMBSTONE OF BOU ABDULLA, the last king of Granada, who surrendered to Ferdinand and Isabella, and died here in exile.

The mairie itself is a phenomenon of ugliness; the central portion is supposed to be decorated with a pediment supported by horns of plenty; but these features are rather suggestive of a tombstone and elephants' trunks.

The **Church** is an exceptionally good one for Algeria. The font is a fine basin of green serpentine, found in the ruins of Mansoura.

The mosque of Abou Abdulla esh-Shoudi, more usually known by the name of **Sidi-el-Halawi**, the Sweetmeat-maker, lies immediately outside the walls. Leave Tlemçen by the gate of the Abattoir, turn to the left, and you come to a small collection of native houses inhabited by negroes, with its own mosque and minaret; keep on above these, and on turning round the N.E. corner of the town wall you will see below you the mosque of Sidi-el-Halawi. As you descend to it take notice of the mosaics on the minaret.

The mosque and its court are decorated with arabesques; but it owes its chief interest to its eight columns of Algerian onyx, with Moorish capitals, and to the richly carved ceilings of cedar over the lateral naves, and the colonnade on each side of the court. The ceiling of the Mihrab should likewise be noticed. The date 754, equal to A.D. 1353, is inscribed over the portal, which is very beautifully decorated with tile mosaics and arabesques.

At least three circles of **ancient fortifications** can be clearly made out. The innermost of these followed the line of the French wall, and there is but little of it left. The walls and towers of the two outer circles are in many places still standing, and, added to the advantages of its situation, must have made the Tlemçen of the Almoahades and early Abd-el-Ouadites a place of great strength. The walls and towers are built of large masses of concrete or pisé (2 to 4 mètres is no uncommon size), which now look like stones, and are almost as durable. The towers, with the exception of two round ones near the N.W. corner, are rectangular; but though these walls are highly picturesque and interesting, it is at Mansoura that the system of Moorish fortifications can be most easily studied.

All visitors to Tlemçen should, if possible, take the two undermentioned walks:—

1. Leave Tlemçen by the gate of the Abattoir, go straight down the hill, and in from 10 to 15 minutes you will come to the minaret, which is all that remains of the mosque of the **Aghadir**. The lower part of this beautiful tower is constructed of large hewn stones from the Roman Pomaria, which occupied the same site as Aghadir, and on several, both inside and outside, Latin inscriptions are found; one is said to bear the name of *Pomaria*. The upper part of the minaret is of brick, doubtless of a later date than A.D. 789, when a mosque was first built here. The fortifications commence a few yards lower down. The arch of the gateway by which the road passes fell down not many years ago. It was called after Sidi Daoudi, the patron saint of Aghadir, whose tomb lies just below. The neighbourhood of this tomb is probably the best point from which to view the fortifications. Tourists are, however, strongly recommended to descend a little farther, taking a path to the right, into the valley of the *Oued Kalia*, and after crossing this brook to turn again to the right. A walk through gardens filled with fruit, ash, elm, and walnut trees, and passing close under the outer or second line of the walls and towers of Aghadir, and within sound of the Oued Kalia, leads in from 5 to 10 minutes to the Oran road; but it will be well to recross the brook just before the highroad is reached, and to follow a path to the right, which will conduct in about 2 minutes to an old Arab burial-ground, with tombs of Marabouts, and an octagonal one of singular elegance. The cemetery is beautifully situated, and elm, and especially ash trees (*Fraxinus Australis*), are here found of a size unusual in N. Africa. One of the latter, still a flourishing tree, measures 4¼ mètres in circumference.

2. Leave Tlemçen by the gate of *Bou Medin*, follow the road to Oran about 150 yards, turn to the right across the bridge over the *Oued Kalia*. The ruin on the left was part of the mint. Immediately after passing the bridge, turn again to the right and follow the path along the edge of the *Oued Kalia*. Extensive **remains of walls and towers** will be met with along the S. side of Tlemçen, to which this path conducts. This side being naturally the most exposed, was most strongly fortified. On the western side there are not many fortifications of importance, except at the north-western angle, where there are the two round towers already mentioned. Visit the Christian cemetery and return by the Porte des Carrières.

A whole morning should be devoted to **Sidi Bou Medin**. About 2 kil. from Tlemçen towards the S.E., and on the slope of a hill, which shelters it from the sirocco, lies a mean-looking Arab village, distinguished at a distance only by its minaret. This is El Eubbad, more commonly called Sidi Bou Medin, which was the home of religion and science when Tlemçen was inhabited by warriors and statesmen. It is in this more fortunate than its neighbour, that its monuments have been better preserved.

Shortly after leaving the gate of Bou Medin the road turns to the right, passes a ruined building which was the ancient mint, nearly opposite the entrance to the public gardens, and traverses the great Arab cemetery, now much circumscribed in extent. Several Koubbas to the right and left, many of which possess a history, and the minaret of a ruined mosque, give interest to the walk. The only one in a good state of preservation is that of *Es-Snousi*, the exterior of which is square with a tiled roof, but the interior is a very elegant dome. After passing through the, to all appearance, poverty-stricken village, the visitor sees before him a Moorish porch of painted woodwork, which gives entrance to the mosque and its dependencies.

To the left on entering is the ruined **Palace** of the founder of all these noble structures, commonly called Abou el-Hassan Ali, or the Black Sultan, but whose name and ancestry, as written in full over the entrance gate of the mosque, is "Our Lord the Sultan Abdulla Ali, son of our Lord the Sultan Abi Saeed Othman, son of our Lord the Sultan Abi Yoosuf, son of Yacoob Abd el-Huk." He was the first of the Merenides and reigned from A.H. 737 till 749 (A.D. 1337 to 1348). The actual date inscribed over the door is A.H. 739. On the tablets below the spring of the arch, at the main entrance to the mosque, his name is written,

Our Lord the Sultan Abou el-Hassan Abdullah Ali."

This was one of his many palaces, and it might well have been his favourite abode. It could not have been very large, but it was richly decorated, and the view from the arcaded terrace, overlooking a wide expanse of plain and mountain, and even the distant sea at Rachgoun, compares favourably even with the far famed Vega of Granada.

It is below the general level of the court, and until 1881 it was covered with earth and rubbish, so that its existence was not suspected; now it has been excavated under the intelligent superintendence of M. Collignon, *Conservateur des Monuments historiques*.

On the same side, also below the level of the court, is the **Koubba of Sidi Bou-Medin**, the patron saint of Tlemçen. His correct name was Shaoïb ibn Hoosain el-Andalousi, surnamed Abou Median, corrupted into Bou-Medin. He was born at Seville in A.H. 520, corresponding to A.D. 1126. He passed over from Spain to Fez, where he devoted himself to the study of theology, and after travelling all over Spain, Algeria, and even as far as Baghdad, he died at Aïn-Tekbalet within sight of Tlemçen, in the 75th year of his age.

The writer ventures to give one earnest recommendation to all visitors. This, to the Mohammedan, is very holy ground; let the visitor remove his shoes at the outer door of the courtyard; and he will have his reward in the increased attention paid to him by the guardians.

A short staircase descends into an antechamber; to the right and left are tombs of persons connected with the mosque, but not of great antiquity. There is nothing remarkable in the architecture of the antechamber; to the right is the entrance to the tomb itself, and an inscription on the door informs us that having been greatly injured by fire it was restored by Sidi Mohammed, Bey of Oran, in A.H. 1208 (A.D. 1792). The koubba itself contains two tombs; to the right is the resting-place of the saint himself, to the left is that of his friend and disciple Sidi Abd-es-Selam of Tunis. The roof and walls retain all their fine old arabesque work, the principal feature of which is the repetition of a cartouch containing the inscription *El-Mulk Lillah*, "The kingdom is God's." The colouring is crude and modern. The whole interior is full of banners of brocade, votive candles, ostrich eggs, and the usual paraphernalia of Arab tombs.

On remounting to the upper court we see before us the principal entrance to the **Mosque** itself, glorious in design and sparkling with the most beautiful tile mosaics; in the best style of Moorish art. These glazed tiles,[1] used in making the mosaic patterns, are supposed to have been made in Fez, or some other parts of Morocco; they are somewhat ruder than those employed in the Alhambra, but exceedingly effective; the square tiles came probably from Spain.

To the right hand is a half ruined building, which, before the French conquest, was recognised as an inviolable sanctuary for criminals or refugees from justice.

Ascending the steps we enter a portico with decorated walls and a roof of honeycombed pendatives, and pass into the open court beyond by large double doors covered with bronze, of which, unfortunately, the lower part has been stolen bit by bit. There is a tradition respecting these doors that they were lost in the sea, but recovered from it and brought to Bou-Medin by the prayers of the saint. It may almost be said that they are to Moorish art what the doors of Ghiberti are to Italian, for purely decorative art was never carried higher. The design is a geometric interlaced pattern.

The mosque itself is worthy of the approach to it. It is divided into five naves, the two lateral ones being prolonged as corridors round the building, so as to enclose an open court—similar in fact to all other mosques in the place. The roofs of these naves are elongated vaults, decorated with plasterwork, in geometric patterns, without tracery, of a design much bolder than that on the rest of the building. It has at one time been painted—a very small fragment of the original painting gives an idea of the style adopted. The pillars are square and perfectly plain, but the whole superstructure, from the spring of the arches to the

[1] (Arabic *Zilaidj*, whence the Spanish *Azulejos*.)

roof, is covered with most delicate lace-like work. So is the mihrab, and the koubba in front of it, the domed ceiling of which is of open work, with stained glass. The painting of this portion of the building is modern, and open to criticism.

The walls of the building have a richly sculptured frieze, but below this they have a very simple pattern excised in the plaster. The ancient mimber was of marble, but it got broken, and the present painted wooden pulpit was given by Abd-el-Kader.

On the two pillars in front of the mihrab are onyx slabs bearing long Arabic inscriptions. These are the original charters by which the lands around were granted in perpetuity to the mosque as *Haboos* or inalienable property. The French Government has taken possession of these, and they have thereby incurred the responsibility of keeping the building in proper order. They have done a good deal of late years; had they begun sooner we should not have had to deplore the irreparable dilapidation of this precious monument.

The traveller should by all means ascend the minaret; he will be rewarded by a magnificent view, and he will be able to inspect closely the manner in which it was decorated.

To the W. of the mosque and attached to it is the **Medrassa** or college, where talebs and scholars taught and studied at the cost of the endowment. In form it is similar to the mosque: the inner chamber has a fine domed roof of open woodwork, below which is a frieze of Arabic inscriptions, also of sculptured wood. The tile mosaics which adorn the entrance are remarkably fine. The building is isolated from the rock behind by a narrow gallery; this got filled up with earth, which entailed the destruction of the plaster work on the walls.

On the E. side of the mosque is the vapour bath and its dependencies.

Mansoura, about 1½ m. to the W. of Tlemçen, is hardly less remarkable than Bou-Medin, and the road to it passes by several interesting objects. It is better to visit it in the afternoon, as the light is then better for seeing the minaret.

Leave Tlemçen by the Fez gate, and about 100 yards farther on will be seen on the right the **Saharidj**, a reservoir, 220 mètres long by 150 broad. It is built with walls of concrete 3·65 mètres high and about 1 mètre thick, strengthened by buttresses; it was constructed, we are told, by Abou Taehfin, the last king of the elder branch of the Abd-el-Ouadites, who was killed at the capture of the Mechouar, in 1337, in order to gratify as far as possible the whim of a favourite wife who wished to behold the sea and ships upon it. It has been partly repaired by the French, but cannot be used as a tank owing to some undiscovered leak. About 1 kil. farther on, the road passes close to what was once a beautiful horseshoe arch called **Bab-el-Khamis**, formerly a gateway in the wall by which Abou Yakoub invested Tlemçen in the first years of the 14th century. It has now lost all its beauty by ruthless restoration. The large ruin which will be noticed on the slope of the hill to the left is an ancient mosque. Beyond the arch the road crosses the eastern wall of **Mansoura**. Its history resembles a tale from the "Arabian Nights." After Abou Yakoub had besieged Tlemçen four years he turned his camp into a city, and surrounded it with walls and towers, of which a large portion now remains. The walls are about 12 mètres high and the towers 37 mètres apart, all built of concrete— a method which Pliny mentions as employed by the people of this country in his time. Though the walls have in places disappeared, the line of towers still marks their direction; they enclosed a nearly perfect square of 250 acres. Ibn Khaldoun says of it:—"It was filled with large houses, immense buildings, sumptuous palaces, and irrigated gardens. It was in 702 (1302) that the king built its walls and that he created a splendid city, famous both for its vast population, its extensive trade, and its massive walls. He included in it baths, caravanserais, a hospital, and a mosque with a lofty minaret." "In a short time," he adds, "it took the first place among the cities of Barbary." Mansoura was, however, evacuated when peace was made in 1306, and deserted till 1329, when it was again occupied during the second siege of Tlemçen. Abou 'l-Hassan, the Black Sultan, after the capture of that city, built a palace at Mansoura, which became a favourite residence. But in 1359 the Merenides were expelled from Tlemçen, and Mansoura was finally deserted. Excepting the walls and the mosque, little remains of its former greatness, which is accounted for by the materials of which Moorish cities are built. Hewn stone and marble were seldom employed, and the concrete and cement with which their places were supplied soon perish when exposed to the weather. The minaret of which mention has been made was built of hewn stone, and one side and a part of two others remain to this day. It is by far the most beautiful architectural monument of Moorish times in Algeria.

Until lately it was in great danger of falling, but now it has been thoroughly strengthened and repaired.

The Arabs of the neighbourhood say that Abou Yakoub, being impatient to complete his tower, employed upon it Mohammedan, Jew, and Christian masons, and that the work of the first only has stood. In this story there is probably a germ of truth, for the general character of the tower is European, but the decoration Moorish. All other minarets near Tlemçen are built either of brick or concrete, with a solid square mass of masonry in the centre, round which runs the staircase, and round this again the outer walls, which are commonly, if not always, of bricks arranged to make peculiar patterns, the solid centre rising several feet or even yards above the walls. The Mansoura minaret is, on the contrary, built hollow in the centre, and constructed of hewn calcareous tufa, the thickness of the walls being about 1½ mètres, and the separate stones 36 cent. in height and usually at least twice that length. It resembles a European church-tower in position, being in the centre of the end opposite the mihrab, and there is an entrance into the mosque through it. Instead of an interior staircase it had a series of inclined planes or ramps up which a horse could mount to the summit. Æsthetically, the tower can hardly be too highly praised. The proportions are perfect, the decoration rich and original, or at least unlike anything else in the neighbourhood. The arches are either circular or pointed, and never horseshoe. Over the entrance arch is a stone projection or porch beautifully carved, and round the arch is written, *Abou Yakoub Yousuf ben Abd-el-Huk commanded this mosque to be built.* The height of the tower is nearly 40 mètres, and the upper part is ornamented with green and blue tiles. Nothing remains of the rest of the mosque except the outer walls, the space within which is oblong, 100 yards by 59.

A small village, with extensive and well-watered gardens around it, appears to occupy a mere spot in the immense area of the ancient city.

The falls of **El-Ourit** or the *Saf-Saf*, 5 kil. from Tlemçen, would be well worthy of a visit, even in a country where waterfalls abound. The road to S. Bel Abbès passes close under them, and the new railway runs just above.

Leave Tlemçen by the gate of Bou Medin, and take the road which branches off to the right, about ½ m. outside the town. It passes through the olive grounds and gardens below Bou Medin, and winds shortly after to the right, round the corner of the hill, and turns again sharply to the left at a bridge, whence the falls are best seen. They are unquestionably beautiful, though not from the quantity of water, or from their height, for though the total fall from the summit of the cliffs where the water is first seen, to the bottom of the ravine below the bridge, cannot well be less than 450 mètres, no single fall seems to be of more than 30; but rocks rise precipitously on either side from steep banks half hidden by wild cherry trees, while huge masses of calcareous tufa, hollowed out in fantastic caverns, cover the ascent in front. The rich green of sloping banks contrasts with the red masses of the stratified cliffs, springing from them, nearly 300 mètres hard and sharp against the sky line; while an immense mass of perpendicular tufa closes in the valley on the left of the upper fall.

The visitor to the stalactite caves of the **Beni Aad** can drive 14 kil. along the road to Sidi bel Abbès, but must leave his carriage and turn off to the right at the 165th kilometric stone. The caves are 5 kil. from the road, but there are Arab encampments at hand where mules may be procured if notice be given beforehand.

The following description of them is from "Through Algeria":—

"Stalactites in every variety of size and form closed in my view above, around, below. No ceiling of human work could exceed in varied beauty the deep-fluted fringes and arches of pale yellowish hue that hung overhead; and not less exquisite were the clustering columns which, shooting up on every side, joined the vault above, or terminated midway in a group of glittering pinnacles. As we threaded our way through overarching aisles, with aisles and aisles seemingly extending into the darkness on either hand, the weird-like fantastic beauty of the scene conjured up my childish visions of fairyland."

The main grotto extends for more than a kil. in length, but it has never been thoroughly explored, and it is supposed that there is a communication between it and other caverns farther down the hill. In visiting this cave the traveller would do well to provide himself with a magnesium lamp, or if that is impossible, a good supply of blue light and red fire, which is easily procurable at Algiers. Facilities for visiting these caves can be obtained by application at the Sous-Prefecture.

The writer saw them illuminated by 200 Arabs carrying flambeaux, some of whom climbed up the highest stalagmites and waved their torches like malignant demons amongst the stalactites depending from the roof. Others ran backward and forward, through the grottoes and forest of columns around; the effect was singularly beautiful, and more like a fairy scene in a pantomime than anything in real life. Such a treat as this can only be enjoyed by special favour, and then the traveller must be prepared to pay a considerable sum in presents to the Arab attendants.

[An excursion may be made to **Sebdou**, and the mountains of the **Beni Snous**. An omnibus runs to and from the former place every day. The road is good; it passes through the village of Mansoura, and then mounts the steep hills south of Tlemçen. The only appearance of European colonisation beyond this is at

14 kil. The poor little village of *Terny*, situated in a plain, the soil of which is of very inferior quality. Mounting the hills above, we come to

22 kil. *Caravanserai of Aïn-Ghoraba*, "The Spring of the Crow." Beyond, the country is more picturesque, and the road passes through the fine oak forest of *Titmokren*, containing park-like glades dotted over with magnificent trees.

35 kil. A *Maison Cantonnière* may be seen on the left side of the road; close to it is a large cavern, called by the Arabs *Aïn-Vemam*, "The Spring of Pigeons," from the number of those birds which frequent it; this is the **source of the river Tafna**. The cave is divided into two stories by a horizontal partition of rock, looking almost like masonry: the lower part contains a pool of cool clear water, which flows underneath the surface of the river bed for a couple of hundred yards, and then appears above ground as the Tafna. After heavy rains the entire cave becomes full of water, which rushes out in a magnificent cascade. The river then flows through a series of rocky gorges to the N.W., till it enters the rich plain of the Tafna, and eventually reaches the sea at Raehgoun.

Beyond the place just mentioned the valley becomes quite narrow, and the road descends into the plain of Sebdou, passing amongst cascades, streams of water, and rich irrigated land. On the opposite side of the plain may be seen the mountains of the Beni Snous, amongst which are a number of rounded mamelons, called by the French "The Twelve Apostles."

43 kil. **Sebdou**. Hôtel de Commerce, 3000 ft. above the sea.

This town is situated on the *Oued Guell el-Kilab*, "Dogs' Ferry," and was once an important military station, with a redoubt and a large entrenched camp, around which a considerable village had sprung up, all the inhabitants of which were more or less dependent on the garrison for their subsistence. But in 1881 it was handed over to the civil authorities, the Bureau Arabe was removed to *El-Aricia*, 50 kil. farther S., and the garrison was gradually diminished, till now it does not number 50 men. There is no land available for colonisation: it all belongs to the Arabs, who cannot be induced to part with it, so that now Sebdou seems menaced with ruin. The only trade which is at all brisk is that of alfa, of which there are usually large depôts waiting to be transported to the coast.

An excursion, which can be made on horseback, starting early in the morning and returning at night, 3 hours' ride each way, is to **Dhara** in the mountains of the Beni Snous, where is the magnificent house of El-Hadj bel Arabi, one of the kaïds of that tribe. The road passes through a fine forest of oak and over wooded hillsides, lighted up in early summer with a profusion of flowers of every colour.

The mother of the kaïd is quite an historical personage, being the widow of Si Mohammed bin Abdulla, Agha of the Beni Snous, who was murdered in 1856 by, or at the instigation of, Captain Doineau, Chief of the Bureaux Arabe at Tlemçen. That officer was sentenced to death for the offence, a punishment commuted into perpetual exile from France. This lady, who goes everywhere by the name of *El-Adjusa*, or "the old woman," is held in the greatest veneration throughout the country. She does the honours of her house with uncovered face, and with the most perfect dignity and cordiality. Travellers should not, however, venture to call upon her without consulting the administrator at Sebdou.]

ROUTE 24.

A Tour through the Centre of Oran to Mascara, Sidi bel Abbès, Tlemçen, Lalla Marnia, Nedroma, and Nemours.

This route is strongly recommended to travellers who do not fear the fatigue of travelling by diligence, and who wish to see something more of the country than is possible by railway. It contains all that is most interesting in the province of Oran, and the traveller, whose eventual destination may be Spain or Gibraltar, can so time his movements as to catch the Transatlantic steamer at Nemours.

It can be done in 5 days' actual travel from Algiers, viz.—

First day—Algiers to Perrégaux by train (Rte. 10).

Second day—Perrégaux to Mascara by train (Rte. 23).

Third day—Mascara to Sidi bel Abbès by diligence in 11 hours.

Fourth day—Sidi bel Abbès to Tlemçen by train.

Fifth day—Tlemçen to Nemours by diligence in 14 hours.

First and second days as above stated.

Third Day.

The diligence starts from Mascara at 6 A.M. For the first 3 kil., as far as the small village of *St. Pierre*, it follows the road to Saida ; there the embranchment to Sidi bel Abbès takes place, and thenceforth the kilometric stones are numbered from 1 onwards as far as Lalla Marnia.

8 kil. The railway station and village of *Tizi*, situated in the wide and fertile plain of *Eghris*. After crossing this we enter the valley of the *Oued Fekan*, still very highly cultivated.

17½ kil. *The Barrage* of that river, embedded in trees ; it irrigates the land between it and

21 kil. The village of *Fekan*, peopled by colonists from Alsace and Lorrain. The road, which has hitherto been S., now turns nearly W., and closely follows the bed of the river, which is richly wooded, especially with large Betoum trees (*Pistachia Atlantica*).

26 kil. The river here falls to a considerably lower level in a fine cascade.

33 kil. *Les Trois-Rivières*, the junction of the *four* streams, the *Oued Fekan*, the *O. Traria*, the *O. Houenet*, and the *O. Melrir*, the united waters of which now form the *Tafna*. After crossing this the road leads through picturesque gorges and more or less barren hillsides to

51 kil. **Mercier-Lacombe**, a very prosperous village, named after a late director-general of civil affairs, who married the daughter of Mr. Bell, H.M. Consul-General. A market is held here every Tuesday. The diligence stops for breakfast at the Hotel de Commerce.

The whole distance between this and Sidi bel Abbès is one continuous stretch of corn, the uniform green of which, in early summer, is only diversified by fields necessarily left fallow, and by the most gorgeous effects of colour caused by wildflowers amongst the growing corn. The country is everywhere well watered, and is one of the richest in the colony.

59 kil. *Mulai Abd el-Kadir*, a small centre of European colonisation, near the marabout of the saint ; there are only a few farms, a school, and the inevitable canteens. Some business is done here in alfa and tan-bark.

71 kil. *Baudens*, formerly called *El-Ksar*, may be seen a few kils. to the S., the name was changed to do honour to an army surgeon.

74 kil. *El-Greiz* Relay.

88 kil. **Sidi bel Abbès**, see p. 269.

Fourth Day.

The railway from Sidi bel Abbès to Tlemçen is not yet (1889) quite complete, but will soon be so.

Proceed along the main line (St. Barbe to Ras el-Ma) as far as *Tabia*, the junction for Tlemçen, where change carriages.

13 kil. from Tabia, *Taffaman*.

24 kil. *Aïn-Tellout*, a magnificent spring of cold clear water issuing from the midst of a thick growth of oleanders.

This was formerly a station on the Roman road between *Albulæ* (Ben Youb) and Tlemçen, and was an outpost of the military fortified camp at *Castra Sereriana* (Lamoricière).

The traveller will find much to admire in the view as he nears Lamoricière.

At Tellout the plain or undulating country suddenly gives place to a deep valley, watered by the Oued Tellout, and dotted here and there with farms and dwellings.

As the road, with windings innumerable, follows the steep sides of the hills and spurs, the valley gradually opens out on the one hand towards Lamoricière and on the other towards the junction of the Isser and Chouli, to the N.W.

Soon the jagged crest of the mountain which rises behind Lamoricière is descried, and presently the pretty village itself appears nestling amid its avenues of trees, at the foot of a rugged hill resembling a hacked and rusty knife with the edge turned uppermost. The picturesque valley of the upper Isser stretches away northwards, hemmed in by hills, and the valley of the Oulad Meimoun extends far below.

33 kil. **Lamoricière**, an important village named after General Lamoricière. Here for the present (1889) the line stops, and the traveller must go on to Tlemçen by diligence.

Just in front and on the left of the road, before the bridge is reached, are the ruins of an old Roman camp and settlement now called *Hadjar Roum* — the Roman stones.

An inscription was found here, of the beginning of the 6th century, proving that this place, instead of being the *Rubræ* or *ad Rubras*, as had hitherto been supposed, is the site of the *Castra SerianaO* mentioned by Morcelli as an episcopal see. The inscription is given *in extenso* by M. Cherbonneau in the "Bull. Acad. Inscrip. et Belles Lettres," 1878, t. vi. p. 30.

The fortified enclosure measured about 400 yds. long and 300 broad, and was rectangular in shape, being placed square with the magnetic N. and S. The village or town appears to have extended as far as the precipice which overlooks the valley of the Oulad Meimoun, and the ground has kept the terrace-like outline which it doubtless then had.

It was evidently a military post, intended to cover the exit from the upper Isser valley which communicates with the High Plateaux. In the same way Albulæ, already mentioned, served to close the valley of the Mekerra.

Little of these remains is at present visible. The ground is covered with stones from the buildings which existed formerly, and a few bearing inscriptions have been found among the débris. The following complete inscription is mentioned by M. MacCarthy:—

DIANAE DEAE
NEMORUM COMITI
VICTRICI FERARVM
ANNVA VOTA DEDI
FANNIVS IVLI
ANVS PRAEFECTVS
COHORTIS II.
SARDORVM

After leaving Lamoricière the road, still skirting the chain of hills, crosses the Isser just past the village; and 12 kil. farther on, the Chouli, a clear stream running over a rocky bed.

The valley narrows in more and more as the road advances. The Chouli comes down through a break in the hills to the S. Some way up its course is the Berber village of Yebdar, situated in a fertile and pretty valley.

163 kil. Auberge Bello—Relay.

165 kil. The path to the caves of the **Beni Aad** branches off to the S.

168½ kil. *Aïn-Fezza*, a small village situated on the most elevated part of the road between Bel Abbès and Tlemçen. Residence of the administrator of the district. The altitude is here 875 mètres above the sea. To the right is seen, half hidden by groves of olive trees, the village of Oujba, entirely native. The road soon after turns into the deep gorge of the Cascades.

173 kil. The *Cascades* (see p. 263).
178 kil. A fine view is here obtained of S. Bou Medin on the left and Aghadir on the right.
179 kil. **Tlemçen** (see p. 255).

Fifth Day.

From Tlemçen a diligence goes to Lalla Marnia and Nemours in one day. Leaving by the gate of Fez we traverse the ruins of Mansoura, and at

184 kil. the last trace of European colonisation is passed. The road now goes through an undulating country, in which there is a little sparse Arab cultivation, and a good deal of scrub, in some places attaining almost the importance of a forest. It is difficult to find any salient points to note ; the following are a few, of no particular interest, save as landmarks :—

192 kil. The *Maison Cantonnière* of *Beni Mister*, near which is an Arab village and a fine grove of olive trees.
194 kil. A stone marking the spot where a Spaniard was assassinated by Arabs in August 1885.
205 kil. *Aïn-Sahra*, a stream of clear water, and the Relay.
210 kil. The *Maison Cantonnière* of *Oued Barbata*. Here begins the forest, if such a name is applicable, of *Tayemsdelt*, composed principally of Thuya trees (*Calitris quadrivalvis*), which extends for the next 10 kil.
222 kil. *Maison Cantonnière*.
223 kil. The road crosses the **Tafna**, one of the most considerable rivers in the province ; its principal source is from a cavern in the mountains overlooking the plains of Sebdou (see p. 264).
230 kil. The old road to Tlemçen branches off to the N.E. at this point. The country here is remarkably fine, park-like, and dotted over with olive trees.
231 kil. **Lalla Marnia**, more properly *Lella Maghnia*, from a female saint, whose tomb is here.

This is a very important strategical and commercial position, only 14 kil. from the frontier of Morocco and 24 kil. from the Moroccan city of Oudjda. It has been identified as the ancient *Syr* by a miliary column, which fixes the distance between it and *Pomaria* (Tlemçen), and to *Siga* at the mouth of the Tafna.

Marnia is an open village, protected by a redoubt, which contains the garrison and military buildings. It is entirely under military government.

It is situated in a rich and fertile district, watered by the barrage of the O. Allou. The town is 365 mètres above the sea.

[34 kil. S. are the disused mines of *Ghar Rouban*, see p. 282.]

Henceforth the road which has hitherto run nearly E. and W. now turns to the N., and the kilometric stones are numbered from Marnia onwards.

5 kil. The *Oued Mouia* is crossed by a wooden bridge. Near this are some thermal springs, much frequented by the inhabitants of the district.

10 kil. The *Maison Cantonnière* of *Sidi Abdulla*. Behind it are two caves with fine stalactites, and an immense supply of guano deposited by the numberless bats which frequent them.

17 kil. A calamine mine has lately been discovered here, but when the writer visited the place in May 1886, although 6000 tons of ore had been extracted, none had been carried away.

The road now ascends the steep range of hills in front, and from the highest point or col, *Bab Tazza*, 820 mètres above the sea, and 20 kil. from Marnia, a splendid view is obtained both towards the N. and S. It dominates the plains of Nedroma, and when the weather is fine one can see as far as the Zaffarine Islands and the Snassen Mountains, within the frontier of Morocco. The inhabitants of this district are Berbers.

From this point the road descends, winding amongst the valleys, till it reaches

32 kil. **Nedroma**. A most interesting Berber city, situated on the lower slope of the hill which we have just

passed, with a magnificent panorama of olive groves and fertile fields in front of it, and rich gardens around. It is exceedingly ancient; its original name was *Medinet el-Botaha;* but in the middle of the 13th century it was rebuilt by Sultan Ghomarasan of Tlemçen, who changed this to its present one, supposed to be a corruption of *Dthud Roma,* "opposite Rome," or perhaps "a barrier against the Christians." The inhabitants speak only Arabic, but their Berber origin would be manifest even if historical evidence of it did not exist. The remarkable beauty of the women is a distinctive characteristic of the Berber race, and here even the passing traveller has an opportunity of judging for himself, as the unmarried girls do not veil their faces. The houses are large, well built, and clean, and the town is surrounded by crumbling walls of concrete, crowned by a ruined citadel, exactly like those of Honai (p. 281).

Until the last few years it was exclusively native, but now a few Europeans have been attracted to it by the fertility of the land and the traffic caused by the new road; the bureau of the administrator of the district has been transferred here from Nemours, and in a year or two it will probably lose its peculiarly Berber character, which now makes it so interesting.

After passing for some distance through the plain the road enters the rich valley of the *Saf-Saf* or river of Trara, one continuous series of market gardens and orchards.

At about 1500 mètres from Nemours there may be seen, in the bed of a river to the left, a pyramid surrounded by an iron railing. This covers the remains of the troops who perished at the combat of Sidi Brahim, 10 kil. to the E., in 1843. This was one of the many gallant but unfortunate actions which threw lustre on French arms during the first years after the conquest.

A column under Colonel Montagnac, consisting of 66 cavalry and 350 infantry, were enticed by Abd-el-Kadir into a skilfully-contrived ambuscade near Sidi Brahim, and almost completely annihilated; one company of reserves managed to force its way nearly to Nemours, but, despite the assistance afforded by the feeble garrison of that place, it shared the fate of the rest. Only one corporal and 12 men of the entire force were rescued.

Abd-el-Kader himself surrendered here two years afterwards.

48 kil. **Nemours** (see p. 282).

ROUTE 25.

From St. Barbe de Tlelat to Sidi Bel Abbès by Railway [thence to Tlemçen], and on to Ras el-Ma.

kil.	Names of Stations.	kil.
..	St. Barbe de Tlelat .	152
6	St. Lucien . . .	146
16	Lauriers Roses . .	136
29	Oued Imbert . .	123
36	Les Trembles . .	116
42	Sidi Brahim . .	110
52	Sidi Bel Abbès . .	100
58	Sidi Lahsen . .	97
64	Sidi Khalid . .	88
71	Bou Kanétis . .	81
75	Tabia . . .	77
83	Chanzy . . .	69
100	Si Slissen . .	52
115	Magenta . .	37
122	Les Pins . .	30
129	Taten-Yaya . .	23
143	Bedeau . . .	9
152	Ras el-Ma . .	..

This line was constructed by Mr. Harding, of Paris, and after its completion it was made over to the Compagnie Ouest Algérien. The works commenced in the spring of 1875, and terminated in May 1877. The country through which it passes is rich and tolerably well cultivated; but one great object in making the line was to tap the alfa districts and bring that produce to the coast. The principal goods carried by it are alfa fibre, wheat, and tan bark. The country slopes gradually up to Bel Abbès, and is picturesque. The line starts from the Tlelat station of the P. L. M. Company (see p. 178).

1 kil. to E. of line is the marabout

of Sidi Bel Khair, after which it follows the general direction of the high road from Oran to Sidi Bel Abbès, crossing it on several occasions.

6 kil. *Arrêt of St. Lucien.* To the E. of the line is a village created in 1876, and named after a child of General Chanzy, who was accidentally killed at Algiers two years before.

8 kil. To the E. are the marabouts dedicated to Sidi Berafor, after which the country becomes more hilly.

9 kil. The line crosses the high road at 38 kil. from Oran.

11 kil. To the E. is a barrage on the Oued Tlelat, constructed in 1872 by military prisoners. It waters a comparatively small area.

13 kil. To the E. the Marabouts of Sidi ben Taib and S. Saiah.

14 kil. W. of line. Djenan el-Meskine, *the garden of the beggar*, a well-watered plantation of fruit trees on the high road.

16 kil. Station of *Lauriers Roses.* To the E. is the Merabet ez-Zeidj; to the W. an old telegraph station and the marabout of S. Mohammed. The village of Lauriers Roses is seen to the W. It consists of but a few houses along the high road.

22 kil. W. An Arab village with a marabout on the top of an isolated mamelon.

22½ kil. *Oulad Ali;* a pretty large Arab market is held here every week.

23 kil. The house of the Kaid of the Oulad Ali to the W. After which the line enters the col of the Oulad Ali.

25 kil. The crossing station of the *Oued Imbert.* This is the highest point on the line, being 508 mètres above the level of the sea. The route to St. Denis du Sig branches off from this place. The country now becomes much more fertile than it has been.

29 kil. Station of *Oued Imbert,* a small village on the W., beyond which is the marabout of S. Machou.

36 kil. *Arrêt des Trembles.* The village is situated on a hill to the E. between the line and the high road; the trees, which give their name to the place, are on the banks of the Mekerra, which flows past the village.

36 kil. The line here crosses the Oued Sarna, and in this neighbourhood the most considerable excavations and embankments in its whole course have been executed. The mountain of Thessalah is seen about 20 kil. to the W. The plain at its eastern base is covered with rich and flourishing farms.

40 kil. To the E. on the Mekerra are the farm and mill of the late M. Bleuze, who, with his housekeeper, was murdered by a party of Arabs in 1875. One of the assassins was executed at S. Bel Abbès in April 1877. The murderers were Arabs to whom he had lent money and subsequently dispossessed of their property.

42 kil. Station of *Sidi Brahim.* The village is an important one, situated on the high road, about a kilomètre to the E. The tomb of the Saint, which gives its name to it, is on a hill some little distance beyond.

46 kil. *Le Rocher.* Several isolated farms and orchards on a bend of the Mekerra form a district rather than a village known by this name. The land is extremely rich and well cultivated.

49 kil. To the E. of the line is a mausoleum surrounded by trees, built by the Marquis de Massol for himself; he was not, however, buried here. Beyond, to the E., is the village of Mulai Abd-el-Kader, whose koubba is on the opposite bank of the river, farther E.

50 kil. Cemetery of Bel Abbès, surrounded by cypress trees.

52 kil. Station of **Sidi Bel Abbès.** Pop., including outskirts, 16,980.

This town occupies the spot where a fort formerly stood, which was erected by the French as a depôt for provisions on the road between Tlemcen and Mascara. It is situated in a plain watered by the *Mekerra,* and is entirely modern. The country around is clothed in the richest verdure, and the soil is exceedingly fertile, producing, among other crops, tobacco of excellent quality; the wheat of this district is in high repute throughout the colony and even in France.

In 1845 an attempt to capture the fort was made by a band of Arabs of the Oulad Brahim tribe, who gained admittance under the pretence of desiring to perform their devotions at the koubba of the Marabout Sidi Bel Abbès, which adjoins the fort. This effort was frustrated, and the Arabs beaten off with great slaughter. With this exception, the history of Sidi Bel Abbès is entirely free from warfare and bloodshed, unlike that of most of the French settlements in Algeria.

The town is surrounded by a ditch and bastioned wall, through which entrance is obtained by means of four *gates* on the roads to Oran, Tlemçen, Daya, and Mascara.

The wide street running between the north and south gates cuts the town into two equal parts; that on the west is the military quarter, and contains barracks and other subsidiary buildings sufficient to accommodate 6000 men. Indeed this may be regarded as one of the most important strategic positions in the province.

It is also the headquarters of the Foreign Legion; the band is said to be one of the best in the French army, and it enlivens the station by playing several times a week.

From a business point of view, Bel Abbès is nearly the most considerable town in the interior of the colony; the land in the neighbourhood is excellent, and it is the principal centre of the alfa trade; 50,000 tons are despatched hence every year, which is about a quarter of the entire quantity of this fibre imported into England.

In summer one can walk all over the town and its immediate neighbourhood in the densest shade. Canals carry the water of the Mekerra through the town, and a supply may anywhere be obtained by digging a few feet below the surface.

At the *Porte d'Oran* a large Arab market is held weekly for the sale of vegetables, fruit, cattle and wool.

The site of Sidi Bel Abbès was formerly a swamp, but the plantations have drained it, and now it is perfectly healthy. The climate is generally cool and bracing, it being 475 mètres above the level of the sea. The environs are more thickly peopled than the town itself; the largest village is Perrin; there is another at the gate of Tlemçen;

there is a Spanish village at that of Mascara, and a negro one near the gate of Oran.

58 kil. Station of *Sidi Lahsen*. The village is on the opposite side of the river; most of the colonists are of Alsatian or German origin.

64 kil. *Sidi Khalid*, a miserable village near the junction of the high roads to Tlemçen and Magenta, but the land is rich and capable of irrigation.

71 kil. *Bou Kanefis*. To the E. of the line before arriving, is a native agricultural penitentiary. The village is surrounded by good land, but it does not seem to have recovered from its almost total destruction, some years back, occasioned by the rupture of the barrage at Tabia, which has never been rebuilt.

75 kil. *Tabia*, a village which, though of recent construction, is doing well.

The barrage before mentioned was constructed to utilise the waters of the Mekerra for the irrigation of the plain of Bel Abbès; but the site was badly chosen, and when full the water cut through the bank, just as occurred at Sig in 1885, and carried away the whole construction with disastrous results.

[The railway to Tlemçen branches off here, traversing the plain of Tifilès in a direct line to Aïn-Tellout, thence passing Lamoricière and Aïn-Fezza, and passing just over the Cascades of the Saf-Saf near Tlemçen. See p. 263.]

83 kil. Passing through a narrow gorge, the line enters the highly cultivated and well-watered valley of **Sidi Ali ben Youb**, now called **Chanzy**, after the popular and distinguished governor-general of that name, the last who combined the civil and military authority in this colony.

The village is about a mile from the station on the right bank of the river. A few hundred yards beyond it are the thermal springs of *Aïn-Skoun;* the temperature is 77° Fahr., and they yield an abundant supply both for drinking and irrigational purposes. There are traces of a Roman piscine;

indeed numerous signs of the Roman occupation are still visible, and the two pillars in front of the Cercle Militaire at Bel Abbès were found here.

Near Chanzy there is a fine quarry of dark-coloured marble.

[Roads branch off to *Tenera* and to *Telagh*, villages on the way to *Daya*, the latter till lately a smala of Spahis, but now a fairly prosperous village.]

Leaving Chanzy, the country becomes more mountainous and wooded, and, especially in the forests of *Djebel Slissen* and *Toumiet*, the scenery is fine.

100 kil. *Si Slissen*. The site of a projected village. Beyond the station there is only a small canteen and some huts; but the traffic here is considerable, as there are roads leading to Daya and Telagh on the E., and to Lamoricière and some important alfa districts on the W.

115 kil. **Magenta**, or *El-Hacciba*, a village created by General Chanzy, but which has never prospered. For a long time it was so unhealthy that the troops were not allowed to pass the summer here, but were removed to the higher and healthier position of Daya, 16 kil. S.E. It is now much more healthy, and as the surrounding lands are fairly good the railway may bring it prosperity.

122 kil. *Arrêt des Pins*, a small station in the valley, near a barrage built for Magenta, but constructed in a place where the water filters through the ground and cannot be retained. There is no traffic here.

129 kil. *Talen-yaya*. The line having now left the region of forests, enters fairly on the high plateaux. This will probably be an important station for the alfa trade but nothing more, as the land offers no inducements for colonisation.

143 kil. *Bedeau*. Near the station is a small redoubt, established here during the last troubles in the S. It is proposed to create an industrial village here, which, as water is abundant, may prosper as long as the alfa trade continues. Indeed it is to this precious fibre that the railway owes its existence, and the province of Oran in a great measure its prosperity. As far as the eye can reach the only vegetation of the high plateaux is that of thickly scattered tufts of alfa grass; it is picked generally by Spaniards, who live for months at a time in these solitudes, and eventually despatched for shipment to Oran and Arzeu.

[Roads branch off hence to *Daya* on the E., to *Sebdou* on the W., and to *El-Arricha* on the S.W.]

152 kil. **Ras el-Ma**. The terminus of the line, at the foot of *Djebel Baghra*, a mountain which dominates the high plateaux, and on the summit of which an optic telegraph station has been established. The view thence is one of utter desolation; with the exception of the line itself, alfa and artemesia, not a sign of habitation or of animal or vegetable life is visible. This forms the western limit of the concession granted to the Cie. Franco-Algérienne. It is hoped that much of the traffic from the S. of Morocco may come here, as it is on the shortest and most direct road from Figuig.

———

ROUTE 26.

From Arzeu to Mascara, Saïda, Mecheria and Aïn-Sefra by Railway.

kil.	Names of Stations.	kil.
..	Arzeu	454
7	Saint-Leu	447
17	Port aux Poules	437
21	La Macta	433
38	Debrousseville	416
51	Perrégaux	203
62	Barrage O. Fergoug	392
71	Oued el-Hammam	383
80	El-Guetna	374
88	Bou Hanefia	366
100	Tizi-Mascara	354
107	Froha	347
113	Thiersville	341
127	Traria	327
140	Charrier	314
145	Franchetti	309
166	Nazreg	288
171	Saida	283
182	Aïn-el-Hadjar	272
191	Garage B. Rached	263
206	Tafaroua	248
215	Kralfallah	239
224	Muley Abd-el-Kader	230
230	El-Beïda	222
236	Modzbah-Sfid	218
248	Tin-Brahim	206
257	Assi el-Madani	197
271	El-Kreider	183
285	Bou-Guetoub	169
299	Rezaina	155
313	Bir-Senia	141
323	El-Biod	131
336	Krebazza	118
352	Mecheria	102
385	Naâma	69
420	Mekalis	34
454	Aïn-Sefra	..

Arzeu. 3072 inhabitants.

Arzeu was occupied by the Romans under the name of *Arsenaria*; it was destroyed by the Arabs on their invasion of Africa, and again built by the sovereigns of Tlemçen. Under the Turks it was the principal place of exportation in the province. During the Peninsular War nearly 300 vessels a year conveyed grain and cattle thence for the use of the English army.

It was besieged and captured by Abd-el-Kader in the year 1831; and in 1833 taken by the French under General Desmichels; and, after again changing hands, was finally ceded to France by the Treaty of the Tafna in 1837.

It occupies a very favourable situation; its harbour is naturally the bes in Algeria, and has been further protected by a solidly-constructed break water, running nearly N.W. and S.E The harbour has an area of 140 hectares and the breakwater a length of 300 mètres. This place is the natural outlet for the produce of the rich valley of the Sig, Habra, Mina and Chelif also the *entrepôt* for the trade o Relizane and Mascara, as well as of th Sahara.

On the 20th December 1873, th governor-general signed a concession granting to the Compagnie Franco Algérienne the permission to construc a railway from Arzeu to Saïda, with th privilege of *exploitation* of alfa in th high plateaux of the subdivision o Mascara, but without any guarante of interest. Some of the most import ant conditions of this grant are:— The Company have the exclusive pri vilege of collecting alfa over nearly million acres of land, without prejudice however, to the Arabs' right of pastur age there. It pays to the State a fixe rate of 15 centimes on every ton export ed, as far as 100,000 tons per annum above which the rate is 25 centimes It has the further privilege to tak from the Government forests whateve wood may be necessary for their works on payment of 2 f. per cubic mètr for pine, thuya and juniper, and 4 f for oak. The concession to last for 9 years. It is generally reported tha this enterprise has not proved a ver successful one, and it is probable tha the Company would have found it diffi cult to continue its operations but fo the impulse that Bou Amama's insur rection gave it. The State gave a sub vention of six million f. to enable i to continue the line right into th desert, and pays large sums for th transport of troops and military stores

Formerly the inhabitants suffere from a want of good water, whic caused the town to become almost de serted, but now the rain-water has bee collected in the ravines of *Ste. Léonie Tazout*, and *Guessiba*, in undergroun galleries, and brought to Arzeu by cemented conduit of 12 kil. in length

The fortifications consist of a new itadel and two old forts. The first mentioned was completed in 1863, and is provided with reservoirs, barracks, tc. It is sometimes used as a political prison. The refugees of Carthagena, 00 in number, were confined here in 874.

A new jetty has been constructed in he harbour, which is now commodious nd safe; on it is a lighthouse with a ed light. There is a fixed light at the nd of the breakwater, and another on little island to the W., 500 mètres om the coast. The beach is clean nd admirably adapted for sea-bathing. he surrounding country is under altivation, and is irrigated with rackish water obtained from "*norias*," r wells supplied with Persian wheels.

In the vicinity are the famous uarries of **Numidian marbles**, which re, however, more easily reached from ran. At Mefessour, on the road from nat town, is the small village of *Kleber*. bove this rises an imposing mountain, marked *Djebel Arousse* on the map, a orruption no doubt of *Djebel er-Roos*, · "Mountain of the Capes," but more merally styled by the colonists *Montagne Grise*, from its arid gray appearance. The central portion, 2000 ft. bove the sea, forms a level plateau, ith a superficies of from 1500 to 2000 res, consisting of an almost uninterrupted mass of dolomitic marble and reccia, mixed with deposits of manunitic iron ore. This s beyond all oubt one of the p ace whence the elebrated **Marmor Numidicum** was btained by the ancient Romans; and regards quantity, beauty, and variety, ese marbles are probably the finest hat the world contains.

The original colour of the rock was eamy white; in the extreme eastern art, where the amount of iron is small, exists very much in its natural condition, only somewhat stained with on, which communicates to it a tint sembling ivory. In conjunction with is is a rose-coloured variety, which is pable of being worked either in large sses or in the finest ornamentation. 'nkets made of it so closely resemble *Algeria*.]

coral as to deceive the casual observer. Here all the rock is of a uniform structure, marble in fact, as distinguished from breccia. In the west of this plateau however, there appears to have taken place some great earth movement; the whole of this side of the mountain has been crushed by pressure into fragments varying in size from large angular masses to the merest dust. This disintegrated mass has subsequently been cemented together by the infiltration of water; the fragments have retained to a certain extent their original rose or yellow colour, while the matrix has been stained of the deepest brown or red owing to the iron oxide and the manganese which has been carried by the water through the fissures, the whole thus forming a beautiful breccia of endless variety and colour. The matrix is as hard as the fragments it contains, so that it takes a uniform polish throughout its whole surface.

Between these two extreme varieties, viz. the white and rose marble on the east, and the breccias on the west, there are many others, such as the well-known yellow called *Giallo Antico*, a *Cippolino* of almost indescribable beauty, a variety which the owner has named *Paonazza*, from its resemblance to a peacock's plumage, and a deep red species, somewhat brecciated, and greatly resembling, if not identical with, the famous *Rosso Antico*. All these owe their colours to the iron and to the greater or less amount of crushing force to which they have been subjected.

These splendid quarries belong to M. Delmonte of Oran; it is much to be deplored that he has not succeeded in working them to the extent they deserve. The writer obtained some blocks with which the English Church at Algiers has been decorated; he also obtained others for the British Museum for the purpose of making pedestals on which to mount the sculptures in the Mausoleum Gallery. Excellent specimens may also be seen in the mineralogical department of the British Museum at South Kensington.

[There is a steam tramway to the

T

Salines of Arzeu for the purpose of bringing in the salt collected there.]

The railway of the Compagnie Franco-Algérienne is a narrow gauge one, the width of the rails being only 1·10 m.

At first the line runs between well-cultivated plains and the sea.

2 kil. It crosses the Oued Magoun, a river which passes between the villages of Kleber and Ste. Léonie. A barrage has been constructed on this stream capable of containing one million cubic mètres of water, but hitherto the soil has been found too permeable to retain it.

7 kil. To the S. is seen the village of **St. Leu.** Close at hand is the Berber village of *Botioua* or old Arzeu, the ancient Roman *Portus Magnus*, mentioned by Pliny, where very interesting ruins still remain.

The most remarkable of these are the ruins of a Roman house, of which the interior disposition is still quite visible. The rooms were paved with mosaics, and in the centre was a court with two *impluvia* to receive rain-water. The most important of these mosaics have been transported to the Museum at Oran.

Shortly afterwards the fertile land gives place to dunes of sand covered with low scrub, amongst which the Forest Department has planted a large number of Aleppo pines, which seem to be thriving.

17 kil. *Port aux Poules.* A hamlet at the small natural harbour formed by the estuary of the Oued Macta.

21 kil. *La Macta.* This is a small village close to where the railway and the high road cross the Oued Macta by contiguous iron bridges. This river has only a course of 4 kil. It rises in the marshy ground to the S. called the Plain of the Macta, and after a sluggish course, caused by the bar at its mouth, falls into the sea at the Port aux Poules. By some this river has been identified as the ancient *Mulucha*, or *Molochath*, which is more generally considered to be the modern *Moulouia*, on the frontier of Morocco. The country round is extremely feverish in the summer months, but not so in winter, and the sport to be had is excellent. The plain abounds in antelope, but, owing to a superstition that a holy man's life was saved by one of them, the Arabs have the greatest objection to their being shot. In addition to these there are bustard, wild ducks, and partridges in abundance. The river is renowned for the large size and excellent quality of its eels.

32 kil. The line here crosses the Oued Tinn. This is a continuation of the Oued Malah, which comes from near Mascara, and falls into the marsh of the Habra. The only way to drain and utilise this country is by cutting a bed for the Macta through this plain, and draining the country by canals on either side into it.

38 kil. *Debrousseville.* It was intended to create an important village here, in the centre of M. Debrousse's concession, but the locality is most unhealthy, and the scheme is never likely to be carried out. The Spaniards have instituted an unusual commerce here of late years, the collection and exportation of snails. Two million kilos. are said to be exported annually, which realise about 20 f. per 100 kilos.

After leaving this the line passes through the skirts of the forest of Mulai Ismael, and then reaches the line from Algiers to Oran at

51 kil. **Perrégaux** (see p. 178).

After leaving Perrégaux the line passes through a narrow valley, bounded by bare and sterile hills, through which winds the river Habra, in a broad bed, overgrown with tamarisk and olive trees.

55 kil. *Col des Juifs.* The valley here widens, and the difficulties of the railway commence. There are here heavy earthworks, and the first of a series of bridges of considerable size, which the company have been forced to make for the passage of the Habra.

62 kil. *Le Barrage* (see p. 178).

An excellent view of the barrage is obtained from the train. After its destruction in 1881 it was restored by the State, but no sooner was the water allowed to collect than infiltrations were perceived in the rock on which the dam abuts. This necessitated the construction of an immense counterfort at the foot of the hill, having a length of 55 mètres, a height of 20 mètres, and an average thickness of 10 mètres.

Beyond this the line crosses and recrosses the Habra, the country becomes more picturesque and better wooded, and eventually emerges into the fertile plain in which is situated

71 kil. *Dublineau*, formerly *Oued el-Hammam*. The name was changed in honour of a colonist of that name who was besieged in his farm by a number of Arabs, whom he repulsed after a heroic resistance. This is a prosperous village situated on the high road between St. Denis du Sig and Mascara, which is here joined by the road from l'errégaux.

[There is a road to Mascara from this point. It crosses the mountainous chain called by the Arabs the *Djebel Tifroura*, and by the French soldiers *Crève-cœur*, and continues alongside of a valley thickly wooded with pine and oak trees. The highest part of the whole route, about 12 kil. beyond Oued el-Hammam, is 2200 ft. above the sea, and commands an extensive view.]

80 kil. *El-Guetna*. About a kil. to the N. of the station, and on the W. side of the river may be noticed an Arab house and a marabout. This is the birthplace of Abd-el-Kadir.

88 kil. *Hammam Bou Hanefia*. The railway here leaves the river, which takes a westerly direction. On its banks, about 2½ kil. from the railway station, are the hot water springs of this name ; they have a temperature of 136° Fahr., and issue from the base of a small hillock. Immediately alongside are cold water springs, coming apparently from the same ground ; the water is slightly saline.

These waters are much appreciated by the Arabs, and considerably used by them, but are rarely visited by Europeans, except by some of the Mascara families who occasionally make a picnic visit.

The baths for Europeans and Arabs are kept quite distinct ; they are fairly commodious, but the caravanserai adjoining offers but few temptations to remain, and unless notice be given beforehand one can count on little or nothing for man or beast. On the mamelon whence the springs burst there is a small natural well, now partly filled up. The heat within is very considerable, and the strong smell of gas renders a long stay in the well impossible. It is common to find small birds dead at the bottom, evidently suffocated by the gas. A few hundred yards higher up there is a Roman burial-ground, some of the inscriptions still exist ; and still higher up, though only separated by a narrow valley, are the remains of a town O, probably a sanitarium attached to the hot springs. It was walled round even on the river side ; the postern door and steps leading to the river are quite distinct. The entrances E. and W., and in fact the streets and some of the houses, are distinguishable. It is believed that the town was destroyed by an earthquake. Nothing of special interest has been found. The railway now mounts a steep gradient, passing by barren clay hills almost without sign of vegetation. This passage was the most troublesome of all the line, owing to the nature of the soil. The works were several times more or less carried away by heavy rains.

100 kil. At *Col Tizi* the extensive plain of *Eghris* is entered at about 12 kil. W. of Mascara. When colonised this plain should give a heavy traffic to the line, though the supply of water is but scanty, and the depth at which it is found is very variable.

A small village has been constructed here, and a branch line of 13 kil. leads to

Mascara. Pop. 11,320. Seat of general commanding subdivision, and of the various subsidiary military and civil offices.

Mascara is finely situated on a slope of the plain of *Eghris*, 1800 feet above the level of the sea, on two small hills separated from each other by the bed of the *Oued Toudman*, which is crossed by three stone bridges.

The general aspect is somewhat imposing, giving the idea of an important and handsome town. The Arabic name of the place is *Maaskera*, which is a corruption of *Omm-el-Asakir*, the Mother of Soldiers. It was built by the Turks on the site of a Roman colony, and during the first years of the French conquest was the favourite residence of the Emir Abd-el-Kader, who was born at *El Guetna*, 16 kil. S. of it.

After the rupture of the treaty Desmichels, Marshal Clauzel recommenced hostile operations and marched against Mascara at the head of a force, one division of which was commanded by the Duc d'Orleans. After a stout resistance the Arabs were dispersed, and the French army entered the town on the 6th of December 1835. The Emir withdrew to the South, taking his family and all his wealth, and three days later Marshal Clauzel retreated to Oran.

Abd-el-Kader returned after their departure, but again retired before General Bugeaud, who finally took possession of the place in 1841. From this date until 1843 there was constant warfare between the French and the Arabs under Abd-el-Kader, who at the end of that year took refuge in Morocco, after which many of his followers submitted to the invaders.

Mascara is now completely a French town, surrounded by a wall of the ordinary type, with the usual squares and rectilineal streets, public buildings, etc.; hardly a vestige remains of the city of Abd-el-Kadir. The only building of any interest is a disused mosque, where the great Emir was wont to preach; it is now used as a powder magazine and storehouse for grain. Another mosque was for years used as a parish church; it is now occupied as a school. The barracks and hospital occupy a prominent position in the town.

There is a purely Arab village 3 kil. to the W.

The principal industry of the place is wine, which is celebrated throughout the colony, and eagerly bought up by agents of Bordeaux houses, especially the white variety. Vineyards are being planted in every available spot.

[An excursion may be made hence to Tiaret, Frenda, and so by railway to Relizane. See Rte. 22.]

107 kil. *Froha*, a flourishing little village in the midst of the plain, whence there is an excellent view of Mascara, and the range of hills on which that town is situated. The line here crosses the main road from Mascara to Saïda, and, winding round a low spur which separates the Plain of *Oued Traria* from that of *Eghris*, recrosses the road, and at 126 kil. arrives at the village of *Oued Traria*, which does not show much sign of prosperity, and at present bears the reputation of being unhealthy. A short distance farther on the valley of the *Oued Saïda* is entered, which is here narrow but well watered and fertile, and widens out on passing

113 kil. *Thiersville*.

127 kil. *Traria*. At 13 kil. E. of the village and at 35 from Mascara are the ruins of *Benian*, O, the ancient *Tasacora*. On ascending the right bank of the Oued Traria the first thing seen is a mausoleum, of which little more than the podium now exists; it is of finely cut stone, almost without cement. The approach to the city was through an avenue of tombs, now completely destroyed. The outline of the city is perfectly visible, it was not large, about 220 mètres square; the gates were guarded by towers.

140 kil. *Charrier*.

145 kil. *Franchetti*, the most important village between Mascara and Saïda. Some kilomètres higher up there is a barrage, which serves this village; and near it, about 1 kil. E. of the road, is *Aïn-el-Hammam*, a pond of hot saline water with a taste of sulphur, and with constant bubbling, from the escape of carbonic acid gas. This is very much frequented by the Arabs, especially by the women.

165 kil. *Nazreg*, a very prosperous village, of rather recent creation, with good land and abundant water for irrigation. The land is here fairly settled and cultivated all the way to

171 kil. **Saïda.** 2902 inhabitants.

Since the opening of the railway this place has sprung up from being simply a military post, and the usual small town or village that always settles round a permanent military establishment, to be a town of some importance and with a good deal of movement. It is pleasantly situated between two small streams, on a slight elevation looking N.; altitude 807 mètres. Thanks to the railway made by the Cie. Franco-Algérienne and to their important exploitation of the alfa lands to the S., Saïda has made more progress during the few past years than any town in the province. A short distance to the S. of the town the limit of the Haut Plateaux is clearly defined. It is here that the old Arab town was situated. It was occupied and fortified by Abd-el-Kader, and held by him for a considerable time during his struggle with the French.

The ground here rises so abruptly that it looks impossible for the railway to pass, and for some time it was not considered practicable; but to avoid a very long detour to the W. it was decided to face the difficulty, and by a system of curves and counter-curves the difficulty was surmounted. There are many Roman remains in the neighbourhood of Saïda,Θ ; the most important is 2 kil. distant, above the ravine of Sidi Salim, exactly opposite the old Saïda of Abd-el-Kader, on a plateau called *Tidernatin*, which forms part of the first steps of the High Plateaux. Here is a sort of fortified camp, protected in part by a natural scarp, and more strongly fortified by a wall and bastions, on the narrow isthmus by which alone access is obtained to it from the country behind. It was in fact the *oppidum* or refuge for the population in case of danger.

[From Saïda there is a track to *Daya*, which lies about 80 kil. to the W.; and another to *Frendah* and *Tiaret*, 150 kil. distant to the N.E.]

182 kil. *Aïn-el-Hadjar*; altitude 1024 mètres. It is here that the Cie. Franco-Algérienne have established their general depôt for alfa and their hydraulic presses. The establishment is very considerable, and capable of turning out fully 30,000 tons per annum. Before they commenced the district was utterly uninhabited, but now there is a thriving village. The climate is rather trying, owing to the great extremes of heat and cold.

This is the highest point on the line; it has an altitude of 1175 mètres.

206 kil. *Tafaroua*; altitude 1150 mètres. The culminating point of the Haut Plateaux has now been passed, and the level gradually descends. The road by the caravanserai of El-Maï to Géryville branches off S.E. To the W. is *Timetlas*, and 5 kil. beyond it the extensive ruins of *Mtalsa*, Θ; they cover an area of about 12 acres, and must have contained a population of not less than 10,000 persons, probably Berbers, during the Roman occupation. The position was no doubt chosen on account of the Oued Timetlas, which afforded it an abundant water-supply. The line has now for some kilomètres passed through a perfectly sterile country, absolutely no vegetation during any season.

215 kil. *Kralfallah*; altitude 1109 mètres. The line continues through sterile country on to

236 kil. *Modzbah-Sfid*. A short branch line to *Markoum* turns to the W. The main line continues to

271 kil. *El-Kreider*, more correctly *El-Khadthera*, the Green; altitude 988 mètres. This station is on the borders of the *Chott el Chergui*, the passage of which has been facilitated by a small island.

Shortly before reaching this place the marabout and village of Sidi Khalifa is passed. The few inhabitants of this small oasis claim descent from the Prophet, and the privilege of passing everywhere without paying tribute of any kind. Kreider is a very important strategical position, as it commands the passage of the Chotts. There is an abundant supply of water, such as it is.

It was here that Colonel Mallaret, during the troubles of 1881, allowed Bou Ammama to pass in open daylight with all his plunder and prisoners, many of the latter being European women. He had been warned of the rebel's proximity the day before, and had a much superior force.

The railway, after passing the Chott, continues through a perfectly barren country till it arrives at
352 kil. **Mecheria**, alt. 1158 mètres. The strategical importance of Mecheria is very great, but it has no interest for the traveller. The extremes of heat and cold make it most trying for the European constitution.
385 kil. *Naâma*.
420 kil. *Mekalis*.
459 kil. **Aïn-Sefra**. This is the present terminus of the line, though the French look forward with hope to its eventual continuation to Figuig within the Moroccan frontier, and on to the banks of the Niger. There is a fort here where the commandant-supérieur and garrison reside, and round it a small village is springing up.

Two interesting excursions may be made from this place, but the traveller will require a special recommendation to the commandant-supérieur.

20 kil. to the E. is the oasis of **Tiout**, of the ordinary Saharan type, and 50 and 60 kil. to the S. are those of **Moghrar Foukani** (the upper) and **Moghrar Tahtani** (the lower). These are totally unlike any oasis in North Africa; they are well-watered valleys with fine scenery, and almost European vegetation. Peaches, apricots, and all the fruits of the north flourish in great perfection.

[From Kralfallah a road branches off in a S.E. direction, crossing the Chott el Chergui farther to the E., passing *Aïn-Sefsifa*, and reaching the military station of **Géryville**. This is as far S. as any held by the French in Algeria, being in just the same latitude as El-Aghonat, to which oasis there is a camel track about 200 kil. in length. A fort encloses the barracks for the garrison, and other military buildings. Outside the fortification is the residence of the Arab chief, and a few other houses which are occupied by the colonists. The place was founded in 1852, on the site of a small Arab town, *El-Biod*, so called from the stream before mentioned.

To the S.W. of Géryville, between that station and the frontier of Morocco, is an extensive tract of country more than 193 kil. in length, consisting of low sandy hills and plains, which, from October to April, affords good and plenteous pasture for the numerous flocks of sheep and camels belonging to the nomade tribes. In the month of May they migrate northwards to their respective territories, where their absence has permitted a new crop to spring up ready for use. Water in the autumn, winter, and spring, is abundant in what are called *ghadirs*, or small lakes, where the rain-water collects and remains till dried up by the summer heat. The word *ghadir* is derived from the Arabic root *ghadara*, to leave or betray, because the water is left by the rain, and frequently betrays those who count too surely on finding it. In this tract occasional springs of pure fresh water have formed green and fertile oases, which appear like islands in the midst of the desert. These are the oases of the *Oulad Sidi Cheikh*.

Some of them are of considerable size, containing many houses, and even occasionally mosques, and have inhabitants to the number of from 500 to 1200. They are each governed by a Cheikh or chief, and a council composed of the principal leaders of the tribe.

25 kil. E. of Géryville is *Aïounet-bou-Bekr*, where Colonel Beauprêtre and the whole of his force were destroyed in 1864. At the first news of the defection of the *Oulad Sidi Cheikh* the garrison of Géryville was reinforced, and Colonel Beauprêtre, Commandant-Superieur of Tiaret, was sent to observe Djebel Amour. Too confident in the fidelity of his *goum*, he allowed himself to be drawn into a position where he was assailed by a large body of insurgents, and both he and every member of his detachment were killed. The enemy, however, sustained great losses, and Si Seliman, the leader of the insurrection, fell.]

ROUTE 27.

From Oran to Beni Saf, Nemours, and the Frontier of Morocco.

From Oran to Aïn-Temouchent by rail (see Rte. 23).

Thence there is a rough road to Beni Saf, passing by Camarata, where is an iron mine, opened out by an English company, subsequently ceded to a French one, now very little worked save during the summer months.

A new road passes near the prosperous village of Les Trois Marabouts (5 kil. from Aïn-Temouchent). It derives its name from an Arab cemetery in which are three conspicuous domed tombs, the largest of which is that of Sidi Rabah Oulad Khalifeh. The village was founded in 1880 for ninety families, and to each a grant of 30 hectares of unusually fertile land was given. Among them are a considerable number of Protestants from the upper Alps, sent over by the Protestant committee of Lyons, by means of funds collected from friends of the Vaudois in France and England.

12 kil. *Aïn-Talba.* A village without inhabitants—speculators bought up the land round about and so prevented the realisation of the scheme which the Government had originated.

25 kil. We enter the small valley of El-Ensor, called "the garden of Beni Saf." It contains several good springs of water, part of which are used for the supply of Beni Saf, and part for the irrigation of market gardens. There are also several establishments for the manufacture of criu végétal.

32 kil. **Beni Saf.**

The iron ore of the district has given rise to a most important industry, and has caused the construction of a new harbour in a part of the coast where it was greatly needed.

The company to which the great iron mines of Mokta el-Hadid, near Bône, belong, acquired the rich mineral basin of Beni Saf, 6 or 7 kil. E. of the mouth of the Tafna and of the island of Rachgoun. They also obtained by purchase a large tract of country round about, containing nearly 2500 hectares, so as to prevent competition, or the establishment of colonists not under their own control.

Here, under the direction of their own engineers, and without State aid, the company have constructed a commodious port of 18 hectares in extent, by means of two artificial moles or breakwaters. The W. mole, after running in a northerly direction for 500 metres, turns abruptly to the E.N.E. and is thus prolonged for about 600 metres, protecting the harbour from all winds from W. to N.E. The mole, which shelters the harbour from the E., is 300 metres long. The entrance faces that direction ; it has a width of 150 metres, and is completely sheltered from E. winds by the coast.

There is only one loading berth, and the ore is brought to it direct from the mines in trucks. The minimum depth of water is 7 mètres.

The amount of hematite iron ore at the Beni Saf mines is immense, it is worked in open quarries close to the sea, and tilted into the vessel's hold ; from 1000 to 2500 tons a day can be put on board. It contains from 58 to 62 per cent of iron and 2 per cent of manganese.

A new town has sprung up here ; the population is about 4000, and consists entirely of those connected with the mines, for the most part Spaniards and natives of Morocco. Everything belongs to the company ; the land around is excellent for cultivation and colonisation, but nothing can be done without their sanction. The banks of the Tafna are easily susceptible of irrigation, and before long a railway from Tlemçen will probably terminate here or in the vicinity.

The harbour is an open one, and is to revert to the State at the option of the Government in 1895, so it is probable that there is a considerable future for the country at no remote period. Private vessels are not excluded if they can find any freight, such as alfa, corn, etc., but they have to pay dues of 2 f. per ton to the company ; they can only use the E. mole.

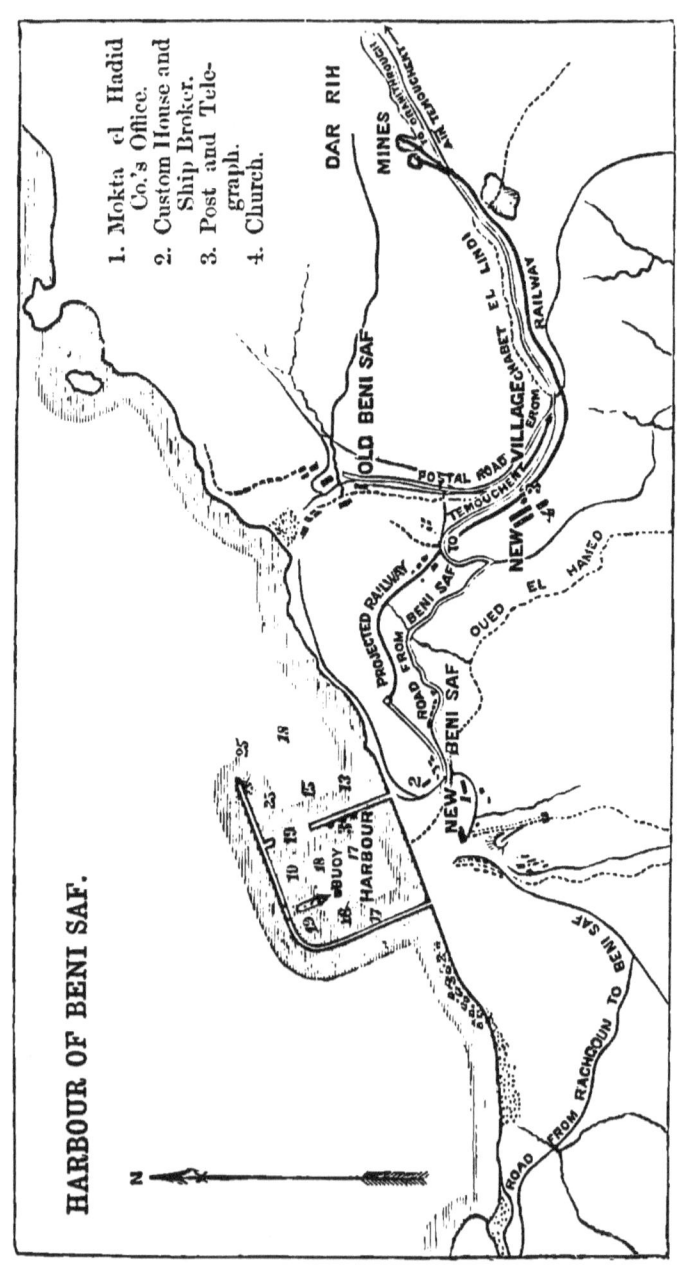

In 1885 311,000 tons of ore were exported, chiefly in British vessels, to Great Britain, the United States, France, Holland, and Belgium.

There are workshops at Beni Saf available for repairs of every kind to vessels.

The island of Rachgoun lies about 1800 mètres from the coast; it is of great value to the port by breaking the force of the sea, all bad weather coming from the W. or N.W.

[There is a good carriage road to **Tlemçen**, distance 63 kil., and a diligence runs every day. It ascends the valley of the Tafna, an important river, having a course of 80 kil. through a rich country, admirably suited for colonisation. The plain is feverish, it is true, but healthy sites for farms and villages could be found on the heights on either bank.

After leaving this valley the road passes *Remchi*, a village founded in 1881, the residence of the administrator of the district, situated in the country of the ZENATA, the aboriginal Berber possessors of Tlemçen; *Aïn - Fekrina* or *Les Trois Marabouts*, marked by a palm tree, near which, on a mamelon, is a tepid spring, which forms a small basin of sweet water, a part of which is used for the supply of Tlemçen, and lastly, *Hennaya*, a prosperous village surrounded by richly cultivated land and olive groves. The whole distance is about 70 kil.]

Proceeding along the coast from Beni Saf towards the W. we reach the mouth of the Tafna. On a hill above its right bank are the remains of the fortified camp built by the French during the expedition which led to the subjugation of this part of the country (see pp. 57, 58). 6 kil. higher up, on its left bank, are the ruins of **Takenbrit**, O, supposed to be the ancient *Siga*, the first capital of Syphax, before he transferred the seat of his government to Cirta (Constantine). A military column was lately found in the river here, bearing the word *Siga*, and stating the fact that it was erected at 1 mile from that place, probably on the road to *Oppidum Timici*. Very little now remains of Roman construction; an Arab city succeeded to it in the 10th century, which was in its turn abandoned after its destruction during the war between El-Ghania and the Almoahides in the 12th century.

Still farther along, and about half way between Beni Saf and Nemours is **Honaï** or *Mersa Honaï*, situated on a small bay formed by Cape *Noë* or *Noun*. It may be visited either from Beni Saf or Nemours. It is about 5 hours' distant from the former place by land and 2½ by boat. From the latter town there is a strategic road made by the engineers in 1845-47 for the purpose of reducing the *Trara* district. The distance is 40 kil. There is no accommodation there of any kind.

Hosn-Honaï is mentioned by El-Bekri as an important city, the birthplace of Abel-el-Moumen, first sovereign of the Almoahides who reigned at Tlemçen from 1145 to 1248. He was a student in a Zaouia here, and after his accession to power he founded a city on the site of his birth, about 1163, and made it the port of Tlemçen. Leo Africanus also describes it as a small but ancient city, surrounded by strong and high walls, frequented by Venetian galleys, which did a good trade with Tlemçen. The houses were fine and well kept up, with trellises of vine in their courts, and decorated with rich mosaics.

On the occupation of Oran by the Spaniards in 1509 it was deserted by its inhabitants, who fled to Tlemçen or Morocco, and it has never been occupied since.

The concrete walls, strengthened at short intervals with square towers, are still standing, and enclose an area of about 7 hectares; they are 6 or 7 mètres in height, and 5 in thickness; some of the interior chambers are more or less entire. In the W. corner of the *enceinte* is the citadel, on more elevated ground. On the hill to the E. is a watch-tower and the marabout of Sidi Braham.

The walls are breached in many places, the crowning parts have everywhere disappeared, and but few traces of architecture remain. Fragments of two of the city gates, however, still exist, and show that they were at one time enriched with elegant Moorish tracery and tile mosaics.

The interior of the ruins is a charming tangle of fig trees and oleanders; when the writer visited it (May 1886) the figs were nearly ripe, the oleanders were in full bloom, the air was fragrant with wild thyme, and there was deep shade everywhere; while running water nearly surrounded the city walls.

The Arabs were accustomed to construct defensive works of concrete; here if they had not known it Nature would have taught them the art. The hills round the bay are composed of conglomerate of indurated sand and waterworn pebbles, so that the materials for their work lay ready to hand; they had only to break up the soft conglomerate and rebuild it in the shape of city walls.

Until very recently there existed within the walls a tower 19 mètres high, with a spiral staircase ascending exteriorly to the top; this was evidently the central portion of a minaret of which the exterior walls had disappeared. The lower portion had been so much worn away that the superincumbent mass appeared to rest on the merest point; thus it had stood since before the memory of man, but it was eventually blown down during a heavy storm in the beginning of 1884.

Three hours by steam from Beni Saf is

Nemours, pop. 2591.

This is the last French town on the coast, and is distant 36 kil. from the frontier of Morocco. It was called *Djamäia Ghazouat* or Mosque of the Pirates, under the Turkish government, and the ruins of the Arab town are still visible on the hill which forms the E. side of the bay. The opposite hill is crowned by a lighthouse. The bay included between these two points is sheltered from all winds except from N.E. to N.W., but as this is the prevailing quarter from which bad weather comes, it is most insecure, and communication with the shore is only possible during very fine weather. There are two curious upright rocks in the bay, known as "Les deux Frères" (*ad fratrem* of the itinerary of Antonine), which are picturesque in appearance, and might be made useful as the limit of a breakwater should a harbour ever be constructed here.

The country on both sides of the frontier of Morocco is rich in mineral wealth: the most important mines which have hitherto been worked are those of argentiferous lead at *Ghar Rouban*, about 80 kil. to the south. The proximity of vast forests permitted the ore to be reduced on the spot, and the pig-lead was sent to Nemours for exportation. But the premises and machinery were destroyed by the Arabs during the insurrection of 1871; the company which owned them failed, and the place is now deserted, save by a few Spaniards. There is also a detachment of French troops there to guard the frontier.

There are other mines of iron, lead, and calamine, but none are being worked to any great extent. A considerable trade is being done in alfa and crin végétal, and in cereals when the harvest is abundant.

Nemours is a military station, and one of the most healthy spots on the coast. The Transatlantic steamer calls here on its way to and from Gibraltar.

The frontier of Algeria is not considered satisfactory by the French authorities, and its "rectification" is a contingency never absent from the official mind. No doubt a great opportunity was lost when Algeria became French. The river Molouia, the ancient *Malua* or *Molocath*, had always been the natural boundary between *Mauritania Cæsariensis* and *Tingitana*, the present empire of Morocco. It is difficult to understand why the commission of 1845 accepted in place of it the Oued Kiss, separated from it only by the sandy beach of Tazagaret, hardly 12 kil. in length; and how they permitted the Zaffarine Islands, which lie off the coast, and which were unoccupied at the period of the conquest, to fall into the hands of the Spaniards.

It is said that the expedition sent from Malaga for this purpose arrived only a few hours before a French one

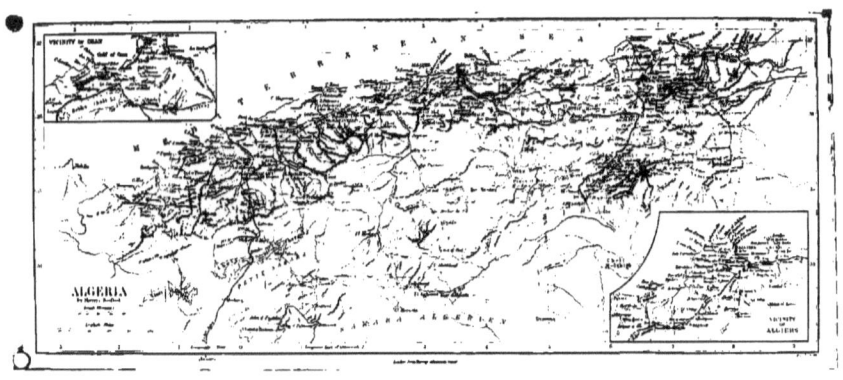

from Oran, and that the latter was not a little surprised to find the flag of Spain already flying there. A strong disposition has been shown of late to rectify this frontier by following the courses of the Molonia and the Oued Gheir, until the junction of the latter with the Oued Msaoura at Igli, and to follow the course of this river to the 29 parallel of latitude, so as to include Timimoun within French territory, as also Oudjda, Igli, Figuig, Beni Abbes, Kezzas, the territory of the Beni Snassen, and many other tribes now subject to Morocco.

SECTION III

REGENCY OF TUNIS.

(*See Historical Notice.*)

THE Regency of **Tunis**, or **Tunisia**, as it has now become the fashion to call it, is simply a prolongation of Algeria. In the former, however, the proportion of hill to plain is much less; the mountain-ranges nowhere attain so great an elevation; the country is less wooded; the rainfall is less; and throughout a great part of the Regency the land is, if not absolutely sterile, capable only of yielding abundant harvests when stimulated to fertility by more than the usual amount of rain. It is naturally divided into four tolerably distinct regions, by parallel lines running N.E. and S.W. The first is the mountain region north of the Medjerda, and the best watered of all, and abounding in forests of oak. The second, or *Tell*, consists of mountains and elevated plateaux enclosed between the Medjerda and a parallel line passing through Hammamet; the third, or *Sahel*, is a region of wide, dreary plains, more or less productive after copious rains; and beyond this is the Sahara.

A survey of the country is in progress, and a map is being constructed at the Depôt de la Guerre on a scale of 1,200,000 or 2·7 geographical miles to the inch. Sheets of a provisional edition are sold at 50 centimes each.

It is extremely difficult to understand how the Sahel could have supported the immense population which it must have contained during the Roman period. It is covered in every direction by the ruins not only of great cities but of isolated posts and agricultural establishments. In many parts one cannot ride a mile in a day's journey without encountering the ruins of some solidly-built edifice.

The Regency corresponds to the most important part of the ancient proconsular province of Africa, excluding the eastern portion, but comprising the Byzacena, Zeugitana, and the territory of Carthage.

Space will not admit of a separate historical sketch; the Roman domination has been sufficiently described elsewhere, and the history of the Mohammedan period is very similar to that of Algeria. It has been well summarised by Mr. Broadley[1] as consisting of three epochs—first, that of Power; second, that of Piracy; and third, that of Decay. To these a fourth may now be added, that of the French occupation.

Until 1881 the government of Tunis was an hereditary Beylick. The Bey acknowledged the suzerainty of the Porte, coined his money in the name of the Sultan, received investiture from him, but paid no tribute. Now, in all but the name, the "Regency" of Tunis is as much a part of French territory as the neighbouring colony of Algeria, and though the government is still carried on in the name of the Bey, that fiction will be maintained only so long as it may suit France to do so. In some respects it is convenient to have such a government to fall back upon.

[1] "The Last Punic War: Tunis Past and Present," by A. M. Broadley, 1882.

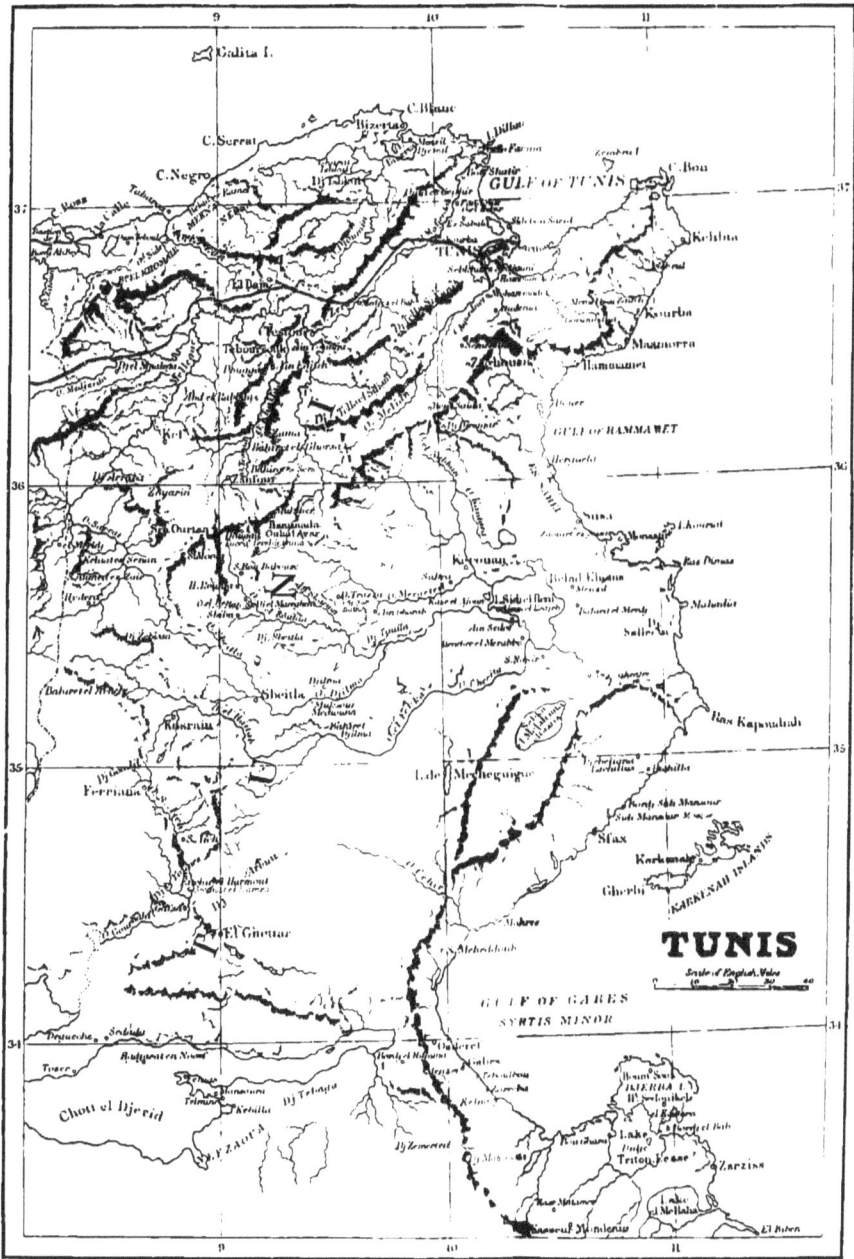

Many things can be done in the name of the Bey which would be difficult under the common law of France; it provides an easy and inexpensive machinery for the government of the native races; and it avoids the necessity for the elaborate governmental system which would become inevitable were the country proclaimed an integral part of the French Republic.

The absorption of Tunis into French territory has long been unavoidable, but it was hastened by the active competition between the Rubattino Company and that of the French Railway for the purchase of the small line between the Goletta and Tunis (see p. 317); and subsequently the Enfida affair (see p. 318) created much sensation, and led to the active interference of M. Roustan, the French Consul-General. This gave rise to what has sometimes been called the "invention" of the Khomair (see p. 305), a predatory and warlike tribe on the frontier between Algeria and Tunis. A French expedition was sent into their mountains, which was supposed to have for its object the punishment of these marauders. Even in France, however, it was hardly believed that this was its ultimate end. No sooner had the invading force commenced its operations than the dreaded Khomair dropped out of sight. Tabarca was occupied, indeed, but so was Bizerta, Kef, and other points in the Regency, which had no connection whatever with the Khomair. General Bréart advanced on the capital, a treaty was presented to the Bey for signature, and two hours were allowed to him to sign a document involving the virtual abandonment of his country to France, under the guise of a Protectorate.

The first military operations were soon over. It was on the 4th April that the French ministers announced their intention to chastise the Khomair; on the 12th of May the treaty of Kasr-es-Saeed was signed; and on the 8th of June the Bey issued a decree constituting the representative of France at Tunis the sole medium of communication between himself and the representatives of foreign powers, and publicly and officially notifying the definitive protectorate of France in Tunis.

M. Roustan, who had been mainly instrumental in getting up the expedition, was made Minister-Resident of France and of the Bey, and virtual ruler of the country. The sensibilities of Italy were deeply wounded, but none of the powers thought it to their interest to oppose this high-handed proceeding. Mohammedan fanaticism was stirred from Tripoli to Morocco; the Bey lost all authority among his people, who refused to obey a ruler who had delivered them over to the foreigner; and when the expeditionary force was somewhat prematurely recalled, a general state of insurrection ensued, and the French found themselves obliged to conquer the country city by city and tribe by tribe, and to send an immense force from the mother country to attain this end.

The holy city of Kerouan was taken, and columns marched all over the country to the very borders of Tripoli. A strong post was established in the heart of the Khomair country, and now every important town and strategical position is in the military occupation of the French.

Mohammed es-Sadik Bey died at his palace of Kasr-es-Saeed on the 28th October 1882, and was quietly succeeded by his brother Sidi Ali, the present Bey.

On the 31st December 1883 Her Majesty Queen Victoria, by an Order in Council, abandoned her consular jurisdiction in Tunis, with a view to English subjects becoming justiciable by French tribunals, under the same condition as French subjects; but, with this exception, all the old treaties with the Regency still remain in force.

Although the country is still governed in the name of the Bey, the French Resident-General is the actual ruler of the country. He is declared to be the depository of the powers of the French Republic in the Regency; the commander of the land and sea forces, and all administrative services are placed under his authority.

THE GOLETTA.

The Goletta, or Port of Tunis, pop. 3000.

The name is a corruption of the Arabic words, *Halk el-Oued*, or *Throat of the Canal*, an artificial passage cutting the town into two portions, and communicating between the sea and the lake of Tunis. In the northern half are the town, fort and battery; in the southern, the Bey's summer palace, the old seraglio, arsenal, custom-house and prison. Vessels are compelled to anchor in the roadstead, as there is not sufficient depth of water in-shore, but they are tolerably well sheltered from all winds except that coming directly from the N. and N.E.

The boat service has been greatly improved of late. Boatmen used formerly to charge pretty much what they pleased; a tariff, however, has now been established, fixing the charge per passenger at 1½ f.; for a trunk or large portmanteau the charge is ½ f. extra; a whole boat costs 9 f.

Steam launches belonging to the Transatlantique Company ply between their vessels and the shore.

The town, like Tunis, has been constructed entirely with the materials of ancient Carthage. The fortress which defends it has been frequently besieged, the most celebrated occasion being that by Charles V (see p. 36).

The *Place* of the Goletta extends along the interior face of the fort, and conducts to the railway station; it is bounded by shops and cafés, where the traveller will be glad to seek refreshment while waiting for the departure of the train.

The town is extending rapidly in the direction of Carthage, the new quarter being much in favour with the Tunisians in summer, on account of sea-bathing. There is, however, very little trade carried on.

The ordinary means of reaching Tunis is by the Italian railway. In summer eight trains run daily each way, four direct, and four call at the Marsa Station; in winter the trains are reduced to five, of which two only call at the Marsa. The distance is 17 kil.

This railway was originally constructed by an English company, and when it was determined to wind this up, a great struggle took place between the French Bône-Guelma and the Italian Rubattino Companies for its possession. Both parties agreed that the railway, with its plant, should be put up to auction in the Vice-Chancellor's chambers in London; it was adjudged to the Rubattino Company for the sum of £165,000.

CITY OF TUNIS.

The city of Tunis stands on an isthmus separating two salt lakes; that to the N.E. communicates with the sea at the Goletta and is called *El-Bahira* or the Little Sea by the natives; it is about 18 kil. in circumference, but nowhere more than 1 or 2 mètres in depth. As it has been the receptacle for all the sewage of Tunis during forty centuries, its bottom is covered with a layer of fetid mud which frequently emits a most pestilential odour. In the centre is an island named *Chekeli*, which contains the picturesque ruins of a mediæval fort.

It is proposed to dig a ship canal from the Goletta to the Marina of Tunis, and to create a port in the lake there. The canal will have a length of 12 kil., with a depth of 7 mètres, and will be excavated by large dredging machines.

The "Société de Construction des Batignoles" have commenced the works, and are (1889) pushing them on actively. It is expected that the whole will be completed by 1894.

The other lake to the S.W. is the Sebkha es-Sedjoumi.

Tunis was certainly known to the ancients by its present name, even before the foundation of Utica and Carthage; it was probably founded by native Africans, and not, like those cities, by Phœnician colonists. Mohammedan authors say that it was at one time called *Tarchich*; it was also called *El-Hathera*, the Green, on account of the beauty of its gardens.

It was originally surrounded by a wall, but a great part of this has now

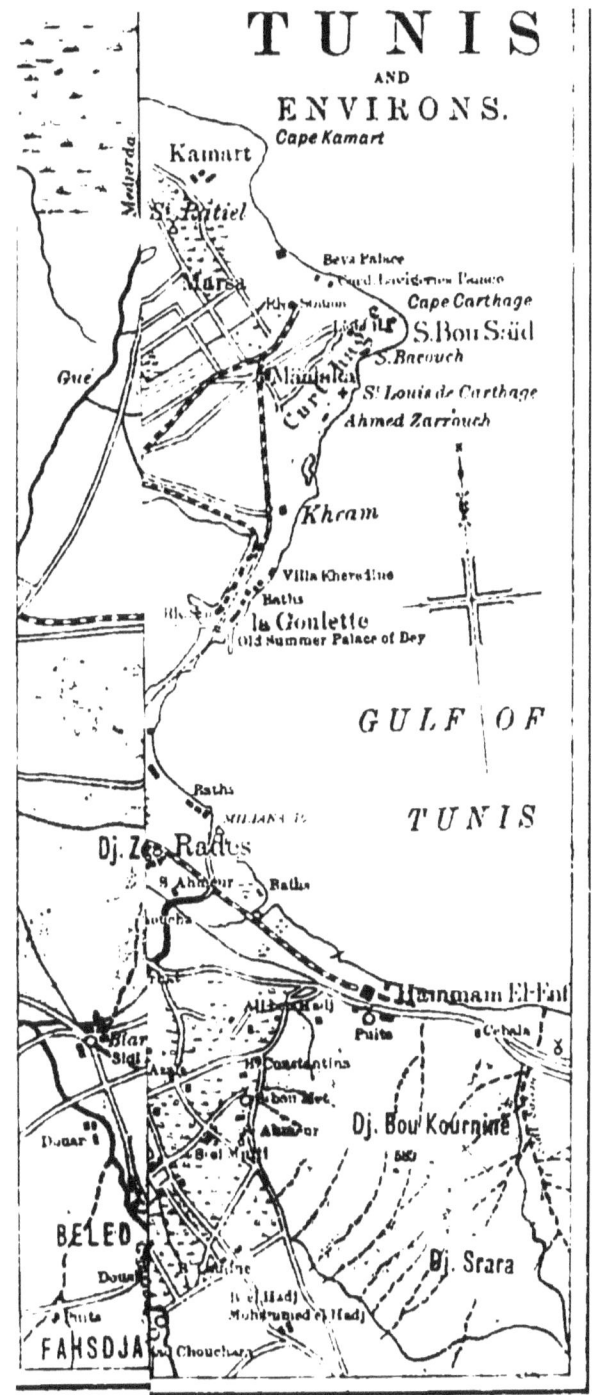

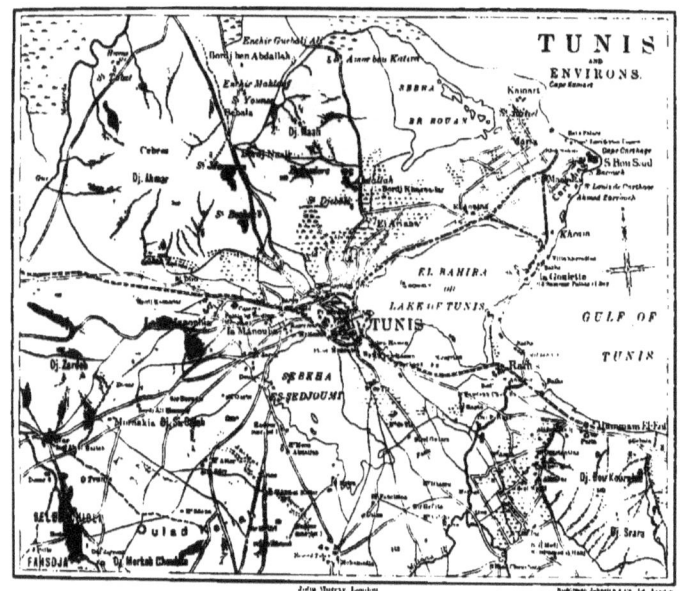

disappeared. The Marine Gate is quite isolated, and the walls on each side only exist in the name of the street, *Rue des Ramparts*.

The other gates are the *Bab el-Hathera*, *Bab Abd-es-Salem*, and *Bab es-Sadjea*, towards the Bardo Palace and the Manouba; the *Bab Sidi Adulla* under the Citadel; the *Bab Sidi Alewa* on the road to Zaghouan; and the *Bab es-Soucka* on that leading to Susa and the coast. In addition to the enceinte there are three forts built in the time of Charles V., called respectively *Bordj Manoubia*, *Bordj Filfila*, and *Bordj er-Rebla*. The last of these is a fine specimen of mediæval military architecture.

Tunis is commanded by two hills in its immediate vicinity, namely, *Sidi bel Hassan* to the S., and the *Belvédère* to the N. The fortress which crowns the former belongs to a time far anterior to the *Bordj er-Rebla*, and its position is unrivalled.

The Belvédère was the first position occupied by the French troops, and the remains of their entrenched camp on the summit are still visible.

Nothing is more attractive to the stranger than the **Native Bazaars**, which, amidst all the manifold changes and ameliorations which have taken place around them, still retain their original character. They are narrow and tortuous, well shaded by the houses themselves, and frequently covered with planks or matting. The trades generally keep together, so that the purchaser has the advantage of comparing the various articles of the same sort in one place. The principal are the *Souk el-Attarin*, or market of the perfumers; *Souk el-Farashin*, where carpets and all manner of gaily coloured garments are exposed for sale; *Souk el-Serajin*, or bazaar of the saddlers, full of splendid embroidery on leather; *Souk el-Turk*, where arms are sold; *Souk el-Bey*, *Souk el-Belad*, and numberless others.

The *Resident Général* has expressed his determination to preserve this part of the town intact, and to create a new city between the marine gate and the lake. This has already made great progress; a wide avenue bordered by stately houses, including the French Residency, the principal hotel, the Roman Catholic Cathedral, banks, public offices, the inevitable cafés, etc., has already been constructed, and wide streets are gradually branching off from it in various directions. In one of these is a fine market-place, and the railway company has laid out part of its land as a public garden. On the N. side of the European quarter is an extensive Maltese quarter, called *Malta es-Segheira*, or Little Malta, inhabited principally by the quiet and industrious natives of that island.

The perimeter is about 8 kil., but the area is not all inhabited. A great deal of space is occupied by cemeteries, ruined houses, and ground not built over.

The population of the Regency is stated to be about 1,110,000, composed as follows:—

French	16,000
Italians	20,000
Maltese	12,000
Other Europeans	3,000
Jews	40,000
Mohammedans	1,019,000
Total	1,110,000

This, however, is a mere estimate; nothing like a regular census has ever been made. The city of Tunis is supposed to contain 20,000 Europeans, 30,000 Jews, and 130,000 Mohammedans.

The costume of the Jews in Tunis differs greatly from that which used to be adopted by them in Algiers before they became "French citizens," or from what actually prevails in Constantine and other less Europeanised parts of Algeria. It is always very trying for the fair sex to appear in skin-tight trousers and short jackets, but the ungracefulness of this is exaggerated by the remarkable corpulence which distinguishes the Jewish ladies in Tunis, and which is supposed to constitute one of their most attractive features.

The Maltese are here a numerous and most valuable class of the community, they work hard, live abstemiously, and frequently succeed in collecting a fair competence with which to retire to their native isle.

The lower part of the city and the faubourgs nearest to it are occupied by Christians and Jews; the upper part is reserved for the Mohammedan population, and is built in the form of an amphitheatre crowned by the Kasba. In front of it is a square, called *Souk el-Islam*, containing the Dar-el-Bey and two handsome rows of shops built in a pseudo-Moorish style, with an astronomical clock in the middle, showing the hour, the day of the month and the moon's age. Enclosed within these four sides is a small garden.

The interior of Tunis presents a confused network of streets and lanes, one or two of which, wider than the others, run nearly through its whole length. A few years ago these were almost impassable, owing to the mud and filth in winter and the dust in summer, but of late years considerable municipal improvements have been carried out, and for a native city they are remarkably clean.

The streets also are well lighted with gas; nearly 1000 public lights have been placed in the town.

English Church.—The English church of St. Augustine is only a few minutes' walk from the Hôtel de Paris; a site was granted by the Bey, and a neat little iron building, lined with wood, was erected by subscription. The E. window was put in by the English community in memory of John Howard Payne.

Roman Catholic Churches. — The Roman Catholic Church in N. Africa is governed by one of its most distinguished prelates, Cardinal Lavigerie. He was for many years Archbishop of Algiers, but in the beginning of 1885 the Pope re-established the archiepiscopal see of Carthage, and the *pallium* of the new dignity was conferred with much solemnity upon him at Algiers. He is also Primate of all Africa.

The *Provisional Cathedral* is situated in the Avenue de la Marine, of the French Residency. There large church in the *Capuchin Co.*, R. Sidi Mourgana; this was origin founded by the Order for the Rede tion of Captives in 1624, but the chuλ at least has been entirely rebuilt since In the establishment of the *Frères de la doctrine Chrétienne*, R. Toweela, is a very ancient chapel, the first one used by free Christians in the city, and till very lately the parish church.

Religious Communities.—There are already many religious communities established in the Regency. The *Dames de Sion* have at Tunis a very superior establishment for the education of girls and boys under seven years. The sisters of *St. Joseph* have nine establishments; two at Tunis, and others at the Goletta, Bizerta, Susa, Monastir, Mahadia, Sfax and Djerba. The sisters of the *Mission d'Afrique* have houses at Beja and the Marsa. The brothers of the *Doctrine Chrétienne* have three schools at Tunis and one at the Goletta. There is also a large asylum for aged people kept by the *Petites Sœurs des Pauvres*, just outside the town, beyond the barracks and the Normal School.

There is also a *Greek Church*, which for two centuries was under British protection.

English Cemetery.—The Protestant cemetery of St. George, belonging to England, but used by other Protestant nations, was formerly situated beyond the inner walls of the town; these have been removed, as the city has greatly extended in that direction, and it is now surrounded by houses in the quarter called *Malta es-Segheira*. The keys can be obtained at the British Consulate. It contains the graves of several English Consuls-General—Mr. Campion, 1661; Richard Lawrence, 1750; James Trail, 1777; Sir Thomas Reade, 1849. The oldest grave is that of Samuel Webbe, a merchant, who died 8th October 1648. The most interesting *was* that of John Howard Payne, Consul for the United States of America, who died at Tunis on the 1st

852. A monument was erected by "his grateful country," and ...rded the fact that "His fame as ...et and dramatist is well known ...rever the English language is ...ken, through his celebrated ballad of ...1ome, Sweet Home,' and his popular ...ragedy of 'Brutus,' and other similar ...roductions."

On the 5th January 1883 the body ...as disinterred and carried to the United States; it was consigned to its ...nal resting-place in Oakhill Cemetery, ...eorge Town, Washington, with much ...olemnity, on the 9th June 1883. A ...1onument has been erected at Tunis ...n the spot where the grave was, ...imilar to that over the new grave ...n America, the expense of the whole ...roceeding having been defrayed by Mr. ...'orcoran of Washington.

As all intramural interments are now ...rohibited, this cemetery is closed, and ... new Protestant cemetery, granted by ...he municipality, has been opened out...ide the town, next to the R. C. one.

Roman Catholic Cemeteries.—There ...re two,—the old one, attached to the ...athedral, and a new and larger one ...utside the Bab el-Hathera. The ...ormer is now closed; in it is an ancient ...hapel, supposed to have been that of ...he Christian slaves. On the altar was . consecration stone bearing the date 659; this has been removed to St. ...ouis. Underneath are vaults where ...n immense number of coffins were ...ound, amongst them was that of the ...ather of M. de Lesseps, who died here ...s Consul-General of France in 1832; ...his also has been removed to St. ...ouis.

This chapel is perhaps the one men...ioned by Père Dan (1635), who says: 'At Tunis there are various chapels in ...he Bagnos, but especially there is a ...ery fine and large one, that of St. Antoine, a little outside the town, ...where all the Christian slaves and free ...nen may go without hindrance to hear ...nass. The French Consul has generally ... priest and a chaplain. There is no ...place in Barbary where the priests and ...those connected with the church are more free, and where the Christian religion is more tolerated than Tunis.'

[*Algeria.*]

Public Instruction.- In 1876 Mohammed es-Sadik Bey during the ministry of Kheir-ed-din Pacha, created a college called *Medressa Sadikia*, in order to educate youth for administrative functions. A great part of the confiscated property of the former minister, Si Mustafa Khasnadar, was appropriated for this purpose. On the fall of Kheir-ed-din the college fell into a condition of complete neglect, and it was only after the French occupation that it was completely reorganised, and placed under the control of the department of public instruction, of which M. Machuel is director. The instruction consists of courses of the Arabic language and literature, French and Italian, mathematics, physics, history and geography. It receives 150 native students gratuitously, who are provided with their morning meal; 50 of these reside entirely within its walls, and are clothed and provided with every necessary.

College of St. Charles.—This is one of the most useful of the many works inaugurated by the Cardinal Lavigerie. In 1875 the "white fathers," *Pères Missionnaires d'Afrique*, were brought by his Eminence from Algiers to Carthage as guardians of the chapel of St. Louis. There the first school was opened, but it was subsequently converted into a seminaire, and the college was transferred to its present site near the cathedral, and named *St. Charles* after the saint whose name the Cardina. bears. About 240 youths of all nations are educated there; French, Italian, Maltese, Jews and Mohammedans live together in perfect harmony, and prepare the way for what the French ever regard as a future possibility, complete assimilation.

The Normal School, or College Alaoui, was founded in 1884 by the present Bey, with the consent of the French Government, for the purpose of educating a class of teachers capable of spreading the French language and influence in the interior of the Regency. The buildings were originally commenced by the Khasnadar for a medressa; they are situated in one of the highest and most healthy parts of the city, commanding a splendid view in every direction.

Library and Museum.—A "*Service des Antiquités, Beaux Arts et Monuments historiques,*" has been instituted under the direction of M. René de la Blanchère, having for its object the study and preservation of historical monuments and works of art throughout the Regency. A museum has been opened in the old Hareem of the Bardo, the great treasure of which is the famous Mosaic pavement from Susa, one of the largest and finest extant. This is well worthy of a visit (see p. 297). The Library is provisionally in one of the rooms of the Ecole Normale.

Mosques.—Throughout the Regency of Tunis, except, strange to say, in the sacred city of Kerouan, Christians are rigorously excluded from entering any of the mosques. The principal one in Tunis is the

Djamäa ez-Zeitouna, "Mosque of the olive tree," a sort of university, where a vast number of youths receive a religious education. It was founded by Hassan el-Ghessani el-Oudjdi in A.D. 698, under the reign of the Khalife Abd-el-Malek ben Merouan, on the site, it is said, of the cell of a Christian anchorite. It is in the very heart of the city, surrounded on every side by bazaars, so that a view at least may be had of the central court from various directions.

Djamäa el-Kasba, the "Mosque of the Kasba," built about 1232. It was formerly entered from that citadel, now it has been walled off from it to prevent intrusion on the part of the soldiers.

Djamäa Sidi Mahrez, in the quarter of the Bab es-Souika, distinguished by its large dome surrounded by smaller cupolas. This building enjoys the privilege of sanctuary. There are innumerable other mosques, medrassas or colleges, zaouias, and tombs of Mohammedan saints. The mausoleum of the Beys, called *Turbet el-Bey,* is situated near the Souk el-Belad ; it is distinguished by its green tiled domes ; the exterior is decorated by plinth, pilasters and entablature of rose-coloured marble, sculptured in the Italian style.

Native Troops.—The Tunisian army has been reduced to a single battalion of honour for the Bey, but the soldiers are well-drilled and equipped, and are no longer to be seen bare-footed and knitting stockings when on guard.

The KASBA, which forms one side of the square in which the Dar el-Bey is situated, at one time contained the ancient palace of the Bey, and immense barracks for the accommodation of Janissaries, as well as bagnios for Christian slaves. It was here that these rose on their keepers when Charles V was attacking Tunis, and greatly contributed to his success. (See p. 37.) The Spaniards strengthened it during their occupation, and built the aqueduct behind the Bardo to supply it with water.

Now all the old buildings have been demolished, and handsome and commodious barracks constructed for the use of the French troops ; nothing but the exterior wall of the ancient Kasba remains.

The **Dar el-Bey**, or town palace, is well worthy of a visit ; the lower rooms are occupied as public offices, and are quite uninteresting, but the traveller can easily obtain permission to view the private apartments of the Bey. His Highness holds receptions here every Saturday, driving over from his residence at the Marsa for the purpose. Some of the older rooms, built by Hamouda Pasha about a century ago, are perfect gems of Moorish decoration, equal to anything in the Alhambra. The principal are the *outer court,* on each side of which is a bedroom for an officer in waiting, called *Beit Dhabit el-Asâa.* The *Beit Wuzir el-Kebir,* or chief minister's apartment, splendidly decorated with tiles and *Nuksh hadida* work, and with a richly painted and gilt ceiling. The *Beit el-Bey,* or audience chamber, leading to his private bedroom. The *Beit el-Fetoor,* or dining-room, with walls of coloured marble and red granite from Carthage, and a roof blazing with gold and colours; and lastly, the *Beit el-Hookem*, or Hall of Judgment, with a domed roof of the most delicate plaster arabesque work.

A long passage, poor in comparison with the more ancient part of the building, but comparatively inoffensive, leads to an immense suite of state rooms, painted in the style of a French café; the walls hung with red damask; gilt chairs and Louis XVI consoles ranged around; everything that is rich and expensive of its kind, but an outrage on the incomparable beauty of the older rooms.

The delicate and intricate arabesque plaster work called *Nuksh hadida*, for which Tunis was once so celebrated, is now almost an extinct art, and is being replaced by European decoration, such as would appear tawdry on a cheap tea-tray.

In this palace Queen Caroline resided during her stay in Tunis, in 1816; as did at a subsequent period the brother of the Emperor William I. of Germany and his daughter, and later still three of our own royal princes were welcomed here by the Bey.

Walks round Tunis.

From the square of the Kasba a very pleasant walk is to the Bab Sidi Abdulla esh-Sherif, near which the water from Zaghouan enters the town through a handsome fountain. Here a cistern has lately been constructed capable of containing 15,000 cubic mètres of water. Outside the gate there is a fine panoramic view of the hills on the east side of the harbour, Zaghouan with its ruined aqueduct on the horizon; the Bardo, two picturesque Spanish forts; and lastly, coming round again to the point of departure, the site of Carthage and the town of Tunis, in which the most conspicuous object is the many-domed mosque of *Djamaa Sidi Mahrez*.

The traveller may continue his walk between the old forts; all around them are *Silos*, or *Rablas*, as they are here called; underground magazines of a bottle-like shape for storing grain, from which the castle obtains its name of *Bordj er-Rabta*. Thence he can join the Bardo road, pass *Bab es-Sadjun*, from which there is a good view of the Spanish aqueduct on the left, also *Bab es-Selam*, and so home to his hotel through the European quarter.

Another beautiful view of the town is from the hill called by the Europeans Belvédère, to the northward of the city. The panorama of the city sloping upwards towards the Kasba, and of the lake and surrounding country, is very fine.

A finer view still is from *Bordj Ali Rais*, on the S.E. of the town, on an elevated hill opposite that on which the tomb of *Sidi Bel Hassan* is situated. Leave Tunis by the *Bab Alawa*, and pass through the cemetery just outside of it. A carriage can drive nearly to the top. The fort is occupied by a small detachment of artillery, and the traveller can easily obtain permission to mount and see the view from the terrace.

EXCURSIONS IN THE NEIGHBOURHOOD OF TUNIS.

To Carthage and the Marsa.

Naturally the first excursion that the traveller will desire to make is to the site of the mighty Carthage—"dives opum, studiisque asperrima belli." He may go by train, the station of Carthage being within half an hour's walk of the chapel of St. Louis; but the preferable course is to hire a carriage and return by the Marsa; the whole may be done in five or six hours.

Carthage.—Carthage is said to have been founded by a Phœnician colony from Tyre, about B.C. 852. They gave to it the name of *Kart-Haduet*, the new city, in opposition to *Utica*, the old. This name became in Greek *Carchedon*, and in Latin *Carthago*.

For the mythological account of its foundation and its ancient history, see Historical Notice, p. 22.[1]

[1] Consult also the valuable work of R. Bosworth Smith, "Carthage and the Carthaginians." London: Longmans, Green, and Co., 1887.

It continued in uninterrupted prosperity and glory for upwards of 700 years, till its destruction by P. C. Scipio, B.C. 146. Thirty years later it was colonised by C. Gracchus, raised to a considerable condition of prosperity by M. Antoninus and P. Dolabella, and rebuilt with much magnificence by Augustus. It subsequently became the chief seat of Christianity in Africa, and many of its most splendid buildings were destroyed with the view of rooting out the last traces of paganism. Its utter destruction, however, did not commence before the Arab invasion in 697, since when one generation after another has continued the operation with unremitting zeal; even as late as the time of St. Louis it still existed as a city; and the narrative of the early Arab historians, such as El-Bekri and El-Edrisi, prove that certain important buildings were still existent and almost intact. But now nothing remains of the great city save a few cisterns and some shapeless masses of masonry; all that is valuable has been carried off either for the construction of the modern city of Tunis or to enrich the public buildings and museums of Europe; and now indeed there can be no doubt that in very truth

"Deleta est Carthago."

The situation of the city was singularly well chosen, on the shores of a magnificent and well-sheltered bay, forming the southern part of an immense gulf, and sheltered from the N.W. and W. by a projecting cape. Carthage consisted, properly speaking, of three different towns, all enclosed within the same wall; namely—*Byrsa*, the citadel; *Cothon*, which included the port and that part of the town occupied by the merchants; and thirdly, *Magaria*. The first occupied the site of the present chapel of St. Louis, the second the lowland between it and the Goletta, and the third stretched in rear of both, from the banks of the lake to the sea-shore, below the village of Sidi Bou-Saeed.

Chapel of St. Louis.—On the 8th of August 1830 a treaty was concluded between Charles X and the Regency of Tunis, containing the following article:—

"We cede in perpetuity to H.M. the King of France a site in the Mäalaka to erect a religious monument in honour of Louis IX on the spot where that Prince died; we engage to respect and to cause to be respected this monument, consecrated by the Emperor of France to the memory of one of his most illustrious ancestors."

It is difficult to determine the exact spot where St. Louis died on the 25th of August 1270, but the spot selected as the site of the chapel was the Byrsa itself, to which place, according to Joinville, St. Louis retreated after his defeat before Tunis, the better to be able to superintend the embarkation of his troops and watch the movements of the enemy. Perhaps the natural desire to occupy so commanding a position was not altogether absent from the mind of the astute French Consul who was empowered to make the selection. Regarding the style and architecture of the chapel the less said the better. Above the entrance is the following inscription:—

LOUIS PHILIPPE, PREMIER ROI DES FRANÇAIS, A ÉRIGE CE MONUMENT EN L'AN 1841, SUR LA PLACE OU EXPIRA LE SAINT LOUIS, SON AIEUL.

Within the chapel has been interred the remains of the Consul-General who negotiated the treaty, father of the celebrated Count Ferdinand de Lesseps; they, together with the original tombstone which once covered them, having been translated from the old chapel near the Cathedral at Tunis.

Close to St. Louis may be seen a neat little chapel, built principally for the use of Maltese pilgrims, and out of compliment to them called by the Maltese name of Notre Dame de la *Meliha*. It contains three stained glass windows in honour of Saints Augustine, Cyprian, and Monica, and two paintings to imitate windows dedicated to Saints Perpetua and Felicitas. Attached to it is a Carmelite convent, a branch of that at Algiers, founded in April 1885, and in immediate proximity to both the Mohammedan Marabout of Sidi Saleh. It is one of Cardinal Lavigerie's most cherished projects to erect a cathedral worthy of the French nation on this spot, to them hallowed ground, and to restore the great city, once the Queen of Africa and the rival of Rome itself.

The Cathedral has indeed been completed, and in it is the tomb of the Cardinal, consecrated by himself, which all well-wishers of Africa trust may long remain untenanted, but the rise of Carthage would mean the fall of Tunis : it is difficult to divert commerce from its ancient channel, and hard to devote so important a city to decay.

Behind the chapel is a college for priests, the *Seminaire*, not only of the "white fathers," who wear the Arab burnous and are destined for missionary labour, but for the ordinary priesthood of the diocese. The novices of the former order reside at the Maison Carrée, near Algiers.

In the lower story of this building is the *Salle de St. Louis*, on the walls of which are paintings representing scenes in the Saint's passage and death at Tunis. The Pope's Legate throughout the series is the portrait of Cardinal Lavigerie. Below are marble tablets containing the arms of descendants of French Crusaders who contributed towards the expense of the Cardinal's various works at Carthage.

Within the enclosure of St. Louis is a most interesting **Museum** formed by the indefatigable explorer and learned archæologist, the Rev. Père Delattre, one of the white fathers and chaplain of St. Louis, who has been occupied in exploring the site of Carthage for many years under the auspices of Cardinal Lavigerie. It is open to the public on Sunday, Monday, Thursday, and Saturday, from 2.30 to 6 P.M., excepting during the hours of divine service, which are usually between 2.30 and 3.30 P.M. Permission to see it can, however, always be obtained by a passing stranger on written application to the director. There is no difficulty in communicating with him, as there is a post and telegraph office within the walls of St. Louis.

An immense number of fragments of sculptured stones, statues, Punic and Latin inscriptions, etc., have been built into the walls around. Of the 500 Punic inscriptions, nearly all are votive tablets, a few only being funereal ; they bear many different symbols, such as the upright hand, the disc of Baal, the crescent of Astarte, palm trees, rams, etc., and inscriptions which vary very little from the following formula :— *To the great lady, Tanith Fen Baal, and to the Lord Baal Hammon, vow made by . . . , son of . . . , son of . . . , that their prayers may be heard.*

Baal was the malignant deity, rejoicing in human sacrifices, and Astarte the Carthagenian Venus, identical with "the abomination of the Sidonians."

The Christian inscriptions generally contain little more than the name of the deceased, generally with the expressions *In pace ; Fidelis in pace ; Innocens in pace*, etc.

The most important objects in the collection are contained in a large hall. The Punic period is here represented by terra-cotta vases, lamps of the most primitive forms, iron and bronze implements, and some really interesting and valuable inscriptions. The rest of the collection consists of objects of the Roman period, pagan as well as Christian. Amongst the most curious is a cippus containing bas-reliefs of the principal occupations of a Roman lady's day—toilet, work, and reading. There is a large collection of lamps, some containing subjects from heathen mythology, others from the Old Testament, such as the colossal bunch of grapes, Daniel in the lions' den, and the seven-branched candlesticks ; while many are distinctly Christian, and contain crosses of many shapes, and the Saviour in various characters.

One very interesting terra-cotta toy represents a man playing an organ, which is worked by hydraulic power.

A glass case contains Carthaginian medals, enabling us to follow the fortunes of that city from its foundation to the Arab invasion, and even to the crusade of St. Louis in 1270, and the expedition of Charles V in 1335.[1]

There are many tombstones from the

---

[1] The museum was broken into in 1888, and nearly the whole collection of coins and medals of inestimable value, was stolen ; fortunately many duplicates were preserved elsewhere.

Cemetery of Slaves of the 1st and 2d centuries; these throw quite a new light on the employment of the slaves and freedmen of the imperial house, and of the constitution of the *tabularium* of Carthage, and of the principal attributions of public functionaries. There are touching epitaphs, such as that which *Ostaria Procula* caused to be engraved for her husband *Aelius*, who lived 76 years, and of whom she had no complaint to make, *De quo nihil questa est*. Finally, there are important Christian inscriptions obtained from the basilica, recording the names of bishops, priests, deacons and readers, which, were they not so seriously mutilated, would have been of the greatest service towards clearing up the history of the early African church.

The **Byrsa** was the first point fortified by the Carthaginians, and around it arose by degrees the houses, public buildings, streets, etc., of this great city. It is the last spur of the natural range of hills which extend westward from Sidi Bou-Saeed, on which were grouped some of the most celebrated public buildings, such as the Palace of Dido, the Temple of Æsculapius, the cisterns, etc. The walls of the fortress themselves were so constructed as to serve as stables for elephants, horses, etc.

The Palace of Dido.—The walls supposed to be those of the Palace of Dido are to the N.E. of the Byrsa. On leaving the chapel the path right ahead is followed for about 100 yards, after which, turning to the left, a few vestiges are found supposed to be the remains of the Palace of Dido, which the Carthaginians subsequently transformed into a temple, and which was again rebuilt by the Romans. The view from this spot is grand and extensive. Dido may well have seen from it the departure of Æneas and his Trojans, and followed them with her eyes as she burnt upon her funeral pile. She might have done this had not the fiction of this gracious queen been entirely effaced by the labours of modern archæologists. Carthage was founded by a band of hardy navigators, who placed the city under the protection of Astarte, who subsequently became humanised under the name of Dido.

Temple of Æsculapius.—The Temple of Æsculapius is situated under the Chapel of St. Louis; four or five small apses are still visible within the wall enclosing the chapel. This building was destroyed at the close of the third Punic War, when the wife of Asdrubal voluntarily perished in the flames with her whole family rather than submit to the Romans. (See p. 24.) It was subsequently restored by them. The building was entirely of white marble, the columns being fluted. Three magnificent halls were excavated by M. Beulé, who estimated that each was at least 50 mètres long and 10 high.

The Forum.—The forum was situated between Byrsa and the sea, close to the military harbour. Here public assemblies were held. Diodorus Siculus says that it was rectangular in shape, and on one side of it was the temple of Apollo. It was from this direction that the army of Scipio penetrated Carthage, and there he established himself for the siege of the Byrsa. Here M. de Ste. Marie found upwards of 2000 Punic inscriptions in 1875, which he despatched to France in the "Magenta" in September of that year. This vessel was burnt in the harbour of Toulon, but fortunately the antiquities on board were saved.

The Harbours.—The site of the ancient ports of Carthage is well known and easily recognisable. On leaving the Goletta by the gate of Tunis the traveller passes over a tongue of land called formerly *Tænia* and *Ligula*. On following this he soon finds himself between the lake of Tunis to the left and the sea to the right. After a walk of twenty minutes he arrives at the house formerly owned by General Kheired-din, the late Prime Minister of the Bey. On continuing his walk for about twenty-five minutes more he arrives at a summer palace of the Bey, now converted into a Lazzaretto. It is on the shore near this that the ports are situated.

Appian says that these two ports communicated with each other and with the sea, the latter entrance being closed with iron chains. The outer one was the mercantile harbour. In the middle of the inner one rose an island, on which, and around the side of the harbour, were immense quays in which were creeks capable of holding 220 vessels, together with storehouses for timber and tackle. Before each separate dock were two Ionic columns, so that the islet and the port presented the appearance of porticoes. The former was the palace of the admiral, who could then see everything that went on in the arsenal. Within this was the military harbour.

From the chapel of St. Louis the traveller can see two little lakes, excavated a few years ago by a late Prime Minister on the site of the ancient ports; but it must not be supposed that the latter were as limited in extent as their modern imitation. They were, however, artificial basins, and both were named *Cothon*, a word used to express a harbour excavated by the hand of man. Like many of the other principal features of Carthage these ports were destroyed by Scipio, restored by the Romans, enlarged by the Byzantines, and subsequently allowed to fall into ruin and be filled up after the Arab conquest.

Of the various other temples to Apollo, Saturn, Astarte, Hercules, etc., few or no remains are visible, and the traveller will look in vain even for their foundations; all that has been written on the subject by Falbe, Beulé, Davis, etc., has not fixed their positions beyond doubt, and the subject is not one likely to interest the ordinary traveller.

Cisterns.—Punic Carthage was supplied with water entirely from cisterns constructed to catch and preserve rainwater. These are found in every direction, but there were two great public reservoirs, one near the sea and the other at Mäalaka. The first of these is situated close to the fort called Bordj El-Djedid. The total length is 139 mètres, and the breadth 37 mètres, they are vaulted and divided into eighteen compartments, two of which contained tanks and circular basins either for distribution or to catch any *debris* brought down by the rain, and allow only clear water to flow into the reservoirs beyond. The cisterns at the *Mäalaka*[1] were very much larger, but are now in a ruinous condition, and the Arabs of the village make use of them as residences for themselves and their flocks; they had a length of 150 mètres, and a breadth of 225.

It is difficult to say for certain whether these are Punic or Roman; probably they, or others on the site of them, were built by the Carthaginians, and restored or rebuilt at a subsequent period. The ground around them was paved with marble for the collection of rain-water, and there is good reason to suppose that the streets of the city were treated in the same manner, in order that none of this precious fluid might be lost.

When the aqueduct from Zaghouan was subsequently constructed, these reservoirs were used for the reception and distribution of the water.

The Mäalaka cisterns are hopelessly ruined, but the others have been restored by the Zaghouan Water Company, and utilised for the supply of the neighbourhood. The water is conducted to them by pipes from Zaghouan, and branches lead thence to the Goletta and the Marsa. Great care has been taken to preserve their original form; this was the more easy as all the portions of them below the ground level, and the vaults of six of the compartments, were in a state of perfect preservation. They are large enough to contain 27,000 cubic mètres of water. Any one wishing to examine the interior should apply *personally* for a card of admittance to Mr. Perkins, the director of the Waterworks' Company, at their offices in Tunis.

Basilica.—Outside the ramparts of the ancient city, where no doubt it was placed before the edict of Constantine, and in a locality called by the Arabs *Damous-el-Karela*, a corruption possibly of *Domus Caritatis*, is the great Basilica. It was a remarkable building, not so much on account of the richness of the material with which it was constructed

[1] The word means in Arabic *ha ıjı ɔ*, or *connected together*.

as for its great size and the peculiarity of its construction. The main body of the building was 65 mètres long by 14 mètres wide. It is divided into nine naves, the central nave and transept being wider than the others and forming a cross; on either side of this there were four smaller ones formed by columns of marble and granite, the bases of which are still in *situ*. The four central pillars were the largest of all, and were destined to support a vault richly decorated with mosaics, some of which may yet be seen in the museum. Instead of the ordinary rectangular *narthex* and *atrium* there is a semicircular court which had an open gallery round, and a fountain in the centre. This terminated in a *trifolium* or *trichorum*, the walls of which were covered with coloured marbles and the dome with mosaics. This contained a tomb, probably of a martyr. The east end terminated in the usual apse. Beyond this was the baptistery, the font being octagonal, within a square, with ten flights of steps to descend into it.

All over the floor of the Basilica were innumerable tombs, generally of squared stones, in which were found skeletons lying on lime. No objects of any kind were found in them, excepting nails, showing that the custom of burying in coffins was common. Sarcophagi, in less number, also existed; they were so placed that the tops were on a level with the floor and served as slabs for the inscriptions. The whole of the pavement was a mass of epitaphs; no less than 12,000 or 13,000 fragments have been found, of bishops, priests, deacons, subdeacons, and readers, *lectores*, as well as holy virgins and martyrs, the last generally recognised by the formula, *Hic sunt reliquiae*.

A considerable number of bas-reliefs have also been preserved of the Virgin and Child, the Good Shepherd, Eve after her Fall, the Miracle of the Loaves and Fishes, etc. All these have been transported to the museum.

This, like the Basilica of Salona in Dalmatia, appears to have been built on land presented to the Church by a convert to Christianity; traces of his residence, and of the columbaria of his family, have been found under the foundations.

Amphitheatre.—The Amphitheatre was entirely of Roman construction. It is situated S.W. of the Mäalaka, and close to the Carthage station of the railway. All that remains, however, is an elliptical excavation, about 12 mètres in depth. The stones have all disappeared. This building measured about 90 mètres in length by 30 in breadth. This was the scene of the martyrdom of Saint Perpetua and her companions on the 7th of March 203.

Circus.—The circus is situated to the S.E. of the Arab village of Douar ech-Chott, and about 3½ kil. from the temple of Æsculapius. Its outline is easily distinguished, and even some vestiges of the Spina, but all the cut stones have been removed. Its length was 675 mètres, and its breadth 90.

Theatre.—Apuleius describes the theatre at considerable length, without specifying its exact site, but El-Edrisi says that it was W. of the sea-baths. Standing at the great cisterns and looking towards the Goletta, the ruins of this building are seen on the left hand near the sea-shore. It was an edifice of great magnificence, but all its beautiful columns of red and black granite have been dispersed in Europe, and it has proved quite a mine of cut stone for the construction of Tunis.

The history of **Christian Carthage** is no less interesting than that of its earlier days. Owing to its constant intercourse with Rome the religion of Christ was implanted here at a very early date. In the second century there were a great many bishops in the proconsular province, and Agrippinus, the first bishop of Carthage, convoked them in council.

The first recorded martyr at Carthage was St. Namphanion, who was killed in 198 under Septimius Severus. Jocundus and Saturninus followed about the same time. St. Perpetua and her companions were thrown to wild beasts in the amphitheatre in 203. St. Cyprian was beheaded in 258; other brilliant names adorn the African Church; Tertullian and Augustine, the latter of whom, born at Tagaste, and partially educated at Medaura, came to Carthage to complete his studies. In his time the see of Carthage numbered 160 churches in the Byzacene, and almost as many in Zeugitana. The names of only twenty-eight bishops of Carthage are, however, recorded, of whom the last, Cyriacus, lived in 1076. To the E. of the chapel of St. Louis, and distant about 3000 mètres from it, is the village of **Sidi Bou-Saeed**, which is esteemed as holy by the Arabs, on account of a tradition that St. Louis became a convert to El-Islam, and was interred there under the name of Sidi Bou-Saeed.

Douar ech-Chott.—To the S., little beyond the foot of the mound on which the chapel is situated, is the little village of Douar ech-Chott, consisting of a few houses and a minaret. Between it and the Goletta are several summer palaces of former dignitaries of Tunis.

The traveller should now continue to the N., to the pleasant district of **Marsa**, where the Bey has a palace, and where several of the principal people of the place, and amongst others the Resident-General and the British Consul, have their summer residences, surrounded by beautiful olive groves. Cardinal Lavigerie has also built a palace on the lower slope of Cape Carthage, the hill on which stands the purely native village of Sidi Bou-Saeed.

Farther to the N. is *Kamart*, where is a palace, now in a ruinous condition, the property of Si Hameida Ben Ayad, and several modern Arab villas.

A drive may be taken from Tunis to the **Ariana**, about 10 kil. to the N. of Tunis, where are numerous fine villas belonging to Arab gentlemen and to a few Europeans, most of them situated in beautiful gardens.

EXCURSION to the GREAT ROMAN AQUEDUCT and the RUINS of OUDENA. This may be done by carriage in a day. They are fully described at pp. 313-15.

EXCURSION TO THE BARDO AND THE ROMAN AQUEDUCT BEYOND MANOUBA.

The **Bardo** is distant about half an hour's drive from the town. It is one of the most characteristic and interesting of all the palaces of Tunis, but is in a condition of great dilapidation and decay. Externally it has the air of a fortress, being surrounded by a wall and ditches, and flanked with bastions and towers. The entrance leads through a street of small shops, few of which are occupied, to a spacious court, where carriages are left. Beyond, there is a second court, in the middle of which is a flight of steps guarded by marble lions; this gives access to the *Beit el-Belar*, or "Hall of Glass," where the Bey used to have audiences every Saturday, and received foreign consuls. The Bey's receptions here are now confined to the two great Mussulman festivals, *Aid el-Kebir* and *Aid es-Seghir*, the great and little festivals. The latter is that which follows the fast of Ramadan, and the former occurs three months afterwards, and is better known as *Courban Bairam*, when multitudes of sheep are sacrificed by pious Mohammedans. On these two occasions his Highness receives in state the principal functionaries of the Regency and the consular body. The *Beit el-Belar* is very handsomely decorated with arabesque plaster work and marble, especially the roof; this is of an open interlaced pattern over mirror, which produces a very bright and pleasing effect. On the same floor there are two other halls, which are not always shown to visitors; the *Beit el-Pasha*, or "Hall of the Pasha," the finest part of the whole, and the only one where there is any quantity of ancient tiles; then comes the *Mahkama*, or "Hall of Justice," where his Highness in person periodically administers the patriarchal but substantially equitable justice which seems far better suited to semi-civilised people than the more elaborate jurisprudence of Europe.

In the upper story is a state saloon, used on the occasion of great fêtes. It is of immense size, but decorated in a very tawdry manner, and hung with pictures, of no artistic merit but interesting from a historical point of view, of European sovereigns, deceased Beys, and Tunisian magnates.

Such was the state of the Bardo, but

it fell into so ruinous a condition that the principal rooms had to be pulled down and rebuilt. The intention was to reconstruct them exactly as they existed formerly, but on the occasion of the author's last visit (Dec. 1888) the work was only in progress.

Close to these public apartments is the *Old Hareem*, which is now repaired and utilised as a museum, under the direction of M. de la Blanchère. It was opened on the 17th May 1888 under the name of **Musée Alaoui**. The halls are of great size, very handsomely painted and gilt, and the walls covered entirely with tiles of native manufacture but of European design.

The *Grande Salle* is an immense rectangle, 19 mètres by 16, surmounted by a dome, gilt and painted in the best style of Arab art. On the floor is the great Mosaic from Susa, 160 mètres square, one of the finest which exists in any country. It represents Neptune in his chariot surrounded with 56 medallions of gods and goddesses, each set in a beautiful garland of foliage. On the walls are other mosaics, most of them being Christian tumulary inscriptions and several fragments of sculpture.

The glass cases contain numerous objects collected throughout the country. Lamps, glass, terra-cotta work, bronzes and pottery of every kind, from the Punic times to those of the Byzantine. On the staircase are arranged a number of votive stones, dedicated for the most part to Saturn, brought from Aïn-Tounga, the ancient *Thignica*.

This leads into the *Patio*, decorated in a very meretricious manner, in which are a great number of inscribed stones, in the Punic, Libyan, and Latin languages. Some are of great interest, such as the inscription from the baths of Carthage, others fixing the names of ancient cities. There are also fragments of sculpture and other antiquities. In the *Salle de Musique* and the *Chambres des Femmes*, as they are called, it is intended to have a museum of Tunisian art. These are in themselves gems of art, being decorated in the most exquisite manner with *nuksh hadid*, or arabesque plaster work.

A catalogue of this interesting collection is being prepared and will be published in 1890.

Excepting the Beylical apartments before described and the museum the whole of the Bardo will probably soon be pulled down.

The only inmates at present are the family of the late Bey, Sidi Mohammed es-Sadik.

Near the Bardo is the palace of the late Bey, the **Kasr es-Saeed**, in which the French treaty was signed, and farther to the W. the *Manouba*, where is the palace once occupied by Kheir ed-din Pacha, then first Minister at Tunis, afterwards Grand Vizier at Constantinople, who sold it, together with his property at the Enfida, to the Compagnie Marseillaise.

EXCURSION TO HAMMAM EL-ENF.

This may be done by railway, several trains running every day, and performing the journey in half an hour. The line passes RADES, the ancient *Maxula*, a small and unimportant village. *Hammam el-Enf*, sometimes erroneously called *Hammam Lif*, "The bath of the nose," from a supposed resemblance to that organ which the hill beyond it bears, is a good deal frequented in summer, but there is no proper establishment there at present. There are several thermal springs, the principal one rising in an old decaying palace built by a former Bey.

The railway goes no farther than this place, but it is intended hereafter to extend it along the coast.

BEST ROUTE FROM TUNIS TO ALGIERS.

The most interesting route from Tunis to Algiers is by Constantine, Setif, and the Chabet el-Akhira. There are many places well worth visiting on the way, all of which are fully described in the body of the work.

First day, alternative routes—

a. Tunis to *Hammam Meskoutine*.
b. Tunis to *Tebessa*.
c. Tunis to *Constantine*.

Second Day—
 a. Hammam Meskoutine to *Constantine.*
 b. Tebessa to *Constantine.*
Third Day—
 Constantine to *Setif.*
Fourth Day—
 Setif to Bougie by the *Chabet el-Akhira.*
Fifth day—
 a. Bougie to *Algiers* by railway.
 b. Bougie to *Algiers* by steamer.

These are the mere days of travel, without taking into consideration the time necessarily spent at each place.

ROUTE 28.

Bône to Tunis by Railway.

Distance in kil. from Bône.	Names of Stations.	Distance in kil. from Tunis.
	BÔNE	355
55	Duvivier	300
65	Medjez-Sfa	290
74	Ain-Tahamimime	281
79	Ain-Afra	276
91	La Verdure	264
97	Ain-Sennour	258
107	SOUK-AHRAS	248
116	Tarja (Halt)	239
124	Sidi Bader	231
140	Oued Mougras	215
156	Sidi el-Hemessi	199
165	GHARDIMAOU	190
176	Oued Meliz	179
187	Sidi Meskine	168
199	Souk el-Arbaa	156
210	Ben Bechir	145
222	Souk el-Khamis	133
235	Sidi Zehili	120
248	BÉJA	107
269	Oued Zargaa	86
289	Medjez el-Bab	66
304	Bordj Toum	51
321	Tebourba	34
330	Djedeida	25
345	Manouba	10
355	TUNIS	

From Bône to Duvivier, see Rte. 19.
55 kil. *Duvivier.* Junction for Constantine and Algiers. After leaving Duvivier the line takes a turn to the westward and follows the right bank of the Oued Melah, an affluent of the Seybouse, till it reaches
65 kil. *Medjez-Sfa*, a small village at the junction of the Oued Sfa and Oued Melah. Here it crosses the old carriage road to Souk-Ahras, and winds, now to the E. now to the W. of it, till
74 kil. *Ain-Tahamimime.* Thence it continues following the general course of the road. The village of *Oued Chaham* is seen to the W., above a deep and densely-wooded glen, through which passes a bright clear stream, one of the most attractive spots on the old carriage road. On a cloudless day even Guelma may be seen in the far distance.

At the 76th kil. the line takes a sudden bend to the E., and runs nearly at right angles to its old course for a distance of 6 kil.

At the 82d kil. it enters the tunnel of *Kef Kerichefa*, 700 mètres in length, and nearly circular in shape, and then returns almost to the place where it had diverged from its general southerly direction. It is most perplexing to observe the features of the landscape, which had been in front of us and on our right hand when we entered the tunnel, now behind us and on our left on emerging from it. To the E. of this bend on the line may be seen at some distance the forest of Kef Djemel, the property of Captain Hope. This is almost the last remaining resort of the red deer in Algeria.

91 kil. *La Verdure.* The village is about a kilomètre and a half to the W. This is about the centre of the beautiful forest of *Fedj el-Makta*, which consists principally of cork oak; but there is a sufficient diversity of other trees to give variety to the tints; while the numerous streams descending from the mountains, among a thick undershrub of heath, bracken, broom and white thorn, delight both ear and eye in a manner not often enjoyed in Africa.

97 kil. *Ain-Sennour.* Not far from this place is an effervescing spring, the water of which is an excellent substitute for soda-water.

107 kil. **Souk-Ahras.** 2430 inhab. 2067 ft. above the sea. The modern

town is in a prosperous condition if we may judge by the size and elegance of its municipal buildings. It has a considerable trade in wool and cattle, and large quantities of alfa fibre are brought by the Tebessa railway. It was formerly the seat of government of the great tribe of *Hanencha*, after whose revolt in 1852 it was created a military post, which became the nucleus of the present town. Its position, 60 kil. from the Tunisian frontier and at the junction of the roads from Tunis to Constantine, Tebessa and Bône, contributed greatly to its prosperity.

It is surrounded by fine forests; there is abundant water power for mills, and other similar industrial establishments; the soil is good, and much of it is capable of irrigation; its climate is temperate and salubrious, so that there is every reason to suppose that it may one day become a place of considerable importance.

In January 1871, after the mutiny of the Spahis at Aïn-Guettar, the Arabs around rose in revolt, burnt the neighbouring farms, assassinated defenceless colonists, and invested the town. The women, children, and sick, were put into the bordj, the streets were barricaded, and every possible precaution made for defence. On the evening of the 26th the insurgents attacked the town, but were driven off after a combat of two hours. The place was relieved on the 31st of January by a column from Bône, under command of General Pouget.

Souk-Ahras was only identified as the ancient Tagaste by an inscription found on the spot, in 1844, when a column under General Randon passed through the district. It seems never to have been of great importance, though it is mentioned by Pliny as one of the free cities. It owes its renown entirely to having been the birthplace of St. Augustine (13th Nov. A.D. 354), whose father Patricius was a person of modest rank, a decurion of the city, and struggled hard to give his son the best education within his means. He died when St. Augustine was only seventeen years of age. He was converted to Christianity by his saintly wife, Monica.

The first years of the Saint's life were passed at Tagaste, and at sixteen he was sent to Medaura (see p. 231), a city which offered greater educational facilities; here he remained a short time, and was then sent to continue his studies at Carthage, in the school of rhetoric, where he soon took the first place.

In 373 he returned to Tagaste, where he taught grammar, and where for nine years he lived in a manner to cause the most profound affliction to his mother, as he tells us in his "Confessions." His old schoolfellow and life-long friend, Alypius, subsequently became Bishop of Tagaste.

There are some Roman ruins round about, but nothing of exceptional interest.

[An interesting excursion from Souk-Ahras is to the ruined Roman city of **Khamisa**, at the source of the **Medjerda** (see p. 233).

This river is formed by two streams, one of which flows from the W. and the other from the S.W. The first of these rises at Khamisa, and the other, called the *Oued Mellegue*, during the greater part of its course, and the *Oued Chabro* near its source, descends from the plateau of Tebessa.

The modern name is a corruption of the Roman one *Bagrada*, and this again is merely a form of the Punic one *Makarath* or *Bakarath*.]

6 kil. After passing Souk-Ahras, the line strikes the Medjerda, which it does not again quit until it approaches Tunis. The river flows through a succession of picturesque gorges, amongst well wooded hills; the line follows generally its left bank, but it crosses the river thirteen times between Souk-Ahras and Ghardimaou.

116 kil. *Tarja*.
124 kil. *Sidi Bader*.
140 kil. *Oued Mougras*.
156 kil. *Sidi el-Hemessi*.
160 kil. The bridge which is here crossed marks the boundary between Algeria and Tunis.
165 kil. **Ghardimaou**, frontier of Tunisia.

This must have been a place of some

importance in Roman times, as an inscription was found here regarding a "Sacerdos provinciæ Africæ," who belonged to the neighbourhood.
176 kil. OUED MELIZ (more correctly *Mehliz*). At 3 kil. to the N. of the line is **Chemtou**, where are fine quarries of *Numidian marble*, second only in importance to those of Arzeu (see p. 273) and the extensive ruins of the Roman **Simittu, Simitthus, or Colonia Simithensium.**

Visitors will find a service of carriages at the station, and rooms and a restaurant at the quarries under the supervision of the administration. Application had, however, better be made beforehand to the office in Tunis, Rue Sadikia, No. 11.

This place is mentioned in the Itineraries as one of the stations on the road from Hippo Regia (Bône) to Carthage, but beyond this nothing is known of its ancient history, and in modern times, until the railway was opened, this part of the country was difficult of access and remote from the usual routes of travellers.

Close to a spot where one of the numerous streams called *Oued el-Melah*, or "Salt River," flows into the Medjerda, is situated a line of small hills covering an area of about 90 hectares, the highest point of which is 260 mètres above the sea level. They are composed almost entirely of marble of various kinds, but principally of Giallo Antico, rose-coloured marble, and a brownish breccia. There can be no doubt that these quarries were extensively worked by the Romans; large excavations made by them exist in various places, and numerous inscriptions have been found on blocks which had been extracted but not carried away. The company has here erected extensive premises; it has constructed a branch railway, crossing the Medjerda by an iron bridge, and joining the main line a little to the E. of the station of Oued Meliz.

The plain on both sides of the hills is covered with extensive Roman remains; the city must have been a very considerable one, owing its existence to its marble quarries. The name of the place is found in several inscriptions, both on tombstones and milliary columns, some of which have been collected in the garden of the director. One of the latter is curious, as it gives the name of a road which passed here:—

VIA
VSOTHA
III

Another is more interesting still, as it indicates the construction by Hadrian of a road destined no doubt for the transport of the marble from Simittu to the sea at Tabarca, probably about A.D. 129.[1]

The most prominent ruin in the landscape is that of a long *aqueduct*, which commenced about 7 kil. distant among the hills to the W., crossed the *Oued el-Achar* by a bridge, still entire, and entered a series of seven vaulted cisterns about 2½ kil. from the marble works. Thence it passed, partly underground and partly on a long line of arches, crossing the Oued Melah by a bridge, now fallen, till it terminated at the *Thermæ*, in the middle of the city. The masonry is not of a particularly fine quality, the plinths of the piers are of large blocks of cut stone, but the masonry above them is of a common rubble, and the voussoirs of the arches are of hammer-dressed stones. Here and there a section of the aqueduct may be seen entirely of cut stone; these mark a reconstruction at a period subsequent to the original work. In one pier may be seen as many as four tombstones, some of them upside down; another pier has one such tombstone, and probably many more were used, the inscriptions of which are turned inwards. The necropolis was in the hills close by, and as there are very few stones now existing there, it is probable that the greater part of them were used for public works.

Close to the end of the aqueduct are the remains of the *Thermæ*, a large building, but of poor construction; the mosaic floor, where visible, is rude, the

[1] These inscriptions have been published in the "Revue Archéologique," by the Rev. Père Delattre, in April and July 1881, and in May and October 1882.

tesserae being of brick, and nearly 5 cent. long by 1½ broad. Farther N. is the *Theatre;* the scena has entirely disappeared, but the cavea is nearly complete. The building is situated close to the river, with a fine view in every direction. There is also an *Amphitheatre* at some distance to the E., but it is in a very dilapidated condition, and could never have been a fine building. There are many other structures more or less ruined, one of which appears to have been a *Basilica*.

But the great feature of the place is undoubtedly the colossal *Bridge* over the Medjerda; it is a work of great magnitude, the southern side is nearly complete, but the rest lies in huge masses, encumbering the bed of the river, as if broken up and tossed about by some great convulsion of nature, to such an extent that it is almost impossible to make out its original plan. It seems to have crossed the river at an obtuse angle, and down stream on the north side there are a number of parallel sluices, with grooves for gates, as if it had also served as a barrage for the irrigation of the plain. The bed of the river has been worn away far below its original level, so that the foundations of the piers are left in the air and entirely exposed. The bridge bears evident proofs of having been rebuilt, like the aqueduct; tombstones having been freely used. The great mass of the masonry is of rubble, almost entirely of waste marble from the quarries, faced with immense blocks of cut stone. Indeed, throughout the whole city there is no appearance of the marble, so near at hand, having been used in blocks for any purpose; probably it was too valuable, and was all exported to Rome. The record of the reconstruction of the bridge is contained on another marble slab now lying in a field on the right bank of the river; an attempt was made to carry it off, but owing to its great weight and size this failed. It proves that the bridge was reconstructed by Trajan from its foundations after he had assumed the title of Dacicus, but before the Arabian and Parthian campaign, probably about A.D. 105. It formed, most probably, the point of departure of a road from Simittu to Sicca Venerea.

187 kil. *Sidi Meskine.* The line now enters a broader part of the valley, still running along the southern side of the river.

199 kil. **Souk el·Arbäa.** An entrenched camp formed by the French on the site of an Arab market held here every Wednesday, hence its name, and now fast rising into an important town. This is a convenient starting-point for various excursions, and there is an auberge at the station, with limited accommodation, where the traveller may put up in comfort. He may visit Chemtou, just described; the Khomair country and Aïn-Draham (see p. 305); and Él-Kef (p. 308). The only attraction in the immediate neighbourhood is the ruined city of **Bulla Regia**, called *Henchir Hummam Durradji* by the natives, situated about 7 kil. from the station, at the foot of Djebel el-Arabia, one of the hills which bound the north side of the valley of the Medjerda. Its position was no doubt determined by a copious spring of sweet water, which, in this region of brackish rivers, was a priceless treasure. It was probably the residence of some of the Numidian kings, and it subsequently became a *liberum oppidum* under the Romans. It is mentioned in the Itinerary of Antonine as a station on the route from Hippo Regia to Carthage; but beyond this little is known of its history, and there are no inscriptions existing on the spot as at Chemtou.

The extent of the ruins can best be seen by ascending the hill for about 300 yards beyond the ruined amphitheatre; they cover an area of many acres, and consist of large buildings and numberless smaller vaulted edifices now buried in the soil, generally above the spring of the arches. In the centre, to the north, is the spring which rose in a large semicircular *nymphaeum* of cut stone, from which leaden pipes issued for the distribution of the water in various directions. Immediately in front of it was an archway built of large blocks of very compact and finely cut limestone. This was destroyed in the most reckless manner to supply building material for the railway. The spring has been enclosed in a *Château d'eau*, and part of its water is conveyed in iron pipes to Souk el-Arbâa, which used to be supplied with water brought from Tunis by rail. The surplus forms a marsh farther down, full of eel and barbel, of great size. Only a small spot on the edge of the reservoir has been cleared to its original level; here a fine mosaic pavement has been discovered, and, to judge by the remains lying about, this must have been a beautiful spot, decorated with temples and colonnades, somewhat like the well-known example at Zaghouan.

Lower down the valley, almost due south of the spring, are the *Thermæ*. Like all the other buildings here, this has been destroyed by an earthquake; huge masses of masonry lie around, disjointed and overthrown, in a manner that could not have been effected by any other agency. One high arch still remains entire. As the rest of the structure is buried in *débris* nearly to the crown of the vaults, there is great hope that valuable works of art may one day be found here; in the meantime the earth and the ruins that encumber it ensure its preservation.

Between the spring and the baths, but a little to the east, is the *Theatre*, also much buried in earth. One can descend in some places into the corridor and form a good idea of the nature of the building. The masonry is of the finest cut stone. The *Auditorium* is entirely filled up; and only one square pier, showing the spring of an arch, exists on the right side of the *scena*.

At a considerable distance farther E. is the *Amphitheatre*, even more destroyed, and apparently of an earlier age. The masonry is of less regular rubble, with only cut stone angles. Like all similar buildings, it commanded a splendid view of the country round.

There are many other edifices, some of great size. One has all its chambers and vaulted roofs in perfect preservation, and was used as a residence by the workmen engaged in laying down the water pipes. Here also is a series of eight contiguous cisterns, of great size, too high to have been filled by the spring; probably they were intended for the collection of rain water, which the Romans in North Africa were more accustomed to use for drinking purposes. After leaving Souk el-Arbaa the line passes to the N. bank of the Medjerda, near its junction with the *Oued Mellegue*, its principal affluent, which also rises in Algeria, N. of Tebessa.

210 kil. *Ben Bechir*, near the confluence of the *Oued Tessaa*.

222 kil. *Souk el-Khamis*.

235 kil. *Sidi Zehili*. The upper plain of the Medjerda terminates here, and the river pursues a more tortuous course through undulating and hilly country.

248 kil. **Beja** (more correctly El-Badja). The station is 12 kil. distant from the town, but a branch line leads to it. In the garden of the station repose the victims of the massacre of Oued Zerga ; a monument has been erected by the railway employés to their memory. The road crosses an old Roman bridge immediately after leaving the station.

Beja is mentioned by Sallust under the name of Vacca or Vaga; the latter was probably the authentic one, as it is found on more than one inscription still existing. During ancient and mediæval times it was renowned for its richness and commerce. Sallust says that it was a regular resort of Italian merchants, *ubi it incolere et mercari consueverant Italici generis multi mortales*.

It has ever been one of the most important corn markets in *Ifrikia*, by which name the northern part of the Regency has always been called since it was the Provincia Africa of the Romans.

El-Edrisi (A.D. 1154) says: "It is a beautiful city, built in a plain extremely fertile in corn and barley, so that there is not in all the *Moghreb* a city so important or more rich in cereals."

El-Bekri calls it the granary of Ifrikia, and says that its soil is so fertile, its cereals so fine, and its harvests so abundant, that everything is exceedingly cheap, and that when there is famine elsewhere, here there is abundance. Every day, he says, 1000 camels and other beasts of burden carry away corn, but that has no influence on the price of food, so abundant is it.

It is situated on the slope of a hill, with a commanding view of the plain beyond. The selection of the site was, no doubt, influenced by the existence of a copious spring of fresh water, which the Romans carefully led to a central position and enclosed within a vaulted chamber of their usual solid construction; this exists uninjured to the present day, but the drainage of the town has been allowed to flow into it and pollute its waters.

The ancient city was surrounded by a wall, flanked by square towers, and on the culminating point of the enclosure was situated the citadel. No doubt this was originally constructed by the Byzantines; the trace was adopted by the Arabs; but as the walls were not continued as the town extended, they soon ceased to surround it, and were allowed to fall into decay.

The old Byzantine citadel has been almost entirely pulled down and replaced by comfortable, if not picturesque, French barracks. Only the central keep remains, formerly the prison, now a depôt for military stores.

A curious discovery has been made at the *Bab es-Souk* or market gate, which shows how much the level of the town has been raised by the ruins of successive ages. One-half of the old Roman double gate has been disinterred below the bottom of the present one, which stands above the other half.

In the outer wall of the Djamäa el-Kebir, or principal mosque, dedicated to Sidna Aissa (our Lord Jesus), is a remarkably interesting inscription, which was first noticed by M. Guérin, proving that this had originally been a Christian basilica, and that it had been restored and embellished during the reigns of the Emperors Valentinianus and Valens, A.D. 364 to 368.

Dyeing is carried on to some extent at El-Badja, but the only distinctive manufactures of the place are wooden sandals used by the women, very tastefully carved out of light wood, generally with an old razor.

In the vicinity of the town is a ruined palace and neglected garden belonging to the Bey, which, like that at Tunis, is called the Bardo. This existed as far back as 1724, when Peysonnel visited the place.

269 kil. OUED ZERGĀA (Gray River). Here took place, on the 30th September 1881, a massacre of railway workmen of a very horrible character by the insurgent Arabs. Having torn up the line on each side of the station, they attacked and burnt the buildings; M. Raimbert, the stationmaster, was burnt alive; and ten other employés, principally Maltese and Italians, were murdered.

Here commence a series of wild gorges and picturesque ravines, through which the Medjerda finds its way from the narrow Beja valley into the broader Tunis plain. It makes a deep curve to the south towards Testour, and both river and line approach each other again at

289 kil. MEDJEZ EL-BAB (Medjez of the Gate). This is a station on the carriage road between Tunis and El-Kef; the town is about 3 kil. from the station, to the S. of the Medjerda. The river is here crossed by a Roman bridge, beyond which is a triumphal arch of the simplest construction, whence the modern name "The Passage of the Gate."

304 kil. *Bordj Toum*.
321 kil. TEBOURBA. *Teburbo Minus* on the left bank of the river.
330 kil. *Djedeida*.
345 kil. *Manouba*. Before reaching this station the line passes through a portion of the great aqueduct of Carthage (p. 313), of which two entire piers and three arches have been wantonly destroyed to enable the line to pass through, whereas by making a very short detour to the right or left this might have been avoided.

This portion of the aqueduct is so different from that met on the way to Zaghouan as to merit a detailed description.

The piers, 4·75 mètres apart, measure 4·60 mètres by 3·68 mètres, constructed of *pisé* or rammed earth, in blocks about 1 mètre thick, and standing on a solid cut stone foundation of varying depth, but faced with a broad square plinth of pisé. The voussoirs, about 0·69 mètre wide, as high as the intrados of the arches, are of cut stone, but the masonry is irregular. The spandrils and the walls of the duct, which was vaulted and lined with cement, are also of pisé. The duct is high enough for a man to pass. There is a band of cut stone at the springing of the arches, but no indications of any mouldings. The construction of the piers is peculiar. There being no quarry sufficiently near for the purpose, the Romans adapted the materials ready to hand. They made a good solid foundation for each pier, and then built the superstructure with carefully-rammed earth mixed with lime in layers of 1·07 mètre. On the upper surface of each layer they formed (while the material was still soft) channels about 0·16 mètre square, laying within them strips of olive wood, about 0·16 mètre wide and 0·03 mètre or more thick. Over these was spread a layer of strong mortar, partly mixed with wood ashes, and from 0·05 mètre thick, wooden pegs 0·16 mètre long being driven through the mortar and laths into the pisé. This kind of framework was repeated to the summit of the aqueduct. The laths and pegs are still undisturbed, and the piers are perfectly true and some of them free from fractures. The aqueduct in the centre of the plain would vary from 21 to 24½ mètres in height. The Arabs have from time to time taken away every bit of lath within reach, and cut away the foundations for the sake of the stones.

The palace of the Manouba was formerly the country residence of Kheir ed-din Pacha; a cavalry station has been built in the neighbourhood.

355 kil. **Tunis** (*q. v.*)

ROUTE 29.

Excursion in the Country of the Khomair.

The country of the **Khomair** (sing. *Khomiri*, incorrectly written *Kroumir*) is situated on the Tunisian side of the boundary line between Algeria and Tunis. It has a breadth of sea coast of about 25 kil., and a depth, in a southerly direction, from Tabarca to Fernana, of 51 kil. In all the maps of Tunis before the French occupation this country was simply a blank space, and little or nothing was known of its inhabitants. Their manners were reported to be almost brutal; and as their territory was inaccessible to any force that the Bey could send against them, no one dared to approach their mountains, or if an expedition did enter, the soldiers were either massacred, or the Khomair themselves dispersed into the interior, where pursuit was impossible; their numbers were reported to be very great, but were much exaggerated, and having but little to lose, they preferred independence and poverty to a more quiet and settled life under Turkish rule. When they were too much pressed by want, they had only to replenish their resources by incursions on either side, and they plundered indiscriminately both the subjects of the Bey and the Arabs of Algeria. Thus, shut in between the two countries, they managed to preserve their independence, a thorn, no doubt, in the flesh of both, but one which was willingly endured by the Algerian authorities till the moment should come when their depredations would give the necessary excuse for the invasion of the Tunisian territories. How the "invention of the Kroumirs" actually did lead to the French protectorate of Tunis, is matter of history.

The author, with one companion, passed through this country in 1876, and he believes that no other European traveller had ever previously been permitted to do so.[1] He again traversed it in April 1884 by excellent roads. Not

[1] See "Travels in the Footsteps of Bruce."

an armed Khomiri was to be seen. The men were all engaged in ploughing the land for next season's crops, while the women were clearing the weeds from among the growing corn; all seemed to have a friendly word or salutation for him, and he saw none of the black looks and scowls which he had noticed on his former journey. The appearance of the people, however, was lean and miserable; they were covered with disgusting rags, and their huts were of the most squalid description, hardly comparable to any save those in use amongst a savage people like the Andaman Islanders.

La Calle should be taken as the starting-point for this expedition, and the traveller may either go to Aïn-Draham by the direct carriage road, or make a detour to Tabarca, and so to Aïn-Draham. The latter cannot well be done, save on horseback, as the carriage road which was commenced, and indeed almost completed as far as Tabarca, never was continued. The latter is highly to be recommended, the scenery is varied and beautiful; but accommodation at Tabarca cannot always be depended on. We give this route, but the traveller should inquire at La Calle if it be practicable.

After leaving La Calle the coast runs E.N.E. through fine cork forests, and then skirts the lake of *Tonga* or *Guerrah el Hout* (Lake of Fish). This is an immense freshwater marsh in summer, although a lake in winter; it is most pestilential, and its influence is felt as far as La Calle.

7 kil. *Oued Messida.* This stream is the communication from the lake into the sea. It forms a small creek much frequented by coral boats; the English steamers anchor off it and take in their cargo of ore, which is brought down from the mines by a line of railway. Beyond is a hill called *Kef Chetob* by the Arabs and *Monte Rotondo* by the Europeans; from its isolation and conical form it is a very prominent feature in the landscape.

13 kil. *Kef om-et-Tcboul.* A little village which has sprung up around the mines of the same name. They produce argentiferous and auriferous lead and zinc ore, all of which is shipped to Swansea. During 1883 twenty steam vessels took on board upwards of 26,000 tons of ore.

Here the direct road to Aïn-Draham continues to the S.E.; that to Tabarca branches off to the N.E. through a wild and mountainous country, intersected by deep ravines, and covered with dense brushwood, with here and there patches of forest containing oak of various species and maritime pine. It crosses the frontier at some distance from the sea, passing over the high range of hills which terminates in Cape Roux; it then descends to the coast, which is here beautifully indented, with charming views of land and water at every turn, till at last the island of Tabarca and the Bordj Djedid, high above the town, come in view.

36 kil. **Tabarca** (see p. 130).

After leaving Tabarca the road ascends the broad valley of the Oued-el-Kebir, nearly due south. The ground, wherever possible, is cultivated, and will one day no doubt be opened out to European colonisation. At present, like all plains in North Africa when undrained and only cultivated in the rudimentary manner employed by the Arabs, it is very unhealthy, but in due time this will be remedied. No places could have been worse or are now better than many parts of the Metidja near Algiers.

All over the country there are ruins of Roman farms or fortified positions; for the most part they are merely heaps of stone, though generally of large blocks finely cut. One of these, 5 kil. from Tabarca, is of a more important character; part of the walls and one-arched gateway are still standing; it is close to the river, and is called *Kasr Zeitoun*, "Palace of the Olive Tree," from a group of gigantic olive trees which grow around it and in its deserted chambers.

17 kil. from Tabarca is the *Oued Kerma*, a beautiful clear stream, so called from a large fig tree growing near it. A road bifurcating to the N.E. leads to the *Camp de Genie*. Beyond the scenery becomes wilder and

more beautiful, consisting of great stretches of oak forest interspersed with glades of cleared and cultivated land.

26 kil. *Col de Babouch.* The junction of this road with that leading up from Kef om-et-Teboul, where is a Tunisian custom-house. The road now passes through a forest of the most splendid oak trees, the branches of which are covered with moss and ferns. The effect of the bright green ferns on the silver gray boughs of these gigantic trees is most striking; indeed the whole route forms a series of studies for a landscape painter. At last Aïn-Draham comes suddenly in sight, perched high above, on a bleak hillside, its regular houses and huts of wood with red-tiled roofs forming by no means a pleasing contrast to the beauty of the landscape through which the traveller has passed.

31 kil. **Aïn-Draham.** This post is situated at 41 kil. from La Calle by the high road passing *Om-et-Teboul, El-Aioun,* and the *Col de Babouch;* it is 800 mètres above the level of the sea, and is well supplied with water from the "Spring of Money," whence its name, and other fountains. Before the French expedition it was perfectly uninhabited, but immediately after that event it was occupied by a garrison of 3000 men under a general of brigade, now it has been reduced to a small detachment, to the despair of the numerous auberge and store keepers who have settled here, and who can have no possible occupation but that of supplying the troops and feeding the officers.

No attempt at defence has been made, no redoubt, no retrenchment, or even the simplest walled enclosure. The barracks of the soldiers and the houses of the settlers cover a considerable extent of ground, and although the Khomair have been disarmed, no one really supposes them to be destitute of weapons. Insurrections have occurred in Algeria under more unlikely circumstances, and it is not impossible that some day a rising of this warlike tribe may temporarily endanger French supremacy.

It is impossible not to be struck by the extraordinary results which have followed the French Protectorate in this once inaccessible region. Admirable roads have been made in all directions, and no serious fears need ever be entertained for the permanent security of the country.

The view from Aïn-Draham is remarkably fine, especially towards the sea; one sees down the whole length of the valley through which the road passes, and the Galita islands, not visible from Tabarca, appear as if they were only a few miles distant.

An excellent road conducts to Souk el-Arbaa; but as carriages are rarely procurable here, the traveller must make his arrangements before leaving La Calle. The first part of the road lies through splendid oak forests; but as it descends these gradually become replaced by brushwood, and finally by open undulating ground more or less cultivated.

5 kil. *Fedj el-Meridj.* A small grassy meadow nestled amongst wooded hills. This evidently was a Roman post, as in the centre of it is a mound of stones; the best have been taken for the construction of the road; but a milliary column has been spared and erected on a plinth. It bears the names of Constantine and Licinius, thus fixing the date prior to the defeat of the latter in A.D. 323. It also bears the number xviii., probably *millia passuum* from Bulla Regia.

20 kil. *Fernana.* This place derives its name from a gigantic cork oak, the only tree within several miles. It is on the southern boundary of the Khomair country, and used to be the extreme limit to which the Bey's camp was permitted to come in its annual circuit for the collection of taxes. Here the chiefs used to meet it and hand over such sums as they felt disposed to pay; if the Tunisian soldiery advanced a step farther the taxes were liable to be paid with powder and lead.

After the occupation of Aïn-Draham a strong column encamped here for many months, and it has left a memorial of its stay in a large and crowded cemetery. There is an auberge or shanty here, at which it is possible to breakfast but not to spend the night.

Close to Fernana, and again at the *douar* below mentioned, are found two milliary columns of Trajan's road to Tabarca. "*Imp. Cæsar divi Trajani Parthic. fil. divi Nervæ nep. Trajanus Hadrianus aug. Pontif. max. trib. potest xiii. Cos. iii. p. p. viam a Simittu usq. Thabracam fec.*"

35 kil. *Dowar ef El-Hadj bel Kassem ben Zorari.* Opposite this a cross country path, but one quite practicable for carriages, branches off to the east, and leads to the important Roman ruins of **Bulla Regia** (see p. 302).

42 kil. **Souk el-Arbäa** (see p. 302).

ROUTE 30.

Tunis to El-Kef via Souk el-Arbäa.

This can be done in one day. Leave Tunis by the early train at 5 A.M., arrive at Souk el-Arbäa at 10.49. Start by diligence at 3 P.M., and arrive at El-Kef about 8 P.M. The diligence has six seats, and is not generally well horsed. The traveller should not fail to take provisions for the way.

The road from **Souk el-Arbäa** runs directly south over the plains of the Medjerda.

9 kil. It crosses the *Oued Mellegue*, an affluent of that river, at a place fordable in summer but in the winter months a ferry boat has to be used. Extensive remains of Roman farmhouses are seen, but nothing of special interest. The road gradually ascends the mountains through a vast tract of heath-land, partly cultivated, and affording pasturage for numerous flocks of sheep and goats. The view of the plain round Bulla Regia and of the Khomair mountains is very extensive.

28 kil. Resting-place for horses in connection with the diligence service.

About a mile to the west is the picturesque Arab village of **Nebeur**, where once stood a Roman *Castellum*, dependant on the colony of Sicca; close by is a magnificent olive grove, and the white koubba of *Sidi Bou Jabar*. On the hill behind the resting-place is the ruined koubba of *Sidi Merzoug*, built of pre-existing Roman work. Several inscriptions have been found here, amongst others one showing that justice was administered here by one of the supreme magistrates of Sicca. There are also many fragments of cornices belonging to the Ionic order, and several moulded stones. From its commanding position this was probably a military post of some importance.

There are two roads from Nebeur to El-Kef; one by the plains, 38 kil., of easy ascent, but little used. The other over the mountains, 18 kil., very bad and steep; in some parts scarcely passable for carriages. A new road has been commenced at the Kef end, but it has apparently been abandoned.

38 kil. Here the road, after a long ascent, becomes more level; scenery wild and mountainous; on the right commences a long range of precipitous limestone rock, rising in some parts nearly 200 feet above the road. Here, at its greatest altitude, the French have established an optical telegraph station, visible at El-Meridj and Aïn-Draham. The panoramic view is most extensive; on the left one overlooks the field of Zama, the exact position of which city is still a mystery; in front the eye traces all the Tunisian frontier.

45 kil. Here the road, still following the precipice on the right, takes a sudden turn towards the west, and the walls of El-Kef come in view, the Kasba only being seen above them.

46 kil. After passing the Arab and Jewish cemeteries, you enter either the upper or lower eastern gate.

El-Kef. The ancient city of SICCA VENERIA, or later *Colonia Julia Cirta Nova*, of which El-Kef occupies the site, was much larger than the modern town; it was one of the most important places in Punic territory long before the Roman conquest of the country, and was probably founded by a colony of Phœnicians, who introduced into it the worship of the Asiatic Venus, which subsequently gave the place so evil a repute. As no traveller should visit the Alhambra without studying Washington Irving's tales, so the visitor to this interesting spot will find a picture of what were probably the manners and customs of the early Christians and their oppressors here, in the pages of Cardinal Newman's beautiful tale, "Callista."

The city, as at present existing, is of irregular shape, enclosed by loopholed walls, and built on the steep slope of a rock (whence its name) facing the S.W., and immediately under the precipitous crag above mentioned. It is a veritable city in the air, a mere excrescence on the rock. It is essentially Arab, the European population numbering under 100, mostly Maltese. The entire population is estimated at 4000. The streets are dirty and ill-paved, but owing to its position, and being well supplied with water, the town is easily washed. The rich plains below have contributed to the prosperity of the inhabitants, but at present many dwellings are unoccupied and in ruins. The town is built entirely with the remains of the Roman city, portions of which still lie below the surface. There are many Roman inscriptions built into the walls of Arab houses, and therefore difficult of access. The principal remains consist of fragments of a *temple* of large dimensions, but of coarse ornamentation; near it were lately found the white marble statues of two emperors and of an empress, but without heads, and two without arms. The *Thermæ* can still be traced, the masonry is of large blocks put together with very little mortar, the openings in the walls being spanned with lintels of great size, many of the stones being more than 2½ mètres long. The walls are fairly perfect up to the spring of the vaulting, and the apsidal end of a chamber, with its flat rib vaulting, is quite perfect, and is now the residence of an Arab.

The *Kasba*, occupied by the French, and forming the pinnacle of the city, is of Roman construction. The town has six gates and six mosques, but of no pretentions exteriorly.

Outside the walls are the old Roman *cisterns*, they are constructed on a platform above the Kasba, and immediately under the precipitous rock before mentioned. They consist of 13 vaulted chambers side by side, 27 mètres long, nearly 7 mètres wide, and 6·40 deep. Except where the vaulting has been broken through they are fairly perfect, the cement lining being in many parts as sound as when it was applied. Some of these chambers are used by the soldiers for gymnastic purposes, one being styled "Salle de billard," and another "Salle d'escrime." These cisterns were supplied from a spring in the rock, and were connected with the fountain within the walls by a short tunnel, which is still perfect, but closed up. The city is now supplied from the same source, and a line of pipes communicate with the fountains. The supply is never ceasing, it comes splashing in at the rate of many thousand gallons a minute, and there is always a busy gathering of men and women, horses and cattle, in the little sloping square in front of it.

Outside the E. gate are *cemeteries*; the tombstones of the small Jewish burial-ground are mostly Roman, some with the Latin inscriptions still legible. The Christian cemetery, close by, is the site of an old Christian basilica, about 27 mètres long and 15 wide. The shafts dividing the nave and aisles appear to have been of gray marble, 0·51 mètre in diameter. The external walls were very thick, those of the apse being 0·50 mètre; all of large blocks from the Roman town, and some of them inscribed.

The French Government has done wisely in erecting barracks for the troops outside the Arab town, on the highest ground, close to the Kasba, and well sheltered between the city walls and the upper range of rocks, forming a plateau at the top of the mountain.

There is a carriage road from El-Kef to Souk-Ahras, and a horse track to El-Meridj.

ROUTE 31.

Excursion to Bizerta and Utica.

The road leaves Tunis by the Bab el-Khadera, passes under the Spanish aqueduct behind the Bardo, the ancient Palace of the Beys, and the Kasr es-Saeed, the late Bey's favourite residence, and soon enters a wood of ancient and extremely picturesque olive trees.

11 kil. A wayside fountain and Arab coffee-shop called *Es-Sabala*, near a palace built by the celebrated Saheb-et-Tabäa, under Hamouda Pacha.

Beyond this commences a long alluvial plain, which, broken up by several low ranges of hills, extends to the very gates of Bizerta; it is of great fertility, and tolerably well cultivated.

23 kil. *El Fonduk*. Here the Medjerda is crossed by a bridge which was built about 1850 on the site of an old Roman one. It is a solid structure of seven arches, with a niche between each pair, pierced so as to admit the passage of water when the floods are high. The original structure was entire when Peysonnel visited it in 1724; it was a tolerably good one, he says, but the arches were badly constructed. This river rises in the beautiful valley of Khamisa, in Algeria, amongst the ruins of Thubursicum Numidarum (p. 233), and traverses some of the richest parts of Tunis—districts rendered celebrated by many of the most stirring events in Roman history. It is none other than the far-famed Bagradas, on the banks of which took place the combat between the army of Attilius Regulus and the monstrous serpent, 225 years before Christ. Pliny repeats the fable as one well known in his day. They besieged it, says he, with ballista and implements of war, as one would have done to a city. It was 120 ft. long, and its skin and jaws were preserved in a temple at Rome until the Numantine war.

The Medjerda has greatly changed its course within the limits of history: indeed, it is constantly cutting through the banks of alluvium, and depositing the *débris* elsewhere. In winter a considerable body of water enters the sea, but after continued rain it becomes a raging torrent, and even a passing shower will sometimes suffice to wash away sheep and cattle, and even travellers.

The plain on the right bank of the river at this place goes by the name of Outa el-Kebir, or the large plain; that on the left is Outa es-Segheir, or the smaller one, while the crossing itself is called El-Fonduk, from an inn on its bank, more dirty and repulsive than such places generally are.

27 kil. A second and smaller bridge is passed, spanning a watercourse running along the southern base of Dj.Zana. From this point the road to Bou-Chater, the ancient **Utica**, branches off.

[The traveller will find it impossible to visit this place and continue his route to Bizerta the same day; he must either make a separate excursion here, or return from Bizerta by Porto Farina and Utica. The former, called by the Arabs Ghar-el-Melah, is situated on the north shore of the *Bahira*, or lake into which the Medjerda now empties itself. This lake was at one time the winter station of the Tunisian Navy, but the alluvium brought down by the river is rapidly filling it up, and now it has been entirely abandoned as a commercial or military port. The Boghaz, or strait connecting it with the sea, has become quite sanded up, so that it is passable only for vessels of the smallest size. These changes in the physical condition of the delta of the Medjerda have taken place within a comparatively recent period. Porto Farina continued to be a place of considerable importance long after the date of Blake's action, one of the most brilliant victories in the history of the British Navy (see p. 43).

The wretched little village of *Bou-Chater* to the S.W. indicates the site of the celebrated city of *Utica*, one of the first founded in Africa; the signification of the name is *The Ancient*. When later Phœnician colonists founded Carthage, Utica still maintained its importance, though it was obliged to submit to the supremacy of the younger city. In B.C. 300 it fell into the power of Agathocles, and it subsequently played an important part in all the Punic Wars, but it is especially famous as being the scene of the unnecessary self-sacrifice of Cato (see p. 25). It continued to exist till the Mohammedan invasion, when it lost not only its being, but its name, and was thereafter known by that of Bou-Chater. The ruins still existing of the ancient city are not very extensive or interesting. A deep excavation marks the site of the amphitheatre. Some fragments of walls exist, the sole remains of the admiral's palace, built on an island in the ancient port, now filled in by the Medjerda, and the whole site is covered with fragments of marble, bricks, and pottery. Some very interesting inscriptions and antiquities were recently found here and exhibited in one of the rooms of the Louvre.[1]]

41 kil. *Bir Attaka*. Beyond Djebel Zana is another wide plain, called Bahirah Gournata, in the middle of which is a well, a convenient halting-place for breakfast.

The hill which bounds the north side of this plain is Djebel Tella; at its foot is a small stream; and from its summit the first view is obtained of the sea and the Lake of Bizerta, along the eastern bank of which the road now runs.

56 kil. *Menzel Djemil*, well named the *beautiful resting-place*, despite the filth with which it is surrounded. The narrow neck of land which here separates the lake from the sea is a perfect garden, covered with plantations of fruit and olive trees and fields of corn.

63 kil. **Bizerta.** Its name is a corruption of the Arab one *Binzerte*, which is as evidently derived from the ancient one *Hippo Zarytus* or *Diarrhytus*, so named to distinguish it from its neighbour, *Hippo Regius*, the modern Bône.

It was an ancient Tyrian colony, and was fortified and provided with a new harbour by Agathocles, in the 4th century B.C. It was subsequently raised to the rank of a Roman Colony, as is testified by an inscription built into the wall of Bordj Sidi Bou-Hadid, containing the ancient name of the place,—COL. IVLIAE. HIPP. DIARR.

[1] Consult Comte d'Hérisson, *Relation d'une Mission Archéologique en Tunisie*. Paris, 4to, 1881. Also, *Recherches sur l'origine et l'emplacement des Emporia Phéniciens*. Par M. A. Daux. Paris, 4to, 1868.

El-Bekri mentions that this place was conquered in A.H. 41 (A.D. 661-2) by Moaonia ibn el Hodaidj. Abd el Melek ibn Merouan, who accompanied him in this expedition, having been separated from the main body of the army, obtained shelter in the house of a native woman. When he became Khalifa, he wrote to his lieutenant in Ifrikia to take care of this woman and all her family - an order which was of course carried out.

Marmol says that although the city contained only 4000 inhabitants they frequently revolted against the kings of Tunis and the lords of Constantine, which was often the cause of their ruin. When Kheir-ed-din took possession of Tunis, they were the first to recognise him, and when he was expelled they killed the governor whom Mulai Hassan had sent with a garrison, and received a Turkish garrison into their fort. Mulai Hassan attacked the place by land, while Andrea Doria co-operated with him by sea, and so the place was taken by assault—"et le Roy chastia rigoureusement les habitans qui s'estoient revoltez trois fois et qui n'avoient jamais gardé la foy ni par amour ni par crainte."

It can hardly be said that Bizerta is in a very flourishing condition; still, the presence of 200 Europeans amongst its population of 5000 souls gives a certain amount of life and commercial activity to it, which no purely Mohammedan city appears to possess.

The situation of the town is extremely picturesque, being built on each side of the canal which connects the lake with the sea, and on an island in the middle of it, principally occupied by Europeans, and joined to the mainland on either side by substantial bridges. The town is entirely surrounded by walls, the entrance to the canal being protected by what in former times would have been considered formidable defences. That on the west is the Kasba or citadel; that on the opposite side is the fort of Sidi el-Hounî, containing the shrine of that holy man. Between these the canal is embanked. The foundations are, no doubt, ancient, though the superstructure is modern.

The west wall is produced as a breakwater, but it is very ruinous, and has evidently projected much farther into the sea than it does at present. Its length is not sufficient to prevent the sand being drifted in by the north-west winds, whereby the canal has been so much filled up as to render it practicable only for light fishing-boats. Near the gate of the Kasba may be seen the chain formerly used to protect the entrance. To the west of the town is an isolated fort called Bordj Sidi Salim, built on a rocky promontory jutting out into the sea.

A few French troops are usually stationed here, some in the old Arab forts, and others in barracks built on the high ground outside the city.

The important feature of Bizerta, however, is its lake, now called *Mazouka* by the Arabs, formerly Hipponitus Pallus, which in the hands of a European power might become one of the finest harbours and one of the most important strategical positions in the Mediterranean. Its length from E. to W. is about 13 kil. and its width 9, but the shallow portion which passes through the town is less than a mile in length, with a depth of from 2 to 10 ft. Beyond, it widens out, and has a depth equal to that of the lake, from 5 to 7 fathoms. A comparatively slight expenditure would be required to convert this lake into a perfectly landlocked harbour, containing 50 square miles of anchorage for the largest vessels afloat. At present the anchorage off the entrance is very insecure; vessels are compelled to remain in the open roadstead and at a considerable distance from the town, and there is no shelter from the prevailing bad winds. The lake teems with excellent fish.

In 1888 the exclusive right of fishing here, at Porto Farina, and the Goletta (the last two places comparatively unimportant), was let by the Tunisian Government for £6750 a year. During two days that the writer remained there, 10,000 dorados, weighing about 10 tons, and worth £400 at Tunis, after deducting all expenses, were caught in the lake; and 5000 large mullets, of about 1¼ lb. each, and worth £100, at the canal of Tinja, between the two lakes.

To the S.W. of this lake is another nearly as large, but with a depth of from 2 to 8 ft. only. It is the ancient Sisara, now called the Gharat Djebel Ishkul, or lake of Mount Ishkul, a remarkable hill of 1740 ft. high, situated at its southern extremity, the Kirna Mons of Ptolemy. This, no doubt, was originally an island, as it is now only separated from the mainland by a stretch of marshy ground. The water is almost sweet in winter, when a considerable body is poured into it by the Oued Djoumin or river of Mater, but in summer, when the level sinks, the overflow from the said lake pours into it by the Oued Tinja, a tortuous canal which connects the two, and then its waters are not potable. The water is generally very turbid, owing to the washing of the clay banks on its margin and the muddy streams flowing in from the plains of Mater. This lake also abounds in fish.

The Oued Tinja is navigable for boats of not more than 2 ft. draught. Its general depth is 6 ft., and its breadth 25 yards, but at the entrance to the lake of Djebel Ishkul there are shallows with a very rapid current, against which a boat has great difficulty in contending. Above the shallows there is a ferry, opposite the marabout of Sidi El-Hasoun, which is completely enveloped by a small grove of trees. This spot appears also to have been the site of an ancient town, as there are Roman remains on both sides of the ferry.

The vicinity abounds in game, and on Djebel Ishkul itself there are a number of wild buffaloes, introduced by a former Bey, which are very strictly preserved.

ROUTE 32.

Excursion to Zaghouan and Oudena.

This expedition can be done in two days, in a carriage and four, which ought not to cost more than 50 f.

There is an inn, *Hôtel Boulanger*, at Zaghouan, where it is quite possible to sleep; it is in a fine old Arab house, with some good tile and plaster work. No provisions of any kind are obtainable on the road.

The traveller leaves Tunis by the Bab Alleoua, by a road which has been cut through an Arab cemetery surrounding the shrine of Sidi Ali ben Ahsan. The heights above are crowned by the picturesque forts, which are prominent objects in the landscape from every point of view round Tunis. The ground being somewhat undulating the great salt marsh or lake, called Sebkha es-Sedjoumi, which extends to 8 kil. to the south-west of the town, is concealed from sight till its southern extremity is approached. During the winter months this contains a considerable body of water, but in summer it becomes little more than a fetid marsh, with a broad efflorescence of salt around its margin.

At 17 kil. from Tunis is the Mohammedia, an immense ruined palace, or rather a mass of palaces, built by Ahmed Bey, who died in 1855, at an expense of many millions of piastres, and decorated with great magnificence, but which since his death has been allowed to go to decay. It has served as an inexhaustible mine for materials with which to build and adorn other palaces; its marble columns have disappeared, its walls have been stripped of their covering of tiles, the roofs have nearly all fallen in, and it is impossible to imagine a more perfect picture of desolation than is presented by this modern ruin.

The aqueduct from Zaghouan passes through one of the courts of the palace, but it is here low, and by no means a striking object.

Beyond, at short distances, may be noticed what seems to be small koubbas; these are inspection chambers, to facilitate the repairs of the aqueduct.

Shortly after leaving the Mohammedia the ruins of the ancient aqueduct come in sight, and at a distance of about 22 kil. from Tunis the road crosses the Oued Melian, the Catada of Ptolemy. Here is seen, in all its surpassing beauty, one of the greatest works the Romans ever executed in North Africa, the aqueduct conveying the waters of Zaghouan and Djougar to Carthage.

During all the time that Carthage remained an independent State the inhabitants seemed to have contented themselves with rain water, caught and stored in reservoirs, both from the roofs of houses and from paved squares and streets. Thirty years after the destruction of this city by Scipio it was rebuilt by a colony under Caius Gracchus; but it was not till the reign of the Emperor Hadrian (A.D. 117 to 138) that the inhabitants, having recovered their ancient wealth, and, having suffered from several consecutive years of drought, represented their miserable condition to the Emperor, who himself visited the city, and resolved to convey to it the magnificent springs of Zengitanus Mons, the modern Zaghouan. This, however, was not sufficient for the supply of the city, and after the death of Hadrian another fine spring at Mons Zuccharus, the present Djebel Djougar, was led into the original aqueduct — probably in the reign of Septimius Severus, as a medal was found at Carthage with his figure on the reverse, and on the obverse Astarte seated on a lion beside a spring issuing from a rock.

It was certainly destroyed by Gilimer, the last of the Vandal kings, when endeavouring to reconquer Carthage, and again restored by Belisarius, the lieutenant of Justinian. On the expulsion of the Byzantines it was once more cut off and restored by their Arab conquerors, and finally destroyed by the Spaniards during their siege of Tunis. It was reserved for the late Bey, Mohammed es-Sadik, once more to restore this ancient work, and to bring the pure and abundant springs which formerly supplied Carthage into the modern city of Tunis.

M. Collin, a French engineer, planned and executed this work. Of course the advanced state of hydraulic science at the present day rendered it unnecessary to make use of the ancient arches. The aqueduct originally consisted, for a great part of its course, of a covered masonry channel, running sometimes quite underground, sometimes on the surface. This was comparatively uninjured by time, and served, with little repair, for the modern work. Where the old aqueduct passed high over the surface of the country iron pipes and syphons have been substituted.

The contract price was 7,800,000 f., but the work cost the Bey nearly 13,000,000 f.; and, useful as it certainly is, there is no doubt that it was the commencement of his financial difficulties.

The original aqueduct started from two springs, those of Zaghouan and Djougar; and to within 26 kil. of the present city of Tunis—namely, to the south side of the plain of the Catada—it simply followed the general slope of the ground without being raised on arches. From this point, right across that plain—a distance of 3 Roman miles, or 7 kil.—with slight intermissions, owing to the rise in the ground, and so on to the terminal reservoir at the modern village of Määlika, it was carried over a superb series of arches—sometimes, indeed, over a double tier. The total length of the aqueduct was 61 Roman m., including the branch from Mons Zuccharus, which measured 22 m.; and it was estimated to have conveyed 32,000,000 litres (upwards of 7,000,000 gallons) of water a day, or 81 gallons per second, for the supply of Carthage and the intermediate country.

The greatest difference is perceptible in the style of construction, owing to the frequent restorations which have taken place. The oldest and most beautiful portions are of finely-cut stone, each course having a height of 0·50 mètre; the stones are bossed, with a squared channel worked at the joints, and the voussoirs are single stones reaching quite to the bottom of the specus, in which there exist, at intervals all along its course, circular manholes, both to admit air and to permit the repair and cleansing of the channel.

A great part of the aqueduct, however, is built in a far less solid manner—of concrete blocks or rubble masonry. In some places, at the angles, or where danger threatened, rough and massive counterforts have been erected to strengthen it. Along the plain of the Oued Melian, in a length of nearly 3 kil., the author counted 344 arches still entire. Since then a number have been destroyed to metal a new military road which has never been completed!

The aqueduct passed the river on a double series of arches. These were all destroyed in order to make use of their foundations for the modern bridge which now carries the water across, and serves at the same time as a viaduct.

From this point to Carthage, along the plains of the Mohammedia, the Manouba, and Ariana, the ancient aqueduct is nearly ruined, and its stones have been used in the construction of Tunis. (See also p. 304.)

Leaving the Oued Melian, the road to Zaghouan follows the line of the aqueduct; but a détour to the east may be made to visit the ruins of **Oudena**, the ancient city of Uthina.

Between the aqueduct and Oudena may be seen a long line of megalithic monuments.

The traveller will be well rewarded by a visit to Oudena. The view from the site of the ancient Uthina commands a vast extent of country. On the N. is the bay of Tunis, the hill of Carthage, and the slopes of Djebel Ahmar; on the S. the rugged Djebel Ressas, constructed by a range of lower hills with the towering Djebel Zaghouan; on the W. is the long broken line of the great aqueduct, in its stately march across the plain.

The present condition of the ruins proves it to have been a place of very considerable importance; they cover an area of several miles, and it must certainly have contained a very large population.

Pélissier imagines this to have been the Tricamaron where Belisarius overcame Gilimer, and where all the hoarded treasure of the Vandals and the piratical spoil of Genseric fell into the hands of the Byzantines.

The central and highest point in the city was crowned by a **Citadel** covering an area of about 60 mètres long and 30 wide. The entrance-gate was on the N.W. front, facing the amphitheatre. The walls were of great thickness and constructed of large blocks of cut stone.

The upper terrace was surrounded by a parapet; below were several chambers with strong vaulted roofs, still nearly entire. The largest of these measures 20 mètres long by 10 wide. The vaults are supported on square piers, with a very bold and massive cornice, each stone being 0·60 mètre in breadth, 0·76 in height, and 0·92 thick. On the northern side is a large arch 7 mètres in diameter, loosely filled up with squared stones. From the centre of this a passage about 0·92 mètre in width runs perpendicular to it, and after a distance of about 5 mètres the passage bifurcates to the right and left, and descends at an angle of 45° till it reaches a vast subterranean apartment, which encircles the whole building, and was no doubt intended to serve as a reservoir. The descent is very difficult, owing to the accumulation of *débris*; but the chamber appears to have been about 4 to 6 mètres high, and nearly as much in width, occupying three sides of a square, of which the passages before mentioned formed the fourth side.

To the N.W. of this building is a very perfect **Amphitheatre**, with an elliptical arena; the major axis is about 70 mètres in length, and the minor one 50. Four principal entrances led into it, and these, together with many of the upper arches, are still in a tolerably perfect condition. No doubt, in the construction of this, advantage was taken of a natural depression on the top of a mamelon in which it is sunk.

Behind this monument, towards the N., may be seen a small **Bridge** of three arches, spanning the bed of a watercourse.

To the S.W. of the citadel are the remains of a **Theatre**, and to the S.E. of it two very magnificent reservoirs, the northern one intended to contain rain-water, but that to the S. was supplied from a well at some little distance, between which and the reservoir are the remains of a solidly-constructed aqueduct.

Perhaps **the most remarkable of the ruins** is one due E. of the citadel; it must have been a building of immense size, but it is impossible from its present appearance to form any conjecture as to its original destination. The walls, which were built of rubble masonry, of great thickness, have been rent asunder into huge masses, too large to have been moved by any mere mechanical power likely to have been employed, and yet they lie scattered about, without any apparent order, in every direction.

Underneath these is a series of reservoirs of immense height and size, separated by partitions, yet connected together by arched passages; access is gained by a very narrow hole in the side of one of them; the masonry throughout is quite perfect; not a trace is visible of any great convulsion of nature, which alone, one would think, could have effected the ruin of the superincumbent building.

Twenty minutes more takes the traveller from Oudena to the southern end of the plain spanned by the aqueduct, where is a domed building, from which the syphon of the modern aqueduct starts; this is 26 kil. from Tunis, and 33 from Zaghouan.

From this spot the road continues through an undulating country overgrown with brushwood. After a few kil. the ruins of a Roman post are passed, called by the Arabs Bab Khalid, the ancient name of which is unknown. At 47 kil. from Tunis is the spot called Magaran, where the two sources from Zaghouan and Djougar unite, and are conveyed in a single stream to Tunis, as they formerly were to Carthage.

The former source will be described hereafter; the latter, Aïn Djougar, is situated 37 kil. farther to the W., close to the village of Bent Saïda, which occupies the site of the ancient Zucchara Civitas. Like the other, this one also issued from a monumental fountain, now in a very bad state of preservation, but when visited by

Shaw the frieze of the building still existed, and bore the following inscription:—

..... RORISII TOTIVSQVE DIVINAE DOMVS EIVS CIVITAS ZVCCHARA FECIT ET DEDICAVIT.

At Magaran there is a very neat house, surrounded by a garden, occupied by the French employé in charge of the waterworks. About 6 kil. farther on, and 53 from Tunis, is the village of **Zaghouan**, the ancient *Zeugis*, which gave its name to *Zeugitana*, or the province of Africa proper. The modern town occupies the same site as the ancient one, the crest of a spur proceeding from the north-east side of the mountain bearing the same name. The only ruin of any importance is the entrance-gate, called Bab el-Goos, which, no doubt, served the same purpose to the ancient city.

After the first destruction of Zaghouan it was rebuilt by a colony of Andalusian Moors from Spain; but, notwithstanding its exceptionally favourable position and the abundance of its water supply, it appears to be falling into decay; half the houses are ruined, and there is no appearance of any modern construction going on.

The principal industry of Zaghouan for many generations has been the dyeing of the red caps worn in all Mohammedan countries throughout the basin of the Mediterranean, and here called *chachias*. In Turkey such a cap is called *fez*, and in Egypt *tarboosh*. This is the only place in the Regency where the operation has ever been performed, and the secret is carefully preserved, and descends from father to son. A military post is established here, which is generally commanded by a captain.

The great interest of the place to the traveller is its vicinity to the springs from which the aqueduct is supplied; the distance is about 2½ kil., and there are two paths, one of which the traveller would do well to take in going and the other in returning, or he may go the whole way in a carriage. The first passes to the S. of the delicious valley which runs east and west behind the town, and close to the spring *Ain Ayat*, which is the cause of its fertility; the other follows its northern border between it and the hill on which the shrine of Sidi Hashlaf is built. This valley is richly cultivated, and produces great quantities of fruit trees; the waters of Ain Ayat are also used to turn a few flour-mills.

The great source, however, which flows into the aqueduct issues from a spot a little farther on, where are situated the remains of a charming Roman temple, known to the natives by the name of El-Kasba, or the fortress.

The building is extremely elegant, and in its original condition must have been one of the most charming retreats which it is possible to imagine. It is situated at the gorge of a narrow and precipitous ravine descending from Djebel Zaghouan, but at a very considerable elevation above the plain at its foot.

It consists of a paved area of a semicircular form, but with the two exterior limbs produced in straight lines as tangents. Round the perimeter was a raised colonnade, and at the end, in the middle of the circular portion, was a rectangular cella, which is still tolerably entire. The walls of this latter building are of rubble masonry, but at the extremity there is a niche lined with cut stone, surmounting what may either have been the base of a statue of an emperor or an altar to a divinity. Probably the former, as the mutilated trunk of such a statue, in white marble, and of colossal size, was actually lying on the ground outside at the time of the writer's visit; this has now disappeared. Above the door are the remains of a beautiful architrave, which doubtless was surmounted by a pediment. To the right and left of this proceeded a lateral gallery, 4 mètres broad. The posterior wall was of finely-cut stone, with thirteen square pilasters on each side, between every alternate pair of which a round-headed niche for statuary was sunk in the thickness of the wall. Towards the interior a Corinthian column corresponded to each of the pilasters, but these have long since been removed, and now decorate the interior of the principal mosque of

Zaghouan. Each end of this colonnade was terminated with a handsome gateway; and from the lower surface of the area on either side a flight of fifteen steps conducted to a basin or nymphæum, shaped like a double horseshoe; in this the spring rose, and was conducted into the aqueduct. The spring is no longer visible, being led into the modern aqueduct before it emerges from the ground.

The colonnade was roofed by one general half-cylindrical vault in the direction of the length of the building, intersected by twelve other transversely directed cylindrical vaults rising from the pilasters in the walls and the columns in front. A cornice of a bold outline ran all round, serving as impost to the vaults and ornamental doorways, and as capitals to the pilasters. A great portion of the vaults supported by the walls still remain, to show the nature of the construction.

The rear of the wall was strengthened exteriorly by a coating of immense blocks of cut stone, to protect it from any rush of water which might flow from the ravine above, after heavy rain. There is also a communication from the colonnade to the exterior by means of a small square-headed door in the posterior wall.

The whole of this monument has now been enclosed within a wall to ensure its preservation, so that the traveller who may wish to visit it must apply to the office of the Company in Tunis for an order to enter; this should be delivered to the employé above-mentioned at Magaran.

A magnificent view is obtained by mounting the hill immediately south of the town, crossing the valley watered by the Aïn Ayat; and a still finer one by climbing to the top of Djebel Zaghouan, which may easily be done by spending an extra day at this place.

A heliographic station has been established on the summit of Djebel Zaghouan, which commands an uninterrupted view of the country round in every direction as far as Susa, Kerouan, etc.

ROUTE 33.

Voyage along the Coast of Tunis from the Goletta to the Island of Djerba.

Excellent steamers of the *Compagnie Transatlantique* and of the *Compagnie Générale Italienne* run from the Goletta every week, visiting the principal ports on the coast as far as Tripoli, and thence crossing to Malta. The days and hours of sailing should be ascertained at Tunis.

Vessels pass between the Island of Zembra and Cape Bon, or Ras Adar, the Hermean promontory, beyond which the Carthaginians so often stipulated that no Roman ships should pass. This is the extreme eastern point of the Dakhul, or large tongue of land which extends in a N.E. direction between the Gulfs of Tunis and Hammamet. On this cape is a remarkably fine red intermittent light, which can be seen for a distance of 25 m.

At a distance of 58 m. from the Goletta, following the vessel's track, is **Kelebia**, a small and clean town, situated about a mile from the sea.

To the N. of the landing-place may still be traced the ruins of the ancient *Clypea*, founded by Agathocles in B.C. 310; the first position occupied by Regulus on his arrival in Africa B.C. 256, and, according to El-Bekri, the last city which remained in the possession of the Christians after the Mohammedan invasion.

This is dominated by a hill 270 ft. high, called *Aspis* by Strabo, on account of its resemblance to a shield. The summit is crowned by the *Kasr Kelibia*, a fine Spanish fortress, the exterior walls of which are in good condition, though the interior is ruinous. In the centre may still be seen part of the Roman Acropolis, a keep of finely cut masonry surrounding a magnificent reservoir, the terraced roof of which is supported by nearly 100 monolithic pillars; its depth is about 8 mètres, and when the writer visited it at the end of the hot season it contained 2½ mètres of water.

On the hill itself are two marabouts, those of Sidi Ali Makadam and Sidi Khurfash, and on the point below, near the ruins of a battery, is a third, dedicated to Sidi Mustafa, which has given its name to the small bay, once a Roman harbour.

Farther along the coast is the village of **Menzel Temim**, to the N. of which is the *Oued Tefkhasid*, the river where Masinissa was defeated by Bocchar, about B.C. 204, and his escort cut to pieces.

At 30 m. from Kelebia is the town of **Nebeul**, also about a mile from the beach, close to the now unimportant ruins of *Neapolis*, of which the modern name is simply an Arab corruption. The land around is very rich, and produces immense quantities of fruit and vegetables. The staple manufactures of the place are pottery and mats. The former is much sought after, and is really curious, owing to the quaint forms employed and the bright yellow and green colours of the glaze.

8 m. farther on is **Hammamet**, a small town of 3700 inhabitants, surrounded by a dilapidated wall and protected by a citadel, clearly of Arab construction. The land in the neighbourhood is well watered, though sandy, and the place once did a considerable trade in lemons, which were sent to Palermo for exportation to America. The modern town is not built on the site of any ancient city.

[Should the traveller decide on making the journey from Tunis to Susa by land, he can do so by carriage in two days; but he should not do so for pleasure, as the road is very bad in many parts, and there are not sufficient objects of interest.

The road is good as far as Hammam el-Enf, but for many miles beyond the track is uncertain and marshy. He can sleep at *Bir el-Bouïta*, nine hours from Tunis, where there is a large fondouk provided with bed settles, but no bedding or provisions. 5 kil. farther on the road passes by a circular Roman edifice, called *Kasr-el-Menara*, 0, built of fine blocks of cut stone; it is about 14 mètres in diameter, and 10½ high, probably the tomb of some distinguished family. The cornice and altars upon it, described by Shaw, have disappeared. They are said by him to have borne the inscriptions:—

L. AEMILIO
AFRICANO
AVVNCVLO

C. SVELLIO
PONTIANO
PATRVELI

VITTELIO
QVARTO
PATR.

There are numerous vestiges of Roman houses near this monument. 8 kil. farther there is a branch back to the right, which the traveller is recommended to take in preference to the direct road, which passes through an immense salt marsh, often impracticable.

The second day's journey lies through the famous property of the **Enfida**, which forms an immense rectangle contained between the towns of Hammamet, Susa, Kerouan, and Zaghouan. Its entire superficies may be estimated at about 120,000 hectares, and it contains a population of nearly 7000 inhabitants.

This property had been granted by the Bey to Kheir-ed-din Pacha, then Prime Minister of Tunis, in consideration of his having obtained from the Sultan the confirmation of the right of succession to the Beylick by members of Sidi Es-Sadik's family.

In 1879, when Kheir-ed-din quitted Tunis for Constantinople he determined to sell all his property in the former country. Having tried in vain to induce his countrymen to become the purchasers he disposed of it to the Société Franco-Africaine.

This was not pleasing to the *entourage* of the Bey, and an endeavour was made to invalidate the sale by the exercise of the Arab custom of *Chefäa*, or right of pre-emption. Several British subjects were concerned in this; but after much litigation and diplomatic action the domain remained in the hands of the original purchasers. Indeed, it may be said that this dispute was one of the principal causes which brought about the French protectorate.]

The vessel now takes a southern course, and after crossing the Gulf of Hammamet, a distance of 33 m., reaches **Susa**, or, according to the modern French orthography, *Sousse.* Pop. 15,000, of whom 5000 are Europeans, including 1000 Maltese.

This is now an important French military station, the camp being located outside the town, west of the citadel. It is admirably constructed and well planted with trees.

It is the ancient Hadrumetum, capital of the province of Byzacium, mentioned by Sallust as having been a Phœnician colony more ancient than Carthage. Trajan made it a Roman colony. It is often mentioned in the Punic and civil wars, and, like many other cities, it was destroyed by the Vandals and restored by Justinian.

After Okba had built the city of Kerouan he remained at Susa during a considerable period. Subsequently, when the Turks took up the profitable trade of piracy, this became one of their favourite haunts, whence they made predatory excursions to the coasts of Italy.

In 1537 Charles V. sent a naval expedition from Sicily against the place, which refused to submit to his *protégé* Mulai Hassan. The command was given to the Marquis of Terra Nova, but after a vigorous assault he was obliged to retire and leave victory in the hands of his enemies. In 1539 another expedition was sent, commanded by Andrea Doria, with better success; but no sooner had he left than it revolted again, and welcomed the celebrated pirate Dragut within its walls.

In all the frequent dissensions between the Arabs and Turks the importance of Susa as a strategic post was so great that its possession was generally the key to supreme power. The town is situated on a gentle slope rising from the sea, and presents a most picturesque appearance from a vessel in the harbour. It is surrounded by a crenellated wall, strengthened at intervals by square towers and bastions. In the interior these walls have arched recesses, which serve as shops and storehouses. At the summit is the Kasba, which has been thoroughly restored by the French, and now contains the residence of the general commanding. The view from the terrace is very fine, and the gates, especially that of the Kasba, are quaintly decorated in distemper. Four gates give entrance to the town, the Bab el-Bahr or Sea Gate, Bab el-Gharbi or Western Gate, and Bab el-Djidid or New Gate, constructed about twenty-five years ago, and a still newer one opening on the quay.

The modern port is simply an open roadstead, very slightly protected by a curve in the coast towards the N., where was the ancient harbour, between the Quarantine Fort and Ras El-Bordj. The remains of the Roman breakwater may still be seen. But the accumulation of sand has rendered the water too shallow to permit vessels to make use of it. A great part of the ancient harbour is, in fact, now dry land. Some land has recently been recovered from the sea; on the S. side the battery has been transformed into a "Cercle militaire."

The principal objects of interest in the town are:—

The *Kasr er-Ribat*, a square building flanked by 7 round bastions, with a high tower built on a square base. It was erected by the third prince of the Aghlabite dynasty, Ziadet Ullah, in A.D. 827, as a convent for *Morabetin* or devotees. El-Bekri mentions it under the name of Mahres er-Ribat.

There is also a curious coffee-shop, called by the Arabs *Kahwat el-Koubba*, or Café of the Dome. It is a small building, square in plan up to about 8 ft. from the ground, thence rising cylindrically for about the same distance, the whole surmounted by a curious fluted dome. The cylindrical portion has four large and four smaller arched niches, with very bold cornices, springing from semicircular pilasters between them. The walls are, however, so thickly encrusted with whitewash, that the architectural details are considerably obscured. A good view of the exterior of the building is obtained by mounting to the top of the *Morestan*, or public hospital, just opposite: the dome is decorated exteriorly by a ridge and furrow fluting, converging at the apex.

There is also a curious old building, either of Roman or Byzantine construction, now used as an oil mill. It consists of a central dome, supported on four arches, three of which give access to narrow chambers, the entrance being in the fourth; beyond the left-hand chamber, on entering, are two parallel vaulted apartments, extending the whole length of the building. The piers of the arches have originally been ornamented with columns, and the ceiling appears to have been decorated with tiles or mosaics.

In the *Babel-Gharbi*, or Western Gate, a marble sarcophagus has been built into the wall, and now serves as a drinking fountain. The inscription is given by Guérin, but at the present day it is quite illegible.

About half a mile outside the gate is the ancient Roman Necropolis.

A very considerable part of the trade is in the hands of Maltese, who are here, as everywhere else in North Africa, the most industrious and frugal, and about the best-behaved class of the population. They almost monopolise the carrying trade, with their *karatonis*, or light carts on two wheels, to which one good serviceable horse or mule is usually harnessed. They also keep horses and carriages for hire at all the principal towns, which are unusually well supplied in this respect. The march of events has forced the Tunisians to abate their intolerance, but people are still alive who remember the time when driving in a carriage with four wheels was the exclusive privilege of the Bey, all others, consuls included, being forced to content themselves with two-wheeled vehicles.

[EXCURSION TO **El-Djem**. This can be done in two days; the writer paid 90 piastres (£2 : 5s.) for the hire of a carriage. There is a fondouk near the amphitheatre, but it is dirty and full of fleas, and nothing short of the magnificence of the view can compensate for a night spent in it. The traveller must take everything he requires with him, including water for drinking purposes.

The road passes for many miles through olive groves of great extent. S. of the village of *Zaouiet-Susa* are the ruins of a Roman fort, O, and beyond, the remains of several cisterns. The views are fine.

The wayside fountain at Menzel is the only water on the road. Beyond this the olive trees cease, and the traveller enters a wide and treeless plain, part of the district called Es-Sahel, or coast region—extremely fertile when an unusual quantity of rain has fallen, but at other times almost uncultivated, and apparently hardly susceptible of cultivation.

There is nothing of interest at El-Djem, save its amphitheatre, which may be said to be all that remains to mark the site of the ancient city of Thysdrus, or Thysdritana Colonia. The modern village is built entirely from its ruins, and all that is visible of the city itself are a few foundations and tombs towards the N.W.

It is first mentioned in history by Hirtius. After the defeat of Scipio at Thapsus it submitted to Cæsar, who condemned it to a fine of corn, proportionate to its small importance. It is also mentioned by Pliny, by Ptolemy, and in the tables of Peutinger. It was here that the proconsul Gordian first set up the standard of rebellion against Maximin, and was proclaimed Emperor in A.D. 238, in his eightieth year. He did not long live to enjoy his exalted dignity; he was defeated in battle by Capellianus, procurator of Numidia; his son was slain, and he perished by his own hands after having worn the purple for less than two months.

The solidity of the masonry and the vast size of this building have induced the Arabs at various periods of their history to convert it into a fortress; it has frequently been besieged, and on each occasion, no doubt, to the great destruction of the fabric. The first instance on record is during the wars of the early Arab conquerors. After El-Kahina had defeated Hassan ibn Naäman, and driven him as far as Tripoli, the latter received considerable reinforcement from Egypt, and again set out for the conquest of Ifrikia, about 693. El-Kahina entrenched herself in the amphitheatre, where she sustained a long siege before being compelled to evacuate it. The name of *Kasr el-Kahina*—the palace, or fortress, of the sorceress—attached itself to the building for many ages after this event.

This edifice offers the same exterior divisions as the principal monuments of a similar kind built elsewhere by the Romans, three outside open galleries, or arcades, rising one above another, crowned by a fourth story with windows. But at El-Djem the architect seems to have tried to surpass, in some respects, the magnificence of existing structures. In the Coliseum at Rome the lower story is decorated with a Doric half-engaged order, the second with an Ionic, and the third with a Corinthian. The fourth story was pierced by windows like this one, but pilasters alone are employed, so that the general aspect is that of three stories, gradually increasing in magnificence as they rise, crowned by a high attic, which supported the masts destined to receive the ropes of the velum. In many other amphitheatres the Doric order is alone employed. But here, at El-Djem, the orders of the first and third galleries are Corinthian; the middle one is composite; the fourth was probably Corinthian also, if it ever was completed.

The windows of the fourth story of the Coliseum are square-headed, as was generally the case in monuments of this kind; but at El-Djem the heads of the windows are neither straight nor semicircular, but segmental, and they are built as true arches, with voussoirs. They are placed at every third interpilaster.

Each of the three lower stories possessed sixty-four columns and arches, and at each extremity was a grand entrance, but the west one is included

[*Algeria.*]

in the breach made by Mohammed Bey in 1697, to prevent the building being again used as a fortress. Since then the work of destruction has gone on rapidly, and now fully one-third of the whole perimeter is destroyed.

The interior of the amphitheatre has suffered much more than the exterior, doubtless from the fact that it has so often served as a fortress, and partly from the material having been taken to block up the lower galleries and to build the modern village.

There are many indications of this great monument never having been completed. The attic story, which was necessary to support the velum, was commenced on the inner wall of the external gallery, but not apparently on the outer wall. Some of the ornamental details also are in an unfinished condition. The keystones of the arches of the lowest order were probably all intended to be sculptured, but they are still in their original rough condition, with the exception of two, one of which bears the head of a human being, and the other that of a lion.

The outside gallery on the ground floor, where most perfect, has been utilised by the Arabs as store rooms for their corn and forage; some of the arches are converted into shops, and there is evidence that the upper galleries also have at some time or other been converted into dwellings, holes in the masonry for the reception of joists being visible in every direction.

Several inscriptions have been found here; the most important has been preserved in the enclosure of the Chapel of St. Louis at Carthage, and has been often quoted; the name of the town is twice mentioned in it—once as Thysdrus, and again as Thysdritana Colonia.

A number of rude Arabic or Cufic inscriptions, accompanied by representations of swords and daggers, have been scratched on the exterior wall above the principal entrance, and one, which is certainly of Berber origin, may date from the era of El-Kahina.

The stone of which the amphitheatre is built was obtained from Sallecta on the sea coast: the Sallecti of the tables

Y

of Peutinger, and the Syllectum of Procopius, the first resting-place of Belisarius in his march from Caput Vada to Carthage. The natives assured the author that between this place and El-Djem the remains of the ancient paved road can easily be traced. The stone itself is of the youngest geological formation, belonging to the raised coast-beaches found at from 60 to 180 mètres above the present level of the Mediterranean. It is a somewhat fine-grained marine shell-limestone, with an admixture of siliceous sand full of fossil shells. Such a material is worked with the utmost facility; indeed, it may be cut with an axe, but it is not susceptible of being dressed with the same precision as more compact stone. The consequence is that the masonry is far inferior to the finest specimens of Roman work in Africa. Mortar has been plentifully used between the joints, and the stones are neither as large nor as closely fitted as usual; the average dimensions are—length 0·96 mètre, and height of courses 0·51 mètre.

Another feature of the construction of this building, never seen in others of the best period of Roman art, is the manner in which the appearance of nearly all the stones has been spoilt by triangular *lewis holes* being cut in their *exterior* faces, for the purpose of raising them into position. This gives the masonry a very slovenly appearance.

The town of Thysdrus, on the S. of the amphitheatre, the site of which is clearly visible from the upper walls of the structure, remains to be unearthed. Judging from the position of the Arab village, it is probable that the walls of the old town will be found from 3 to 4·50 mètres below the present surface. Fragments of marble and pottery are seen everywhere.

The traveller can make a short excursion from El-Djem to the ruins of ROUGA, Θ, known as **Caraga**, or can take the carriage road to *K'sour-es-Sif*, 29 kil., walk to Sallecta, and then drive to Mahadia, 12 kil. farther, whence he can take the steamer either to Sfax or Susa. Susa is the best place from which to make an excursion to **Kerouan.**]

12 m. farther on is **Monastir**, the *Ruspina* of the Romans, and the *Misteer* of the Arabs. It is situated on a promontory, with a few small islands lying off it, which affords some shelter from the N.W. winds. A quay and custom-house have been built by the French. To the S.E. is an extensive spit of shallow and dry banks, extending 10 m. from the coast, at the extremity of which are the Kuriat islands. To the N. of the landing-place is an Arab fort, the Bordj el-Kebir, and a country house belonging to the family of the late Si Osman of Tunis, a Greek renegade. The three islands off the point are Djezirat el-Hammam, el-Ghadamsi or the Tonnara, and El-Oustani. The town is about a mile from the shore, connected with it by a good carriage road; it is of the usual Tunisian type, surrounded by a crenellated wall, strengthened by a citadel, which Guérin believes to have given its name to the place. El-Bekri mentions the fact that it contained lodgings for a number of holy men who had quitted their families to seclude themselves from the world.

En-Nasri calls it "the best of sepulchres and the worst of habitations," in allusion to the tombs of Imam ibn Yoonus and El-Mazeri, learned Mohammedan doctors, which it contains. The country around is extremely fertile, and contains fine olive groves, the principal wealth of the district. Date trees commence to be seen here, and ripen their fruit, which they do not farther N.

After leaving Monastir the steamer rounds *Ras Dimas*, the ancient *Thapsus*, celebrated for the decisive victory which Cæsar won under its walls against Scipio and Juba I., and anchors at **Mahadia**, 31 m. from Monastir. This is the site of *Turris Hannibalis*, or country seat of Hannibal, whence he is said to have embarked after his flight from Carthage. The modern city, at one time the seaport of Kerouan, was built in 912 by Obeidulla el-*Mahadi*, a descendant of Ali, Khalifa of the West, whence its name. It is frequently called Africa in ancient chronicles. This place is interesting to Englishmen as being the scene of the very first expedition against North Africa in which we took a part. It is thus described by Froissart and Holinshed:—

"In the thirteenth year of the reign of Richard II. [1390] the Christians took in hand a journey against the Saracens of Barbary, through the suit of the Genoese, so that there went a great number of lords, knights, and gentlemen of France and England, the Duke of Bourbon being their general. Out of England there went John de Beaufort, bastard son to the Duke of Lancaster, also Sir John Russell, Sir John Butler, Sir John Harcourt, and others. They set forward in the latter end of the thirteenth year of the king's reign and came to Genoa, where they remained not very long, but that the galleys and other vessels of the Genoese were ready to pass them over into Barbary, and so about midsummer in the beginning of the fourteenth year of the king's reign, the whole army being embarked, sailed forth to the coast of Barbary, where, near to the city of Africa, they landed, at which instant the English archers stood all the company in good stead with their long bows, beating back the enemy from the shore, which came down to resist their landing. After they had got to land they environed the city of Africa, called by the Moors Mahadia, with a strong siege, but at length, constrained by the intemperancy of the scalding air in that hot country, breeding in the army sundry diseases, they fell to a composition on certain articles to be performed in behalf of the Saracins, and so, sixty-one days after their arrival, they returned home."

Mahadia is situated on a narrow promontory extending about a mile to the E. ; it has anchorage to the N. and S. sides according to the direction of the wind, but it is entirely exposed to the E. The southern side is that generally used, and a small harbour has been made there, which shelters coasting craft in all weather. This place has risen from its ruins in a remarkable manner since the French occupation ; the old and dilapidated ramparts have been pulled down, and their material used for the breakwater of the harbour ; so that now the town is thoroughly ventilated from every direction. The Arab quarter, on the N. of the promontory, remains untouched, but a new one, containing many important buildings, including barracks for the French troops, is springing up to the S.W.

At the extreme E. of the cape is the old Spanish citadel. This was recently a mere ruin, now it has been thoroughly repaired, and forms not only a precious monument of the past, but excellent quarters for the French commandant. It rose within the fortified position which occupied the entire eastern part of the promontory, and was admirably chosen both for defence and on sanitary conditions, being surrounded by the sea on three sides. Under its walls is an ancient *Cothon* or harbour, in a perfect state of preservation. It is a rectangle excavated out of the rock, about 147 mètres long by 73 broad, with an opening to the sea of about 13, once no doubt secured by a chain. This was very probably of Phœnician origin, but the retaining walls show signs of reconstruction, in which old Roman columns and stones have been used.

A large number of Phœnician tombs may be visited both to the N. and S. of the town.

Leaving Mahadia the steamer passes **Salekta**, the *Syllectum* of Procopius, the first stage of the march made by Belisarius from Caput Vada to Carthage. The landing-place of the Byzantine army was at the modern **Kapoudiah**, or Ras Khadidja, a low rocky point 11 m. farther to the S.E., on which is built a remarkable tower nearly 49 mètres high.

The voyager, however, will see nothing of this coast, as the vessel has to give a wide berth to the extensive banks which surround the **Kerkena Islands**, the *Circinæ Insulæ* of the Romans. The principal ones are *Cherka* or *Ramleh* to the E. and *Gharba* to the W. They are low, and covered with date and olive trees. Cereals are grown in some places, but the inhabitants, of whom there are about 3000, live to a great extent on the produce of the sea, and by making mats and baskets.

The dangers of these islands have been to some extent mitigated by luminous buoys, which enables vessels to go between them and the coast in fine weather.

Sfax is 116 m. from Mahadia. This is the ancient *Taphroura*, and the most important city in the regency, after Tunis. The modern name is said to be derived from the Arabic word for a cucumber. It has a population of 42,000, of whom 2000 are Europeans, and of the latter 1200 are Maltese.

The anchorage is at least 2 m. from the shore, and there is a rise and fall of 6 ft. in the tide at springs; at Gabes the rise is 8 ft. The lesser Syrtis is almost the only place in the Mediterranean where there is any tide at all.

Sfax may be said to consist of three distinct portions. The European town to the S., along the seashore, in which many important improvements are being carried out by the municipality, such as roads, piers, etc.; then comes the Arab quarter, surrounded by a picturesque wall flanked by towers, some round and others square; and beyond this again the French military camp.

The distinctive feature of Sfax is the suburb, consisting of gardens and country houses, which extends for 6 or 8 kil. to the N. and W. Nearly every family has an orchard or garden, with a little house in it, where the owner passes at least the summer, frequently the entire year, riding to town and out again every day from his work.

One of the most interesting sights of the place is the series of several hundred bottle-shaped reservoirs for collecting rain-water, within a walled enclosure almost as large as the Arab town itself.

This is the only place on the coast where there was anything like a serious resistance to the French.

By the end of May 1881 the whole country was in a state of revolution; and the fanaticism of the people of Sfax was thoroughly excited against Christians in general, but against the French in particular, who, however, had fewer representatives amongst the European colony than any other nation. About the 25th of the month the Bey proposed to man the forts with Tunisian soldiers; this excited the suspicion of the populace, who, on the 28th, broke out and proclaimed a *Jehad*, or holy war. Almost all the Europeans went on board French men-of-war, or other vessels in the roads. The ironclad *Alma*, and the postal-steamer *Mustafa*, arrived on the 29th with 1500 Tunisian soldiers, but it was found inexpedient to land them. In the evening H.M.S. *Monarch* and *Condor* arrived, to the great satisfaction of the British community.

On the afternoon of the 5th July the bombardment commenced by the French gunboats and two ironclads; the Sfaxiots returned the fire as best they could, but entirely without effect; desultory firing continued for more than a week. On the 14th of July more French vessels arrived, and there was now a squadron of four gunboats and nine ironclads. On the 15th the bombardment commenced in earnest; on the 16th the boats were sent on shore, under cover of the ships' guns, and a landing was effected, though not without some loss; the Kasba was occupied by 8 A.M., every house in the town was broken open and ransacked, the doors in the markets, mended with wood, unpainted like the rest, bear witness to the fact at the present day. By the middle of August the town had resumed its usual quietness, and the French soldiers were busily engaged in clearing away the ruins and repairing the damage caused by the bombardment. The town had to pay a war indemnity of £250,000, and an international commission was formed to recompense Europeans for the losses they had sustained. The Arabs of the town soon returned to their occupations, but the Bedouins fled to Tripoli, leaving the whole of the southern portion of the Regency nearly depopulated. They did not return for several years.

This is one of the centres of the sponge trade.

After leaving Sfax, the Italian steamer proceeds direct to Djerba, but the French one touches at Gabes, the ancient *Tacape*. Two-thirds of the way from Sfax to Gabes is the little port of Skira, just opened to commerce, which has been chosen by the Franco-English Esparto Company as its emporium for the exportation of that fibre.

Before the French Protectorate only one solitary building existed at the landing-place of Gabes, but now this has become an important military station; barracks for a large number of troops have been built; about forty other houses have sprung up; a pier upwards of 200 mètres long has been constructed, and a considerable French town will soon exist.

Gabes can hardly be called a town, like the other principal places on the coast, but rather an assemblage of villages scattered through a beautiful oasis of palm trees.

The most important are *Dhara* and *Menzel*, purely Arab towns, of no particular interest; the houses appear to be constructed, to a great extent, with the cut stone and broken columns of the ancient Tacape. Before the French occupation they were at constant feud with each other, and a fort had to be built between them to keep both in awe of the Tunisian authority. The population is said to be 16,000, of whom 460 are Europeans, and of these latter 200 are Maltese. The number of date-palms is 400,000. A considerable trade is carried on in alfa, oil, and dates.

It is impossible, within the limits of such a work as this, to go into full details regarding the daring scheme of the late Commandant Roudaire, for the creation of an inland sea, by the submersion of the Sahara. Still it is hardly possible, when speaking of Gabes, to pass it over in silence. The project was conceived before the French Protectorate, but it is hardly probable that it will ever be carried out, now that its originator is no more.

Between a place 70 kil. S. of Biskra and the sea, exists an immense depression, 375 kil. long, occupied by three *chotts* or salt lakes, all of which are below the level of the sea. The isthmuses which separate them are of varying heights, but both considerably above the sea level. The whole of this area is separated from the sea by a third isthmus, also considerably above the Mediterranean.

Some geographers assert that this depression is the site of the ancient lake of *Triton*, that it communicated with the sea down to a very recent period, and that partly by the upheaval of its bottom, and partly owing to the difference between the quantity of water which entered, and the amount of evaporation and absorption, the sea gradually disappeared, leaving the existing chotts the only evidence of the former condition of things.

Others maintain that there never was an inland sea here at all, and that the Tunisian chotts have the same origin as the more elevated Sebkhas of Algeria, the salt therein existing entirely from the washing of the higher ground by rain, which has no means of exit except by evaporation.

The quantity of water necessary to flood this depressed area would be 193 milliards of cubic mètres. M. Roudaire proposed to cut through the narrowest portion of the inland isthmuses, thus leaving the three basins prepared to receive the waters of the Mediterranean. He then intended to cut a canal between it and the sea, about 15 kil. N. of Gabes, at a place where the work would be facilitated by the presence of another small chott, and by the depression through which the Oued el-Melah flows into the sea.

There is no reason to imagine that at the present day there can be any insuperable difficulties in carrying out such a project, except that of obtaining the necessary amount of capital; but it is difficult to conceive any appreciable advantages as likely to result from it. There might perhaps be some slight modification of climate, though the area which this sea would occupy would hardly be larger in proportion to the rest of the Sahara than a single spot on the traditional panther's skin. Ships also might be able to circulate, but in a region which produces nothing save dates; and many groves of these invaluable trees would certainly be sacrificed to produce a very doubtful benefit to humanity.

The company which was got up for the creation of an inland sea received important concessions from the Tunisian Government, authorising it to create a port at Oued el-Melah, and to sink a number of artesian wells. One has already been finished; it is delightful to witness the column of water it throws up into the air, equal to 10,000 tons a day, a quantity sufficient to redeem 600 hectares of land from sterility, and irrigate 60,000 palm trees. This is the true solution of the story of an inland sea, a sea of verdure and fertility, caused by the multiplication of artesian wells, which never fail to bring riches and prosperity in their train.

After leaving Gabes the steamer crosses the *Syrtis Minor* and anchors off **Djerba**, immortalised by Homer as the "Island of the Lotophagi." The distance is 36 m., but the sea is so shallow that vessels cannot approach nearer than 4 m. At that distance a light vessel has been stationed by the Compagnie Transatlantique, and passengers, by the Italian steamers at least, can generally be taken on shore in the steam launch belonging to the agent; but even thus they must look well after the tide, as at dead low water the smallest boat cannot approach the shore. The rise and fall is 7 ft.

The population of the island is about 35,000, of whom 360 are Europeans, and 300 of these are Maltese. There is a large Jewish community, who inhabit two separate villages, *Harat el-Kebira*, close to the capital, and *Harat es-Sogheira*, nearer the centre of the island. The Mohammedans are to a great extent of Berber origin, and some of them are Wahabite, professing the tenets of the Beni M'zab in Algeria.

Djerba is mentioned by many ancient writers. Herodotus and Eratosthenes call it the *Island of the Lotophagi*; Strabo and Pliny, *Meninx*; Scylax, *Brachion*; Aurelius Victor (3d century) mentioning the fact of two Emperors, Gallius and Volusianus, having been raised to the purple here, gives both the second of these, and that used at the present day, *Creati in insula Meninge quæ nunc Girba dicitur*.

Much controversy has arisen regarding the lotus of the Odyssey. "Now whosoever did eat the honey-sweet fruit of the lotus had no more wish to bring tidings nor to come back, but there he chose to abide with the lotus-eating men, ever feeding on the lotus, and forgetful of his homeward way." Most writers have been content to follow Shaw, who identifies it as the *Seedra* of the Arabs, or the *Ziziphus lotus* of botanists, a fruit which in its wild state is hardly eatable, and even when cultivated is quite unworthy of immortality, a fruit moreover which does not exist upon the island at all. It seems unnecessary to go out of one's way to search for the Homeric food, the island is covered with it, no greater blessing than it was ever bestowed by Providence on man, and no other fruit is so all-sufficient for human sustenance as the "honey-sweet" lotus of the ancients, the DATE of the modern Arab.

The ordinary landing-place at Djerba is on the N. side of the island, close to the modern capital *Houmt es-Souk*; a good pier has been built, and a carriage road made to the town. Close to the former is the old fort, *Bordj Kebir*, the scene of many sanguinary struggles between Christians and Mohammedans. Near it was the celebrated *Bordj er-roos*, or pyramid of skulls, which was seen and described by Sir Grenville Temple in 1832. It was 20 ft. high, and 10 ft. broad at the base, tapering towards a point, and composed entirely of skulls resting in regular rows on intervening layers of the bones appertaining to the bodies. These, no doubt, were the remains of the unfortunate Spanish garrison commanded by Don Antonio d'Alvaro, who were overpowered and exterminated by the Turks in 1560. The Viceroy of Sicily and Andrea Doria were of the number, but they managed to effect their escape in a small boat. In 1848, at the instance of the Christian community of Djerba, supported by the consuls at

Tunis, this monument was pulled down, and the bones interred in the Catholic cemetery close by.

The principal villages in Djerba are *Houmt es-Souk*—the capital, *Midoun*, and *Cedrien*, 13 and 16 kil. to the S.E. of it. *Houmt Ajim*, on the S.W. coast, *Gullala* to the S., celebrated for its pottery, and *Cedouiksh*, on the way from the capital to El-Kantara. The island is very flat, the highest point being only 36 mètres above the sea. The soil is sandy but fertile, covered in every direction with olive and date trees; the former are particularly fine, and fruit of various kinds is cultivated in enclosed gardens round all the villages. A considerable trade is done in sponges, which are fished up by Maltese and Greeks; the former use iron graines, the latter frequently employ a diver's dress. The principal manufactures are bornouses and coloured blankets, which are in great request in North Africa.

The most remarkable feature of Djerba is the great bight or inland sea which separates it from the mainland. This forms a large lake of irregular shape, the greatest length being 17 kil., and the greatest breadth 13 kil. It communicates with the Syrtis Minor to the W., by means of a narrow strait, 2½ kil. broad, and with the sea to the E. by a longer and broader one, the narrowest part of which is 3 kil. The channels in these are narrow and rather intricate, but both they and the lake itself are perfectly navigable for vessels of about 200 tons burden.

At El-Kantara, about the middle of the larger strait, are the ruins of what must have been a magnificent city, probably *Menina*, certainly the most important place on the island. Although this was accessible to trading vessels in ancient times, the water was still sufficiently shallow to admit of a causeway being built to the W. of it, connecting the island with the mainland; this probably had an opening to permit the passage of vessels. Even now it is possible to cross at low tide over what is called the *Tarik El-Djemil*, or "road of the camel."

In the middle of the eastern strait is a fort called *Bordj Castille*, connected with the shore by a long sandy spit. This is said to have been built by the Aragonese of Sicily in 1289.

The ruins of El-Kantara have not been sufficiently explored; some fine things have been found, and immediately carried away, but enough remains to show that Meninx must have been a place of unusual magnificence. This may be judged by the wealth of richly-coloured marbles employed, capitals, shafts, vases, sculptured stones of immense size, broken sarcophagi, etc., of the richest varieties of coloured marbles and breccias, all of Greek origin. These testify to the riches and importance of the place, and to the extent of its foreign commerce.

Other important Roman remains exist. Bou-Ghara, ancient *Gightis*, to the S.W. of the lake, and indeed everywhere on that part of the mainland as far as *Zarzis*, the last port on the Tunisian coast. In the map which has been issued by the Depot de la Guerre, upwards of fifty places are marked with the letters R.R., indicating the existence of Roman ruins. They prove beyond all doubt that this small inland sea was at one time a place of considerable importance, a haven of safety, and perfectly navigable for the vessels then in use. It answers in all material points to the description which Scylax, at least, gives of **Lake Triton**, and there can be little doubt that it is here, and not in the region of the chotts, that we must look for the position of that famous lake.

Zarzis is very little frequented except by sponge fishers. The anchorage is protected by a natural breakwater like that at Mahadia. The salubrity of its climate and the presence of sweet water, not less than its geographical situation, make it a better station than Gabes for the troops intended to protect the south part of the Regency.

ROUTE 34.

Susa to Kerouan.

The easiest way of visiting Kerouan is by carriage from Susa; the journey can be done in 6 hours, and the traveller, if not too fastidious, will find accommodation which he can put up with. There is also a horse tramway. This belongs to the military, but is now open to the ordinary traveller.

The journey is over a desolate and uninteresting plain, to the north of the Sebkha of Sidi el-Hani.

Next to Mecca and Medina no city was, till the French occupation, so sacred in the eyes of Western Mohammedans. It was founded by Okba ibn Nafa in the 50th year of the Hedjira (A.D. 670). He proposed to his troops to found a city which might serve him as a camp, and be a rallying point for Islamism till the end of time. He conducted them to where Kerouan now is, and which was then infested with wild beasts and noxious reptiles. Ibn-Khaldoun states that he collected around him the 18 companions of the Prophet who were in his army, and called out in a loud voice, "Serpents and savage beasts we are the companions of the blessed prophet, retire! for we intend to establish ourselves here." Whereupon they all retired peaceably, and at the sight of the miracle many of the Berbers were converted to Islamism. Okba then planted his lance in the ground and called out—" Here is your **Kerouan**!" (caravanserai or resting-place) thus giving the name to the new city. He himself traced out the foundations of the Governor's Palace and the great mosque; the true position of the *Kiblah*, or direction of Mecca, is believed by Mohammedans to have been miraculously communicated to him by God.

Before the French Protectorate no Christian could enter its walls without a special order from the Bey, and a Jew did not dare even to approach it. The sacred character of the city, however, did not exempt it from its full share of war and violence. Even the great mosque has more than once been almost totally destroyed by the Mohammedans themselves, though it was never absolutely polluted by a Christian invader.

When Tunis was occupied by the French, formidable preparations were made for the attack of the Holy City, where a desperate resistance was anticipated, and the occupation of which was considered the only means of controlling the fanaticism of the Tunisians. Three Corps d'Armée were ordered to arrive at once under its walls. The first sent from Tunis, taking the route by Zaghouan, was commanded by General Logérot, under the superior orders of General Saussier. The second started from Tebessa, commanded by General Forgemol, and was composed of soldiers from Algeria and Arab *Goums*. The third, under General Etienne, marched from Susa. The last-named found the gates open to him, and entered the city without opposition. Not a blow was struck. The Governor voluntarily surrendered the town, the French force defiled through it and encamped under the walls, one regiment having occupied the citadel.

This is the only place in the Regency of Tunis where Christians are permitted to visit the mosques and religious edifices, but to do this an order is required from the French commanding officer. The first Englishman who ever visited them was Mr. A. M. Broadley, who has given the best description yet published,[1] and of which we have liberally availed ourselves.

Kerouan is of an irregular oblong figure, surrounded by a crenellated brick wall, strengthened by towers and bastions, and pierced by five principal gates, and four posterns, now closed. The chief suburbs are to the south and west; they contain several important shrines and three great cisterns. The largest of these is generally attributed to the Aghlabite dynasty, who ruled towards the close of the 8th century. It consists of three portions—a large

[1] "The last Punic War—Tunis Past and Present." 1882.

polygonal reservoir of 64 sides, containing 5800 cubic mètres of water; a smaller one above, with 17 sides, and a capacity of 4000 cubic mètres, intended to receive any *débris* that may be washed down by the stream and allow only the clear water to flow into the main receptacle; and lastly, two reservoirs lower down, containing each 450 mètres, from which the inhabitants of the city may draw water. This has been restored by the French in connection with the works for supplying the city with water from the Oued Merguelil and the springs of Cherchira. There are two other reservoirs, but in a ruinous condition.

The names of the gates are *Bab el Tunis*, Tunis Gate; *Bab el-Khaukh*, Gate of the Peach; *Bab el-Djelladin*, Tanners' Gate; *Bab el-Kasba*, Gate of the Fort; and the *Bab el-Djidid*, or New Gate.

The **Great Mosque** of Sidi Okba is the principal object of attraction, and occupies nearly all the northern angle of the town. It consists of a rectangle divided off into three parts, 1*st*, the Maksoura, or prayer chamber, exclusively reserved for worship; 2*d*, the vestibule adjoining it; and 3*d*, a great cloistered court, from which rises the minaret. The effect on entering the maksoura is very grand. It forms a rectangle consisting of 17 naves, each of 8 arches, supported by coupled marble and porphyry columns, the spoil of the chief Roman edifices in North Africa. There are 296 in this portion of the building, and 439 in the entire mosque. The capitals are of every style of Roman architecture, and some have a distinctly Christian character, the majority belonging to what is known as the Composite order—a combination of the Ionic and Corinthian. The central nave is wider than the others, and the columns there are arranged three and three. It leads from the *Bab el-Behou* or "Beautiful Gate" to the *Mihrab* or sacrarium. The former is of beautifully sculptured wood, with a long inscription in relief, containing an extract from the Koran and the record of its construction. The latter has the archivolt supported by two columns of alabaster sent by one of the Byzantine emperors to Hassan ibn Naâman in A.D. 689. The walls are of exquisitely painted plaster work, through the openings of which the original mihrab of Sidi Okba can still be seen when it is lighted up.

To the right of this is the *mimbar* or pulpit, 6 mètres high, of splendidly carved wood, every panel being of different design; and near it is an enclosure of the same kind of work, called the *Beit el-Edda*, giving access to several chambers, the room of the Imam, and what ought to be the library. It bears a long cufic inscription in a single line, recording its construction by Abou Temim el-Moez ibn Badis, one of the Sanhadja Emirs, whose reign commenced in A.D. 1015.

The shafts of the columns which support the dome are of porphyry, and measure about 12·6 mètres in height. This great chamber is dimly but effectively lighted by coloured glass in the dome.

The court is surrounded by a double arcade with coupled columns, and under it is an immense cistern occupying the entire area. On the north-west side, facing the Bab el-Behou, rises the minaret or *minar*, as it is called, a high quadrangular tower of three stories, each decreasing in height and breadth. Several pieces of Roman sculpture and inscriptions are built into the base, and the steps are mostly of slabs of marble from Roman buildings. A very fine view is obtained from the summit.

The most striking peculiarity of the mosque is the grand simplicity and cathedral-like aspect of the interior. There is nothing little or tawdry about it; everything speaks to the Moslem of the solemn character with which he invests his Jehovah.

Close to the mosque is the **Zaouia of Sidi Abd el-Kadir el-Djilani**, whose confraternity has so many votaries in North Africa, although its headquarters are in Baghdad. It consists of a lofty cupola, with the usual cloisters, leading to a number of conventual cells. The principal apartment is lighted by stained glass windows.

In the centre of the town is the **Djamäa Thelatha Biban**, or Mosque of the Three Gates, one of the most ancient in the city. The façade is decorated with Cufic inscriptions recording its construction by Mohammed ibn Kheiroun el-Maäferi in the 3d century of the Hedjira, and its restoration in 844 of the same era. Its interior is a single chamber supported by 16 Roman columns.

Perhaps the finest specimen of Moorish architecture within the city is the **Zaouia of Sidi Abid el-Ghariani**, who died about A.D. 1402. He was one of the Almoravides (*El-Marabbitin*). The hereditary governor of Kerouan is one of his descendants, and guardian of the sanctuary in which his ancestors are buried.

The entrance is a false arcade of white and black marble, in which is a square door, opening into an interior court of two stories; each side of this court, on the ground floor, has three arches supporting an upper colonnade. The interior is divided off by ancient columns. Beside the first arch is a second, surrounded by an arcade, supported on Roman columns. In the upper story are about 30 cells for dervishes or other holy men.

In the centre of the town is the sacred well **El-Barota**, supposed to have a communication with Zemzem at Mecca; it is enclosed within a domed building, and is the only one in the city.

Outside the city are many interesting religious edifices. Near the Bab el-Djidid is the **Djamäa ez-Zeitoun**, or mosque of the olive tree, a very ancient building. Not far from it is the conspicuous **Djamäa Sidi Amar Abada**, built in the form of a cross, and surmounted by seven cupolas, the interiors of which are decorated with Arabic inscriptions. This is of very recent construction. The person whose name it bears passed as a saint, and amused himself by fabricating gigantic swords, chandeliers, pipes, etc., covered with rude Arabic inscriptions. One of these contained a curious prediction of the French occupation. His object appears to have been to establish a reputation with posterity for being of gigantic stature and able to use the fantastic objects he passed his life in accumulating. He was greatly in favour with the Bey, who even consented, at his request, to bring up some large anchors from Porto Farina to Kerouan.

Half a mile beyond this, and to the N.W. of the town, is the most important building of Kerouan, the **Djemaät es-Sehebi**, wherein is interred one of the companions of the prophet, *Abdulla ibn-Zemäa el-Beloui*, whence its familiar name, "Mosque of the Companion." With him are buried, what he always carried about him in life, three hairs of the prophet's beard—one under his tongue, one on his right arm, and the third next his heart. This has given rise to the superstition amongst Europeans that he was one of the prophet's barbers!

The Zaouia is entered through a doorway near the base of a minaret, in the angle of a spacious court. The exterior of this minaret is faced with tiles, and on each side of its upper portion is a window of two lights, separated by a marble pillar. The roof is of green tiles, terminating in a gilded crescent. The door enters through a vestibule, lined with *faïence* and Moorish plaster work. A second door from this opens into a cloister, the arches being supported by marble columns, and the walls decorated in the same manner as the vestibule. This leads into another vestibule crowned with a fluted cupola, also decorated with tiles, *Nuksh hadida* work, and stained glass of great beauty, but not apparently of great antiquity, probably not earlier than the 18th century. A door on one side communicates with a mosque and two other cloisters, surrounded by cells for marabets and pilgrims to the shrine. Beyond this domed chamber is a broad court splendidly adorned with tiles and plaster work, and surrounded by an arcade of white marble columns, supporting a richly-painted wooden roof. From this one enters the shrine of "The Companion." It is about 6 mètres square, and dimly lighted by four small windows with coloured glass; a fine chandelier of Venetian glass hangs from the dome, and there are the usual accompaniments of smaller lamps, balls, ostrich eggs, etc.

The catafalque is surrounded by a high grating and covered with two palls—one of black velvet, adorned with Arabic inscriptions, in silver, presented by Ahmed Bey, and the other of coloured brocade, sent by Sidi Es-Sadik Bey.

An adjoining chamber contains the catafalque of Abdullah-ben Sherif, an Indian saint.

The whole of this mosque has been altered from time to time, and almost reconstructed. The upper part of the walls of the shrine are in the worst possible taste.

To the S.W. of the city is the **Cemetery**, covering an immense extent of ground, and full of the most interesting Cufic and Arabic inscriptions, which have not yet been sufficiently studied.

Continuing to the E., and passing the suburb of *Kubleych*, we come to the **Zaouia of the Aissaouia**, near the Tanners' gate. Most of the natives of Kerouan are affiliated to this powerful confraternity. They practise the same mystic and revolting rites as at Algiers, the guiding principle of which appears to be the utmost amount of self-inflicted bodily torture rendered supportable by religious frenzy.

There are many other interesting buildings in Kerouan, but the traveller will generally be satisfied with those just described.

ROUTE 35.

Excursion from Kerouan to Sbeitla.

This is a journey in which some privation must be expected, but the traveller will be rewarded by seeing the most beautiful, the most extensive, and the best-preserved ruins in North Africa.

It can be made in a carriage, obtainable at Kerouan, but it would be better to hire it at Susa. The cost of the carriage with four horses will be 20 f. a day; return journeys are always paid for at the same rate. This includes the food of the horses, but not of the driver.

The traveller must provide himself with bedding and provisions, as there are no habitations on the road, the population living in tents.

Kerouan to Hadjeb el-Aioun . . . 50 kil.
Hadjeb el-Aioun to Oued Gilma . . . 21 kil.
Oued Gilma to Sbeitla . 25 kil.

The track for more than 32 kil. is over the dreary plain that isolates Kerouan like an oasis. A few kil. farther is a broken bridge and a spring with a fondouk close by, where shelter can be obtained. The scenery on approaching the mountains is heathlike and more cheerful. The country appears quite deserted, except by large flocks of sheep and goats, and numerous coveys of partridges. It is only at nightfall, when the Arab fires are lighted for the evening meal, that one becomes aware of a considerable scattered population living entirely in tents. The track once again is on lower ground, which is marshy at all seasons of the year, and after heavy rains is impassable for carriages. The camp newly formed at *Hadjeb el-Aioun* is now visible on the hillside. Here, by permission of the Commandant, to whom a written introduction is advisable, shelter can be had for the night and provisions purchased at the canteen. The country west of this must have been at one time thickly populated. There are remains of numerous Roman villages, and cut stones of large size are standing in all directions. Oued Gilma, so called after a stream of that name, is an abandoned French camp, where there are a large number of unroofed dwellings. The traveller cannot expect to find shelter here. There is an Arab settlement close by. This is the site of the ancient *Chilma*, or *Oppidum Chilmanense*, which does not appear to have played a very important part in history.

The track then crosses a number of water-courses, and then, winding round the hill sides, reaches

Sbeitla. There is no accommodation here beyond a half ruinous and deserted fondouk. This name, like so many others, is merely an Arab corruption of the ancient one, *Sufetula*. No city in Africa possessed finer specimens of Roman architecture, and even as late as the Arab invasion it continued to be one of the most important cities in Byzacene.

Here took place the first great and disastrous encounter between Christianity and Mohammedanism in North Africa, when the army of the Exarch Gregorius was utterly exterminated by Abdullah ibn-Saad, and so much booty was taken that, according to the Arab historians, every horseman got 3000 dinars, and every foot-soldier 1000.

One of the most remarkable features of this part of the country, and which evidently led to its selection as the site of the ancient city, is its excellent water-supply. Here the **Oued Sbeitla**, which for a great part of its course is lost in the sand, flows in a clear and beautiful stream, never dry even in summer.

The form of the ancient city is still perfectly apparent, and many of the streets can be traced in their entire course.

To the S. of the town is the *Triumphal Arch of Constantine* (A.D. 305), which bears not only his name, but also that of Maximian, by whom he was adopted. It has a single opening, and the four Corinthian columns that decorated its principal façade were entirely isolated from the walls; these have now fallen down, and lie in fragments at the base of the monument.

The most important of the ruins is the **Hieron**, so called, or enclosure, on the N.W. side of which are the magnificent remains of **Three Temples**, partly attached, and together forming one design. It is about 92 mètres in length and 70 in width. It had on the S.E. side, facing the temples, but not in the axis of any one of the three, being nearly 6 mètres out of the central line, a triumphal gateway of very excellent design. Within the gateway was a large portico, the roof being supported by shafts of the Corinthian order, and communicating with a colonnade which appears to have been carried round three sides of the enclosure. On the S.W. side was a series of shops built against the enclosing wall. On the opposite side was another entrance to the Hieron, and two archways connecting the first and third temples with the central one gave access from a street running along the back wall of the three temples. The porticoes, each of which was supported by six monolithic shafts of great size, were on a splendid scale of design, and, judging from sculptured fragments lying on the ground, must have been of a very decorative character. The paving of the porticoes appears to have been on the same level, there being separate flights of steps to each temple. The external walls of the *cellæ* of the side temples were enriched by pilasters of the Corinthian order, those of the central temples by engaged shafts of the Composite order. The surfaces of those attached to the walls were raised and rusticated, giving a bold character to the design. The entire structure, about 36 mètres from end to end, was raised on a high stylobate of bold design. The enrichments of the cornices and soffits were beautifully chiselled, and owing to the extreme hardness of the limestone, which was quite white when quarried but assumed a golden-brown tint after a lapse of time, the decorative work is in a fairly perfect condition. The *Hieron* itself was paved with very large flat stones, as smooth as marble. The triumphal gateway before referred to was enriched with rusticated engaged shafts, corresponding with those of the central temple.

Wilmauns, writing of this place in 1880, says:—"*De fortuna civitatis cujus ruinae et magnae et pulchrae jure ab omnibus qui eas viderunt celebrantur nihil scimus.*"[1]

It is to be hoped that not only in

---

[1] Since the above was written, Sufetula has been carefully explored by Lieutenant Boyé, and the results published in the *Comptes Rendus des Séances de l'Académie des Inscriptions et Belles-Lettres*, 1884, pp. 367-373; also, in the *Bulletin de Géographie et d'Archéologie d'Oran*, 1885, p. 114. Mr. Graham also has published beautiful illustrations of it, see *Bibliography*, 1885.

the Hieron but in other parts of the city excavations will be made. The entire façades of the three temples with their inscriptions, and probably much sculptured ornament, are now buried in the soil, within a confused mass of gigantic masonry. In other parts of the city, the streets of which are clearly defined, there is little doubt that excavations, judiciously conducted, would be attended with surprising results.

The *Amphitheatre* is at the N. of the city. It was circular in form, but is now entirely destroyed.

Many other important ruins exist, but they sink into insignificance when compared with the temples.

There is absolutely no limit to the excursions that may be made on horseback, but they should only be undertaken by people in good health and prepared to encounter a considerable amount of inconvenience. Horses and mules can readily be hired for about 4 or 5 f. a day, and local guides will be supplied by the kaids of the various districts, who are always courteous and obliging, especially if the traveller has letters of introduction to them. Accommodation of the roughest description, often no better than an Arab *gourbi*, is procurable; but the traveller is sure to be rewarded, often by beautiful scenery, always by Roman remains of surpassing interest. It is altogether beyond the scope of such a work as the present to give itineraries of such journeys as are not likely to be undertaken by the ordinary traveller.

APPENDIX.

LIST OF BRITISH CONSULS IN ALGERIA AND TUNIS.

As the Consulates of Algiers and Tunis are amongst the first ever established by England, it may be interesting to give a complete list of the various Consuls-General and Consuls, as far as can be ascertained. This has not been compiled without much difficulty and research.

ALGERIA.

1580. John Typton was certainly Consul-General at Algiers prior to 1580. He is believed to be the first native-born Englishman ever appointed Consul. In 1585 Tunis and Tripoli were added to his jurisdiction.

1600. John Audellay. The Pacha of Algiers, in a letter to Queen Elizabeth, alludes to this person, "who says he is your Majesty's Consul here."

1606. Richard Alline or Allon was appointed Consul on behalf of the Levant Company. In 1618 the Pacha complained to Sir Robert Mansel that he had escaped to Bougie in a British vessel; that he had there enticed the governor and several other people on board, and had carried them off to slavery at Leghorn.

1620. William Henry Ward. It is doubtful whether he was a Consul, often described as *Residens* in Latin; or a mere resident at Algiers; his tombstone was as follows:—
Hic jacet sepultus Willelmus Henricus Wardus armiger et mercator Anglicanus Residens in Argel, ubi decessit 4 die Maii anno domini 1620.

1620. Richard Ford. A sailor appointed by Sir Robert Mansel, to please the Dey, "a common man well cloathed by the name of a consull."

1622. James Frizell, agent to Mr. Leath, deputy of the Turkey Company, appointed by Sir Thomas Roe, in March 1622, "as consul, on account of and at the charge of the Turkey Company." He was still here in 1643.

1646. Humphrey Oneby was Consul during the mission of Casson; all that is known of him is that he died on the 18th July 1653.

1646. Edmond Casson, Envoy from the Parliament for the Redemption of Captives; died at Algiers 5th December 1654.

1656. Robert Browne, died of plague at Algiers, 1664.

1664. Captain Nicholas Parker, R.N., commanding H.M.S. *Nonesuch*, temporarily appointed by Sir Thomas Allen; recalled 1667.

1666. Mr. John Dobson, appointed Consul; he never joined his post.

1666. William Lear, appointed in succession to Parker; it is not certain that he ever actually took charge.

1667. John Ward, a merchant at Algiers; relieved Parker on 25th April 1667.

1668. Robert Crofftes, factor of William Bowtell, appointed by Sir Thomas Allen, but he never took charge. Ward continued to act some time longer; after giving up the Consulate he was cut in pieces by order of the Dey for having shot a Jew in his presence, on the 20th July 1674.

1672. Samuel Martin appointed, but he did not join his post till 1674. He ceased to be Consul in 1680.

1682. Captain John Neville, R.N., temporarily appointed by Admiral Herbert.

1683. Philip Rycant, appointed Agent and Consul-General 23d April 1683; revoked 26th October 1684.

1684. John Erlisman, appointed 16th June 1684; died 8th February 1690.

1690. Laurence Wise, servant of Erlisman, acted for a short time.

1690. Robert Cole, a merchant, was entrusted with the Consulate by the Dey.

1691. Thomas Baker, who had been ten years Consul-General in Tripoli, assumed charge 15th June 1691; he resigned 10th August 1694, and returned to Tripoli as Special Envoy.

1694. Robert Cole, many years a merchant at Algiers, appointed Consul-General 10th August 1694. He died there 13th November 1712.

1712. Thomas Thomson, a merchant, selected by the Dey to take charge on Cole's death. He held the office till the arrival of his brother.

1713. Samuel Thomson, who assumed charge 13th November 1713; he left for England February 1716.

1716. Thomas Thomson again acted *ad interim*.

1720. Charles Hudson, a merchant, appointed 8th January 1720. He went to France for the benefit of his health 24th July 1728, and died at Montpellier 14th May 1729.

1728. Edward Holden, partner of Mr. Hudson; acted for him during his absence.

1729. Charles Black arrived at Algiers as Consul-General 7th September 1729. The Dey refused to receive him, and he left on the 26th of the same month.

1729. George Logie appointed by the Dey to take charge of the Consulate till H.M. pleasure should be known.

1730. Charles Black sent back to Algiers with a squadron under Admiral Cavendish. He was recalled in 1738.

1739. Edward Holden, who had acted in 1728, was now appointed Agent and Consul-General; he died on the 25th November of the same year.

1739. Mr. John Ford was appointed by the Dey to act ad interim, which he did till the arrival of

1741. Ambrose Stanyford, on the 30th January 1741. He died at Algiers 19th April 1752.

1752. Robert White, the Vice-Consul, assumed charge.

1754. Stanhope Aspinwall arrived as Agent and Consul-General 29th July 1754. He was recalled in 1761.

1761. John Ford, who had acted in 1739, was appointed, but he died before leaving England.

1762. Simon Peter Cruize acted as Consul.

1763. James Bruce, the traveller, arrived as Agent and Consul-General 19th March 1763. He left to carry out his explorations 17th June 1765.

1765. Robert Kirke assumed charge 17th June 1765; he was shortly afterwards recalled.

1766. John Le Gros was named, but the state of his health prevented him from leaving England.

1766. James Sampson was appointed 29th July 1766; he arrived 10th May 1767, and was almost immediately afterwards recalled.

1767. Hon. Archibald Campbell Fraser, Consul-General at Tripoli, was sent to Algiers, where he arrived 16th October 1767. He hauled down his flag and left 26th October 1773. He was sent back 22d April 1774, with the Mediterranean Squadron, under Sir Peter Denis, but the Dey refused to receive him. He was pensioned.

1776. Edward Bayntun, Agent and Consul-General at Tripoli, was transferred to Algiers; arrived 23d April 1776; died 1st November 1777.

1777. John Woulfe, his Vice-Consul, assumed charge.

1780. Nathaniel Davison arrived as Agent and Consul-General 5th April 1780. In consequence of the Dey's arbitrary conduct he left in February 1783.

1783. John Woulfe again acted.

1785. Charles Logie appointed Consul-General 20th May 1785. He was pensioned in November 1791.

1792. Charles Mace appointed 1st June 1792; arrived at Algiers 2d January 1794. He was turned out by the Dey 20th October 1795.

1796. Francis Vidau held charge of the Consulate for a short time.

1796. Richard Masters arrived as Consul-General 26th November 1796. Owing to the arbitrary conduct of the Dey he was forced to quit Algiers in January 1798.

1798. Isaac Bensamon, a Jewish broker, remained in charge.

1800. John Falcon, who had been Mr. Masters's secretary, was now appointed, and reached Algiers about the 1st June 1800. He was turned out of Algiers at a moment's notice by the Dey, on the 23d April 1803, and not again permitted to return.

1804. Richard Cartwright was nominated Consul-General about the 12th October 1804, and arrived at Algiers on the 3d January 1805. He felt it necessary to leave Algiers on the 22d February 1806.

1806. Henry Stanyford Blanckley appointed Agent and Consul-General 26th May 1806; arrived 9th October; recalled 24th May 1812.

1812. Hugh M'Donell arrived at Algiers as Pro-Consul 1st April 1812; appointed Agent and Consul-General 11th July 1814. He left Algiers owing to the Dey's conduct, on the 29th January 1824, after which he retired on a pension, and died 23d June 1847.

1824. William Danford was Pro-Consul from 27th July till the 29th of January following.

1825. Morris Thomas acted from that date till the arrival of

1827. Robert William St. John, on the 6th December. He was the last Agent and Consul-General accredited to the Regency, and was at Algiers at the time of the French Conquest. He retired in 1851, and died shortly afterwards at Pau.

1851. John Bell was appointed Consul-General on the 22d of July, and died at Algiers in June 1863, immediately after his retirement.

1863. Henry Adrian Churchill, C B., succeeded 23d April. Left 15th June 1867, and died at Palermo in 1886.

1867. Lieut.-Colonel Robert Lambert Playfair was appointed Consul General in Algeria 20th June 1867. His jurisdiction was extended to Tunis in 1885, and so remained till 1889; he was created a K.C.M.G. in 1886.

TUNIS.

1585. John Typton appointed Consul-General

1626. Thomas Brown, mentioned as Consul by Sir John Lawson 15th June 1626. A letter of Charles II alludes to his having been "outed" during the Commonwealth and restored by him.

1650. Samuel Booth Rowse appointed under the Commonwealth. He is mentioned by the Levant Company, 1656, as having well discharged his duty as Consul, was forced from his Consulship, and anxious to return.

1656. Thomas Brown re-appointed by Charles II. In 1661 Brown mentions in one of his despatches that "Campion" is to succeed him.

1661. Campion succeeded about the middle of 1661, and died on 1st October of the same year. His tomb still exists in the cemetery of St. George.

1663. Thomas Rowse appointed Agent and Consul by Charles II on the 20th August 1663.

1662. John Erlisman assumed the offices of Agent and Consul-General on the 16th February 1662. He left Tunis on the 4th October 1676. He subsequently died as Consul-General at Algiers.

1674-75. Francis Baker, kinsman of Erlisman, had acted for him since the 5th January 1674-75; he now succeeded him. Charles II, in his letter of the 27th August 1683, gives him leave to return to England.

1683. Thomas Goodwyn appointed Agent and Consul-General 27th August 1683. The last Act signed by him in the archives is dated 4th October 1697.

1700. John Goddard appointed Agent and Consul-General 20th June 1700. The last Act signed by him is dated 22d May 1708, after which date his chancellor, John Waldeck, seems to have had charge of the Consulate-General.

1712. Richard Lawrence succeeds the foregoing on the 13th November 1712. Before his death, being very ill, he gave over charge of his office to

1750. John Wrightman, partner of the newly-appointed Consul-General,

1750-51. Charles Gordon, who assumed charge 3d January 1750-51. He delivered over charge to Mr. Traill on the 10th April 1766. He and his wife are both buried in the English cemetery.

1766. James Traill assumed charge on the above date, that of his arrival in H.M.S. Œolus, Hon. Captain Leveson-Gower. He died in 1785, and is buried in the English cemetery.

1785. Robert Traill, son of the preceding, acted until the arrival of the new Consul-General,

1790. Perkins Magra, in January 1790. He had several times leave of absence, when Louis Hargreaves and Henry Clark acted for him. He finally left Tunis for Malta in 1802.

1804. Richard Oglander appointed Agent and Consul-General 26th October 1804; retired on a pension 3d June 1824; and died in the Isle of Wight, 9th April 1857.

1824. Alexander Tulin, the Vice-Consul, acted at various times during the absence of Mr. Oglander, and until the arrival of his successor.

1825. Sir Thomas Reade, K.C.B., who was appointed 1st January 1825. He was the first non-trading Agent and Consul-General. He died 29th July 1849, and was buried in St. George's cemetery.

1849. Vice-Consul Louis Ferrière assumed charge on the death of Sir Thomas Reade, and acted till the arrival of

1850. Sir Edward Baynes, K.C.M.G., on the 26th March 1850. He died there 22d July 1855, and was interred in the Roman Catholic cemetery.

1855. Richard Wood, now Sir Richard Wood, G.C.M.G., C.B., was appointed Agent and Consul-General 30th August 1855. He arrived in Tunis 20th January 1856, and retired on a pension 31st March 1879.

1879. Thomas Fellowes Reade, son of Sir Thomas Reade; the last Agent and Consul-General; appointed 23d June 1879, arrived at Tunis 10th September in the same year. Retired on a pension 7th January, and died in England 24th March 1885.

1885. On the death of Mr. Reade, Tunis having passed under French protection, the appointment of Agent and Consul-General was abolished and Lieutenant-Colonel Sir R. Lambert Playfair, K.C.M.G., Consul-General in Algeria, had his Consular jurisdiction extended to Tunis also, on the 16th March 1885. Thomas B. Sandwith, C.B., was named Consul at Tunis.

1888. Mr. Sandwith was promoted to the Consulate-General of Odessa, and on the 1st July George Thorne Ricketts was appointed Consul.

1889. He resigned in July 1889, whereon the Consulate was restored to the independent position it had previously held, and R. Drummond Hay was appointed Consul.

BIBLIOGRAPHY OF THE MOST IMPORTANT WORKS ON ALGERIA AND TUNIS.[1]

1556. Leo Africanus, *De Totius Africae Descriptioni*, lib. ix. The author was an Arab of Granada, named El-Hassan, who visited a great part of Africa; was taken by corsairs, and baptized by Leo. X. His original work was in Arabic, but it has been translated into Latin, and into nearly all the modern languages of Europe. In English it is to be found in *Purchas's Pilgrims*, vol. ii.

1573. L. Marmol-Caravajal, *Description General de Africa*. Granada, 3 vols. folio. Marmol was a native of Granada, served in the expedition of Charles V against Algiers, was taken prisoner, and travelled during seven years and eight months over a great part of North Africa. A French translation was published by D'Ablancourt at Paris in 1667.

1612. Fray Diego de Haedo, *Topographia e Historia General de Argel*. Valladolid, folio. A French translation by Dr. Monnereau and M. Berbrugger was published in the *Revue Africaine*, 1870, p. 364 et seq. The author was a Benedictine monk, and dedicated his work to his relative the Archbishop of Palermo. It contains an account of the martyrdom of Jeronimo.

1637. Rev. Père Dan, *Histoire de Barbarie et de ses Corsaires*. Paris, folio. This gives an account of the Baltimore captives.

1725. Laugier de Tassy, *Histoire des Etats Barbaresques*. Amsterdam, 12mo. The author was Commissaire de la Marine for the King of Spain in Holland. His work was pirated in English in 1750, under the title of *A Complete History of the Piratical States of Barbary*, and it has been translated into several other languages.

1728. J. Morgan, *History of Algiers, to which is prefixed an epitome of the General History of Barbary from the earliest times*. London, second edition, 4to, 1731.

1738. Thomas Shaw, D.D., F.R.S., Fellow of Queen's College, Oxford, *Travels and Observations relating to several parts of Barbary and the Levant*. Oxford, folio, second edition, quarto. Dr. Shaw was chaplain to the Consulate at Algiers. This is one of the most valuable works ever written on North Africa.

1783. Major W. Dalrymple, *Travels through Spain and Portugal in 1774, with an account of the Spanish Expedition (O'Reilly's) against Algiers in 1755*. London, 4to.

1791. Abbé Poiret, *Voyage to Barbary, or Letters written from Numidia (1785-86) on the Religion, Customs, and Manners of the Moors and Bedouin Arabs, with an Essay on the Natural History of the Country*. Translated from the French edition of 1789. 2 vols. 12mo.

1811. Thomas Macgill, *An Account of Tunis, of its Government, Manners, Customs, and Antiquities, especially of its Productions, Manufactures, and Commerce*. Glasgow: Longman, Hurst, Rees, Orme, and Brown; 8vo.

1814. William Lithgow, *Travels and Voyages through Europe, Asia, and Africa for 19 years*. Leith: Longman, Hurst, Rees Orme, and Brown; 8vo.

1816. W. Janson, *A View of the Present Condition of the States of Barbary; or an account of the Climate, Soil, Produce, Population, Manufactures, Naval and Military strength of Morocco, Fez, Algiers, Tripoli, and Tunis. Also, a Description of their Mode of Warfare, interspersed with Anecdotes of their Cruel Treatment of Christian captives, illustrated by a new and correct hydrographical Map, drawn by J. J. Asheton*.

1818. Fil. Pananti, *A Geographical and Historical Narrative of a Residence in Algiers*, etc., with Notes and Illustrations by Edw. Blaquiere. London, 4to.

1819. A. Salama, *A Narrative of the Expedition to Algiers under the command of the Right Hon. Viscount Exmouth*. London, 8vo. Mr. Salama was Oriental interpreter to Lord Exmouth.

1826. W. Shaler, U.S. Consul-General at Algiers, *Sketches of Algiers, Political, Historical, and Civil*. Boston, 8vo. An exceedingly valuable and rare work. A French translation was made of it in 1830 by Bianchi, which was used as a handbook by the French expeditionary force that took Algiers. Paris: Librarie Ladvocat.

1830. Edward Blaquier, *Narrative of a Residence in Algiers*. London, 4to.

1833. C. C. Falbe, *Recherches sur l'Emplacement de Carthage*, 8vo, with atlas of six plates in folio. The author was a captain in the Danish navy and Consul-General at Tunis. In conjunction with M. Pricot de Sainte Marie he published a map of the Regency of Tunis, the only reliable one existing prior to the French protectorate.

[1] For all that has ever been written regarding the Eastern Barbary States, consult the three last works in this list.

1835. Rev. Michael Russell, LL.D., D.C.L., afterwards Bishop of Glasgow and Galloway, *History and Present Condition of the Barbary States*. Edinburgh, 12mo.

1835. Sir Grenville Temple, *Excursions in the Mediterranean: Algiers and Tunis*. London: Saunders and Otley; 2 vols. 8vo. An admirable and scholarly account of his journeyings in the two countries during 1832-33. The original drawings made during his expedition are numerous and of great interest. One of them was published in the work above quoted, and thirteen others in *The Shores and Islands of the Mediterranean*, Rev. G. N. Wright. London: Fisher and Son; 1839, 4to. The originals are in the possession of Sir Lambert Playfair.

1837. Thomas Campbell (the Poet), *Letters from the South during his Residence in Algeria*. London, 2 vols. 8vo.

1838. Dureau de la Malle, *Voyages dans les Régences de Tunis et d'Alger, par Peyssonnel et Desfontaines*. Paris: Librarie de Giele; 2 vols.

1841. Mrs. Broughton, *Six Years' Residence in Algiers*, 1806-12. London: Saunders and Otley; 8vo. Mrs. Broughton was daughter of Mr. Blanckley, H.M. Agent and Consul-General. The most valuable part of this volume consists of extracts from her mother's diary.

1842. Colonel Scott, *Journal of a Residence in the Esmala of Abd el-Kader, and of Travels in Morocco and Algiers*. London.

1844. W. B. Hodgson, *Notes on Northern Africa, the Sahara, and the Soudan*. New York, in 8vo. This work contains a bibliography of works on the Berbers and their dialects.

1844-54. *Exploration Scientifique de l'Algérie pendant les Années 1840-44, Publié par Ordre du Gouvernement*. Paris: Imprimerie Royale; 17 vols. A magnificent work, illustrating the geography, natural history, archæology, and architecture of the country.

1846. Captain J. C. Clark Kennedy, *Algeria and Tunis in 1845*. London: Henry Colburn; 2 vols. 8vo. An account of his journey through the two countries with Viscount Fielding.

1847. Lieutenant Spratt, R.N., *Remarks on the Lake of Benzerta in the Regency of Tunis in 1845*. See *Jour. Roy. Geog. Soc.*, vol. xii.

1851. Jos. Eug. Daumas, *Les Chevaux du Sahara*. Paris: Chamerot; 8vo. General Daumas acted as Consul of France at Mascara with Abd el-Kadir from 1837 to 1839, and was subsequently attached to the Bureau de la Guerre at Paris. He wrote many valuable works and papers on North Africa.

1852-56. Ibn Khaldoun, *Histoire des Berbers et des Dynasties Musulmanes de l'Afrique Septentrionale*. Translation française par le Baron MacGlucken de Slane. Algiers 4 vols. The original work is a general, history of the Mohammedan world, and is unsurpassed in Arabic literature as a masterpiece of historical composition. It was printed at Bulac, in 7 vols. royal 8vo, in A.D. 1284. He was a native of Tunis; taught at Tlemçen; was first the captive and subsequently the friend of Timur, and died at Cairo in A.D. 1406.

1853. E. Pellissier de Reynaud, *Description de la Régence de Tunis avec carte*. This forms part of the Exploration Scientifique de l'Algerie, in which work the author took an active part. He wrote numerous other works and papers on North Africa. He was attached to the Bureau Arabe at Algiers in 1833, and subsequently French Consul at Malta.

1853. Hon. Charles Sumner, *White Slavery in the Barbary States*. London: Sampson Low, Son, and Co.; 8vo.

1854. John Reynell Morell, *The Geography and History, Political, Social, and Natural, of French Africa*. London, 8vo.

1856. James Hamilton, *Wanderings in North Africa, comprising Scenery, Agriculture, Slave Trade*, etc. Several plates, 8vo.

1857. Abou Obeid el-Bekri, *Description de l'Afrique Septentrionale*. Texte Arabe, publée par le Baron de Slane. Alger et Paris, 8vo. A translation by the same author in the *Journal Asiatique*, 1858-59.

1858. H. M. Walmsley, *Sketches of Algeria during the Kabyle War*. London, 8vo.

1858. Eug. Fromentin, *Un été dans la Sahara*. Fromentin was a distinguished artist, born at La Rochelle in 1820. He travelled in Algeria, and published numerous articles in the feuilleton of the *Pays* and elsewhere. He subsequently published the above, which is superbly illustrated, and also another—*Une Année dans le Sahel*, 1859. Paris: Michel Lévy Frères.

1859. Rev. J. W. Blakesley, *Four Months in Algeria, with a Visit to Carthage*. Cambridge, 8vo, with maps and illustrations.

1859. Charles Brosselard, *Les Khouan, de la Constitution des ordres religieux Musslemans in Algérie*. Paris: Challamel; brochure in 8vo.

1860. Dr. N. Davis, *Carthage and her Remains, being an account of the Excavations and Researches on the site of the Phœnician Metropolis of Africa, and other adjacent places*. Conducted under the auspices of H.M. Government. London, 8vo.

1860. Rev. H. B. Tristram, *The Great Sahara*. London, 8vo.

1862. V. Guerin, *Voyage Archéologique dans la Régence de Tunis*. Paris, 2 vols. 8vo, with maps. This valuable work was published under the auspices of Duc Albert de Luynes.

1863. Dr. N. Davis, *Ruined Cities within Numidian and Carthagenian Territories*. London, 8vo.

1863. *Through Algeria.* By the author of "Life in Tuscany." London, 8vo.

1864. **John Ormsby,** *Autumn Rambles in North Africa.* London: Longmans, Roberts, and Green; 8vo.

1864. *Mémoires de la Congrégation de la Mission, dite de St. Lazare,* vols. ii. and iii. Paris, à la Maison Principale de la Congrégation de la Mission, Rue de Sèvres, 95. This work is printed for the exclusive use of the congregation. It contains most valuable contemporary correspondence from the missionaries of St. Vincent de Paul at Algiers, from the beginning of the 17th century.

1864. **Alphonse Rousseau,** *Annales Tunisiennes ou aperçu Historique sur la Regence de Tunis.* Alger: Bastide; 8vo.

1865. **Mrs. G. A. Rogers,** *A Winter in Algeria,* 1863-64. London, 8vo.

1866. **G. A. Sala.** *A Trip to Barbary by a roundabout Tour.* London, 8vo.

1867. **Colonel Churchill,** *Life of Abd el-Kader, from his own dictation, and compiled from other authentic sources.* Crown 8vo.

1867. **Miss M. B. Edwards,** *Winter with the Swallows.* London, 8vo.

1868. **Mrs. Lloyd Evans,** *Last Winter in Algeria.* London, 8vo.

1868. **M. A. Daux,** *Recherches sur l'origine et l'emplacement des Emporia Phéniciens.* Paris, 4to.

1871. **Lieut.-Colonel the Hon. C. S. Vereker,** *Scenes in the Sunny South.* London: Longmans and Green; 2 vols. 8vo.

1872. **Lady Herbert of Lea,** *A Search after Sunshine.* London, 8vo.

1872. **Hanoteau et Letourneux,** *La Kabylie et les Coutumes Kabyles.* An exhaustive work on Kabylia by General Hanoteau and M. Letourneux, Conseller à la Cour l'Appel. Paris: Challamel; 3 vols. large 8vo.

1874. **C. Home Douglas,** *Searches for Summer, showing the anti-Winter Tactics of an Invalid.* London and Edinburgh, 8vo.

1875. **George Gaskell,** *Algeria as it is.* London, 8vo.

1877. **Lieut.-Colonel (now Sir Lambert) Playfair,** *Travels in the Footsteps of Bruce in Algeria and Tunis.* London: C. Kegan Paul; 4to. Bruce the traveller was Consul-General at Algiers from 1763 to 1765. He subsequently made extensive explorations in Algeria and Tunis, and magnificent architectural drawings of all the Roman remains he visited, but he left no account of his journey. These drawings are in the possession of his descendant Lady Thurlow. The author has published an account of his journey over the ground traversed by Bruce, illustrated by fac-similes of his drawings. This work is now very rare, as the remaining copies of the edition were destroyed by fire in Kegan Paul's premises in 1883.

1877. **Edward Rae,** *Barbary, the Country of the Moors; a Journey from Tripoli to the Holy City of Kairwan.* London: Murray; crown 8vo, with maps and six etchings.

1878. **R. Bosworth Smith,** *Carthage and the Carthagenians.* London: Longmans, Green, and Co.; 8vo. A most careful and exhaustive study of ancient Carthage and her two greatest citizens—Hamilcar Barca and Hannibal.

1879. **V. Largeau,** *Le Pays de Rirha Ourgla, Voyage à Rhadames.* Paris: Hachette.

1880. **Paul de Tchihatchef,** *Espagne, Algérie et Tunisie.* Lettres à Michel Chevalier. Paris: J. B. Baillière et Fils; large 8vo.

1881. **E. Cosson,** *Compendium Florae Atlanticae, seu Expositio Methodica Plantarum in Algeria.* Paris: Imprimerie Nationale (in course of publication).

1881. **Alexander A. Knox,** *The New Playground, or Wanderings in Algeria.* London: C. Kegan Paul; 8vo.

1881. **Comte d'Herrisson,** *Relation d'une Mission Archéologique en Tunisie.* Paris: Société Anonyme de Publications Periodiques; 4to, with illustrations and a plan of Utica.

1881. **Louis Piesse,** *Itineraire de l'Algérie, de Tunis et de Tanger.* Paris: Hachette et Cie.; small 8vo, 7 maps. This excellent work forms one of the series of *Guides Joanne.*

1882. **Edgar Barclay,** *Mountain Life in Algeria.* London: crown 4to, with 8 full-page illustrations by Photogravure from drawings by the author.

1882. *Association Française pour l'Avancement des Sciences.* Compte Rendu de la 10e Session à Alger, 1881. Paris: 8vo, 1241 pp.; maps and illustrations.

1882. **A. M. Broadley,** *The last Punic War or Tunis Past and Present.* Edinburgh: William Blackwood and Sons; 2 vols. 8vo. The author was a barrister at Tunis, and correspondent of the *Times* during the war which resulted in the French Protectorate. His visit to the Holy City of Keroaun is especially interesting.

1882. **Ernst von Hesse-Wartegg,** *Tunis: The Land and the People.* Translated from the German. London: Chatto and Windus; 8vo, illustrations.

1884. **Charles Tissot,** *Géographie Comparée de la Province Romaine d'Afrique.* Tome Premier, Géographie Physique—Géographie Historique Chorographie. Paris: Imprimerie Nationale; 4to.

1884. **Lieut.-Colonel (now Sir Lambert) Playfair,** *The Scourge of Christendom: Annals of British relations with Algiers prior to the French Conquest.* London: Smith, Elder, and Co.; 8vo, with illustrations. Algiers is the first Consulate ever established by England. A nearly complete collection of the correspondence of diplomatic agents and consuls, and royal letters from 1600, are preserved in the Public Record Office. There is a break during the Commonwealth, but the letters of this period exist in the Rawlinson MSS. in the Bodleian. It is principally from these sources that the author has obtained his information. The great interest of the work is the subject of Christian slavery.

1885. **Rev. Alexander A. Boddy**, *To Kairwân the Holy; Scenes in Mohammedan Africa*. London: Kegan Paul, Trench, and Co.; post 8vo, maps and illustrations.

1885. **Alexander Graham, F.R.I.B.A.**, *Remains of the Roman Occupation in N. Africa, with special reference to Algeria*. Illustrated. Trans. Royal Inst. Brit. Architects. New series, vol. i.

Also another paper, by the same author and on the same subject, in 1866, with special reference to Tunisia, both most valuable and instructive papers.

1889. **Georges Balut**, *Indicateur Tunisien*, containing much interesting information regarding Tunisia.

1887. **Alexander Graham, F.R.I.B.A.**, and **H. S. Ashbee, F.S.A., F.R.G.S.**, *Travels in Tunisia*, with a glossary, a map, a Bibliography, and 50 illustrations. London: Dulau and Co.; 8vo.

The Bibliography has been completed to 1888, published separately, and forms Part II. of the general *Bibliography of the Barbary States*.

1889. **Sir R. Lambert Playfair, K.C.M.G.**, *Bibliography of the Barbary States*. Part I. *Tripoli and the Cyrenaica*. Supplementary Papers of the R.G.S., p. 58.

1888. **Sir R. Lambert Playfair, K.C.M.G.**, *Bibliography of the Barbary States*. Part III. *Algeria*, from the Expedition of Charles V in 1541 to 1887. Supplementary Papers of the R.G.S., vol. ii. part ii. pp. 130-430. Contains about 5000 articles.

INDEX AND DIRECTORY.

Abd-el-Kader.

A
ABD-EL-KADER, 55, 276.
ABDI, OUED, 213.
ABDOUNA, DJ., 184.
EL-ACHAR, OUED, 301.
EL-ACHIR, 160.
AD DIANAM, 127.
ADELIA, 170.
Road for Milianah; omnibuses meet every train *from* Algiers, 3¼ hr., 1 f.
EL-ADJIBA, 158.
AFFREVILLE, 170.
Buffet at station. *H. de Vaucluse*, good, moderate. *Omnibus* to Milianah, 1½ hr., 1 f.; to Teniet-el-Ahd to meet morning train, 8 hrs., 6 f. *Carriages* to Teniet, 20 f. *per diem.*
EL-AFFROUN, 168.
AFIA, CAPE, 118.
EL-AFIA, island, 116.
L'AGHA, 108, 155.
AGHADIR, ruins of, 259.
EL-AGHOUAT, 153; palm-gardens, 153; rocher des Chiens, 153.
AGOUMI-N-TESELLEND, 147.
AGRICULTURE, SYSTEM OF, 86.
AGRIOUN, OUED, 201.
AHL KSAR, caverns at, 158.
AÏN-ABID, 237.
AÏN-ADGEL, 164.
AÏN - AMARA, or EL-MARRAH, 239.

Aïn-Meimoun.

AÏN-ARNAT, 161.
AÏN-AYET, river, 316.
AÏN-AZOUAGHA, 228.
AÏN - BARBAR, copper mines, 121, 126.
AÏN-BARID, 163.
AÏN - BEIDA (CONSTANTINE), 234.
AÏN-BEIDA (ORAN), 246.
AÏN-BEINAN, 109.
AÏN-BESSEM, 164.
AÏN-BOU-ARREREDJ, 160.
AÏN-BOU-DINAR, 248.
AÏN-BOU-M'RAOU, 118.
AÏN-CHEGGA, 218.
AÏN-DRAHAM, 307.
Hôtel des Pacificateurs, poor.
AÏN-EL-ARBAA, 255.
AÏN-EL-BORDJ, 234.
AÏN-EL-ESNAM, 158.
AÏN-FEKRINA, 281.
AÏN-GHORABA, Caravanserai of, 264.
AÏN-EL-GHORAB, 165.
AÏN - EL - HADJAR, 200, 277.
AÏN - EL-HAMMAM, 147, 276.
AÏN-EL-IBEL, 152.
AÏN-ESH-SHANIA, 229.
AÏN-ET-TURK, 184.
AÏN-FAKROUN, 234.
AÏN-FEZZA, 266.
AÏN-GUETTAR, 229.
AÏN-KERMAN, 164.
AÏN - KHENCHLA, 213, 236.
AÏN-KHIAL, 255.
AÏN-MAGHRAMMA, 200.
AÏN-MAKLOUF, 150.
AÏN-MEIMOUN, 213.

Aït-el-Ahsen.

AÏN-MELILA, 205.
AÏN-M'KEBRITA, 80.
AÏN-MOKRA, iron mines, 126.
AÏN-MOUDJARAR, 150.
AÏN-MOUDJEBAR, 150.
AÏN-MOULABER, 234.
AÏN - OMM - EL - ALLEUG, 157.
AÏN-OUERROU, 152.
AÏN-OUSSERA, 151.
AÏN-REGADA, 237.
AÏN-SABA, 151.
AÏN-SAHRA, 267.
AÏN-SEFSIFA, 278.
AÏN-SEFRA, 278.
AÏN-SENNOUR, 299.
AÏN-SKOUN, 270.
AÏN - SUEFRA, ravine, 247.
AÏN-TAHAMIMIME, 299.
AÏN-TALBA, 279.
AÏN-TASSERA, 160.
AÏN-TÉDELÈS, 249.
AÏN-TEKBALET, 255.
AÏN-TELLOUT, 266.
AÏN - TEMOUCHENT (ORAN), 255.
Hôtel de Londres.
AÏN-TOUKRIA, 142.
AÏN-TOUNDA, ravine, 175.
AÏN-YAGOOT, 205.
AÏOUN SAAD, 185.
AÏOUN SRAKNA, 105.
AÏOUNET - BOU - BEKR, 278.
AÏSAI. OUED, 145.
AISSAOUI, religious dances in Algiers, 100.
AÏT-BOU-YOOSUF, 145.
AÏT-EL-AHSEN, 146.

Aït-Iraten.

AÏT - IRATEN, tribe, the, 145.
AÏWENAT, or AÏOUN-ED-DIAB, 230.
AKBOU, 204, 244.
AKBOU, mamelon of, 158, 204.
ALFA - FIBRE, 85, 151, 271.
ALGERIA, description of, 12; tours in, 112.

ALGIERS, 93.

	PAGE
Aïssaoui, the	100
Aqueducts	101
Cemeteries	101
Churches—	
English	96
Cathedral	98
Notre Dame des Victoires	99
Ste. Croix	99
St. Augustine	99
Jesuits	99
French Protestant	99
Clubs	101
Educational Establishments	102
Environs	105
Fortifications	104
Gates	102
Harbour	103
Historical Notice	94
Hospital, Civil	102
Hospital, Military	102
Houses	95
Jews' Synagogue	99
Kasba, or Citadel	104
Library and Museum	102
Lyceum	102
Moorish Houses	95
Mosques—	
The Grand	99
The New	100
Djamâa Safir	100
Zaouia of Abd-er-Rahman eth-Thalebi	100
Observatory	106
Palace	103
Population	93
Public Buildings	101
Shops, Bazaars	96, 103
Streets and Squares	94, 95

H.B.M. Consul General, Sir R. Lambert Playfair, K.C.M.G.
Vice-Consul, Geo. W. Crawford, Esq.
Consulate, 12 Rue du Hamma.

Algiers.

Hours of attendance, 8 to 11 A.M., 1 to 3 P.M.
Consul U. S. A., Charles Grellet, Esq., 3 Rue Roland de Bussy.

Hotels in Town. These are convenient when the traveller intends making only a short stay. *H. d' Europe*, the best; *H. de l'Oasis*, good; both on the *Boulevard National*, overlooking the sea. *H. de la Régence*, an old established house on the Place du Gouvernement, good; *H. des Étrangers*, Place Bresson, excellent cuisine. Second class hotels: *H. du Louvre; de Paris; de Genève.* Cost from 10 to 15 f. per day, including attendance and wine.

Hotels at Mustafa Supérieur—all good. In every way preferable for a lengthened stay, the higher up on the hill the better is the air. In this order they are:—
H. St. George. Open November 1889, under the management of a Swiss hotel-keeper. 12 f. 50 c. per day, including attendance and wine. 70 bedrooms. *H. Kirsch*. From 12 f. 50 c. to 15 f., including attendance, without wine. 50 beds. *Grand Hôtel de Mustafa Supérieur*. From 12 f. to 15 f. including attendance, without wine. *Hôtel d'Orient*,[1] *Hôtel Continental*.[1] The two last are nearest the town, and are under the same management.

[1] These hotels have not furnished information regarding terms.

Algiers.

Pensions: *Villa du Palmier*, kept by an English lady, Mrs. Jennings, excellent. *L'Olirage*, kept by an American lady, Mrs. Whitcombe, excellent. *P. Val Riant*, Campagne Jolly, fair. *P. Victoria*, L'Agha, comfortable and cheap. *P. Anglo-Suisse*, Village d'Isly, fair. The cost of Pensions may be put down as a little less than hotels, 8 to 12 f. a day, including wine.

Restaurants. All the hotels in town have restaurants also; in addition there are *Taverne Grüber*, Boulevard de la République; *Cosmopolitan Bar*, R. du Laurier—sends out breakfasts and dinners. Several *Fish Restaurants* for déjeûner, near the Fish Market, at S. corner of New Mosque.

Cafés: *Café de la Bourse; d'Appolon;* both on the Place du Gouvernement; *Grüber*, B. de la République; and many others.

Means of Communication. Always consult time-tables of various companies.
A. *Compagnie Général Transatlantique*, see p. 1.
I. Daily departures from Marseilles to Algiers, 12.30 P.M. Return daily, noon. The passage by the fastest boats occupies about 24 hours. II. Port-Vendres to Algiers, Tues. 6.30 P.M. Return from Algiers Thurs. noon. III. Marseilles to Oran direct, Sat. and Tues. 4 P.M. Return from Oran

Algiers.

Wed. and Frid. 5 p.m. IV. Marseilles to Cette, Port - Vendres, Carthagena (fortnightly), and Oran, Tues. 11 p.m. Return from Oran, twice a month, *via* Port-Vendres and Cette, and twice by Port-Vendres *vid* Carthagena. The former, Mond. 5 p.m. ; the latter, 10 p.m.

Cost of Passage to Algiers, 100 f. first class, 80 f. second class.

V. Algiers along the coast to Tunis, Frid. noon.

B. *Compagnie de Navigation Mixte (Touache)*. 1. From Algiers to Marseilles and Cette, Thurs. 6 p.m. ; fare, 50 f. Return Thurs. 6 p.m. II. Algiers to Bône and other ports on coast, Tues. 8 p.m.

C. *Soc. Gén. de Transports Marit. à Vapeur*. Marseilles to Algiers, Tues. and Sat. 5 p.m. Return Tues. and Sat. 5 p.m.

Cabs. Every public conveyance is bound to produce a table of fares. For a whole day (12 hrs.), 20 f. ; half a day (6 hrs.), 11 f. By the hour, in town, 2 f. ; outside, from 2.40 to 3 f. By the course, from 1 to 7 f. according to distance. See table.

Omnibuses. Good services run in all directions. To *Plateau Saulière* and *Mustafa Inférieur* every few minutes. To *Mustafa Supérieur* every ½ hr. († to and ¼ past) ; return at ½ hrs. To *Colonne Voirol* every hour. There are others to *Hussein Dey*, St.

Algiers.

Eugène, Pointe Pescade, El-Biar, etc. Fares from 10 c. to 40 c.

Railway Station (terminus of all lines), on the quay. Passengers for Mustafa Supérieur may get out at the previous station on the line, that of *L'Agha*, but should arrange beforehand for a carriage.

Theatres. *Municipal*, in the Place Bresson, a handsome edifice capable of containing nearly as many people as the Grand Opera in Paris. *Variétés*, Rue d'Isly, good.

Societies : Société historique ; d'Agriculture ; de Climatologie.

Architects : *English*, Benj. Bucknall, Campagne Stephann ; *French*, George Ginauchain.

English Doctors: Dr. Thomson, Villa Belvedere ; Dr. Gardner, Villa Regina ; Dr. Stanley Stevens, Grand Hotel de Mustafa ; all at Mustafa Supérieur.

French Doctors. Those most in the habit of attending English are Dr. Stephann, 16 Boulevard de la République ; Dr. Bruch, No. 3 Rue Arago.

English Dentist : Mr. Clark, Place Bresson.

Nurses. The nearest place where nurses can be obtained is the Holland Nursing Institution, Villa Estradié, Monté de Cimiez at Nice (telegraphic address, "Woodcock, Nice"), strongly recommended. Les Sœurs de Bon Secours, Rue de la Fonderie.

Chemists : *Obrecht*,

Algiers.

Rue Bab-Azoun ; *Monnet*, Place du Gouvernement.

Banks : *Banque de l'Algérie, Crédit Foncier et Agricole, Crédit Lyonnais*, all on the Boulevard de la République ; *Compagnie Algérienne*, Place Bresson ; *French Private Banker*, M. Deglaire, Rue Juba. Cheques on England cashed by *Messrs. Burke and Delacroix*, Boulevard de la République.

English Merchants · Messrs. Burke and Delacroix, 4 Boulevard de la République, agents for Lloyds, for the British India S.N. Company, for Holt's ocean line, and for Moss of Liverpool. Travellers will probably obtain better exchange for cheques and circular notes here than at the banks.

Shipping Agents : Stuart Bankhart, 36 Rampe Chasseloupe Laubat ; Desseigne, 4 Boulevard de la République.

Markets : There are markets for the sale of articles of daily consumption held every morning in the Place de la Lyre and Place de Chartres. It is well worth while to visit these before breakfast, to see the beautiful fresh fruit, flowers, and vegetables just brought in from the country.

The fish-market is held beneath the Boulevard de la République, nearly opposite the Place du Gouvernement.

The market for Arab commodities and provisions is in the Place d'Isly.

Algiers.
House and General Agents: *Messrs. Dunlop and Tustes*, 15 Rue d'Isly. They have also a grocery store and a butcher's shop. Send provisions of all kinds to villas at Mustafa, and generally are most useful to travellers.

Churches: *Anglican*, see p. 96. *Chaplain*, Rev. H. B. Freeman. *Presbyterian*, Mustafa Supérieur, built entirely at the expense of Sir Peter Coats, see p. 98. Information as to hours of services posted up at hotels and consulate. *Roman Catholic, Cathedral*, see p. 98; *Nôtre-Dame-des-Victoires*, Bab-el-Oued, formerly a mosque, built in the 17th century by Ali Bitchenin, a Christian renegade; *Sainte Croix*, also an old mosque near the Kasbah; *St. Augustin*, built in 1878, in the Rue de Constantine; *Jesuit Church*, in the Rue des Consuls. *French Protestant Temple*, Rue de Chartres. *Synagogue*, Rue Caton. *Mosques*, see p. 99.

Libraries: *Government Library and Museum*. Open every day after 1 P.M. R. de l'État Major. See also p. 102. *English Circulating*, in connection with the church. The terms are very low, and visitors are strongly advised to subscribe to it. *University*, in the École Supérieur des Lettres, etc., at the Agha.

Shops. The best shops are in the Bab-Azoun. The bazaars where Arab

Algiers.
articles are sold are in the passages leading from the Place du Gouvernement, the Rue de la Lyre, and the Place de la Cathedral.

Beautiful **Arab Embroideries** are made at the establishment of Madame Luce Benaben, Rue Bruce. **Old Embroideries and Curiosities** of various kinds are to be had of Mr. Bucknall (architect), Campagne Stephann, Fontaine Bleue, Mustafa. Monsieur Marlier, Rue Jenina, makes exquisite **brasswork**.

Booksellers: *Gavault St. Layer*, Rue Bab-Azoun; *Jourdan*, Place du Gouvernement.

Photographers: *Famin*, Rue Bab-Azoun, unequalled for views; *Geyser*, on stairs leading to Place du Chartres from Rue Bab-Azoun; excellent for likenesses.

Livery Stables: Mame, 24 Rue d'Isly; Moise, 43 Rue d'Isly.

Newspapers, etc. There are many daily newspapers published in Algiers, the most important of which are the "Moniteur de l'Algérie," the "Akhbar," the "Dépêche," the "Vigie Algérienne," and the "Petit Colon." Amongst the reviews are, the "Revue Africaine," journal of the proceedings of the Algerian Historical Society, in which, and in the similar publication of Constantine, "Recueil des Notices et Mémoires de la Société Archéologique," and that

Algiers.
of Oran, "Bulletin de la Société de Géographie et d'Archéologie," are many valuable papers on Algeria.

Baths. The best European baths are, *Bains du Hamma*, Rue du Hamma, next theatre; *Bains du Square*, Rue Arago.

Moorish Bath: Rue de l'État Major, open for men from 5 P.M. till noon next day.

Sea Baths at the Agha.

Club: *English* (see p. 102). Members' subscriptions, 125 f. per annum. Season subscriptions, 125 f. and 10 f. entrance. Monthly subscriptions, 40 f. Weekly subscriptions, 20 f. For rules and all other information apply to honorary secretary or manager at the Club. *Cercle d'Alger*, Boulevard de la République, entrance R. de Palmyre.

Government Library and Museum, see Libraries, and page 102.

Thomas Cook and Son have a branch office in the Square Bresson, where tickets to and from England may be obtained, also for tours in Algeria and Tunis, and in any part of the Mediterranean. **Murray's hand-books on sale**.

Courier and Guide: Joseph Bordj, care of Messrs. Dunlop and Tustes.

Post and Telegraph Offices: *Head-Office*, Boulevard de la République. *Branch*, E. side of the Place du Gouverne-

Algiers.

ment. *Another Branch at Governor's Palace, Mustafa, officially styled Mustafa Palais.*
Dressmakers: Madame Adler, Rue du Soudan. Madame Philoch, 7 Rue Rovigo.
Shoemaker: Moreaux, Place du Gouvernement.
Confectioners: *Fille,* 2 Rue Bab-Azoun; *Reiffel,* 15 Rue Bab - Azoun (5 o'clock tea may be had at either).
Algiers to Aumale and Bou Saâda, 163.
Algiers to Cherchel and Tipasa, 133.
Algiers to Constantine by rail, 155.
Algiers to el-Aghouat, 147.
Algiers to Coleah and the Tombeau de la Chrétienne, 137.
Algiers to Cape Matifou and the Ruins of Rusgunia, 111.
Algiers to Oran by rail, 165.
Algiers to Philippeville, Bône, and Tunis by sea, 113.
Algiers to Rovigo and the Baths of Hammam Melouan, 140.
Algiers to Ténès by Orleansville, 246.
Algiers to Teniet-el-Ahd, 141.
Algiers to Tizi-Ouzou and Fort National, 143.
ALLAGHAN, 204.
ALLALA, OUED, 246.

ALMA, 155.
Hôtel d'Orient.
ALYPIUS OF TAGASTE, 90, 300.
AMEUR EL-AIN, 133.
AMIMIN, OUED, 127; hot springs, 127.
AMINS, the, 16.

Auberge du.

AMMI MOUSSA, 175.
LES AMOUCHA, 200
EL ANASSER, 160.
ANCHIR DAMOUS, 230.
ANNOUNA, OUED, 239.
AOUINET-ED-DIEB, 221.
AQUÆ CALIDÆ, 169.
AQUÆ TIBILITINÆ, 238.
AQUEDUCTS: Roman, 134, 149; Ain-el-Bled, 227; Ain-Chela, 227; Simittu, 301.
ARAB INVASIONS, 32, 90.
ARABIC WORDS, Glossary of, xi.
ARABS, THE, 8, 9.
EL-ARBA, 163.
EL-ARBÂA, 212.
L'ARBAL (GHABAL), 179.
ARBATACH, 111.
ARCH OF CONSTANTINE, 332.
ARCHÆOLOGY, 89.
ARCHITECTURE, DOMESTIC, 95.
AREG, the, 19.
EL-ARIA, 198.
ARIANA, 297.
LES ARIBS, 171.
Army, the, 66.
AROUSA, OUED, 174.
ARRÊT OF ST. LUCIEN, 269.
ARRÊT DES PINS, 271.
ARRÊT DES TREMBLES, 269.
EL-ARROUCH, OUED, 185.
ARSENARIA, 272.
Artesian Wells, 18, 219, 221, 326.
ARZEU, 272.
ARZEU TO MASCARA, SAIDA, AND GERYVILLE, 272.
ARZEU, OLD, 274.
EL-ASSAFIA, 154.
ASSEL, DJ., 200.
EL-ATEUF, 154.
ATLAS MOUNTAINS, 13, 103.
ATMENIA, OUED, 162.
LES ATTAFS, 172.
AUBERGE DU 108 KIL., 150.

Barral.

AUBERGE BELLO, 266.
AUBERGE DES DEUX PONTS, 149.
AUBERGE DU NADOR, 149.
AUBERGE DE LA RAMPE, 141.
AUBERGE DU ROULAGE, 150
AUMALE, 164.
Hôtel de Roulage.
Diligence from Algiers every second day, 17 hrs. 20 f. A better route from Bordj Bouira.
AURÉS MOUNTAINS, 17, 211.
AUSUM, 244.
AUZIA, 164.
AZIB - BEN - ALI - CHERIF, 203.
AZIB-ZAMOUN, 143.
AZROU-N-TCHOUR, 245.

B

BAB EL - KHAMIS, arch, 262.
BAB TAZZA, 267.
BABA ALI, 166.
BABOR, ascent of, 118, 200.
EL-BADJA, 303.
BAHIRA - ET - TOWILA, 234.
BAHIRAH GOURNATA, 311.
BAHR EN-NISSA, 119.
BAHRS, or GOUFFRES, 19, 74.
BAINS DE LA REINE, 80, 183.
EL-BALI, 213.
BARBAROSSA, the brothers, 34.
BARBER, DJ., 176.
BARDO, excursion to the, 297.
LE BARRAGE, 172.
BARRAGES OF THE KHAMIS, 111; the Chelif, 172; the Habra, 178; the Sig, 170.
BARRAL, 241.

Bastion de France.
BASTION DE FRANCE, 130.
BATNA, 206.
Hôtel des Étrangers, bad; H. de Paris, said to be better; both quite unworthy of such an important place.
Carriages can be hired for Timegad, 30 f.; and mules for cedar forest.
BATNA, cedar forest, 211.
BATNA, OUED, 206.
BAUDENS, 265.
BEAUFORT, DUC DE, expedition, 117.
BEAUPRÈTRE, COL., massacre of, 278.
BEDEAU, 271.
BEGHRA, DJ., 271.
BEGRADAS, 233.
BEJA, 303.
BEL ABBÈS SIDI, 269.
BEL-HACEL, 249.
BEL KEFIF, 221.
BELLE-FONTAINE, 155.
BELLEVUE, 249.
BEN AKNOUN, 106.
BEN ALI CHERIF, 60, 144, 204.
BEN BECHIR, 303.
BEN CHICAO, 150.
BEN HINNI, gorge, 156.
BENI BIZAZ, 118.
BENI ILLILTEN, 245.
BENI ISGUEN, 154.
BENI ISMAILI, 201.
BENI MANISSAR, 62.
BENI MANSOUR, 158.
BENI MELEKUCH, 244.
BENI MERED, 166.
BENI MISTER, 267.
BENI M'ZAB, 11, 154.
BENI OURTILAN, 160.
BENI AAD, stalactite caves, 263, 266.
BENI AMRAN, 156.

BENI SAF, 279.
Brit. Vice.-Consul, T. O. Stewart, Esq.
No decent hotel.

Biskra.
Means of Communication by Sea: The steamers of the Transatlantique Co. touch every fortnight on their way from Oran to Nemours, Melila, Malaga, Gibraltar, and Tangier, and vice versâ.
IRON MINES, 279; harbour, 280.
BENI SALAH, mountains, 167; village, 167.
BENI SNOUS, mountains, 264.
BENI YENNI, 146.
BENIAN, 276.
BENT SAIDA, 315.
BERBERS, the, 7.
BERD, OUED, 200.
BERDA, hot springs, 241.
BERDI, OUED, 158.
BEROUAGIA, 150.
BERRIAN, 154.
EL-BETHOM, 163.
EL-BIAR, 106, 213.
BIBANS, 159; see Portes de Fer.
BIBLIOGRAPHY of the most important works on Algeria and Tunis, 337.
BIDA COLONIA, site of, 147.
EL-BIOD, 278.
BIR-EL-ARCH, 162.
BIR ATTAKA, 311.
BIR EL-BOUÏTA, 318.
BIR REBALOU (AKBA-LOU), 163.
BIR ROGAA, 234.
BIR TOUTA, 166.
BIRDS OF ALGERIA, 69.
BIRKET-EL-FARAS, lake, 229.
BIRKHADEM, 107.
BIRMANDRAIS, 107.

BISKRA, 215.
Hôtel Victoria, close to the station, one of the best in the colony. H. du Sahara, an old house,

Boghari.
less favourably situated, cheaper.
Diligence to Tuggurt every second day; takes 3 days; cost 100 f. Bad.
PAGE
Oasis of Gaddecha and Filiah . . . 215
Fort St. Germain . 215
Market-place . . 215
Climate, M. Landon's Garden . . . 215
Hot Baths . . . 216
Oasis and Date Palms 216

Biskra to Tuggurt, 217.
BISKRA, OUED, 215.

BIZERTA, 133, 311.
Hôtel de France, poor.
Carriage from Tunis 20 f. a day.
BIZERTA, excursion to 309.
BIZOT, 185.
BLAD GUITOUN, 143.
BLAKE, ADMIRAL, at Tunis, 43.

BLIDAH, 166.
Hôtel d'Orient, good; Hôtel Gerond, comfortable.
Railway Station a short distance from town. Omnibus fare, 1 f.
Hospital for civil and military, near the Porte d'Alger.
PAGE
History . . . 166
Situation . . . 167
Gates, Hospital, Theatre 167
Cavalry Barracks . 167
Promenade . . 167

Koubra of Sidi Abd-el-Kader, 168.
BOAR, WILD, HUNTING, 68.

BOGHAR, 151.
Hôtel Celestine.

BOGHARI, 151.
Hôtel des Messageries tolerable.
Omnibus to Boghar.

INDEX AND DIRECTORY 347

Bône.
BÔNE, 121.
  Brit. Vice - Consul :
Abel Delacroix.
  Hôtel d'Orient, in the Cours Nationale, good ; *H. de Commerce* (Marius). Rue des Volontaires.
Station of *Eastern Telegraphic Company*.
Railway to Constantine and Tunis.
  Means of Communication : A. *Compagnie Gén. Transatlantique*. I. From Marseilles, direct, Sat. 4 P.M. Return Tues. 4 P.M. II. Marseilles *viâ* Ajaccio to Bône, Mond. 4 P.M. Return Sat. 5 P.M. III. Marseilles *viâ* Philippeville to Bône, Wed. 4 P.M. IV. To La Calle and Goletta, Mond. 3 P.M. V. To Philippeville, Djedjelli, Bougie, and Marseilles, Thurs. 9 A.M. VI. Along the coast to Algiers, Sund. 11 P.M.
  B. *Compagnie Navig. Mixte* (Touache) weekly between Algiers and Bône.

	PAGE
History	121
Streets	121
Squares	123
Cathedral, Church, Mosque	123
Kasba, Barracks, Military Hospital, Theatre, Roman Remains	123
Harbour, Quays	123
Excursions	123

Bône to Constantine, by rail, 236.
Bône to Tunis by rail, 299.
BORDJ BENI MANSOUR, 158.
BORDJ BOGHNI, 157.
BORDJ BONI, 242.

BORDJ BOU - ARREREDJ, 160.
  Hôtel des Voyageurs.

Bou Tafsa.
BORDJ BOUIRA, 157.
  Hôtel de la Poste, poor.
  II. de la Colonie.
  Diligence to Aumale, 5 hrs.
BORDJ CASTILLE, 327.
BORDJ KAID EL-AKHDAR, 228.
BORDJ EL-KALA, 127.
BORDJ MEDJANA, 242.

BORDJ MENAÏEL, 143.
  Hôtel de la Colonie.

BORDJ SABATH, 237.
BORDJ SEBAOU, 143.
BORDJ TOUM, 304.
BORDJ ZIKRI, 234.
BOTIOUA, 274.
BOUAC, Cape, 114.
BOU-CEDRAIA, 151.
BOU CHATER, 133, 310.
BOU DRIECEN, DJ., 213.
BOU FAIMA, 143.
BOU-GHAZOUL, 151.
BOU GUELFA, 143.
BOU HADJAR, 255.
BOU HAMMAMA, 213.
BOU HAMDAN, OUED, 240.
BOU ISMAIL, 137.
BOU JAGAR, or BOU-DJABAR, DJ., 229.
BOU KADIR, 174.
BOU KANEFIS, 270.
BOU KOTAN, OUED, 159.
BOU KSAIBA, 121.
BOU LIFFA BAY, 129.
BOU MEDFA, 169.
BOU MEDIN, 260.
BOU MERZOUG, OUED, 197.
BOU NOUARA, 236.
BOU NOURA, 154.
BOU ROUMI, 133.

BOU-SÂADA, 165.
  No decent *hotel*.

BOU SAR, 142.
BOU SELAM, river, 200.
BOU SELLAM, OUED, 161.
BOU SFER, 184.
BOU TAFSA, 200.

Brédéah.
BOU TLELIS, 254.
  A good *inn*.
BOU ZAINA, OUED, 213.
BOU ZAREA, 106.
BOU ZHOUAR, 142.
BOU ZIGZA, 111.
BOUDOUAOU, 155.

BOUFARIK, 166.
  Hôtel Benoit, *H. Mazagran*, *Cercle Civil*, frequented by colonists ; bedrooms.
BOUGIARONE, 118.

BOUGIE, 114.
  Hôtel de France, excellent ; *H. d'Orient et de la Marine*, not recommended.
  Direct railway communication with Algiers.
  Carriage for Sétif through Chabet, 120 f.
  Means of Communication by Sea. A. *Compagnie Transatlantique.* I. From Algiers along coast to Tunis. Leaves Algiers Frid. noon. Ar. Bougie Sat. Return, for Dellys and Algiers, Tues. 8 P.M. II. To Marseilles direct, Frid. 8 P.M. III. Marseilles, Ajaccio, Bône and Philippeville to Bougie, Mond. 4 P.M.
  B. *Compagnie de Navigation Mixte*. From Algiers to Bougie and on to Bône, Tues. 8 P.M.

	PAGE
Population	114
History	114
Kasba, Forts	115
Amphitheatre	116
Roman remains	116

BOUGIE TO BENI MANSOUR, 202.
BOUJAT, COL DE, 211.
BOUNDARIES, 12.
BOURKIKA, 133.
BOUTAN, river, 170.
BRAO, DJ. SIDI, 162.
BRÉDÉAH, 254.

INDEX AND DIRECTORY

Bugeaud.
BUGEAUD, village, 125.
BULLA REGIA, 302.
BUREAU ARABE, 65.
BUSTARD-SHOOTING, 69.

C

CALCEUS HERCULIS, 213.
CAMARATA, 279.
CAMEL, THE, 71.
CAMP DES CHÊNES, 141, 149.
CAMP DE GÉNIE, 306.
CAMP DU MARÉCHAL, 143.
CAMP DES ZOUAVES, 150.
CAMPBELL, THE POET, at Bougie, 114.
CAP CAXINE, 109.
CAP DE FER, OR RAS EL HADID, 121.
CAP FILFILA, 121.
CAP DE GARDE, 121.
CAP NEGRO, 132.
CAP OKAS, 202.
CAP ROSA, 127.
CARAGA, 322.
CARBON, CAPE, OR EL-METKOUB, 114; lighthouse, 116.
CARPETS at El Kalâa, 176.
CARTENNA, 246.
CARTHAGE, 291.

	PAGE
Situation	292
Chapel of St. Louis	292
Palace of Dido	294
Temple of Æsculapius	294
Forum	294
Harbours	294
Cisterns	295
Basilica	295
Amphitheatre	296
Circus, Theatre	296
History	296
Martyrs	296
Douar esh-Chott	297

CASTELLUM AUZIENSE, 164.
CASTELLUM MEDIANUM, 242.
CASTELLUM, TINGITANUM, 173.
CASTIGLIONE, 137.
Hôtel de Tapis Vert, excellent. Other hotels

Chott el-Chergui.
principally for summer bathers.
CATTLE, NATIVE, 71.
CAVALLO, CAPE, 116.
CAXINE, CAPE, 109.
CEDAR FOREST AT BATNA, 211; at Beni Salah, 167; at Teniet, 141.
CEREALS, THE, of Algeria, 83.
CHABET-EL-AKHIRA GORGE, 200.
CHABET EL-AMEUR, 143.
CHABRO, OUED, 221.
CHACHIAS, manufacture of, 310.
CHANZY, 270.
CHAPEAU DU GENDARME, 153.
CHARRIER, 276.
CHÂTEAU NEUF, 106.
CHAWIA TRIBE, the, 7, 212.
CHAWI PATOIS, 212.
CHEGGA, 218.
CHELIF, plain of the, 81, 141.
CHELIF, river, 142, 171.
CHELLATA, 244.
CHELLATA, COL DE, 245.
CHELLIA, ascent of, 213.
CHEMTOU, 301.
CHÉNIA, 160.
CHENNOUA, DJ., 134.
CHERAGAS, 108.

CHERCHEL, 135.
Hôtel de Commerce, excellent.
Carriage to El-Affroun, 18 f. To Coleah, 2 days, 45 f.

	PAGE
History	135
Amphitheatre	135
Museum	136
Military Hospital	136

Cherchel to Tenes on horseback, 136.
CHERF, OUED, 240.
CHETMA, 217.
CHIFFA, river, 148.
CHOTT EL-CHERGUI, 277.

Constantine.
CHOTT MELGHIGH, the, 18, 218.
CHOTTS, the, 277.
CHOTTS, or SEBKAS, 77.
CHOULI, river, 266.
LES CINQ PALMIERS, 246.
CLIMATE, 2.
CLOTHING, 5.
CLYPEA, the ancient, 317.
COL DES BENI AÏCHA, 155.
COL DE BABOUCH, 307.
COL DES JUIFS, 274.
COL DES OLIVIERS, 185.
COL DES PINS, 158.
COL DE SABLE, 154.
COL DE TIROURDA, 147.

COLEAH, 137.
Hôtel de Paris.
COLLO, 119; bay, 118.
COLONIA AUGUSTI, 246.
COLONISATION, 81.
COLUMN FOUND AT PERRÉGAUX, 178.
CONDÉ SMENDOU, 185.
CONFLAGRATION OF FORESTS, 89, 126.

CONSTANTINE, 185.
Hôtels d'Orient, de Paris, and *du Louvre*, all fairly good.

	PAGE
History	185
Situation	187
Gates	188
Abattoir	189
The Sidi Rachid, Hill of Mansoura	189
Barracks	189
Bridge of El Kantara	189
Warm baths of Sidi Mecid	191
Tomb of the silversmith	192
Koubba of Sidi Mohammed el-Ghorab	192
Tomb of Salah Bey	193
Streets and squares	193
Churches and mosques	193, 194
Palace of Constantine	194
Harem of Salah Bey	194
Kasba hospital	195
Roman remains	195
Garden of the Artillery	196
Palais de Justice, Museum	196

INDEX AND DIRECTORY 349

Constantine.

PAGE
Subterranean Passages 196
Aqueduct, Stone Pyramid to Comte Damrémont . . . 196
Markets, Manufactures 197
Excursions . . 197
Megalithic Monuments 197
Arch of . . . 327

Constantine to Algiers, 199.
Constantine to Batna and Biskra, 204.
Constantine to Bône by rail, 236.

CONSULS, BRITISH, in Algeria, 334; in Tunis, 336.
COPPER MINES, 121, 235, 246.
CORAL FISHING, 127.
CORBELIN, Cape, 114.
CORK TREE, THE, 88.
CORSO, OUED, 155.
COTTON, 84.

D

DAHRA, the, 174; population, 175.
DAKLA, PITON DU, 150.
DAOUDA, 137.
DATE PALM, THE, 84; at el-Aghouat, 153; Biskra, 216; el-Kantara, 214; Tuggurt, 220.
DAYA, 271.
DEBBA, 177.
DEBROUSSE, M., 178.
DEER, RED, 71.
DELLYS, 61, 113.
Hôtels de la Colonie, de France.
DESBROUSSEVILLE, 274.
DESCRIPTION, GENERAL, OF ALGERIA, 12.
DHARA, 264.
DIVISIONS, NATURAL, 13.
DJAMÂAT-ES-SAHARIDJ, 146.
DJEBEL FILFILA, 121.
DJEBEL GARCA, 235.
DJEBEL HAMIMAT, 235.
DJEBEL RIGHIS, 235.

Duzerville.

DJEBEL TEMOULGA, 172.
DJEDAR (tombs), 251.
DJEDEIDA, 304.
DJELFA, 152.
EL-DJEM, 320; history, 320; amphitheatre, 321.
DJEMÂA, the, 15.
DJEMÂA, OUED, 140, 163, 202.
DJENAN EL-MESKINE, 269.
DJER, OUED, 168.
DJERBA, 326.
  British Cons. Agent, M. Joseph Parienti. No *hotel.*
EL-DJERDA, promontory, 119.
LA DJIDIOUIA, or ST. AIMÉ, 175.
LA DJIDIOUIA, OUED, 175.
DJIDJELLY, 116.
DJILALI BEN AMER, *Caravanserai,* 250.
DJINET, Cape, 196.
DJURDJURA, DJ., 145; ascent of, 245.
DOLMENS, 199; *see* Megalithic.
DOUAR ECH-CHOTT, 297.
DOUARS, 9.
DOWAR EL-HADJ BEL KASSEM BEN ZORARI, 308.
DRA-BEN-KEDDA, 143.
DRA-EL-MIZAN, 143, 157.
  Hôtel de la Jeune France, fairly good.
DREA, 221.
DUBLINEAU, 275.
DUPERRÉ, 171.
DUVIVIER, 241.
  Junction for Tunis. Village 2½ kil. from railway station. Of the two *hotels* that of Marius Lavagne is the least bad.
DUZERVILLE, 242.

El-Kef.

E

EARTHQUAKES, 58, 80, 117, 168.
EDDOUS, OUED, 158.
EDOUGH, DJ., 121; ascent, 124.
EGHRIS, plain, 265, 275.
EL-AFFROUN, 168.
  Diligences to Marengo and Cherchel meet every train *from* Algiers.
  Hôtel de la Gare, at station; *H. du petit frère,* in village; no sleeping accommodation.
EL-AGHOUAT, 153.
  Hôtel du Sud.
  Diligences from Medea in 2 days, 80 f.
  Carriage, 400 or 500 f., and to the Oases of the Beni Mzab.
EL-ARBA, 163.
  Hôtel des Étrangers, fairly good.
EL-ENSOR, 279.
EL-ESNAM, 158,
EL-EUBBAD, 260.
EL-GUERRAH, 163.
  Junction for Biskra. No *hotel.* A wretched buffet.
EL-KANTARA, 213, 327.
  Hôtel d'Orient.
EL-KANTARA, bridge of, 214.
EL-KANTARA, 213; Oasis, 214.
EL-KANTARA, OUED, 214.
EL-KEF, 308.
  The accommodation for European travellers is of the roughest kind. Lodgings can be had at several houses dignified as *hôtels.*
  Hôtel de Kef; H. de France; H. Messageries Guiraud. All bad.

El-Kef.
Service of omnibuses with Souk el-Arbāa.
EMIGRATION TO ALGERIA, 82.
ENFIDA, the, 318.
ER-RAHEL, 254.
ESH-SHAM, DJ., 141.
EUCALYPTUS, the, 89.
EULMA, tribe, 162.
EXMOUTH, LORD, at Algiers, 51, 52.

F

FAID, OUED, 200.
FALCONRY, 69.
FAMINE IN ALGERIA, 58.
FEDALA, OUED, 213.
FEDJ-EL-MEKTA, forest, 297.
FEDJ-EL-MERIDJ, 307.
FEIDJET EL-GHOUSSA, 228.
FEKAN, OUED, 265.
FEMALES, POSITION OF, 10.
FEMME SAUVAGE, valley, 107.
FER, CAP DE, 121.
FER, LES PORTES DE, 159.
FERGOUG, OUED, 178.
FERKATS, 9.
FERMATOU, village, 200.
LA FERME, 246.
FERNANA, 307.
FESDIS, 206.
FEZARA, lake, 126.
FIGS, 83.
FILFILA, Cape, 121.
FILIAH, oasis, 215.
FIRIS, plain, 213.
FISH, 72; ejected by Artesian Wells, 73.
FLORA, THE, OF ALGERIA, 86.
FODDA, OUED, 172.
FONDUK, 111.
EL-FONDUK, 310.
FONTAINE DES GAZELLES, 214.
FONTAINE DU GÉNIE, 136.
FONTAINE DES PRINCES, 125.

Ghardimaou.
FOOD, NATIONAL, 10.
FORESTS, 87.
FORT DE L'EAU, 111.
FORT DE L'EMPEREUR, 104.
FORT GÉNOIS, 124.
FORT-NATIONAL, 145.
Hôtel des Touristes, poor.
Excursions from, 146.
FORTASSA, 250.
Diligence to Mascara, 6 hrs., 4.50 f.
FRAIS VALLON, 105.
FRANCHETTI, 276.
FRARAH, 241.
FRECHIH, OUED, 248.
FRENDA, 254.
Hôtel Maestracci, poor.
LES FRÊNES, or EL-BETHOM, 163.
FROHA, 276.
FRUITS, 83.

G

GABES, 325.
British Cons. Agent, F. Calleja.
No *hotel*.
GADDECHA, oasis, 215.
GALITA, island, 132.
GAMRHA, 219.
GARCA, DJ., 235.
GARDE, CAP DE, 121.
GAZELLE HUNTING, 69.
GELÄA, 243.
GELDAMAN HILLS, 204.
GEOLOGY, 75.
GERYVILLE, 278.
GHABAL, 179.
GHADIRS, 278.
GHAR EL-DJAMÄA, 238.
GHAR EL-MELAH, lake, 133.
GHARBA, 323.
GHARAT DJEBEL ISHKUL, lake, 312.
GHARDAIA, 154.

GHARDIMAOU, 300.
Examination of luggage at custom-house.
Buffet.

Goletta.
GHAZAL, DJ., 216.
GHEIR, OUED, 203, 218.
GHORFA DES OULAD MIRIAM, 164.
LA GLACIÈRE, farm, 167.
GOUSSIMET, OUED, 200.

GOLETTA (Port of Tunis), 286.
Brit. Vice - Consul, M. Joseph Cubisol.
No Hotels. Numerous *Cafés*.
Railways, see Tunis.
Boat hire for landing, 2½ piastres (f. 1.50).

Means of Communication: A. *Comp. Gen. Transatlantique.* I. From Marseilles, direct, Mond. Wed. and Frid. 4 P.M. Return same days and hour. II. To Susa, and along coast of Tunis, to Tripoli and Malta, Thurs. 5 P.M. Return from Malta Tues. 5 P.M. III. For Bizerta, La Calle, Bône, Philippeville, Algiers, and Port Vendres, Sat. noon. IV. Bône, Philippeville, and so to Algiers, Sat. 5 P.M. V. For Malta, Mond. 10 A.M. Return Thurs. 1 P.M.

B. *Navig. Gen. Italiana.* I. To Cagliari, Leghorn, and Genoa, Wed. 1 P.M. Return Thurs. 9 P.M. II. To Pantellaria, Marsala, Favignana, Trapani, and Palermo, Frid. 8 P.M. Return, Tues. 10 P.M. III. Along the coast of Tunis to Tripoli and Malta, Wed. 5.30 P.M. Return, Wed. 10 A.M.

C. *Transp. Marit. à Vapeur*. Departure from Marseilles, direct. Wed.

INDEX AND DIRECTORY 351

Goletta.

5 P.M. ; from Goletta *viâ* Bône, Sund. noon. Passage, 60 f.
Goletta to the Island of Djerba by sea, 317.
GOURAÏA, 116.
GOURAYA, 137.
GOVERNMENT, 65.
EL-GREIZ, 265.
GROTTE DES VEAUX MARINS, 183.
GROUS, hot springs, 163.
GUÉ DE CONSTANTINE, 140, 166.
GUEBAR BOU AOUN, 242.
GUELMA, 240.
  Hôtel Auriol or *d'Orient*, tolerably good ; *Grand Hôtel*, Rue St. Louis ; *H. de l'Univers*, Rue de Bône, nearest to the railway station, which is about 300 mètres from the town.
  Buffet at station.
GUELT-EL-KILAB, 264.
GUELT-ES-STEL, 151.
GUERAH EL-HOUT, lake, 129, 306.
GUERAH-EL-MELAH, 129.
GUERAH - EL - OUBERA, lake, 129.
GUERRARA, 154.
EL-GUETNA, 275.
GUYOTVILLE, 106, 108.

H

L'HABRA, barrage of, 178.
L'HABRA, OUED, 274.
EL-HACHEM, OUED, 134.
HADDAD, SHEIKH EL, 16, 61.
EL-HADJAR, 185.
HADJAR-EL-MELAH, 152.
HADJAR ROUM, old Roman camp, 266.
EL-HADJEB, 168.
HADJEB EL-AÏOUN, 331.
HAKOUM, OUED, 150.
EL HAMELIA, 161.
HAMMAT, DJ., 235.
EL-HAMMA, 185.

Haracta.

EL-HAMMAM, 150, 159 ; hot springs, 159.
HAMMAM BÈRDA, 241.
HAMMAM BOU HADJAR, 255.
HAMMAM BOU HANEFIA, 275.
HAMMAM EL-ENF, 133, 298.
HAMMAM GERGOUR, 200.
HAMMAM GROUS, 163.
HAMMAM KSANNA, 164.
HAMMAM MELOUAN, 80, 140.
  Établissement Thermal. Poor accommodation ; opens 1st May.
  Carriage road from Rovigo.
HAMMAM MESKOUTIN, 80, 238.
  Hôtel comfortable. Engage rooms by letter to M. Rouyer, Guelma. Cost about 12 f. a day.
  Post Office on the establishment.
HAMMAM R'IRHA, 80, 169.
  Thermal Baths : Establishment of M. Alfonse Arlès - Dufour. Good, terms moderate.
  A *public conveyance* meets trains at Bou Medfa. 2 f. each person. (For private carriage 15 f. ; write beforehand.)
  Mules and donkeys can be hired at the hotel.
HAMMAM SALAHIN, 216.
HAMMAM SIDI ABDELI, 255.
HAMMAM SIDI ALI BEN-YOUB, 270.
HAMMAMET, 318.
  Brit. Cons. Agent, A. Cacchia.
HAOUCH, BOU - KAN-DOURA, 163.
HARACTA, tribe, 235.

Isserville.

HARRACH, river, 140.
HAUSSONVILLERS, 143.
HENCHIR HAMMAM DAR-RADJI, 302.
HENNAYA, 281.
HERBILLON, 121.
HIERON, 332.
HIGH PLATEAUX, THE, 13, 16.
L'HILLIL, 176.
HIPPODROME, 163.
HIPPONE, 123 ; St. Augustine at, 123.
HISTORICAL NOTICE OF ALGERIA, 20-65.
HONAI, 281.
HORSES, 71.
HÔTEL GESSIN, 111.
HÔTEL DES VOYAGEURS, or CAMP DES CHÉNES, 149.
HOTELS, 6.
HOUENET, OUED, 265.
HOUMT-ES-SOUK, 326.
HULFA, OR ESPARTO GRASS, 85 ; *see* ALFA.
HUSSEIN DEY, 155, 166.
HYDRA, ruins of, 228.
HYDROGRAPHICAL SYSTEM, 14.

I

ICHERRIDHEN, 146.
ICOSIUM, 93.
IGHIL ALI, 244.
IGHZER-AMOKRAN, 203.
IGILGILIS, 117.
ILLIL, OUED, 176.
IMESSEBELEN, the, 8.
INKERMANN, 174.
INSURRECTION of 1871, 59, 62.
IRIL, 158.
IRISH IMMIGRANTS, 242.
IRON MINES, of Aïn-Mokra, 126 ; of Soumah, 166 ; Beni Saf, 279.
ISSER, river, 143, 150, 156, 255, 266 ; gorge, 156.
LES ISSERS, 143.
ISSERVILLE, 143.
  Hôtel de l'Étoile.

Jardin d'Essai.

J

JACKSON, DR., on the climate of Algiers, 3.
JARDIN D'ESSAI, 107.
JEMMAPES, 127.
JEWELLERY, Kabyle, 146.
JEWS, 11.
JOL, 135; see Cherchel.
JULIA CÆSAREA, 135.

K

KABYLE GOVERNMENT, 15.
KABYLE LANGUAGE, 12.
KABYLE VILLAGE DESCRIBED, 144.
KABYLIA, 7.
KABYLIA OF DJURDJURA, excursion through, 242.
KAID HASSEN, bordj, 201.
KAID MANSOUR, bordj, 200.
KAIDS, 8.
EL KALÄA, 176.
KALÄA (GELÄA), 243.
KALÄAT ES-SANAN, 229.
KALAMA, 240.
KALIA, OUED, 259.
KAMART, 297.
KAMETA, 133.
EL KANTOUR, DJ., 185.
KAOUA, 175.
KAPOUDIAH, 323.
KARGUENTAH (ORAN), 179.
KASR BAGHAI, ruins of, 235.
KASR BINT-ES-SULTAN, 172.
KASR EL-AHMER, 230.
KASR EL-KEF, 308.
KASR EL-MENARA, 318.
KASR TEMOUCHENT, 162.
KBOUR-EL-ABBAS, 214.
EL-KEBIR, OUED, 118, 132, 167.
KEF; see El-Kef.
KEF-EL-AKHDAR, 218.

Kulb, Dj.
KEF ER-RAKHM, 230.
KEF KERICHEFA, tunnel, 299.
KEF SIDI OMAR PEAK, 172.
KEF OUM-ET-TEBOUL, 130, 306.
KELEBIA, 317.
 Brit. Cons. Agent, F. Conversano.
 No *hotel*.
KERKENA ISLANDS, 323.
KERMA, OUED, 306.
KEROUAN, 328.
 Kerouan to Sbeitla, 331.
KEROUIA, forest, 178.
KHAMIS, OUED, 111.
KHAMISA, 232.
                PAGE
 Ruins of ancient city. 232
 Triumphal Arch,
  Basilica . . . 232
 Theatre . . . 232
 Tombs . . . 233
 Arab legend of . . 233
EL KHAMZA, OUED, 185.
KHARATA, 200.
KHAROUBA,' DJ., 213.
EL-KHENEG, 198; dolmens, 199.
KHOMAIR, tribe, the, 305.
KHOOSHADA, 228.
KIRBA, 246.
EL-KISSA, ruins, 228.
KLEBER MARBLE QUARRIES, 273.
KOTAN, OUED BOU, 159.
KOUBBA, village of, 107; ecclesiastical college at, 107.
KOUBBA VIEUX, 107, 140.
KOUKOU, 147.
KOULOUGLIS, 11.
KRALFALLAH, 277.
EL-KREIDER, 277.
KRISTEL, 184.
LE KROUB, 163.
EL KSEUR, 203.
KSOUR-ES-SIF, 322.
KUBR-ER-ROUMIA, 138.
KULB, DJ., 230.

Les Lacs.

L

LA CALLE, 127.
 Hôtel d'Orient.
 Diligence daily to and from Bône. Carriage road to Aïn-Draham and on to the Tunisian railway.
                PAGE
 Coral Fishery . . 127
 History . . . 127
LA CHIFFA, 148, 168.
 Diligence for Medeah.
 Café de la Gare. Good meals may be had.
LA CHIFFA, gorge, 148.
LA CHIFFA, river, 148.
LA MORICIÈRE, 266.
 Hôtel de l'Univers.
 Arab Market on Monday.
 Railway from Tabia completed so far; the travellers must go on to Tlemçen by diligence.
LADY KHADIDJA, shrine of the, 158.
LALLA FATIMA, 147.
LALLA MARNIA, 267.
 Hôtel de France, excellent.
LALLA OUDA, OUED, 174.
LAMBESSA, 206.
LAMIDA, 164.
LAND TENURE, 9.
LANDON'S, M., garden, 215.
LANGUAGES, NATIVE, 12.
LAURIER'S ROSES, stat., 269.
LAVARANDE, 171.
LE KROUB, 163.
 Hôtel de France, tolerable.
LELLA SETTA, mountain, 256.
LES LACS, 205.
LION HUNTING, 68.

Locusts.

LOCUSTS, 58, 74.
LODGINGS, 5.
LODI, 150.
LOLLIUS, tomb of, 198.
LONDON TO ALGERIA, I.
 See p. 312.
LOURMEL, 254.
LULLY RAYMOND, 114.

M

EL-MAADER, 206 ; OUED, 206.
MAADTHER, DJ., 230.
MAALIKAIN, mountains, 157.
LA MACTA, 274.
MADID, 165.
MAFRAG, river, 127.
MAGARAN, 316.
MAGENTA, 271.
MAGHAIER, 218.
MAGOUN, OUED, 274.

MAHADIA, 322.
 Brit. Cons. Agent, C. Violante.
 No hotel.
MAHADJIBA, ruins, 198.
MAHMEL, DJ., 213.

MAILLOT, 158.
 A fairly good inn.
MAISON BLANCHE, LA, 111, 155.
MAISON CANTONIÈRE, 247, 267.
MAISON CARRÉE, LA, agricultural establishment at, 110, 166.
MAKHEIREGA, DJ., 230.
MALAH, OUED, 254.
EL MANÄA, 213.
MANOUBA, 304.
MANSOURA, 261.
MANSOURA, 159.
MANSOURA, hill, 193.
MANSOURIA, promontory of, 116.
EL-MAOUNA, 241.
MAP, NEW, 113.
MARABOUTS, THE, 15.
MARBLE QUARRIES, 121, 273, 301.

[*Algeria.*]

Medeah.

LA MARE D'EAU, 179.
MAREGH, OUED, 159.

MARENGO, 134.
 Hôtel d'Orient, poor ;
 Hôtel Marengo, rather better.
MARKOUNA, ruins of, 208.
MARMOR NUMIDICUM, 273.
MARSA, 297.

MASCARA, 275.
 Grand Hotel, fairly good ; *H. du Louvre*.
 Branch railway to main line.
 Diligence to Oran by night, 12 hrs., 12 f. To Frenda, 13 hrs., 10 f. To Sidi Bel Abbés (see Rte. 24).
MASCULA, the ancient, 213, 235.
MASSIN, caravanserai, 141.
MASSIN, OUED, 141.
EL MATEN, 203.
MATIFOU, Cape, 112.
MAURITANIA, 21 ; derivation of the word, 21.
MAUSOLEUM, ROMAN, 204.
MAZAFRAN, river, 137.
MAZAGRAN, 249.
MAZALA, DJ., 236.
MAZOUKA, lake, 312.
MAZOUNA, 175.
MDAOUROUCH, 221, 230.
MÉCHÉRA-SFA, 250.
MECHERIAH, 278.
MECHTA EL-ARBI, 162.
MEÇID, DJ., 191.
MEDABIAH, the, 154.

MEDEAH, 149.
 Hôtel d'Orient ; *Hôtel Louis*.
 Mules can be hired.
 Arab Market on Tuesday.
MEDEAH, aqueduct, 149.

El-Metkoub.

MEDLÆ, or AD MEDIAS, 149.
MEDJANA PLAIN, 160.
MEDJERDA, OUED, 233, 302, 310.
MEDJEZ-AMAR, 240.
MEDJEZ-EL-BAB, 304.
MEDJEZ-SFA, 299.
MEDRASSEN, monument, 205.
MEGALITHIC REMAINS, 89, 109, 142, 152, 165, 197, 208, 216, 234, 236, 239, 250.
MEHARI (the camel), 71.
MEKALIA, 249.
MEKALIS, 278.
MEKERRA, river, 269.
MEKLA, 144, 146.
MELAB-EL-KORAN, 163.
MELAGOU, plain, 213.
EL MELAH, OUED, 301.
MELGHIGH, CHOTT, 218.
MELIKA, 154.
MELLEGUE, OUED, 221, 230, 303, 308.
MELOUAN, hot springs, 140.
MELRIR, OUED, 265.

MÉNERVILLE, 155.
 Hôtel Blanchard.
MENZEL, 325.
MENZEL DJEMIL, 311.
MENZEL TEMIM, 318.
MERCIER-LACOMBE, 265.
MERDJA, 174.
EL MERIDJ, 229.
MEROMAN, 218.
MERS-EL-KEBIR, 183.
MERSA ED-DEBBAN, 109.
MERSA ED-DEJAJ, 155.
MERSA EL-KEBIR, 181.
MERSA TOUMLILIN, 113.
MESKIANA, 221.
MESKOUTIN, hot springs, 238.
MESLOUG, 160.
EL-MESRAN, 151.
MESRATA, 177.
EL-MESSEN, 158.
METIDJA, plain, 94, 140, 166.
EL-METKOUB, 114.

2 A

Metlili.

METLILI, 153.
METLILI, DJ., 213.
MEURAD, OUED, 134.
MEZA BERZIG, 219.

MILIANAH, 170.
Hôtel de Commerce, good.
Reached by omnibus either from Adalia or Affreville, stations on railway.

	PAGE
History	170
Barracks, Military Hospital	171
Church, Koubba of Sidi Moh-ben-Yussef	171
Environs	171

MILITARY FORCE, 66.
MILLESIMO, 241.
MINA, river, 176, 249.
MINERALOGY, 79.
MINES, MERCURY, 213; calamine, 267; *see* Iron.
MIRA, 145.
MIRABEAU, 143.

MISSERGHINE, 254.
A fairly good inn.

MODZBAH-SFID, 277.
MOGHRAR FOUKANI, 278.
MOGHRAR TAHTANI, 278.
MOHAMMED ED-DIBBAH, KOUBBA OF, 155.
MOHAMMEDIA, ruined palace, 313.
MOKRANI, rebellion of, 61.
MOKTA EL-HADID, ironworks, 126.
MOKTA EL-OUST, 153.

MONASTIR, 322.
Brit. Cons. Agent, F. Portelli.
No *hotel*.

MONDOVI, 242.
MONKEYS, 70.
MONTAGNE GRISE, 273.
MONTAGNE ROUGE, 248.
MONTAGNE DE SEL, 214.
MONTENOTTE, 246.

Nemours.

MOORS, 10.
MORSOTT, 221.

MOSTAGANEM, 247.
Hôtel de France, fairly good. *H. des Messageries*.
Diligences: To L'Hillil 3 times a day, 4 hrs., 4 f. To Perrégaux, 4 hrs., 3 f. To Oran, 10 hrs., 8.15 f. To Cassaigne, 7 hrs., 3 f.

MOUIA, OUED, 267.
MOULAI ISMAIL, forest, 179.
MOUNTAINS, HEIGHT OF, 14.
MOUZAÏA, DJ., 149.
MOUZAÏA LES MINES, 150.
MOUZAÏAVILLE, 168.
MTALSA, 277.
MULAI ABD-EL-KADER, village, 265.
MUSTAFA INFÉRIEUR, 108.

MUSTAFA SUPÉRIEUR. For *Hotels* see Algiers, 105.
English Club near the Governor's palace.

M'ZAB COUNTRY, 154.
MZA SEDIRA, 208.
MZITA, 159.
MZOURI SALT LAKE, 205.

N

NAÂMA, 278.
NADOR, DJ., 149, 255.
LE NADOR, zinc mines, 241.
NAZREG, 276.
NATIVE TROOPS, 66.
NEBEUL, 318.
NEBEUR, 308.
NEDROMA, 267.
NEGRIER, 255.
NEGRO, Cape, 132.

NEMOURS, 282.
Hôtel de France, fairly good.

Oran.

NOE, Cape, 281
NOIR, Cape, 114.
NOTRE DAME D'AFRIQUE, 110; peculiar ceremony after vespers, 110; silver statue of the archangel Michael, 110.
NOVI, 136.
NUMIDIA, 21
NUMIDIAN MARBLE QUARRIES, 273.

O

OAK TREE, THE, 88.
OKAS, Cape, 202.
OLIVE TREE, THE, 88.
OMAR-DRA-EL-MIZAN, 157.
OMM-EL-ASHERA, 213.
OMM-EL-BOAGHI, 234.
ONYX, ALGERIAN, 255.
OPPIDUM NOVUM, 171.
OPPIDUM TIMICI, 255.
ORAN, 179.

	PAGE
Population	179
History	179
Situation, Harbours, Trade	181
Churches, Mosques	181
Theatre, Museum	182
Citadel, Forts	182
Subterranean Galleries	183
Hospitals, Negro Quarter	183
Environs	183

Hotels: *Continental*, the best in the colony. *H. de la Paix. H. de l'Univers.*
Restaurant: Café de Létang.
British Vice-Consul: A. Boozo.
French Baths: Boulevard Oudenot.
Moorish Baths: Rue de la Mosquée.
Carriages have all their scale of charges.
Boats: The charge for landing is 50 c. for each passenger, and 40 c. for each package.

Oran.
Means of Communication by Sea: A. *Compagnie Général Transatlantique* (see Algiers). From Oran to Tangiers, viâ Nemours, Malaga, and Gibraltar, Frid. 8 P.M. B. *Comp. Nav. Mixte* (Touache). For Cette and Marseilles, Wed. 8 A.M.
C. *Comp. Cuillol Het. St. Pierre*, Marseilles, Wed. 8 A.M.
D. *Compagnie Salinas.* For Carthagena and Alicante, Tues. 4 P.M. For Alicante, direct, Frid. 4 P.M. For Almeria, Tues. 4 P.M.
E. *Compagnie Acuña.* For Almeria, Tues. 4 P.M. *Oran to Beni Saf, Nemours, and the Frontier of Morocco*, 279.
Oran to Tlemçen, 254.
ORAN, a tour through, 265.
ORANGES, 83.

ORLEANSVILLE, 172.
Hôtel de France, good.
Markets: Saturday and Sunday.
Omnibus to Ténès daily, 5½ hrs., 6 f.
Carriage to Ouarensenis, 20 f. per diem.
ORPHANAGES, 106.
OSTRICHES, 72.
OUACHE, DJ. (Wahash), 197.
OUARANSENIS, peak, 172.
OUARCE, 232.
OUARGLA, 59.
OUDENA, ruins of, 314.
OUED ALLALA, 246.
OUED AMIMIN, 127.
OUED AMISEUR, 203.
OUED ATMENIA, 162.
OUED BARBATA, 267.
OUED BESBES, 242.
OUED BOU DJEMAA, 242.
OUED BOUKTENA, 150.

Oulad Rahmoun.
OUED CHAHAM, 299.
OUED CHOUK, 221.
OUED CORSO, 155.
OUED DJER, 168.
OUED EL-HAMMAM, 159.
OUED EL-KHEIR, 249.

OUED FODDA, 172.
Hôtel de la Gare, poor.
Carriage may be had for Barrage. 2 hrs., 10 f.
OUED FRARAH, 241.
OUED GHEIR, plain, 218.
OUED HAKOUM, 150.
OUED HAMIMIM, 163.
OUED IMBERT, 269.
OUED KHAMIS, 111.
OUED KHELLONG, 249.
OUED MALAH, 177.
OUED MELAH, 152, 325.
OUED MELIZ, 301.
OUED MESSELMOUN, 136.
OUED MESSIDA, 306.
OUED MOUGRAS, 300.

OUED RIOU, 174.
Station for Inkerman.
Hôtel d'Inkerman, fairly good.
Diligences daily to Ammi Mousa (N.), and Renault, in the Dahra (S.)
OUED ROUINA, 171.
OUED SEDEUR, 152.
OUED SLY, 174.
OUED SMAR, 155.
OUED TAGA, 208, 213.
OUED TAGHIA, 172.
OUED ZEBOUDJ, 170.

OUED ZENATI, 237.
A service of diligences daily to Aïn-Beïda.
OUED ZERGAA, 304.
OUENZA, DJ., 221.
L'OUGASSE, 179.
OUJBA, 267.
OULAD ABD-EN-NOUR, tribe, 162.
OULAD ALI, 269.
OULAD BOU-ALI, 158.
OULAD MIZIAN, 174.
OULAD OU-KASAI, 144.
OULAD RAHMOUN, 163.

Philippeville.
OULAD RIAH, caves, 248; tragedy in, 248, 249.
OULAD SEAD, 200.
OULAD SIDI CHEIKH, 278.
OULAD SIDI EL-AKHDAR, 174.
OUMACH, oasis, 217.
EL-OUIRICIA, 200.
EL-OURIT, FALLS OF, or the Saf-Saf, 263.
OURLANA, 219.
EL OUTAÏA, 214.

P
PALÆSTRO, 156.
Hôtel de Commerce.
Terrible tragedy at, 156.
PALMIERS, LES CINQ, 246.
PALMIERS, LES TROIS, 246.
PANTHER HUNTING, 68.
PARTRIDGE SHOOTING, 70.

PERRÉGAUX, 178.
Junction for Saïda and Arzen.
Hôtel des Colonies, tolerably good.
Arab Market on Thursday.
PÉLISSIER, 248.
PETIT, 241.
PHILIPPEVILLE, 119.

	PAGE
Harbour	119
City	119
Archæological Treasures	120
Ancient Baths	120

British Vice-Consul, M. Henri Tessier.
Hotels: *H. d'Orient*, in the Square. *H. Gibraud*, in the street behind it, very good.
Means of Communication: *Comp. Transatlantique.* 1. From Marseilles, direct, Mond.

Philippeville.

and Frid. 4 P.M. Return from Philippeville, Sund. 6 P.M. II. Marseilles, *vid* Ajaccio and Bône, Wed. 4 P.M. III. Philippeville to Djedjelli, Bougie and Marseilles, Thurs. 11 P.M. IV. To Bône, Goletta, and Marseilles, Sund. 10 P.M. V. To Bône, Ajaccio, and Marseilles, Frid. 11 P.M.

Philippeville to Constantine by rail, 184.
PINE, THE ALEPPO, 88.
PITON, D'AKBOU, 204.
PLAGUE, THE, 47, 49.
PLATEAUX, the High, 13, 16, 277.
POINTE PESCADE, or MERSA - ED - DEBBAN, 109.
POLLASTRO, island, 132.
POMARIA, 256.
PONT DE CHELIF, 248.
PONT D'ISSER, 255.
PONTEBA, 172.
POPULATION AND RACES, 6.
PORT-GUEYDON, 114.
PORT AUX POULES, 274
PORTE, LA PETITE, 159.
PORTES DE FER, LES, 159.
PORTO FARINA, lake, 133.
PORTUS MAGNUS, 274.
POTTERY, KABYLE, 146.
PRÆCILIUS, TOMB OF, 192.
PRE - HISTORIC MONUMENTS ; *see* Megalithic.
PUNIC WAR, first, 21 ; second, 22 ; third, 24.

R

RADES, 298.
RAILWAYS, 6.
RAINFALL, TABLE OF, 4.
RAMPE, AUBERGE DE LA, 141.
RANDON, 242.
RAPIDI, 164.

Rovigo.

RAS BOU-FHAL, 127.
RAS DIMAS, 322.
RAS EL HADID, 121.
RAS EL KEBIR, 118.
RAS EL-MA, 162, 271.
RAS ER RAJEL, 132.
RAS EZ ZEBIB, 133.
RAS SIDI ALI EL-MEKHI, 133.
RAS TAKOUCH, 121.
LA RASSAUTA, 111.
RAT À TROMPE, the, 152.
RATS, GERBOA, 218.
LA REGHAÏA, 155.

RELIZANE, 176.
Junction for line from Mostaganem to Tiaret.
Buffet. Hôtel de la Paix, indifferent.

REMCHI, 281.
RENAULT, 174.
RENTS, 6.
RESIDENCE, CHOICE OF, 5.
RESSAS. DJ., 133.
LA RÉUNION, 203.
RIGHIS, DJ., copper mines, 235.
RIO SALADO, 254.
R'IRHA (Righa), hot springs, 80, 169.
RIVERS, 14, 18.
ROBERTVILLE, 184.
ROCHER, LE, 269.
ROCHER DE SEL, LE, 152.
ROCHER DES CHIENS. 153.
ROKNIA, 239.
ROMAN BATH, remains of, 162.
ROMAN RUINS, 90.
ROMAN STAT., ruins of, 235.
ROMRI, 177.
ROSA, Cap, 127.
ROUGA, ruins of, 322.
ROUIBA, 155.
ROUINA, OUED, 171.
ROUMADIA, mountain, 119.
ROUMMEL, OUED, 191.
ROUTES, 1, 113.
ROUX, Cape, 130.
ROVIGO, 140.

Sainte Barbe de Tlelat.

RUISSEAU, 107.
RUISSEAU, DES DEUX PONTS, 149.
RUISSEAU DES SINGES, 148.
RUSAZUS, 114.
RUSCURIUM, 114.
RUSGUNIA, ruins of, 111.
RUSUBEESER, 114.

S

SÄADA, 218.
ES-SABALA, 310.
SABLE, COL DE, 154.
SAF-SAF, river, 255, 268.
SAF-SAF, stat., 184.
SAHARA, upper and lower, 17-20.
SAHEL, the, 93.
ES-SAHEL, OUED, 158, 202, 244.
SÄIDA, 276.
SÄIDA, OUED, valley, 276.
SAINT AIMÉ, 175.
SAINT ANDRÈ, 184.
SAINT ARNAUD, 162.
SAINT AUGUSTIN, at Hippone, 123 ; at Medaura, 231 ; birthplace, 300.
SAINT CHARLES, 184, 239.
SAINT CYPRIEN DES ATTAFS, 171.
SAINT DENYS DU SIG, 178.
SAINT DONAT, 162.
SAINT EUGÈNE, 110.
SAINT GÉROME, 184.
SAINT GERONIMO, martyrdom of, 98 ; discovery of his skeleton, 99.
SAINT JOSEPH, 241.
SAINT LEU, 274.
SAINT PIERRE, 265.

SAINTE BARBE DE TLELAT, 179.
Junction for Sidi-bel-Abbès, Tlemçen, Ras-el-Ma.

INDEX AND DIRECTORY 357

Sainte Barbe de Tlelat.
Hôtel de la Gare, tolerable.
Sainte Barbe de Tlelat to Bel Abbès and Tlemçen, 268.
SAINTE CLOTILDE, 184.
SAINTE LÉONIE, 274.
SAKAMODI, 163.
SALAH BEY, oasis, 192.
SALAHIN, hot springs, 216
SALEKTA, 323.
LES SALINES, 176.
SALLUST, 191.
SALT MOUNTAIN, 214.
SALTO DEL CAVALLO, 183.
SANEDJA, river, 121.
SARNA, OUED, 269.
SBEITLA, 332.
SBEITLA, OUED, 332.
SCULPTURE ILLUSTRATED BY MOORISH ARCHITECTURE, 95.
SEASON FOR TRAVELLING, 5.
SEBÄA ROUS, the, 142, 151.
SEBAKH, zone, 162.
SEBAOU BORDJ, 143.
SEBAOU, river, 143.
SEBDOU, 264.
SEBKAS, 77.
SEBKHA, 158.
SEBKHA. of Oran, 254.
SEBKHA ZAHREZ, salt lakes, 151.
SEBT BENI YAHIA, 147.
SEBT, OUED, 137.
SELIL, 218.
SENAN, OUED, 255.
SEN-EL-LEBBA, DJ., 152.
LA SENIA, 179, 183.
SEQUESTRATION OF LAND, 62, 82.
SERIANA, 215.
SERSOU, 17, 142.

SETIF, 160.   PAGE
Citadel . . . 161
Climate, Position . 161
Market . . . 161
Hôtel de France, *H. d'Orient*; neither as good as might be expected.

Sidi Khalid.
Diligence and carriages for Bougie, *viâ* the Chabet el-Akhira.
SEYBOUSE, river, 240.
SFAX, 324.
Brit. Vice - Consul, Joseph Leonardi, Esq.
Hôtel de France; *H. Transatlantique*, both poor.
SHEBBA, OUED, 159.
SHEEP, 71.
SI MOH. BIN NASIR, tomb, 202.
SI SLIMAN, OUED, 174.
SI SLISSEN, 271.
SICCA VENERIA, the ancient, 308.
SIDI ABD-EL-KADER, El-Djilani, koubba of, 168.
SIDI ABD-EL-KADER, tomb of, 246.
SIDI ABDULLA, 267.
SIDI AICH, 203.
SIDI AISSA, 164.
SIDI, AKKACH, koubba of, 121.
SIDI ALI BEN-YOUB, village, 270; hot springs, 270.
SIDI BADER, 300.
SIDI BEL ABBÈS, stat., 269.
SIDI BEL ABBÈS, town, 269.
SIDI BOU JUBAR, 308.
SIDI BOU MEDIN, tomb, 260.
SIDI BOU-SAEED, 297.
SIDI BOU ZAIN, salt lake, 176.
SIDI BRAHIM, stat., 159, 221, 269.
SIDI BRAO, 162.
SIDI EMBAREK, tomb of, 137.
SIDI FERUCH, or FURRUDJA, 109.
SIDI HAMANA, Zaouia of, 163.
SIDI EL-HEMESSI, 300.
SIDI KHALID, 270.

Souk Ahras.
SIDI KHALIFA, 277.
SIDI-KHELTAB, 249.
SIDI LAHSEN, 270.
SIDI MAMMAR BEN-MOKHALA, tomb, 246.
SIDI MAKLOUF, 153.
SIDI MAKLOUF, koubba of, 153.
SIDI MEÇID, 191.
SIDI MERZOUG, 308.
SIDI MESKINE, 302.
SIDI MOH. EEN AOUDA, 249.
SIDI MOH. EL-GHORAB, tomb, 192.
SIDI MOH. BEN ABD-ER-RAHMAN BOU KOBERAIN, 108.
SIDI MOH. BOU KOBERAIN, 203.
SIDI MOUSSA, 140, 163.
SIDI NAAMAN, koubba of, 106.
SIDI OKBA MOSQUE, 216.
SIDI RACHID, 219.
SIDI RAHEL, oasis, 219.
SIDI REHEUR, 202.
SIDI YAHIA, tomb of 162.
SIDI ZEHILI, 303.
SIG, river, 178.
SIGA, ancient, 281.
SIGUS, ruins of, 234.
SIMITTU, ruins of, 301.
SIROCCO, the, 3.
SKIRA, port of, 325.
SMENDOU, OUED, 185.
SNAKES, 74.
SOCIÉTÉ PROTECTRICE ALSACIENNE-LORRAINE, 82, 143.
SOCIÉTÉ GÉNÉRALE ALGÉRIENNE, 108.
SOFS, the, 15
SOLOMON, 222.
SOUF, 19.
SOUFLAT, 61.

SOUK AHRAS, 299.
Junction for **TEBESSA**.
Hôtel de Tagaste;

Souk Ahras.

Grand Hôtel, both fairly good.
Buffet at station.

SOUK EL - ARBÄA (Tunisia), 302.
Hôtel at the station.
Diligence to El-Kef.
SOUK EL-DJEMÄA, 143.
SOUK EL-HAAD, 156.
SOUK EL-KHAMIS, 303.
SOUMA BINT-EL-ABRI, 228.
SOUMAH, 197.
SOUMAH, iron mines, 166.
SOUMAM, OUED, 202.
SOUMAR, 245.
SOUMAT - EL - KHENEG, 228.
SOUR GHOZLAN, 164.
SPAHIS, 66.
SPORT, 67.
SPRATT, REV. D., his diary, 42.
SPRINGS, hot, 80; Aminin, 127; Bains de la Reine, 183; Berda, 241; Bou Hadjar, 255; El-Hamma, 185; El-Hammam, 159; Hammam Bou Hanefia, 275; Fontaine de la Gazelle, 214; Grous, 163; Melouan, 140; Meskoutin, 238; R'Irha, 169; Salahin, 216; Sidi Ali ben-Youb, 270.
SRIGINA, island, 119.
STAOUËLI, battle of, 109; plain, 108; la Trappe, 108; Notre Dame de, 109.
STEAMERS, 1.
STORA, 119.
SUBTERRANEAN LAKES, 19, 73.
SUFETULA, 332.

SUSA, or **SOUSSE**, 319.
  Brit. Vice - Consul, William Galea, Esq.
Hôtel de France, fairly good.
  Boat for landing, 1.50.

Tarf.

Railway to Kerouan.

	PAGE
History	. 319
Gates, Port	. 319
The Kasr er-Ribat	. 319
The Bab el-Gharbi	. 320
Population, Trade	. 320

Susa to Kerouan, 328.
SYR, the ancient, 267.

T

TA-BABORT, ascent of, 118.
TABARCA, island of, 130; history, 130.
TABIA, 266, 270.
TABLAT, 163.
TADMITZ, forest of, 152.
TAFFAMAN, 266.
TAFNA, treaty of, 57.
TAFNA, river, 264, 267.
TAFAROUA, 277.
TAGASTE, 300.
TAGDEMPT, or **TAKDEMT**, 251.
TAGEMSDETT, forest, 267.
TAGHIT, mercury mines, 213.
TAGRAMARET, 254.
TAGURA, 229.
TAKENBRIT, ruins of, 281.
TA KITOUNT, col de, 200.
TA KITOUNT, fort, 200.
TAKSEBT, 114.
TALET MIZEB, 145.
TAMALA, OUED, 200.
LES TAMARINS, 213.
TAMDA, 145.
TAMERNA, 219.
TAMGOUT LALLA KHADIDJA, DJ., 146, 158.
TAMOUDA, 144.
TANARAMUSA CASTRA, 150, 168.
TAOURA, 229.
TAOURIRT AMRAM, 147.
TAOURIRT MAIMON, 146.
TAOURIRT EL HADJ, 146.
TAOURIRT TEIDILI, 147.
TAOURIRTE, 158.
TARF, 14.

Thessalah.

TARJA, 300.
TATEN-YAYA, 271.
TAZA, OUED, cave of, 118.
TAZMALT, 204.
TEBESSA, 222.

	PAGE
History	. 222
Temple of Jupiter	. 223
Triumphal Arch of Caracalla	. 224
Basilica	. 225
Roman Aqueduct	. 227
Excursions	. 228

Hôtel Métropole. H. Calama, both bad.
Tebessa to Souk-Ahras, 228.

TEBOURBA (Teburbo Minus), 304.
TEDLES, Cape, 114.
TEFKHASID, OUED, 318.
TELERGMA, 162.
TELL, the, 14, 162.
TELLA, DJ., 311.
TELLIA APODA, the, 163.
TEMACIN, 220.
TEMDA, OUED, 174.
TEMOUCHENT, OUED, 255.
TEMOULGA, 172.
TEMPERATURE, TABLE OF, 4.

TÉNÈS, 246.
Hôtel de la Poste, poor.

TENIET-EL-AHD, 141.
Hôtel de Commerce, good.
CEDAR FOREST, 141.
TERNATEN, 253.
TERNY, 264.
TESSÄA, OUED, 303.

THAYA, 237.
  A *Buffet*, where it is just possible to sleep. *Mules* may be hired for excursion to the caves.

THERMAL SPRINGS; *see* Springs.
THESSALAH, mountain 269.

Theveste.

THEVESTE, 223 ; *see* Tebessa.
THIERS, 157.
THIERSVILLE, 276.
THUBURSICUM NUMIDARUM, 232.

TIARET, 251.

Hôtel de Commerce, in the fort, inconveniently situated. *Café d'Orient*, in the new town, close to post and diligence station, better ; neither very good, but will no doubt be improved as Tiaret becomes more known.

Diligence to Frenda, 8 hrs., 6 f.

Carriage to Djedars, 20 f.

Arab Market, Monday.

TIBILIS, ruins of, 239.
TICHY, 202.
TIFESH, 231 ; valley, 231.
TI FILKOUTH, 245.
TIFROURA, DJ., 275.
TIGAUDA, MUNICIPIUM, 172.
TIGHAOUT, river, 174.
TIGZIRT, ruins of, 114.
TIJDID, 247.
TIKLAT, 203.
TILIOUANET, 177.
TIMEGAD, ruins of, 208.
TINGURTIA, 251.
TINJA, OUED, 312.
TINSILT, salt lake, 205.
TIOUT, oasis of, 278.

TIPASA, 134.

Hôtel des Bains de Mer, fairly good.

TIRILTE, 158.
TIROURDA, COL DE, 147.
TITMOKREN, forest, 264.
TIXTER, 160.
TIZAIRT, 244.
TIZI, 265, 275.
TIZI-BART, 245.
TIZI-N-DJAMA, 147.

Tuggurt.

TIZI-OUZOU, 143, 203.
Hôtel des Postes.

TIZI RACHED, 146.
TIZI-RENIFF, 143
LE TLÉLAT, river, 179.
TLEMÇEN, 255.

	PAGE
Situation	256
History	256
Mosques	257
Museum	258
Fortifications	259
Mosque of Aghadir	259
Arab Cemetery	260
Bou Medin	260
Arab College, or Medrassa	261
The Sahariḍj	262

Hôtel de France; H. de la Paix.

Route either by Oran, and Ain-Temouchent, or by St. Barbe de Tlelat, Sidi-Bel-Abbès and Lamoricière.

TOBACCO, 84.
TOMBEAU DE LA CHRÉTIENNE, 138 ; legend of, 138.
TOMBEAU DE LA NEIGE, 203.
TOMBS NEAR MÉCHÉRA, 250.
TONGA, lake, 306.
TORRE CHICA, 109.
TOUDMAN, OUED, 275.
TOUMLET, DJ., 185, 271.
LA TRAPPE DE STAOUËLI, 108.
TRARIA, OUED, 265, 276.
TRAVELLING, SEASON FOR, 5.
LES TREMBLES, 164.
TRITON, lake, 325.
LES TROIS MARABOUTS, 279.
LES TROIS PALMIERS, 246.
LES TROIS RIVIÈRES, 265.

TUGGURT, 59, 219.

A very rude *hotel*.

Diligence runs from Biskra every second day,

Tunis.

occupies 3 days. Cost, 100 f. Bad.

	PAGE
Mosques	220
Date Palms	220

TUNIS, 284.

	PAGE
Regency of	284
Historical Sketch	284
The Goletta	286
City	286
Situation	286
Population	287
Streets and Lanes	288
Cemetery	288
Churches	288
Colleges	289
Mosques	290
Native Troops	290
Dar-el-Bey	290
Kasba Walls	290
Excursions	291

H.B.M. Consul, R. Drummond Hay.

Hotels : *Grand Hôtel* on the Esplanade of the Marine ; good. *H. de Paris*, R. Bab Zira, under the same management. *Hôtel Gigino* in square next to British Consulate.

Baths : There are excellent French baths close to the marine gate. Three Turkish ones are available for Christians — *Hammam el-Kashashin, Hammam Dar el-Djild*, and *Hammam Souk el-Djizna*. The usual cost is about 2 piastres (a shilling) for each person.

Means of Communication ; see Goletta.

English Church of St. Augustine (Iron), Rev. C. J. W. Flad.

Public Carriages : Tramways through the town. Ordinary Carriages, 15 f. a day ; f. 1.80 per hr. in, and 2.10 outside the town. Course 1 to 3 f.

Tunis.

Railways: The *Italian Rly.* to the Goletta and Marsa, behind Cathedral. *French Rly.* to Algeria, with branch to Hammam-el-Enf on opposite side of Marina.
    Tunis to Algiers, 298.
    Tunis to El-Kef viâ *Souk el-Arbâa*, 308.
TURCOS, 66.
TURKS, 11.

U
UTICA, 133, 310.

V
VALLÉE DES CONSULS, 110.
VALMY, 179.
VEGETABLES, 83.

Zaghouan.

LA VERDURE, 299.
VERECUNDA, 208.
VESOUL BENIAN, 170.
VILLE DES MINES, 150.
VINE, CULTIVATION OF THE, 85.
VOILE NOIRE, rock, 121.
VOIROL COLONNE, the, 107.

W
EL-WADHAHA, 213.
WAHASH, DJ., 197.
WARNIER, 246.
WELLS, OR SAINTS' TOMBS, 245.

Y
YEBDAR, 266.

Z
ZAGHOUAN, 316.
    PAGE
Aqueduct . . . 313, 314

Zurich.

ZAGHOUAN *Continued*.
    PAGE
Amphitheatre . . . 315
Theatre, Reservoirs .. 315
History . . . 316
El-Kasba . . . 316
ZAIAM, OUED, 158.
ZAKKAR, mountain, 170.
EZ-ZAN, OUED, 132.
ZANA, DJ., 311.
ZAOUIET-SUSA, 320.
ZARZIS, 327.
ZEBECHA, DJ., 153.
ZEMBRA, island, 133.
ZENATA, country, 281.
ZENATI, OUED, 237.
ZERALDA, 137.
Z'HOUR, OUED, 119.
ZIAMA, 116.
ZIBAN, 17, 216.
ZOOLOGY, 70.
ZOUAOUA TRIBE, THE, 147.
ZURICH, 62, 134.

THE END

Murray's Handbook

ADVERTISER,

1890-1891,

CONTAINING

USEFUL INFORMATION FOR TRAVELLERS,

RAILWAY

AND

STEAMBOAT COMPANIES,

HOTELS,

AND

MISCELLANEOUS ADVERTISEMENTS.

COMPAGNIE
DES
MESSAGERIES MARITIMES.
FRENCH POSTAL STEAMERS.
FROM MARSEILLES TO
AUSTRALIA AND NEW CALEDONIA.
On the 1st of every month for Mahé (Seychelles) King George's Sound, Adelaïde, Melbourne, Sydney, Noumea, transhipping at Mahé for Reunion and Mauritius.
EAST COAST OF AFRICA.
On the 12th of every month for Port-Saïd, Suez, Obock, Aden, Zanzibar, Mayotte, Nossi-be (branch line for the West Coast of Madagascar), Diego-Suarez, St. Marie, Tamatave, Reunion and Mauritius.
CHINA AND JAPAN.
Every alternate Sunday on and after 4th May for Alexandria, Port-Saïd, Suez, Aden, Colombo, Singapore (branch line for Batavia), Saïgon (branch line for Quin-hon, Tourane, Haï-phong), Hong-Kong, Shang-haï, Kobe and Yokohama.
CORRESPONDING EVERY FOUR WEEKS.
1° at Colombo for Pondichery, Madras and Calcutta.
2° at Saïgon for Manilla.
KURRACHEE, BOMBAY.
Branch line from Aden to Kurrachee and Bombay corresponding with the East Coast of Africa and Australian lines.
MEDITERRANEAN.
For Constantinople and Odessa every other Saturday (on and after 10th May).
Constantinople and Black Sea ports every other Saturday (on and after 17th May).
Alexandria, Port-Saïd, Syrian Ports, Smyrna, Salonica, Piræus (on and after 10th May).
Piræus, Salonica, Smyrna, Syrian Ports, Port-Saïd, Alexandria (on and after 17th May).
LONDON.
Weekly from Marseilles to Havre and London (merchandise only).
FROM BORDEAUX TO
ATLANTIC OCEAN.
1° On the 5th of each month for Lisbon, Dakar, Rio Janeiro, Montevideo and Buenos Ayres.
2° On the 20th of every month for Corunna or Vigo, Lisbon, Dakar, Pernambuco, Bahia, Rio Janeiro, Montevideo and Buenos Ayres.
3° On the 12th of each month (steerage passengers and merchandise only), for La Corogne, Vigo, Las Palmas, Montevideo, Buenos Ayres, Bahia Blanca.
4° On the 28th of each month (steerage passengers and merchandise only) for Las Palmas, Montevideo, Buenos Ayres and Rosario (calling occasionally at Passages, Marino, Corunna and Vigo).

OFFICES { PARIS: 1, RUE VIGNON.
MARSEILLES: 16, RUE CANNBIERE.
BORDEAUX; 20, ALLÉES d'ORLEANS.

NORDDEUTSCHER LLOYD,

BREMEN.

Imperial and United States Mail Steamers.

THIS COMPANY ARE THEIR OWN INSURERS.

The following magnificent Clyde-built Express Steamers—
"Lahn," "Saale," "Trave," "Aller," "Ems," "Eider,"
"Werra," "Fulda," "Elbe," of 5500 tons, 8000 horse power,
which are amongst the fastest and most luxuriously fitted
vessels afloat,

ARE APPOINTED TO SAIL BETWEEN

BREMEN AND NEW YORK,

Calling at Southampton for Passengers and Mails. From Bremen
every Wednesday and Saturday; from Southampton every Thursday
and Sunday; from New York every Wednesday and Saturday.

FARES TO NEW YORK FROM

	Bremen.	Southampton.	Havre.	Paris.
1st Class:	300 to 525 Mks.	285 to 495 Mks.	300 to 510 Mks.	315 to 525 Mks.
2nd „	200 to 300 „	200 to 270 „	200 to 285 „	205 to 300 „

FARES FROM NEW YORK TO

Bremen, Southampton, London, or Havre. { 1st Class: 75 to 175 $
{ 2nd „ 50 to _65 $.

The above-named prices are determined by the season of the year and the position of state-room.

This Company has regular Mail and Passenger Steamers between
Bremen and the following ports: BALTIMORE (direct), weekly; Bahia,
Rio de Janeiro, and Santos, *viâ* Antwerp and Lisbon, monthly; Monte
Video and Buenos Ayres, twice a month.

ALSO MONTHLY MAIL AND PASSENGER SERVICES TO

EASTERN ASIA
(CHINA AND JAPAN),
AND
AUSTRALIAN PORTS.

Full particulars on application to the Company in Bremen or to the
undermentioned Agents.

AGENTS IN LONDON:

KELLER, WALLIS, & Co., 32 Cockspur Street, Charing Cross; 5 and 7 Fenchurch Street, E.C.
PHILLIPPS and GRAVES, Botolph House, Eastcheap, E.C.

Agents in Southampton.................KELLER, WALLIS, and Co.
„ Paris and Havre ....LHERBETTE, KANE, and Co.
„ New York ....OELRICHS and Co., No. 2 Bowling Green.
„ Baltimore ....A. SCHUMACHER and Co.
„ Antwerp.......................H. ALBERT DE BARY and Co.
„ Lisbon...........................KNOWLES, BAWES, and Co.

DUBLIN AND GLASGOW STEAM PACKET COMPANY.

The Company's First-Class Saloon Paddle Steamers,
Duke of Argyll, Duke of Leinster, Lord Gough, and the First-Class Screw Steamer **General Gordon,** or other Steamers, Are intended to Sail as per Monthly Sailing Bills, unless prevented by any unforeseen occurrence, from

DUBLIN TO GLASGOW

Every MONDAY, WEDNESDAY and FRIDAY, and every alternate TUESDAY, THURSDAY and SATURDAY. From

GLASGOW TO DUBLIN

Every MONDAY, WEDNESDAY and FRIDAY, and every alternate TUESDAY, THURSDAY and SATURDAY, calling at Greenock both ways, except Saturday Boat from Dublin, which proceeds direct to Glasgow.

	£	s.	d.		£	s.	d.
Cabin Fare (including Steward's Fees)	0	13	9	Return Ticket to Edinburgh (2 Months)	1	10	0
Return Tickets (6 Months)	1	0	0	Single Ticket to Edinburgh (3rd Class and Deck)	0	7	6
Steerage	0	5	0	Return Ticket to Edinburgh (2 Months) (3rd Class and Deck)	0	12	0
Return Tickets (6 Months)	0	8	0
Single Ticket to Edinburgh	0	18	6

Passengers can travel between Greenock and Edinburgh Direct, without change of carriage, by either Caledonian or North British Railway, according to the Ticket they hold. The Caledonian Railway Stations are Cathcart Street, Greenock; and Prince's Street, Edinburgh. North British Company's—Lyndoch Street, Greenock; and Haymarket and Waverley Stations, Edinburgh.

☞ Passengers are also Booked Wellington Street, Through between Dublin and the principal Railway Stations in Scotland.

AGENTS.—HENRY LAMONT, 70, Wellington Street, Glasgow. JAMES LITTLE & Co., Excise Buildings, Greenock.

DUBLIN OFFICES.—Booking Offices for Passengers—1, Eden Quay; where Berths can be secured up to 2 o'clock p.m., on day of Sailing.

CHIEF OFFICE AND STORES.—71, NORTH WALL.

Further particulars, Monthly Bills, &c., on application to { A. TAYLOR, Secretary. B. MANN, General Manager.

GENERAL STEAM NAVIGATION COMPANY.

From and to Irongate and St. Katherine's Wharf, near the Tower.

LONDON AND OSTEND.—From London.—Wednesday and Sunday.—From Ostend—Tuesday and Friday. FARES, Chief Cabin, 10s. or 7s. 6d. Return, 15s. or 11s. 3d.

LONDON AND ANTWERP.*—Twice a week. See Time-tables.

LONDON AND HAMBURG.—Viâ Thames. Every Thursday and Saturday. From Hamburg—Monday or Tuesday and Thursday or Friday. Viâ Harwich Wednesday and Saturday from each end. FARES, viâ Thames. Chief Cabin, 30s. and 20s. Return Tickets, 45s. and 31s.
" " Harwich (Parkeston Quay), 1st Class Rail and Saloon. Single, 37s. 6d. Return, 56s. 3d. 2nd Class Rail and Saloon. Single, 35s. 9d. Return, 52s. 9d. 2nd Class Rail and Fore Cabin. Single, 25s. 9d. Return, 38s. 9d,

LONDON AND BORDEAUX.—Every Friday. From Bordeaux—Every Friday. FARES Chief Cabin, 50s. and 35s. Return Tickets, Chief Cabin, 80s. and 60s. Excursion, 70s.

LONDON AND ITALY.—Genoa, Leghorn, Naples, Messina, and Palermo.

LONDON AND OPORTO.—Every three weeks. FARES, 84s., Chief Cabin only; Ladies, 10s. extra

LONDON AND EDINBURGH (GRANTON PIER).—Every Wednesday and Saturday. From Edinburgh (Granton Pier)—Every Wednesday and Saturday. FARES, Chief Cabin, 22s.; Fore Cabin, 16s. Return, 34s. and 24s. 6d. Deck (Soldiers and Sailors only), 10s.

LONDON AND HULL.*—Every Wednesday and Saturday, at 8 morn. From Hull—Every Wednesday and Saturday. FARES, Saloon, 10s.; Fore Cabin, 7s. Return Tickets, 15s. and 11s.

Steward's Fees are included in above Fares and Return Tickets are available for two months, excepting on the Edinburgh Station, where they are available for twelve months.

* Summer Service only.

YARMOUTH, MARGATE, RAMSGATE, DEAL AND DOVER.—From London Bridge Wharf. During the summer there are special Passenger Services.

For Bank Holiday arrangements see Special Advertisements.
During the season Excursion Tickets to the near Continental Ports are issued at reduced fares.

For any alterations that may be made, and further particulars, apply to the Secretary.
55, *Great Tower Street, London, E.C.,* or 14, *Waterloo Place, S.W.*

SPLENDID SEA TRIPS.

GLASGOW and BRISTOL CHANNEL.

The First Class Steamers *HUMBER, MEDWAY, SOLWAY, AVON*, and *SEVERN*, will Sail as under (calling at Greenock, Prince's Pier)—
Glasgow to Bristol *via* Belfast every Monday and Thursday at 2 p.m.
Glasgow to Cardiff and Swansea *via* Belfast every Friday at 2 p.m.
Glasgow to Newport *via* Belfast every alternate Friday at 2 p.m.
Bristol to Glasgow *via* Belfast every Monday and Thursday evening.
Cardiff to Glasgow *via* Swansea every Monday p.m. tide.
Swansea to Glasgow *via* Belfast every Wednesday evening.
Newport to Glasgow *via* Swansea and Belfast every alternate Tuesday p.m. tide.

These Steamers have very superior accommodation for Passengers, carry Stewardesses, and afford a favourable opportunity for making Excursions from West of England to Ireland and Scotland.

Fares—Glasgow: Cabin, 20s. Steerage, 12s. 6d.
    „ Belfast: „ 17s. 6d.   „ 10s.

Returns issued at Fare-and-Half, available for Two Months, and can be used to return from any of the ports.
Circular Tours can be made *via* London and East Coast in connection with Carron Co.'s Steamers to Grangemouth; London and Edinburgh Shipping Co.'s Steamers to Leith; and General Steam Navigation Co.'s Steamers to Granton. Cabin Fare, 35s. Also per Dundee, Perth and London Shipping Co.'s Steamers from London to Dundee. Cabin Fare, 37s. 6d. And per Aberdeen Steam Navigation Co.'s Steamers from London to Aberdeen. Cabin Fare, £2 5s. These Fares are exclusive of all Railway Fares for Rail parts of the Journey.

Guide Books and further Particulars on application to—
    WILLIAM SLOAN & CO., 8, Gordon Street, Glasgow.

ALGIERS. MUSTAPHA - SUPERIOR.
Sanitary Station.
Hotel d'Orient and Hotel Continental.

First-class Houses. Full south. Situated in a large park and pine forest. Magnificent views. Omnibus in attendance at the arrival of steamers.

LAWN TENNIS.

REICHERTER & HILDENBRAND, Proprietors.

AMIENS.
GRAND HOTEL DU RHIN,
PLACE ST. DENIS.

FIRST-CLASS HOTEL, the nearest to the Cathedral and Railway Station. Much frequented by English and Americans. Spacious Apartments and airy Bed Rooms. Private and Public Saloons. Warm Baths. Large Garden. Omnibus to and from each Train. English Interpreter.

CH. FICHEUX, Proprietor.

AMIENS.

GRAND HOTEL DE L'UNIVERS.—First-Class, Hotel recently enlarged, facing St. Denis' Square, near the Railway Station. Three minutes' walk to the Cathedral. Drawing and Bath Rooms. English Interpreter.
Omnibus of the Hotel at every Train.

AMIENS.
HOTEL DE FRANCE, D'ANGLETERRE, AND DE L'EUROPE.
BRULÉ, Proprietor.

FIRST-CLASS HOTEL, close to the Cathedral, the Museum, and other Public Buildings. Having been recently newly furnished, it offers great comfort. Families and Single Gentlemen accommodated with convenient Suites of Apartments and Single Rooms.
Omnibus at the Station.   English spoken.

AMSTERDAM.
AMSTEL HOTEL.

THIS Magnificent FIRST-CLASS HOTEL is situated near the Zoological and Botanical Gardens, the Crystal Palace, Museums, &c. Cheerful views on the Amstel river. It is provided with every Comfort, and contains 200 well-furnished Rooms and Saloons, Reading and Smoking Rooms, and a special Ladies' Saloon. First-rate Table and Choice Wines.

Terms Moderate.   Lift.
Railway, Telegraph Offices, and Stables attached to the House.
R. SEQUEIRA, jun., Manager.

ANTWERP.
HOTEL ST. ANTOINE.
PLACE VERTE, OPPOSITE THE CATHEDRAL.

THIS excellent First-Class Hotel, which enjoys the well-merited favour of Families and Tourists, has been Newly Furnished and Decorated. Great Comfort, Superior Apartments, and Moderate Charges. Elegant Sitting, Reading and Smoking Rooms; fine *Salle à Manger*, excellent Table d'Hôte and choice Wines.

English, American, and French Papers.
TELEPHONE.
BATHS IN THE HOTEL.

ANTWERP.	AVIGNON.
GRAND HOTEL.	**GRAND HOTEL DE L'EUROPE.**
REOPENED by, and under the direction of Mr. Schoefter Wiertz, the well-known proprietor of Hotel de l'Univers, Brussels.	**VERY GOOD.**

AVRANCHES.
GRAND HOTEL DE LONDRES.
MOREL, new Proprietor. First Class House. Near Post and Telegraph. Apartments and Rooms for Families. Smoking Room. Large Garden. Moderate Prices. Omnibus to all the trains.

AVRANCHES.
GRAND HOTEL D'ANGLETERRE.
Recently reconstructed and newly furnished throughout with large additions, and every possible Comfort. Celebrated Cellar. English Papers. Moderate Prices. Omnibus at Station. Carriages for Mount St. Michel and Excursions.
A. HOULLEGATTE, Proprietor.

BADEN - BADEN.
VICTORIA HOTEL.
Proprietor, Mr. FRANZ GROSHOLZ.

THIS is one of the finest-built and best-furnished First-Class Hotels, main front with Morning Sun, situated in the new Promenade nearest the Kursaal and the famous Frederic Baths; it commands the most charming views, and is reputed to be one of the best Hotels in Germany. Principally frequented by English and American Travellers. Highly recommended in every respect, very moderate charges. Table d'hôte at 1 and 6 o'clock. English and other Journals. Beautiful airy Dining Rooms, Ladies' Drawing Room, Reading and Smoking Rooms. Pension in the early and latter part of the season.
Hydraulic Lift. Bath Rooms. Sanitary Arrangements perfect.

BADEN-BADEN.
First-class Establishment, NEAREST CONVERSATION HOUSE and NEW VAPOUR BATHS. Now surrounded by ITS OWN BEAUTIFUL PARK.

HOLLAND HOTEL
With DEPENDANCE "BEAU SÉJOUR."

OPEN ALL THE YEAR
Charges strictly moderate.
Special arrangements for a prolonged stay. Pension.
HYDRAULIC LIFT IN BOTH HOUSES.
A. RÖSSLER, Proprietor.

BÂLE.
HOTEL EULER.
FIRST CLASS HOTEL.
Opposite the Central Station.

BASLE.
HOTEL SCHRIEDER ZUM DEUTSCHEN HOF.
OPPOSITE the Baden Railway Station. Comfortable accommodation. Moderate Charges.
M. ERNE, Proprietor.

BAYEUX.
HOTEL DU LUXEMBOURG.
REPUTED the best. Situated in the centre of the town, close to the Cathedral and public buildings. Breakfast, 2 fr. 50 c.; Dinner, 3 fr. Rooms from 2 fr. Table d'hôte. Restaurant à la carte. Garden. Billiard room. Recreation Ground. Carriages for Excursions.
ENGLISH SPOKEN.

BELFAST.
THE IMPERIAL HOTEL.
Just Re-decorated and Enlarged. First-Class. Best Situation.
Omnibuses meet all Trains and Steamers.
W. J. JURY, Proprietor.

BERLIN.

GRAND HOTEL DE ROME,

UNTER DEN LINDEN, 39, *opposite the Royal Palace*.

This old, reputed, first-class Hotel, has the best situation in the Town, close to all the principal sights and Royal Theatres. Lately re-furnished throughout.

Splendid **RESTAURANT**, looking out over the "Linden."

"CAFE." DRAWING ROOM FOR LADIES. BATHS. LIFT.

TABLE d'HOTE. ELECTRIC LIGHT.

Newspapers in all Languages. Omnibus at Stations. Moderate Charges.

Proprietor: **ADOLF MÜHLING,**

Purveyor to the Imperial Court.

BAYONNE.
GRAND HOTEL ST. ETIENNE.
FIRST-CLASS HOTEL.
Most highly recommended to Families as being the best in Bayonne. Aristocratic Hotel.

BERLIN.
HOTEL ROYAL,
F. LANGE, Proprietor.
UNTER DEN LINDEN,
No. 3, *WILHELMSTRASSEN-ECKE.*
Only a Few Minutes Distance from the Stadtbahnhof Friedrichstrasse.

BILBAO.
GRAND HOTEL D'ANGLETERRE.

BEST SITUATED FIRST-CLASS HOTEL. — Near the Station and Theatre. Close to the Post and Telegraph Offices, on Promenade. Interpreter. Omnibus at the Station.   **L. MONET.**

BLOIS.
GRAND HOTEL DE BLOIS.
H. GIGNON.

Highly recommended to Strangers.

VERY COMFORTABLE TABLE D'HÔTE AND PRIVATE DINNERS.

Apartments for Families. Close to the Castle of Blois.

Comfortable Carriages for visiting Chambord and the Environs.

BATHS IN THE HOTEL.
OMNIBUS AT THE STATION.   ENGLISH SPOKEN.

BIARRITZ.
GRAND HOTEL VICTORIA.
GRANDE PLAGE.

THIS new Hotel is built with all the latest improvements of comfort. Near the British Club, in the centre of all the best Promenades. 100 Rooms and Saloons. Facing the Sea, and full South. Renowned Cuisine. Moderate Charges.

J. FOURNEAU (*from the Hôtel de France*).

| LIFT.] | BONN. | [LIFT. |

GRAND HOTEL ROYAL.

ON the Banks of the Rhine. European repute. 200 Rooms and Salons. Situation without equal, facing the Rhine, Seven Mountains and Park. Near the Landing-place and Railway Station. Extensive English Gardens. Reading, Smoking and Billiard Rooms. Ladies' Salons. Arrangements on the most moderate terms for Pension. Warm and Cold Baths in the Hotel. **L. VOGELER.**

BORDIGHERA.
HOTEL ANGST.

First-Class Hotel with every modern comfort, situated in the middle of a large beautiful garden on the Strada Romana. Sheltered position. Magnificent view. Best drainage-system by the English Sanitary Co.

Conducted by the Propri tor, **A. ANGST** (Swiss).
Formerly **Grand Hôtel de Bordighera.**

BOULOGNE-SUR-MER.
BERRY'S (late ROBERT'S)
English and French Boarding Establishment and Family Hotel,
96, 98, 100, & 102, RUE DE BOSTON,

OPPOSITE the Casino Bathing Establishment, near the Steam Packets and Railway Station, and having a splendid Sea View from the extensive gardens of the Hotel. Terms moderate, and special arrangements for the Winter Season, by day, week, or month. Single Boarders received. Established 50 years.

BOULOGNE-SUR-MER.
HOTEL DES BAINS ET DE BELLE VUE.
MM. MESUREUR & CO., Proprietors.

FIRST CLASS HOTEL, situated Rue Victor Hugo (late Rue de l'Ecu), and on the Port facing the Railway Station and Steamers.
Hot and Cold Sea Baths and Vapour Baths in the House.

BOULOGNE-SUR-MER.
GRAND HOTEL CHRISTOL & BRISTOL.
First-class Hotel.

Best Situation in the Town. Highly recommended for Families and Gentlemen.

Carriage in Attendance on Arrival of all Trains and Boats.
SAGNIER and F. CHRISTOL, Proprietors.

BOULOGNE-SUR-MER.
HOTEL DERVAUX,
73 to 80, GRANDE RUE; and 24, RUE DES VIEILLARDS.

THE most healthy part of Boulogne, near the Post Office, English Church, Theatre, and Market. The Hotel is now carried on by Mr. ALPHONSE DERVAUX, son of the founder. Arrangements by the day, week, or month. Reduced prices during the winter months.

BOULOGNE-SUR-MER.
BRIGHTON AND MARINE HOTEL
JACQUES LECERF, Proprietor.

A large first-class Hotel, best situation in the Town, facing the Sea and the "Etablissement des Bains," the Garden of which is separated from the Hotel by the road only. Visitors to this Hotel have the advantage of hearing, from their own rooms, the Military Band which plays in the Garden. The Hotel has been newly furnished.

BOULOGNE-SUR-MER.
HOTEL DU PAVILLON IMPÉRIAL.
First-class Hotel.
The only one facing the Sea.
VERMERSCH, Proprietor.

BRUNSWICK.
HOTEL DEUTSCHES HAUS.
(HOTEL, GERMAN HOUSE.)
FIRST-CLASS HOTEL, GOOD ATTENDANCE, COMFORTABLE.
ENGLISH SPOKEN.
ROBERT SCHRADER.

BRUSSELS.
GRAND HOTEL GERNAY.
Moderate Charges. Ancien Propriétaire de l'Hôtel de Portugal à Spa.
This Hotel is close to the Railway Station for Ostend, Germany, Holland, Antwerp, and Spa, forming the Corner of the Boulevards Botanique et du Nord.
Baths in the Hotel. Telephone.

BRUSSELS.
HOTEL DE SUÈDE.
FIRST CLASS.
CENTRAL PART OF THE TOWN.
GOOD CUISINE. CHOICE WINES.
VAN CUTSEM.

BRUSSELS.
HOTEL DE LA POSTE,
28, RUE FOSSE AUX LOUPS, NEAR THE PLACE DE LA MONNAIE.
FAMILY HOTEL SPECIALLY RECOMMENDED TO ENGLISH TRAVELLERS.
Omnibus—Telephone. Ladies' and Smoking Rooms. English Spoken.
HYACINTHE TILMANS, Proprietor.

BRUSSELS.
HOTEL MENGELLE
Hydraulic Lift. **(RUE ROYALE).** *Hydraulic Lift.*
B. MENGELLE, Proprietor.

THIS large and beautiful First-Class Hotel is situated in the finest and most healthy part of the Town, near to the Promenades the most frequented, and is supplied with every modern accommodation and comfort. Table d'Hôte at 6 and 7.15, five francs. Restaurant à la carte, and at fixed prices, at any hour. Excellent Cuisine and Choice Wines. *The Largest and Finest Dining-Room in the Town.*
HYDRAULIC LIFT.
Baths, Smoking Room, Reading Room, Billiard Room.
Arrangements made with Families during the Winter Season.

BRUSSELS.	BRUSSELS.
HOTEL DE L'UNIVERS. (CENTRAL.) *First Class. Moderate Prices.* Table d'Hôte, Restaurant, Salon, Smoking Room, Garden. Omnibus at Station. M. Shoffler-Wiertz has taken also the management of the Grand Hotel, Antwerp.	**Murray's Handbook for Belgium and Holland.** *Twenty-first Edition. With Maps and Plans. Post 8vo. 6s.* JOHN MURRAY, Albemarle Street.

BUXTON HYDROPATHIC and WINTER RESIDENCE
(MALVERN HOUSE),
BUXTON, DERBYSHIRE.

The largest and most complete Hydro in the neighbourhood. Central and Sheltered situation. Close to Mineral Wells and Baths. Every comfort for Invalids and Visitors. Sanitary, ventilating, and heating arrangements on the most approved principles.
Two BILLIARD TABLES, SMOKING ROOM, splendidly appointed BALL ROOM.
The BATHS have been wholly refitted with all the most recent appliances, and there has been added as complete a system of Baths for MASSAGE TREATMENT as engineering skill has been able to devise.
For terms, etc., apply to the PROPRIETOR. Telegrams—"*Buxton Hydro., Buxton.*"

CAEN.
GRAND HOTEL D'ESPAGNE.
(CYCLIST TOURING CLUB)

FIRST-CLASS, and one of the best frequented. Newly furnished. Near the Race Course, Post and Telegraph Office, and the Boat for Havre. E. RENAUX, Proprietor.
Recherché table, good family cookery. Table d'hôte déjenner 2 fr. 50 c.; Dinner 3 fr. Service at separate tables for families at the same price. *The most recommended.* English spoken. Man spricht Deutsch. Special information on the Curiosities of the Town.

CAEN.

HÔTEL  D'ANGLETERRE,
Rue St. Jean, Nos. 77, 79, 81.

Situated in the Centre of the Town. Rendezvous of the best Society.

100 *Elegantly Furnished and Comfortable Bed Rooms and Sitting Rooms.*

BREAKFASTS À LA CARTE.
TABLE D'HÔTE BREAKFASTS AT 3 FRANCS.

DINNER AT TABLE D'HÔTE, 4 FRANCS.
SUITES OF APARTMENTS FOR FAMILIES.

ENGLISH AND SPANISH SPOKEN.

L. MANCEL, Proprietor.

CARLSBAD.
ANGER'S HOTEL (Branch, RHEIN HOTEL).

THESE Two First-Class Hotels offer special comfort to English and American Travellers, who will find them most desirable residences.

Charges Moderate; deservedly recommended.
ENGLISH & AMERICAN NEWSPAPERS. BATHS, CARRIAGES, OMNIBUS, LIFT.
Mr. and Mrs. Anger speak English.

CARLSBAD.
HOTEL GOLDENER SCHILD.
WITH DEPENDENCE (TWO GERMAN MONARCHS).

THIS HOTEL has European celebrity, is very beautifully situated, with large Garden, and is newly furnished and decorated. Travellers will find here every comfort at *moderate prices*. English, French, and German Newspapers. Open all the year. English Attendance.

F. ROSCHER, Hotelier.

CARLSBAD.
WIESINGER'S HOTEL NATIONAL.
On the Neuen Gartenzeilstrasse. First-Class Hotel. Open all the year.

THIS HOTEL, situated next to the City Park, and only four minutes from all the Mineral Springs, commands a splendid view of the Mountains; is recommended to families and travellers in general. Large Dining Rooms and shady Garden. Good German and French Cooking. Moderate Charges.

The Proprietor, **Ant. Wiesinger**, has left his Hotel "Drei Fasanen" on account of his increasing business in the above Hotel.

CHESTER.
THE GROSVENOR HOTEL.

FIRST-CLASS. Situated in the centre of the City, close to the CATHEDRAL and other objects of interest. Two Large Coffee Rooms and Ladies' Drawing Room for the convenience of Ladies and Families. Open and close Carriages, and Posting in all its Branches. The Hotel Porters and Omnibuses, for the use of Visitors to the Hotel, attend the Trains. Tariff to be had on application. A Night Porter in attendance.

DAVID FOSTER, Manager.

COBLENTZ.
GIANT HOTEL—HÔTEL DU GÉANT.

THE best situated First-Class Hotel, just opposite the landing-place of the Steamboats and Fortress Ehrenbreitstein. Excellent Cuisine and Cellar. Moderate Charges. Reduction for a long residence.

PROPRIETORS, **EISENMANN BROS.**

COBLENTZ.
GRAND HOTEL DE BELLE VUE.

FIRST-CLASS. Commanding a splendid view of the Rhine and the Fortress of Ehrenbreitstein.

Moderate Charges.

COLOGNE.
HOTEL DU DÔME.

TH. METZ EBBEN.—This old and excellent House has been enlarged by an elegant New Building, and comfortably fitted-up; it is advantageously situated in the centre of the City, near the Cathedral and the Central Railway Station. Table d'Hôte 1 and 5 o'clock. Splendid Dining Room, Ladies' Saloon, Smoking Room, &c. Recommended to English Tourists. Moderate Charges.

COLOGNE.
HOTEL DISCH.

First-Class House. Near Cathedral and Central Station. Greatly enlarged. Every comfort found. 200 Rooms with 300 beds. Omnibuses meet every Train and Steamer. Choice wines for wholesale. Hydraulic Lift. Electric Light, Coloriferes in winter. T. CHRISTOPH, Proprietor.

CONSTANCE.
HOTEL & PENSION INSELHOTEL AM SEE.

FIRST-CLASS HOUSE, considerably enlarged by new buildings. Commanding a magnificent view on the Lake of Constance and the Alps. Beautiful Garden. Warm baths as well as baths in the lake and river.

A. Gutzschebauch, *Director*.

COPENHAGEN.
HOTEL KONGEN of DENMARK.

THIS FIRST-CLASS HOTEL, much frequented by the highest class of English and American Travellers, affords first-rate accommodation for Families and single Gentlemen. Splendid situation, close to the Royal Palace, overlooking the King's Square. Excellent Table d'Hôte. Private Dinners. Best attendance. Reading Room. Hot Baths. Lift.
English, French, German and American Newspapers.
ALL LANGUAGES SPOKEN.   **MODERATE CHARGES.**
Ladies' Drawing Room.   **Vienna Coffee House.**
CARRIAGES IN THE HOTEL.
R. KLÜM, Proprietor.

COPENHAGEN.
HOTEL PHOENIX.
First-Class Hotel in the Centre of the Town.
CHARGES MODERATE.
N.B.—Patronized by His Majesty the Emperor of Russia.
C. E. SÖDRING, Proprietor.

BAD-CREUZNACH.
HOTEL ORANIENHOF.

LARGEST First-Class House. Finest situation in own grounds. Visited by the Crown Princess of Germany. The Oranienspring, strongest mineral spring at Kreuznach, belongs to Hotel.
H. D. ALTEN, Proprietor.

COUTANCES.
HOTEL DES TROIS ROIS
H. SIFFAIT, Proprietor.
First-class House. Apartments and Drawing Room (Piano) for families. Terrace. Near the Cathedral. Moderate Prices.
Omnibus to all the Trains.

CUXHAVEN (North Sea Bath).
DÖLLE'S HÔTEL BELVÉDÈRE.
E. DÖLLE, Proprietor.

FIRST-CLASS HOTEL, newly built, with a brilliant view on the Sea and Port, newly and comfortably fitted up, good Cuisine, Choice Wines, Warm Sea-Baths in the house. Two minutes' from the Railroad Depot, fifteen minutes' to the new Sea-bathing Establishment.
HOTEL-CARRIAGE AT THE STEAMBOAT LANDING.

DINANT-SUR-MEUSE.
HOTEL DE LA TÊTE D'OR.
ALEXIS DISIÈRE, Proprietor.

FIRST-CLASS, upon the GRAND PLACE. Is to be recommended for its comfort. Pension from 7 francs 50 centimes per day.

DRESDEN.
VICTORIA HOTEL.
ON THE PUBLIC PROMENADE,
Five Minutes from the Central Station.

Proprietor, C. WEISS.

EISENACH (THURINGIA).
HOTEL RAUTENKRANZ.
Most beautiful view on the Wartburg. First and largest Hotel in the City; favourably known for its Moderate Prices, Excellent Cooking, and Choice Wines.
W. OPPERMANN.

ENGELBERG.
THE VALLEY OF ENGELBERG (3200 ft. high) with its
KURHAUS AND HOTEL SONNENBERG.

THE property of Mr. H. HUG. Summer stay unrivalled by its grand Alpine scenery, as well as by the curative efficacy of the climate against lung and chest diseases, coughs, nervous ailments, &c., &c. Clear bracing air, equable temperature. Recommended by the highest medical authorities. The HOTEL SONNENBERG, in the finest and healthiest situation facing the Titlis and the Glaciers, is one of the most comfortable and best managed hotels in Switzerland. Lawn Tennis Ground. Excellent and central place for sketching, botanising, and the most varied and interesting excursions. The ascent of the Titlis is best made from here. Shady Woods. Vapour and Shower Baths. Waterspring 5° R.; 200 Rooms; Pension from 7 fr. a day upwards. Because of its so sheltered situation specially adapted for a stay in May and June. Resident English Physician. English Divine Service.

ENGELBERG, SWITZERLAND.
KURHAUS HOTEL ET PENSION TITLIS.

THIS First-Class Hotel, in the best situation of the valley, in the middle of an extensive garden, has been recently much enlarged and improved. 200 Beds. Lofty Dining Saloon. Large Saloon de Réunion, with Veranda. Smoking-Room. Reading-Room. Billiards. Salle de Musique. Lift. Electric Lighting in all Rooms. Bathin the Hotel. Good attendance, with Moderate Charges.

English Chapel in the garden of the Hotel.

ED. CATTANI, Proprietor.

EXETER, DEVON.
POPLE'S NEW LONDON HOTEL.

FOR Families and Gentlemen. Re-furnished and Re-decorated. Large covered Continental Courtyard. This First-Class Hotel has long stood pre-eminent, and is patronised by the leading County Families. Adjoining Northernhay Park, and within three minutes walk of the Cathedral. General Coffee Room. Drawing-room Suites of Apartments. Table d'Hôte at 7 o'clock. Night Porter. Omnibuses and Cabs meet every Train.

POSTING ESTABLISHMENT.
Also Proprietor of the Globe Hotel, Newton Abbot.

FRANKFORT-ON-MAIN.
PENSION VORSTER.
FAMILY PRIVATE HOTEL.
Lindenstr. 17 (West End).

FRANZENSBAD.
THE KÖNIGSVILLA,
FIRST-CLASS FAMILY HOTEL.

Unrivalled Situation.		Special Care paid to
Home Comforts.		Kitchen, Cellar,
12 Salons. Balconies.		and
60 Bedrooms.	New Park with splendid Lawn Tennis Ground.	Attendance.

Under the superintendence of the Proprietor himself, **Mr. F. F. KOPP**, late of "Cosmopolitan Hotel," Nice.

FREUDENSTADT. (2,600 feet above sea.)
BLACK FOREST HOTEL.
RAILWAY-LINE STUTTGART, OFFENBURG, STRASSBURG.

FIRST-CLASS HOTEL situated on a charming hill, and surrounded by a very extensive and beautiful Park. 60 very comfortable Bedrooms and Saloons, with 15 Balconies. Water and Milk cures. Electricity. Massage. Pine needle and Soole Baths.

BEST CENTRAL RESIDENCE FOR EXCURSIONS.
Elegant Coaches and Landau Carriages at the Hotel.
TROUT FISHING, AND VERY GOOD SHOOTING.
Moderate Charges. Pension.

ERNEST LUZ, Junior, *Proprietor.*

GENEVA.
GRAND HOTEL BEAU RIVAGE.
THE LARGEST AND BEST IN GENEVA.
MAYER & KUNZ, Proprietors.

GENEVA.
GRAND HOTEL METROPOLE.
ONLY FIRST-CLASS HOTEL OPPOSITE THE JARDIN ANGLAIS, AND VIEW OF THE LAKE.
OPEN ALL THE YEAR. LIFT. BATH-ROOMS.
Moderate charges and special arrangements for prolonged stay.
ADOLPHE DURINGER, Proprietor.

GENEVA.
GRAND HOTEL NATIONAL.
THE LARGEST AND BEST.
200 Rooms overlooking Lake and Mont Blanc.
LIFT. GARDEN. CONCERTS.
ARMLEDER & GOERGER, Proprietors.

GENEVA.
HOTEL PENSION VICTORIA
(FORMERLY HOTEL FLAEGEL).
Finest situation, near the English Garden. Splendid view on the Lake and the Alps. Moderate charges. No charge for light and attendance. Omnibus at the Station. Lift. Baths. **W. NIESS, Proprietor.**

GENEVA.
RICHMOND FAMILY HOTEL.
FACING LAKE AND MONT BLANC.
TERMS FROM SEVEN TO TEN FRANCS PER DAY,
ALL INCLUDED. LIFT.

GENEVA.
HOTEL-PENSION BELLEVUE,
RUE DE LYON.

HEALTHY Situation. Most extensive and shady grounds. Comfortable apartments and single rooms. Highly recommended. Pension from 5 francs per day.
JEAN SUTTERLIN.

GENEVA.
HOTEL DE LA POSTE.
Best sanitary arrangements. 100 well-furnished rooms, from 2 to 3 francs the bed. Table d'Hôte Dinner, 3½ francs and 4 francs, wine included; Supper, 3 francs. Pension, for stay, 7 to 10 francs. Lift.

GENOA.
HOTEL DE LONDRES
(Opposite to Rubattino's Office)
ET
PENSION ANGLAISE.
The nearest to the Central Station.
First Class. Full South. Moderate Prices.
FLECHIA & FIORONI.

GENOA (ITALY).
GRAND HOTEL ISOTTA.
HYDRAULIC LIFT AND RAILWAY OFFICE.

Only FIRST-CLASS HOUSE built for an Hotel; in the healthiest position in the town.

G. BORGARELLO & CH. SON.

GRENOBLE.
HOTEL MONNET.

THIS splendidly-situated First-Class Hotel, which is the largest in the Town, and enjoys the well-merited favour of Families and Tourists, has just been considerably enlarged and Newly Furnished. The Apartments, large and small, combine elegance and comfort, and every attention has been paid to make this one of the best Provincial Hotels. Public and Private Drawing-rooms; English and French Papers. Table d'Hôte at 11 and 6. Private Dinners at any hour. Excellent Cuisine. Moderate Charges.

The Omnibuses of the Hotel meet all Trains.

L. TRILLAT, Proprietor.

First-Class Carriages can be had at the Hotel for Excursions to the Grande Chartreuse, Uriage, and all places of interest amongst the Alps of Dauphiné.

URIAGE-LES-BAINS.
HOTEL RESTAURANT, MONNET.

Founded in 1846. English Visitors will find every comfort and luxury in this First-Class Establishment. Private Rooms for Families. Excellent Cuisine and Wines. Table d'Hôte, 11 and 6. Carriages and Horses can be had in the Hotel for Excursions and Promenades.

GIJON (Spain).
GRAND HOTEL FRANCAIS, LA IBERIA.

MAGNIFICENT SITUATION, between the two Beaches. View on the Port and open Sea. Apartments for Families. Table d'Hôte and Restaurant.
L. MALET, Proprietor.

HEIDELBERG.
HOTEL DE DARMSTADT.

Three Minutes' from the Station. This Hotel, beautifully situated on the Bismarck Square, Two Minutes from the new Neckar Bridge, is well known for its good keeping and very moderate prices.
H. KRALL, Proprietor.

THE HAGUE (Holland).
HOTEL DES INDES,
VOORHOUT, 56.

THIS magnificent First-Class Hotel is the largest in the city. Charmingly situated near the Theatre, Park, Museum, Telegraph, and the most frequented Promenades. It is supplied with every modern accommodation and comfort.

TABLE D'HÔTE AT SIX O'CLOCK.

Restaurant a la carte at any hour.

EXCELLENT CUISINE AND CHOICE WINES.

SMOKING ROOM, READING ROOM, BATH, AND CARRIAGES.

Rooms from 2 florins a day.

Arrangements made with Families during the Winter Season.

P. WIRTZ, Proprietor.

HAMBURG.
HOTEL DE L'EUROPE.

RENOWNED FIRST-CLASS HOUSE, patronized by H.R.H. the Prince of Wales, and by most of the Imperial and Royal Families of Europe. Splendid situation, overlooking the Alster-Bassin. 180 Rooms and Apartments. Elegant Reading and Smoking Rooms. Baths. Lift. Table d'Hôte. **BRETTSCHNEIDER & BANDLI, Proprietors.**

HANOVER.
GRAND HOTEL HARTMANN.

FIRST-CLASS Hotel, opposite the Central Station and Post Office, with a beautiful "Restaurant and Café." Rooms from 2 Marks. Light and Service included. Carriage in the House.
CHRISTIAN HARTMANN, Proprietor.

HARROGATE.
"THE GRANBY."

FIRST-CLASS FAMILY HOTEL, facing the Stray. Every accommodation for Visitors and Tourists. Carriages to Wells and Baths every morning free of charge. Good Stabling. Carriages on Hire. Tennis Court in the Grounds.
W. H. MILNER, Proprietor.

GRAND HOTEL AND BAINS FRASCATI.
Open all the year.   *Table d'Hôte.*   *Restaurant facing the Sea.*
Arrangements for Families. Pension from 12 fr. all the year round.
TH. FOTSCH, Directeur.

HEIDELBERG.
HOTEL VICTORIA.
FIRST-CLASS HOTEL in every respect. Exceedingly well Situated. Beautiful Veranda and large Garden at the back of the House. Advantageous arrangements made with families intending a longer stay. Highly recommended.

BATHS OF HOMBURG.
HOTEL BELLE VUE.—First-Class Hotel, exceedingly well situated, opposite the Music Pavillon, and close to the Springs. Families, and Single Gentlemen, will find this Hotel one of the most comfortable, combining excellent accommodation with moderate Charges. Best French and English Cooking. Excellent Wines. Café Restaurant. Mineral, Pine, Shower, Cold, and Warm Baths Indoors.
W. FISCHER, Proprietor.

HILDESHEIM.
HOTEL WIENER HOF.
FIRST-CLASS, in the centre of the town, near the Cathedral and all the curiosities, to which latter the Hotel itself, with its old wood-carvings, belongs in the first place. Garden adjoining the house. Omnibus at the Railway Station. *Old German Beer-room newly opened.* ENGLISH SPOKEN.   **CARL WESEMANN, Proprietor.**

HILDESHEIM.
HOTEL D'ANGLETERRE.
FIRST-CLASS House, considerably enlarged by an additional building, situate in the centre of the city. Table d'Hôte at 1 o'clock; meals *à la carte* at all hours. Omnibus to all Trains. Garden adjoining the Hotel.
ENGLISH NEWSPAPERS.   *On parle français.*   *English spoken.*
C. HEERDT, L. KÖSEL'S NACHFOLGER, Proprietor.

BATHS OF HOMBURG.

MINERAL SPRINGS

very salutary for DISEASES of the STOMACH and LIVER and ATTACKS of GOUT.

UNRIVALLED SUMMER CLIMATE.

SOVEREIGN CURE in NERVOUS DEBILITY.

MINERAL, PINE and MUD BATHS, highly recommended for RHEUMATISM.

LAWN TENNIS GROUNDS.

All kinds of Amusements. Comfortable Hotels and Private Houses at moderate prices.

MAGNIFICENT KURHAUS, with the well-known RESTAURANT.

HOMBURG.

ROYAL VICTORIA HOTEL.—Patronised by H.R.H. the Prince of Wales and several other Royal Personages. Highest and Driest Position. First-Class Hotel, close to Springs and Kursaal, with fine view of Taunus Mountains. Quiet Apartments. Newly enlarged by Three spacious Villas. At early and later part of Season arrangements made on very reasonable terms. Best Stag Shooting, as well as Trout Fishing, free for guests of Hotel. Lawn Tennis. Fournisseur to H.R.H. Prince of Wales and H.R.H. Duke of Mecklenburg Strelitz.   GUSTAVE WEIGAND, *Proprietor*.

HOMBURG.

HOTEL DES QUATRE SAISONS, and VILLA, with the finest views of the Taunus, kept by Mr. W. SCHLOTTERBECK.—This first-rate House is exceedingly well situated near the Sources and the Kursaal. It combines every comfort desirable with moderate charges. It has a beautiful Garden for the use of Visitors. Highest position, and one of the best Table d'Hôtes in the Town. Arrangements at Moderate Prices at the early and later part of the Season. Patronised by H.M. the Emperor Frederic, H.M. the Empress Victoria and H.I.H. Princess Victoria of Germany.

HYÈRES.
HOTEL CONTINENTAL,
ET
HOTEL DES ILES D'OR.

These large and beautiful Establishments are situated in the finest and most healthy part of the Town, surrounded by charming Gardens, with Orange, Lemon and Palm Trees. Commanding magnificent views of the Sea, the Isl.s of Hyères and the Mountains. Extensive Dining Saloons, decorated with Pictures by one of the first country Painters of France, Conversation Saloons with beautiful Winter-Garden, Smoking Rooms, Billiard Saloons, Baths on every floor, combining the elegance and luxury of the most important and attractive Hotels in Europe. Moderate charges. N.B. Pension from 9 francs per day.

OMNIBUS AT THE STATION.

E. WEBER, Proprietor

ILFRACOMBE HOTEL.—*Thoroughly Furnished, Equipped, & Decorated.*
250 Apartments, Noble Dining Rooms, Elegant Drawing Rooms, Large Reading Room, Capacious Billiard Room (Two Tables), Comfortable Smoking Room, Ornamental Grounds extending to the Sea, Eight Lawn Tennis Courts, Table d'Hôte Dinner, at separate tables, from 6 to 8 o'clock. There is attached to the Hotel one of the Largest Swimming Baths in England, also Private Hot and Cold Sea and Fresh Water Baths, Douché, Shower, &c. Full Descriptive Tariff of MANAGER, Ilfracombe, North Devon. The attractions of Ilfracombe, and the Places of Interest in the neighbourhood, point to it as the natural centre to be chosen by the Tourist who desires to see with comfort all the beauties of Coast and Inland Scenery which North Devon affords. There is also easy access into South Devon and Cornwall. *Tourist Tickets to Ilfracombe for Two Months are Issued during the Season at all principal Railway Stations.*

ILFRACOMBE.
ROYAL CLARENCE
FAMILY AND COMMERCIAL HOTEL.
(*Old Established.*)

HAS recently been rebuilt with extra Bed Room accommodation. Commodious Coffee Room and Ladies' Drawing Room. Billiards.

Omnibus meets every Train.

TARIFF ON APPLICATION.   *CHARGES MODERATE.*

CHAS. E. CLEMOW, Proprietor.
At Anderton's Hotel, Fleet Street, London, and "Peacock" and "Royal," Deal n. Lincolnshire.

INTERLAKEN.
HOTEL-PENSION,
JUNGFRAU.
F. SEILER-STERCHI, Proprietor.

THIS Establishment, with two Branch Houses, is situated in the centre of the Höheweg, and enjoys a splendid view of the Jungfrau and the entire range of the Alps. It recommends itself for its delightful position, as well as for its comfortable accommodation.

TABLE D'HÔTE AT 2 AND 6.30 O'CLOCK.
DINNERS À LA CARTE.

CARRIAGES, GUIDES, AND HORSES FOR MOUNTAIN EXCURSIONS.

OMNIBUS WAITING AT ALL THE STATIONS.

INTERLAKEN.
RUGEN HOTEL, JUNGFRAUBLICK.

FIRST-CLASS Hotel and Pension, 150 Beds. Situated in the healthiest position, 30 metres higher than Interlaken, with Splendid View on the Jungfrau and Silverhorn, &c. Surrounded by Terraces and Gardens. Pension from 10 to 15 francs, according to Room. Reduced Prices in May, June, and after 15th September. Season, May to October.   J. OESCH-MÜLLER, *Proprietor.*
Also proprietor of the Hotel St. George, at Mustapha Superieur, Algiers.

INNSBRUCK.

THE beautiful and sheltered situation of Innsbruck renders it a very agreeable place of residence all the year round. In Spring as well as in Autumn it is especially to be recommended as a stopping place between the different watering places. It is also to be recommended after a sojourn at the seaside.

HOTEL TYROL.

CARL LANDSEE, Proprietor.

THREE FIRST-CLASS HOTELS.

Opposite the Railway Station.

INNSBRUCK is the centre from which many splendid excursions can be made in every direction, and of any length. Attractive walks in the immediate neighbourhood of the town, and the different elevations, render it a good place for walking cures after the system of Dr. Oertel.

HOTEL DE L'EUROPE.

JOHANN REINHART, Proprietor.

ARRANGEMENTS MADE.

MODERATE CHARGES.

POST AND TELEGRAPH OFFICES.

THE climate in Winter, dry, strengthening, sunny, free from cold winds and fogs, has attracted many visitors of late years, and among those who have found the greatest relief are weak, convalescent, nervous, appetiteless and sleepless persons.

N.B.—University, Grammar, Music, and other Schools. Private lessons of every kind are available, so that studies can be continued and the education of children carried on.

HOTEL ZUR GOLDENEN SONNE.

CARL BEER, Proprietor.

INTERLAKEN.
GRAND HOTEL VICTORIA.

Magnificent First-class Family Hotel; the best situated at Interlaken.

400 BEDS.

ELEVATOR.

Special arrangements made for a stay of some time.

ED. RUCHTI, Proprietor.
Also Proprietor of "HOTEL DES ANGLAIS," Cannes.

INTERLAKEN.
HOTEL "BEAU SITE" PENSION.

Rooms from 1 fr. 50 c.; Dinners at 2 fr. 50 c.; Pension from 6 fr. Excellent Cooking. Good Wines. Fresh Milk and Whey. Unparalleled, most desirable situation, with view of the Glaciers of the Jungfrau, Moench and Eiger.

BEAUTIFUL AND SHADY GARDEN.
No charge for Omnibus to the principal Promenades, to the Kursaal, and to the Churches.

Open from APRIL.   Omnibus at the Station.

HIGHLY RECOMMENDED.   **ED. RUCHTI, Proprietor.**

KARLSRUHE.	LAKES OF KILLARNEY.
HOTEL GERMANIA. *BEST SITUATED.* **FIRST-CLASS HOTEL.** Omnibus at the Station. F. LEERS, Proprietor.	*By Her Gracious Majesty's Special Permission.* **ROYAL VICTORIA HOTEL.** Magnificently situated on the Lower Lake. Patronised by H.R.H. the Prince of Wales, H.R.H. the Duke of Connaught, the principal Royal Families of Europe, and leading American Families. *Reduced Tariff during Winter Months.*

LAUSANNE.
HOTEL and PENSION VICTORIA.

THE above Hotel has been recently greatly improved, and supplied with every modern comfort. Board and Lodging from 6 to 7 frs. Beautiful gardens commanding extensive and charming views.

LS. DESPLAND, Proprietor.

LAUSANNE.

HOTEL GIBBON.

One of the very Best First-Class Hotels of Switzerland.

BEAUTIFUL LARGE GARDEN & SHADED TERRACE.

FULL VIEW OF LAKE LEMAN FROM EACH WINDOW.

IN WINTER PENSION.

EMILE RITTER, Proprietor.

LE MANS.
GRAND HOTEL
(Formerly HOTEL DIOT ET DE LA BOULE D'OR).

Magnificent Situation. **30, RUE DUMAS.** Comfortable Bedrooms and Sitting Rooms for Families and Tourists. Salons. Baths. Special Omnibus to the Station. English spoken.   **J. CHANIER, Proprietor.**

LIMOGES.
GRAND HOTEL DE LA PAIX.

FIRST-CLASS HOUSE. Specially recommended to Families and Tourists. Omnibus to Station. English spoken.

J. MOT, Proprietor.

LOCH LOMOND.
TARBET HOTEL

IS the most commodious on the Lake. Parties Boarded on Moderate Terms.

A. H. MACPHERSON, Proprietor.

LISBON.
BRAGANZA HOTEL.

THIS First-Class well-known Family Hotel, lately renovated by the Royal House of Braganza, and fitted up by the new Proprietor, VICTOR C. SASSETTI, highly recommendable for its large, airy, and Comfortable Apartments, commanding the most extensive and picturesque views of the River Tagus, as well as of Lisbon. Superior Cuisine, and carefully-selected Wines.

LLANGOLLEN.
ROYAL HOTEL.

THE above First-class Hotel is now under the Proprietorship of JAMES S. SHAW (several years with Mr. MEHL, at Queen's Hotel, Manchester, and at County Hotel, Carlisle) and is now second to none in North Wales for its comfort, catering, and lovely situation. **HOTEL OMNIBUS MEETS ALL TRAINS.**

LOCARNO.
TERMINUS of the GOTHARD RAILWAY on LAGO MAGGIORE.

BEST STOPPING PLACE on the ITALIAN LAKES.
4 hrs. from Milan. 7 hrs. from Genoa. 6 hrs. from Lucerne.

THE GRAND HOTEL

OPEN the whole year. Most luxurious and comfortable home for all the seasons in Italy or Switzerland. Patronized by the Royal Families of Europe. Unrivalled situation in the mildest and most constant climate of Europe; without snow, wind or fog, but with plenty of sunshine. **Entirely adapted for winter residence.** Open fire places, calorifères and majolica stoves. Beautiful walks and mountain excursions. English Church, Doctor, Society. Lift. Private Steamer and Carriages for visitors. Exquisite Cuisine. Moderate charges.

Messrs. BALLI, Proprietors.

LONDON.
FOREIGN BOOKS AT FOREIGN PRICES.

TRAVELLERS may save **expense** and **trouble** by purchasing Foreign Books in England at **the same Prices** at which they are published in Germany or France.

WILLIAMS & NORGATE

have published the following CATALOGUES of their Stock:—

1. **CLASSICAL CATALOGUE.**
2. **THEOLOGICAL CATALOGUE**
3. **FRENCH CATALOGUE.**
4. **GERMAN CATALOGUE.**
5. **EUROPEAN LINGUISTIC CATALOGUE.**
6. **ORIENTAL CATALOGUE.**
7. **ITALIAN CATALOGUE.**
8. **SPANISH CATALOGUE.**
9. **ART-CATALOGUE.** Art, Architecture, Painting, Illustrated Books.
10. **NATURAL HISTORY CATALOGUE.** Zoology, Botany, Geology, Chemistry, Mathematics, &c.
11. **NATURAL SCIENCE CATALOGUE.** Mathematics, Astronomy, Physics, Chemistry, Technology.
12. **MEDICAL CATALOGUE.** Medicine, Surgery, and the Dependent Sciences.
13. **SCHOOL CATALOGUE.** Elementary Books, Maps, &c.
14. **FOREIGN BOOK CIRCULARS.** New Books, and New Purchases.
15. **SCIENTIFIC-BOOK CIRCULARS.** New Books and Recent Purchases.

ANY CATALOGUE SENT POST-FREE FOR ONE STAMP.

WILLIAMS & NORGATE, Importers of Foreign Books.
14, HENRIETTA STREET, COVENT GARDEN, LONDON, and
20, SOUTH FREDERICK STREET, EDINBURGH.

LONDON.
THE CHEQUE BANK, Ltd.,
ESTABLISHED 1873.

4, **Waterloo Place, Pall Mall, London.** *City Office:* 3, **George Yard, Lombard St., London.** *United States Agency for sale of Cheques:* 2, **Wall St., New York.**

CIRCULAR NOTES FOR FOREIGN TRAVEL.

Cheque Bank Cheques are largely used in place of Circular Notes by Travellers on the Continent, the Colonies, the United States, and all over the World.

The Cheque Bank has correspondents in all parts of the World, by whom the Cheques are cashed at the current rate of exchange without deduction.

More convenient than Circular Notes.   *No evidence of identity required.*

Cheque Bank Cheques are well known to Hotel Keepers and generally accepted by them as cash.

Cheque Bank Cheques will also be found very convenient for Foreign and Inland Postal Remittances.

Fry's PURE CONCENTRATED Cocoa

Lancet.—"Pure, and very soluble."
Medical Times.—"**Eminently suitable for Invalids.**"
SIR C. A. CAMERON, President Royal College of Surgeons, Ireland.—"**I have never tasted Cocoa that I like so well.**"

Half a tea-spoonful is sufficient to make a cup of most delicious Cocoa.

Be careful to ask for "FRY'S PURE CONCENTRATED COCOA."

43 Prize Medals awarded to
J. S. FRY & SONS, Bristol, London & Sydney.

DINNEFORD'S MAGNESIA.

A Pure Solution.
For Acidity of the Stomach.
For Heartburn and Headache.
For Gout and Indigestion.
Safest Aperient for Delicate Constitutions, Ladies, Children, and Infants.

DINNEFORD & CO., 180, New Bond Street, London.
Sold by Chemists throughout the World.

LUCERNE.
GRAND HOTEL NATIONAL.
PFYFFER, SEGESSER & Co., Proprietors.

OPEN ALL THE YEAR.

THIS large and splendid HOTEL is one of the most comfortable in Europe. Situated in front of the Lake, with the finest Views. Every attention paid to Tourists.

A LIFT FOR THE USE OF VISITORS.

LUCERNE.
HOTEL D'ANGLETERRE.

First-Class Hotel, Splendid View on the Lake and Mountains.

Proprietor, **F. T. STEFFEN.**

LUCERNE.
SCHWEIZERHOF AND LUZERNERHOF.

First-Class Hotels.
IN THE BEST SITUATION on the LAKE and PROMENADE.

600 BEDS.

LIFT AND ELECTRIC LIGHT IN BOTH HOTELS.
ARRANGEMENT *EN PENSION* WITH PROTRACTED STAY (EXCLUSIVE OF JULY AND AUGUST).
SCHWEIZERHOF OPEN ALL THE YEAR.
WITH GOOD WARMING SYSTEM.
Proprietors, HAUSER BROTHERS.

LUCHON, BAGNÈRES DE, PYRÉNÉES.
GRAND HOTEL RICHELIEU.
(*Hotel de S. M. le roi de Hollande.*)
200 Rooms, 10 Salons. Splendid view.
Villa Gracieuse, to Let. Omnibus at all Trains. **LOUIS ESTRADE, Proprietor.**

LUCERNE.	LUXEMBOURG.
HOTEL DU RIGI.	**GRAND HOTEL BRASSEUR.**
Comfortable, pleasant situation.	FIRST-CLASS HOTEL. Highly recommended for its comfort and good situation. English spoken. Omnibus at all Trains.
Open from 15th APRIL, to 6th OCTOBER.	BRASSEUR, Proprietor.

LUGANO.
MONTE S. SALVATORE RAILWAY COMPANY.

(15 *Minutes from the Town.*)

WIRE-ROPE-RAILWAY worked by Electricity.
(SYSTEM ABT.)

"ONLY A HALF HOUR'S JOURNEY."

Excellent Restaurant on the Kulm.

Situated 2,925 feet above the sea.

MAGNIFICENT VIEW.

LYNTON, NORTH DEVON.
ROYAL CASTLE FAMILY HOTEL.

Patronised by the English and Continental Royal Families.

FIRST-CLASS HOTEL, especially favourite and attractive. Table d'hôte. Reading and Drawing Rooms. New Smoking and Billiard Pavilions, all Facing the Sea. Magnificent Views, and Ornamental Grounds of Twelve Acres. Private Hotel and Boarding House attached.

THOS. BAKER, Proprietor.

LYONS.
HOTEL UNIVERS,
FACING PERRACHE STATION.

THE MOST COMFORTABLE.

First Class.   Full South.

MRS. DUFOUR IS ENGLISH.

LYONS.
GRAND HOTEL DE LYON.
PLACE DE LA BOURSE.
FIRST-CLASS HOTEL.
Moderate Charges.

MACON.
GRAND HOTEL DE L'EUROPE.
Five minutes' from the Station.

F IRST-CLASS, and well situated, with view of Mont Blanc. Recommended to Families. Interpreters. Carriages. Omnibus.
Mme. Vve. BATAILLARD, Proprietress.
Macon, the most favoured Station for hours of arrival and departure, is the most central stopping-place from Paris for Switzerland, Italy, the Mediterranean, and terminus for direct trains for Tours and Bordeaux.

MALAGA.
ROYAL VICTORIA HOTEL
(ANCIEN HOTEL DE LONDRES),
ALAMEDA 14
First-Class Establishment. Splendid View, Full South. Charges Moderate. Interpreters.

MALMÖ (SWEDEN).
HOTEL HORN.

F IRST-CLASS HOTEL, completely renewed, in the centre of the town, commanding a fine view, opposite the Railway and Post Office. Comfortably furnished. Good cooking. Restaurant and Café. Cold and warm Baths. Private Dinners. Moderate charges.
I. F. H. HORN, Proprietor.

MALMÖ (SWEDEN).
HOTEL KRAMER.

F IRST-CLASS HOTEL, the Largest and most Comfortable in the Town, new and richly fitted up, 100 rooms. Situate on the great square, in the vicinity of the Railway Stations and Steamboat Landings. One of the most commodious, and respecting charges, one of the cheapest hotels in Scandinavia. Rooms from 1 krona, upwards. Baths and carriage in the hotel. Meals à la carte, at all hours. Prompt and polite attendance. Dinner kept ready for passengers.

MARIENBAD.
HOTEL KLINGER.

F IRST and Largest Hotel, with private houses, HALBMAYR'S HOUSE, MAXHOF No. 100, and the recently opened HOTEL KLINGER, late Stadt Dresden, "connected with the Old House," most beautiful situation of the Spa, situate at the corner of the Promenade on the Kreuzbrunnen and the Park, commanding a charming view. Newly and elegantly furnished. 350 Rooms and Saloons. Reading, Conversation, and Smoking Rooms. Lift. Table d'hôte and à la carte. Meals sent out into private houses.
Carriages at the Hotel. Omnibus at the Station.
In answer to several inquiries, the Proprietor begs to intimate that he does not keep Tonters, and therefore begs to warn Travellers against any false statements respecting his Hotel being full, etc.
J. A. HALBMAYR, Proprietor.

MARIENBAD.
HOTEL WEIMAR.

F IRST-CLASS HOUSE, patronised by English. Elevated position, near the Springs and Bath Establishments. Single Rooms and Family Apartments, furnished with every modern comfort and luxury. Carriages for Excursions. Omnibus at all Trains.
HAMMERSCHMID, Proprietor.

MAYENCE.
HOTEL DE HOLLANDE.

WELL-KNOWN FIRST-CLASS HOTEL. Thorough Comfort, excellent Cooking, Choice Wines, at Moderate Charges. Since the removal of the railway, the Finest and Best Situated Hotel in the Town, affording an open view of the river. Favourite and quiet stopping place for excursions into the neighbourhood Special arrangements for Winter abode. Opposite the landing place of the steamers. Omnibus meets all trains. Proprietor: RUDOLPH SEIDEL, *for years Manager of this Hotel.*

MAYENCE.
RHINE HOTEL.

FIRST-CLASS Hotel. Finest Position and Splendid View of the Rhine. Especially recommended to English and American Travellers. Rooms, including Light and Attendance, from 2 francs 50 centimes. Omnibus at Station.

W. SCHIMMEL.

MENTONE. (1st CLASS HOTEL).
HOTEL DE BELLE VUE.

THIS well-known ESTABLISHMENT is beautifully situated in the best quarter of the Town, with a vast Garden, and affords every English comfort.
Lawn Tennis Court. Ascenseur. Lift.

G. ISNARD, Proprietor.

MILAN.
HOTEL DE ROME.

ADMIRABLY situated, full South, on the Corso, a few steps from the Duomo, Scala, and Galleries. This Hotel, comfortably furnished and fitted up with the greatest care, is warmly recommended to English travellers for its comfort and moderate charges.
Branch House—PIAZZA FONTANA, 8 and 10.

BORELLA BROTHERS, Proprietors.

MOSCOW.
HOTEL SLAWIANSKY BAZAR.
THE LARGEST FIRST-CLASS HOTEL THE TOWN.
NEAR THE KREMLIN.

SPLENDID RESTAURANT, READING AND BATH ROOMS.

Telephone, Post and Telegraph Offices in the house.

MUNICH.
WIMMER & CO.,
GALLERY OF FINE ARTS,
3, BRIENNER STREET,

Invite the Nobility and Gentry to visit their GALLERY OF FINE ARTS, containing an Extensive Collection of

MODERN PAINTINGS
by the best Munich Artists.

Correspondents in England, Messrs. J. & R. McCRACKEN, 38, Queen Street, Cannon Street, E.C., London. Correspondents in the United States, Messrs. BALDWIN BROS. & Co., 53, Broadway, New York.

NEUHAUSEN-SCHAFFHAUSEN, Falls of the Rhine.
HOTEL SCHWEIZERHOF.
F. WEGENSTEIN, Proprietor.

FIRST-CLASS HOTEL, replete with every comfort, in the best position opposite the Falls of the Rhine, and Five minutes' walk from Neuhausen Station.

NO GRATUITIES to the SERVANTS. 200 ROOMS.

Splendid View of the Rhinefalls, the Castle of Laufen, and the Swiss Alpine Chain.

FINE PARK AND GARDEN.

RAILWAY TICKETS ISSUED AT THE HOTEL.

Special arrangements for a stay of some time.

The English Church Service is at the Schweizerhof.

Omnibuses at Neuhausen and Schaffhausen.

By means of Electricity and Bengal Lights, and *directed from the Schweizerhof,*

THE FALLS OF THE RHINE ARE ILLUMINATED
Every Night during the Summer Season.

MUNICH.
SEDELMAIER & SCHULTZ,
OPTICIANS,
17, THEATINER STRASSE,
Near the THEATINER CHURCH.

Largest selection of Optical goods in Munich. Specialities: Opera glasses, double Field glasses, Perspectives, Compasses, Altimetres, Pedometres, patent Eye glasses—the best existing. All Tourist's Instruments.
Prices exceedingly reduced.

NANTES.
HOTEL DE FRANCE.
PLACE GRASLIN.   VERY FINE.
FIRST-CLASS Hotel. Entirely renovated. Large and Small Apartments for Families. Sitting Rooms. Bedrooms from 2 fr. Table d'hôte. Restaurant. Omnibus and Carriages. *English spoken.*   DOUET, Proprietor.

NUREMBERG.
HOTEL GOLDEN EAGLE.
FIRST-CLASS HOTEL, well situated, opposite the Kriegerdenkmal, newly re-built, contains 110 elegantly furnished Rooms and Saloons, and is much frequented by English and American families. Arrangements made with Families and Single persons. Baths in the house. Carriages. Omnibus to and from the Station.
L. SCHLENK, Proprietor.

OSTEND.
HOTEL DE LA PLAGE.
FIRST-CLASS HOTEL FACING THE BATHING PLACE.
Open from the 1st June to 15th October. Highly recommended.
J. and O. THOMA, Proprietors.

PALERMO.
HOTEL DE FRANCE.
FREQUENTED by English and American families; has many sunny rooms; in the healthiest position in Palermo, facing the beautiful Garden Garibaldi, Piazza Marina, near the Botanical Garden and Villa Giulia. First-rate Cuisine.
English and American Newspapers. MODERATE CHARGES.
P. WEINEN.

PAU.
HOTEL DE FRANCE.
THIS FIRST-CLASS HOTEL, situated on the Place Royale, commands the most splendid view of the whole chain of the Pyrénées, and is adjoining to the English Club.
GARDÈRES FRÈRES, Proprietors.

OSTEND.
MERTIAN'S
FIRST-CLASS
FAMILY HOTEL AND PENSION.
Close to the Sea and Kursaal. Telephone.

PISA.
ROYAL VICTORIA HOTEL.
Clean.   Great Attention.
RECOMMENDED.

ORAN.
HOTEL CONTINENTAL.
F. GARCIN, *Proprietor.*

PLACE D'ARMES BOULEVARD SÉGUIN and
PROMENADE DE L'ETANG.

WINTER QUARTERS. Exceptional situation, with fine view of the Sea and Environs; 120 rooms and Salons. Table d'hôte. Restaurant à la Carte. Moderate Prices. Private Rooms. Reading Room. Baths and Hydropathy. Omnibus to all the Trains and on the arrival of the Boats.

PAU.
GRAND HÔTEL BEAU SÉJOUR.

FIRST-CLASS. Recommended for its Comfort. Incomparable position for beauty of the Panorama. Apartments for Families, with view embracing the Pyrénées. Excellent Cooking and irreproachable attendance. **BOURDETTE**, *Proprietor.*
— The Drainage perfected under the most modern system.

PISA.
GRAND HOTEL.
Moderate Charges.
W. GARBRECHT.
SPEAKS GOOD ENGLISH.

PLYMOUTH.
Only Hotel with Sea View.
GRAND HOTEL.
(ON THE HOE.)
Facing Sound, Breakwater, &c. Mail Steamers anchor in sight. Public Rooms, and Sitting Rooms, with Balconies. JAMES BOHN, *Proprietor.*

POITIERS.
GRAND HOTEL DE FRANCE.—First-Class and recommended to Families and Tourists for its comfort and good management. The most central of the Town, near the Hotel de Ville, Prefecture, Telegraph, Post Office, Museum, Historical Monuments, and Promenades. Speciality of Fowls and truffled Pâtés of all sorts. Carriages for Drives. Railway Omnibus calls at Hotel.
ROBLIN-BOUCHARDEAU, Proprietor.

RAGATZ.
BATH AND CURATIVE ESTABLISHMENT OF RAGATZ-PFÆFERS, SWITZERLAND.
(Warm Thermal Springs of 28—30° R., same as Wildbad and Gastein.)
GRAND HOTEL QUELLENHOF
GRAND HOTEL HOF RAGATZ
Beautiful position. Large fine Parks. Walks of any altitude. Healthy Climate. Bath Installations of highest perfection connected with both hotels by covered ways. Station for Travellers going to and coming from Upper and Lower Engadine. Comfortable Carriages to all places, same Tarif as in Coire. Pension and Tourist-Prices very reasonable.

RENNES.
GRAND HOTEL.
JULLIEN, Proprietor. GRIVOIS, Successor.
FIRST-CLASS, well recommended. English Spoken, and English Newspapers. Omnibus at the Station.

RHEIMS.
HOTEL DU LION D'OR.
THE most aristocratic of the town, and the only one actually in front of the Cathedral. Housemaids for Ladies. Very nice Garden.
English spoken.

RIGI.
HOTEL AND PENSION RIGI-SCHEIDEGG.
TERMINUS Station of the Rigi Kaltbad-Scheidegg Railway. Excellently suited for Tourists and Pensioners. Pension by a stay of not less than four days, 7 francs to 12 francs, Room included. Liberal treatment. View on the Alps as beautiful as at Rigi Kulm. English Service. Lawn Tennis Grounds.
Dr. R. STIERLIN-HAUSER.

CAIRO (Egypt).

HOTEL DU NIL.

H. FRIEDMANN.

CAIRO, EGYPT.
HOTEL CONTINENTAL.

THIS-First Class Hotel, newly built and handsomely furnished, is situated in the finest and healthiest part of the Ismaillieh quarter, close to the English and Catholic churches. Perfect English sanitary arrangements. Large Verandah, Drawing and Ladies' Saloons, Reading, Smoking and Billiard Rooms. Terms moderate. Best cooking in Cairo.

GEORGE NUNGOVICH, Proprietor.

CANNES.

HOTEL BEAU SITE
AND
HOTEL DE L'ESTÉREL.

BOTH situated at the West End of Cannes, in the midst of a most splendid Garden, and adjoining Lord Brougham's property; the healthiest part of the Town.

300 Rooms and Private Sitting Rooms.

Enlarged Drawing Room, separate Reading Room, Smoking and Billiard Room, with Thurston's Tables.

BATH ROOM.   LIFT WITH SAFETY APPARATUS.

THREE LAWN TENNIS COURTS,
CONSIDERED THE FINEST AND LARGEST IN CANNES.

GEORGES GOUGOLTZ, Proprietor.

CASINO DE CHERBOURG.
HOTEL DES BAINS DE MER.

ONLY ESTABLISHMENT on the Sea Shore. Hot and Hydropathic Baths, with Sea Water.

Open 1st June till 1st October.

Director, Ls. MERTZ.

ROME.
HOTEL ROYAL MAZZERI
Via Venti Settembre.

THIS New Hotel, opened in 1888, is situated full South, on the Highest and Healthiest part of Rome, near the English Embassy and the Royal Palace. A short distance only from the Railway Station.

ST. PETERSBURG.
HOTEL DE FRANCE.
Kept by E. RENAULT.

BEST situation in the Town, Great Morskaïa, right opposite the Winter Palace, Hermitage, Foreign Office and Newski Prospekt. Oldest Hotel. Tramways in all directions. Fashionably frequented, especially by English and Americans. Elegant Reading Room, with French, English, American, German, and Swedish Papers. Greatly to be recommended for its cleanliness, comfort, and superior *cuisine*. Dinners 1 r. 50 k. and 3 r. The charge for Apartments is from 1 to 20 roubles. All languages spoken. Warm and Cold Baths. Post and Telephone on the Premises. The English Guide, Charles A. Kuntze, highly commended.

☞ The Hotel is recommended in *Murray's Handbook of Russia*.

The HOTEL BELLE VUE, opposite to HOTEL DE FRANCE, belongs to the same Proprietor.

ST. PETERSBURG.
FIRST-CLASS RESTAURANT.
A. CONTANT.

MOIKA 58.

Renowned for its Wines and Cookery.

SPLENDID GARDEN.

An Orchestra performs during Meals.

ST. GERVAIS-LES-BAINS, VILLAGE
(Hte. SAVOIE.)
HOTEL DU MONT BLANC.
(2,450 feet above Sea level.)

Bracing air, best situated Hotel in place, near Post and Telegraph. Lovely views, excursions, glaciers, &c. English spoken.

A. CHAMBEL, Proprietor.

SALISBURY.
THE WHITE HART HOTEL,
Nearly opposite the Cathedral. The LARGEST and PRINCIPAL HOTEL in the CITY.

THIS old established First-Class Hotel contains every accommodation for Families and Tourists. A Ladies' Coffee Room. Billiard and Smoking Rooms and spacious Coffee Rooms for Gentlemen. Table d'Hôte daily, during the season, from 6.30 to 8.30 p.m., at separate tables. Carriages and Horses on Hire for Stonehenge and other places of interest. Excellent Stabling, Loose Boxes, &c. Tariff on application to H. T. BOWES, Manager, *Posting-Master to Her Majesty*.

SALZBURG.
HOTEL DE L'EUROPE.

OPPOSITE the Station. First-Class Hotel, surrounded by a large Park, and offering the best view on the Mountains. PENSION: until the 15th of July and after the 15th of September, from 4 florins upwards; from the 15th of July until the 15th of September, from 5.50 florins upwards. Lawn Tennis Grounds.

ELECTRIC LIGHT.   *HYDRAULIC LIFT.*

Moderate Charges.

G. JUNG, Proprietor.

SAUMUR.
HOTEL BUDAN.
The only one on the banks of the Loire.
SPLENDID VIEW.

SENS (Yonne).
GRAND HOTEL DE PARIS.
FIRST-CLASS. Situated near the Cathedral and Promenades. Specially recommended to Families. English spoken. Omnibus to Station.

LEMOINE-AUDY, Proprietor.

SENDIG SCHANDAU,
SAXON SWITZERLAND.
Pension from 6 marks, everything included.

HOTELS AND PENSIONS HIGHLY RECOMMENDED

SPA.
Grand Hotel Britannique.
F. LEYH, Proprietor.
PATRONISED BY THE ROYAL FAMILY OF BELGIUM,
And maintains a high reputation among the Aristocracy of Europe.
SITUATED IN THE HEALTHIEST PART OF THE TOWN.
LARGE GARDEN AND SWIMMING BATHS.
Adjoining the Boulevard des Anglais and the English Church.

ENGLISH SPOKEN.

OMNIBUS AT EACH ARRIVAL.

SPA.
GRAND HOTEL DE L'EUROPE.
First-class House, close to the Mineral Springs, Casino, and Anglican Church.
FAMILY HOTEL. HIGHLY RECOMMENDED.
HENRARD-RICHARD, Proprietor.

SPEZIA (RIVIERA DI LEVANTE).
GRAND HOTEL et HOTEL ROYAL CROIX de MALTE.
FIRST-CLASS, full south, overlooking the Bay, view of the Carrara Mountains. Favourite winter resort. Lovely excursions to Portovenere (Byron's Grotto). S. Terenzo (Shelley's House). La Foce (Cornice Road).
COATES & Co., Proprietors.

STRASBOURG.
HOTEL D'ANGLETERRE.
BEST-SITUATED NEWLY REBUILT FIRST-CLASS HOTEL. Near the Station and Cathedral. Close to the Post and Telegraph Offices. Baths. Moderate Charges. Rooms from 2 marks, light and attendance included. Omnibus at the Station.
CH. MATHIS, Proprietor.

STRASBURG.
HOTEL NATIONAL.
THE only one opposite the Railway Station. New FIRST-CLASS HOTEL, combined with every Comfort. Large and Small Apartments for Families and Single Gentlemen. Baths and Lift system improved. Best Cuisine. Moderate Charges. **L. OSTERMANN, Proprietor.**
Formerly Manager of the Hotel "Ville de Paris."

STOCKHOLM, SWEDEN.

GRAND HOTEL.

THIS Handsome Building is situated in the finest part of the City, between Charles the XIIth's Square and the National Museum, on one of the Principal Quays, just at the confluence of the Lake Mälar and the Baltic.

The Royal Palace, one of the stateliest in Europe, faces the Hotel on the opposite side of the Harbour. The Royal Opera and the Principal Theatres are in close proximity.

The balconies and roof of the Hotel command the most extensive Views of the City.

The House is replete with every modern improvement and convenience, and no expense has been spared to render it one of the first and most comfortable Hotels on the Continent.

The Building contains Four Hundred Sleeping Apartments, besides Dining Rooms, Sitting Rooms, Coffee and Reading Rooms, a Billiard Room, a Telegraph and Post Office, Baths, Retiring Rooms, a Laundry, and other accommodations. The several flats can be reached by Steam Lifts.

All European Languages spoken. Guides and Conveyances supplied to all places of interest in the City and Neighbourhood. *Terms* will be found to compare favourably with those of other first-class Hotels.

The Hotel Rydberg.
GUSTAF ADOLF'S TORG.

THIS Old-established House has long been favourably known to Travellers. It contains One Hundred and Fifty Sleeping Apartments.

The Proprietor of these Two First-Class Hotels is in a position to offer every advantage to strangers visiting the Swedish Capital.

R. CADIER,
Proprietor of the Grand Hotel and the Hotel Rydberg.

STOCKHOLM.
HOTEL CONTINENTAL.

THIS comfortable Hotel is situated opposite the Central Railway Station and in the Centre of the City, with 100 Elegant Apartments. Good Dining Room and Coffee Room. English Newspapers, English Attendance. Moderate Charges. Baths Hot and Cold.
C. BAYOUD, *Proprietor.*

STUTTGART.
HOTEL MARQUARDT

IS situated in the finest part of the Town, in the beautiful Place Royal, adjoining the Railway Station, near the Post Office, the Theatre, the Royal Gardens, opposite the Palace, and facing the Königsbau. This Hotel will be found most comfortable in every respect; the Apartments are elegantly furnished, and suitable for Families or Single Gentlemen. Table d'Hôte at 1 and 5 o'clock. French and English Newspapers.
GME. MARQUARDT, Proprietor.

SWEDEN.
Imperial Quarto, half bound, Morocco, £5 5s.
THE CHURCHES OF GOTTLAND,
BY
MAJOR ALFRED HEALES, F.S.A., F.R.S.L., Hon. A.R.I.B.A.

Dedicated by Special Permission to His Majesty the King of Sweden and Norway.
Illustrated by Twenty-seven Copyright Photographs.
Issue strictly limited to 50 Copies.

London: ROWORTH & CO., Limited, Newton Street, High Holborn, W.C.

THUN (Switzerland).
HOTEL THUNERHOF.

A FIRST-CLASS HOUSE, one of the largest and most comfortable in Switzerland. The only one with a Lift in the place, and especially adapted for a long sejour. The Terrace of the Hotel, which has no rival in Switzerland, is worth a visit. There is also an English Library.

Pension, during the whole Season, by staying Five Days, from 8 francs, everything included.

CH. STAEHLE,
Also Proprietor of the Hotel du Paradis at Cannes.

TOULOUSE.
GRAND HOTEL DU MIDI.

Patronized by the Duke of Norfolk and Duc d'Aumale.
BEAUTIFULLY SITUATED ON THE PLACE DU CAPITOLE.
FIRST-CLASS ESTABLISHMENT,
Offering the same comforts as the largest Hotels in France. *Frequented by the highest Class of English and American Travellers.* English spoken. Restaurant and Table d'Hôte. Rich Reading Room and Conversation Salon. "The Times" Newspaper.

EUG. FOURQUIER, *Proprietor.*

TOURS.

GRAND HOTEL DE L'UNIVERS.

ON THE BOULEVARD, NEAR THE STATION.

European Reputation.

Highly recommended in all the French and Foreign Guide Books.

EUGENE GUILLAUME, Proprietor.

TOURS.

HOTEL DE BORDEAUX.

Proprietor, CLOVIS DELIGNOU.

Patronized by His Royal Highness the Prince of Wales, and the European Courts.

IN FRONT OF THE STATION AND UPON THE BOULEVARD.

Splendid Apartments.

TARRAGONA.
HOTEL DE PARIS.
FIRST-CLASS: frequented by English and American Tourists. Excellent accommodation and every convenience. Italian proprietors.
PRIMATESTA FRATELLI.

TURIN.
Murray's Handbook for North Italy, the Italian Lakes, &c., &c.
Maps and Plans. Post 8vo., 10s.

John Murray, Albemarle Street.

VENICE.
HOTEL D'ITALIE
AND BAUER.

FIRST-CLASS HOTEL, near St. Mark's Square, on the Grand Canal, facing the Church of St. Maria della Salute. Patronised by English and Americans.

FIRST-RATE ATTENDANCE.

Celebrated for its **Grand Restaurant** *&* **Vienna Beer**

JULES GRÜNWALD, Proprietor.

VENICE.
HOTEL D'EUROPE.
FIRST-CLASS HOTEL.
SITUATED IN THE BEST POSITION ON THE GRAND CANAL.

Has just been repaired and greatly improved. New large Dining Room on the Ground Floor overlooking the Grand Canal.
SMOKING AND READING ROOMS. BATHS.
Patronised by the most distinguished Families.
HYDRAULIC LIFT.
MARSEILLE BROTHERS, Proprietors.

VERONA.
GRAND HOTEL DE LONDRES
and HOTEL ROYAL DES DEUX TOURS.

THE ONLY FIRST-CLASS HOTEL IN VERONA, In the centre of the Town. Great comfort and moderate charges. English Church Service in the Hotel. All Languages spoken. Omnibus at the Stations. Highly recommended.

A. CERESA, Proprietor.   G. CAVESTRI, Manager.

VICHY.

GRAND HOTEL DES AMBASSADEURS, Situated in the Park.—
This magnificent Hotel is now the first in the town. It is managed in the same style as the largest and best hotels on the Continent. By its exceptional situation, the house presents three fronts, from which the most beautiful views are to be had; and from its balconies is heard twice a day the excellent Band of the Casino. The management of its large and small apartments is very comfortable. Every room has a Dressing Room. Special wire going from all apartments to the private servants' rooms. Beautiful Reading, Drawing, and Smoking Rooms. Billiard Tables. English spoken. Omnibus of the Hotel at all Trains. The Hotel is open from the 15th of April. Post and Telegraph Offices adjoining the Hotel.

ROUBEAU, Proprietor.

VICHY.
GRAND HOTEL DU PARC,
and GRAND HOTEL.
THE LARGEST AND MOST COMFORTABLE IN VICHY.
A FIRST-CLASS HOTEL, situated in the Park, facing the Baths, Springs, and Casino.

PRIVATE PAVILION FOR FAMILIES.

GERMOT, Proprietor.

VIENNA.
HOTEL ARCHDUKE CHARLES,
KÄRNTHNERSTRASSE (the favourite Street).

ONE OF THE MOST RENOWNED FIRST-CLASS HOTELS, with good Restaurant. English cooking in the House. Bath Rooms. Reading Rooms, etc.

Pension.   Prices Moderate.

B. SMITH, Proprietor.

VIENNA.

J. & L. LOBMEYR,
Glass Manufacturers,

Appointed Purveyors to the Imperial Court of Austria,

No. 11, KÄRNTHNERSTRASSE.

The most extensive Establishment for BOHEMIAN CRYSTAL, FANCY GLASS, and Chandeliers.

Every variety of Glass for Household use, Ornament, and in Art Workmanship. Specialities in Engraved Glass and Looking-Glasses. Chandeliers, Candelabras, in Crystal and Bronze.

LARGE SHOW-ROOMS UPSTAIRS.

The prices are fixed, and are very moderate.—English is spoken.

Their Correspondents in England, Messrs. J. & R. M'CRACKEN, No. 38, Queen Street, Cannon Street, E.C., London, will transmit all orders with the greatest care and attention.

VIENNA.
HOTEL CONTINENTAL, PRATERSTRASSE.
300 ROOMS.

FIRST-CLASS. Good Food; Garden; Restaurant; Situated on the Danube. Visited by the Ministers and Members of Parliament. A nice Front Room from 1¼ gulden. CH. SCHMITT, Manager, formerly at the Clarence Hotel, Manchester.

VIENNA.
HOTEL SACHER.
Opposite the Imperial and Royal Opera House.

MOST elegant and frequented quarter of the Capital. Arrangements made for Pension. Baths on all floors. Hydraulic Lift. First Restaurant in Austro-Hungary. English Cooking.

VIENNA.
Murray's Handbook for Southern Germany, Austria-Hungary, &c.

New Edition. In two parts. Post 8vo., 12s.

JOHN MURRAY, Albemarle Street.

WIESBADEN.
HOTEL BELLE VUE.

THIS FIRST-CLASS FAMILY HOTEL is situated in the finest part of Wiesbaden, and patronized by Their Royal Highnesses the Prince and Princess of Wales, and by Royal Families of several Courts. Has just been Repaired and greatly Improved. New elegant Dining Room. New Smoking and Reading Rooms, with a beautiful Garden.

Pension. Bath. Prices Moderate.
VICTOR KLEEBLATT, *Proprietor.*

WIESBADEN.
HOTEL AND BADHAUS VICTORIA.
NEW MANAGEMENT.

FIRST-CLASS HOTEL, beautifully situated opposite the Stations. Entirely renovated. Private Mineral Spring. Pension all the year round. Hydraulic Lift.   SCHWEISGUTH BROS., Proprietors.

WIESBADEN.
HOTEL ET BAINS DE NASSAU.
(NASSAUER HOF.)

Messrs. GOETZ BROTHERS, Proprietors.

FIRST-CLASS HOTEL of old and good reputation, opposite the Curhaus, Colonnades, Parks, and next the Theatre. Splendid Dining and Reading Rooms. Table d'Hôte at One and Five o'clock. Mineral Baths of Own Hot Spring.

HOTEL VILLA NASSAU.
Annexe of the HOTEL DE NASSAU.   Proprietors also Messrs. GOETZ BROTHERS.

FINEST FAMILY HOTEL in Town, with all Modern Comfort, in beautiful situation next the Hot Springs, Theatre, Curhaus, Colonnades, etc.

WIESBADEN.
ROSE HOTEL AND BATH HOUSE.

SPLENDID First-Class Establishment, surrounded by its own large Gardens, best situation, opposite the Promenades and the Park. An elegant Bath-House attached, supplied with Mineral Water direct from the principal hot spring (the Kochbrunnen). Drawing, Reading, Smoking and Billiard Rooms. Table d'Hôte at One and Six o'clock. Hydraulic Lift.

                                                   H. HAEFFNER.

WILDBAD.

HOTEL KLUMPP,
Formerly HOTEL DE L'OURS.

MR. W. KLUMPP, PROPRIETOR.

THIS First-Class Hotel, containing 45 Saloons and 235 Bed Rooms, with a separate Breakfast and new Reading and Conversation Rooms, as well as a Smoking Saloon, and a very extensive and elegant Dining Room; an artificial Garden over the river; is beautifully situated in connection with the old and new Bath Buildings and Conversation House, and in the immediate vicinity of the Promenade and the New Colonnade. It is celebrated for its elegant and comfortable apartments, good *Cuisine* and Cellar, and deserves its wide-spread reputation as an excellent Hotel. Table d'Hôte at One and Five o'clock. Breakfasts and Suppers *à la carte*. Exchange Office. Correspondent of the principal Banking-houses of London for the payment of Circular Notes and Letters of Credit. Omnibuses of the Hotel to and from each Train. Elevators to every floor. Fine Private Carriages when requested. Warm and Cold Baths in the Hotel. Reduced prices for Rooms in the months of May, September and October.

EXCELLENT ACCOMMODATION.

ZURICH.
HOTEL BAUR AU LAC.
**FIRST-CLASS HOTEL. BEST SITUATION.
BEAUTIFUL GARDEN. HYDRAULIC LIFT.**
ELECTRIC LIGHT IN EVERY ROOM.
PATRONISED BY ENGLISH AND AMERICAN FAMILIES.
Not to be confounded with Hotel Baur (in the Town).
Proprietor, C. KRACHT.

FRENCH, GERMAN, ITALIAN.
DR. WM. SMITH'S MANUALS.
FRENCH COURSE.

French Principia, Part I.
A First French Course, containing Grammar, Delectus, Exercises, with Vocabularies, and materials for French Conversation. (202 pp.) 12mo. 3s. 6d.

Appendix to French Principia, Part I.
Containing Additional Exercises, with Examination Papers. (110 pp.) 12mo. 2s. 6d.

French Principia, Part II.
A Reading Book, containing Fables, Stories, and Anecdotes, Natural History and Scenes from the History of France. With Grammatical Questions, Notes, and Copious Etymological Dictionary. (376 pp.) 12mo. 4s. 6d.

French Principia, Part. III.
Prose Composition. Containing Hints on Translation of English into French, the Principal Rules of the French Syntax compared with the English, and a Systematic Course of Exercises on the Syntax. 12mo. 4s. 6d. (376 pp.)

The Student's French Grammar.
A Practical and Historical Grammar of the French Language. By C. HERON-WALL. With Introduction by M. LITTRÉ. (490 pp.) Post 8vo. 6s.

A Smaller Grammar of the French Language.
For the Middle and Lower Forms. Abridged from the above. (230 pp.) 12mo. 3s. 6d.

GERMAN COURSE.

German Principia, Part I.
A First German Course, containing a Grammar, Delectus, and Exercise Book, with Vocabularies and materials for German Conversation. New and revised Edition. (224 pp.) 12mo. 3s. 6d.

German Principia, Part II.
A Reading Book, containing Fables, Stories, and Anecdotes, Natural History and Scenes from the History of Germany. With Grammatical Questions, Notes, and Dictionary. (272 pp.) 12mo. 3s. 6d.

Practical German Grammar.
With a Sketch of the Historical Development of the Language and its Principal Dialects. (240 pp.) Post 8vo. 3s. 6d.

ITALIAN COURSE.

Italian Principia, Part I.
A First Italian Course, containing a Grammar, Delectus, Exercise Book, with Vocabularies. By Signor Ricci. (218 pp.) 12mo. 3s. 6d.

Italian Principia, Part II.
A First Italian Reading Book, containing Fables, Anecdotes, History, and Passages from the best Italian Authors, with Grammatical Questions, Notes, and a copious Etymological Dictionary. 12mo. 3s. 6d.

JOHN MURRAY, ALBEMARLE STREET.

USEFUL BOOKS FOR TRAVELLERS & STUDENTS.

CHAMBERS'S PRACTICAL AND CONVERSATIONAL POCKET DICTIONARY OF THE ENGLISH, FRENCH AND GERMAN LANGUAGES. 6s.

CROWE AND CAVALCASELLE'S LIVES OF THE EARLY FLEMISH PAINTERS. Woodcuts. 7s. 6d.

——— Life and Times of Titian, with some account of his Family. Illustrations. 2 Vols. 8vo. 21s.

——— Raphael; His Life and Works. 2 Vols. 8vo. 33s.

DENNIS (GEORGE). Cities and Cemeteries of Etruria. 20 Plans and 200 Illustrations. 2 Vols. Medium 8vo. 21s.

DÜRER (ALBERT); his Life and Work. By Dr. THAUSING. Edited by F. A. Eaton, M.A. With Illustrations. 2 Vols. Medium 8vo. 42s.

FORD (RICHARD). Gatherings from Spain. Post 8vo. 3s. 6d.

GEORGE (ERNEST). The Mosel; Twenty Etchings. Imperial 4to. 42s.

——— Loire and South of France; Twenty Etchings. Folio. 42s.

GLEIG (G. R.). Story of the Battle of Waterloo. Post 8vo. 3s. 6d.

GORDON (Sir ALEX.). Sketches of German Life, and Scenes from the War of Liberation. Post 8vo. 3s. 6d.

——— Lady Duff. The French in Algiers. Post 8vo. 2s.

HAYWARD (A.). The Art of Dining, or Gastronomy and Gastronomers. Post 8vo. 2s.

JAMESON (Mrs.). Lives of the Early Italian Painters—and the Progress of Painting in Italy—Cimabue to Bassano. With 50 Portraits. Post 8vo. 12s.

KUGLER'S HANDBOOK OF PAINTING.—The Italian Schools. A new Edition, Revised. By Sir HENRY LAYARD. With 200 Illustrations. 2 Vols. Crown 8vo. 30s.

——— The German, Flemish, and Dutch Schools. Revised. By J. A. CROWE. With 60 Illustrations. 2 Vols. Crown 8vo. 24s.

LANE (E. W.). Account of the Manners and Customs of Modern Egyptians. With Illustrations. 2 Vols. Post 8vo. 12s.

LAYARD (Sir A. H.). Nineveh and its Remains. With Illustrations. Post 8vo. 7s. 6d.

——— Nineveh and Babylon: Discoveries in the Ruins, with Travels in Armenia, Kurdistan, &c. Illustrations. Post 8vo. 7s. 6d.

MICHAEL ANGELO, Sculptor, Painter, and Architect. His Life and Works. By C. HEATH WILSON. Illustrations. 8vo. 15s.

TOCQUEVILLE'S State of Society in France before the Revolution, 1789, and on the Causes which led to that Event. 8vo. 12s.

WILKINSON (Sir J. G.). Popular Account of the Ancient Egyptians. With 500 Woodcuts. 2 Vols. Post 8vo. 12s.

JOHN MURRAY, ALBEMARLE STREET.

Murray's Magazine.
PUBLISHED MONTHLY, 1/-

Contents.
TOPICS OF THE DAY.
SPORT AND TRAVEL.
FICTION.
LITERATURE AND ART.
POPULAR SCIENCE PAPERS.
MISCELLANEOUS.

The Magazine is supplied Monthly, by post, to any part of Great Britain and Ireland, or the Continent of Europe, for 13s. (16fr. 30c.) per annum, prepaid.

MARCIA.
The New Novel for 1890.
By W. E. NORRIS,
Author of "Major and Minor," &c.

CONTENTS FOR JUNE.
MARCIA. Chaps. 21-24. By W. E. Norris, Author of 'Thirlby Hall,' &c.—(*To be continued.*)
COURT FUNCTIONS. By A. Débutante.
SIR CHARLES DILKE ON IMPERIAL DEFENCE. By Admiral Colomb.
EARLY DAYS RECALLED. By Mrs. Ross.—(*To be continued.*)
CAROLINE. By Miss Daintrey.
EARLY SUMMER AT THE CAPE. By the Rev. W. Greswell.
THAT FIDDLER FELLOW. Chaps. 4-6. By Horace Hutchinson.—(*To be continued.*)
NOTES OF THE MONTH, FROM LONDON AND PARIS.
CORRESPONDENCE.
OUR LIBRARY LIST.
SHORT CRITICISMS ON CURRENT BOOKS.
&c. &c. &c.

LONDON: JOHN MURRAY, ALBEMARLE STREET.

By Appointment to H.R.H. the Prince of Wales.

ALLEN'S PORTMANTEAUS

AND STRONG DRESS BASKETS,

37, WEST STRAND, LONDON.

New Illustrated Catalogue of Articles for Home or Continental Travelling, Post Free.

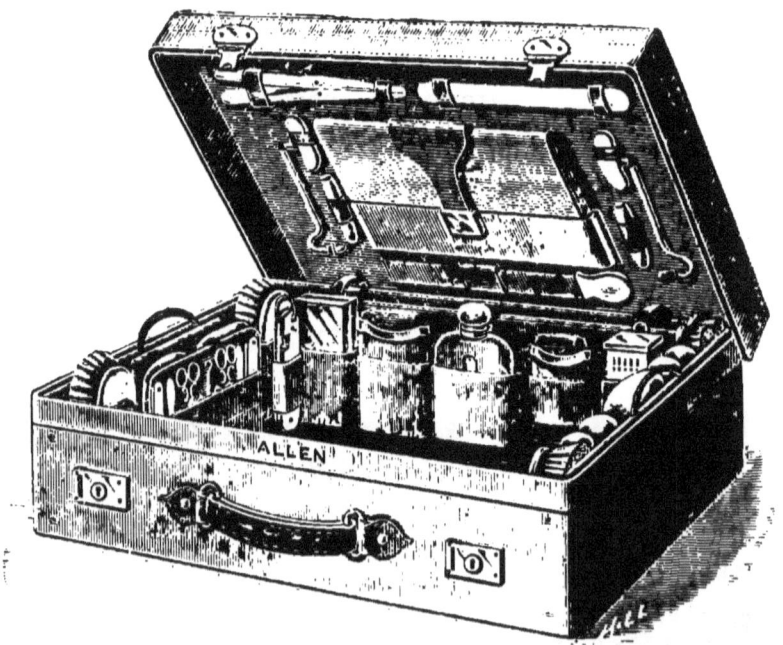

SOLID LEATHER SUIT CASES
OVERLAND TRUNKS,
STRONG DRESS BASKETS,
GLADSTONE BAGS, &c.

DISCOUNT FOR CASH 10 PER CENT.